Flash™ MX 2004

ETHAN WATRALL | NORBERT HERBER

SAN FRANCISCO | LONDON

SYBEX®

Associate Publisher: Dan Brodnitz

Acquisitions Editor: Mariann Barsolo

Developmental Editor: James A. Compton

Production Editor: Mae Lum

Copyeditor: Laura Ryan

Technical Editors: Tai U, Scott Balay

Production Manager: Amy Changar

Cover, Interior, and Technical Illustration Designer: Caryl Gorska, Gorska Design

Compositor: Chris Gillespie, Happenstance Type-O-Rama

Graphic Illustrator: Caryl Gorska, Gorska Design

Proofreaders: Laurie O'Connell, Amy J. Rasmussen, Nancy Riddiough

Indexer: Ted Laux

CD Coordinator: Dan Mummert

CD Technician: Kevin Ly

Cover Designer: Caryl Gorska, Gorska Design

Cover Photographer: Robert J. Birnbach

An earlier version of this book was published under the title *Flash MX Savvy* © 2002 SYBEX Inc.

Library of Congress Control Number: 2003115475

ISBN: 0-7821-4284-2

About the Authors

Given the fact that Ethan is an archaeologist by training, people often ask "what the heck is an archaeologist doing writing books about interactive design?" Well, to understand this, you need to understand that he has two great loves in his academic life. The first, which represents a culmination of years of archaeological experience, is household craft production in Predynastic Egypt. He has worked at both Nabta Playa (an extremely large Neolithic habitation site in the Egyptian Western Desert) and Hierakonpolis, where he has excavated such cool things as prehistoric wells, clay mines, households, animal enclosures, pottery kilns, and cemeteries.

The second, and here comes the answer to the big question, is the place of interactive media in archaeology. Whether from the standpoint of an educational tool, a method for scholarly publication, or simply an issue deserving academic discussion, Ethan has dedicated himself to expanding the dialog surrounding the use of interactive media in archaeology. He is particularly interested in the role that interactive entertainment plays in the public perception of archaeology—a topic on which he has published and delivered papers targeted to both professional archaeologists and professional game designers. Not content to simply comment on the situation, Ethan practices what he preaches: active involvement on the part of academics in the interactive entertainment industry.

He is currently a visiting faculty member in the Department of Telecommunications at Indiana University, where he teaches classes in interactive new-media design, the social aspect of new information and communication technologies, and interactive entertainment. He has written several books including *Dreamweaver 4/Fireworks 4 Visual Jump-Start*, *Dreamweaver MX: Design and Technique*, and *Flash MX Savvy* (co-authored with Norbert Herber). His next book, *Dreamweaver MX 2004: Solutions*, will be published by Sybex in January 2004.

Ethan's digital alter ego can be found hanging out at www.captainprimate.com.

Norbert Herber is an audio and interactivity architect. His interests are focused on the use of audio in interactive environments, nonlinear music composition, and the effects of the sound+picture relationship in both linear and nonlinear media. When he's not writing books, you can find him composing music and sound effects for websites, CD-ROMs, generative audio applications, and live performance. When he's not doing those things, he's probably out walking his dog.

Norbert is a Visiting Lecturer at Indiana University, Bloomington, where he teaches classes in the areas of multimedia development and scripting, interactive design, and digital audio. He co-authored *Flash MX Savvy* (Sybex, 2002) with Ethan Watrall.

For information on Norbert's current and past projects, visit www.x-tet.com.

Dedication

To my son Sam. Who would have thought that something that poops so much and robs his mother and myself of so much sleep would bring me such incredible joy?

—ECW

To my family.

—NFH

Acknowledgments

As with any book, especially one of this length, there are quite a number of people who deserve thanks for their help in bringing this project to fruition. ■ First and foremost, I must extend my thanks to my friend, coauthor, and partner in many digital shenanigans: Norb Herber. A book covering an application whose complexity actually extends over two versions in which two authors share writing duties is an undertaking rife with possibilities for disaster. Instead, we managed to create a book with some serious neckwear punch. Here's to many more fruitful collaborations! ■ To all those who graciously gave us permission to use their work as Inspirational Design Models or in the Color Gallery (there are way too many folks to list by name—they know who they are), I offer my profound thanks. I especially want to thank Paul Corrigan at Oddity Studios whose contributions and help were above and beyond the call of duty. ■ On a more personal level, as always I want to express my profound love and gratitude to Jenn. She graciously put up with my lunacy and long hours on the computer during the year that this book was being written, rewritten, revised, re-revised, and so on, and so on. Thanks, as always, to my daughter Taylor. Thanks also to both Mom and Dad for their support during this project. Finally, a special thank you (and a good tummy rub) to my dog, Oscar; nothing brings you down to earth like a pooch who wants nothing more in life than to play. ■ Lastly, my sincere apologies to anyone whom I managed to forget. Thanks, everybody!

Ethan Watrall

Not only was this book a team effort by two authors, each of us had our own "support staff" to help us through the writing process. Thanks to Mom and Dad, Genevieve, Lyla, Susan, Hasan, and, most of all, my dearest Jenny. I think it's time for a vacation! ■ Cheers to those who shared their work as Inspirational Design Models and/or in the color gallery, especially Paul D. Miller, a.k.a. DJ Spooky that Subliminal Kid; Éric Gagnon of Sarbakan; Justin Mysza from NPFC; Harry Gottlieb and Amanda Lannert from Jellyvision; Molly Z, Pall Thayer, Rick Goldsworthy, and Steve Ragatz at Academic Edge; and Scott McCloud. Your work is a constant reminder of why I fell in love with Flash. ■ Thanks also to my colleagues in Chicago—Tim Arroyo and Bernie

Mack at IADT—for their contributions to this book, and Brian Hrastar at Optimus for sharing his video footage. ■ I'd like to offer a huge thanks to my partner in crime, Ethan Watrall. We made it! Now let's get some degrees. Thanks for reminding me not to sweat the little stuff. ■ Finally, thank *you* for reading this!

Norbert Herber

Both of us want to acknowledge lots of other people who helped make this book a reality. ■ Many thanks go to our agent, David Fugate of Waterside Productions, Inc. As always, we are forever in his debt for all the work he put in and for the advice he provided during this project. At Sybex, Jim Compton, Mae Lum, Dan Schiff, Dan Mummert, Laura Ryan, and Maureen Forys deserve praise for all their help and hard work. Kudos to technical editors Scott Balay and Tai U for their many insights. ■ Without the help of Mariann Barsolo, our acquisitions editor at Sybex, this project might well have exploded very early. She was always there with great advice, tons of help, and an incredibly understanding attitude, especially during the really nutty periods. ■ We also want to extend our profound gratitude to those individuals who helped with the software and hardware that either appears on the CD or was used while we were writing the book: Karina Bessoudo (Toon Boom Studios); William Reeb (Wacom); Philip Staiger (Eovia); Alisa Popolizio, Silke Fleischer, and Patrick Wallace (eHelp); Carrie Cochrane (Electric Rain); Eric Ott (WebAssist); and Zac Wheatcroft (BIAS).

Contents

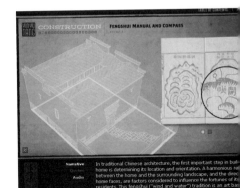

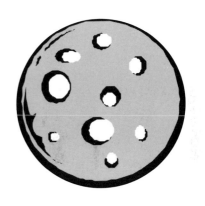

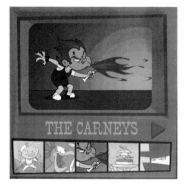

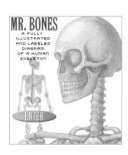

Introduction

In the summer of 1996, a little-known company named FutureWave shipped a small program called FutureSplash Animator, a relatively simple application that was designed to create linear, vector-based animations. After its release, the application attracted considerable attention when it was used in the design of both Microsoft's Web version of MSN and Disney's subscription-based Disney Daily Blast. In November 1996, Macromedia approached FutureWave about the possibility of working together. For FutureWave, which was still a tiny company of six employees, this was an incredible opportunity. So, in December 1996, FutureWave sold the technology to Macromedia, who released Flash 1 in early 1997. The rest, as they say, is history.

Fast-forward to 2004. Seven versions later, Macromedia has split Flash into two programs: Flash MX 2004 and Flash MX Professional 2004.

Two Versions of Flash?

This release of Flash is truly unique in that for the first time, users can choose between two versions of the application: Flash MX 2004 or Flash MX Professional 2004. Flash is arguably one of the most popular interactive authoring applications. As such, Flash has become a different kind of application to different kinds of developers.

To support the myriad needs of their users, Macromedia elected to separate the application into two versions. Each has been designed in ways that Macromedia believes serves the interests of an incredibly diverse user base. Flash MX 2004 represents the next step for Flash as an authoring tool and offers enhanced features to streamline many of the most important tasks performed in the application. Flash MX *Professional* 2004 is the new release on steroids. It includes all the enhancements of the regular version plus additional features that support project-based Flash development, server communication technologies, enhanced streaming-media support, improved video compression, and PowerPoint-style authoring; all in an environment that is conducive to online application development.

The professional version provides more tools for big-picture development and has a few advantages to offer over the regular version. You will be able to do the same kinds of work with one that you do with the other. The main difference is that with the Pro version, some tasks can be made easier or more efficient. It offers tools that will be welcome to developers of large-scale Flash projects and applications. If your work requires exchanges of data between Flash and a server or you need to code an application from the ground up, the Pro version is for you. If you like Flash as is and are interested in interface enhancements and functionality improvements, you'll probably feel more comfortable with the regular version.

With both versions of Flash MX 2004, you can create not only unbelievably cool-looking animations, but also incredibly complex interactive experiences that feature rich media and the integration of dynamic, database-driven applications.

Not only are today's Web-based Flash creations a quantum leap beyond anything that could have been conceived previously for online media, but they are pushing the boundaries of interactive digital media. Although Flash was originally intended for the Web, its sheer popularity (and phenomenal power) has taken it far beyond the online domain. These days, you can see the integration of Flash as an authoring tool in mobile devices, broadcast media, and console games.

To really understand the penetration of Flash into the world of interactive digital media, you need only look at the number of people who have downloaded the Flash Player over the years: more than 436 million. Yup, that's right, nearly half a billion! Need we say more?

About This Book

This book was written with a lot of love, blood, sweat, and tears…seriously. We don't want to give you the impression that we are "tortured authors," holed up in a dingy loft pouring over manuscripts and surrounded by bottles of wine and take-out containers. However, we did put a lot of thought and planning into the writing process. Our objective was to create the most intuitive, learning-focused Flash reference imaginable.

Unlike many Flash books, this one was written not only to explain *how* to work with Flash but *why*. Knowing why you do things is a crucial step in the learning process because it gives you the means to creatively apply your newfound skills to original ideas of your own. The techniques outlined in this book will give you the basic concepts to create an enormous variety of things in Flash. Additionally, all techniques are presented with the assumption that this is just the beginning. Our hope is that you will use these lessons as a point of departure for your own creative ideas. As educators, we approached this book in much the same way we would approach a class.

This book will be equally effective for Macintosh and Windows users. As a writing team, we are split: Norbert is "the Mac guy" and Ethan "the Windows guy." As much as possible, we present a balanced approach so that regardless of your platform, this book will fit your specific needs and illustrate each technique clearly.

Who Needs This Book?

Every man, woman, and child on the planet needs this book!

But seriously, it's impossible to write a book that is all things to all people. That said, we did our best to write a book that is many things to a lot of different people. We carefully selected the topics and crafted the way we discussed them so that many different types of people with varying levels of expertise and different goals could pick up this book and find it useful. Granted, if worse comes to worst, this book is large enough to to prop up the wobbly leg on your bed or serve as a pretty decent doorstop.

The range of people who will get the most out of this book will vary from the savvy computer user who "gets" Flash but has never actually worked with the program to someone who is thoroughly grounded in the basics of Flash and wants to move on to intermediate and moderately advanced skills.

We feel strongly that although this book isn't really written for people who already have advanced Flash skills, we certainly don't want to discourage any interested individual from using the book—quite the contrary! It covers topics that even the most advanced user might not be familiar with, including several chapters each on ActionScript, working with audio, and integration with other software. However, we feel that those more-experienced Flash users might not find in this book exactly what they are looking for, and would therefore be disappointed—something we definitely don't want.

Truly advanced users who are looking to explore the ActionScript stratosphere, or investigate the possibilities of integrating Flash with server-side scripting and database technologies will not find what they're looking for. With this book, focusing on core topics was particularly important because Flash is now two different programs with different features. The topics we had to exclude are all pretty high-end, and we're sure that nearly all readers will find everything they might want to do with Flash covered here. Still, we don't want anyone looking for one of these topics to buy the book and be disappointed.

So, here is an abbreviated list of major topics that we didn't cover:

- Creating form-based applications with Screens (Flash MX Professional 2004 feature)
- Using Unicode and the Strings panel to publish in multiple languages
- Data Binding and Web Services
- Writing Programs in ActionScript 2.0

Having said this, anyone eager to take part in the Flash revolution and become a dyed-in-the-wool "Flasher" should read this book! That includes any student wanting to put their class project on the Web, any animator or artist wanting to go digital with their creations, anyone who is frustrated by the inherent design limitations of HTML, anyone enamored with the "wow" factor of vector animation and interactivity—in short, anyone who is excited about the endless possibilities and phenomenal power of Flash but a little befuddled about where to start or a bit unsure of their skills. If you're one of these folks, this book is for you!

How This Book Is Organized

There is a natural progression of skills involved in working with Flash MX 2004 and Flash MX Professional 2004. The chapter-by-chapter structure of this book is designed to emulate this progression. Although each chapter builds on the previous one, this book can also be used as a reference for those wishing to tackle specific problems.

 We've been careful to point out which features are new in Flash MX 2004; this will be useful if you've used Flash MX and are completely new to both the regular and Professional versions of MX 2004. Be on the lookout for the handy "new to MX 2004" icon shown in the margin.

Some topics covered here pertain only to features available in Flash MX Professional 2004. They can be quickly identified with the "Pro only" icon shown in the margin.

Here's a quick look at what you can expect to explore in each chapter.

PART I: Getting to Know Flash

Part I sets the stage for all your future work in Flash. In **Chapter 1**, you'll start off by getting a nice introduction to the world of Flash. You'll bone up on the venerable history of Flash (including the advances in each version), explore the difference between vectors and bitmaps, and get a snapshot of what kinds of cool stuff are being created with Flash. In **Chapter 2**, you'll explore the great updates that Flash MX 2004 and Flash MX Professional 2004 feature. Finally, in **Chapter 3**, you'll delve deeply into the Flash interface and get your hands dirty exploring how you can manipulate your working environment.

PART II: Creating and Manipulating Visual Content

Part II is geared toward teaching you the fundamentals of creating and manipulating all things visual in Flash MX. In **Chapter 4**, you'll become intimately familiar with all of Flash's painting and drawing tools. From there, **Chapter 5** covers the process of creating and manipulating text. In **Chapter 6**, you'll learn how to use objects (a blanket term for just about anything graphical in Flash) to your advantage. **Chapter 7** features an in-depth discussion about working with reusable content—primarily symbols and the Library. **Chapter 8** explores how to work with layers—a vital subject if you want to create animations having any degree of complexity. Finally, **Chapter 9** explores the incredibly handy new project-management tools available in Flash MX Professional 2004.

PART III: Animating with Flash

Part III is designed to teach you just about everything you need to know about creating animation in Flash. First, **Chapter 10** thoroughly explores how to use the Timeline to add the dimension of movement to your Flash creation. From there, you'll learn how to work with Movie Clips—arguably one of the most important elements in Flash—in **Chapter 11**.

Finally, **Chapter 12** will teach you how to work with scenes, a vital tool for partitioning and organizing animated content. The last chapter in Part III, **Chapter 13**, will look at how you go about creating interactive presentations with Slides—a new feature available in Flash MX Professional 2004.

PART IV: Adding Basic Interactivity

This section of the book will introduce you to one of the most compelling and important aspects of Flash development: interactivity. **Chapter 14** introduces you to behaviors, the built-in commands that allow you to control the interactivity of your movies. **Chapter 15** presents a discussion on the creation and design of interactive controls, an essential part of any interactive experience. **Chapter 16** covers components, ready-made modules that can be added to a Flash movie to facilitate user-input and interactivity.

PART V: Creating Advanced Interactivity with ActionScript

If you love Flash but have hesitated to take the plunge into the world of Flash-based scripting, Part V is for you. **Chapter 17** discusses some beginning concepts of programming and explains how ActionScript works inside a Flash movie. **Chapter 18** provides details on the syntax, structure, and elements of ActionScript, while **Chapter 19** discusses managing multiple Timelines in a single movie, one of the most important aspects of Flash development. **Chapter 20** presents a variety of inspiring and useful in-context examples that use Action-Script to add all sorts of functionality to your Flash movies. We feel that it's important to keep this book realistic; as a result, **Chapter 21** discusses the techniques and tools that you can use to troubleshoot ActionScripts that aren't performing as expected.

PART VI: Working with Audio

Part VI covers one of the most important (and sadly neglected) aspects of multimedia development: audio. **Chapter 22** provides useful information on the basics of digital audio and serves as a primer for anyone who is new to working with sound and music on their computer. With the essentials of digital audio under your belt, you can read **Chapter 23** to learn how audio works inside Flash and how to publish "sonified" Flash movies. Because getting your audio to synchronize with any variety of events is a crucial part of animation and interactive development, **Chapter 24** discusses the various techniques for audio-visual synchronization. Finally, **Chapter 25** ups the ante, showing you how to control audio elements interactively via ActionScript.

PART VII: Integrating Flash with Other Programs

In Part VII, you'll learn how you can integrate Flash with other useful applications. **Chapter 26** discusses Flash in the context of Macromedia's other multimedia powerhouse: Director. In **Chapter 27**, you'll learn how to integrate Flash with the latest incarnation of Macromedia's popular WYSIWYG web-development program, Dreamweaver MX 2004. **Chapter 28** discusses different ways that you can use third-party audio applications to edit sounds, compose music, and engineer your digital audio files before integrating them with your Flash masterpiece. Finally, in **Chapter 29**, you'll get a taste of how to integrate 3D with your Flash creation. The chapter covers both third-party 3D software and techniques for simulating 3D with Flash's painting and drawing tools.

PART VIII: Publishing and Distributing Flash Movies

Part VIII focuses on how you go about actually getting your beautiful Flash creations to your audience. In **Chapter 30**, you'll learn how to publish your Flash movies to several formats that are suitable for distribution. **Chapter 31** discusses the techniques involved in publishing Flash movies that include video and in publishing Flash movies *as* digital video in either QuickTime or AVI format. **Chapter 32** discusses the ins and outs of developing Flash movies for delivery on CD-ROM. And finally, **Chapter 33** will introduce you to the techniques involved in creating Flash content for mobile devices running the Pocket PC operating system.

Inspirational Design Models

Every creative endeavor—and that includes a Flash movie—definitely benefits from a little inspiration now and then. Let's face it, even the most innovative person on the planet sometimes feels a bit creatively constipated.

To help, we've included an Inspirational Design Model (IDM) at the end of almost every chapter. Each IDM highlights a notable Flash creation and (loosely) relates to the subject of the chapter. For example, in Chapter 23, "Flash Audio Basics," the IDM is DJ Spooky's *Errata Erratum*, a provoking fusion of sound, animation, and artwork by Marcel Duchamp. Ultimately, the IDMs give you not only helpful nudges along the path of creativity, but also a good feel for the terribly groovy possibilities of the application.

Hands On Sections

This book offers eight Hands On sections. As the name suggests, these put your skills to work on projects that are larger and more in-depth than those within the chapters. **Hands On 1** shows you how to create your own custom panel layout in Flash. **Hands On 2** features a step-by-step tutorial on using Flash's painting and drawing tools to create a static seascape. **Hands On 3** walks you through the creation of a short science-fiction animation. **Hands On 4** shows you how to create a favorites application for your website using components and ActionScript behaviors. **Hands On 5** incorporates ActionScript and shows you how to create a modular movie that uses multiple SWF files and pop-up windows. **Hands On 6**, which focuses on audio, demonstrates how you can use Flash to create a mixing-board application. **Hands On 7** shows you how to create an animated 3D preloader and place it in an HTML document. And to top it all off, **Hands On 8** teaches you how to synchronize streaming video to a Flash animation.

Color Gallery

The Color Gallery contains some of the most innovative, beautiful, and interesting Flash work on the Internet today. Pieces were selected not only because they are visually stunning, but because they demonstrate the true potential of this application, from concept and artistry to interactivity and entertainment.

CD Bonus Chapters

This book's companion CD-ROM contains several full-length bonus chapters (in Adobe Acrobat PDF format) on a variety of topics. **Bonus Chapter 1** explores how to make Flash dynamic (either alone or with other database-driven technologies) by sending data out or bringing data in. **Bonus Chapter 2** discusses integrating Flash with Macromedia's vector-illustration application, Freehand MX. **Bonus Chapter 3** offers step-by-step tutorials for features that didn't quite fit into other parts of this book. These tutorials show you how to create some of the coolest Flash widgets and doohickeys (such as navigational widgets and preloaders) as well as how to create an interactive Flash-based software tutorial with eHelp's Robodemo. The **Bonus Hands On** outlines the steps of burning a cross-platform CD-ROM with Toast 6 Titanium.

ActionScript Reference

The ActionScript Reference on this book's CD-ROM provides you with the correct syntax, contextual examples, and tips for working with many ActionScript terms. This isn't a complete reference; rather, it contains what we consider to be *essential* ActionScript elements. It should prove to be very helpful when you're composing scripts from the ground up.

How to Use This Book

This book can be used in two ways. The first, as mentioned earlier, depends on the fact that the material presented follows a logical learning curve. As a result, you can easily read this book from cover to cover, confident that when you're finished, you'll have a solid foundation in basic, intermediate, and some advanced Flash development techniques.

This book can also be used as a reference. If you want to solve certain problems or learn specific skills, you can simply locate the information you desire by using the index or the table of contents.

The bottom line is that whatever way you decide to use this book, you'll learn the skills necessary to continue your journey in the wonderful world of Flash MX 2004 and Flash MX Professional 2004.

About the CD

As with many computer books, *Flash MX 2004 Savvy* comes with a handy-dandy companion CD-ROM, which is compatible with both Macintosh and Windows platforms. Although the CD would probably make a pretty decent Frisbee, we've gone to great lengths to include some really useful stuff.

First, you'll find a whole bevy of demo and trial software. Most, if not all, of these applications were chosen because they are discussed in this book; some of them are needed for the successful completion of the Hands On tutorials. Second, the CD contains all the necessary support and example files that are used in the chapters and the Hands On sections. Third (as described earlier), there are several bonus chapters that we couldn't fit into the printed pages of the book you're holding.

 Anytime we want to point you toward files on the CD, the cool little CD icon shown in the margin will appear next to the text. Feel free to use these files as starter files for your own unique Flash creations. We recommend that you open all Flash MX 2004 documents (FLA files) from within Flash. Simply choose File → Open and browse to the file that you need.

Getting in Touch and Staying Connected

We have developed a community resource for the readers (and potential readers) of this book. Visit www.vonflashenstein.com to learn about Flash in the laboratory of Dr. Helmut von Flashenstein and his faithful lab assistant, Müvie Klip. In the depths of his lab, Dr. von Flashenstein will introduce you to various Flash oddities, lessons, and other material in support of this book.

The website includes:

- An expanded Inspirational Design Model section
- An "ActionScript laboratory" with sample code and source FLA files
- Opportunities to sign up for receiving news and events via e-mail
- Access to bonus tutorials and articles

We said that this book was constructed like a class, but there's one exception: You can't raise your hand to ask a question or offer feedback. So, in case you want to get in touch with us, here are our addresses:

norbert@vonflashenstein.com
ethan@vonflashenstein.com

We get a lot of mail from our readers, so please forgive us if it takes a while to respond to your questions.

PART I

Getting to Know Flash

Flash began its career humbly as a great tool for adding low-bandwidth animations to websites. Since those hallowed days, the application has grown by leaps and bounds! Yes, Flash can still animate, but it can also be used to create amazingly complex, interactive products, dynamic and data-driven websites and online applications, cartoon serials, online (and offline) games, music videos, music players, instant messengers…the list goes on and on. Flash has evolved from "simple animator" to "multimedia authoring juggernaut" in no less than 7 years. In fact, it would be hard to imagine the Internet today without Flash and what it offers to the world of interactive digital media.

Part I of this book will take you on a guided tour of Flash. You'll learn about the history of the software, explore its role in interactive digital media today, and get a brief glimpse of the directions the application might take in the future. Of course, you'll also be introduced to Macromedia's latest additions to the Flash pedigree: Flash MX 2004 and Flash MX Professional 2004. Whether you're a veteran Flash developer or a first-time user, this section of the book will show you the now, then, and possibly the tomorrow of Flash.

CHAPTER 1

Introduction to Flash

As one of the most popular and versatile applications for creating digital multimedia, Flash continues to wear many hats. Flash has always been at the cutting edge of technology for delivering compelling animated content. As a vector-based medium, Flash is also able to deliver the goods at a fraction of the bandwidth required by other animated media. What many people don't realize is that Flash can do much more than simply create bandwidth-efficient vector animation. As the application continues to evolve, its scope broadens more and more. Flash is now one of the most flexible interactive digital-media authoring tools available, offering the capabilities to run not only on the Internet and desktop computer platforms, but on game consoles and mobile devices as well. It is truly *multi*media.

To get a sense of Flash's true identity, it's helpful to become familiar with its historical lineage, makeup, and current applications. In this chapter, you will explore:

- **The history of Flash**

- **The differences between raster and vector formats**

- **The many faces of Flash**

A History of Flash

Before you dig into today's Flash, it's a good idea to cast your eye back and get an idea of how this virtual revolution in interactive multimedia came about. Besides, it's a cool story.

So, turn the "way back" machine to the late 1980s. The stage for our little story has been set with four companies. The first, Macromind, was a Chicago-based software company whose primary product was an application called VideoWorks. The second, Paracomp, based in San Francisco, was best known for its Macintosh 3D application, Swivel3D. The third company was Authorware, a Minnesota-based company best known for its CBT/multimedia authoring application, Authorware. In 1991, Macromind, which had moved to San Francisco, merged with Paracomp to form Macromind-Paracomp. Authorware then moved from Minnesota and joined Macromind-Paracomp in Redwood Shores, California, to found the mighty Macromedia—the beginning, so to speak.

As you might have noticed, this accounts for only three of the four players in our story. To learn about the fourth member of the cast, we look back to January 1993. Jonathan Gay, who had put himself through college writing such venerable early Mac games as *Dark Castle* and *Beyond Dark Castle,* convinced his buddy Charlie Jackson (founder of Silicon Beach Software) to invest some money and help form a company called FutureWave. The whole point of the company, whose first product was an application called Go, was to produce software that would dominate the pen computer market. Well, unfortunately, the early pen computers failed to really catch on, and there was some corporate interference by AT&T, so Go became an application without a market.

So FutureWave found itself in serious trouble. It was a small software company with no income and had spent a year developing an application that would never see the light of day. Their salvation came in the form of a small drawing program called SmartSketch that they had developed as a sideline to Go. FutureWave began marketing SmartSketch as a computer-based drawing solution for both Macintosh and Windows platforms. It wasn't long before people were asking why FutureWave didn't turn SmartSketch into a 2D animation program. In perhaps one of the most stunning examples of technological foresight, FutureWave shifted the focus of SmartSketch from a static image-creation program to an animation program. This shift was based solely on the hope that the Internet—something that everyone was beginning to talk about—would be a great medium for delivering 2D animation.

After both Adobe and Fractal Design declined to buy the technology (they must be kicking themselves now!), FutureWave shipped its FutureSplash Animator in the summer of 1996. FutureSplash Animator was a relatively simple application for creating linear vector-based animations. After its release, the application gained some attention when it was used in the design of both Microsoft's web version of MSN and Disney's subscription-based Disney Daily Blast. In November 1996, Macromedia approached FutureWave about the possibility of the two firms working together. For FutureWave, which was still a tiny company with only six employees, this was an astonishing opportunity. So, in December 1996, FutureWave sold the technology to Macromedia, which released the first Flash in early 1997. The rest, as they say, is history.

Once it was picked up by Macromedia, Flash began to evolve as a software tool. Each new version offered significant advances in the application's capabilities and usability:

Flash 1 Flash 1, which was really just a rebranded version of FutureWave's FutureSplash, featured very basic (by Flash MX's standards) timeline-based vector animation. Its primary strength was that, with the help of either a Netscape plug-in or an Internet Explorer ActiveX control, the user could mount animations on the Web for anyone to view and enjoy.

Flash 2 Flash 2 was a major step for the application. Generally speaking, it began the transformation of Flash from a straight linear-vector animation program to an interactive media-design program. The shift resulted from the integration of such features as reusable button symbols, embedded graphics, vector fonts, very basic actions, and stereo audio. Flash 2 also supported the import of an impressive selection of file formats, including EPS, GIF, JPEG, AutoCAD DXF, BMP, Enhanced Metafile, AIFF, Windows Metafile, and Shockwave.

Flash 3 One of the most significant additions to Flash 3, besides the continual improvement to the user interface, was the increasing importance and integration of actions. Based loosely on JavaScript, actions (which would later evolve into ActionScript) enabled users to add a certain measure of control and interactivity into their movies. In addition, the integration of masks, shape tweening, and transparency allowed users to exert much more control over how their Flash creations actually looked.

Flash 4 One of the most exciting improvements in Flash 4 was the ability to implement compressed MP3 audio files in the context of a Flash movie. Flash 4 also boasted improved ActionScript, which made it easier to create interactive games and interfaces. Other enhancements included editable text fields, an improved user interface, and a simplified publishing process.

Flash 5 The greatest advance in Flash 5 was definitely ActionScript. By aligning itself with the ECMA-262 standard, Macromedia announced to the world that Flash and Action-Script were ready to compete with the "big dogs." Other changes in this version were in the user interface: additional art tools, the introduction of panels, the Movie Explorer, the Macromedia Dashboard (for online help and updates), and user-customizable keystrokes for common tasks and functions.

Flash MX Flash MX was a major step forward for Flash. While this newest version of Flash was really just the sixth incarnation of the program, Macromedia replaced the numerical version name with the *MX* moniker. Why the new name? Well, according to Macromedia, they made the switch to *MX* to inform developers that the software presents integrated solutions to Internet-based digital media. Because Macromedia's tools (Flash, Dreamweaver, ColdFusion, and so on) can be so tightly integrated, the company felt it was only appropriate that the various applications carry the same name. *MX* is simply a label used for this family of Macromedia tools. The initials don't actually stand for anything in particular, and the Flash community simply had to accept this change at face value—despite the fact that some were somewhat grumpy about the name change.

In terms of the program features, Flash MX was definitely a worthy upgrade. The most notable was the new, more streamlined and usable user interface. The program also featured components—drag-and-drop widgets and doohickeys—that under normal circumstances would take a very long time to create by hand. In addition, the integration of a host of new visual design tools, such as the free transform tool, the envelope modifier, enhanced text support, and an enhanced Color Mixer, allowed Flash authors to exert far more control over how they grant interactive creation looked. Finally, Flash MX featured enhanced support for rich media, such as audio, digital video, and external images.

Flash has clearly come a long way. Features that once seemed amazing and unbelievable in one version pale in comparison to the possibilities offered in subsequent upgrades. As you will soon discover, Flash MX 2004 and Flash MX Professional 2004 are another significant step forward. Like the upgrades that came before it, Flash MX 2004 and Flash MX Professional 2004 offer options and features that will continue to keep Flash at the forefront of digital media and Internet development.

Raster vs. Vector Formats

Computers can store and display graphics in two main formats: *vector* and *raster*. To better understand how Flash works and why it presents advantages over other kinds of animation applications, it's vital that you understand the differences between these two graphic formats.

One of the aspects of Flash that makes it unique is its use of *vectors* to display much of its animated content. Vectors are line representations of an image. Like cartoons, they resemble an actual image but don't look completely realistic. The vectors that create an image give it shape and color. The curves of the vectors give an object its shape and contour. Every vector has two color properties: stroke (or outline) and fill; these properties (see Figure 1.1) give a vector image both its outline and overall color.

> The kicker about vector images is that stroke and fill are calculated mathematically. This is very important when it comes to animation.

Raster images, which are sometimes referred to as bitmap images, are very different from vector images. A raster image is created by a collection of pixels. A *pixel,* which is a hybrid word combining *picture* and *element,* is a colored dot or tile. A raster image, which can contain millions of pixels, works like a mosaic. Each little colored tile, which consumes a fixed amount of your computer's memory, plays a role in creating the overall color makeup and detail of the image. For an illustration of raster format, see Figure 1.2.

One of the major differences between vector and raster images is in their scalability. Because the components of a vector image (stroke, fill, and so on) are calculated mathematically, they can be scaled, stretched, and manipulated by the computer without any loss of the image's clarity or resolution. The same, however, is not true for raster images. They have a preset grid configuration, so any change in size alters the grid. When the size of a raster image is increased, the computer must interpolate (make an educated guess for) the additional pixels needed to make a larger grid. This can result in unwanted "chunkiness" or "blockiness" in the enlarged raster graphic.

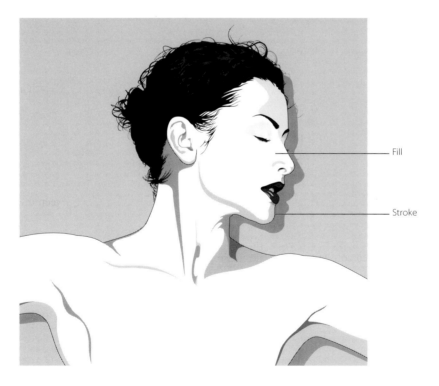

Fill

Stroke

Figure 1.1

The stroke and fill of a vector image give it its overall graphic properties.

Figure 1.2

A raster image is created using a series of colored tiles, or pixels, arranged in a grid format.

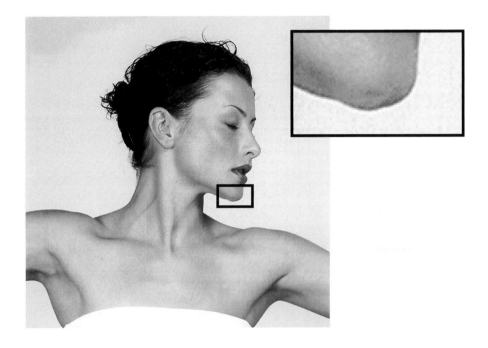

The Many Faces of Flash

As you probably know by now, Flash isn't just an animation tool. So, what *is* it, then? Rather than try to define Flash, it's better to exemplify what it can do. Its presence and application around the world speak volumes.

Broadcast Media

Even though Flash is probably most "at home" on the Web, it has also made its way to broadcast media in recent years. This transition shouldn't come as a surprise. After all, Flash has proven to be a powerful animation tool and can be exported to a variety of file formats.

Flash has been used for several broadcast applications, both in Europe and in the United States. In the U.K., the web design firm Kerb developed one of the first broadcast cartoon series that was created entirely in Flash. You can check out the series, *Hellz Kitchen,* an irreverent and hilarious look at a group of slightly deranged talking vegetables, by visiting Kerb's website (`www.kerb.co.uk`).

Though it has since gone off the air, Flash could be seen in the United States in the intro animation of *The Rosie O'Donnell Show.* Another great example of Flash in broadcast media is the Spike TV (formerly TNN) show *Gary the Rat.* Created entirely in Flash, *Gary the Rat*

chronicles the escapades of an attorney (voices by Kelsey Grammer) so unscrupulous that he actually turned into a rat. To check out the show's website, visit `www.spiketv.com/shows/animation/gary_the_rat/index.jhtml`.

> For more information on this and other uses of Flash as a "convergent media," see `www.macromedia.com/macromedia/proom/pr/2000/converge.html`.

Mobile Computing/Communications

As computers continue to become both smaller and more communicative, Flash will be part of the revolution. The Flash Player is poised to deliver content to a wide variety of web-ready gadgets and mobile devices. This includes business applications news services, games, educational applications, maps and geographical aids, event guides, entertainment, wireless applications, and so much more—the works!

One of the first mobile platforms to support Flash was Microsoft's Pocket PC. You can read more about Flash for the Pocket PC platform at `www.macromedia.com/software/flashplayer/pocketpc`. For those who use handheld mobile devices that feature the Palm OS operating system, don't despair! While the Flash player is almost always associated with the Pocket PC operating system, the most recent models of Sony's popular Clié handheld (which runs on Palm OS) includes the Flash player.

The science fiction doesn't stop there. Flash is also being developed for implementation on mobile phones and other handheld or portable computing devices. For more information, see `www.macromedia.com/software/flashplayer/resources/devices`.

For an introduction to the ins and outs of developing Flash content for the Pocket PC operating system, check out Chapter 33.

Gaming Consoles

Arguably one of the most unexpected applications of Flash has been in the interactive entertainment industry—console games, to be precise.

The most noteworthy example was the use of Flash to create the user interface for LucasArts' popular *Star Wars: Starfighter* game for PlayStation 2 and Xbox. Although LucasArts had designed the in-game/heads up display (HUD) interface for *Starfighter*, they encountered a serious problem near the end of their development cycle when they realized that they were lacking a functional out-of-game user interface. Enter Macromedia Flash. LucasArts partnered with two companies, Secret Level (`www.secretlevel.com`) and Orange Design (`www.orangedesign.com`), to design the out-of-game interface using Flash. Released in February 2001, first for PlayStation 2 and then for Xbox, the game served as a milestone in Flash history.

For more information on how Flash was used in *Star Wars: Starfighter*, see the Gamasutra article at www.gamasutra.com/features/20010801/corry_01.htm.

Excited by the possibilities of using Flash content in console and PC games, Secret Level began development of a software development kit (SDK) called Strobe. Designed to provide hardware-accelerated Flash-content rendering for games, Strobe's core engineering supported 60fps playback on both Playstation 2 and Xbox. Unfortunately, in June 2001, Strobe's development was put on hold pending the finalization of licensing terms with Macromedia.

Interestingly, in May 2001, Macromedia and Sony announced a partnership geared toward bringing the Flash Player to Sony PlayStation 2. Facilitating in-game visual design like that featured in *Star Wars: Starfighter* was high on the partnership's list of goals. Offering a complete range of Flash-facilitated connected entertainment experiences in the emerging broadband era was also an important focus for the new partners. Unfortunately, since the announcement, both companies have been totally silent about any kind of successful completion of any collective goals that have emerged from the partnership.

However, this series of rather disheartening events did not spell the end of Flash content on game consoles. Pleased with the process of Flash content integration in *Star Wars: Starfighter*, LucasArts once again teamed up with Orange Design to develop a Flash-based out-of-game interface for *Star Wars: Starfighter*'s sequel, *Star Wars: Jedi Starfighter*. Released in March 2002 for Playstation 2 and in May 2002 for Xbox, *Star Wars: Jedi Starfighter* showed that console games were an excellent place for Flash content.

Hopefully, future Flash/game console collaborations will open new avenues for Flash and Flash developers alike.

The Internet

Flash started as a tool for deployment of animated content on the Internet and, well, some things will never change. No matter how Flash continues to advance in the areas of connectivity, media authoring, and audience interactivity, it will always be a web development tool at heart. To get a sense of this tradition, see the Inspirational Design Model sections throughout this book. Most of these projects are web-based and present a very rounded view of the possibilities that this application presents.

In addition to delivering information and entertainment, Flash is used for advertising. To read how Flash can track advertisements, see the article at www.macromedia.com/resources/richmedia/tracking.

Edutainment

As the Web has become more complex, more easily accessed, and more plentiful in rich media, it has increasingly become a destination for those wanting to be educated and entertained at the same time. Edutainment is a subset of media (online or offline, interactive or not) that presents science, history, or culture in a compelling and entertaining manner. This is where Flash-based edutainment enters the picture. Flash allows for the creation of nonlinear, self-motivated, educational, exploratory experiences that feature compelling and powerful use of sound, video, imagery, and interactivity. While there are a select group of outstanding examples of Flash-based edutainment, there is little doubt in my mind that the über example is *Becoming Human* (www.becominghuman.org).

Developed jointly by NeonSky Creative Media (www.neonsky.com) and Terra Incognita (www.terraincognita.com) for the Arizona State Institute for Human Origins, *Becoming Human* is an original interactive Flash documentary that explores human evolution from our earliest ancestors to the emergence of *Homo sapiens. Becoming Human* features a host of innovative and interactive tools (such as interactive exhibits) that allow you to go beyond the Flash documentary itself and pursue your personal exploration into the fascinating world of human evolution.

Becoming Human is partitioned into several sections that allow you to explore questions about culture, hominid anatomy, archaeological evidence, and lineage. Each section features not only a spectacular linear Flash documentary narrated by the prestigious paleoanthropologist Dr. Donald Johanson, but also topical discussions by many other prominent scholars in the field of human evolution. The combination of the linear documentary and the interactive exploratory tools (both of which are created totally in Flash) makes *Becoming Human* one of the most interesting, innovative, and cutting-edge Flash creations out there.

This book contains several additional excellent examples of Flash-based edutainment for you to discover and experience, including *Yin Yu Tang: A Chinese House* (Chapter 7), The Theben Mapping Project (Chapter 4 and the color section), and *Langlevelater* (Chapter 10).

Flash isn't just for edutainment, it's also used in educational settings. Not only does the new Slides feature allow instructors to create interactive presentations, but there are also third-party applications for creating educational Flash-based applications. Easily one of the most interesting (and innovative) applications is from eHelp (www.ehelp.com). Based in San Diego, California, eHelp (which will become part of Macromedia in December 2003) makes RoboDemo for creating interactive Flash-based software simulations. In addition, they make RoboPresenter, incredibly cool software to allow you to convert PowerPoint presentations into low-bandwidth Flash movies. On this book's accompanying CD, you'll find demo versions of RoboDemo and RoboPresenter, as well as a tutorial on how to create Flash-based software simulations with RoboDemo (in Bonus Chapter 3).

Web Games and Cartoons

Flash is great for creating multimedia and interactive navigation, but it is *superb* for creating fun stuff! Why do we try to pass Flash off as such a "serious" application, when a large portion of its development community is dedicated to doing work that is meant to be anything but serious! Games and cartoons are another important part of the Flash oeuvre.

FLASHTOON TOOLS

As Flash webtoons and animated shorts have become more and more popular, a spate of tools have cropped up to facilitate their creation. As with all things digital, some tools are better than others. Arguably one of the most mature, usable, and feature-rich is Toon Boom Studio (www.toonboomstudio.com). Developed by the Montreal-based company Toon Boom (www.toonboom.com), Toon Boom Studio is a 2D animation application that facilitates the creation of compelling animation targeted to the Web, digital video, wireless devices, and beyond. Among many other things, the program features powerful and intuitive 3D scene planning, advanced camera manipulation, lip sync tools, and project management. The great thing about Toon Boom Studio, beyond its robust features, is that it's one of the best-priced 2D animation solutions for short-form or "flash"-style productions. All in all, Toon Boom Studio is a great product for Flashers who are looking for a great way to bring their animated aspirations to life.

A demo copy of Toon Boom Studio (for both PC and Mac) has been included on this book's accompanying CD.

Kiosk Development

A *kiosk* is a piece of custom computer hardware that delivers a fixed body of information, usually through a very user-friendly interactive interface. Kiosks are most commonly used in situations where an organization wants to let the user control the access to information (usually through a touch screen or a mouse-driven interface) that would traditionally be delivered by a receptionist or another such individual. Because Flash can create powerful interactive experiences that are both complex and beautiful, it naturally lends itself to creating kiosks.

Although it would be difficult to provide a representative list of all the kiosks that have been developed with Flash, there are a few very noteworthy examples that we absolutely must mention. In late 2000, Moccu (www.moccusite.com) presented the prototype for a touch screen, Flash-based petrol pump at CeBit in Hannover, Germany. Designed to let motorists search for information on travel routes and traffic situations, browse special shop offers, and even send e-mail while they're filling their tank, the CeBit pump proto-type has yet to be implemented. It will be an outstanding and exciting example of the possibilities of merging Flash content with nontraditional computing environments such as kiosks (and even web-enabled appliances).

While commercial kiosk applications are a great place for Flash to spread its wings, kiosks are equally common in museum exhibits and galleries. One of the most eloquent experts in cultural kiosk Flash design is Second Story Interactive. Based in Portland, Oregon, Second Story Interactive (`www.secondstory.com`) has created a string of Flash-based kiosks that range from the educational and entertaining to the highly compelling.

Arguably one of their most entertaining (as well as educational) was the *Inventions & Inspirations: History of Recorded Sound* kiosk. From Thomas Edison to Public Enemy, from gramophones to digital sampling, this interactive kiosk tells the epic story of the individuals and innovations that transformed how we create and experience music. Housed in the Sound Lab of Seattle's Experience Music Project, *Inventions & Inspirations: History of Recorded Sound* traces the evolution of making and capturing sound, and features visionaries with their inventions and influential musicians who embraced invention in their artistry, as well as each innovation's impact on audience experience. The kiosk also includes interactive modules that demonstrate what sound is and how we're able to record it.

Digital Art

Some Flash work defies description and needs no explanation. As the audience, you can take away from the experience whatever you like. Works of this nature can be called only one thing: art.

There are many individuals who are pushing the boundaries of Flash in ways that challenge current thinking about interactive, digital media. Two of these individuals are featured in this book: Maruto (Josh Davis), and Yugo Nakamura. See this book's color section for a glimpse into their work and for links that will allow you to experience it firsthand at your computer.

CHAPTER 2

What's New in Flash MX 2004 and Flash MX Professional 2004

Well, it's official: both new versions of Flash have some truly cool features. With both releases, Macromedia has upheld its longstanding tradition of producing meaningful software updates. By introducing a horde of new and exciting features, Macromedia has once again managed to push the boundaries of cutting-edge interactive design tools. This chapter details the latest and greatest additions.

Topics covered include the following:

- **Robust usability and productivity improvements**

- **New tools for enhancing typographic freedom and creativity**

- **Rich video integration**

- **Project management and version control**

- **Application development and ActionScript advances**

- **Extensibility**

Robust Usability and Productivity Improvements

Great software is easy to use. As such, Macromedia has included the following additions in both Flash MX 2004 and Flash MX Professional 2004 to increase its usability and streamline your workflow:

Halo interface The improved interface (called Halo) is featured in both Flash MX 2004 and Flash MX Professional 2004. While not really a radical change, the Halo interface is primarily visual in nature—designed to give Flash MX 2004 and Flash MX Professional 2004 a little extra visual appeal.

Start Page The Start Page is a handy utility that acts as a central location for the logical first tasks that a user would likely choose when they open up Flash to start a work session. For more information on the Start Page, check out Chapter 3.

Improved user interface Flash MX 2004 and Flash MX Professional 2004 feature the new and improved, tabbed, multiple-document interface. Now, you can have multiple Flash movies open at any given time, and seamlessly move between them for maximum productivity. To learn more about the improved interface, check out Chapter 3.

Timeline Effects Sometimes creating a simple animation can be tedious (especially if you have to repeat the process over and over again). Timeline Effects simplify the animation process. With them, you can create complex animations without ever having to work with traditional flash animation techniques such as keyframes or tweening. If you want to learn more about Timeline Effects, turn to Chapter 10.

Templates Templates were introduced back in Flash MX, but Flash MX 2004 and Flash MX Professional 2004 have taken them to the next level. Now you can select from a plethora of new templates that allow you to bypass many of the common tasks required to create a great-looking Flash movie. For more information on the new templates available, check out Chapter 3.

Spell Checker Now you no longer have to be a slave to bad spelling! The new Spell Checker allows you to check the spelling of all aspects of your Flash movie. You can read more about the Spell Checker in Chapter 5.

Improved Flash Player performance Macromedia has been working hard on improving the Flash Player's overall performance. Runtime performance of the Flash Player has been improved by two to five times for video, scripting, and general display rendering.

Find and Replace The new Find and Replace tool is extremely powerful, allowing you to search your entire Flash movie for text, specific fonts, colors, sounds, symbols, video, or bitmaps. If you want to learn more about the Find and Replace tool, check out Chapter 9.

Improved external file import support Despite the fact that Flash's painting and drawing tools are fairly robust, there are definitely times when you'll want to import external files for inclusion in your grand Flash creation. With these two new versions of Flash, Macro-media has included high-fidelity import of Adobe PDF and Adobe Illustrator 10 files. For more information on the new external file import support, flip to Chapter 6.

Behaviors Taking a hint from Director and Dreamweaver, behaviors simplify the creation of ActionScript so that even beginners can easily add advanced interactivity to their Flash movies, all without writing a line of ActionScript by hand. Behaviors are covered in detail in Chapter 14.

Integrated help feature Macromedia knows that learning Flash can be a complex process. As a result, it has included a new, fully integrated help system that features an in-context reference, a language guide, and extensive tutorials. For more information on how to get help in Flash MX 2004 and Flash MX Professional 2004, refer to Chapter 3.

Publishing Profiles Now, with the help of Publishing Profiles, you can save your publish settings for a given project, and then reuse them whenever you need to publish a similar project but don't want to go through the trouble of manually setting the necessary proper-ties. To learn more about Publishing Profiles, read Chapter 30.

History Panel The History Panel allows you to record your interaction with the program. The recorded steps can then be converted into Commands for future use. The History Panel is covered in depth in Chapter 9.

Components For developers who create highly interactive or content-driven movies, Components are a welcome addition. They enable you to add standard interface controls through a simple drag-and-drop procedure. Both Flash MX 2004 and Flash MX Profes-sional 2004 have a series of cool new UI- and scripting-related Components that make your life easier. To learn more about Components, turn to Chapter 16.

International language character support No longer are you limited to creating Flash movies with language characters native to the operating system upon which you are work-ing. Now, full Unicode support throughout the product allows international language character sets to be used within any version of the application running on any operating system. In addition, the Strings Panel allows strings to be isolated for efficient localization into multiple languages.

Screens The Screens authoring mode allows users to create Flash movies in a new and tremendously exciting way. Now, you can quickly and easily create either interactive pre-sentations (Slides) or form-based applications (Forms). The Screen Outline Pane shows the overall structure of your screen-based project in a graphical/hierarchical manner, and allows you to manipulate the screens in your Slide- or Form-based project with maximum efficiency. In addition, a series of Screens specific behaviors allows you to create effective navigation and interesting transitions. To learn more about creating interactive presenta-tions with Slides, turn to Chapter 13.

New Tools for Enhancing Typographic Freedom and Creativity

Flash MX 2004 and MX Pro 2004 include a series of new tools for enhancing your typographic freedom and creativity during the Flash creation process:

Aliased text Ideal for use on mobile devices, aliased text produces crisp and legible text optimized for small size representation. Text is first rastered to a non-anti-aliased state, and then converted to a vector representation, thus ensuring a highly legible font at small display sizes. Aliased text is covered in detail in Chapter 5.

Cascading Style Sheets (CSS) support With the help of the new ActionScript `setStyleSheet` method, you can format the text in your Flash movie using an external style sheet or internal style information.

Rich Video Integration

What is Flash without rich media? In Flash MX, Macromedia introduced a host of new tools for video integration. With Flash MX 2004 and Flash MX Professional 2004 , the application has taken a whopping step forward in its ability to work with imported digital video.

Video Import Wizard When importing video clips, this new multi-step wizard provides additional control over frame ranges to be imported, reusable encoding settings and new capabilities for cropping color correction. For more information about the Video Import Wizard, check out Chapter 31.

External Flash Video (FLV) support You can now play FLV files back from disk directly from an FLV (without the need to pack video into a SWF). This eliminates file duration limitations, and optimizes delivery so long videos can be played back with limited RAM and without having to download the entire file from the web server. External FLV support is covered in Chapter 31.

 Video application integration The new QuickTime FLV Export plug-in enables third-party products that support QuickTime to export video files directly to FLV format. Supported products include Avid, Final Cut Pro, Cleaner, After Effects, Combustion, and the QuickTime Movie Player. If you want to learn more about video application integration, see Chapter 31.

 Enhanced video quality and screen recording Through the use of the Quicktime FLV Exporter, a new encoder is now available that offers greater encoding control and superior image quality for video with larger frame sizes and higher frame rates. For more information about enhanced video recording and screen recording, check out Chapter 31.

Streaming media components Three new components allow FLV and MP3 files to quickly be connected to an interactive controller within your movie. In addition, an event model allows video to trigger other events in your project. Streaming media components are discussed in Hands On 8.

Project Management and Version Control

Flash Project file The Flash Project file (.flp) is a new file type that allows you to group related files (.fla, .as, .jsfl, and other media files such as digital video and audio) into a project that can share common properties. The Flash Project files are then manipulated using the Project Panel. The new Flash Project file format is discussed in Chapter 9.

The Project Panel The Project Panel is a centralized location from which you can manage the properties of a Flash project. With it, you can upload your Flash project to a web server (using the Remote Site model and an FTP client much like that in Dreamweaver) and manage and manipulate the individual files that make up your Flash project. In addition, the Project Panel acts as a powerful version control system, ensuring that the correct file versions are used during editing, and to prevent accidental overwriting. For more information about the Project Panel, refer to Chapter 9.

Application Development and ActionScript Advancements

Flash's scripting language, ActionScript, is probably one of the most powerful tools at your fingertips during the creative process. You'll see incredible enhancements to ActionScript in Flash MX 2004 and Flash MX Professional 2004. In addition, Flash MX Professional 2004 features a series of incredibly robust and powerful tools for application development.

ActionScript 2.0 Arguably one of the most noteworthy ActionScript enhancements in Flash MX 2004 and Flash MX Professional 2004 is the introduction of ActionScript 2.0, the next generation of ActionScript. ActionScript 2.0 features greatly improved support for object-oriented programming and a more robust programming model. For those Flashers who aren't inclined to the intricacies and complexities of the kind of high-level object-oriented programming that characterizes ActionScript 2.0, the original ECMA-26 ActionScript featured in Flash MX (now known as ActionScript 1.0) is available for use in Flash MX 2004 and Flash MX Professional 2004.

Data integration Easily one of the most progressive and exciting features for Flash developers, Flash MX Professional 2004 now boasts a full-featured set of tools that allows you to connect and work with external data sources as never before. Through the use of data binding, you can connect to web services or XML data sources, and then manipulate and display the data through the use of a series of new data-specific components or ActionScript.

Extensibility

Macromedia has always been committed to extensibility. It shows in all of their products, and Flash is hardly any different. Whether you want to create new Components or customize the program's working environment, the tools have always been available to make Flash *more* than the program it was when it was released.

JavaScript Application Programming Interface (JSAPI) The JSAPI is the Holy Grail of extensibility. With it, you can develop new Components, Timeline Effects, behaviors, and even program modules that fit right into Flash's program architecture.

CHAPTER 3

A Tour of the Flash Interface and Getting Started on Your Movie

After you've double-clicked the Flash program icon, you'll face a multitude of panels and windows. Have no fear, fellow Flasher, for by the end of this chapter, you'll be well acquainted with the Flash interface and know how to bend it to your will! To accomplish this amazing feat, you'll start by exploring the main program menu, the toolbars, and the Toolbox. From there, you'll look at the areas of the interface where you'll produce the majority of your creative masterpieces: the Stage and the Timeline. Then you'll look at the myriad of panels in Flash that help you streamline your workflow and leverage your creative potential. After you get a really good idea of how the interface behaves, you are going to learn how to create and manage a new Flash document. Finally, you'll delve into customizing Flash and using the Flash help system.

Topics in this chapter include:

- **The main menu bar**
- **Using the Toolbar on a Windows computer**
- **The Toolbox**
- **The Stage and the work area**
- **Exploring the Timeline**
- **Taking advantage of the Property Inspector**
- **Working with panels**
- **Customizing panels**
- **Working with documents in Flash MX 2004 and Flash MX Pro 2004**
- **Customizing keyboard shortcuts**
- **Getting help in Flash MX 2004 and Flash MX Pro 2004**

Getting Comfortable with the Flash MX 2004 and Flash MX Pro 2004 Workspace

One of the great joys of both Flash MX 2004 and Flash MX Pro 2004 is their interfaces. The programs boast an incredible collection of tools, all of which can be at your fingertips at a moment's notice. The interface, which accommodates a wide range of expertise and working styles, lets you maximize what's really important: creativity. So, let's launch Flash and explore the tools you'll be using.

> By default, Flash loads with a preset configuration of tools. Don't worry about this for the moment because, by the end of the chapter, you'll have learned how to get the interface looking exactly how you want.

The Main Menu Bar

Like many other programs, the main program menu bar lets you access many of Flash's functions, tools, and commands. The main program menu bar appears at the top of the program's interface (see Figure 3.1).

> Many of the commands in the main program menu bar have hot keys associated with them— all of which are customizable. For more information on customizing keyboard shortcuts, see the "Customizing Keyboard Shortcuts" section later in this chapter.

File Menu

The File menu contains many of the primary file-related operations. Because most, if not all, of your Flash projects will either start or finish with one of the options in the File menu, it's good to become familiar with it. The File menu contains the following commands (many of which are covered in subsequent chapters): New, Open, Open from Site, Open Recent, Close, Close All, Save and Compact, Save as Template, Save All, Revert, Import, Export, Publish Settings, Publish Preview, Publish, Page Setup, Print Preview, Print, Send, Edit Sites, and Exit.

Edit Menu

The Edit menu contains commands that let you handle data and manipulate the Flash environment to one degree or another. The commands include Undo, Redo, Cut, Copy, Paste in Center, Paste in Place, Paste Special, Clear, Duplicate, Select All, Deselect All, Find and Replace, Find Next, Timeline (with submenu commands for Cut Frames, Copy Frames, Paste Frames, Clear Frames, Remove Frames, and Select All Frames), Edit Symbols, Edit Selected, Edit in Place, Edit All, Preferences, Customize Tools Panel, Font Mapping, and Keyboard Shortcuts.

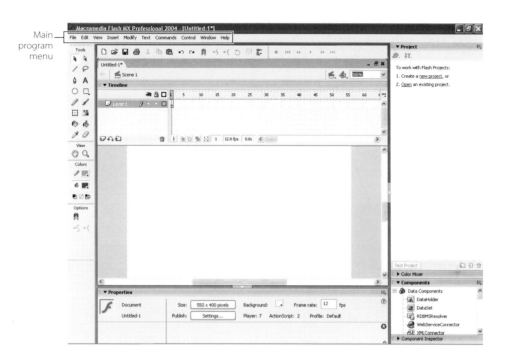

Figure 3.1

Flash MX 2004 and Flash MX Pro 2004's main menu bar

View Menu

The View menu gives you access to a number of commands that let you control how movies (as well as some tools) are viewed. These commands include Goto (with submenu commands First, Previous, Next, Last, and Scene), Zoom In, Zoom Out, Magnification (with submenu commands Fit in Window, 25%, 50%, 100%, 200%, 400%, 800%, Show Frame, and Show All), Preview Mode (with submenu commands for Outlines, Fast, Anti-Alias, Anti-Alias Text, and Full) Work Area, Rulers, Grid (with submenu commands Show Grid and Edit Grid), Guides (with submenu commands Show Guides, Lock Guides, Edit Guides, and Clear Guides), Snapping (with submenu commands for Edit Snap Align, Snap Align, Snap to Grid, Snap to Pixels, and Snap to Objects), Hide Edges, Show Shape Hints, and Show Tab Order.

Insert Menu

The Insert menu lets you add the elements that make a Flash animation. The Insert menu includes New Symbol, Timeline (with submenu commands for Layer, Layer Folder, Motion Guide, Frame, Keyframe, Blank Keyframe, and Create Motion Tween), Timeline Effects (with submenu commands grouped under three categories: Assistants, which contains Copy to Grid and Distributed Duplicate; Effects, which contains Blur, Drop Shadow, Expand, and Explode; and Transform/Transition, under which are, not surprisingly, Transform and Transition), and Scene.

Modify Menu

While the Insert menu lets you insert various elements of a Flash project, the Modify menu enables you to alter those elements. The Modify menu contains the following commands: Document, Convert to Symbol, Break Apart, Bitmap (with submenu commands for Swap Bitmap and Trace Bitmap), Symbol (with submenu commands for Duplicate Symbol and Swap Symbol), Shape (with submenu commands for Smooth, Straighten, Optimize, Convert Lines to Fills, Expand Fill, Soften Fill Edges, Add Shape Hint, and Remove All Hints), Timeline (with submenu commands for Distribute to Layers, Layer Properties, Reverse Frames, Synchronize Symbols, Convert to Keyframes, Clear Keyframe, and Convert to Blank Keyframe), Timeline Effects (with submenu commands for Edit Effects and Remove Effects), Transform (with submenu commands for Free Transform, Distort, Envelope, Scale, Rotate and Skew, Rotate 90 Degrees Clockwise, Rotate 90 Degrees Counterclockwise, Flip Vertical, Flip Horizontal, and Remove Transform), Arrange (with submenu commands for Bring to Front, Bring Forward, Send Backward, Send to Back, Lock, and Unlock All), Align (with submenu commands for Left, Vertical Center, Right, Top, Horizontal Center, Bottom, Distribute Widths, Distribute Heights, Make Same Width, Make Same Height, and To State), Group, and Ungroup.

Text Menu

The Text menu contains the commands for manipulating text attributes and alignment. These include the following: Font (with a submenu of all the available fonts on your system), Size (with a submenu of point sizes), Style (with submenu commands Plain, Bold, Italic, Subscript, and Superscript), Align (with submenu commands Align Left, Align Center, Align Right, and Justify), Tracking (with submenu commands Increase, Decrease, and Reset), Scrollable, Check Spelling, and Spelling Setup.

Commands

The Commands menu, which is new to Flash MX 2004 and Flash MX Pro 2004, contains options that let you manage, manipulate, and run Commands. These include Manage Saved Commands, Get More Commands, and Run Command. In addition, if you have any previously saved commands, they will appear at the bottom of this menu.

Control Menu

The Control menu contains all the commands that you'll need to control the playback of your Flash movie. These include Play, Rewind, Go to End, Step Forward One Frame, Step Backward One Frame, Test Movie, Debug Movie, Test Scene, Test Project, Loop Playback, Play All Scenes, Enable Simple Frame Actions, Enable Simple Buttons, Enable Live Preview, and Mute Sounds.

Window Menu

The Window menu gives you access to some of Flash's most important tools—primarily panels and dialog boxes. It includes the following commands: New Window, Toolbars (with submenu commands Main, Status, and Controller), Project, Properties, Screens, Timeline, Tools, Library, Design Panels (with submenu options for Align, Color Mixer, Color Swatches, Info, Scene, and Transform), Development Panels (with submenu options for Actions, behaviors, Components, Component Inspector, Debugger, Output, and Web Services), Other Panels (with submenu commands for Accessibility, History, Movie Explorer, Strings, and Common Libraries), Hide Panels, Panel Sets (with submenu commands Default, Training Layout, and any Layouts you have previously saved), Save Panel Layout, Cascade, and Tile. A selection list of currently open windows appears at the bottom.

Help Menu

The Help menu offers you access to a myriad of resources to help you out. These include Help, How Do I, What's New, Using Flash, ActionScript Dictionary, Using Components, Flash Exchange, Manage Extensions, Flash Support Center, Transfer Your Software License, and About Flash.

Using Toolbars on a Windows Computer

Flash's toolbars are available only on the Windows operating system (sorry, no toolbars on the Mac). The series of toolbars contain shortcuts for popular menu commands.

> As you can easily access many of the commands in the toolbars through the main program menu, you can easily leave them turned off to conserve precious screen real estate.

Main Toolbar

The Main toolbar (see Figure 3.2), accessible through Window → Toolbars → Main, is similar to the edit/production toolbar of many graphics programs. The default tools (from left to right) include the following: New, Open, Save, Print, Print Preview, Cut, Copy, Paste, Undo, Redo, Snap to Object, Smooth, Straighten, Rotate, Scale, and Align.

Figure 3.2

The Main toolbar

> Although the default location of the Main toolbar is just above the Timeline, it can also float free of the interface or be placed along the left or the right side of the interface. To move it from its default location, simply click it (anywhere off its various buttons) and drag it to the desired location.

> Many of the commands in the Main toolbar (Copy, Cut, Paste, Smooth, Straighten, Rotate, and Scale) are accessible only if you have an object selected on the Stage.

Controller Toolbar

The Controller toolbar (see Figure 3.3), accessible through Window → Toolbars → Controller, gives you access to a series of VCR-like buttons, which enable you to control and test your animation in the Flash Movie Editor.

> Like the Main toolbar, the Controller toolbar can also float free of the interface or be placed along the left or the right side of the interface. To move it from its default location, simply click its surface (avoiding its various buttons), and drag it to the desired location.

Figure 3.3

The Controller toolbar

From left to right, the buttons in the Controller toolbar are Stop, Rewind, Step Back One Frame, Play, Step Forward One Frame, and Go to End.

> If the symbol or scene you are editing doesn't actually feature any kind of animation, the buttons in the Controller toolbar won't be accessible.

The Edit Toolbar

The Edit toolbar (see Figure 3.4), which is located just below the document's title, provides information and controls for editing symbols and scenes. In addition, the Edit toolbar lets you increase or decrease the magnification of the Stage. While, strictly speaking, the Edit toolbar is not a new feature to Flash MX 2004 and Flash MX Pro 2004, it has been renamed and changed so that it can be hidden. In previous versions of Flash, the Edit toolbar was known as the Scene and Symbol bar.

Figure 3.4

The Edit toolbar

Digging into the Toolbox

Imagine you are a cross between an artist and a handyman (or handywoman…or handyperson?). I know the idea is a little silly, but for this section, it's apt. Now, to carry out your job, you need all manner of tools designed both to create art as well as to repair and modify your creations. Where would you find such an odd set of tools in one place? Look no further, for the Flash Toolbox is just what you need!

Macromedia has always had problems with how they name the Toolbox. In some places, it's referred to simply as Tools, while in others it's referred to as the Toolbar. For the sake of this book, we're going to stick with calling it the Toolbox—which is an old-school reference from back in the day (Flash 4), but is still used rather frequently.

Essentially, the Flash Toolbox (Windows → Tools, shown in Figure 3.5), which is partitioned into four sections, is a central location for a whole host of drawing, painting, selection, and modification tools. Let's have a look at each of the sections separately.

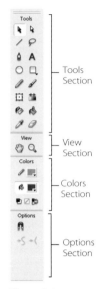

Figure 3.5

The Toolbox

Tools Section

This section of the Toolbox contains tools for drawing, painting, and selecting. Don't worry about understanding how each of the individual tools work at this point: they'll all be covered in subsequent chapters.

View Section

The View section of the Toolbox contains the necessary tools for zooming in on and panning your Flash movie. For more information on how to put the tools in the View section to good use, flip forward to the "Discovering the Stage and the Work Area" section later in this chapter.

The Hand tool is "handy" for panning your movie if you've magnified the Stage to such a degree that all of it isn't visible. A little confused as to what exactly the Stage is? See the "Discovering the Stage and the Work Area" section to find out.

Colors Section

As you would expect, the Colors section of the Toolbox deals exclusively with colors. The functionality of the Colors section, which allows you to set both stroke and fill color, is duplicated in the Stroke and Fill controls in the Property Inspector. Don't worry about how you can use the tools in the Colors section just yet; we'll cover the use of color in Flash in Chapter 4.

Options Section

The Options section of the Toolbox, unlike the previous three sections discussed, doesn't contain a set of static tools. Instead, it contains modifiers for tools selected in any of the other three sections. For example, when you select the Rectangle tool from the Tools section of the Toolbox, the Round Rectangle Radius button appears in the Options section.

At this point, don't worry too much about figuring out how each of the modifiers work, as they'll all be covered in subsequent chapters.

Customizing the Toolbox

While the Toolbox is fairly handy because of what it contains, it itself has not been particularly customizable—until now. In Flash MX 2004 and Flash MX Pro 2004, Macromedia has given you the ability to customize the Toolbox so that it suits your needs. Let's take a look at how.

First, you can easily remove unused tools from the Toolbox by following these steps:

1. Choose Edit → Customize Tools Panel to open the Customize Tools Panel dialog box (see Figure 3.6).

Figure 3.6

The Customize Tools Panel dialog box

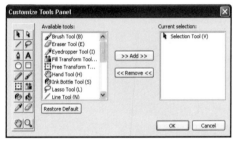

2. Select the tool that you want to remove from the mock-up of the Toolbox located on the left side of the dialog box. You'll notice that two things happen.

   - First, the tool you selected in the mock-up is highlighted in red.

   - Second, the tool appears in the Current Selection list box. If, for example, you selected a tool group (a tool with multiple tools nested below it), all of the tools will appear in the Current Selection list box.

3. Select the tool in the Current Selection list box that you would like to remove from the Toolbox, and click the Remove button `<< Remove <<`.

4. If you are finished, simply click OK to be returned to the main workspace.

Now, if you want to replace one tool with another (effectively reorganizing the Toolbox), just follow these steps:

1. Follow steps 1 through 3 outlined previously to remove a tool from the Toolbox.

2. Select the empty slot (which was just created by removing a tool from the Toolbox). You'll notice that the empty slot is highlighted in red.

3. Select a tool from the Available Tool list box that you want to put in the empty slot.

4. Click the Add button `>> Add >>`. You'll notice that the new tool that you selected now occupies the empty slot.

5. If you are finished, click the OK button.

A tool group is a series of tools that occupy the same space in the Toolbox. You can identify a tool group by the fact that the lead tool (the one that actually appears in the Toolbox) has a small black down arrow in its bottom-right corner. To access other tools in the tool group, simply click and hold down your mouse button over the lead tool and a pop-up menu opens, giving you access to the other tools in the group.

If you want to nest one tool below another (thereby creating a tool group), just follow these steps.

1. Select the tool that you want to convert into a tool group in the Toolbox mock-up on the left side of the Customize Tools Panel dialog box.

2. From the Available Tools list box, select a tool you want to nest below the selected tool.

3. Click the Add button.

4. If you want to add more tools to the tool group, simply repeat steps 1 and 2.

Discovering the Stage and the Work Area

Much as in a play, the Stage is where it all happens in Flash. This is where you craft your eye candy, where all your animations do their thing, and all your creations come to life. Ultimately, what happens on the Stage is what your audience sees after you've exported your movie.

The work area is the gray expanse that surrounds the Stage. You can think of the work area as "backstage," if you want to continue the theatrical metaphor. You can actually place elements in the work area as you would place them on the Stage. The difference is that they won't be visible in the Flash movie itself when it's exported or tested. The great thing is that all the elements placed in the work area behave in exactly the same way as if they were on the Stage. As a result, you could create an animation where a small sphere begins its journey in the work area and ends its journey on the Stage. Figure 3.7 shows the Stage and the work area.

Figure 3.7

The Stage and the work area

You can toggle the visibility of the work area by choosing View → Work Area. Alternatively, you can use the shortcut Cmd+Shift+**W** (Mac)/Ctrl+Shift+**W** (Win).

> Like many of the "toggleable" features in Flash, a check mark next to its command in the View menu indicates that the work area is visible.

Customizing the Stage's Size

The Stage starts out as a blank slate upon which you create and choreograph your glorious Flash creation. As one would expect, the Stage certainly wouldn't be good to anyone if you couldn't mold it to look exactly how you wanted. Flash wouldn't be that exciting if everyone's movie had to be the same size or color. Never fear, Macromedia has built in the ability to change the Stage's size and color.

Figure 3.8

The Document Properties dialog box

To change the Stage's size, follow these steps:

1. Choose Modify → Document or use the shortcut Cmd/Ctrl+**J** to open the Document Properties dialog box (Figure 3.8).

2. Enter pixel values into the Width and Height fields, hit OK, and the dimensions of the Stage will immediately change.

Customizing the Stage's Color

Now, to change the background color of the Stage (and as a result, the background color of the movie), you follow almost the same steps. But, instead of entering a value into the Width and Height fields, click the Background Color swatch and choose a color from the Color Picker.

Alternatively, you can use the Property Inspector to change the look of the Stage. To do this, follow these steps:

1. If it isn't open already, open the Property Inspector by choosing Window → Properties or using the shortcut Cmd/Ctrl+F3.

2. If you don't have any other object selected on the Stage, the Property Inspector will display the Stage's properties.

3. To change the Stage's background color, just click the Background swatch in the Property Inspector. When the color palette opens, select the color you want.

4. Click the Size button to open the Document Properties dialog box. From there, you'll be able to change the dimensions of the Stage by entering a pixel value into the Width and Height fields.

> If you want the changes that you've made to be the default for all the Flash movies you create, click the Make Default button in the Document Properties dialog box.

Adding a Grid to the Stage

During ancient Egyptian times (especially during the New Kingdom, 1550–1070 B.C.), grids were employed during the decoration of tombs to make sure that all of the proportions in the paintings (particularly those of the humans and humaniform gods) were accurate. In the digital age, grids are just as useful for visual designers, illustrators, and of course, Flash designers. You can very easily add a grid to your Stage (see Figure 3.7, shown earlier) so that your illustrations remain proportioned or your objects line up.

To display a grid on your stage, just select View → Grid → Show Grid.

You can just as easily change the properties of the grid when it's displayed. To do so, follow these steps:

1. Choose View → Grid → Edit Grid to open the Grid dialog box (Figure 3.9).

2. To change the color of the grid, simply click the Color swatch, and choose a color from the Color Picker.

3. To dynamically toggle the grid on and off, click the Show Grid radio button.

4. If you want placed objects to snap to the grid (that is, automatically line up with horizontal and vertical axes), click the Snap To Grid radio button.

5. To edit the size of the grid (that is, the distance in pixels between the lines), enter a value into the horizontal field (represented by the left/right arrows) and the vertical field (the up/down arrows).

> If you want to preview how your new grid size will look without having to exit the Grid dialog box, simply toggle the Show Grid option by clicking the Show Grid radio button.

6. To set the accuracy of the snapping, select one of the options from the Snap Accuracy drop-down menu.

7. When you've finished setting the properties of the grid, click OK. If you want the changes that you've made to become the default properties of the grid whenever it's turned on in *any* document, simply click the Save Default button.

Figure 3.9

The Grid dialog box allows you to change the properties of the Stage's grid.

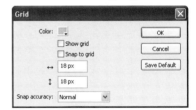

Adding Rulers to the Stage

By default, the Stage doesn't offer any way to get an idea of absolute size (in terms of units of measurement). You can easily change this by turning on a set of rulers that are displayed along the top and left sides of the Stage (see Figure 3.10).

To turn on the rulers, simply choose View → Rulers.

Zooming In on the Stage

The ability to zoom in on your movie is particularly handy. For example, if you were working with a large or complex movie, you could zoom in on a specific location to better isolate a particular detail. To zoom in on a specific location in your movie, follow these steps:

1. Select the Zoom tool from the View section of the Toolbox (or simply hit either the M or Z key).

2. Move the Zoom tool over the Stage, click and drag the mouse so that the line encloses the area you want to magnify, and release the mouse button.

Figure 3.10

The rulers appear on the left and top of the Stage.

To zoom out, simply hold down the Option/Alt key. You'll notice that the magnifying glass icon changes to contain a minus sign instead of a plus sign. From here, click your mouse button until you are zoomed out to where you want. Alternatively, instead of using the Option/Alt key to zoom out, you can click the Reduce button (the one with the minus sign), which appears in the Options section of the Toolbox when the Zoom tool is active.

Panning Your Flash Movie

To pan your Flash movie, follow these steps:

1. Select the Hand tool from the View section of the Toolbox (or simply hit the H key).

2. Click anywhere on the Stage, hold down your mouse button, and drag the Stage to the location you want. When you are finished, release your mouse button.

Exploring the Timeline

If the Stage is where "it all happens," the Timeline is what "makes it happen." The Timeline, which is discussed in depth in Chapter 10, is the tool you employ when you add any kind of change over time to your Flash movie (see Figure 3.11).

Without going into too much depth, the Timeline, by default, occupies the uppermost portion of the Flash interface and is broken up into three primary elements: the playhead, frames, and layers.

The Timeline, like many other interface elements within Flash MX, can be both minimized and docked/undocked. For more information on how to dock, undock, and minimize the Timeline, see the "Customizing Panels" section later in this chapter (the Timeline isn't a panel *per se*, but the same principles apply). You can also get a step-by-step tutorial about how to create a custom panel layout in Hands On 1.

The Playhead

When you play your Flash animation, the playhead travels across the Timeline (horizontally) at a consistent rate. As the playhead moves through each of the individual frames, the contents are displayed on the Stage, thereby creating the animation.

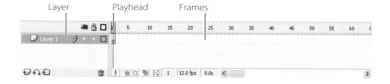

Figure 3.11

The Flash Timeline

Although Chapter 10 covers the ins and outs of the Timeline and the playhead, it's important to know that you can move the playhead manually. You can either click the frame's location on the Timeline header (the strip on the top of the Timeline where the frame numbers—in increments of five—are located), or drag the playhead to the desired location.

Frames

Frames are pretty much the heart and soul of the Timeline. Each frame represents a moment of time in an animation. In addition, each frame can contain unique content that changes from frame to frame.

Strictly speaking, what are referred to as *frames* in the Timeline are not actually frames, but *cells* (which is a word purloined form traditional pen-and-paper animation). However, not only will you not hear any other Flash users refer to them as cells or the word *cells* used in any other book, but Macromedia doesn't ever really use the word. So, for the purposes of this book, we'll use the term *frames* as well.

As the playhead moves across the Timeline, the content of each of the frames appears on the Stage.

Your animation's frame rate determines the actual speed at which the animation plays. For more information on frame rate, see Chapter 10.

Layers

Flash animations are not just constructed horizontally (with frames) but also vertically with layers. Each layer contains a single element or animation. As a result, you can have many layers with many different elements and animations, thereby creating a complex movie.

Layers give you the ability to separate content. For especially complex Flash movies, this is a good way to keep track of your work. To learn more about layers and how you can alter their appearance, see Chapter 8.

Taking Advantage of the Property Inspector

The Property Inspector (see Figure 3.12), which was introduced back in Flash MX, is a tool you'll undoubtedly find yourself using quite frequently during the creative process. Essentially, it serves as a doorway to the properties of any given object (be it some text, a shape, a button, a Movie Clip, or a component).

Figure 3.12

The Property Inspector is a dynamic tool that displays the properties of any currently selected object.

Like many other interface elements within Flash MX 2004 and Flash MX Pro 2004, the Property Inspector can be both collapsed/expanded and docked/undocked. For more information on how to dock, undock, and minimize the Property Inspector, see the "Customizing Panels" section later in this chapter (the Property Inspector isn't a panel *per se*, but the same principles apply). You can also get a step-by-step tutorial about how to create a custom panel layout in Hands On 1.

Its power is that it's a dynamic tool. By *dynamic*, I mean that the options displayed change depending on what sort of object you select. For example, if you select a string of text, you'll be able to change its font, color, and size. On the other hand, when you click a shape, you'll be able to change its stroke, fill, and dimensions. So, you see, it's a pretty powerful and useful tool. To access the Property Inspector, all you need to do is select Window → Properties or use the shortcut Cmd/Ctrl+F3.

To access less common attributes of a given object, all you need to do is click the expander arrow (the Down arrow in the bottom-right corner of the Property Inspector).

Working with Panels

Panels are arguably one of the most important aspects of both the Flash MX 2004 and Flash MX Pro 2004 interfaces. With them, you can access a whole bevy of incredibly powerful tools that work with any number of elements within Flash MX.

One of the coolest things about panels in Flash is that they can be integrated into the overall interface (as opposed to *floating* around the workspace). *Docking*, as the process is called, makes it considerably easier for you to access tools and information while maximizing your workspace (see Figure 3.13).

To learn more about docking panels (as well as their many other workspace-streamlining features), see the "Customizing Panels" section later in this chapter. In addition, you can check out a step-by-step tutorial on customizing panels in Hands On 1.

Figure 3.13

The default Flash interface complete with docked panels

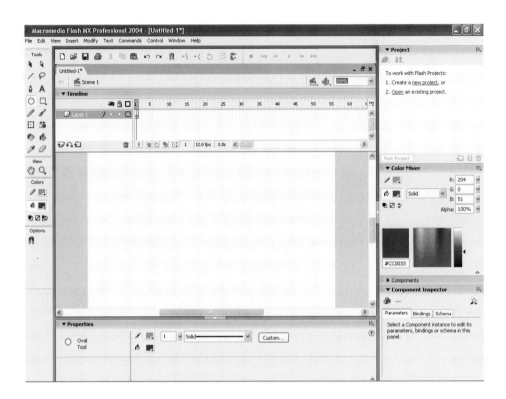

On top of this, you can easily open, close, move, and resize panels to streamline your work environment (and therefore your creative process).

Each panel, regardless of its purpose, has an Options drop-down menu accessible by clicking the icon in its upper-right corner. Although some panels won't have many options in this menu, there will be some that have many options.

It's extremely important to remember that, due to the differences between the two versions of the program, Flash MX Pro 2004 has some additional panels that aren't available in Flash MX 2004.

At this point, it's a good time to explore each of the panels available in Flash.

When you initially open Flash (regardless of which version of the most recent release), you'll see the default organization of preset docked panels. If you open any new panels, they won't appear docked, but instead they will be free floating. Don't worry, you can easily dock them if you so desire.

Project Panel

The Project panel (see Figure 3.14), which you access by choosing Window → Project (or Shift+F8), provides you with a centralized location for managing and manipulating Flash projects. For more information on the Project panel or Flash projects, check out Chapter 9.

Figure 3.14

The Project panel

Align Panel

The Align panel (see Figure 3.15), which you can open by choosing Window → Design Panels → Align (Cmd/Ctrl+**K**), enables you to align objects (or groups of selected objects) according to a series of preset criteria—each of which is represented by a button. For more information on using the Align panel, see Chapter 6.

Figure 3.15

The Align panel

Color Mixer Panel

The Color Mixer panel (see Figure 3.16), accessible by selecting Window → Design Panels → Color Mixer (Shift+F9), gives you the ability to create colors, using RGB, HSB, or Hexadecimal Code, and save them as swatches to the Color Swatches panel. The Color Mixer panel also enables you to assign colors to either the stroke or fill. For more information, see Chapter 4.

Figure 3.16

The Color Mixer panel

Color Swatches Panel

The Color Swatches panel (see Figure 3.17), accessible by choosing Window → Design Panels → Color Swatches (Cmd/Ctrl+F9), helps you organize, load, save, and remove individual colors from the currently used color palette. For more information on using the Color Swatches panel, see Chapter 4.

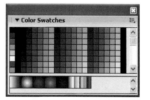

Figure 3.17

The Color Swatches panel

Info Panel

The Info panel (Figure 3.18), which is accessible by going to Window → Design Panels → Info (or by using the shortcut Cmd/Ctrl+**I**), gives you the ability to numerically change the dimensions (in the Width and Height fields) and the position (in the X and Y fields) of a given selected object. The bottom portion of the Info panel contains information about the point your mouse cursor is currently placed over. The lower-left corner displays the color of the point under the mouse cursor (in RGB format), and the lower-right corner of the panel provides information (in X/Y coordinates) as to the mouse's exact current position.

Figure 3.18

The Info panel

Figure 3.19

The Scene panel

Scene Panel

The Scene panel (see Figure 3.19), accessible by choosing Window → Design Panels → Scene (or Shift+F2), gives you the ability to navigate between, rename, add new, and delete scenes. To learn more about scenes and the Scene panel, see Chapter 11.

Figure 3.20

The Transform panel

Transform Panel

Similar to the Info panel, the Transform panel (see Figure 3.20) gives you the ability to numerically manipulate a selected object. The top portion of the panel includes two fields that allow you to scale an object horizontally or vertically. You can open the Transform panel by selecting Window → Design Panels → Transform or by using the shortcut Cmd/Ctrl+**T**.

When scaling an object with the Transform panel, you can constrain the proportions by clicking the Constrain check box.

The bottom portion of the Transform panel allows you to either rotate or skew, in degrees, the currently selected object.

Actions Panel

The Actions panel (see Figure 3.21), which can be opened by choosing Window → Development Panels → Actions or by using the shortcut F9, is where you attach ActionScripts to either objects or frames. The Actions panel enables you to either choose from a preset list of ActionScripts or manually write your own. For more information on the Actions panel, see Chapter 14.

Figure 3.21

The Actions panel

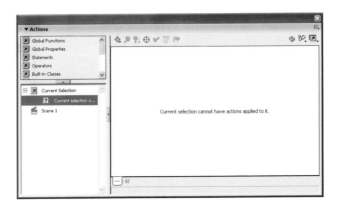

Behavior Panel

The Behavior panel (see Figure 3.22), which is new to Flash MX 2004 and Flash MX Pro 2004 and can be accessed by choosing Window → Development Panels → Behaviors (or Shift+F3), provides a centralized location for adding and manipulating behaviors, which are premade chunks of ActionScript that allow you to add interactivity to your Flash movie without ever having to write a single line of code.

Figure 3.22

The Behavior panel

ActionScript Debugger

Because ActionScript is a scripting language, it's natural that Macromedia would include a debugger. The ActionScript Debugger (see Figure 3.23), which was introduced in Flash 5 and is accessible by choosing Window → Development Panels → Debugger (or Shift+F4), lets you troubleshoot troublesome ActionScript. Chapter 22 explores the ActionScript Debugger in detail.

Movie Explorer

The Movie Explorer (see Figure 3.24) is a handy little tool introduced in Flash 5. Accessible by choosing Window → Other Panels → Movie Explorer, or by using the shortcut Option/Alt+F3, the Movie Explorer provides central access to all your movie's assets. From this central location, you can search for an object or element by name, display and alter the properties of a given element, and replace all instances of a font with another font. For a better look at the Movie Explorer, see Chapter 9.

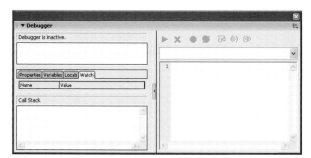

Figure 3.23

The ActionScript Debugger

Figure 3.24

The Movie Explorer

Figure 3.25

The Output window

Output Window

The Output window (see Figure 3.25), which cannot be docked with other panels, is a snazzy little tool that, once you've exported your Flash movie, provides you with a read-out of the file size for all scenes, objects, text, symbols, and instances. You can open the Output window by choosing Window → Development Panels → Output, or by pressing the F2 key.

Figure 3.26

The Web Services panel

Web Services Panel

The Web Services panel (see Figure 3.26), which you access by choosing Window → Development Panels → Web Services, is the gateway to bringing dynamic data into your Flash movie. With this panel, you designate sources of external data (such as XML or a web service) that can then be bound to Flash MX Pro 2004's new data components.

Figure 3.27

The Accessibility panel

Accessibility Panel

Introduced in Flash MX, the Accessibility panel (see Figure 3.27) is an incredible step forward in making Flash content accessible to audiences with a variety of disabilities (who use a range of different technologies to access the Web). You can open the Accessibility panel by choosing Window → Other Panels → Accessibility. The Accessibility panel will be discussed in Chapter 30.

Figure 3.28

The Components panel

Components Panel

The Components panel (see Figure 3.28), accessible by choosing Window → Development Panels → Components, is the central repository for Flash's specialized, premade, complex Movie Clips with already defined parameters. Components are extremely handy if you want to create relatively complex user interface components (such as scrollable windows or drop-down menus) with a minimum of muss and fuss.

Component Inspector Panel

The Component Inspector panel (see Figure 3.29), accessible by choosing Window → Development Panels → Component Inspector, is the tool by which you edit the parameters of Components that you've added to your movie using the Components panel. In addition, the Component Inspector panel lets you bind data from another component or an external data source such as a web service or XML to a given component for use within your Flash movie.

Figure 3.29

The Component Inspector panel

Start Page

The Start Page (see Figure 3.30) is a handy utility that acts as a central location for the logical first tasks that a user would likely choose when they open up Flash to start a work session. With it, you can open a recent document, create a new document, or create a new document based on a template. In addition, the Start Page provides you with links to various helpful places on the Macromedia website.

Library

The Library (see Figure 3.31), which can be opened by choosing Window → Library (or Cmd/Ctrl+**L**), is a repository of all of the symbols that you create or use for your Flash movie. Whether a Movie Clip, Button, or Graphic symbol, the Library has it all. For more information on the Library, see Chapter 9.

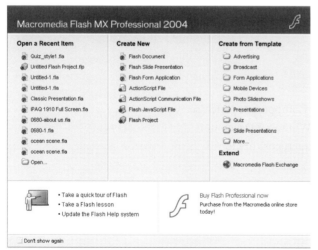

Figure 3.30

The Start Page

Figure 3.31

The Library

Common Libraries

The Common Libraries, which are accessible by choosing Window → Other Panels → Common Libraries, are slightly different from the Library itself. Where the Library contains only those symbols associated with the currently open Flash movie, the Common Libraries contain a series of symbol groups (Buttons, Learning Interactions, and Sounds). Each symbol group has a bunch of premade symbols that come with Flash. The Common Libraries give you lots of symbols so that you don't have to create them yourself.

History Panel

Easily one of the most powerful features in both Flash MX 2004 and Flash MX Pro 2004, the History panel (see Figure 3.32), which you access by choosing Window → Other Panels → History, shows a list of the steps that you've performed in the active document since you created or opened that document. You can use the History panel to undo or redo individual steps or multiple steps at once. In addition, you can apply steps from the History panel to the same object or to a different object in the document. Beyond using the recorded steps within the same document, you can save the steps (or any subset of steps within the overall sequence) as commands that can be used in any other document.

Figure 3.32

The History panel

Strings Panel

The Strings panel (see Figure 3.33), which you access by choosing Window → Other Panels → Strings, is a new feature to Flash MX 2004 and Flash MX Pro 2004 that facilitates multilingual support. The panel facilitates the publication of multilingual movies by tracking strings for localization.

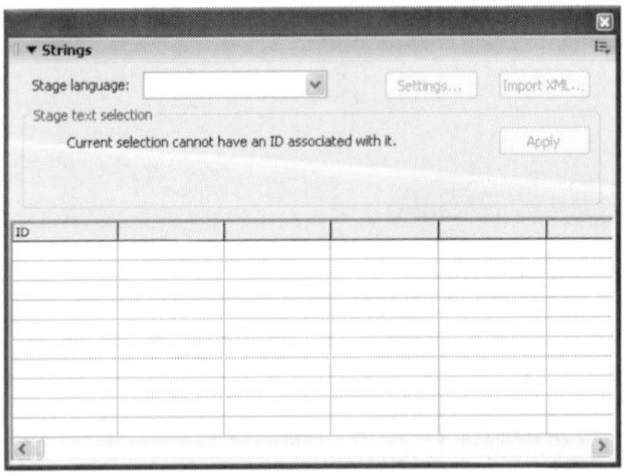

Figure 3.33

The Strings panel

Customizing Panels

One of the great things about the Flash MX 2004 and Flash MX Pro 2004 user interfaces is that they have evolved to such a point that all elements fit seamlessly and efficiently together to create an extremely usable work environment. This is no great surprise because, with the increasing complexity of Flash itself, screen real estate has become increasingly precious.

One of the most obvious features of the interfaces is that their panels, as mentioned before, are dockable and collapsible/expandable.

When you dock a panel, you physically combine it with another element of the interface. If you dock two floating panels, you create a floating "mega" panel (see Figure 3.34).

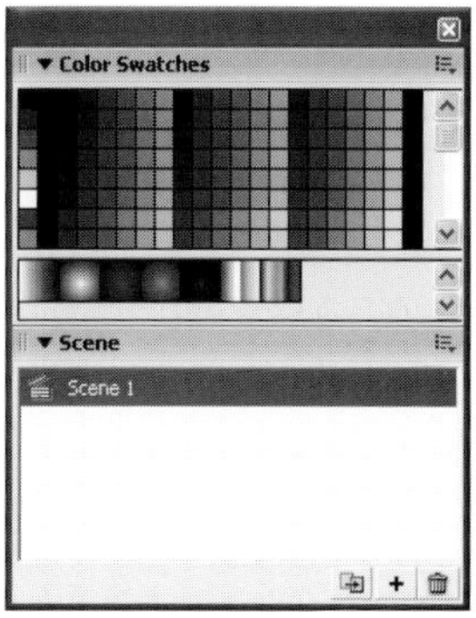

On the other hand, as illustrated in Figure 3.35, you can also dock a panel with a section of the underlying interface (underlying in the sense of what is below a floating panel) to create an area where all of your commonly used panels reside. Ultimately, docking panels makes it considerably easier for you to access tools and information while maximizing your workspace.

Given the sheer amount of tools in Flash MX 2004 and Flash MX Pro 2004, the interface has become a little crowded. As a result, Macromedia has provided users with the ability to expand and collapse panels, thereby economizing on space while still keeping the necessary tools at their fingertips (see Figure 3.36).

Figure 3.34

The Scene panel and Color Swatches panel have been combined to form a floating "mega" panel.

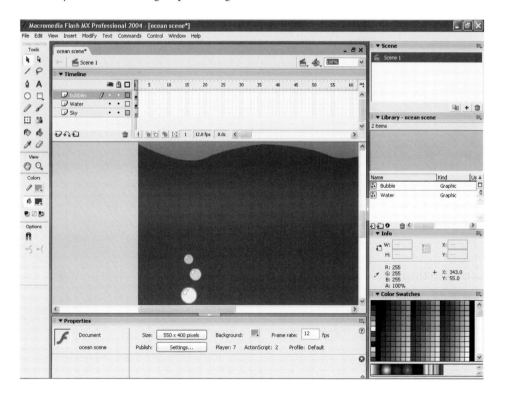

Figure 3.35

Flash MX interface with docked panels

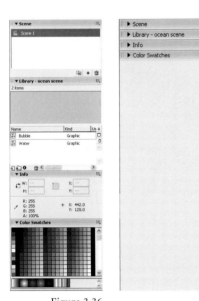

Figure 3.36

The left screen shows a series of panels that have been collapsed, and the right one shows the same panels expanded.

With all of the docking/undocking and collapsing/expanding that can go on in Flash MX 2004 and Flash MX Pro 2004, there is any number of permutations for interface elements. You can certainly experiment and develop an interface layout that best suits your needs.

To learn more about customizing panels, see Hands On 1, which follows this chapter.

Working with Documents in Flash MX 2004 and Flash MX Pro 2004

Arguably one of the most fundamental things you need to learn about working with any program for the first time is the various ways you go about creating and saving documents. Flash is hardly any different. Even though it might seem a little elementary to some, it's a good idea to get a solid understanding of how to create, open, and save documents in Flash. Beyond the basics, Flash also offers some additional related topics that are important to learn if you are just starting out.

In this section of the chapter, you are going to learn how to create a new document, work with Flash templates, open a recently created document, navigate between multiple open documents, save your document, and revert to a previously saved version of your document.

Creating a New Document

Obviously, one of the most elemental things you need to do when first starting to work with a program is to create a new document. Unless you've turned it off, the Start Page will automatically open when you launch Flash. From there, you'll be able to choose from a list of common tasks (opening a recent document, creating a new document, and creating a template-based document). However, if you've turned off the Start Page (which you accomplish by clicking the Don't Show Again check box located in the lower-left corner), Flash MX 2004 and Flash MX Pro 2004 always create a new document for you when you launch the program. However, there are definitely times when you are going to want to create a new document manually.

Strictly speaking, while the act of creating a new movie in Flash is not something new to Flash MX 2004 and Flash MX Pro 2004, the process by which you do it has changed from previous versions of the program.

To create a new document in Flash, just follow these steps:

1. Choose File → New.

2. When the New Document dialog box opens (see Figure 3.37), choose from the file types listed in the Type list box.

> For a description of the different file types (file extensions, uses, and so on), simply keep an eye on the Description section of the New Document dialog box as you click on the various options.

3. When you've made your selection, click OK.

Creating a New Flash Movie from a Template

While not *really* a new feature, the number of templates has been greatly increased in Flash MX 2004 and Flash MX Pro 2004. So, what exactly are templates? Well, templates are files that allow you to bypass many of the common tasks required to create a great-looking Flash movie. Depending on which template you select, there might already be a detailed layout and design (complete with interactivity) into which you just need to drop your custom content.

To create a new Flash movie based on a template, just follow these steps:

1. Choose File → New. The New Document dialog box opens.

2. Click the Templates tab in the New Document dialog box.

3. The templates section of the New Document dialog box (see Figure 3.38) gives you access to a series of templates organized into categories. From here, select one of the types of templates located in the Category list box.

4. From here, select one of the specific types of templates that appear in the Templates list box.

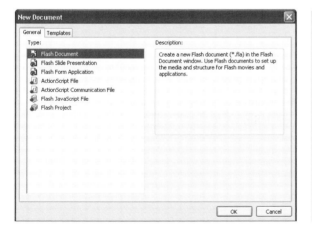

Figure 3.37

The New Document dialog box lets you choose the type of new file you want to create.

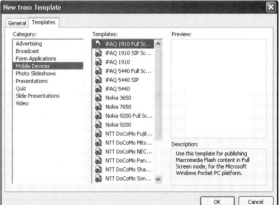

Figure 3.38

Access the templates section of the New Document dialog box by clicking the Templates tab.

> You'll notice that when you select a template from the Templates list box, a description appears.

5. Once you've made your selection, click OK, and you'll be pushed back to the Stage.

> Not only will the actual template display on the Stage, but instructions, located on a guide layer of the Timeline, will also appear. Click each of the keyframes in the guide layer to get a different set of instructions.

Opening a Recent Document

As the number of Flash movies you are working on at any given time increases, you are going to want to switch back and forth between them. Instead of the regular route of using the Open command in the File menu, Macromedia has provided somewhat of a shortcut for opening recent documents. Let's take a look at how:

1. Choose File → Open Recent.
2. Select the file that you want to open from the submenu that opens.

Navigating Between Multiple Documents

One of the most important enhancements to the Flash interface (in both versions of the program) is the addition of the multiple document interface. Taking a note from Dreamweaver MX, this new tabbed interface (see Figure 3.39) lets you open multiple documents at any given time, and then move fluidly between them simply by clicking their associated link to bring them into focus.

Saving Your Document

Obviously, the whole point of creating a Flash movie is so that you can keep it. This entails saving. To save your document, just follow these steps:

> When a document contains unsaved changes, an asterisk (*) appears after the document name in the document title bar, the application title bar, and the document tab. When you save the document, the asterisk is removed.

1. Open the File menu, and choose one of the Save options:
    - Select Save if you just want to save the current document you are working on.
    - Select Save and Compact if you want to reduce the overall size of your Flash file.

- Select Save As if you want to save a file that you've already saved under a new filename.
- Select Save All if you want to save all of the currently open documents.

2. When the Save As dialog box opens, navigate to the location in which you want to save the file, enter a filename into the File Name field, and click Save.

> If you want to save your file as a Flash MX file (instead of a Flash MX 2004/Flash MX Pro 2004 file), select Flash MX Document (*.fla) from the File Type drop-down menu in the Save As dialog box.

Reverting to a Previously Saved Document

Hey, we all make mistakes. You are going to make mistakes (or a whole series of mistakes) when you are learning to work with Flash—it's a fact of life. The frustrating thing about many programs is that if you find you've walked down a path in your design that no longer seems fruitful, or even if you've royally screwed something up, you cannot throw all of those changes out and go back to a version of the file in which you hadn't messed things up. The super-cool thing about Flash MX 2004 and Flash MX Pro 2004 is that you *can.* Here's how: Choose File → Revert.

Document Tabs

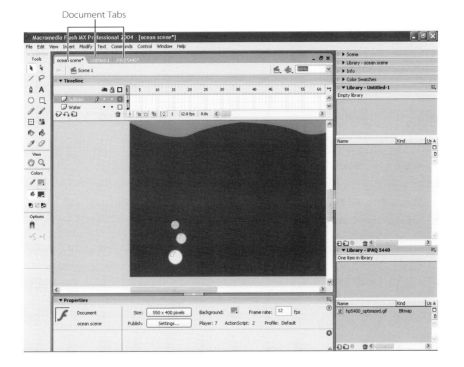

Figure 3.39

The multiple document interface lets you have numerous documents open at the same time and navigate fluidly between them.

Saving a Flash Movie as a Template

Figure 3.40

The Save As Template dialog box

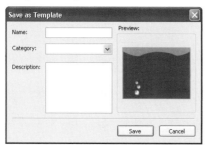

Earlier in this section, you learned how to create a new Flash movie based on one of the premade templates that Flash MX 2004 and Flash MX Pro 2004 ship with. The neat thing about Flash is that you can go in the *other* direction: turning a Flash movie that you're working on into a template for future use. To do this, just follow these steps:

1. Choose File → Save as Template.

2. When the Save As Template dialog box appears (Figure 3.40), enter a name for your template into the Name field.

3. Select a category for your new template from the Category drop-down menu.

4. Enter a description of your new template into the Description field.

> The Preview section of the Save As Template dialog box shows what your template will look like when you preview it in the Templates section of the New Document dialog box.

5. When you've finished, simply click the Save button.

Customizing Keyboard Shortcuts

Keyboard shortcuts are a quick and easy way to access a program's functions. Up until now, however, most programs offered the user only an immutable set of shortcuts. But Flash MX 2004 and MX Pro 2004, as well as many of the other Macromedia programs, offer a Keyboard Shortcuts editor that lets you use existing shortcuts, create your own shortcuts, and edit existing shortcuts. To customize Flash's keyboard shortcuts, just follow these steps:

To redefine a command's shortcut:

1. Choose Edit → Keyboard Shortcuts to open the Keyboard Shortcuts editor.

2. If it isn't already selected, choose Macromedia Standard from the Current drop-down menu at the top of the Keyboard Shortcuts editor (Figure 3.41).

3. Click the Duplicate Set button 🔳 just to the right of the Current set drop-down menu.

4. When the Duplicate dialog box opens, enter a name into the Duplicate Name field, and click OK. Notice that the name of the duplicate set that you've just created appears in the Current drop-down menu.

5. Now choose the specific group of commands that you want to work with from the Commands drop-down menu.

6. If you've chosen Drawing Menu Commands or Test Movie Menu Commands, click the plus sign to expand the command category (File, Edit, View, Insert, and so on) that you want to work with. If you've chosen Drawing Tools or Actions Panel Commands, skip to step 9.

7. Select the specific command that you want. Notice that the existing shortcuts attached to that command appear to the right of the command (the shortcut will also appear in the Shortcuts text box just below).

8. Select the command's existing shortcut in the Shortcuts text box.

9. Click the Remove Shortcut (−) button ⁻ to strip the command's existing shortcut.

10. Press the Add Shortcut (+) button ⁺; the Press Key field will automatically go live.

11. Press the key combination that you want to add; the key combination appears in the Press Key field.

12. Click the Change button to assign the new shortcut to the command.

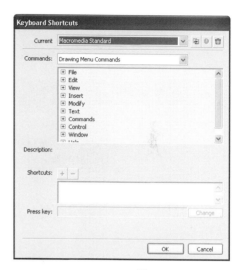

Figure 3.41

The Keyboard Short-cuts editor

> If your key combination is already assigned to another command, Flash will alert you and let you either reassign the shortcut or simply cancel it.

13. When you've finished, click OK, and the new keyboard shortcut will be assigned.

Using Flash Help

Macromedia has provided Flash users with a panopoly of resources for when you're in a jam and can't quite figure something out. You can access many help options through the Help menu, including:

Help (Help → Help) Provides centralized help function with content that is accessible through a content list, an index, or a search engine.

ActionScript Dictionary (Help → ActionScript Dictionary) Provides a syntactical reference (organized alphabetically) to the ActionScript language.

How Do I (Help → How Do I) Provides a topically-based help function designed to aid you in addressing specific tasks.

Using Components (Help → Using Components) Provides a complete guide for working with Components.

Flash Exchange (Help → Flash Exchange) Takes you to the Flash Exchange at Macromedia's website. There, you can find and download hundreds of components of all types authored by Flash developers from around the world.

Manage Extensions (Help → Manage Extensions) Launches the Macromedia Extension Manager, a handy little app that keeps track of any additional component libraries you have installed.

Flash Support Center (Help → Flash Support Center) Provides up-to-date information on the latest Flash developments and technical issues. (It's sometimes referred to as the *Developers Resource Center.*)

Inspirational Design Model

For those whose lives revolve around interactive digital media, promoting yourself online is important. The kicker is that there are so many personal promotion sites out there that it's hard to get noticed. Well, it's hard if you don't do something outstandingly creative, that is.

A great example (chockful of inspiration goodness) of an amazingly creative self-promotional Flash site is RixK (see Figure 3.42). Created by Ki Wan Kim, RixK (www.rixk.com) features a simple (yet very effective) interface full of the kinds of detailed, whimsical touches that separates good Flash design from great Flash design.

Figure 3.42

RixK

© RixK.com

Creating your Own Custom Panel Layout

As mentioned in the previous chapter, Flash MX 2004 and Flash MX Professional 2004 have remarkably malleable interfaces. Not happy with which panels are visible, where they are located, or if they are docked or floating? You can easily change the interface to suit your needs. In this Hands On, we're going to take a look at the steps that you need to take to create a customized interface. At the end of the Hands On, you are going to learn how to save your customized interface so that you can load it up whenever you want.

Docking Two Panels to Create a Mega Floating Panel

To dock two panels to create a mega floating panel (Figure H1.1), follow these steps:

1. Open any two panels by using the Window menu.

Figure H1.1

You can combine two or more panels to create a mega floating panel.

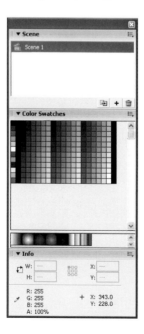

Remember that when you initially open up Flash, the panel or panels you want to use to create your mega floating panel might be docked with the interface. To undock them, follow the
instructions later in this Hands On.

2. Click the gripper region of the panel's title bar (represented by the small dots on the
   left side of the title bar) and drag it toward the target panel (Figure H1.2). Notice that
   a ghost image of the panel appears as you drag your mouse.

You'll notice that your cursor changes when it moves over the gripper region of the panel's
title bar.

3. Move your cursor over the target panel.

4. When a black highlight appears in the target area (Figure H1.3), release the mouse
   button.

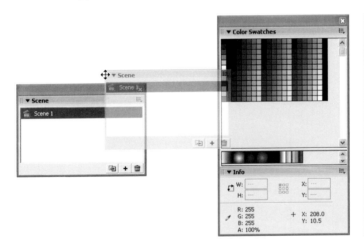

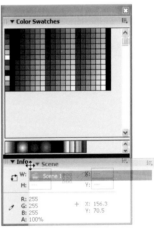

Figure H1.2

**When you're combining two
panels, a ghost image of the
dragged panel appears as
you're moving it toward the
target panel.**

Figure H1.3

**When you see a black highlight
appear in the target area, release
your mouse button to combine
the two panels.**

Docking a Panel with the Underlying Interface

To dock a panel with the underlying interface, follow these steps:

1. Use the Window menu to open the panel that you want to dock with the underlying interface.

2. Click the gripper region of the panel's title bar and drag it over the area of the interface you want to dock it with.

> Flash MX 2004 and Flash MX Pro 2004 let you dock a panel to the left, bottom, and right of the interface.

3. When the black highlight appears in the target area (Figure H1.4), release your mouse button and the panel will automatically dock.

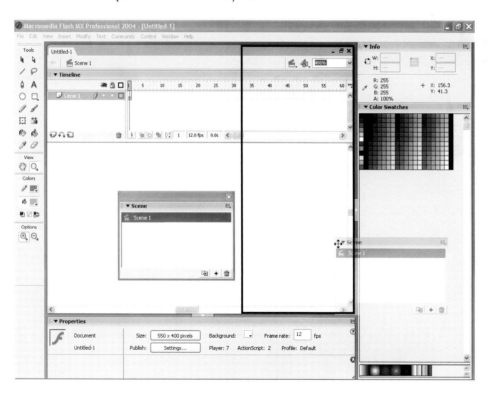

Figure H1.4

Regardless of where in the interface you want to dock the panel, a black highlight will appear indicating the target region.

Undocking a Panel

While we've looked at combining two panels to make a mega floating panel as well as how to dock a panel with the underlying interface, we haven't explored how you can undock a panel from the underlying interface, thereby making it a floating panel. Let's take a look at that now.

1. Open the docked panel that you want to undock from the interface.

2. Click the gripper region of the panel's title bar and drag it away from the docked area out into the middle of the Stage.

3. When you've reached an area of the interface where you don't get a black highlight (Figure H1.5), simply release your mouse button.

Figure H1.5

When you drag your docked panel away from the underlying interface to an area where you don't get a black highlight, release your mouse button, and you'll be rewarded with a floating panel.

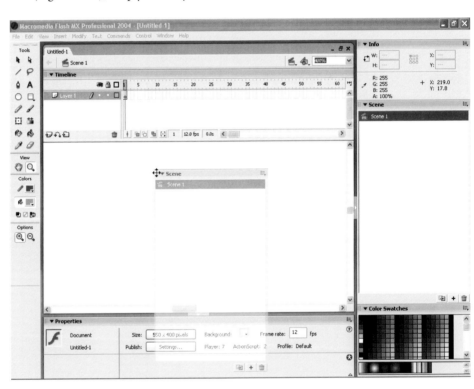

Saving a Custom Panel Layout

After working with Flash MX 2004 and Flash MX Pro 2004 for a while, you'll get to the point where you develop a panel layout most conducive to your working style. So you don't want to have to constantly re-create the layout every time you fire up the program, Flash MX 2004 and Flash MX Pro 2004 let you save your layout so it is accessible from the same location as a preset panel layout. Let's take a look at how:

1. Using the techniques outlined in the previous section of this Hands On, create a panel layout that is most conducive to your working style.

Figure H1.6

The Save Panel Layout dialog box

2. Choose Window → Save Panel Layout. The Save Panel Layout dialog box opens (see Figure H1.6).

3. In the Save Panel Layout dialog box, enter a name for your custom layout in the field.

4. When you've finished, click OK.

5. From here, you can access your custom panel layout by choosing Window → Panel Sets.

PART II

Creating and Manipulating Visual Content

As you *learned in Chapter 1, both Flash MX 2004 and Flash MX Professional 2004 can create an incredible array of exciting interactive products. Be it traditional websites, webtoons, kiosks, or other more adventurous applications, the common thread is that the overwhelming majority are visually based. This is no great surprise as one of the greatest aspects of Flash MX 2004 and Flash MX Pro 2004 is that they are vector based as opposed to bitmap based, allowing you to create some truly stunning visual imagery.*

Ultimately, this means that you'll be spending a fair amount of your creative energy focusing on crafting the visual aspects of your beautiful Flash creation. As a result, Macromedia has included an extremely wide variety of tools designed to create, manage, and manipulate all the visual aspects of your Flash movie.

CHAPTER 4

Creating Static Content with the Painting and Drawing Tools

The good people at Macromedia have molded Flash into a topnotch animation program as well as a graphics program of surprising power. The program boasts a whole bevy of powerful and usable tools for creating both vector and bitmap graphics. In this chapter, you'll spend time exploring these tools. You'll start off by looking at the various selection tools that are available. Then, you'll learn about the line and shape drawing tools: the Pencil tool, the Brush tool, the Pen tool, the Ink Bottle tool, the Paint Bucket tool, and the Dropper tool. In addition, you'll learn how to work with the Eraser tool and manipulate stroke and fill with the Property Inspector. You'll close the chapter by exploring how to create and manipulate digital color in Flash.

- Selecting static content for manipulation

- Drawing lines

- Drawing shapes

- Using the Pencil, Brush, Pen, Subselection, Ink Bottle, and Paint Bucket tools

- Sampling with the Dropper tool

- Using the Eraser tool

- Changing a shape's stroke with the Property Inspector

- Altering a shape's fill with the Property Inspector

- Working with digital color

Selecting Items for Manipulation

Flash MX 2004 and Flash MX Pro 2004 pride themselves on having a fairly extensive set of tools that you can use to select lines, shapes, text, groups, symbols, buttons, and a multitude of other items to place on the Stage. Every item you place on the Stage has a tool to select it (or parts of it). In this section, you'll quickly explore each of the various selection tools available, including the Arrow tool, the Subselection tool, and the Lasso tool.

> Because the Pen tool and the Subselection tool are intrinsically connected, it is difficult to separate them in a discussion such as this. A more in-depth discussion of the Subselection tool's functionality (especially in conjunction with the Pen tool) is provided in the section "Drawing with the Pen Tool" later in this chapter.

Using the Arrow tool to Select Content

Located in the top-left corner of the Toolbox, the Arrow tool ▶ lets you select and move single or multiple items about the Stage. The Arrow tool also allows you to change the shape of an unselected line, stroke, or object.

> Selecting an object with the Arrow tool is the first step in editing an object's properties with the Property Inspector.

Selecting Content

Selecting an object with the Arrow tool is actually quite simple: Just point and click. However, a few tips and tricks will help you better take advantage of its functionality. First, when you select an ungrouped object, a checkered pattern appears over it to indicate that it is currently selected.

> If you're interested in learning more about the difference between a grouped and an ungrouped object, as well as how you group and ungroup objects, see Chapter 6.

Figure 4.1

The top three are ungrouped objects selected with the Arrow tool, and the bottom three are grouped objects selected with the Arrow tool.

On the other hand, a grouped object that has been selected has a thin rectangular box around it. Figure 4.1 illustrates the difference between grouped objects that have been selected with the Arrow tool and ungrouped objects selected with the Arrow tool.

Many objects, especially if they have been drawn with one of the shape tools, usually have both a fill and a stroke. Therefore, if you want to select the entire object, you'll need to select both the fill and stroke separately. You can also double-click an object's fill to select both the fill and stroke. Alternatively, you can select both the stroke and fill, and then group them together by selecting Modify → Group. After grouping them, you only need to click the object to select the group.

Figure 4.2

The Arrow tool changes when you move it close to the unselected line, stroke, or shape.

To deselect an item that you've selected with the Arrow tool, click anywhere else on the Stage, choose Edit → Deselect All, hit your Esc key, or use the keyboard shortcut Cmd+Shift+**A** (Mac)/Ctrl+Shift+**A** (Win).

Moving Content

To move an object with the Arrow tool, select it, drag it to the desired location, and release your mouse button. If you have grouped a series of objects, the process works the same way when you want to move the group.

Many objects are made up of both a stroke and fill. If you don't select both and attempt to move the object, the unselected portion of the object will be left behind.

Figure 4.3

You get a preview of the new position of the line, stroke, or shape.

Changing the Shape of an Object

Although you can alter the shapes of objects more easily with other Flash tools, the Arrow tool is a quick way to fiddle with the form of an unselected line, stroke, or shape:

1. Select the Arrow tool from the Toolbox. Make sure you have an ungrouped object on the Stage (this example shows a simple circle). Make sure the object itself is unselected.

2. Move the Arrow tool close to the edge of the circle and notice that the cursor changes slightly (see Figure 4.2).

3. When the cursor changes, click and drag the line to where you want it. Notice that you get a ghost-like preview of the line's position (see Figure 4.3).

4. When the line, edge, or shape is altered as you want, release your mouse button, and the shape change is automatically applied (see Figure 4.4).

Figure 4.4

The shape change is automatically applied when you release your mouse button.

Working with the Arrow Tool's Snap To Object Option

When you toggle Snap To Objects, which is located in Toolbox's Options section when the Arrow tool is selected, you cause the selected objects to snap to other objects on the Stage. You can snap selected objects to just about anything: lines, freeform paths, shapes, and so on. In addition, you can even snap objects to the Stage's grid. Using the Snap To Objects option is useful when you want to make sure the objects on the Stage line up or arrange them in a consistent manner.

Figure 4.5

A small circle appears in the center of the selected object when you move it with the Arrow tool.

> To view the grid, select View → Grid → Show Grid. To snap objects to the grid, choose View → Grid → Snap To Grid. Finally, if you want to edit the grid properties, select View → Grid → Edit Grid.

When you've got the Snap To Objects option toggled, you'll notice that a small circle appears in the center of the selected object when you move it with the Arrow tool. This small circle is called the *transformation point* or *registration point* in Flash (see Figure 4.5).

The transformation point, and not the object itself, is doing the snapping; however, this is pretty much moot as the transformation point and the object are the same. When you move the transformation point of one object (and therefore the object itself) over another object (a straight line drawn with the line tool, for instance), the transformation point enlarges to about twice its size and snaps to the object.

Although a full understanding of transformation points isn't yet vital, your curiosity might be piqued. If this is the case, see Chapter 6 for an in-depth discussion of transformation points and how you manipulate them.

> Snap To Objects is most useful when you are creating a tweened animation along a path. For more information on tweening along a path, see Chapter 10.

Snapping to Pixels

In addition to employing the Snap To Objects options, you can also use the Snap To Pixels option. Although it's not accessible in the Options section of the Toolbox when the Arrow tool is selected, the Snap To Pixels option is best explored at this stage of the discussion.

Essentially, when the Snap To Pixels option is turned on (View → Snapping → Snap To Pixels), a pixel grid (visible only if the Stage is magnified to at least 400 percent) appears to which all objects will snap.

> To temporarily make the pixels grid invisible, press X. When you hold down the X key, the grid will disappear, reappearing when you release the button.

Using the Arrow Tool's Smooth Option

The Arrow tool's Smooth option ⁺ʃ, which is located in the Toolbox's Options portion when you've got the Arrow tool selected, reduces the number of bumps in a selected curve. The result is a smoother curve than you had previously.

To use the Smooth option, select a curve with the Arrow tool and click the Smooth button. Alternatively, you can select the curve with the Arrow tool and choose Modify → Shape → Smooth.

> The Smooth option does not work with grouped objects.

Using the Arrow Tool's Straighten Option

The Arrow tool's Straighten option ⁺⟨, located in the Toolbox's Options portion next to the Smooth button, takes the curve out of relatively straight lines, making them perfectly straight.

To use the Straighten option, select a line with the Arrow tool and click the Straighten button. Alternatively, you can select the curve with the Arrow tool and choose Modify → Shape → Straighten.

> The Straighten option doesn't work with grouped objects.

Selecting with the Lasso Tool

While the Arrow tool selects individual objects, the Lasso tool ℘ selects all the objects (or parts of objects) in a specific area.

> You can select portions of individual ungrouped objects (say, the corner of a large square) with the Lasso tool. That area will be selected independently from the rest of the object and can therefore be moved with the Arrow tool, creating the illusion that you took a pair of scissors, cut off the corner, and then moved it away from the square.

The Lasso tool contains three options in the Toolbox's Options section: Magic Wand, Magic Wand Properties, and Polygon mode. Much like the Arrow tool, the Lasso tool is amazingly easy to use. All you need to do is click and drag the tool to draw a line around the area you want to select.

> For selection purposes, the Lasso tool automatically closes an area that you don't close yourself.

Selecting with the Lasso Tool's Polygon Mode

Polygon mode  lets you assert a great deal more control over selection than you'd get if you were simply using the Lasso tool.

Essentially, Polygon mode lets you select an area by drawing multiple connected straight edges. Make sense? In Polygon mode, the Lasso tool draws a straight line. Every time you hit your mouse button, a selection point is created. You can then draw another straight line (which is attached to the selection point you just created). The process is repeated until you encircle the entire selection area. When you double-click your mouse button, the area is selected. Figure 4.6 illustrates Polygon mode in action.

Figure 4.6

Polygon mode in action

> Just as with the Lasso tool when it isn't in Polygon mode, an unclosed area is automatically closed when you finish your making your selection.

Working with the Magic Wand

The Lasso tool's Magic Wand option selects similar colors in a bitmap image that has been broken apart.

> When you break apart a bitmap (which isn't the same as tracing a bitmap), you are simply telling Flash to regard the image as a collection of individual color areas. For more information on how to work with bitmaps in Flash MX 2004 and Flash MX Pro 2004, refer to Chapter 6.

After the bitmap image has been broken apart (which is accomplished by selecting the image and then choosing Modify → Break Apart), you can then click individual colors with the Magic Wand to select them.

> A color area selected with the Magic Wand is overlain by a checkerboard pattern to denote its selection.

SETTING THE PROPERTIES OF THE MAGIC WAND

The Magic Wand Properties button , which is located in the Toolbox's Options portion when you have the Lasso tool selected, allows you to set the properties of the Magic Wand. When you click the Magic Wand Properties button, the Magic Wand Settings dialog box (see Figure 4.7) opens and you can make the appropriate adjustments to the Magic Wand. The options are as follows:

Threshold Defines the degree to which the Magic Wand will select similar (but not identical) colors. Choices range from 0 to 200. For example, if you use a threshold setting of 0, only identical colors will be selected. As you increase the threshold setting, the amount of similar colors that are selected will increase.

Smoothing Determines how edges of a selection should be smoothed. The choices include Normal, Pixels, Rough, and Smooth.

Figure 4.7

The Magic Wand Settings dialog box

Creating Static Visual Content with Flash's Drawing Tools

Now that you've looked at how to use Flash's various selection tools, it's time to create something that can be selected. Flash boasts a whole of host of great tools that allow you to draw anything you imagine. Want to create a Picasso-like portrait of yourself (remember, both eyes on one side of your face) or a drawing of your favorite flower? In this section, you'll look at the tools you need to draw these types of images.

As with the previous tools discussed in this chapter, all the tools you need are located in the Toolbox (see Figure 4.8).

> When you select one of the following drawing tools from the Toolbox, you can manipulate the drawn object's stroke and fill using the Property Inspector before you draw it.

Drawing Straight Lines with the Line Tool

Unlike the freeform Pencil tool, which will be discussed shortly, the Line tool creates single straight lines.

To use the Line tool, click where you want the line to begin, drag until it is the desired length, and release your mouse button. You can set the thickness and style of the Line tool using the Property Inspector. To learn more about manipulating an object's stroke, see the section "Changing a Shape's Stroke with the Property Inspector" later in this chapter.

> Holding the Shift key down while you're using the Line tool will constrain the line to angles in multiples of 45 degrees.

Drawing Shapes

Flash provides you with three tools for drawing basic shapes: Oval, Rectangle, and Polygon. Although fairly similar, each has particular characteristics you should explore.

Figure 4.8

Most of your painting and drawing needs in Flash will be met with tools located in the Tools section of the Toolbox.

Drawing a Rectangle

Located in the Toolbox's Tools section, the Rectangle tool ▢ lets you draw rectangles and squares. Much as with the Oval tool, you can create a rectangle by selecting the Rectangle tool from the Toolbox, clicking your cursor on the Stage where you want the shape to start, dragging until you have created the desired shape and size, and then releasing your mouse button. A rectangle, like an oval, is composed of both a stroke and a fill. To find out more about how you can adjust a rectangle's stroke and fill, see the sections "Changing a Shape's Stroke with the Property Inspector" and "Altering a Shape's Fill with the Property Inspector" later in this chapter.

Holding down the Shift key while drawing your rectangle creates a perfect square.

CHANGING RECTANGLE CORNER RADIUS

The Rectangle tool has one available option in the Toolbox's Options portion: Round Rectangle Radius ⌅ . There will certainly be instances when you'll want to round the corners of the rectangle or square you create. This is where the Round Rectangle Corner Radius option comes in.

When you click the Round Rectangle Radius button, the Rectangle Settings dialog box

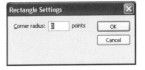

Figure 4.9

The Rectangle Settings dialog box

opens (see Figure 4.9). From here, you can enter a value (from 0 to 100) in the Corner Radius field. The higher the value, the more rounded the corners of your rectangle become. Give it a try and see what kind of results you get.

Using the Oval Tool

Located in the Toolbox's Tools section, the Oval tool ○ helps you draw ellipses and circles. To use the Oval tool, click your mouse where you want the shape to start and then drag until you have created the desired shape and size. When you are finished, release your mouse button. An oval is composed of both a stroke and a fill. To find out more about how you can adjust an oval's stroke and fill properties, see the sections "Changing a Shape's Stroke with the Property Inspector" and "Altering a Shape's Fill with the Property Inspector" later in this chapter.

Holding down the Shift key while drawing your oval creates perfectly round circles.

Drawing a Polygon

In the newest versions of Flash, Macromedia has introduced a new shape drawing tool: the Polygon ⬠ . By default, the Polygon tool is grouped under the Rectangle Tool in the

Toolbox. To access it, click the Rectangle Tool and hold down the mouse button until a menu opens, from which you can select the Polygon tool.

Once you've found the Polygon tool, using it is very easy. Click your mouse where you want the Polygon to start, drag until you have created the desired shape and size, and then release your mouse button. As with all the other shapes we've discussed thus far, a Polygon is composed of both a stroke and a fill. To find out more about how you can adjust a Polygon's stroke and fill properties, see the sections "Changing a Shape's Stroke with Property Inspector" and "Altering a Shape's Fill with the Property Inspector" later in this chapter. You can adjust the properties of the polygon by clicking the Options button in the Properties panel.

Creating a Freeform Path with the Pencil Tool

The Pencil tool ✏ creates single lines. Unlike the Line tool, however, the Pencil is a free-hand tool. With it, you can draw shapes that range from straight lines to incredibly squiggly doodles.

Using the Pencil tool is almost as simple as using an actual pencil. All you need to do is select the Pencil tool from the Toolbox, click the area of the Stage where you want your line to begin, hold down the mouse button, and draw the shape you want. When you're finished, just release the mouse button. Figure 4.10 illustrates the Pencil tool in action.

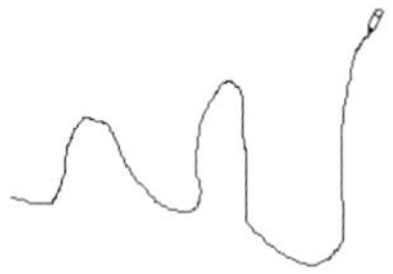

Figure 4.10

The Pencil tool in action

Setting Pencil Mode

The Pencil mode ↳, which is the Pencil tool's only option, contains three properties: Straighten, Smooth, or Ink. The specific Pencil mode you choose is applied to the line you draw *as you draw it.* However, you can straighten or smooth an already drawn line by selecting the target line and then choosing Modify → Shape Smooth or Modify → Shape → Straighten. Alternatively, you can also click either the Smooth or Straighten button after having selected the already drawn line. The Pencil modes include the following options:

Straighten ↳ Straightens all curves in the lines you draw. This creates a line angular in nature.

Smooth S Smooths out any angularities in the lines you draw. Unfortunately, you have no real control over the degree to which Flash smoothes out your lines.

Ink ✎ Ensures that your line is displayed exactly how you've drawn it—no smoothing and no straightening.

Drawing with the Brush Tool

The Brush tool ✏ , much like the Pencil tool, creates single freeform lines. Unlike the Pencil tool, however, the shapes created with the Brush tool are all fill. As a result, to change the color of the brush stroke, you'll need to use the Property Inspector (discussed in the section "Altering a Shape's Fill with the Property Inspector" later in this chapter).

The cool thing about the Brush tool is that, as with the Pencil tool, you can smooth or straighten a stroke that you create. To do this, select the already created stroke with the Arrow tool and hit the Straighten or Smooth buttons. Alternatively, you can choose Modify → Shape → Smooth or Modify → Shape → Straighten.

Using the Brush tool is as easy as using the Pencil tool. Just select the Brush tool from the Toolbox, click the area of the Stage where you want your line to begin, hold down the mouse button, and draw the shape you want. When you're finished, just release the mouse button.

Selecting Brush Size

The Brush tool certainly wouldn't be that useful if you were stuck with one size. Well, fear not, Macromedia has provided you with a series of different brush sizes, all of which are accessible through the Options portion of the Toolbox when you've got the Brush tool selected.

Brushes ranging from tiny to huge are accessible through the Brush Size drop-down menu ●⌄. To change the brush size, just make your choice from the drop-down menu *before* you draw your line. You cannot dynamically change a line's size by choosing a different brush size after you've drawn it.

Setting Brush Shape

Flash also allows you to set your brush's shape. Much like setting brush size, you need to choose a brush shape, all of which are accessible from the Brush Shape drop-down menu ●⌄, *before* you draw your line.

Unfortunately, Flash still doesn't give you the ability to create your own custom brush shapes, so you'll have to make do with what is available.

Setting Brush Mode

Brush mode ◉ , which is accessed through a drop-down menu in the Toolbox's Options section, is perhaps one of the most interesting aspects of the Brush tool.

Essentially, Brush mode lets you specify exactly how your brush stroke affects an existing drawn or painted element. Figure 4.11 illustrates the effects of the different Brush modes.

Figure 4.11

Each Brush mode has a different effect on how your brush stroke interacts with other shapes on the Stage.

Paint Normal   Paint Fill   Paint Behind   Paint Selection   Paint Inside

There are five Brush mode options:

Paint Normal Applies a stroke from the Brush tool on top of existing elements—just as if you took a can of spray paint to the Mona Lisa (yikes!).

Paint Fill Applies your brush stroke only to areas made up of fills while leaving the strokes of shapes unaltered.

Paint Behind Applies the strokes from your Brush tool behind any existing element.

Paint Selection Applies your brush stroke only to areas of fill that have been previously selected.

Paint Inside Applies brush strokes only in the same area they were initiated. Paint Inside mode will not paint over existing elements other than the one in which you started the stroke.

Using a Graphics Tablet with the Brush Tool

One of the cool things about the Brush tool is that if you're using a graphics tablet, such as those produced by Wacom, you can dynamically vary the weight of the stroke. Two graphic tablet–specific options are available when you're using the Brush Tool: Use Pressure and Use Tilt.

The Pressure modifier, which you access by clicking the Use Pressure button ✎ , varies the width of brush strokes as you vary the pressure on the stylus (see Figure 4.12). The Tilt modifier, which you access by clicking the Use Tilt button ⤢ , varies the angle of brush strokes when you vary the angle of the stylus on the tablet. The Tilt modifier measures the angle between the top (eraser) end of the stylus and the top (north) edge of the tablet. For example, if you hold the pen vertically against the tablet, the Tilt is 90°.

Figure 4.12

A Brush stroke drawn with a Wacom graphics tablet

Drawing with the Pen Tool

The Pen tool ✒ is the primary tool for creating freeform vector art within Flash. Granted, the vast majority of the drawing tools in Flash (such as the Line or the Pencil) create vector graphics. However, the Pen tool is by far the most useful and powerful.

> The Pen tool works closely with the Subselection tool, which is covered later in this chapter starting with the section "Modifying a Point's Position with the Subselection Tool."

If you're familiar with illustration programs such as Macromedia FreeHand or Adobe Illustrator, you'll recognize the Pen tool. Designed to build precision paths, the Pen tool works by creating points that are connected by paths to form a segment. The line segments can be either straight as an arrow or curved as a mountain path. One of the many joys of

Figure 4.13

Any complex line (which is more than one segment long) is composed of paths linked by a series of points.

the Pen tool is that the points (which are created each time you click the mouse button) act as anchors that can be moved around to alter the characteristics of any of the line segments (see Figure 4.13).

Setting Pen Tool Preferences

Before you tear off and start learning how to put the Pen tool to work, you need to become familiar with its preferences, which you access by choosing Edit → Preferences and clicking the Editing tab. From here, you have three choices (all located in the upper-left corner of the Editing tab):

Show Pen Preview Lets you preview line segments as you draw. A preview of the line segment is displayed as you move the pointer around the Stage.

Show Solid Points Specifies that unselected anchor points appear as solid dots and selected anchor points appear as hollow dots.

Show Precise Cursors Specifies that the Pen tool pointer appears as a crosshair cursor, rather than the default Pen tool icon.

Drawing a Straight Line with the Pen Tool

Drawing a straight line is quite easy with the Pen tool. All you need to do is select the Pen tool from the Toolbox, click a place on the Stage where you want to begin the line (which creates a point), and then move your mouse and click again to define the endpoint of the line. Whammo, you've just created a straight line with the Pen tool. Figure 4.14 shows a simple one-segment line drawn with the Pen tool.

Figure 4.14

A simple, one-segment line drawn with the Pen tool; notice that it ends and begins with a point.

Drawing a Curved Line with the Pen Tool

Drawing a curved line is where the Pen tool really begins to shine! Drawing a straight line is easy (and can be accomplished with many other drawing tools in Flash), but creating (and manipulating) curved segments is what the Pen tool is really good at.

When you draw a curve with the Pen tool, you create curve points. When you draw a straight-line segment, you create corner points.

To create a curved line with the Pen tool, follow these steps:

1. Select the Pen tool from the Toolbox.

2. Click anywhere on the Stage where you want your curve to begin.

3. Move the cursor to the location where you want the curve to end.

4. Click to add the end point in the segment. However, instead of releasing your mouse button, keep it pressed down and move the mouse a little bit in any direction. You'll notice that as you move your mouse away (with the button still held down), two things happen:

   - First, your cursor is actually dragging one of two tangent handles that are linked to the final point in the segment.

   - Second, the farther away you drag one of the tangent handles away from the original point, the more extreme your curve gets (see Figure 4.15).

5. To adjust the characteristics of the curve, simply move the selected tangent handle.

6. When the curve is exactly how you want it, release the mouse button. Notice that the tangent handles disappear.

Figure 4.16 illustrates the resulting curved segment.

Figure 4.15

The resulting curve that is created as you move the selected tangent handle away from the original end point. Note that the tangent handle stretches out the farther you drag it away.

Adding a Point to a Line

Each time you click your mouse button when you use the Pen tool, you add a point to a path. When you are finished, you have a series of points and the segments that run between them. The points themselves really determine the way in which the line looks. As you'll see later in this section, you can move points around to alter the shape of the line. Given this, it's pretty obvious that the Pen tool wouldn't be all that useful unless you could add more points along the path *after* you've drawn it.

> It's very important to note that you can't actually add a point to a segment that resides between two corner points, only a segment that exists between two curve points (or a corner point and a curve point).

Figure 4.16

The resulting curve

Follow these steps to add points to a path:

1. Make sure that a curved path already exists on the Stage and that you have the Pen tool selected. (To learn how to make a curved path, see the section "Drawing a Curved Line with the Pen Tool" earlier in this chapter.)

2. Move the Pen tool over the area of the path you want to add the point. Notice that the cursor changes from a pen with a small *x* to its right (which is the default cursor when you are pointing anywhere on the Stage) to a pen with a small plus (+) to its right (see Figure 4.17).

3. Click to add the point.

Figure 4.17

When you move the cursor over a curved path, the icon changes to a pen with a plus (+) next to it. This indicates that you can add a point.

Removing a Point from a Stroke

Removing a point from a stroke is as easy as adding one; follow these steps:

1. Make sure a multipoint path already exists on the Stage and you have the Pen tool selected.

> Removing a curve point is a two-step process. First, you actually convert the curve point to a corner point and then you remove the corner point. If you want to remove a corner point, it's simply a one-step process.

2. Move the Pen tool over the point that you want to remove. Notice that the cursor changes from a pen with a small *x* to its right (which is the default cursor when you are pointing anywhere on the Stage) to a pen with a small caret (^) to its right (see Figure 4.18).

3. Click once. This converts the curve point to a corner point. Once you do this, you'll notice that your cursor changes to a pen with a small minus (–) to its right (see Figure 4.19).

4. Click the point once again to remove it entirely.

Using the Subselection Tool to Change the Position of a Point

Because the points in a path act as a sort of skeleton, moving any of the given points alters the structure of the path itself. To move a point with the Subselection tool, follow these steps:

Figure 4.18

When you move the cursor over a path, the icon changes to a pen with a small caret (^) next to it.

1. Make sure you've got a multi-segmented path on the Stage. Also, make sure you select the Subselection tool, which is located just to the right of the Arrow tool in the Toolbox's Tools section.

2. Click the path with the point you want to move to select it (notice that the path changes color when selected).

3. Move your cursor over the point you want to move. Notice the cursor turns from an arrow with a small black box to its right, which is the default for the Subselection tool, to an arrow with a small empty box to its right, which indicates that you are over an editable point.

Figure 4.19

Once you convert the curve point to a corner point, your cursor changes to a pen with a small minus (–) to its right.

4. Click and drag the point to the desired location.

5. When the point is at the desired location, simply release your mouse button.

> If the point you've selected is a curve point, the tangent handles appear when you select it with the Subselection tool.

Changing the Curve of a Segment with the Subselection Tool

As discussed previously, it's pretty painless to create a curved segment with the Pen tool. But what happens if you want to edit the curviness, for example, of the curve after you've created it? Well, this is where the Subselection tool comes in. To alter a curve with the Subselection tool, follow these steps:

1. Make sure that you have a curved path on the Stage. Also, make sure that you select the Subselection tool ⬦ , which is located to the right of the Arrow tool in the Toolbox's Tools section.

2. Click the path with the point you want to move to select it (notice that the path changes color).

3. Click the curve point once (remember that the curve point is usually the second point in the curved segment because that was the one whose tangent handles were used to modify the curve's shape). Depending on whether the curve point is at the end or in the middle of the path, either one or two tangent handles will be displayed (see Figure 4.20).

4. Click the point at the end of the tangent handle and drag it to adjust the curve's shape.

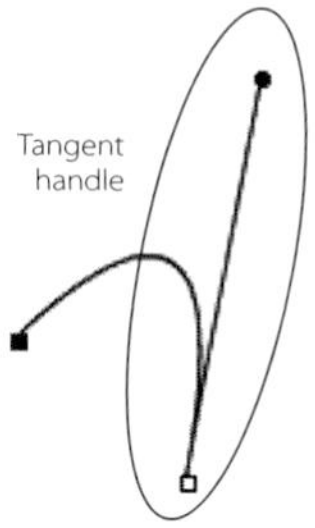

Converting a Corner Point to a Curve Point

Corner points are all well and good when you're drawing angular paths with the Pen tool. However, they are limited in that they can't be fiddled with to produce (or adjust) a curve. This is a little annoying if you have spent a couple of hours creating a perfect image only to find that you need to make a slight curve in a straight line. Fortunately, Flash has the ability to turn a corner point into a curve point:

1. With the Subselection tool ⬦ , select the corner point that you want to convert. When it's selected, the corner point will turn from a hollow square to a filled square.

2. Once it has been selected, hold down the Option/Alt key.

3. Click the corner point that you want to convert, and then drag it slightly. Notice that two tangent handles immediately appear.

4. You can then click and drag either tangent handler to adjust the shape of the curve.

Changing a Shape's Stroke with the Ink Bottle Tool

Located in the Tools section of the Toolbox, the Ink Bottle 🐦 changes a stroke's color, width, and style. The benefit of using the Ink Bottle, as opposed to just selecting the individual stroke and then using the Property Inspector, is that you can use it to make it easier to change the stroke attributes of multiple objects simultaneously.

Tangent
handle

Figure 4.20

After clicking the desired curve point with the Subselection tool, either one or two tangent handles will appear, depending on whether the point is at the end or in the middle of the path.

Using the Ink Bottle involves becoming familiar with the workings of the Property Inspector. For more information, see the section "Changing a Shape's Stroke with the Property Inspector" later in this chapter.

To use the Ink Bottle, follow these steps:

1. Without anything selected on the Stage, select the Ink Bottle tool from the Tools section of the Toolbox.

2. If it isn't already, open the Property Inspector by choosing Window → Properties. Notice that the Property Inspector displays the Ink Bottle options (see Figure 4.21).

3. Choose a stroke color, stroke height, and stroke style.

To learn how you go about creating a custom stroke, see the section "Changing a Shape's Stroke with the Property Inspector" later in this chapter.

4. Now, move your cursor (which has changed into an ink bottle) over any stroke that you want to change and click once. The target stroke will automatically change to reflect the options you chose in the Property Inspector.

Once you've set the properties of the Ink Bottle tool, it remains "filled." This means that you could continue clicking other strokes on the Stage and they would all change to reflect the options you set in the Property Inspector.

Altering a Shape's Fill with the Paint Bucket Tool

While the Ink Bottle tool changes the character of an object's stroke, the Paint Bucket tool 🪣 fills an area with color. It can both fill empty areas as well as change the color of already filled areas. You can paint with solid colors, gradient fills, and bitmap fills. One of the neat things about the Paint Bucket tool is that it can fill areas that are not entirely closed.

Much as in the case of the Ink Bottle tool, using the Paint Bucket tool requires at least a basic understanding of how the Property Inspector works. See the section "Altering a Shape's Fill with the Property Inspector" later in this chapter.

To use the Paint Bucket, follow these steps:

1. Without anything selected on the Stage, select the Paint Bucket tool from the Tools section of the Toolbox.

2. If it isn't already, open the Property Inspector by choosing Window → Properties. Notice that the Property Inspector displays the Ink Bottle options (see Figure 4.22).

3. Choose a fill color.

4. Now move your cursor (which has changed into a paint bucket) over the inside of an empty shape or an existing fill and click once. The target area will automatically "fill up" with the new color you set using the Property Inspector.

Figure 4.21

The Property Inspector with the Ink Bottle's Properties displayed

Figure 4.22

The Property Inspector with the Paint Bucket's properties displayed

Setting the Paint Bucket Gap Size Option

As mentioned previously, the Paint Bucket tool can actually fill objects that aren't entirely closed. The Gap Size option , which you access through the Toolbox's Options section, lets you set the gap size at which the Paint Bucket will still fill an open shape.

To set the gap size, just choose from one of these options in the drop-down menu: Don't Close Gaps, Close Small Gaps, Close Medium Gaps, or Close Large Gaps.

Using the Paint Bucket Lock Fill Option

The Paint Bucket's Lock Fill option 🔒 comes into play when you're using gradients as fill (see the section "Working with the Color Mixer Panel" later in this chapter). Located in the Toolbox's Options section when you've got the Paint Bucket selected, this creates the illusion that all filled areas (regardless of whether they are side by side or far apart) are all part of the same, continuous gradient. Figure 4.23 illustrates the Lock Fill option.

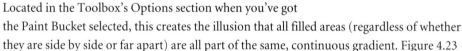

Figure 4.23

When used in conjunction with a gradient fill, the Lock Fill option creates the illusion that filled objects are part of the same, continuous gradient.

To use the Lock Fill option, just follow these steps:

1. Select or create a gradient fill using the Color Mixer panel.

> To learn how you go about creating and manipulating gradient fills, see the section "Working with the Color Mixer Panel" later in this chapter.

2. Select the Paint Bucket tool.

3. Select the Lock Fill option 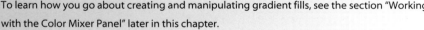.

4. Move your cursor (which has changed into a paint bucket with a small padlock icon to its right) over the inside of an empty shape or an existing fill and click once. The target area will automatically "fill up" with the gradient you mixed.

5. Repeat step 4 to fill additional areas until you achieve the illusion that the filled areas are all part of the same, continuous gradient.

Figure 4.24

The bounding box that appears for a linear gradient when you're working with the Fill Transform Tool

Using the Fill Transform Tool

The Fill Transform tool , which used to be part of the Paint Bucket option but was turned into a tool in its own right back in Flash MX, lets you adjust the visual properties of a gradient or bitmap fill.

> This discussion hinges on understanding how you use the Color Mixer panel to create gradient and bitmap fills. Before continuing, you might want to read the section "Working with the Color Mixer Panel" later in this chapter.

Let's take a look at how you can use the Fill Transform tool:

1. Select the Fill Transform tool.

2. Click an area filled with a gradient or bitmap fill. Notice that when you select a fill for editing, a bounding box with handles and a center point appears. You'll find that, depending on whether you are working with a linear gradient, a radial gradient, or a bitmap fill, you'll get different handles.

Figure 4.25

The bounding box that appears for a bitmap fill when you're working with the Fill Transform Tool

- In the case of a linear gradient fill, the bounding box that appears is rectangular with a center point, a circular handle in the upper-right corner, and a square handle on the right (see Figure 4.24).

- However, if you are working with a bitmap fill, the bounding box appears with two separate sets of handles (see Figure 4.25): four circular ones (one on top, one in the top-right corner, one on the right, and one in the center) and three square ones (one on the left, one in the bottom-left corner, and one on the bottom).

- On the other hand, if you're working with a radial gradient fill, the bounding box is oval in shape, with a square handle in the middle, and three circular handles along the edge of the oval (see Figure 4.26).

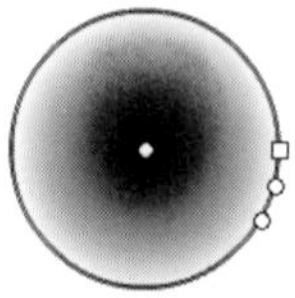

> When your pointer is over any of these handles, it changes to indicate the handle's specific function.

Figure 4.26

The bounding box that appears for a radial gradient when you're working with the Fill Transform Tool

3. From here, you can perform several distinct actions:

   - **Reposition the center point of a gradient (either radial or linear)**: Simply click and drag the center point to a desired location within the bounding box (see Figure 4.27).

   - **Change the width of the linear gradient or bitmap fill**: Click and drag the square handle on the side of the bounding box (see Figure 4.28).

Figure 4.27

Repositioning the center point of a radial or linear gradient

Changing the width of the gradient or bitmap fill resizes only the fill and not the object itself.

   - **Change the height of a bitmap fill**: Click and drag the square handle at the bottom of the bounding box (see Figure 4.29).

   - **Rotate the linear gradient, radial gradient, or bitmap fill**: When you're working with a linear gradient or bitmap fill, drag the circular rotation handle in the corner (see Figure 4.30).

Figure 4.28

Changing the width of a linear gradient or a bitmap fill

As with adjusting the width, when you adjust the height of a gradient or bitmap fill, you are not adjusting the height of the actual filled object.

On the other hand, if you are working with a radial gradient, drag the bottommost circular rotation handle.

   - **Stretch or compact a linear gradient or a bitmap fill**: Drag the square handle at the right of the bounding box (see Figure 4.31).

     However, if you are working with radial gradient, click and drag the first circular handle (just below the square handle).

   - **Skew or slant a bitmap fill**: Drag one of the circular handles on the top or right side of the bounding box (see Figure 4.32).

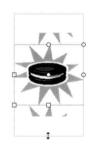

Figure 4.29

Changing the height of a bitmap fill

Sampling with the Dropper Tool

The Dropper tool ✐, which is located in the Toolbox's Tools section, lets you sample the fill or stroke from one object and then apply it to another.

To sample the stroke of an object:

1. Make sure that you have the Dropper tool selected and you have an object with a stroke on the Stage.

2. Move the Dropper over the stroke. You'll notice that the cursor changes from a simple dropper to a dropper with a small pencil to its right (see Figure 4.33).

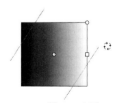

Figure 4.30

Rotating a linear, gradient, or bitmap fill

Figure 4.31

Stretching (top) or compacting (bottom) a linear gradient or bitmap fill

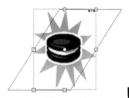

Figure 4.32

Slanting a bitmap fill

Figure 4.33

When you move the dropper over a stroke, it changes to a dropper with a small pencil to its right.

3. Click your mouse button once. Notice that the Dropper instantly changes to the Ink Bottle tool. This means you are ready to apply the sampled stroke color to the stroke of another object.

4. Move the Ink Bottle cursor over another stroke and click once—voila! The stroke of the second object is changed to that of the first.

To sample the fill of an object:

1. Make sure that you have the Dropper tool selected and you have an object with a fill on the Stage.

2. Move the Dropper over the fill. You'll notice that the cursor changes from a simple dropper to a dropper with a small brush to its right (see Figure 4.34).

3. Click your mouse button once. Notice that the Dropper instantly changes to the Paint Bucket tool. This means you are ready to apply the sampled fill (whether it is a color, gradient, or bitmap) to the fill of another object.

4. Move the Paint Bucket cursor over another fill and click once.

> If you hold down the Shift key when you click an object with the Dropper tool, the color sampled is applied to both the fill and stroke and can be applied to another object.

Using the Eraser Tool

To use the Eraser tool, which is a heck of a lot easier than using a real eraser (no little rubber shavings), select it from the Toolbox, move it to the location on the Stage you want to erase, and click and drag until you've erased to your heart's content. Yup, it's that easy.

Selecting Eraser Mode

Much like the Brush tool, the Eraser has several different modes, all of which are accessible by clicking the Eraser Mode button in Toolbox's Options section when you've got the Eraser selected.

Essentially, the five Eraser modes let you specify exactly how your Eraser affects an existing drawn or painted element:

Erase Normal Erases any fills or strokes over which you drag the Eraser tool.

Erase Fills Constrains the Eraser so it erases only fills and empty areas without erasing any strokes over which it passes.

Erase Lines Erases only strokes and lines. Any fills your cursor passes over will not be affected.

Erase Inside Erases within the constraints of a shape. When this mode is selected and you start your stroke in a filled area, only the section inside of that area is erased.

Erase Selected Fills Affects only fills that are selected at the time when you begin erasing.

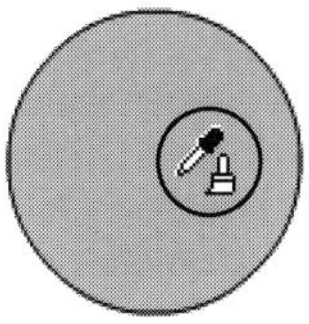

Working with the Faucet Option

The Faucet option , which is located in the Toolbox's Options section when you've got the Eraser selected, automatically deletes any fill or stroke that you click. Just select the Faucet option, point and click, and say "bye bye" to the offending fill or stroke.

Selecting the Eraser Shape

As with the Brush Size mode, you can specify the size and shape of your Eraser. The available Eraser shapes and sizes range from small to large and are accessible through a drop-down menu in the Options section of the Toolbox when the Eraser is selected.

To change the Eraser shape and size, make your choice from the drop-down menu *before* you use the Eraser.

Changing a Shape's Stroke with the Property Inspector

As mentioned in Chapter 3, stroke is the character of the line formed when you draw an object. Whether you want to change the character of a line drawn with the Pencil tool or the border of a rounded rectangle, you'll need to use the Property Inspector.

> As already discussed, you can use the Color Mixer panel to manipulate stroke color. However, if you want to fiddle with other stroke attributes, such as height and style, you need to use the Property Inspector.

With it, you can change the height, style, and color of an object's stroke. Let's take a look at how:

1. If it isn't open already, open the Property Inspector by choosing Window → Properties.

2. Now, select the object whose stroke you want to manipulate.

> If you want to change the stroke of an ungrouped object, make sure you don't just select its fill. The easiest way to avoid this is to select the Arrow tool and click and drag so that the selection box encompasses the entire object.

3. Click the Stroke Color swatch. When the color palette opens, select the color that you want to use for the object's stroke (see Figure 4.35).

Figure 4.34

When you move the dropper over a fill, it changes to a dropper with a small brush to its right.

4. From here, you can set the stroke's height (thickness) either by adjusting the slider (accessed by clicking the little down arrow to the right of the Stroke Height field) or by simply typing in a numerical value into the Stroke Height field (see Figure 4.36).

> The minimum stroke height is 0.1, and the maximum is 10.

5. Now you can set the stroke's style by choosing one of the options from the Stroke Style drop-down menu (see Figure 4.37).

6. If you aren't happy with the preset stroke styles that Flash offers, you can create your own by clicking the Custom button to the right of the Stroke Style drop-down menu. The Stroke Style dialog box (see Figure 4.38) that opens initially lets you set the type and thickness of the custom stroke.

   Your choices are automatically shown in the preview window in the left-hand portion of the dialog box. To get a good feel for how this dialog box works, experiment with the various options and see what kinds of results you get. Depending on the stroke type you've chosen, you will have access to a far wider range of unique options in the Stroke Style dialog box.

Figure 4.35

Changing the stroke's color

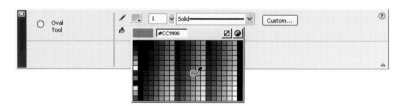

Figure 4.36

Changing the stroke's height

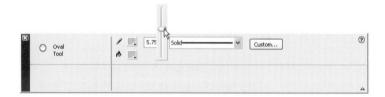

Figure 4.37

Changing the stroke's style

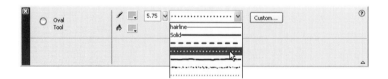

You can also set an object's stroke color through the Stroke Color well in the Toolbox's Colors section—represented by the color swatch just to the right of the Pencil icon. Click the color swatch and then choose the color you want from the color-picker that opens.

Altering a Shape's Fill with the Property Inspector

You have two ways of setting fill color. One will be discussed in the section "Working with the Color Mixer Panel" later in this chapter. The other, discussed in this section, involves using the Property Inspector. In all honesty, using the Property Inspector is a little limiting because you have access only to solid color. With the Color Mixer panel, you also have access to gradient and bitmap fills.

Figure 4.38

The Stroke Style dialog box

To set an object's fill using the Property Inspector, follow these steps:

1. If it isn't open already, open the Property Inspector by choosing Window → Properties.

2. Now, select the object whose fill you want to manipulate.

3. Click the Fill Color swatch. When the color palette opens, select the color you want to use for the object's stroke (see Figure 4.39).

Using the Fill Color well in the Toolbox works exactly the same as if you were to use the Color Mixer panel or the Property Inspector; it's just accessed from a different location. All you need to do is toggle the Fill Color button, click the color swatch, and then choose the color you want.

Working with Digital Color

Like any other visual medium (such as painting, photography, film, or 3D modeling), color is an extremely important factor in crafting something with impact in Flash. Unless you are targeting your work toward an audience of visually impaired individuals (a process that involves specialized knowledge and experience), you need to spend a great deal of time thinking about how you'll effectively maximize color in Flash. In this section, you'll explore some specific color-oriented topics.

Figure 4.39

Changing the fill's color

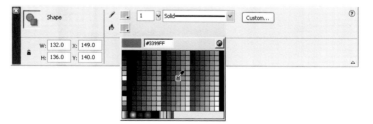

Until the Web came along, all computer-oriented graphic designers created images and artwork specifically for print. When it comes to print, color is composed using a system designed to make sure that the color displayed on a computer monitor translated accurately into the ink in a printer. Called CMYK (Cyan/Magenta/Yellow/Black), the system defines individual colors as a percentage of each of these four colors. For example, the CMYK abbreviation for the color black would be 0-0-0-100.

When it comes to designing specifically for the screen, CMYK has no real place. Instead, color is composed using the RGB (Red/Green/Blue) system, which defines an individual color in terms of a combination of these three colors.

When it comes to the Web, there is an additional color system of which you need to be aware. *Hexadecimal notation* (sometimes just referred to as *Hex*) is less of a real color system and more of a way to describe RGB color in an alternative format. Used by HTML, Hex notation is composed of six characters (00DDFF, for example). The first two characters represent the red color channel (R), the middle two the green channel (G), and the last two the blue channel (B). Each of the numeric characters (0–9) and each of the letters (A–F) represent an integer from 0–16. As a result, the Hex notation translates neatly into an RGB value. When it comes to using color in conjunction with web-oriented media (HTML, Flash, digital video, and so on), there are some things you need to know.

Most computers can display at least 256 colors (most can display millions). The problem, however, is that you can't be exactly sure *which* 256 colors. This would normally cause some rather frustrating problems for web designers. Fortunately, the majority of web browsers (Netscape Navigator and Microsoft Internet Explorer are the most popular) all share a fixed-color palette: the *browser-safe palette* or *web-safe palette,* as it's sometimes called. So, if you choose a color from the browser-safe palette, you are guaranteed your design will look exactly the same (at least when it comes to color) from system to system.

If you use a color outside the web-safe color palette, the browser converts the odd color to the closest color it can find in its system palette. As a result, you run the risk of having your colors look slightly different from machine to machine if you stray from the web-safe color palette.

Working with the Color Swatches Panel

Each Flash movie contains its own color palette, stored in the architecture of the file itself. Flash displays a file's palette as swatches (small squares of color) in the Color Swatches panel (see Figure 4.40).

Although the Color Swatches panel (Window → Design Panels → Color Swatches) displays the web-safe palette by default, you can add, delete, edit, and duplicate colors as you need. You can also import and export custom-created palettes. You do all these operations through the Color Swatches panel's Options pop-up menu, which again, you access by clicking the icon in the panel's top-right corner.

The options include the following:

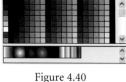

Figure 4.40
The Color Swatches panel

Duplicate Swatch Automatically duplicates the currently selected swatch.

Delete Swatch Deletes the currently selected swatch.

Add Colors Lets you import color palettes that have been saved in the CLR (Flash Color Set) or ACT (Color Table) file format. After choosing the option from the drop-down menu, just navigate to the file on your hard drive and select it.

Replace Colors Lets you replace the current palette with an imported palette. Just choose the option from the drop-down menu, navigate to the CLR file, and select it.

Load Default Colors If you've manipulated your current palette, use the Load Default Colors option to revert back to the web-safe palette.

Save Colors To export a color palette, choose Save Colors from the drop-down menu. When the Export Color Swatch dialog box opens, navigate to the location where you want to save the palette, choose a desired file type from the Format menu (Mac) or Save as Type drop-down menu (Win), enter a desired name, and click Save.

Save as Default Designates the current palette as the default palette to be loaded when you use the Load Default Colors option in the drop-down menu.

Clear Colors Automatically removes all the colors from the current palette besides black and white.

Web 216 Switches the current palette to the web-safe palette.

Sort by Color Rearranges the color swatches by hue, allowing you to better locate a given color in the current palette.

Working with the Color Mixer Panel

While the Color Swatches panel displays the individual colors in the current palette, the Color Mixer panel (see Figure 4.41), which is accessible by choosing Window → Design Panels → Color Mixer, creates and edits solid colors.

It is also used to create gradient and bitmap fills. We've talked a bit about this before, but now we'll go over it in more detail.

The primary purpose of the Color Mixer panel is to exert complete control over both fill and stroke color. To do this, just select either the Stroke Color icon (indicated by the pencil) or the Fill Color icon (indicated by the paint bucket) and follow the color-mixing procedures detailed next.

Figure 4.41
The Color Mixer panel

Because you cannot create or edit gradient or bitmap fills using the Property Inspector, you'll find it's preferable to use the Color Mixer panel to do all your fill work.

Mixing Solid Colors

You can use the Color Mixer panel to create solid RGB (Red, Green, Blue), HSB (Hue, Saturation, Brightness), or Hexadecimal notation colors using a series of different methods (all of which are explored in this section). Once you've created colors, you can add them to the current palette and have them displayed in the Color Swatches panel.

One of the great things about using the Color Mixer panel is that you can dynamically apply fill. This means you can change and manipulate an object's fill either before or after it is created. If you want to change the fill of an existing object, make sure it has been selected (with the Arrow tool) and then make the desired changes in the Color Mixer panel.

Let's take a look at how you use the Color Mixer panel to create and mix solid colors.

When you've mixed a color using any of the upcoming procedures, all you have to do is select the Add Swatch command from the Color Mixer panel's Options menu. The color will automatically be added to the Color Swatches panel.

MIXING AN RGB COLOR

To mix an RGB color, follow these steps:

1. If it isn't open already, select Solid from the Fill Style drop-down menu (see Figure 4.42).

2. Choose RGB from the Color Mixer panel's Options menu.

Figure 4.42

By selecting Solid from the Fill Style drop-down menu, you can then begin to mix solid colors.

3. From here, simply enter numerical values into the R, G, and B fields (see Figure 4.43). Alternatively, you can use the sliders to the right of the individual color channel fields.

   You can also choose a color by clicking anywhere in the color box with your cursor. The appropriate RGB code automatically appears in the color channel fields.

4. If you want to manipulate the color's transparency, enter a value into the Alpha field (or adjust the slider) to specify the degree of transparency—0 for complete transparency to 100 for complete opacity.

MIXING AN HSB COLOR

The process for mixing an HSB color works exactly the same as mixing an RGB color. Choose HSB from the Color Mixer panel's Options menu (below left). From there, enter values (in percent) into the H, S, and B fields. You can also choose a color by clicking anywhere in the color box with your cursor. You can also enter a value into the Alpha field (or adjust the slider).

Figure 4.43

The R (red), G (green), and B (blue) fields in the Color Mixer panel

MIXING A HEX COLOR

Mixing a Hex color is just as easy as mixing either an RGB or an HSB color. Simply enter the appropriate Hex values into the Hex field (see Figure 4.44).

The Hex value of any color you create using RGB or HSB is automatically displayed in the Hex field.

You can also choose a color by clicking anywhere in the color bar with your cursor.

Figure 4.44

The Hex Color field and the Color Box

Using the No Fill Style

When you choose None from the Fill Style drop-down menu, any object you draw (oval, rectangle, and so on) will have no fill (see Figure 4.45).

Unlike the other choices in the Fill Style drop-down menu, you can't dynamically change an object's fill to None after it has been drawn. As a result, if you don't want an object to have a fill, select None from the Style drop-down menu before drawing it.

Figure 4.45

If you select None from the Fill Style drop-down menu, any shape you draw will have no fill.

Creating a Linear Gradient

A linear gradient is a fill that gradually changes from one color to another, in a continuous fashion, either vertically or horizontally (see Figure 4.46).

Let's take a step-by-step approach to creating and editing a linear gradient with the Color Mixer panel:

Figure 4.46

A linear gradient

1. With the Color Mixer panel open and an object selected, choose Linear from the Fill Style drop-down menu.

> Alternatively, you can choose Linear from the Fill Style drop-down menu *before* you draw the object. By doing this, your object, when it's drawn, will be filled with the linear gradient you selected and edited beforehand.

Figure 4.47

**The gradient defini-
tion bar pointers
determine the start-
ing and ending col-
ors of the gradient.**

2. To change a color in the selected gradient, first click one of the pointers below the gradient definition bar. As a gradient slowly changes from one color to another, the pointer you choose determines either the starting color or the ending color (see Figure 4.47).

3. Once you have one of the pointers selected, click the color swatch just above the gradient's definition bar. This will open the color palette from which you can choose a new color (see Figure 4.48).

4. To change the character of the gradient, click and drag either pointer. The farther apart the pointers are, the more gradual the gradient will appear. Conversely, the closer together the pointers are, the more abrupt the gradient will be (see Figure 4.49).

As you move the pointers around or change the gradient colors, your changes will automatically preview in both the gradient definition bar and the gradient preview.

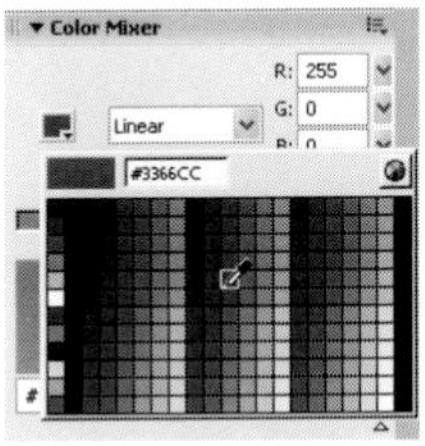

Figure 4.48

**The color palette
from which you can
choose a new color**

5. You can increase the complexity of the gradient by adding additional colors. To do this, click just below the gradient's color definition bar to add an additional pointer. Once it has been added, you can change the pointer's color by following the process outlined in step 4.

6. Once you've finished editing the gradient, you can add it to the Color Swatches panel (so it can be used whenever you want). To do this, select Add Swatch from the Color Mixer panel's Options drop-down menu.

To transform a gradient fill of any kind (either linear or radial), you can use the Fill Transform tool described in the section "Working with the Fill Transform Tool" earlier in this chapter.

Figure 4.49

**The closer the gradi-
ent pointers, the
more abrupt the
gradient will be.**

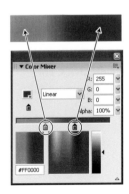

Creating a Radial Gradient

A radial gradient is quite similar to a linear gradient. However, instead of the fill changing from one color to another in a linear pattern, it changes in a circular pattern (see Figure 4.50).

Beyond that detail, creating and editing a radial gradient is exactly the same as if you were working with a linear gradient.

Creating a Bitmap Fill

You can use the Color Mixer panel to create a fill that is a bitmap image (as opposed to a solid color or a gradient). Let's take a look at how:

1. With the Color Mixer panel open and an object selected, choose Bitmap from the Fill Style drop-down menu.

Figure 4.50
A radial gradient

> Alternatively, you can choose Bitmap from the Fill Style drop-down menu *before* you draw the object. By doing this, your object, when it's drawn, will be filled with the bitmap you selected and edited beforehand.

2. If you haven't already imported another bitmap into your movie, the Import to Library dialog box will open. Navigate to where the bitmap you want to use as fill is located, select it, and then click Open.

Imported bitmap

Figure 4.51
Imported bitmaps are displayed in the Color Mixer's Bitmap Fill window.

3. If you've already imported a bitmap (or bitmaps), they are displayed in the Bitmap Fill window (see Figure 4.51).

4. Select the bitmap that you want to use as fill from the thumbnails displayed in the Bitmap Fill window.

5. To manipulate the way in which the bitmap fill is displayed, use the Fill Transform tool, discussed in the section "Working with the Fill Transform Tool" earlier in this chapter.

Inspirational Design Model

Created by Second Story Interactive (www.secondstory.com), the Theban Mapping Project site (www.thebanmappingproject.com) features an incredible example of interactive Flash Edutainment (The Atlas of the Valley of the Kings) that lets people explore the Valley of the Kings—where, from 1500 B.C. to 1000 B.C., ancient Egyptian pharaohs were buried in expansive underground complexes. From professional Egyptologists to school children, this site serves the needs of a wide and diverse audience. Visitors unfamiliar with the Valley of the Kings can go on a virtual tour of a 3D tomb, or watch narrated movies. For experienced academics, the site offers the opportunity to research the architecture and decoration of every chamber in every tomb in the Valley of the Kings.

The Interactive Atlas (see Figure 4.52), which is a stand-alone multimedia experience, displays compelling movies, dynamic information, and gripping images in context with detailed maps and measured drawings of the tombs within the Valley of the Kings.

Figure 4.52

The Theban Mapping Project

© Second Story Interactive Studios

CHAPTER 5

Creating and Crafting Text

Even though the Web is becoming an increasingly more visual medium by the second, the majority of the information is still textual.

Beyond the textual content that you can transmit, however, the type itself is an extremely powerful tool for giving your digital creation extra life and meaning. Because of Flash's vector animation tools, text—especially if it's properly crafted—can have an incredible impact on your visitors. Taking the time to choose the right type for your textual content can turn a good Flash site into a great Flash site.

In this chapter, you'll explore the following topics:

- **Understanding text, type, and fonts**
- **Working with Flash's font limitations**
- **Adding type with the Text tool**
- **Using the Property Inspector to manipulate text**
- **Breaking apart text**
- **Changing the shape of characters**
- **Creating a Font symbol**
- **Checking your Movie's spelling**

Understanding Text, Type, and Fonts

When you work with text in Flash MX 2004 and Flash MX Professional 2004 (or any other graphics program for that matter), you'll find that the words *text, font,* and *typeface* are often used interchangeably. Don't be fooled, however; there is a big difference among the three.

Text refers to any combination of characters that make up a written document of some sort (whether a word, a sentence, or a book). A *font,* on the other hand, is a complete set of characters in a particular size and style. This includes the letters, the numbers, and all of the special characters that you get by pressing the Shift, Option, or Cmd/Ctrl keys. A *typeface* contains a series of fonts. For example, the typeface Arial contains the fonts Arial, Arial Bold, Arial Italic, and Arial Bold Italic.

For more information about the art of text, type, fonts, and just about anything else typographic, try these great resources: www.rsub.com/typographic and http://counterspace.motivo.com.

Working with Flash's Font Limitations

Although Flash has some font-related issues that need to be discussed, they are nowhere near as complicated (and limiting) as those related to fonts and HTML-based design. However, they are important and ultimately will impact your Flash creations.

Flash movies can use Type 1 PostScript fonts, TrueType fonts, and bitmap fonts (on the Macintosh only). To use PostScript fonts, you must have Adobe Type Manager (ATM) installed on your system.

If you're using Windows 2000, you don't need to install ATM to use Type 1 PostScript fonts.

For the most part, when you publish your final product, Flash embeds the necessary information about fonts, thereby allowing your audience's computers to display them properly. However, in some cases, fonts might still appear incorrectly in your Flash creation when your audience views it because they many not have that font installed on their machine.

You can avoid this problem in two ways. First, if you are not picky about the actual font you use, employ the _sans, _serif, or _typewriter fonts available in the Font drop-down menu of the Property Inspector (see the "Using the Property Inspector to Manipulate Text" section later in this chapter). Essentially, when you use these fonts (which are called *device fonts*), you are telling the Flash movie to use the equivalent fonts installed on your audience's computers. This way, you always know that your text will appear correctly. Essentially, device fonts are the fonts that your operating system employs to display its textual information.

Second, to keep your fonts from displaying incorrectly when your Flash creation is viewed, you can break apart the given text and turn it into shapes instead of text. The process for breaking apart text will be covered later in this chapter in the "Breaking Apart Text" section.

Besides the problem of users not having a certain font installed, there are some other specific font issues of which you should be aware. When it comes to Windows machines, PostScript fonts are prone to display incorrectly. As a result, it is strongly suggested that Windows users limit themselves to TrueType fonts.

Mac users need to be cautious when employing Adobe PostScript fonts. For the most part, PostScript fonts function properly, but there are situations where they cause problems. Sometimes, PostScript fonts will display properly while you are creating your Flash movie but will display incorrectly when the movie is actually published.

Creating Type with the Text Tool

Now that you've explored the limitations of Flash-based text, you can explore the process of creating text by using the Text tool **A**, which is located in the Tools section of the Toolbox.

Although the vast majority of your text editing in Flash will be facilitated by the Property Inspector (which you'll explore later in this chapter), you always need to start off by actually creating some text—a process made possible by the Text tool.

To use the Text tool, select it from the Toolbox, click anywhere on the Stage, and begin typing. Don't worry too much about how the text appears at this early stage of creation; you'll learn how you can get it to look exactly how you want in the "Using the Property Inspector to Manipulate Text" section later in this chapter.

> To edit text, simply click a text block with the Text tool (or double-click it with the Arrow tool) and make the changes that you want. When finished, click anywhere outside of the text box.

Understanding Text Boxes

Flash creates text in blocks called *text boxes* (see Figure 5.1). The text blocks themselves become editable objects that you can move about the Stage at will.

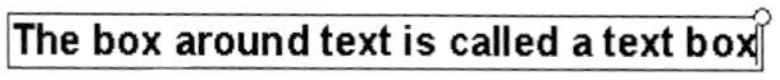

There are actually three distinct types of text boxes (see Figure 5.2), each with a particular function within the process of creating and manipulating text in Flash.

- An Extending text box extends as you type. You can easily recognize these by a small circle in the upper-right corner. The Extending text box is the default type of text box in Flash.

| The box around text is called a text box |

Figure 5.1

As you're typing the text, notice that it is contained in a rectangle with a small circle in the upper-right corner. This is a text box.

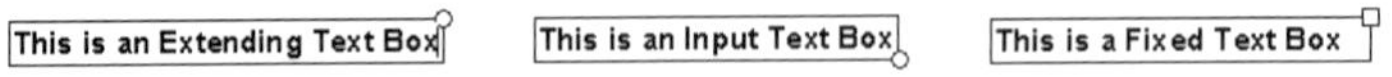

Figure 5.2

There are three distinct types of text boxes: Extending (left), Input (center), and Fixed (right).

This is an Extending Text Box   This is an Input Text Box   This is a Fixed Text Box

- An Input text box contains Dynamic Text that can be changed by anyone viewing your Flash movie.

> For more information on how to create and work with Dynamic Text, see the section "Working with Dynamic Text" later in this chapter.

- A Fixed text box doesn't increase horizontally. To create a Fixed text box, which is recognizable by a small square in its upper-right corner, choose the Text tool from the Toolbox, click anywhere on the Stage, and drag the text block to the desired size. Notice that you can only drag horizontally. When you type, your text will automatically wrap, extending the size of the text block vertically, but not horizontally.

Say, for instance, that you wanted to create a field where someone types a password to access a restricted area of your site. You would accomplish this (at least in part) by creating an Input text block. Unlike the other two types of text boxes, the Input text box, which is recognizable by a small circle in the lower-right corner of the text box, is not, strictly speaking, created with the Text tool. Instead, you need to choose Dynamic Text or Input Text from the Text Type drop-down menu in the Property Inspector (see the following section).

Using the Property Inspector to Manipulate Text

The Text tool is the primary method for *creating* text, and the Property Inspector is the primary tool for *editing* and *manipulating* it. Unlike pre-MX versions of Flash, which used several different panels to control various aspects of Flash text, Flash MX 2004 and Flash MX Pro 2004 use the all-powerful Property Inspector to manipulate text. You can access it by choosing Window → Properties.

Before learning how to manipulate text with the Property Inspector, however, there is a single detail that needs to be discussed. In Flash MX 2004 and Flash MX Pro 2004, there are three distinct types of text: Static Text, Dynamic Text, and Input Text. Each type, which will be discussed in the following sections, has its own place and function within a Flash creation.

Let's take a look at the process that you need to follow to create and edit each of the three types using the Property Inspector:

1. If you haven't already, insert some text onto the Stage using the Text tool.

2. If the text box that you've just created is still "live" (or, still editable), select the text using your cursor. If you've deselected the text box, simply reselect it with the Arrow tool (a light blue box will appear around the selected text block).

3. If it isn't already, open the Property Inspector by choosing Window → Properties.

4. Select the specific type of text that you want to create from the Text Type drop-down menu (see Figure 5.3).

Text Type drop-down menu

Figure 5.3

The Text Type drop-down menu in the Property Inspector lets you select the type of text that you want to work with.

From here, the Property Inspector will change to reflect that text type's specific properties, all of which are described in the following sections.

> This step-by-step process describes how you can manipulate text *after* it's already been created. If you want to create some text with the Text tool whose properties have already been set, just select the Text tool from the Toolbox, open the Property Inspector, set the text properties (all of which are described next), and then insert the text onto the Stage. The inserted text will automatically have all the properties (font, color, size, and so on) that you set with the Property Inspector.

Working with Static Text

Although you are going to spend time exploring and discussing Dynamic Text and Input Text a little later in this section, it's important to recognize that Static Text, which is automatically created when you insert text using the Text tool, is the default type of text in Flash. In other words, when you create text with the Text tool, it is automatically Static Text.

> When you want to work with Static Text, you really don't have to follow the steps in the previous section because Static Text is already chosen in the Text Type drop-down menu.

Beyond its innate ability to convey textual information, Static Text doesn't do anything special. As a result, you'll find that you'll probably use it the most. As a result, it's good that you become intimately familiar with all the following Static Text options accessible through the Property Inspector (see Figure 5.4).

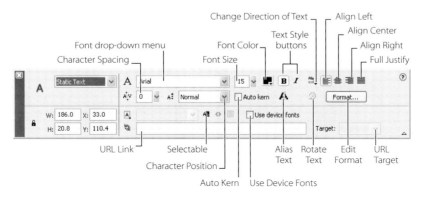

Figure 5.4

Static Text properties displayed in the Property Inspector

The options are as follows:

Font drop-down menu Displays the current font when the Text tool is active. The list shows every font currently installed on your computer. You can either choose a font with the Font drop-down menu before you begin typing or select existing text within a text block (or the text block itself) and change its font with the Font drop-down menu.

> You can also change the font of selected text by choosing Text → Font and then picking from the list of fonts installed on your machine.

Font Size field Sets a font's size. You can either enter a value (in point size) into the Font Size field or use the Font Size slider (which is accessible by clicking the small Down arrow to the right of the field).

> You can also change the font size by choosing Text → Size and picking from the list of sizes available.

Text style buttons Sets the text to either bold or italic. As with the rest of the options in the Property Inspector, you either select a block of text with the Arrow tool or use the Text tool to select the text when the text block is "live." Then click one of the style buttons. You can also click either of the style buttons before you create a new string of text.

> Unfortunately, the Property Inspector offers a limited array of style options. For more (though not much more) options, select Text → Style and choose a style from the list.

Text Color swatch Opens the Text Color palette so you can set your text's color. If you are unhappy with the available color choices, mix your own using the Color Picker (accessible by clicking the small color wheel in the top-right corner of the Text Color palette).

Character Spacing value Represents the distance between characters in a string of text. The higher the Character Spacing value, the farther apart the characters will be. Figure 5.5 illustrates different Character Spacing values, also referred to as *tracking*.

The Property Inspector lets you set the Character Spacing for any given text block (either before or after it has been created). If the text has already been created, all you need to do is select the text block or the actual text and enter a value in the Character Spacing field. Alternatively, you can use the Tracking slider, which is accessible by clicking the small Down arrow just to the right of the Tracking field, to adjust the amount of tracking.

Figure 5.5

The top line of text has a character spacing of 0, the middle line has a character spacing of 2, and the bottom line has a character spacing of 5.

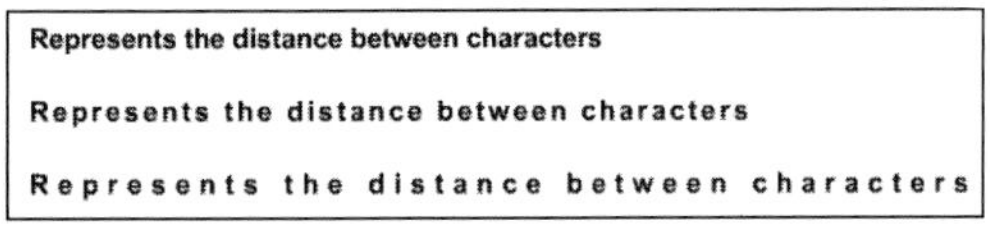

Represents the distance between characters

Represents the distance between characters

Represents the distance between characters

As with all of the other options in the Property Inspector, you can also set the tracking *before* you create text with the Text tool.

Character Position value   Character Position, which is also referred to as *baseline shift* in graphic design, refers to how closely the text sits above or below its natural baseline (the bottom of the letters). By changing a text block's Character Position value, you can create superscript or subscript characters. Unlike most graphic design programs that allow you to set an exact baseline shift value, Flash gives you only three default settings: Normal, Superscript, and Subscript (see Figure 5.6).

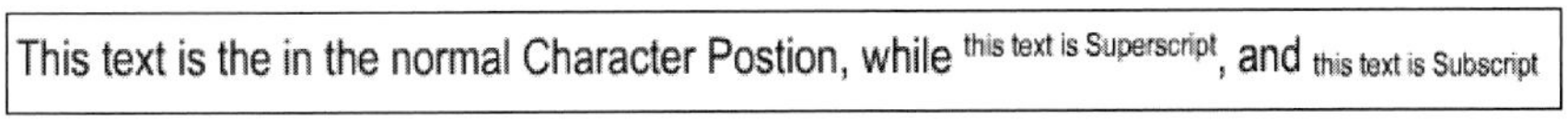

This text is the in the normal Character Postion, while this text is Superscript, and this text is Subscript

Figure 5.6

The three baseline shift presets

To set the character position, select a string of already created text, and choose one of the three baseline shift options from the Character Position drop-down menu. As with all of the other options in the Property Inspector, you can also set the baseline shift *before* you create text with the Text tool.

In addition to changing some text's Character Position value, you can also create superscript or subscript by choosing Text → Style → Superscript or Subscript.

Auto Kern option   Evens out the spacing between individual characters in a string of text. When you select the Auto Kern option, you activate the built-in kerning option of many (but not all) fonts.

If you want to apply the Auto Kerning feature, a font must have kerning information built into the file; this is why some fonts will auto kern and others won't.

Change Orientation of Text button   Accesses a drop-down menu with a series of options that change the direction of the selected text. The default Horizontal option makes the text flow from left to right horizontally. The two remaining options—Vertical, Left to Right and Vertical, Right to Left—make the text flow vertically. The difference between the two is that if you apply the Vertical, Left to Right option to a block of text with more than one line, the first line will remain the first vertical line. However, if you choose the Vertical, Right to Left option, the last line in a text block with more than one line of text will be the first vertical line.

Rotate Text button   Changes the text's orientation (only on vertical text). With rotation turned off, individual characters will face to the right.

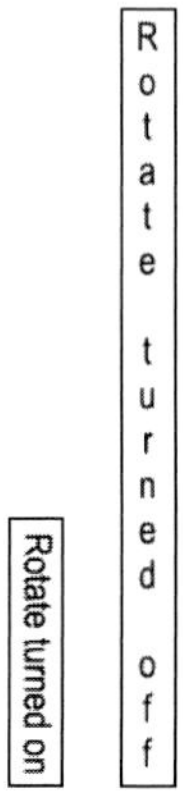

Rotate turned on Rotate turned off

Figure 5.7

The text on the left has the rotation turned on, while the text on the right has the rotation turned off.

On the other hand, if you turn the rotate option on, the individual characters will face downward. The differences between text with the rotation turned on and text with the rotation turned off is illustrated in Figure 5.7.

URL Link field Flash offers several different ways in which to link to a URL. The easiest method uses the URL Link field in the Property Inspector.

> Any Flash text to which you've attached a URL will appear on the Stage with a dotted underline.

Simply select a string of text that you want to turn into a link, and type a URL into the URL Link field.

> You can add a URL only to horizontal text.

URL Target field Because it's entirely possible that your Flash movie be delivered in a framed HTML document, the Target drop-down menu lets you set the location in which the URL loads. There are four default options:

- Choosing _blank loads the link in a new browser window, maintaining the window in which the hyperlink was located just below the newly opened window.

- If you choose _parent, the document, when loaded, will occupy the entire area of the frameset document in which the link resides.

- Choosing _self (which is the default link target) simply opens the document in the frame where the link resides.

- If you choose _top, the document will be loaded into the uppermost (hierarchically speaking) frameset—wiping out all frames and nested framesets.

You can also manually enter a frame name into the Target drop-down menu/field if you want to target a specific named frame in the HTML document.

Selectable button Under normal circumstances, Static Text is part of the Flash movie and is therefore not selectable as text would be in an HTML document, for example. However, if you want your audience to be able to select the Static Text in your movie (and therefore copy and paste it), make sure the Selectable button is toggled.

Use Device Fonts option By selecting the Use Device Fonts option, you tell Flash not to embed the font used in a given text block. Instead, Flash will look at the user's computer and employ the most appropriate font on their system to display the text. Ultimately, because the font information is not embedded, the SWF file's size will be slightly smaller.

You can evoke the Use Device Fonts option only when you're working with horizontal text.

Alignment buttons The right side of the Property Inspector offers you four alignment options: Align Left, Center, Align Right, and Justify (see Figure 5.8). To align text, select a text block (or a string of text within a text block) and click one of the alignment buttons.

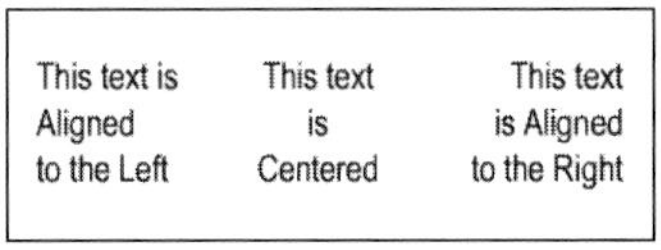

This text is Aligned to the Left	This text is Centered	This text is Aligned to the Right

Figure 5.8

The results of the four alignment options from left to right: Align Left, Center, and Align Right.

Formatting options By clicking the Edit Format Options button, you get access to a Format Options dialog box (see Figure 5.9), which contains a series of options that affect the way in which an entire text block looks (opposed to individual characters within the text block).

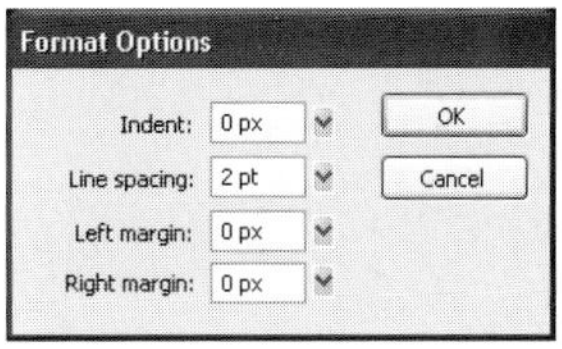

Format Options

Indent:	0 px	OK
Line spacing:	2 pt	Cancel
Left margin:	0 px	
Right margin:	0 px	

Figure 5.9

The Format Options dialog box

When you set the left margin of a text block, you set the distance, in pixels, between the left side of the text box and the text itself. Enter a value numerically into the Left Margin field or use the Left Margin slider (accessible by clicking the small Down arrow to the right of the Left Margin field).

When you manipulate the right margin, you set the distance, in pixels, between the right side of the text box and the text itself. Enter a numerical value into the Right Margin field or use the Right Margin slider (accessible by clicking the Down arrow to the right of the Right Margin field).

The Indent setting changes the distance, in pixels, between the left side of the text box and the first line of text.

The Line Spacing setting represents the vertical distance, in points, between lines in a text block. To set the line spacing, enter a value numerically into the Line Spacing field, or use the Line Spacing slider.

Alias text The Alias text feature, which is new to Flash MX 2004 and Flash MX Pro 2004, is ideal for use on mobile devices as it produces crisp and legible text optimized for small size representation (Figure 5.10). Text is first rastered to a non-anti-aliased state, and then converted to a vector representation, thus ensuring a highly legible font at small display sizes.

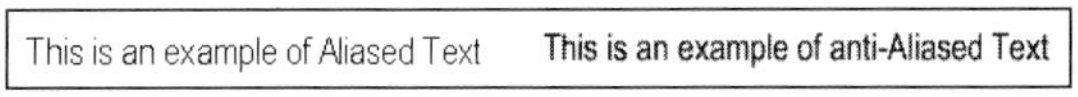

This is an example of Aliased Text	This is an example of anti-Aliased Text

Figure 5.10

The text on the left is an example of aliased text, while the text on the right is an example of anti-aliased text.

Working with Dynamic Text

When you create Dynamic Text, you produce a text box with content dynamically updated from another source, say, a database or text file on your server. So, Dynamic

Text is not really fixed or unchanging *per se*, even though it's created in the same way as Static Text. Instead, it's sort of like a text container with contents that can change. With this in mind, one can easily come up with some genuinely interesting uses. You could create a constantly changing list of your favorite jokes or your daily itinerary—the possibilities are endless.

If you are interested in using Dynamic Text to create dynamic content, see Bonus Chapter 1 (on this book's accompanying CD).

If you want to create and manipulate Dynamic Text, you have to go through an extra step that you wouldn't normally have to go through if you were working with Static Text: You'll need to manually select Dynamic Text from the Property Inspector's Text Type drop-down menu.

From there, you'll get access to the specific Dynamic Text properties in the lower-right corner of the expanded Property Inspector (see Figure 5.11), each of which is described next:

Line Type drop-down menu Displays three choices: Single Line, Multiline, and Multiline No Wrap. Single Line displays the text as one line, and both Multiline and Multiline No Wrap display it as more than one line. The difference between the two Multiline options is that Multiline No Wrap will break a single line into more than one line only if the last character is a breaking character, such as Return/Enter.

Instance Name field Contains the name of the text block so that dynamic content intended for that specific text block will know exactly where it needs to go.

Make sure that the name you enter into the Instance Name field is unique.

Variable field Introduced in Flash 5, the Variable field allows you to enter the name of the ActionScript variable associated with a particular string of Dynamic Text. Since the introduction of the Instance Name field, however, this field has seen less and less use for reasons that will become more apparent as you become more familiar with Flash.

For more information on Variables, check out Chapter 18.

Figure 5.11

Dynamic Text properties displayed in the Property Inspector

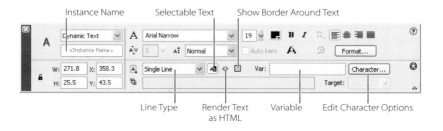

Selectable Text button Allows your audience to select the text within the Dynamic Text box, much as in the case of the Static Text option.

Render Text as HTML button Tells Flash to allow you to use certain HTML tags in the text box for formatting its contents. Now, don't get all wild and crazy, thinking that you can use every HTML tag under the sun. Unfortunately, there are only a limited number of HTML tags (including bold, italic, underline, font face, font color, paragraph break, and font size) that are supported.

Show Border around Text button Tells Flash that you want the text box to be surrounded by a visible border.

Edit Character Options button When you click the Edit Character Options button (shown as Character), the Character Options dialog box opens (see Figure 5.12).

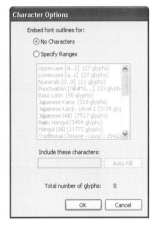

Figure 5.12

The Character Options dialog box

From here, you can determine exactly how many characters of the font are embedded in the file. Embedding a character in the file allows Flash to "remember" how to render it when the movie is played back on a system that does not have the specific font you specified for the text box. The Edit Characters dialog box refers to characters as *glyphs* to remind us of the fact that elements of a font are not necessarily characters (after all, they could be ideograms from a Chinese font or Elvis heads from a clipart font).

By selecting the No Characters option at the top of the Character Options dialog box, you are instructing Flash not to store the shapes of any characters. The option beneath it, Specify Ranges, enables the other fields in the Edit Characters dialog box, which you can use to specify which characters you would like to have embedded into your Flash movie. The list box in the center of the Edit Characters dialog box contains several pre-defined sets of characters that allow you to quickly embed groups such as Numerals and Uppercase Letters. You can also include specific characters by typing them into the Include These Characters field. If you press the Auto Fill button, Flash reads all the text inside the text box and files each character appearing in its contents in the Include These Characters field. At the bottom of the Edit Characters dialog box, you will find a running total of the number of characters that you have instructed Flash to store within the Flash movie. The fewer characters of a font you embed, the smaller the resulting Flash movie file will be, so keep an eye on this number!

Working with Input Text

Input Text is almost exactly the same as Dynamic Text. The only real difference lies in the fact that data is traveling in the other direction—from the user's computer to a server, rather than from the server to the computer. Simply put, while you can't enter text into a Static text box or a Dynamic text box, you can enter text into an Input text box. As a result, most of the options available once you select Input Text from the Text Type drop-down menu in the Property Inspector (see Figure 5.13) are exactly the same as described previously.

Figure 5.13

Input Text properties displayed in the Property Inspector

There are, however, two additional options:

Password option Beyond the Single Line, Multiline, and Multiline No Wrap options in the Line Type drop-down menu, you have a fourth option: Password. Use the Password option to display the on-screen text as asterisks to maintain password security.

> Selecting the Password option affects only the display of the text entered by the user. To make the password work, you are going to have to use ActionScript to pass the information to a server-side application. For more information about integrating database-driven applications and Flash, see Bonus Chapter 1 (on this book's accompanying CD).

Maximum Characters field Entering a numerical value into the Maximum Characters field limits the number of characters that a user can enter into a given text field.

Breaking Apart Text

As you've probably noticed, when you create text, it's inserted onto the Stage as a block. Whether a letter, a word, or an entire Shakespearean soliloquy, you can't independently manipulate (scale, skew, move, and so on) individual portions of the text block.

> You need to be aware of two problems when you break apart text and turn it into shapes. First, broken-apart text increases your Flash creation's file size considerably. Second, once text is broken apart, you can no longer edit it as you would other text.

Although this is especially irksome, there is a rather easy way around the problem. Essentially, you break the text block down into its parts. Let's take a look at how:

1. Select a text block with the Arrow tool.

2. Choose Modify → Break Apart.

3. The result will be that the text block will be broken into its individual characters, each of which can be edited, moved, and manipulated independently of the others (see Figure 5.14).

> Breaking apart text is especially handy if you want to animate individual characters of a larger text block.

Manipulating Text Shape

One of the really neat things that you can do with Flash is manipulate the shape of the individual characters of a given font. If you don't like how the *G* looks in Arial, you can change it to look exactly how you want. The process involves taking the text and breaking it apart several times. To accomplish this, follow these steps:

Figure 5.14

The same block of text as it appears normally (left) and after it has been broken apart (right)

> When you use the Break Apart command, you can affect only TrueType fonts. Bitmap fonts disappear when you break them apart. PostScript fonts can be broken apart only on Mac systems running ATM.

1. Make sure the Stage has some already created text.

2. Select the text box with the Arrow tool.

3. Choose Modify → Break Apart. At this point, the text should break down into a group of several selected items, each of which is composed of one character.

4. Without deselecting anything, again choose Modify → Break Apart.

5. Deselect the shape by clicking anywhere else on the Stage or by choosing Edit → Deselect All.

6. By doing this, you convert the text into a shape like any other. From here, you can use the Arrow tool to manipulate the shape of the character(s), as illustrated in Figure 5.15.

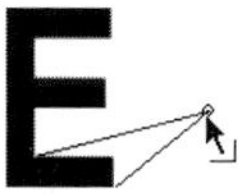

Figure 5.15

Once you've completely broken apart the text, you can manipulate the shape of the individual characters with the Arrow Tool.

> One of the coolest things about text that has been broken apart is that you can use the Ink Bottle to add an outline around the individual characters.

Creating a Font Symbol

If you are planning on creating and using a Shared Library (discussed in Chapter 7), you would do well to become familiar with *Font symbols*. Essentially, a Font symbol allows you to stick any font into a Shared Library, which sits on a server somewhere. From there, any number of Flash movies can link to the Shared Library and use the font without it having to be embedded in their files, thereby reducing their overall sizes.

To create a Font symbol, follow these steps:

1. Open the movie that you want to house the Shared Library.

2. If it isn't open already, choose Window → Library to open the Library.

3. Choose New Font from the Library Options menu. The Font Symbol Properties dialog box opens (see Figure 5.16).

Figure 5.16

The Font Symbol Properties dialog box

4. Enter the name for the font that will appear in the Library into the Name field.

The name that you give isn't the official name of the font itself, just an identifier that you assign for your own purposes.

5. Select the actual font from the Font drop-down menu.

6. Choose whether you want the Font symbol to be bold or italic.

7. When you are finished, click OK.

For more information on Shared Libraries, see Chapter 7.

Checking Your Movie's Spelling

Easily one of the most underrated, but extremely powerful, new tools in Flash 2004 and Flash 2004 Pro is the spell checker. It's completely mind-boggling why Macromedia didn't introduce a spell checker into Flash before this version. Just because Flash doesn't produce reams and reams of text doesn't mean that the text that it does produce can't be misspelled. Hey, even the best spellers among us misspell a word or two now and then, and need the occasional help of a spell checker. For those of us who can't spell our way out of a paper bag (myself included), the spell checker is that much more of a blessing.

The process by which you check your document's spelling involves two steps. First, you've got to set the properties of the spell checker. Then you actually run the spell checker, which involves dealing with any misspelled words that don't appear in your chosen dictionary.

Figure 5.17

The Spelling Setup dialog box

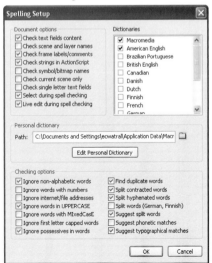

Setting Up the Spell Checker

Before you can actually run the spell checker, you need to set its properties. Let's take a look at how:

1. Choose Text → Spelling Setup. The Spelling Setup dialog box opens (see Figure 5.17).

2. Set the scope of the spell check by selecting one (or more) of the options from the Document Options section (in the top-left corner of the dialog box).

3. Select the dictionary to be used during the spell check from the Dictionaries list box.

> While you can choose as many dictionaries as you like, you need to choose at least one for the spell checker to work.

4. To use a personal dictionary (a text file composed of words that you have designated), click the Browse for Personal Dictionary File button  next to the Path field. When the Open dialog box displays, navigate to where the text file you would like to use as the designated personal dictionary is located, select it, and click the Open button.

> Creating a personal dictionary is a very handy thing if your Flash movie uses specialized words that aren't normally found in the generic dictionaries that are available.

5. To add words to your personal dictionary, click the Edit Personal Dictionary button. When your personal dictionary is open in the Edit Personal Dictionary dialog box (see Figure 5.18), you can change the spelling of existing words and add new words. When you've finished editing your personal dictionary, click the OK button.

6. To specify how the spell checker checks your document, select any of the choices in the Checking Options section of the Spelling Setup dialog box.

7. When you've finished setting the properties of the spell check, click OK.

Checking your Document's Spelling

Once you've used the Spelling Setup dialog box to set all the properties of the spell checker, you are free to check the spelling of your movie. To do so, just follow these steps:

1. Select Text → Check Spelling.

2. If you have any misspelled words (based on the search criteria that you set in the Spelling Setup dialog box), the Check Spelling dialog box opens (see Figure 5.19).

Figure 5.18

The Edit Personal Dictionary dialog box

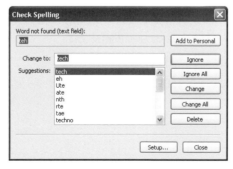

Figure 5.19

The Check Spelling dialog box lets you decide how to deal with misspelled words that were found during the spell check.

3. From here, you have several options as to how you want to deal with misspelled words that were identified:

Click the Setup button in the Check Spelling dialog box if you want to open the Spelling Setup dialog box to change the way in which your document's spelling is checked.

- If the word that was brought up is in fact spelled correctly (but simply doesn't appear in the dictionary or dictionaries that you selected in the spell checker's properties), you can click the Add to Personal button.
- Click the Ignore button if you want the spell checker to ignore that single instance of the misspelled word.
- Click the Ignore All button if you want the spell checker to ignore all instances of the misspelled word.
- To change the spelling of the word, select one of the options from the Suggestions list box. If you want, you can manually enter a correction into the Change To field. From there, click the Change button to make the correction. If you want to correct all instances of the misspelled word, click the Change All button.
- If you want to remove the misspelled work entirely from the movie, click the Delete button.

4. To end the spell check, you have two options:
- If you want to cancel the spell check before it reaches the end of your document, click the Close button.
- Continue spell checking until Flash tells you that it's finished checking your document. Click the Yes button to have Flash go back to the beginning of your movie and start checking again. If you want to close the spell checker, click the No button.

Inspirational Design Model

There is little doubt that sound digital typography gives a well-designed site that extra creative punch. Let's face it, folks: Type is power! Because of its foundation in vector technology, Flash gives you the opportunity to leverage typographic power. No site illustrates this more elegantly than typographic (www.typographic.com). Designed by Jimmy Chen, an astounding visual designer who lives in Los Angeles, typographic takes web design beyond the realm of the commercial, the corporate, and the everyday into something far more potent (see Figure 5.20). Every square centimeter is packed with beautiful digital typographic design. The visual subtleties of typographic are quite stunning and create a visual space that easily holds your attention for long periods of time.

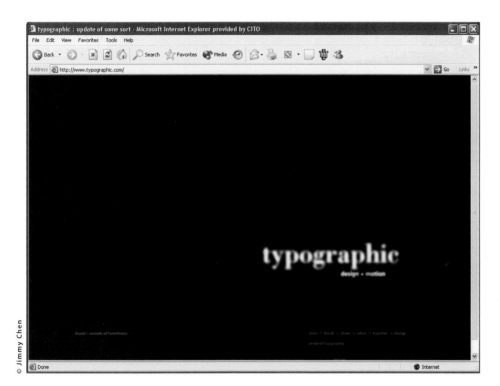

Figure 5.20

Jimmy Chen's typographic

CHAPTER 6

Working with Objects

In the previous chapters, you learned how to create various elements in Flash. Whether shapes, text, or color, you've spent a fair amount of time wading into the process of visual creation. To a certain degree, you've also learned how to manipulate the elements you've created.

The success of your Flash creation depends, at least partly, on your ability to exert complete control over the way in which your objects look. So, what exactly is an object? Well, simply put, an *object* is another word for anything visual you either create or import in Flash. This means that, for example, blocks of text, imported bitmaps, and shapes drawn in Flash are all referred to as *objects*.

The great thing about working with objects is that Flash offers a whole host of tools with which to manipulate and modify them. Whether you want to modify their shape, move them about the Stage, or group them with other objects, this chapter explores all the ways in which you can exert control over the look of the objects in your Flash creation.

In this chapter, you'll explore the following topics:

- **Understanding objects**
- **Working with external bitmaps**
- **Working with external vector files**
- **Grouping and ungrouping objects**
- **Moving, manipulating, and arranging objects**
- **Transforming objects**
- **Working with transformation points**

Understanding Objects

Objects are the heart and soul of Flash. Anything you draw, paint, or import onto the Stage is considered an object. So, an object can range from an imported JPEG of your dog Zippy to an illustration of the solar system that you created with the painting and drawing tools (and everything in between).

In the following sections, you're going to explore the plethora of tools and procedures that let you manipulate the appearance of individual objects.

The term *object* is also used in ActionScript. However, don't be fooled; an ActionScript object and the kind of object discussed in this chapter are totally different. For more information on ActionScript objects, see Chapter 17.

Working with External Bitmaps

Although Flash is designed to work primarily with vector-based art, it also handles bitmaps relatively well. The program boasts a virtual plethora of tools designed to import and manipulate bitmaps. Beyond getting acquainted with these tools, however, it's vitally important to understand the nature of bitmaps and how Flash deals with them. In Chapter 4, you learned how to use bitmaps as fill. Now you're going to learn how bitmaps factor into the greater pantheon of Flash objects.

Bitmaps, which are also sometimes called *raster graphics*, are images composed of individual pixels that have a fixed size and take up a set amount of computer memory. The quality of a bitmap image is determined by its resolution. For the most part, resolution is expressed as dots per inch (dpi). A bitmap with a higher resolution (say, 300dpi) will be better quality than one with a lower resolution (say, 72dpi).

One of the other characteristics of a bitmap image is that it is resolution dependent. When the resolution and size is set, its quality is fixed. As a result, changing a bitmap's dimensions can drastically affect its quality. One of the most obvious manifestations of this quality change is something called *jaggies*. If you take a bitmap image and enlarge it, you'll be able to see its individual pixels. The edges of the image will have a jaggy appearance because the number of pixels per inch cannot change. A similar vector image, on the other hand, would simply recalculate the mathematical equations that define its shape and preserve a smooth edge at any size. Figure 6.1 illustrates bitmap jaggies and the lack thereof in vector images.

Figure 6.1

The individual pixels of the bitmap (on the left) are visible, and the edge of the vector image (on the right) is smooth.

All of these characteristics make bitmaps larger and more memory intensive than vectors. As a result, it behooves you to use vector-based art as much as possible when orchestrating your Flash creation. However, sometimes bitmaps have a distinct advantage over vectors. Although vectors are smaller in file size, they are generally unable to efficiently display complex photorealistic images or images with continuous color tones.

As everything you create in Flash with the painting and drawing tools is vector-based, Flash doesn't have the ability to actually create bitmaps. However, Flash can easily import many different types of bitmap files. After being imported, they can then be manipulated to minimize the amount of memory they'll consume in your Flash creation.

Importing External Bitmaps

You can import bitmaps into Flash in two ways: by using the Import command or simply pasting an image onto the Stage.

> Flash can import the following raster/bitmap files: Windows Bitmaps (BMP/DIB), GIF (GIF), JPEG (JPG/JPEG), PNG (PNG), and PICT (PCT/PIC). Flash can import the following bitmap/raster files *only* if you've got QuickTime 4 or above installed: MacPaint (PNTG), Quick-Time Image (QTIF), Photoshop (PSD), Silicon Graphics Images (.SGI), TGA (TGA), and TIFF (TIF).

A copy of QuickTime 6 has been included on this book's CD-ROM.

To import a bitmap, follow these steps:

1. Choose File → Import → Import to Stage or use the shortcut Cmd/Ctrl+**R**.

> Alternatively, you can select File → Import → Import to Library if you want the bitmap to be placed in your movie's Library. For more information on the Library and what it is used for, refer to Chapter 7.

2. When the Import dialog box opens, navigate the file you want to import, select it, and click the Open button.

> Use the Files of Type drop-down menu at the bottom of the Import dialog box to display only files of the exact type you are trying to import.

3. When the bitmap is imported into Flash, it is automatically placed both on the Stage and in the Library (as a symbol).

Importing a TIFF file requires QuickTime. If you have QuickTime on your system, and you are trying to import a file called `image.tiff`, for example, you might get a rather odd prompt: "Flash doesn't recognize the file format of `image.tiff`. Would you like to try importing via QuickTime?" The prompt isn't much to worry about. If you select Yes, your imported image won't be adversely affected. On the other hand, if you do not have Quick-Time on your system, you will get the message: "One or more files were not imported because there were problems reading them."

> Although Flash will import a PNG created in any program, if you're importing a Fireworks PNG, you get the Fireworks PNG Import Settings dialog box. From here, you can set a series of options, including whether you want the various layer in your image to be flattened into a single layer.

To copy a bitmap from another application:

1. Copy the intended bitmap from the other application by choosing Edit → Copy or using the shortcut Cmd/Ctrl+**C**.

2. Return to Flash, and paste the bitmap onto the Stage by choosing Edit → Paste in Center or using the shortcut Cmd/Ctrl+**V**.

Tracing an Imported Bitmap

The Trace Bitmap option lets you take a bitmap and convert it into a native Flash vector file format with discrete areas of color. This is a definite advantage if you want to manipulate the bitmap image as you would a vector image. While tracing a bitmap might decrease its original file size, tracing a bitmap that has complex color and shapes will almost always increase its file size (sometimes drastically so). Under most circumstances, tracing a bitmap and turning it into a vector image also decreases its file size.

> When you trace a bitmap, the link between the image and the symbol in the Library is severed. If you want to place the traced bitmap back into the Library, simply convert it to a symbol—a process discussed thoroughly in Chapter 7.

Figure 6.2

When you trace a bitmap, you are not going to get a perfect vector copy of the original bitmap. The results are often not what you might expect. The image on the left is the original bitmap, while the image on the right is the traced version of the bitmap.

Don't get too excited, however, because when you trace a bitmap, the results are not necessarily what you would expect. It is nearly impossible to convert an image into a vector so that it looks the same as it did when it was a bitmap. The difference between the original bitmap and its traced version is illustrated in Figure 6.2. This having been said, let's explore how you go about tracing an image:

1. With the Arrow tool, select a bitmap image on the Stage.

2. Choose Modify → Bitmap →Trace Bitmap to open the Trace Bitmap dialog box (see Figure 6.3).

From here, you can set the various Trace Bitmap properties:

Color Threshold Determines the number of colors in the bitmap after it has been traced and turned into a vector image. When you trace a bitmap, the colors of adjacent pixels in the bitmap are compared. If the difference between the RGB color values of the adjacent pixels is lower than that

Figure 6.3

The Trace Bitmap dialog box

entered in the Color Threshold field (which can be a number from 1 to 500), then the adjacent pixels' colors are considered the same. By doing this, the process averages out the colors in the bitmap. The higher the color threshold, the fewer colors will be in the traced bitmap. On the other hand, if you enter a lower value into the Color Threshold field, the traced image will have more colors. Figure 6.4 illustrates the results of different Color Threshold values.

Minimum Area Sets the minimum amount of area a block of color in the bitmap must cover (in pixels) to be traced out as its own shape by Flash. By entering a very large value, the resulting vector image will be composed of larger, more solid blocks because Flash will ignore small patches of color. By entering a very small value such as 10, Flash will draw these smaller areas out into the resulting vector image. As you might have guessed, smaller values will generally result in more detail being preserved. However, tracing large, complex bitmaps at low Minimum Area settings can be a very strenuous task for your computer, so work your way down the range from 1,000 until you achieve the desired effect.

Curve Fit Determines how closely to the edges of the pixels in your bitmap the outlines of the traced bitmap are drawn. Options include Pixels, Very Tight, Tight, Normal, Smooth, and Very Smooth. By selecting Pixels, you are telling Flash to draw its lines sharply along the edges of the pixels. The resulting image will have a very boxy, pixilated look to it. If your image has many curves that you want to maintain while avoiding pixilation, select Tight or Very Tight. On the other hand, if you aren't that worried about preserving the exact shapes in your image, select Smooth or Very Smooth from the Curve Fit drop-down menu.

Figure 6.4

The image on the left is the original bitmap image. The other three images have a Color Threshold value of 25, 50, and 75, respectively.

Corner Threshold Determines how many corners and points the tracing process uses when drawing vector shapes from portions of your bitmap image. Choosing Many Corners from the drop-down menu preserves complex, twisting shapes in the image, and choosing Few Corners smoothes them out by telling Flash to draw them in shapes with as few corners as possible.

To create a traced bitmap that looks as close as possible to its original bitmap form (given the constraints of the tracing process), set a Color Threshold of 10, a Minimum Area of 1 pixel, the Curve Fit to Pixels, and the Corner Threshold to Many Corners.

Setting the Properties of an Imported Bitmap

Each bitmap you import into Flash MX 2004 or Flash MX Professional 2004 has a series of properties you can manipulate.

When you set bitmap properties, you have to work with the Library. Don't worry too much about the intricacies of the Library yet because it will be covered in detail in Chapter 7.

To manipulate a bitmap, follow these steps:

1. Open the Library by choosing Window → Library or use the shortcut Cmd/Ctrl+**L**.

2. To open the Bitmap Properties dialog box, select the bitmap in the Library, and do one of the following:

   - Click the Properties icon, which is the third icon from the left at the bottom of the Library (the small blue circle with an *i* in it).

   - Ctrl+click (Mac) or right-click (Windows) and choose Properties from the context menu.

   - Choose Properties from the Library's Options drop-down menu.

3. When open, the Bitmap Properties dialog box (see Figure 6.5) has several options:

   Preview window Gives you a preview of the selected bitmap. If the bitmap itself is larger than the preview window, a hand icon (which appears when you move your cursor over the preview window) lets you pan the image.

   Name field Displays the name of the bitmap and lets you change it if you want.

When you change the name of the bitmap in the Bitmap Properties dialog box, you aren't actually changing the filename, just the name given to the bitmap in the Library.

   Path, Date, and Dimensions areas Display the bitmap's path, date of creation, and dimensions.

Allow Smoothing option Instructs Flash to *anti-alias* (or smooth) the image when checked.

Compression drop-down menu Gives you two choices:

- By choosing Photo (JPEG), you compress the image in JPEG format. To use the image's default compression quality, click the Use Imported JPEG Data check box. To choose a new quality compression setting, deselect Use Imported JPEG Data and enter a value between 1 and 100 in the Quality field. A higher value preserves greater image quality but results in a larger file size.

- By choosing Lossless (GIF/PNG), you maintain the image "as is" by not discarding any of its data. Although Lossless compression maintains image quality, it results in a far larger image size.

Figure 6.5

The Bitmap Properties dialog box

Use Imported JPEG Data option Ensures that the image maintains its original quality. This option is unavailable if you've selected Lossless (GIF/PNG) from the Compression drop-down menu.

Test button Allows you to check the file's compression. The results, which include the file sizes of the original and the compressed images, are displayed at the bottom of the Bitmap Properties dialog box.

Update button Checks to see if any changes have been made to the original file. If there have been changes, the imported file will update to reflect the changes to its parent.

4. Once you've set the bitmap's properties, click OK.

Editing an Imported Bitmap

Flash gives you the ability to launch an external image-editing program. From here, you can make any changes you want to a given bitmap and then have Flash reflect the changes.

> If you are editing a Fireworks PNG file that's been imported as a flattened image (by choosing the Flatten Image option from the Fireworks PNG Import Settings dialog box), you can choose to edit the PNG source file for the bitmap. If you've imported a PNG as an editable object, you won't be able to edit it with an alternate image-editing program.

To edit a PNG with Macromedia Fireworks 3 or later:

If you don't have a version of Macromedia Fireworks installed, you won't have access to the Edit with Fireworks option.

1. Open the Library by choosing Window → Library or using the shortcut Cmd/Ctrl+**L**.
2. Ctrl+click (Mac) or right-click (Windows) and choose Edit with Fireworks from the context menu.
3. When the Edit Image dialog box opens, specify whether the PNG source file or the bitmap file is to be opened.
4. When Fireworks opens, make the desired changes to the file.
5. When finished, choose Select → Update, and Fireworks automatically updates the file. If you are using Fireworks 4 or later, simply click on the Done button in the upper-left corner of the Document window, and the file will automatically be updated in Flash.

If you want to edit a bitmap with an image-editing program other than Fireworks:

1. Open the Library by choosing Window → Library or use the shortcut Cmd/Ctrl+**L**.
2. Ctrl+click (Mac) or right-click (Windows) and choose Edit With.
3. When the Select External Editor dialog box opens, navigate to the program file of the external editor you want to use, and select it.
4. After the external editor opens, make the desired changes to the image and save it.
5. To automatically update the file in Flash, do one of the following:
   - Select the bitmap's icon in the Library and choose Update from the Library Options menu.
   - Ctrl+click (Mac) or right-click (Windows) the bitmap in the Library and select Update from the context menu.

Figure 6.6

The Update Library Items dialog box

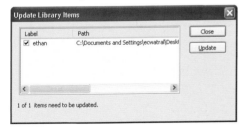

6. From here, an Update Library Items dialog box (see Figure 6.6) opens, giving you a list of all the items that can be updated. Click the check box next to those items you want to update, and click the Update button.
7. Click the Close button.

Importing an External Vector File

Even though Flash's painting and drawing tools are fairly powerful, you might want to import a vector file created with another program. This is especially true for illustrators and graphic designers who work with vector illustration programs (such as Freehand or Illustrator) in conjunction with Flash.

> For more information on integrating Flash MX 2004 and MX Pro 2004 with Macromedia Freehand, check out Bonus Chapter 2, "Working with Flash and Freehand," on this book's accompanying CD.

In this section, you're going to look at how to import vector files from two of the most popular vector illustration programs: Adobe Illustrator and Macromedia Freehand.

> The process of importing an EPS file into Flash is exactly the same as importing an Adobe Illustrator file.

Importing an Adobe Illustrator File

The ability to import an Adobe Illustrator file is a new feature to Flash MX 2004 and Flash MX Pro 2004; let's take a look at how:

> Flash MX 2004 and Flash MX Pro 2004 are able to import only Adobe Illustrator 10 (or earlier) files.

1. Choose File → Import to Stage (or File → Import to Library if you want to import the vector file directly into your movie's library).

2. When the Import dialog box opens, navigate to where the file is located, select it, and click Open.

3. From here, the Illustrator Import Options dialog box opens (see Figure 6.7).

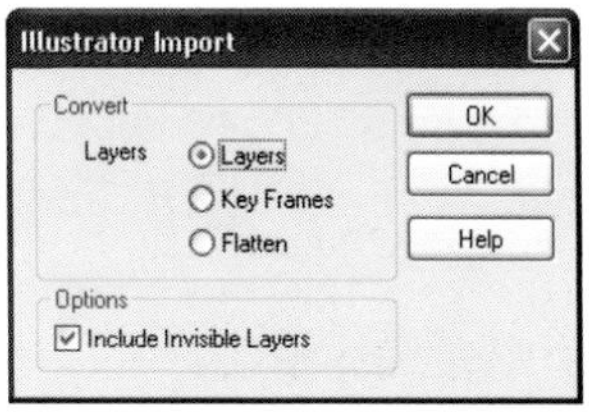

4. Select one of the options in the Convert Layers To section of the Illustrator Import dialog box to determine how Flash will deal with a multilayered Illustrator document:

   • Select Layers if you want each layer of the Illustrator file to be converted into a discrete layer in the Flash movie.

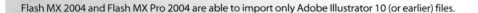

Figure 6.7

The Illustrator Import dialog box

- Select Key Frames if you want each layer in the Illustrator file to be converted into a discrete keyframe in your movie's Timeline.

- Choose Flatten if you want all the layers in the Illustrator file to be flattened into a single layer in your movie.

5. From here, select Include Invisible Layers to import all of the Illustrator document's layers regardless of whether they are visible or not.

6. When you've finished setting the properties of the imported Illustrator file, click OK.

Importing a Macromedia Freehand File into Flash

Freehand is extremely powerful when you're working in concert with Flash. Because both programs are made by the same company, and Macromedia is in the habit of making applications that work *very* well together, Freehand has a whole series of tools that actually allow you to craft Flash content before you even start working with Flash.

> For more information on integrating Flash MX 2004 and Flash MX Pro 2004 with Macromedia Freehand, check out Bonus Chapter 2, "Working with Flash and Freehand," on this book's accompanying CD.

In addition, you also have a more detailed level of control over how Flash deals with imported Freehand files.

> Flash can import Freehand MX or earlier files.

To import a Freehand file into Flash, just follow these steps:

1. Choose File → Import to Stage (or File → Import to Library if you want to import the vector file directly into your movie's library).

2. When the Import dialog box opens, navigate to where the file is located, select it, and click Open.

3. The Freehand Import dialog box opens (see Figure 6.8).

4. In the Mapping section of the Freehand Import dialog box, select how you want Flash to deal with a multipage Freehand document:

- Select Scenes if you want each page to be converted into a discrete Scene in your Flash movie.

- Select Keyframes if you want each of the pages into the Freehand document to be converted into a discrete keyframe in your movie's Timeline.

5. Then you need to choose how you want Flash to convert a multilayered Freehand file. In the Mapping section of the Freehand Import dialog box, select one of the following options:

   - To convert each layer in the Freehand document into a discrete layer in your Flash movie's Timeline, select Layers.

   - If you want each of the layers in the Freehand document to be converted into a discrete keyframe in your movie's Timeline, select Keyframes.

   - To convert all the layers in the Freehand document into a single layer in your movie's Timeline, select Flatten.

Figure 6.8

The Freehand Import dialog box

6. If you want to import all the pages in the Freehand document, select the All option in the Pages section. Alternatively, if you want to import only a specific range of pages from a multipage Freehand document, select the From option, and then specify the first and last pages in the sequence.

7. At this point, you need to set document-specific options for your imported Freehand file in the Options section:

   - Select Include Invisible Layers to import all the Freehand document's layers regardless of whether or not they are visible.

   - Choose Include Background Layer to include the background layer when you bring the Freehand document into Flash.

   - Select Maintain Text Blocks, if you want all the text within the Freehand file to remain fully editable after you import it into your movie.

8. When you've finished setting the properties for the Freehand file to be imported, click OK.

If the Freehand file you are importing is composed using CMYK colors, Flash automatically converts it to RGB.

Grouping and Ungrouping Objects

When you combine multiple objects into one unit, it's called *grouping*. The process itself is useful for a number of reasons. Say you wanted to create a flower to use in your Flash movie. You can get a lot more visual detail and control over the way the flower looks if you draw the individual parts separately. So, you could draw the petals, the stem, the leaves, and then arrange them on the Stage exactly how you want. However, what happens when you want to move the *whole* flower? Well, you could select each of the elements and then move them with the Arrow tool. However, what if you accidentally forgot to include a vital part of the flower (say, the stem) in the selection? When you moved the flower, the stem would stay behind, putting your beautiful creation out of whack.

Don't laugh; this kind of thing happens all the time to even the most accomplished Flashers. How could you avoid this potentially calamitous situation? This is where grouping comes in. When you group a series of objects, they are treated as one unit. So, in our silly flower example, if you had grouped all of the elements, you'd be able to select and move them all as one unit, leaving no part behind.

> As discussed in Chapter 4, you can also group the stroke and fill of a given object to avoid moving one independently of the other.

To group objects, follow these steps:

1. With the Arrow tool, select any objects on the Stage you want to include in the group. Remember, you can select anything on the Stage: text, shapes, bitmaps, and so on.

> To select multiple objects, hold down the Shift key and click any items you want included in the selection.

2. With the various objects selected, choose Modify → Group or use the shortcut Cmd/Ctrl+**G**. Figure 6.9 illustrates a series of grouped objects.

> The Property Inspector will identify an object (or objects) as being grouped.

Ungrouping objects is just as easy as grouping them:

1. Select the grouped objects with the Arrow tool.
2. Choose Modify → Ungroup or use the shortcut Cmd/Ctrl+Shift+**G**.

One of the great things about the way Flash deals with grouped objects is that you can edit individual elements (for instance, the petals in our flower example) without having to ungroup them. This is quite helpful if you've created a particularly detailed image with which you don't want to go through the entire grouping process again. Let's take a look at how:

1. Select a group with the Arrow tool.
2. Choose Edit → Edit Selected. Alternatively, you can also simply double-click on an object in an already selected group. Notice that everything else on the Stage that isn't part of

Figure 6.9

At the top is a series of ungrouped objects. At the bottom, the same objects have been grouped. Notice the line that surrounds the entire group as if its parts were all one object.

the group changes color slightly; this signals their temporary inaccessibility. Also, notice that the Edit toolbar, which is located along the top of the Stage, indicates that you are currently editing the group (usually represented by the default name of Group).

3. From here, make any changes you want to any of the objects within the group.

4. When finished, simply choose Edit → Edit All, double-click anywhere outside the group with the Arrow tool, or click the scene name in the Edit toolbar.

Moving Objects

When it comes to working with objects, you'll often need to move them around the Stage. You can move objects in four ways: with the Arrow tool, with the arrow keys, through the Property Inspector, or with the Info panel.

To move an object with the Arrow tool, just follow these steps:

1. Select an object. To select a series of objects, hold down the Shift key and click.

2. With the Arrow tool, click and drag the object (or series of objects) to the desired position on the Stage. If you want to constrain its movement vertically or horizontally, hold down the Shift key while moving the object(s).

> If you hold down the Option/Alt key while dragging, Flash creates a copy of the object(s) and moves the copy instead of the original.

To move an object with the arrow keys on your keyboard:

1. Select an object or group of objects that you want to move.

2. Use the arrow keys on your keyboard to move the selected object 1 pixel at a time in any direction. If you want to move the selected object 8 pixels at a time, hold down your Shift key while using the arrow keys.

To move an object or a group of objects with the Property Inspector or the Info panel, follow these steps:

1. Open the Property Inspector by choosing Window → Properties or open the Info panel by choosing Window → Design Panels → Info.

2. Select the object or objects you want to move. Notice that there is an X field and a Y field in the lower-left corner of the Property Inspector (see top of Figure 6.10) or at the right side of the Info panel (see bottom of Figure 6.10). These represent the vertical (Y)

and horizontal (X) coordinates of the currently selected object. The X/Y coordinate system is relative to the upper-left corner of the Stage—the location of which is 0/0.

3. Type a value into each of the fields to change the position of the selected object.

Figure 6.10

Both the Property Inspector and the Info panel have X and Y fields, which represent the vertical (Y) and horizontal (X) position of the selected object on the Stage.

The units of measure used in the Info panel's X/Y coordinate system are determined by what you specified in the Ruler Units that you set in the Document Properties dialog box. To change them, choose Modify → Document (or use the shortcut Cmd/Ctrl+J) and choose an alternate one from the Ruler Units drop-down menu.

Manipulating Objects with the Align Panel

The Align panel, which is accessible by selecting Window → Design Panels → Align (or by using the shortcut Cmd/Ctrl+**K**), is a handy tool that lets you do all manner of interesting things. Figure 6.11 illustrates the Align panel and all of its options.

Figure 6.11

The Align panel has four sets of buttons: Align, Distribute, Match Size, and Space.

Beyond aligning objects on the Stage, the Align panel also lets you distribute, match the size of, and space objects. In the following section, you'll look at each of these options separately.

If you want to align objects to the Stage (opposed to other objects), click the Align/Distribute to Stage button in the right portion of the Align panel.

Aligning Objects

The top section of the Align panel contains a series of buttons that lets you align selected objects horizontally or vertically. From left to right, the buttons let you align objects by their left edges, horizontally by their center points, and by their right edges. The second set of buttons, from left to right, lets you align objects by their top edges, vertically by their center points, and by their bottom edges.

Flash aligns objects according to their bounding boxes, not any feature of the object itself.

To align a series of objects, follow these steps:

1. With the Align panel open, select the objects that you want to align. Remember, you can select multiple objects by clicking and dragging with the Arrow tool and surrounding them with the bounding box or selecting them individually with the Arrow tool (remember to hold down the Shift key to select multiple objects).

2. Select one of the alignment options from the Align panel. Figure 6.12 illustrates the effects that the various alignment options have on images.

When aligning to the left, Flash uses the left edge of the leftmost object in the selection for the alignment. The same applies when you are aligning to the top, bottom, or right; Flash uses the edge of the topmost, bottommost, or rightmost object for the alignment.

Figure 6.12

The first row is an illustration of three unaligned objects. The bottom row illustrates the three same objects aligned horizontally to the top edge.

Distributing Objects

Beyond alignment, the Align panel gives you the ability to distribute selected objects. This comes in handy if you want to evenly space three or more selected objects. From left to right, the buttons in the Distribute section of the Align panel let you distribute objects evenly by their top edges, their center points vertically, and their bottom edges. The next distribute buttons, from left to right, let you distribute objects evenly by their left edges, their center points horizontally, and their right edges.

To distribute a series of objects, follow these directions:

1. Select a series of objects (distributing less than two won't have any visible effect, so remember to select three or more).

2. Click one of the distribute buttons in the Align panel. Figure 6.13 provides an example of the Distribute option's effects.

Figure 6.13

The left row of objects is undistributed. The right row, however, contains the same objects after they've been distributed vertically to their center points.

Matching Object Size

When you use the Match Size buttons in the Align panel, you can resize a series of selected objects so that their horizontal or vertical dimensions match those of the largest in the selection. From left to right, the Match Size buttons in the Align panel let you match two objects' width, height, or both width and height.

To match the size of objects, follow these steps:

1. Select two or more objects on the Stage.

2. Click one of the Match Size buttons in the Align panel. Figure 6.14 illustrates the Match Size option's effects.

Figure 6.14

The top two objects are unaltered. The bottom two are examples of the same objects after their heights have been matched. As the one on the left was the larger of the two, it has remained unchanged. The right object, however, has been stretched.

Spacing Objects

The Space buttons in the Align panel allow you to space selected objects out vertically or horizontally. So, what exactly is the difference between the Space options and the Distribute options? Although you won't see much difference between two similarly-sized objects if they were either spaced or distributed, the difference is obvious when you're working with differently-sized objects.

When you use the Space Evenly Horizontally or the Space Evenly Vertically buttons, you are guaranteed that there will be a fixed number of pixels between each object. When you distribute objects of varied sizes, you'll find that the larger the object is, the less space there will be between it and the next one. This is primarily because the Distribute options use a central reference point to arrange the objects. As a result, you might want to use the Space option in the Align panel instead.

To space objects, follow these steps:

1. Select two or more objects on the Stage.

2. Click one of the Space buttons in the Align panel. In Figure 6.15, you'll see an example of the Space Evenly Horizontally option.

Arranging Objects

Figure 6.15

The top four objects are unaltered. The bottom four show what happens when you use the Space Evenly Horizontally option in the Align panel.

Although you can use layers (something we'll talk about in depth in Chapter 8) to position objects in your Flash creation vertically, you can also stack them within a single layer using the Arrange option. The result of both methods is that some objects appear to be either behind or in front of other objects.

So, what exactly is the difference between using layers to stack items and using the Arrange option? Well, as you'll come to learn in Chapter 8, layers provide you a great deal more control over the Z (depth) organization of your movie. However, in cases where all the elements in your movie exist within a single layer, the Arrange options are your best bet for manipulating the stacking order of your objects.

The Arrange options, which are accessible by selecting Modify → Arrange, allow you to change the position of any selected object in the stack, thereby moving them in front of or behind other objects. The options in the Arrange menu are pretty straightforward; let's take a look at each:

Bring to Front Moves the selected object to the absolute top/front of the stack in the currently selected layer.

Bring Forward Moves the currently selected object one increment forward/up in the stack of the currently selected layer.

Send Backward Moves the currently selected object backward/downward one increment in the stack of the currently selected layer.

Send to Back Moves the currently selected object to the absolute bottom/back of the stack of the currently selected layer.

Lock Locks the position of all the objects in the stack of a given layer.

Unlock All Unlocks the stack of the currently selected layer.

Transforming Objects

In previous versions of Flash, the tools with which you could manipulate an object's shape, size, and orientation were all accessible in the Options section of the Toolbox when the Arrow tool was selected. However, in Flash MX, Macromedia introduced a discrete tool, called the Free Transform tool, with which you can manipulate all aspects of a given object.

Located in the Tools section of the Toolbox, the Free Transform tool ⊞ has a series of *modifiers* that let you transform a selected object. These modifiers are accessible in the Options section of the Toolbox when the Free Transform tool is selected.

Although you can specify the action that you want to take on an object by selecting a specific transform modifier, the Free Transform tool also lets you manipulate an object without selecting any of the options. All you need to do is select the Free Transform tool, click the object you want to manipulate, and then move your cursor over any of the handles on the object's bounding box. Depending on the transform that you can perform on that specific handle, your cursor will change accordingly.

> The following sections show you how to use the Free Transform tool in conjunction with its various modifier options.

Never content to provide you with only one way to perform an action, Flash also allows you to do many of the same types of transformations with the Transform panel (which is accessible by choosing Window → Design Panels → Transform).

Figure 6.16

The Free Transform tool's bounding box

In the following sections, you'll explore how to scale, rotate, flip, skew, distort, and edit the envelope of a selected object. You'll also learn how to restore a transformed object.

Scaling an Object

By scaling an object, you change its size (either horizontally, vertically, or uniformly). You can scale an object with either the Free Transform tool or the Transform panel.

To scale an object with the Free Transform tool, follow these steps:

1. Select the desired object with the Arrow tool, then choose the Free Transform tool ⊞ from the Toolbox. Alternatively, click the desired object with the Free Transform tool to select it.

2. From here, you'll notice that a bounding box with handles appears around the selected object (see Figure 6.16).

3. Select the Scale button ⊡ in the Toolbox's Options section (accessible when you've selected the Free Transform tool). Alternatively, you can select Modify → Transform → Scale.

Figure 6.17

Scaling an object horizontally

> Remember, because of the nature of the Free Transform tool, you can bypass step 3 if you want and go straight to step 4.

4. To scale horizontally, click one of the transform handles on the left or right of the bounding box and drag until the object reaches the desired size (see Figure 6.17).

5. To scale vertically, click one of the transform handles on the top or the bottom of the bounding box and drag until the object reaches the desired size (see Figure 6.18).

Figure 6.18

Scaling an object vertically

6. To scale vertically and horizontally at the same time, click one of the corner transform handles and drag until the object reaches the desired size. By doing this, you'll also maintain the object's proportions (see Figure 6.19).

7. When you've finished, click anywhere off the object to hide the transform handles.

You can also scale an object with the Transform panel:

1. Select the object that you want to scale.

2. Choose Window → Design Panels → Transform to open the Transform panel (see Figure 6.20).

3. To scale the object horizontally, enter a value (in percent) into the Width field.

4. To scale the object vertically, enter a value (in percent) into the Height field.

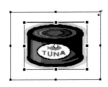

Figure 6.19

Scaling an object horizontally and vertically

5. To scale the object both horizontally and vertically, click the Constrain check box and then enter a value (in percent) into either the Width or Height field.

> The value that you enter into the Width or Height field can range from 1 to 4,000, depending on how large the selected object originally was.

6. When you've finished, click anywhere off the object to hide the transform handles.

Rotating an Object

When you rotate an object, it turns around its registration point. Don't worry too much about registration points yet because they're covered in the "Working with Transformation Points" section later in this chapter. For the time being, just recognize that they are a central point that acts as a pivot for rotation.

Figure 6.20
The Transform panel

As with many of the transformation operations, you can rotate an object with the Free Transform tool or the Transform panel. To rotate an object with the Free Transform tool, follow these steps:

1. Select the desired object with the Arrow tool, then choose the Free Transform tool ⊞ from the Toolbox. Alternatively, click the desired object with the Free Transform tool to select it.

2. From here, you'll notice that a bounding box with handles appears around the selected object.

3. Select the Rotate and Skew button ⟳ in the Toolbox's Options section (accessible when you've selected the Free Transform tool). Alternatively, you can choose Modify → Transform → Rotate and Skew.

> Remember, because of the nature of the Free Transform tool, you can bypass step 3 if you want and go straight to step 4.

4. Move your cursor over one of the *corner handles*. If the selected object is not a group, you'll notice that your cursor changes to an icon with arrows that form a circle (see Figure 6.21).

5. From here, click and drag in a circular motion to rotate your object.

6. When you are finished, click anywhere off of the object to hide the transform handles.

Figure 6.21
Note the cursor change when you move your movie over the corner handle of an object that has been selected with the Free Transform tool.

   To rotate an object with the Transform panel, follow these steps:

1. Select the object that you want to rotate.

2. Choose Window → Design Panels → Transform to open the Transform panel (see Figure 6.20, shown earlier).

3. Click the Rotate radio button.

4. Enter a value (in degrees) in the Rotate field.

5. Click Return/Enter to apply the rotation to the selected object.

> You can also rotate a selected object 90° clockwise or counterclockwise by choosing Modify →
> Transform → Rotate 90° CW or Rotate 90° CCW.

Flipping an Object

Flash lets you flip a selected object horizontally or vertically without changing its relative position on the Stage.

1. Use the Arrow tool to select the object that you want to flip.

2. Select Modify → Transform → Flip Horizontal or Flip Vertical. Figure 6.22 illustrates the effects of the Flip Horizontal and Flip Vertical options.

Skewing an Object

Skewing slants an object along its vertical or horizontal axis. As with many of the operations already discussed in this chapter, you can slant an object in two ways.

To slant an object with the Free Transform tool:

Figure 6.22

Three copies of the same object. The one at the top shows the original position. The middle illustrates the object after it has been flipped horizontally. The one at the bottom illustrates the same object after it has been flipped vertically.

1. Select the desired object with the Arrow tool, then choose the Free Transform tool ⊡ from the Toolbox. Alternatively, click the desired object with the Free Transform tool to select it.

2. Click the Rotate and Skew button 🗇 in the Toolbox's Options section (when you have the Free Transform tool selected).

> Remember, because of the nature of the Free Transform tool, you can bypass step 2 if you
> want and go straight to step 4.

3. When the handles appear, move your cursor over one of handles in the middle of the sides of the bounding box. Notice how your cursor changes into a pair of arrows pointing in opposite directions, oriented either vertically or horizontally (depending on which handle you moved your cursor over).

4. As illustrated in Figure 6.23, click and drag horizontally or vertically (depending on which handles you are manipulating).

5. To finish, click anywhere off the object to hide the transform handles.

To skew an object with the Transform panel, follow these steps:

1. Select the object that you want to skew.

2. Choose Window → Design Panels → Transform to open the Transform panel (see Figure 6.20, shown earlier).

3. Click the Skew radio button.

4. To skew the object vertically, enter a value (in degrees) in the Skew Vertically field.

5. To skew an object horizontally, enter a value (in degrees) in the Skew Horizontally field.

6. When you are finished, press Return/Enter.

Figure 6.23

Simply drag horizontally or vertically to skew the selected object.

Distorting an Object

When you apply a distort transformation, you can change the position of either the corner or side handles of an object's bounding box (see Figure 6.24).

This process not only changes the position of the selected handles (and therefore the shape of the object itself), but it also changes its adjoining edges (see Figure 6.25).

> It's worth noting that the Distort transformation won't work on a group (Modify → Group), but it works just fine on a group of individually selected objects.

If you hold down the Shift key while applying a distort transformation, the object will be tapered.

Unlike the previous transformations discussed, you can distort an object only by using the Free Transform tool. Here's how:

1. Select the object you want to distort with the Arrow tool.

2. Select the Free Transform tool ⊡ .

3. Click the Distort button ▱ in the Toolbox's Options section (when you have the Free Transform tool selected). Alternatively, you can also choose Modify → Transform → Distort.

4. When the bounding box appears, move your cursor over any of the handles. Notice how your cursor changes to a larger white pointer.

5. Click and drag the handle. When you've reached the location on the Stage where you would like the handle to be moved, simply release your mouse button. Your object will distort accordingly.

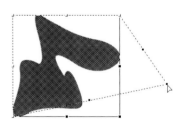

Figure 6.24

Distorting an object

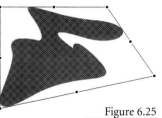

Figure 6.25

Distorted object

Manipulating an Object's Envelope

An *envelope* is the bounding box that surrounds one or more *ungrouped* objects. With the Edit Envelope transform, you can effectively manipulate this envelope and thereby warp an object with a fair amount of precision.

The Edit Envelope transformation does not work on grouped objects, symbols, bitmaps, gradients, or text.

To manipulate an object's envelope, follow these steps:

1. Select the object (or objects) whose envelope you want to edit with the Arrow tool.

Although the Edit Envelope transformation won't work on a group (Modify → Group), it works just fine on a group of individually selected objects.

2. Select the Free Transform tool ⊡ .

3. Click the Envelope button in the Toolbox's Options section (when you have the Free Transform tool selected). Alternatively, you can also choose Modify → Transform → Envelope.

Remember, if the object is grouped, you won't have access to the Envelope button.

4. When the bounding box opens, move your cursor over any of the handles. Notice how your cursor changes to a larger white pointer.

You'll note that there are two types of handles: square and circular. The square handles are the points along the object's bounding box that you can directly manipulate, and the circular handles are tangent handles.

Figure 6.26

Editing the envelope of an object

5. Click and drag the handle (see Figure 6.26). When you've reached the location on the Stage where you want the handle to be moved, simply release your mouse button. Your object will warp accordingly.

6. Notice that when you click and drag one of the envelope handles, tangent handles will appear. Much as in the case of path created with the Pen tool, you can manipulate the tangents (by clicking and dragging the handle at the end of the tangent) to further warp the object's envelope (see Figure 6.27).

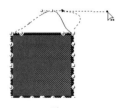

Figure 6.27

Manipulating an object's envelope tangents

7. When you've finished distorting the object's envelope, deselect it by clicking anywhere else on the Stage.

Restoring Transformed Objects

As you can see, you can apply a number of transformations to any given object. It would be quite easy to go wild and transform an object beyond all hope of returning it to its previous state. You'd be surprised how far away an object can wander from its initial appearance, leaving you totally stumped as to how it originally looked. But there is an easy way to restore objects to their pre-transformed state:

1. Select the object that you want to restore.

2. Choose Modify → Transform → Remove Transform. Alternatively, you can click the Reset button in the bottom-right corner of the Transform panel ⊞.

Working with Transformation Points

A registration point is a reference that Flash uses when it carries out all of the previously mentioned transformations. When you rotate an object, you rotate it around the registration point. When you align or distribute objects, the registration point acts as a reference for the procedure.

Unfortunately, you can't directly manipulate an object's registration point. However, you can change the position of an object's *transformation point,* which is like a temporary registration point that appears when an object is being transformed. Ultimately, by moving the position of the transformation point, you can get better control over the result of any given transformation. Say, for instance, you want an object to rotate not around its center, but instead around its upper-right corner. Well, all you would need to do is move the object's transformation point from the center to the desired location in the upper-right corner.

> When you move an object's transformation point, its new location is merely temporary. As soon as you apply a new transformation, the transformation point will reset to its default location, which is in the center of an object.

Let's take a look at how you go about moving an object's transformation point:

1. Select the object whose transformation point you want to manipulate.

2. Initiate any transform (either with the Free Transform tool or choosing Modify → Transform). This will cause the bounding box to appear around the selected object.

3. Click and drag the transformation point (which appears in the center of the object as a white circle) and drag it to the desired location (see Figure 6.28).

4. When the transformation point is in the desired location, carry out the desired transformation.

> To reset the transformation point to its default location manually, double-click it.

Figure 6.28

Moving an object's transformation point

Inspirational Design Model

Created by Brian Taylor, Rustboy (www.rustboy.com) is a promotional site for a short film of the same name that is currently in production and will ultimately be distributed online. Rustboy (the primary character of the film) began life as a simple 2D creation, but has since been thrust into the glorious world of 3D. The site (see Figure 6.29), which is a great example of simple yet stylish Flash design, features a tirelessly updated diary on current Rustboy milestones, beautifully illustrated story boards and concept art, short QuickTime teasers, and insights into the creation of the film. The site itself is designed in such a way that it perfectly captures the slightly dark feeling of Rustboy, and the world in which he lives.

Figure 6.29

Rustboy

CHAPTER 7

Reduce, Reuse, and Recycle: Working with Symbols

Imagine if you created a Flash movie in which all the elements were variations on the same theme. Until now, you would have to spend a great deal of time painstakingly creating each element individually. With the help of *symbols,* however, you will never have to toil in vain, oppressed under the weight of backbreaking digital labor. You will be able to create one master image and then base all subsequent images upon it, making specific changes to each as you go. Symbols help streamline the creative process and maximize your artistic juices. The purpose of this chapter, therefore, is to explore the glorious world of symbols.

The chapter covers the following topics:

- Understanding symbols
- Creating native Flash symbols
- Using the Library to work with symbols
- Working with symbol instances

Understanding Symbols

Essentially, symbols are reusable elements that reside in the Library. You can use them repeatedly in either the same Flash creation or another one entirely. Whenever you create a symbol, it is automatically placed in the Library, where it is stored for future use. When you drag a symbol out of the Library (discussed in the section "Adding a Symbol to the Stage" later in this chapter) onto the Stage, the symbol itself is not placed on the Stage. Instead, Flash creates a copy, called an *instance,* and places it on the Stage. You can change instances as many times or in as many different ways as you want without altering the original symbol. There will always be a copy of the original symbol residing in the Library.

Animation of any significant complexity can be accomplished only with symbols. As a result, it's important that most, if not all, of the graphical elements you create in Flash MX 2004 and Flash MX Professional 2004 are either converted to symbols or created as symbols right off the bat. Don't worry about how symbols are animated with the Timeline; that will be covered in Part III. For now, the only important things to understand are the differences between the various types of symbols.

Symbols fall into one of two categories: native Flash symbols and imported symbols. Native Flash symbols are created directly within Flash, while imported symbols are created in another program and imported into Flash.

In Flash MX 2004 and Flash MX Pro 2004, native symbols are also referred to as *symbol behaviors.* This is due to the fact that, as you'll soon discover, there are three types of native Flash symbols, all of which behave and have different purposes within your movie.

Symbols are beneficial for a couple of reasons. The first, which has already been discussed briefly, is that they allow you to streamline the creative process. When it comes to native Flash symbols, all you need to do is create one object and then manipulate its instance on the Stage to create multiple variations without having to re-create the object from scratch every time. The second reason that symbols are so powerful is that they help you reduce the overall file size of your Flash creation. Each time a symbol is used, Flash simply refers to the profile of the original in the Library. If you're using multiple instances based on a single symbol, Flash needs to save only the information about their differences. If you were to use a different symbol for each of the various objects, each would be included in the Flash file, increasing the overall file size.

Introducing Native Flash Symbols

Let's explore the three different types of native Flash symbols:

Graphic symbols Graphic symbols ⊞ are static graphic objects created with the various Flash drawing and painting tools. They work in conjunction with the main movie and are most commonly used as elements in Timeline animations.

Button symbols While the Graphic symbols are static elements, Button symbols ⊞ are dynamic, altering their appearance when clicked. Buttons are one of the most popular interactive elements you can create in Flash. Although you'll explore Button symbols (and how you make them) in Chapter 15, it's important to know they are made up of four different static images (referred to as *states*). Each state is visible based on how the user interacts with the button: when the button is up (the *up* state), when the user's mouse is over the button (the *over* state), and when the user clicks the button (the *down* state). The fourth button state, the *hit* state, is not a visible element in the button. Instead, it acts more like a hotspot that determines the active area of the button.

One of the most important things about Button symbols, at least in terms of creating interactivity, is that they can be tightly integrated with ActionScript.

Movie Clip symbols It's no exaggeration to say that Movie Clips ⊞ are probably one of the most important aspects of Flash itself. Movie Clips are smaller, self-contained movies that you can place within another movie. They are infinitely nestable so you could have a Movie Clip within a Movie Clip within a Movie Clip, and so on.

Movie Clips, which are in no way limited in their composition, run *independently* of the Timeline. They can also be placed within other symbols, so you could insert a Movie Clip into one of the previously mentioned Button symbol states, creating an animated button.

> If you're really interested in finding out how you can create and manipulate Movie Clips, see Chapter 11.

Movie Clips become even *more* powerful when you realize that they can be controlled using ActionScript. As a result, you could have any number of Movie Clips in your movie and send various commands to them (based on either user interaction or some purely non-user-based occurrence in your movie) using ActionScript.

> To learn more about ActionScripting for movies with multiple Movie Clips (referred to as *multiple timelines*), check out Chapter 20.

Introducing Imported Flash Symbols

Now that you've looked at the three native Flash symbols, you can move on to look at the various types of imported symbols:

Bitmaps You've already looked at how you import a bitmap into Flash. What you haven't learned is that when bitmaps are imported into Flash, they're automatically inserted in the Library and converted into symbols for your use.

Audio Unlike graphical elements, audio files can't be seen. As a result, when they are imported, they're placed only in the Library (and not also on the Stage like imported bitmaps). Because audio is such a large topic, at this point, there is little more you need to know other than audio files are one of the many types of nonnative Flash symbols.

> For more about audio and Flash, see Part VI.

Digital Video One of the great things about Flash is that it lets you import and use a series of different digital video formats. If you have QuickTime 4 (or above) installed on your computer, you can import QuickTime files (MOV), Audio Video Interlace (AVI) files, Digital Video (DV) files, and Motion Picture Experts Group (MPEG) files.

> You can also import sound-only QuickTime movie files and place them in the Library as symbols.

If you're working in Windows and you have DirectX 7 (or above) installed, you'll be able to import AVI, MPEG, and Window Media Files (WMV/ASF).

> When imported, all digital video files are automatically placed in the Library to be used as symbols.

In addition, both Flash MX 2004 and Flash MX Pro 2004 users can import and use the Macromedia Flash Video (FLV) format.

> For more information on importing and working with digital video (especially the new FLV features in Flash MX 2004 and MX Pro 2004), check out Chapter 31.

Creating Native Flash Symbols

There is little doubt that symbols are one of the most important elements of Flash. Mastering their creation and manipulation will open up a world of incredible creative possibilities for you. In this section, you'll look at the two primary ways to create Graphic symbols: creating from scratch and converting from existing graphics.

Button and Movie Clip symbols are discussed in future chapters, so this section deals exclusively with creating Graphic symbols. For more information on creating Movie Clips, refer to Chapter 11. To learn more about creating Button Symbols, see Chapter 15.

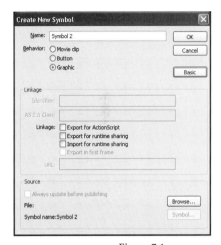

Figure 7.1

The Create New Symbol dialog box

Creating Symbols from Scratch

When it comes to Graphic symbols, it's more than likely that you'll create most within Flash with the painting and drawing tools:

1. Make sure you don't already have an object selected on the Stage.

2. Choose Insert → New Symbol or use the shortcut Cmd/Ctrl+F8. The Create New Symbol dialog box opens (see Figure 7.1).

> You can switch between basic and advanced options in the Create New Symbol dialog box by clicking the Basic/Advanced button. The options available in the Advanced section relate to creating a Shared Library, which is discussed in the section "Working with Shared Symbol Libraries" later in this chapter.

3. In the Create New Symbol dialog box, make sure the Graphic radio button is selected, enter a name for your symbol into the Name field, and click OK.

> If your Flash creation will use a great deal of graphics, it's a good strategy to give each symbol a distinct name so you won't get confused. By default, if you don't name the symbol, Flash MX 2004 and Flash MX Pro 2004 will use the name *Symbol X*, where *X* is a sequential number.

4. From here, Flash adds the symbol to the Library and switches you to Symbol Editing mode (see Figure 7.2). The name of the symbol appears in the Edit Toolbar bar, just to the right of the name of the scene you're currently working in. For reference, the symbol's registration point is represented by the crosshairs in the middle of the Symbol Editor.

> The Symbol Editor is a little tricky in that it looks almost exactly like the regular Flash environment. Don't get confused, though; you can tell the difference because the symbol's name is displayed in the Edit Toolbar just to the right of the actual scene's name, and a small cross, representing the symbol's eventual registration point, appears on the Stage.

Figure 7.2

Symbol Editing mode enables you to create your symbol with the same painting and drawing tools you use in the Stage.

Figure 7.2

Symbol Editing mode enables you to create your symbol with the same painting and drawing tools you use in the Stage.

5. Use the painting and drawing skills you mastered in Chapter 4 to create the desired symbol.

6. When you're finished, you need to exit Symbol Editing mode. To do this, either choose Edit → Edit Document or click the scene name in the Edit Toolbar.

Scenes are a way to break your Flash creation into manageable chunks. To find out more, see Chapter 12.

Converting Existing Objects to Symbols

Although many of your Graphic symbols will be made from scratch in the Symbol Editor, you might come upon a situation where you need to convert an existing graphic (something you didn't create in the Symbol Editor) into a symbol:

1. On the Stage, select the object you want to turn into a Graphic symbol.

2. Choose Modify → Convert to Symbol.

3. When the Convert to Symbol dialog box opens, make sure you select the radio button appropriate for the type of symbol you want to create.

4. Enter a name for your symbol in the Name field.

5. From here, you can set the location of your symbol's registration point. To do this, click one of the nine small boxes in the registration point diagram. Each box represents the location of the symbol's registration point within its square bounding box (see Figure 7.3).

6. When you're finished, click OK and the symbol is automatically added to the Library. The original object that you converted on the Stage is switched into an instance with a parent symbol residing in the Library.

Using the Library to Manage Symbol Assets

The Library, accessible by choosing Window → Library (also by using the shortcut F11 or Cmd/Ctrl+L), is the repository for all symbols in a given Flash movie. Whether you're using Graphic symbols, Button symbols, Movie Clips, or any of the various imported symbols in your Flash movie, the Library is where they'll be. The Library also enables you to preview animations and sound files quickly and easily.

The Library has a second cousin called the Common Library, which you access by selecting Window → Other Panels → Common Libraries. There you'll find four groups of premade symbols—Buttons, Classes, Learning Interactions, and Sounds—that you can use in your own movie. With this basic introduction to the Library, you can begin to take advantage of its power and versatility.

Registration point diagram

Figure 7.3

The Convert to Symbol dialog box; note the Registration Point diagram.

> For more information on using the Button Common Library, refer to Chapter 15.

Exploring the Library

The Library is packed with information and tools designed to make managing and manipulating symbols considerably easier (see Figure 7.4). The only way to get a handle on them is to explore each individually.

The Sort Window Columns

The Sort window displays information about each symbol in the Library in columns. Under normal circumstances, you can make all the columns visible only if you resize the Library horizontally (by clicking its left edge and dragging). Alternatively, you can also click the Wide Library View button in the right portion of the Library (just above the vertical scroll bar).

Figure 7.4

The Library

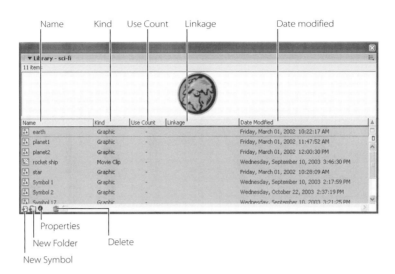

Clicking any aspect of a symbol (name, icon, linkage, date modified, and so on) will display a preview of it.

The Sort window contains the following columns:

Name Shows the name you assigned each symbol. The Name column also displays the filename for imported files such as audio files and bitmaps. The Name column is sorted alphabetically. To reverse the sort order, click the Sort Order button to the right of the Library window.

Kind Indicates whether the symbol is a Button, Bitmap, Graphic, Movie Clip, or Sound. To group items in the library by the type, click the Kind column header.

The type of symbol is also indicated by the small icon to the left of the name.

Use Count Tracks exactly how many times each symbol has been used. This is especially helpful if you're working on a particularly large project and you want to determine which symbols have actually been used in the final movie.

Linkage Indicates whether a symbol is being shared with another movie or imported from another movie.

Date Modified Indicates the last time a symbol or imported file was updated.

Library Panel Buttons

In addition to the Sort window columns, the bottom portion of the Library features several important buttons:

New Symbol   Opens the Create New Symbol dialog box, allowing you to create new symbols directly from within the Library.

New Folder   Allows you to set up folders in the Library so you can better organize your content. This feature is amazingly useful when working with large, complex movies that need to be well organized. To add an item to a folder, click the item and drag it to the folder. To expand a folder, double-click it.

Properties   Opens the Symbol Properties dialog box. From there, you can change any of the selected symbol's properties.

Delete   Lets you delete symbols from the Library. Just click the symbol you want to delete and click the Delete button to remove it from the Library.

The Library Options Menu

The Library Options menu, accessible by clicking the menu icon in the upper-right corner of the Library, allows you to manage all aspects of the Library. A subset of these options is also available by Ctrl+clicking (Mac) or right-clicking (Win) a Library item.

> The New Symbol and New Folder options were discussed in the previous section.

The following settings are available in the Options menu:

New Symbol   Like the New Symbol button at the bottom of the Library, the New Symbol option in the Library's Options menu opens the Create New Symbol dialog box, allowing you to create new symbols directly from within the Library.

New Folder   The New Folder option, like the New Folder button at the bottom of the Library, allows you to create a folder that can be used to organize your movie's symbol assets.

New Font   Lets you create font symbols that are stored in a shared Library. This is beneficial because you no longer have to embed a font directly in your Flash movie.

> To learn more about Font symbols, see Chapter 5.

New Video   Inserts an empty Video symbol into the Library. To fill the symbol, double-click the Video symbol's icon. When the Embedded Video Properties dialog box (see

Figure 7.5) opens, click the Import button. From there, navigate to where the desired video file is located, select it, and click OK.

Rename Allows you to rename a symbol directly within your Library. Select the symbol that has the name you want to change, choose the Rename option from the Options menu, and type a new name in the Sort window.

You can also double-click the symbol's name in the Sort window to change it.

Move to a New Folder Automatically creates a new folder on the Sort window into which it will move the currently selected symbol.

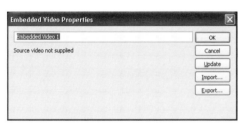

Figure 7.5

The Embedded Video Properties dialog box

Duplicate Makes an exact duplicate of the currently selected symbol. Select a symbol in the Sort window, choose Duplicate from the Options menu, and make any adjustments when the Duplicate Symbol dialog box opens.

Delete Works exactly the same as the Delete button at the bottom of the Library. Just select the unwanted Library item and select Delete from the Options menu.

Edit Opens the currently selected Graphic, Movie Clip, or Button in Symbol Editing mode. From there, you can make any changes you want, and the symbol in the Library will change accordingly.

Edit With The Edit With option opens the currently selected bitmap or sound with an external application. If you have Fireworks installed on your machine, Flash launches Fireworks for bitmap editing. Changes made using Fireworks do not affect the original bitmap file you imported; they appear only within Flash. When it comes to audio files in the Library, a dialog box appears, prompting you to choose a sound editor.

Properties Opens the Symbol Properties dialog box for the selected symbol. From there, you can change the symbol's type, edit its name, and manipulate its Linkage properties.

Linkage Lets you set several options needed to create a Shared Library. For more information on creating Shared Libraries, see the section "Working with Shared Symbol Libraries" later in this chapter.

Component Definition Lets you control the parameters of a Flash MX 2004 and Flash MX Pro 2004 UI Component through the Component Definition dialog box.

For more information about Components, see Chapter 16.

Select Unused Items Automatically selects any symbols not currently used in the Flash project.

Update Automatically updates a bitmap or audio file that you've altered in an external program rather than having to re-import it.

> If you choose the Edit With option in conjunction with Macromedia Fireworks to make a change to artwork, you do not have to use the Update option; the process is automatic.

Play Plays any selected Movie Clip, Sound, or Button symbol.

> You can also play a Movie Clip, Sound, or Button symbol by clicking the Play button in the upper-right corner of the preview window.

Expand Folder Automatically expands any selected folder so that all of its contents are visible.

Collapse Folder Collapses the currently selected folder so that none of its contents are visible—the opposite effect as the Expand Folder.

Expand All Folders Expands all the folders in the current Library so all of their contents are visible.

Collapse All Folders Collapses all the open folders in the current Library so that their contents are not visible.

Shared Library Properties Opens the Shared Library Properties dialog box, allowing you to assign a URL for a given shared Library.

Keep Use Counts Updated Tells Flash to continuously update the use counts.

> Evoking the Keep Use Counts Updated option eats up a lot of your computer's processing power, often resulting in a drastic slowdown.

Update Use Counts Now Lets you manually update the use counts.

Using the Library to Work with Symbols

Now you'll take your knowledge about symbols and put the Library to work. In this section, you'll start by looking at how you add symbols to the Stage. You'll also explore how to use various Library options to manage and manipulate your symbols.

Adding a Symbol to the Stage

The Library is a two-way street: You can place symbols on the Stage just as easily as you can add them to the Library.

> Remember that when you place a symbol onto the Stage, you're creating an *instance*. An instance is a copy of the parent symbol that you can change and manipulate without altering the original symbol.

To add a symbol to the Stage, follow these steps:

1. Open the Library by choosing Window → Library or use the shortcut F11 (or Cmd/Ctrl+**L**).

2. Click and drag the desired symbol onto the Stage.

Changing a Symbol's Name

When you initially create a symbol, you give it a name. There are actually a number of different quick and easy ways to change that name:

1. Open the Library (Window → Library, F11, or Cmd/Ctrl+**L**).

2. Select the symbol that has the name you want to change.

3. Do one of the following:

    - Cmd+click (Mac) or right-click (Win) and choose Rename. When the current name is highlighted in the Sort window, type a new name.

    - Choose Rename from the Options menu. When the current name is highlighted, just type a new one.

    - Choose Properties from the Options menu (or click the Properties button in the bottom of the Library) to open the Symbol Properties dialog box. From here, type in a new name into the Name field.

    - Double-click the symbol name (not the symbol icon) and type a new name.

Duplicating Symbols

Flash enables you to duplicate symbols in the Library with a minimum of trouble. You might find this handy if you've created a complex symbol that you wanted to copy, alter, and then add to the Library. Instead of jumping through a series of hoops, you can duplicate the symbol and then edit the copy in whatever way you want. Also, duplicating a symbol allows you to create a new symbol (to which you can make any changes) without actually changing any of that symbol's instances on the Stage. Further, it's a great process if you want to make drastic experimental changes to a symbol without risking the original.

To duplicate a symbol, follow these steps:

1. Open the Library (Window → Library , F11, or Cmd/Ctrl+**L**).

2. Select the symbol you want to duplicate.

3. Do one of the following:

    • Cmd+click (Mac) or right-click (Win) and choose Duplicate.

    • Choose Duplicate from the Options menu.

4. When the Duplicate Symbol dialog box opens, enter a new name. If you want to retain its original format, make sure to select the appropriate radio button. If you want to turn the duplicate symbol into an alternative format, click the desired radio button.

5. Click OK. The duplicated symbol is automatically placed in the Library.

6. From here, you can edit the duplicate symbol and make any changes you want.

Editing a Symbol

You might find yourself in a situation where you want to make more significant changes to a symbol that go beyond changing its name. All you need to do is follow these steps:

1. Open the Library (Window → Library , F11, or Cmd/Ctrl+**L**).

2. Select the symbol that you want to edit.

3. Do one of the following:

    • Double-click the symbol's icon (to the left of the symbol name in the Sort window).

    • Cmd+click (Mac) or right-click (Win) and choose Edit.

    • Choose Edit from the Library's Options.

    • If the symbol you want to edit is a bitmap or audio file, select Edit With to open the appropriate external editor.

4. When Flash switches to the Symbol Editor, make any changes you want.

5. When you're finished, you need to exit Symbol Editing mode. To do this, either choose Edit → Edit Document or click the Scene button in the Edit toolbar.

When you change a symbol, all its associated instances automatically change as well.

Organizing Your Library

As your experience with Flash develops, you'll find that many of your projects use a large number of symbols. This can certainly lead to some workflow and organizational problems. To avoid this problem, you can do several things.

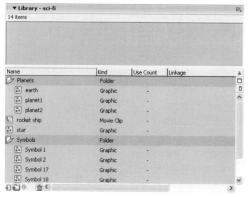

The first solution involves creating various folders to keep similar symbols in (see Figure 7.6). Just as you can create folders in a website to better organize your files, you can make folders in a Flash Library to better organize your symbols, bitmaps, and sounds.

To create a folder, click the New Folder button in the bottom-left corner of the Library window. You can also choose New Folder from the Library Options menu. From here, simply click and drag the various symbols into their intended folders. Alternatively, you can also select a symbol and choose Move to New Folder from the Library's Options menu.

Figure 7.6

You can organize your Library by creating various folders to keep common or similar symbols in.

The second way to organize your Library, which has decidedly less of an impact on the Library's overall organization (but is nonetheless useful), involves using the Sort window columns. By clicking the name of either the Date Modified or Name column, the contents of the Library are reorganized in descending order.

Opening External Flash Libraries

One of the great things about Flash is that you're not limited to the Library being used in your current Flash project; you can also open other Flash movie Libraries by using the Open External Library option.

> External Libraries aren't a different kind of file. Essentially, they're just regular FLA files, the Library contents of which you've taken and put in your Library. Because of this, there's no special procedure for creating an external Library; you just need to create a Flash movie like any other.

Follow these steps:

1. Open the Library (Window → Library, F11, or Cmd/Ctrl+L).

2. Choose File → Import → Open External Library.

3. When the Open as Library dialog box opens, navigate to the FLA file that has the Library you want to access, select it, and click Open. The external Library appears as another Library panel in your movie (see Figure 7.7).

If you have not moved your original Library window, the new Library window might open directly on top of the old one. Drag the new Library window until you can see both windows.

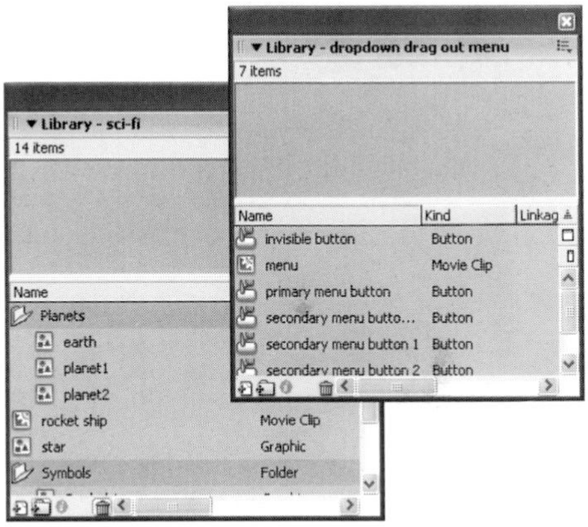

Figure 7.7

The original Library is on the left, and the Library on the right has been opened from an external Flash file.

4. Click and drag any symbol from the newly opened Library to your current movie's Library. This automatically copies the desired symbol from the imported Library into your current movie's Library, to be used as any other symbol would.

Working with Shared Symbol Libraries

As Flash development teams become larger and projects become more complex, sharing assets becomes important. With Shared Symbol Libraries, also referred to as *Shared Library Assets* or *Shared Libraries,* you can use graphics, buttons, movies, audio files, and other assets in your movie by linking to the Library of a centrally located SWF file (on a web server, for example). The result is that a Flash movie no longer has to have its own individual Library.

The beauty of Shared Symbol Libraries is that teams can share a standard set of symbols across multiple movies. You can make any final modification to a symbol in the Shared Library. After the Shared Library has been published, any other movies that use the Library are updated automatically. In addition, when you draw your symbols from a Shared Symbol Library, your final movie doesn't need any embedded symbols and therefore is smaller.

Although Shared Symbol Libraries are beneficial to large projects, they have, unfortunately, proven to be somewhat unreliable and unpredictable. We strongly suggest that if you find the need to use Shared Libraries, you limit their use to storage of relatively small (in terms of file size) elements.

Before you learn how to create and work with Shared Symbol Libraries, you need to learn about the two models for Shared Libraries: *runtime* and *author-time.*

- In a runtime Shared Symbol Library, assets are loaded into the destination movie from a source movie when the movie actually plays. Although the source movie (the movie you're drawing the symbols from) doesn't have to be accessible when you initially author the movie, it must be posted to a web server and be accessible for the destination movie to draw the symbols at runtime. Using a runtime Shared Symbol Library is really appropriate only when you're distributing your Flash movie on the Web; this way, it will have access to the actual Shared Symbol Library.

- In an author-time Shared Symbol Library, you can replace any symbol in the movie you're currently working on with a symbol from another movie. Although the symbol in the destination movie retains its original name and properties, its contents are replaced. For example, you could use an author-time Shared Symbol Library when you want to integrate symbols into your movie that were created by someone else. The primary difference between an author-time Shared Symbol Library and a runtime Shared Symbol Library is that the source movie must be accessible on your local network (or on your own hard drive). Because you integrate symbols from a Shared Symbol Library into your own movie when it's being created, author-time Shared Symbol Libraries can be used whether you're distributing your movie over the Web or by some other means.

Figure 7.8

The Font Symbol Properties dialog box

Creating a Runtime Shared Symbol Library

Creating and using a runtime Shared Symbol Library involves two discrete steps. The first involves creating the source movie (in which the Shared Symbol Library resides) and identifying symbols (through the use of unique names) within the source movie. The assignment of unique identifiers for symbols in the Shared Symbol Library is vital so that the destination movie can successfully locate and acquire the symbols it needs to run properly.

> If you plan to use runtime Shared Symbol Libraries, get into the habit of using the same name for the unique identifier as you did for the symbol's actual name; this might avoid some confusion in the long run.

The second part, which you do when you create the destination movie, involves telling Flash that the symbols being used will be drawn from a source movie at runtime.

Let's start by looking at how you create a runtime Shared Symbol Library:

1. Create a new Flash file by choosing File → New (or by using the shortcut Cmd/Ctrl+**N**) and selecting the Flash Document option from the New Document dialog box.

2. Create or import all the elements that you want to include in the final runtime Shared Symbol Library and add them to the currently active movie's Library. For how to create either native Flash symbols or imported Flash symbols, see the section "Understanding Symbols" earlier in this chapter.

3. If you want to include an entire font in your Shared Symbol Library, choose New Font from the Library Options menu. When the Font Symbol Properties dialog box (see Figure 7.8) opens, type a name for the font you want to include, locate the font in the Font menu, and select the style you want to be included.

4. Delete all objects from your Stage that will be included in the final Shared Symbol Library.

Now that you've included all the symbols that will ultimately reside in the final runtime Shared Symbol Library, you need to assign a unique identifier to each so that they can be successfully located and used by the destination movie:

1. Select one of the symbols in the Library that you're working on.

2. From here, you have a couple of different options:

   - Choose Linkage from the Library Options menu or from the Ctrl+click (Mac) or right-click (Win) context menu.

   - Select Properties from the Library Options menu or from the Ctrl+click (Mac) or right-click (Win) context menu. In the Symbol Properties dialog box that opens, click the Advanced button to access the Shared Symbol Library options (see Figure 7.9).

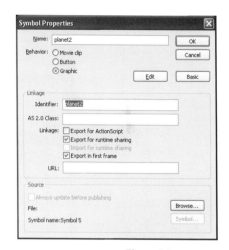

Figure 7.9

The Symbol Properties dialog box with Shared Symbol Library options displayed

> If the item that you've selected is not a native Flash symbol (Button, Movie Clip, or Graphic), you won't have access to the properties.

3. Select the Export for Runtime Sharing option.

4. Type a unique name (without any spaces) into the Identifier field.

5. Enter the URL for the place where the source SWF file will be located in the URL field.

> The URL that you enter into the URL field must be absolute (for example, `http://someURL.com/movies/mymovie.swf`, not `/movies/mymovie.swf`). If you don't place the source movie in the location you set or enter the correct URL, the destination movie will not be able to locate and draw the necessary symbols.

6. Repeat the process for each symbol that will ultimately be included in the final Shared Symbol Library.

> Although the process of tagging each symbol with a unique identifier is tedious (especially if you've got a lot of symbols), it is necessary. Any of the symbols that aren't assigned a unique identifier will not work properly in the final Shared Symbol Library.

7. When you've finished identifying all the desired symbols as assets within the runtime Shared Symbol Library, click OK.

Now that you've set up all the properties of the source movie (which will act as the runtime Shared Symbol Library), save and publish it by following these steps:

1. Save the currently open Flash file (that contains the Library you've been working on) by choosing File → Save. Alternatively, you can use the shortcut Cmd/Ctrl+**S**. So you don't get confused, make sure you give the file a distinct name that will identify it specifically as containing a runtime Shared Symbol Library.

2. From here, publish the FLA file as a SWF file (Flash's web format). All you need to do is select File → Publish Settings. Make sure that Flash is the only format chosen in the Formats tab. Beyond that, you don't need to set any of the other options.

3. Once you've finished adjusting the necessary Publish Settings, click OK. Then choose File → Publish (or use the shortcut Shift+F12). The SWF file will be saved to the same directory where you saved the original FLA file that you were working on.

4. Take the SWF file (which includes the tagged symbols) and upload it to the server with the URL that corresponds to what you entered into the URL field.

> For a far more detailed and thorough look at publishing your Flash movie, see Chapter 30.

Linking to a Runtime Shared Symbol Library

Now that you've gone through the process of creating a runtime Shared Symbol Library (the source movie), you can use its assets in another Flash movie (the destination movie).

The effect of linking to a runtime Shared Symbol Library is something like opening external Flash Libraries. The most important difference is that when you change a symbol in your runtime Shared Symbol Library (source movie), it changes all the linked symbols in the destination movies that use it.

> Unless you've got a copy of the symbol you want to draw from the runtime Shared Symbol Library (source movie) in the destination movie's Library, you won't be able to do any linking at all. Although this seems a little counterproductive (what's the point of drawing the symbol from a runtime Shared Symbol Library if it's already in the destination movie?), it's important to realize that the symbol won't actually get exported if it has been linked to a runtime Shared Symbol Library. It really just acts as a placeholder in your movie.

Now follow these steps to link to a Library:

1. Create a new Flash movie (or open an existing one) to act as the destination movie.

2. Open the movie's Library by choosing Window → Library.

3. Make sure that copies of the symbol that you want to draw from the runtime Shared Symbol Library (source movie) are in the Library of the newly created movie. You can do this by opening both Libraries and then dragging the symbols from the source movie into the target movie.

4. Select the Graphic, Movie Clip, or Button symbol, and open the Symbol Properties dialog box by choosing Properties from the Library's Options menu. If the Symbol Properties dialog box isn't expanded, click the Advanced button.

5. Select the Import for Runtime Sharing option.

6. Enter the unique identifier for the symbol you're drawing from the runtime Shared Symbol Library (source movie) into the Identifier field.

> If you don't put the exact identifier into the field, the destination movie will not be able to locate the symbol you want to use.

7. Enter the exact location for where the runtime Shared Symbol Library (source movie) is posted into the URL field.

> If you don't put in the exact URL, the destination movie won't be able to locate the source movie or access the required symbol.

8. When you've finished, click OK.

Severing the Link to a Runtime Shared Symbol Library

Although linking to a runtime Shared Symbol Library is definitely a handy technique, you might find yourself in a position where you want to sever the link between your destination movie and the source movie. Here's how:

1. Open the destination movie that contains the symbol you want to de-link.

2. Open the Library by choosing Window → Library.

3. Select the Movie Clip, Button, or Graphic symbol you want to de-link.

4. Open the Symbol Properties dialog box by selecting Properties from the Library Options menu.

5. De-select the Import for Runtime Sharing option.

6. Click OK.

Linking to an Author-Time Shared Symbol Library

As mentioned before, when you employ an author-time Shared Symbol Library, you can replace any symbol in the movie that you're currently working on with a symbol from another movie entirely.

> When you're working with an author-time Shared Symbol Library, the source movie must be directly accessible at the time you publish your movie, either over a local network or on your own computer.

Remember that although the symbol in the destination movie retains its original name and properties, its contents are replaced by those of the symbol you're drawing from the source movie.

> Any asset that the symbol from the source movie uses (such as an audio file in a Movie Clip) is also copied over to the destination movie.

To replace a symbol in a destination movie with one drawn from an author-time Shared Symbol Library, just follow these steps:

1. Open the movie that has the symbol you want to replace.

2. Open the Library by choosing Window → Library.

3. Select the symbol you want to replace.

4. Open the Symbol Properties dialog box by selecting Properties from the Library Options menu.

5. Click the Browse button located at the bottom of the Symbol Properties dialog box.

6. When the Locate Macromedia Flash Document File dialog box opens, navigate to where the FLA file containing the symbol you want to use as the replacement is located, select it, and click Open.

Figure 7.10

The Select Source Symbol dialog box

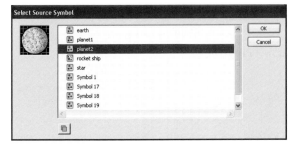

7. When the Select Source Symbol dialog box (see Figure 7.10) opens (which lists all the symbols in the FLA file you picked), select the symbol that you want to use as the replacement.

8. Click OK.

9. When you are returned to the Symbol Properties dialog box, click OK again. Note that the contents of the symbol have been replaced.

To replace one symbol for another in the same movie, click the Symbol button in the Source section of the Symbol Properties dialog box to access the Select Source Symbol dialog box.

Working with Symbol Instances

You've already learned that when you drag a symbol from the Library to the Stage, you're not really adding the symbol *per se*. Instead, you're creating a copy (called an *instance*) that you can alter without changing the parent symbol (which remains in the Library). As such, an instance can be changed to look quite different than its parent symbol. Although editing the symbol in the Library updates all its instances, editing an instance of a symbol updates only that instance.

In the next section, you'll investigate how you can manipulate the various visual characteristics of symbol instances.

Modifying the Appearance of Instances with the Property Inspector

Instances have a series of properties that you can manipulate to change the instance's visual character. You'll find that many, if not all, of these instance properties are particularly important when it comes to animation. You can animate each property—including transparency, brightness, and color—to create a change in the instance's visual appearance over time. For example, you could animate an instance's transparency so it appears to fade in over time.

For more information on how to animate an instance's visual properties, see Chapter 10.

This section of the chapter will make you familiar with the tools to change the overall appearance of any given symbol instance.

When it comes to the visual character of an instance property, you'll rely exclusively on the Color drop-down menu in the Property Inspector (see Figure 7.11) to make any changes.

1. Select the symbol instance that has the visual properties you want to manipulate.

2. If the Property Inspector isn't already open, choose Window → Properties.

Figure 7.11

The Property Inspector's Color drop-down menu

3. Select one of the options from the Color drop-down menu (each of which has unique properties).

> The alterations you make to a symbol instance's visual properties in the Property Inspector will be dynamically applied to the selected symbol instance.

Let's take a look at each option individually:

None Leaves the symbol instance unaltered. Applying the None effect is a good way to revert a symbol instance back to its original form after you've fiddled with its visual properties.

Brightness Changes the relative brightness of the selected symbol instance when you input a value (in percent) into the Brightness field (or use the Brightness slider) (see Figure 7.12). The value can range from 100 percent (white) to –100 percent (black).

> Setting the Brightness to 0 percent retains the original color of the symbol instance.

Tint Offers several ways to alter the color of the selected symbol instance. You can click the Tint swatch (which opens the Color Picker) and choose a color. Alternatively, you can mix your own RGB color by entering a value into the R, G, and B fields (see Figure 7.13).

> Remember, you can also use the sliders (accessed by clicking the down arrow just to the right of each field) to adjust the value of the individual RGB channels.

Finally, you can adjust the amount of tint by entering a value (in percent) between 0 and 100 into the Tint field.

Figure 7.12
Brightness properties

Figure 7.13
Tint properties

Figure 7.14
Alpha properties

Figure 7.15
Advanced properties

Like the R, G, and B fields, you can manipulate the Tint amount by adjusting the slider (accessed by clicking the down arrow just to the right of the field).

Alpha Lets you adjust the transparency of a selected symbol instance. Enter a value into the Alpha field or use the slider (accessed by clicking the down arrow to the right of the field) to adjust the value. The value can range from 0 (totally transparent) to 100 (no transparency) (see Figure 7.14).

Advanced When you select Advanced from the Color drop-down menu (see Figure 7.15) and click the Settings button in the Property Inspector, you open the Advanced Effect dialog box (see Figure 7.16), where you can change the color and transparency of an object simultaneously.

In the Advanced Effect dialog box, you'll notice that there are two sets of Tint and Alpha controls. The four controls on the right (R, G, B, and Alpha) change the color and transparency of a selected symbol instance by an absolute value. The four controls on the left change a symbol instance's Tint and Alpha value by a relative amount (percentage).

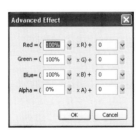

Figure 7.16
Advanced Effect dialog box

Replacing One Instance with Another

You might find yourself in a situation where you want to swap one instance for another. This is particularly useful when you have a complex scene where you want to swap one symbol instance with another but want to make sure the new one is placed in the exact same location as the old one. To do this, follow these steps:

1. Select the symbol instance you want to replace.

2. Choose Window → Properties.

3. Click the Swap button .

4. When the Swap Symbol dialog box (see Figure 7.17) opens, select the symbol that you want to swap, and click OK.

Transforming an Instance on the Stage

Symbol instances are exact copies of their parent symbols in the Library. You can transform them without changing the parent. As such, you're probably going to transform symbol instances on a regular basis. To do this, follow these steps:

1. On the Stage, select the symbol instance you'd like to edit.

2. From here, use any of Flash's transformation tools to manipulate the symbol instance.

> To transform every aspect of the symbol instance, you'll probably have to break it down into its parts—a process accomplished by selecting the symbol instance and then choosing Modify → Break Apart.

If you want to edit the parent symbol of a given instance, you can open the Library, select the symbol, and choose Edit from the Library Options menu. Alternatively, you can double-click the symbol, which opens the Symbol Editor, where you can make any changes you want.

> Remember, when you change the parent symbol, all its associated symbol instances also change.

Figure 7.17

The Swap Symbol dialog box

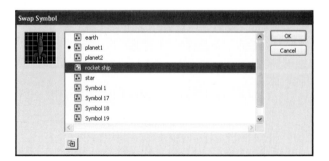

Inspirational Design Model

Originally located in a small, remote village in the southeastern region of Huizhou in China's Anhui province, Yin Yu Tang is an elegant, rural home. Built in the late Qing dynasty (1644–1911), the house was home to the Huang family for more than 200 years. In 1997, the remaining members of the Huang family, most of which had long since moved away from their ancestral home, authorized the house to be transported across the world to the Peabody Essex Museum in Salem, Massachusetts.

The exhibit itself is complemented by a spectacular interactive experience (mounted on the Web at www.pem.org/yinyutang and on kiosks through t the exhibit itself) designed to allow users to explore the house and discover a rare example of the region's architecture and learn about the daily life of the Huang family. Created by Second Story Interactive (www.secondstory.com), the heart of the interactive experience (see Figure 7.18) is composed of five thematic sections that provide a unique lens through which the house can be examined: Orientation, Construction, Ornamentation, Belongings, and Preservation. Content is segmented into distinct "scenes" within each theme; as visitors navigate between scenes, a persistent 3D model view of Yin Yu Tang reacts to reveal different features of the house. A visual interactive family tree, dozens of audio interviews, hundreds of historical and contemporary photographs, and many videos are sprinkled throughout the experience to make this Chinese home "a living house."

Figure 7.18
Yin Yu Tang

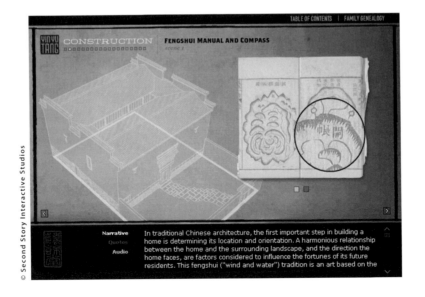

© Second Story Interactive Studios

CHAPTER 8

Adding Depth to Flash Movies with Layers

Up until this point, all of the painting, drawing, and manipulating of visual elements that you've done has taken place on one layer. Well, prepare yourself for the third dimension! Don't get too excited, you're not going to look at creating 3D images in Flash until Chapter 29. However, now is a perfect time to start exploring how you can create 2D visual content in discreet planes stacked one upon another.

Like many other graphics programs, Flash lets you create any number of individual layers in your movie. If you are confused as to what layers are, it's easiest to think of them as invisible levels where you can create and place objects. Layers let you partition your movie when you're building complicated or composite images and animations so that you can focus on each element independently. Layers are also extremely important when it comes to animation—a topic covered in Chapter 10. In this chapter, you're going to explore all aspects of layers.

Topics covered include:

- Understanding and exploiting the power of layers
- Creating a new layer
- Adding content to a layer
- Distributing objects to layers
- Working with layer properties
- Creating and manipulating layer folders
- Editing layers
- Creating guide layers
- Creating mask layers

Understanding and Exploiting the Power of Layers

Each layer in a Flash movie acts like a transparent sheet upon which any number of individual objects reside. Ultimately, your final Flash movie will consist of a stack of layers. Although individual layers are not really recognizable on the Stage, they are displayed horizontally across (and accessible from) the Timeline (see Figure 8.1).

The way in which each layer is displayed in relation to other layers in the Timeline is important. Because the layers (and therefore the content on the layers) are stacked, the topmost ones appear in the foreground of the movie, and the bottommost ones appear in the background of the movie. Although this might be a little difficult to grasp in the abstract, look at it this way: Say you had two different images in two separate layers that occupied the same space on the Stage. The image in the top layer of the Timeline would appear in front of the image in the bottom layer.

Layers come in a number of different "flavors," all of which play distinct roles in Flash. Don't worry too much about the types of layers right now, as you'll learn all about them later in this chapter (see the sections "Creating Guide Layers" and "Creating Mask Layers"). In addition, each layer has a series of different options accessible through the Timeline. You'll get a chance to explore these options shortly (see the section "Working with Layer Properties").

> Selecting a layer is as simple as clicking its name in the Timeline. You'll notice that when it is selected, the layer is highlighted and a small pencil appears to the right of its name. This indicates that the layer is active, and that any objects you add to the Stage will be assigned to it.

Although layers play an integral part in the creation of static content, they become even more important when you start learning about animation, covered in Chapter 10. For the time being, however, it's important to familiarize yourself with creating and manipulating layers.

Figure 8.1

The Timeline

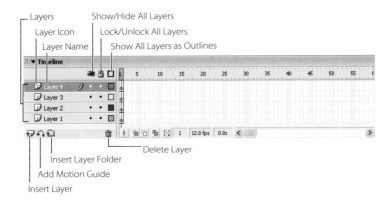

Creating a New Layer

When you create a new Flash document, one layer appears in the Timeline. You certainly don't *have* to add more layers to your movie. However, once you are creating extensive (and, of course, amazingly brilliant) Flash movies, you'll find that working in one layer is not only confusing, but it might result in some functionality problems.

Without getting too much ahead of things, let's take a look at a short example. When it comes to creating complex animations, you'll find that you are going to want to create one layer for each discreet object or symbol. By doing this, you can exert greater control over each object (moving, manipulating, and so on) and therefore your overall animation. The bottom line, for a number of different reasons, is that it's wise to use many layers for each distinct object (or group of objects). The number of layers that you can create is limited only by the amount of available memory on your computer.

> Because Flash flattens all of the layers upon export, you don't have to worry about increasing the file's size resulting from many different layers.

Do one of the following to create a new layer:

- Click the Insert Layer button ⬚ in the bottom-left corner of the Timeline.
- Choose Insert → Timeline → Layer.
- Cmd+click (Mac) or right-click (Win) any layer in the Timeline and choose Insert Layer from the pop-up context menu.

When you carry out any of these procedures, Flash automatically adds the new layer above the existing one.

> If you have more than one layer, Flash inserts the new layer above the currently selected one.

Adding Content to a Layer

You'll find that through the course of creating your Flash masterpiece, you will add layers as you need them. Adding new layers is all well and good, but what about adding content to those layers? The process itself is quite simple; all you need to do is select the layer by clicking it and insert any content you want onto the Stage (by using the painting and drawing tools or dragging a symbol instance from the Library). As long as that particular layer stays active, all content that you add will automatically be placed in it.

As you add content to a layer, you'll notice that the small black outline of a circle (which always occupies the first frame of a newly created layer and is called a *blank keyframe*) will fill up and become a small solid black circle; this is called a *keyframe*.

You are going to learn all about frames, keyframes, and blank keyframes in Chapter 10, so all you need to know right now is that when a keyframe appears, it means that content has been added or manually changed in that frame.

Distributing Objects to Layers

As mentioned previously, it's wise to limit a single object or symbol to a single layer when you are working with complex composite images or animations. However, you might find yourself in a situation where you end up with multiple objects or symbols on a single layer.

> When you import many types of vector files (such as those from Adobe Illustrator or Macromedia FreeHand), the image will comprise many different ungrouped objects.

As a result, Flash MX 2004 and Flash MX Professional 2004 have a handy option that allows you to select multiple objects and distribute them so that they each occupy their own discreet layer.

Flash gives all the newly created layers a unique name. In the case of letters in a string of text that has been broken apart (discussed in Chapter 5), each layer is named with the particular character (F, L, A, S, or H, for example). In the case of a layer that contains a Library object (such as a symbol, bitmap, or video clip), Flash gives the layer the same name as the object itself. In the case of a layer containing a symbol instance, Flash gives the layer the same name as the instance. Finally, when a layer contains a graphical object created using Flash's Painting and Drawing tools, Flash gives the layer a default name of Layer 1, increasing sequentially (Layer 2, Layer 3, and so on).

To distribute objects to layers, follow these steps:

1. Select the objects on the Stage that you want to distribute to layers. Remember, you can select objects across multiple layers.

2. From here, with all of the objects still selected, you can either choose Modify → Timeline → Distribute to Layers or access the context menu by Ctrl+clicking (Mac) or right-clicking (Win) and selecting Distribute to Layers.

Working with Layer Properties

Figure 8.2

The layer properties icons appear to the right of the layer's name in the Timeline.

Now that you've learned how to create and add content to layers, you can learn how to work with layer properties. Each layer has a series of properties represented and accessible through the icons to the right of the layer's name (Figure 8.2).

In this section, you'll explore how to turn layer visibility on/off, view layer objects as outlines, change the layer outline color, and lock/unlock a layer.

Turning Layer Visibility On/Off

One of the great things about layers in Flash is that they can be "turned off." By doing this, you make the content of any given layer invisible. Ultimately, this helps to unclutter the Stage and allows you to focus better on the objects on a particular layer. When you're done with whatever you were doing, you simply "turn the layer back on," and it becomes visible again. To change a layer's visibility, perform one of the following tasks:

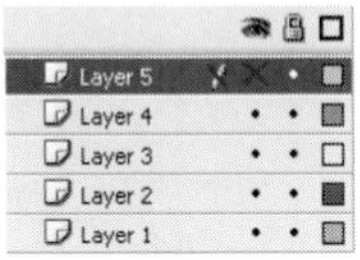

- Click the small dot in the layer's eye column. A red X automatically appears, denoting the layer's hidden state (see Figure 8.3). To turn the layer visibility back on, click the red X.

- To hide all the layers at the same time, click the eye icon. To reverse this process, click the eye icon again, or Cmd+click (Mac) or right-click (Win) and choose Show All from the pop-up context menu.

- To hide all the layers except one, Option/Alt+click the small dot in the layer's eye column that you want to stay visible. Alternatively, you can Cmd+click (Mac) or right-click (Win) and choose Hide Others from the pop-up context menu.

Figure 8.3

When a layer is hidden, a red X appears to the right of its name.

Figure 8.4

Viewing a layer's objects as outlines

Viewing Layer Objects as Outlines

Viewing layer objects as outlines allows you to alter all of the layer's objects so they appear as colored outlines (see Figure 8.4).

This is particularly useful if you want to speed up the display of your movie when editing or testing animations.

To view layer objects as outlines, you have three options:

- Click the layer's outline icon (represented by a colored box). The box icon will become hollow, indicating that the layer's objects are currently displayed only as outlines. To turn the option off, click the hollow box icon. Figure 8.5 shows both states of the layer's outline icon.

- To display the content of all layers as outlines, click the Timeline's box icon (located above the layers themselves). To reverse the process, click the icon again.

- To view all layer objects as outlines except one, just Option/Alt+click the layer's outline icon whose objects you want to remain "solid."

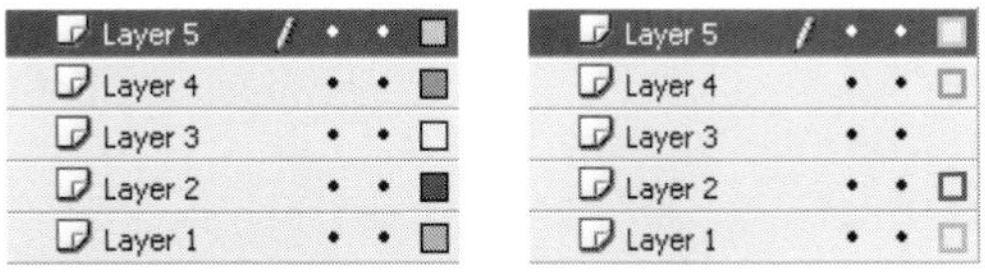

Figure 8.5

The left image displays the outline icon as it appears when you have the View Layer Objects as Outlines option turned off. The right image shows the outline icon as it appears when you have the option activated.

Changing the Layer Outline Color

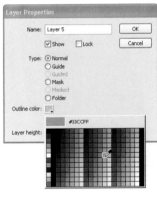

You'll notice that each of your layer's outline box icons is a different color, each of which represents the color of the layer's objects if they were to be reduced to outlines using one of the procedures described in the previous section. So, if your outline box icon is red, your objects are represented as red outlines. You certainly aren't stuck with the default color, though:

1. First, to open the Layer Properties dialog box, do one of the following:

   • Double-click the layer icon (to the left of the layer name).

   • Cmd+click (Mac) or right-click (Win) the layer and choose Properties from the pop-up context menu.

   • Select the layer whose outline color you want to change, and choose Modify → Timeline → Layer Properties.

2. When the Layer Properties dialog box opens, click the Outline Color swatch and choose the color you want (as illustrated in Figure 8.6).

3. When you've finished, click OK.

Locking/Unlocking Layers

When you first create a layer in Flash, it is automatically unlocked; otherwise, you wouldn't be able to add to or edit the layer. However, the tricky thing about layers is that you don't need to have them selected to actually manipulate their contents. As a result, you could inadvertently modify the content of one layer while working on the content of another. This can be particularly frustrating if the movie that you're working on took a great deal of time to create, and the mistaken displacement of any given object would result in lost work hours. To avoid this sort of unfortunate situation, Flash lets you lock layers. You have a few ways to lock/unlock a layer:

• Click the small dot in the layer's lock column (represented by a padlock). A little padlock automatically appears, denoting the layer's locked state (as illustrated in Figure 8.7). To unlock the layer, click the padlock.

• To lock all layers at the same time, click the Timeline's padlock icon. To reverse this process, click the padlock icon again.

• To lock all the layers except one, just Option/Alt+click the small dot in the layer's eye column that you want to remain visible. Alternatively, you can Cmd+click (Mac) or right-click (Win) and choose Lock Others from the pop-up context menu.

Creating and Editing Layer Folders

One of the exciting features of Flash, at least in terms of layers, is the ability to create what are called *layer folders*. Essentially, layer folders are folders in the Timeline (see Figure 8.8) into which you can place multiple layers, thereby organizing your Timeline.

For instance, say you had an animation with a series of cartoon characters. If you've planned your movie correctly, each discreet part of the characters (arm, head, leg, floppy ears, and so on) occupies an individual layer. To cut down on the confusion in your Timeline, you could organize the body parts for each character into a layer folder—a Goofy folder, a Daffy folder, a Bender folder, and so on.

One of the cool things about layer folders is that you can expand and collapse them, thereby hiding all of the associated layers in the Timeline without affecting what is visible on the Stage.

> Although layer folders don't manifest themselves in the Timeline like layers do, they have many of the same properties (lock/unlock, visibility, name, and outline color)—all of which you can manipulate in the same way as you would if you were working with a regular layer.

In the following sections, you are going to learn everything you need to know about layer folders. You'll explore how to create them, edit them, add layers to layer folders, and expand and collapse them.

> You can change the position of a layer folder in the same way that you can move a layer—a procedure we'll talk about shortly.

Layer Folder

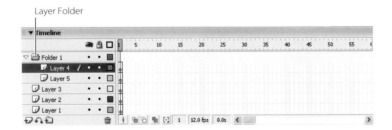

Figure 8.8

Layer folder

Creating a Layer Folder

The process by which you create a layer folder is really quite easy; just do one of the following:

- Click the Insert Layer Folder button in the bottom-left corner of the Timeline.
- Choose Insert → Timeline → Layer Folder.
- Cmd+click (Mac) or right-click (Win) any layer in the Timeline and choose Insert Folder from the pop-up context menu.

When you carry out any of these procedures, Flash automatically adds the new layer folder above the selected layer.

> You can also convert a selected layer to a layer folder by changing its type from Normal to Folder in the Layer Properties dialog box (accessible by selecting the layer and then choosing Modify → Timeline → Layer Properties).

Adding a Layer to a Layer Folder

The purpose of layer folders is to act as containers for layers. As a result, you need to learn how to add layers to layer folders:

1. Make sure that you've already created a layer folder using the procedure described in the previous section.

2. As illustrated in Figure 8.9, click and drag the desired layer to the layer folder's icon (notice that the folder icon will be highlighted when your cursor is directly over it).

3. Release your mouse button.

4. The layer will move so that it's just below the layer folder. It will also be indented slightly, indicating its position within the layer folder (Figure 8.10).

Figure 8.9

Moving a layer into a layer folder

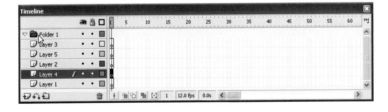

Figure 8.10

Layer added to layer folder

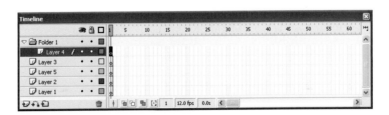

Expanding and Collapsing a Layer Folder

As mentioned previously, one of the benefits of a layer folder is that it can be expanded to show its contents and collapsed to hide them. Ultimately, this lets you unclutter your Timeline without actually removing the collapsed layer folder's associated objects/symbols from the Stage.

To either collapse or expand a layer folder, just click the small arrow to the left of the layer folder name. When the arrow is pointing down and the layer folder's associated layers are visible (see Figure 8.11), you know that it is expanded.

On the other hand, if the arrow is pointing to the right, and the layer folder's associated layers aren't visible, you know it has been collapsed (see Figure 8.12).

Editing Layers

Now that you've looked at how to manipulate a layer's properties, it's time to explore how to edit layers. You've already mastered the finer points of creating layers, adding content, and setting properties. In this section, you'll learn how to move a layer, copy layers, delete layers, rename a layer, and change a layer's height.

Moving a Layer

As you've already learned, the position of a layer within the stack determines whether its associated objects or symbols either overlay other layer content or are overlaid by the content from other layers. Because of this, you are going to want to be able to change the position of a layer within the stack, thereby changing the way in which objects and symbols on the Stage interact visually with one another. Here's how:

1. Select the layer that you want to move.

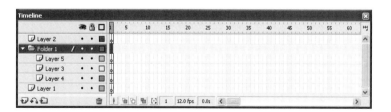

Figure 8.11

Expanded layer

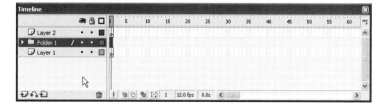

Figure 8.12

Collapsed folder

2. Click and drag the layer to its intended place within the Timeline's layer stack. Notice that a thin black bar appears, highlighting the projected position of the layer.

3. When the highlighted line reaches the location where you want to move the layer, simply release your mouse button.

Copying a Layer

You might find yourself in a situation where, instead of inserting a new layer, you want to copy an existing layer (along with all of its content). This process is a little cumbersome. You really don't copy the layer itself; you copy its content (frame by frame) and then paste it into a newly created layer. Follow these steps:

1. Select the layer that you want to copy by clicking its name; this selects the entire layer.

2. Cmd+click (Mac) or right-click (Win) any of the selected frames in the layer, and choose Copy Frames from the pop-up context menu. Alternatively, use the shortcut Cmd/Ctrl+Option/Alt+**C** or choose Edit → Timeline → Copy Frames; this copies all the content in each of the layers' frames.

3. Create a new layer. If you are having trouble remembering how to insert a new layer, see the "Creating a New Layer" section earlier in this chapter.

4. Select the newly created layer by clicking its name.

5. Cmd+click (Mac) or right-click (Win) the target layer's first (empty) keyframe, and choose Paste Frames from the pop-up context menu. Alternatively, choose Edit → Timeline → Paste Frames, or use the shortcut Cmd/Ctrl+Option/Alt+**V**.

Deleting a Layer

Deleting a layer is just as simple as creating one:

1. Select the layer you want to delete by clicking its name.

2. Do one of the following:

   • Click the Delete button 🗑 .

   • Click and drag the layer to the Delete button.

   • Ctrl+click (Mac) or right-click (Win) and choose Delete Layer from the pop-up context menu.

When you delete a layer, you also delete all of its content from the Stage. Therefore, make sure you want to do this because Flash doesn't ask you whether you *really* want to go ahead with the procedure.

Renaming a Layer

As you've already seen, each layer is created with a distinct name. Granted, the name *Layer 1* isn't all that imaginative, but Flash lets you change the layer name to anything you want.

> When renaming a layer, it's a good idea to give it a name that describes its content. This makes it easier for you to identify the layer's content as your Flash creation gets more complex.

You have a few ways to rename a layer:

- Double-click the layer's name (not its icon) and then enter a new name when the editable field appears (see Figure 8.13).

- Double-click the layer's icon (located to the left of its name). When the Layer Properties dialog box opens, enter a new name into the Name field. Alternately, you can choose Modify → Timeline → Layer Properties to open the Layer Properties dialog box.

Figure 8.13

Double-clicking a layer's name will make it editable.

> If the entire layer name isn't visible, simply click and drag the bar that separates the area of the left part of the Timeline (where the layer name is) and the right part of the Timeline (where the frames are).

Altering Layer Dimensions

When layers are created, they are a default height. However, you might find yourself in a position where you want to change the height of the layer. For instance, when it comes to working with audio in Flash (covered in Part VI), you can add sounds to the Timeline. Unlike other objects that you work with in conjunction with the Timeline, the audio files are represented by the sound's waveform, which is easier to see when the layer's size is larger (Figure 8.14).

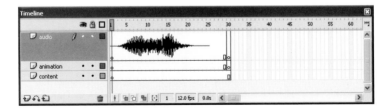

Figure 8.14

Increasing the dimensions of the layer makes a sound's waveform more visible.

> Although this section discusses how you can change a layer's height, you are going to learn
> how to manipulate the appearance of the frames within the layer (and thereby the layer
> itself) in Chapter 10.

To increase the height of a layer, follow these steps:

1. Open the Layer Properties dialog box. If you are having trouble remembering how, see the section "Working with Layer Properties" earlier in this chapter.

2. As illustrated in Figure 8.15, choose one of the options from the Layer Height drop-down menu (100%, 200%, 300%).

3. When you are finished, click OK.

> You might find that the number or size of your layers inhibits the number of layers that
> you can see simultaneously in the Timeline. There are a few ways to work around this.
> First, you can use the Timeline's scroll bar to scroll down to lower layers. Alternatively,
> you can click and drag the bar that separates the Timeline from the Stage to increase the
> amount of visible layers.

Creating Guide Layers

As mentioned, layers come in several different flavors. A *guide layer* is one of the various types in which a layer comes, and there are two different kinds of guide layers: regular guide layers and *motion guide layers*. You can fill a regular guide layer with content (lines, shapes, and so on) that help with layout and positioning (kind of like customizable, irregular graph paper). You can use a motion guide layer, on the other hand, to help create the complex motion path of an animation.

This section teaches you how to designate an existing layer as a guide layer and how to create a motion guide (without actually creating the animation proper). You'll get into how to create the animations in Chapter 10.

> The cool thing about guide layers, whether you are using them for layout or to create a path
> for complex animation, is that they don't appear in the final Flash movie after it has been
> published.

To create a guide layer, follow these steps:

1. Select the layer that you want to designate as a guide layer.

2. From here, you have several choices:

- To create a regular guide layer (not a motion guide), Cmd+click (Mac) or right-click (Windows) and choose Guide from the pop-up context menu. As illustrated in Figure 8.16, the Guide Layer icon will then appear to the left of the layer's name.

- To add a motion guide layer, you have three choices: Click the Add Motion Guide icon in the lower portion of the Timeline, choose Insert → Timeline → Motion Guide, or Ctrl+click (Mac) or right-click (Win) and choose Add Motion Guide from the pop-up context menu. An additional layer is created just above the current layer. You can identify the motion guide layer by the special symbol (which looks like an arc with a circle on top of it) just to the left of the layer's name (see Figure 8.17).

Figure 8.15

You can customize the height of your layer by selecting one of the options in the Layer Height drop-down menu.

You can also create guide layers or motion guide layers by clicking the appropriate option in the Layer Properties dialog box.

After their creation, both types are immediately usable. When it comes to the regular guide layer, you can create any visual element (by painting and drawing or importing) to aid in your layout. When it comes to a motion guide layer, you can create a motion path for an animation. As mentioned before, the next step in using motion guide layers is beyond the scope of this chapter. If you are eager to learn about creating animation paths with a motion guide layer, see Chapter 10.

Guide Layer Icon

Figure 8.16

A guide layer is des-ignated by the Guide Layer icon, which appears to the left o the layer's name.

Creating Mask Layers

Mask layers are the second type of layer that you'll look at in this chapter. Essentially, you use mask layers to create a hole through which the contents of the underlying layer are vis-ible. Imagine looking through a keyhole at a complex scene. Because of the shape of the keyhole, you can see only a limited portion of the scene itself. This is essentially how a mask layer works. In Flash, you create the size and shape of the "hole" through which the scene beyond (or, because of the nature of layers, *below*) is visible. Figure 8.18 illustrates a mask layer in action.

One of the neat things about mask layers is that you can animate the mask so that it moves. Mask layers are useful for creating all sorts of effects such as a scene viewed through a telescope or a landscape revealed by a spotlight—the possibilities are endless.

Motion Guide Layer Ic

Figure 8.17

A guide layer is des ignated by the Motion Guide Laye icon, which appear to the left of the layer's name.

Unfortunately, you cannot mask layers inside Button symbols.

Because you'll be exploring the process of animating mask layers in Chapter 10, you're going to spend this section of the chapter learning how to create a static mask layer.

Let's take a look at how you go about creating a mask layer:

1. Select the layer with the content that will be visible through the mask you create.

Figure 8.18

The image on the left illustrates a non-masked imaged. The image on the right illustrates the same image with a circular mask.

Remember that a mask layer works only on the layer immediately below it.

2. Insert a new layer by clicking the Insert Layer button in the Timeline or by selecting Insert → Timeline → Layer.

3. In the newly created layer, which is placed above the layer with the content you want the mask applied to, draw the "hole" through which the other layer will be visible. Although the hole doesn't have to be circular (it can be any shape), it *must* be filled. When the layer is converted into a mask layer, all areas composed of a solid fill will be transparent. On the other hand, all areas not composed of a solid fill will be opaque.

4. Ctrl+click (Mac) or right-click (Win) the layer's name and choose Mask from the pop-up context menu.

5. The layer is automatically turned into a mask layer. Note that both the mask layer's and the masked layer's icons change (see Figure 8.19).

Figure 8.19

After creating a mask layer, the icons of both the mask layer and masked layer change.

Inspirational Design Model

A creepy old swamp in which Inbred Boy whips his three lowly mouse slaves into shape and forces them to show the user around? Sound like the premise for a cutting-edge Flash site? If you said yes, you'd be right. The brainchild of Montreal-based illustrator, designer, and interactive guru Cameron Wilson, Inbred Boy (www.inbredboy.com) is a wickedly humorous (not to mention slightly off-kilter), self-promotional site that is a feast for the eyes.

Inbred Boy (see Figure 8.20) is not only incredibly creative in its design, illustration, and construction, but it also showcases a whole host of Cameron Wilson's other cool work—including traditional print design, Flash cartoons, and other interactive experiments.

Illustration, animation, and design by Cameron Wilson. Programming by Christian Ayotte. Sound design by Matthew Lafontaine.

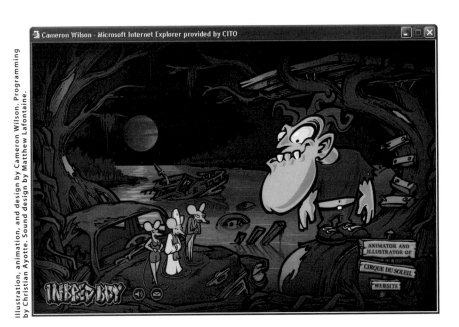

Figure 8.20

Inbred Boy

Managing Your Flash Movie Project

Let's face it: the process of creating a Flash movie is fairly complex. With each passing version, Flash has become a more intricate authoring tool. Now, not only is there more you need to master in the Flash authoring environment, you also have to be able to manage the multitude of assets generated during the authoring process. In addition, given the complexity of the tool, you need to come up with ways to streamline the production process so that you don't waste time on pointless or unnecessarily repetitious tasks.

Fortunately, the folks at Macromedia recognize that it takes a lot more efficiency and skill to create a great Flash movie than it did back in the early days, when the program was little more than a glorified version of the FutureSplash animator. As such, they've included a whole host of tools (some of which are new to Flash MX 2004 and Flash MX Professional 2004) that help you address the complex nature of the program and the authoring process.

In this chapter, you'll look at these tools and learn how to think about your Flash movie more in terms of a project than a simple single file. Topics that will be covered include the following:

- **Working with a Flash Project**
- **Using the Movie Explorer to manage and manipulate movie-wide assets**
- **Using the Find and Replace function**
- **Automating tasks with commands**

Working with a Flash Project

A Flash Project is a new and exciting feature in Flash MX Pro 2004. Essentially, a Flash Project enables you to manage and manipulate multiple document types (such as SWFs, FLAs, ActionScript files, and external Flash Video files) and files that make up a complex movie from a centralized location: the Project panel. A Flash Project, which is little more than a specialized kind of XML file with an `.FLP` extension, simply references all the documents you've defined as being part of the project.

Besides centralized management, there are many benefits to creating and working with a Flash Project. First, any changes you make to any of the files in the project are automatically updated to the FLP file. There is no need to save the Project file as it is automatically always kept current. Second, you can test your project directly from within the Project panel. Under normal circumstances, without the benefit of the Project panel, you would need to individually export each of the files that make up your movie, and then test them.

Third, you can set the default publishing settings, and then publish all the files in your project directly from within the Project panel. This is especially helpful if, for example, you are working with more than just one SWF file. Under normal circumstances, you would have to set the publish properties for each of the FLA files separately, and then export each of them to SWF separately—a process that could become fairly time consuming. However, when you are working with a Flash Project, you simply set the default publish settings for all files of a specific type, and then when you are ready, publish them all from within the Project panel.

The final benefit to working with a Flash Project is the fact that multiple authors (who can be in the same place or different places entirely) can simultaneously work on the same Flash Project. In this kind of situation, you can also establish version control to make sure that each author who is working on a Project file is always using the latest version of a file, and that multiple authors on a Project do not overwrite each other's work.

In this section, you'll explore all aspects of a Flash Project. First, you'll learn how to create a Flash Project. From there, you'll look at using the Project panel to manage and manipulate a Flash Project. Then you'll finish by learning how to maintain version control over your Flash Project.

Creating a New Flash Project

Before you can start grouping files into a project, you need to create a Flash Project file. You can do this starting from the New Document dialog box or the Project panel. Let's explore each.

To create a Flash Project file from the New Document dialog box, follow these steps:

1. Choose File → New.

2. When the New Document dialog box opens (see Figure 9.1), make sure the General tab is active, select Flash Project from the Type list box, and click OK.

3. When the New Project dialog box opens, navigate to the location on your hard drive where you want to save the Project file, enter a name for the file into the File Name field, and click Save.

   Remember, the Flash Project file, which has an .FLP extension, is just a specialized XML file that references all the other physical files in the Project.

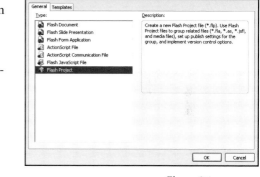

Figure 9.1

The New Document dialog box

Beyond using the New Document dialog box to create your Flash Project file, you can also use the Project panel itself. All you need to do is follow these steps:

1. Open the Project panel by choosing Window → Project.

2. When the Project panel (see Figure 9.2) opens, click the New Project link in the main window of the Project panel.

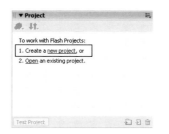

Figure 9.2

Click the New Project link to open a new Flash Project file.

3. When the New Project dialog box opens, navigate to the location on your hard drive where you want to save the Project file, enter a name for the file into the File Name field, and click Save.

If you've already created a Project file, and want to create a new one from within the Project panel, the steps are a little different:

1. With the Project panel open (Window → Project), click the Project button 🔷 in the panel's upper-left corner.

2. Select New Project from the subsequent drop-down menu.

3. When the New Project dialog box opens, navigate to the location on your hard drive where you want to save the Project file, enter a name for the file into the File Name field, and click Save.

When you create a Flash Project file from directly within the Project panel, you'll see the Project file displayed within a panel's main work area.

Opening an Existing Flash Project

Opening an existing Flash Project is an easy process. All you need to do is follow these steps:

1. Choose File → Open.

2. When the Open dialog box opens, navigate to where the Flash Project (.FLP) file is located, select it, and click Open.

3. The Flash Project file automatically opens in the Project panel.

You can also open a Flash Project file directly from within the Project panel. To do so, just follow these steps:

1. Make sure the Project panel is open (Window → Project).

2. If you already have an existing Project file open, click the Project button 🔅 and select Open Project from the subsequent drop-down menu.

3. If you don't have an existing Project file open in the Project panel, click the Open link in the panel's main window (see Figure 9.2, shown earlier).

4. When the Open dialog box opens, navigate to where the Flash Project (.FLP) file is located, select it, and click Open.

> You can have only one Flash Project open at a time. If you try to open a second Flash Project, you'll be prompted to confirm the action.

Managing and Manipulating Your Flash Project

As your Flash Project increases in size and complexity, it will include more files. If you don't maintain total control, things can easily spiral out of control, and you'll be left with nothing more than a disorganized mess and a dizzying array of files, many of which were originally created for good reason, but now only confuse and confound. To prevent this, you need to do everything you can while building the Project to maintain order so that you can maximize and streamline your workflow and save yourself frustration and wasted time.

In this section, you'll look at how to use the Project panel to manage and manipulate your Project. You'll learn how to handle the basic tasks of adding files to your Project, using folders to organize Project files, opening files from within the Project panel, deleting Project files, and finding lost Project files.

Adding Files to a Flash Project

After you have created a Flash Project file, you need to start building the Project by adding files. To add files to your Flash Project, just follow these steps:

1. Make sure that you've either created a new Project file or opened an existing Project file (by following either of the processes described earlier) and that you have the Project panel open (Window → Project).

2. From here, you have two ways of adding files:

   - Click the Add Files to Project button ⊞ in the bottom-right corner of the Project panel.

   - Ctrl+click (Mac) or right-click (Win) on the Flash Project file that you've just opened or created and choose Add File from the context menu.

3. When the Add Files to Project dialog box opens, navigate to the location on your hard drive (or other storage device) where the file is located, select it, and click the Add button. The file is added to the Project panel underneath the Project file (see Figure 9.3).

> You can add a given file to a Project only once. If you attempt to add the same file a second time, you will get an error message.

Organizing Your Flash Project with Folders

Every computer user knows (or should know) the value of organizing files into a logical folder structure; and with large, complex Flash Projects, this organization is particularly important. The Project panel allows you to create folders within a Project and to store files within them. You can also nest folders within folders, increasing your Project's organization. In this section, you'll explore how to add folders to the Project panel, move folders, and add files to a folder.

Figure 9.3

When you add a file to a Flash Project, it appears indented just below the Project file itself.

ADDING A FOLDER TO THE PROJECT PANEL

Adding a folder to organize your Project is actually a really easy process—and might well save you a lot of hardship down the road. Let's take a look at how.

1. Make sure that you've either created a new Project file or opened an existing Project file and that you have the Project panel open (Window → Project).

2. From here, you have two ways of adding a folder:

   • Click the Add Folder to Project button ⊡ in the bottom-right corner of the
     Project panel.

   • Ctrl+click (Mac) or right-click (Win) on the Flash Project file that you've just
     opened or created and choose Add Folder from the context menu.

3. When the Project Folder dialog box opens (see Figure 9.4), enter a unique name for
   the folder into the Name field and click OK. A new folder is added to the Project
   panel below the Project file (see Figure 9.5).

> Folders that occupy the same level of the Project's structure *must* each have a unique name.
> If you try to create a new folder with the same name as an existing folder at that level of the
> Project, you'll get an error message. However, because folder names are case-specific, you
> can have two folders with the same name but at least one letter in a different case.

MOVING FOLDERS

Because you can nest folders within folders, it's a good idea to become familiar with how
you move folders from one location in the Project hierarchy to another.

> When you move a folder from one location to another in the Project hierarchy, the contents
> of the folder move as well.

To move a folder, follow these steps:

1. Select the folder that you want to move.

2. Without releasing your mouse button, drag the folder to where you want to move it.
   As you drag it, a small document icon appears next to your cursor and the location
   you move your mouse over is highlighted (see Figure 9.6).

3. When the cursor/file icon/highlight is over the desired location, simply release your
   mouse button.

> If you attempt to move a folder to a location in the Project's hierarchy that has an existing
> folder with exactly the same name, the folder that you are moving will be deleted and its
> contents placed in the existing, identically named, folder.

ADDING FILES TO FOLDERS

Of course, the purpose of creating folders in a Project is to organize related files in them.
The important thing to remember is that when you organize files in your Project, you

aren't changing the structure of your computer's physical file system. Let's start by looking at how you add a new file to an existing folder:

1. Make sure that you've created the folder that should include your file.

2. Select the folder you want to place the file in.

3. From here, you have two ways of adding a file:

   • Click the Add Files to Project button ⊕ in the bottom-right corner of the Project panel.

   • Ctrl+click (Mac) or right-click (Win) on the target folder and choose Add File from the context menu.

4. When the Add Files to Project dialog box opens, navigate to the location on your hard drive (or other storage device) where the file is located, select it, and click the Add button.

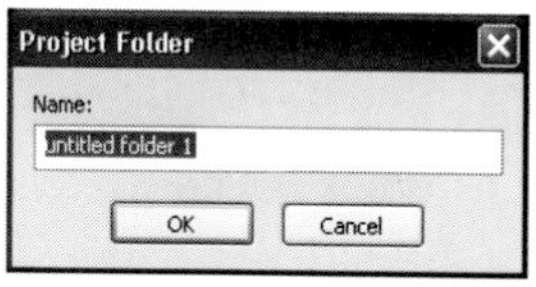

Figure 9.4

The Project Folder dialog box

Figure 9.5

When you add a top-level folder to a Flash Project (as opposed to a folder nested within another folder), it appears indented just below the Project file itself.

Now, what if you wanted to move an existing file from one folder to another within a Project? The process is really quite easy; just follow these steps:

1. Select the file that you want to move.

2. Without releasing your mouse button, drag the file over the folder you want to move it to. As you drag it, a small document icon appears next to your cursor and the location you move your mouse over is highlighted (see Figure 9.7).

3. When the cursor/file icon/highlight is over the desired folder, release your mouse button.

Figure 9.6

Moving a folder in the Project panel

OPENING AND EDITING PROJECT FILES

A Flash Project, as you have already learned, is simply a group of files referenced by a specialized XML file (with an .FLP extension). Because of this, the vast majority of the time when you work on your Flash Project, you are really working only on the files in the Project. Given this, it's a good thing to learn how you go about opening and editing files from directly within the Project panel; here's how.

It's very important to note that while a Flash Project can contain many different types of files, you can open and edit only native Flash files (SWFs, FLAs, AS files, FLVs, and so on). When you are working from within the Project panel,

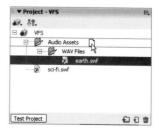

Figure 9.7

Moving a file between folders in the Project panel

non-native file types (such as Quicktime MOV files, PNG files, and GIFs) will automatically open in the application that your operating system associates with that specific file type.

To open and edit Project files:

1. Make sure a Flash Project is open in the Project panel (Window → Project).

2. Double-click the file you want to edit.

3. When the file opens on the Stage, make any changes you want.

4. Choose File → Save to save the file.

5. If you want to remove the edited file from the Stage, choose File → Close.

DELETING FILES FROM A FLASH PROJECT

As you continue to work with a Flash Project, you are obviously going to encounter a situation where you would like to remove a file from the Project. To do this, follow these steps:

1. Make sure you have a Project open in the Project panel (Window → Project).

2. Select the file you want to delete.

3. From here, you have two ways of deleting a file:

   • Click the Remove from Project button 🗑 in the lower-right corner of the Project panel.

   • Ctrl+click (Mac) or right-click (Win) on the target folder and choose Remove from the context menu.

Once you've deleted a file from a Project, you cannot undo the process, so be absolutely sure you want to remove the file before you do it. However, it's important to remember that when you delete a file from a Project, you are removing the reference to the FLP file, not deleting the file from your system.

FINDING LOST FILES

We've already learned that a Flash Project is a specialized kind of XML file that simply references all the other files that you've added to your Project. The next thing you need to know is that, when added, the files aren't actually embedded in the Project file. Instead, they stay where they are, and a link is created between them and the Project file. The link, much like a URL, is severed if an external file (or the Project file itself) is moved (or deleted). When this happens, the external file, while still listed in the Project panel, is not included when the overall project is tested or exported. If this happens, it's up to you to reform that link between the Project file and the external file. Here's how:

1. Make sure the project with the missing file is open in the Project panel (Window → Project).

2. Select the missing file, which is designated with a special icon 🖼 .

3. Click the Project button  in the upper-left corner of the Project panel and select Find Missing File from the subsequent pop-up menu.

4. When the Find Missing File window opens, navigate to the location of the missing file, select it, and click Open.

RENAMING A PROJECT OR FOLDER

There is definitely going to be a point when you want to go back to a Project you've been working on and either change its name or the name of one of its associated folders. The process is really quite easy; just follow these steps:

1. Make sure that you have a Project open in the Project panel (Window → Project).

2. Depending on what you want to rename, select either the folder or the Project name.

Figure 9.8

On the right is the Rename Project Folder dialog box; on the left, the Rename Project dialog box.

3. From here, you've got a couple of choices:

   • Click the Project button  in the top-left corner of the Project panel and select Rename from the subsequent pop-up menu.

   • Ctrl+click (Mac) or right-click (Win) on the target folder and choose Rename from the context menu.

4. When the Rename Project Folder dialog box or Rename Project dialog box opens (depending on whether you're renaming a folder or a Project file), enter a new name in the Name field (see Figure 9.8).

5. When you've finished, click OK, and the folder or Project file is automatically renamed.

Testing Your Flash Project

A Flash Project is more than a simple movie; it's a collection of files that work together to create an overall interactive experience. So you need to be able to make sure that all the parts work together, and you need to do that testing directly from within the Flash authoring environment. The good news is that you can very easily test your entire Project from within Flash.

Before you can test your Project, you have to designate a FLA file as the default file. What's the point of a default file? Well, it's the FLA file that is the "central" movie that launches, controls, or displays all the other files in the Project. Setting a file as the default is quite easy; let's take a look at how:

1. Make sure you have the Project you want to test open in the Project panel (Window → Project).

2. Ctrl+click (Mac) or right-click (Win) on the FLA that you want to make the default file of the Project and choose Make Default Document from the context menu. Notice that the file's icon changes from the regular FLA icon to the default file icon ⬇.

Once you've set one of the FLAs as the Project's default file, you can then go ahead and test the Project. Follow these steps:

1. Make sure the Project you want to test is open in the Project panel (Window → Project).

2. Select the Project file you want to test.

3. From here, you've got three ways of testing:

   - Click the Test Project button ⌈Test Project⌉, which is located in the lower-left corner of the Project panel.

   - Ctrl+click (Mac) or right-click (Win) on the Project file and choose Test from the context menu.

   - Click the Project button 🔧 in the top-left corner of the Project panel and select Test Project from the subsequent pop-up menu.

From here, Flash publishes the default document as well as all the other FLA files so that you can try out your entire Project.

> If no FLA has been designated as the Project's default file, the Default Document Required dialog box will be displayed. Click the Select button, choose the file you want to act as the default from the Select Default Document dialog box, and click OK. Flash will then publish your Project using the selected FLA file as the default.

Publishing Your Flash Project

Once you've tested your Project (and you are satisfied with the results of your labors), it's time to Publish.

> What exactly is Publishing? Well, it's the process by which you take a raw FLA file and convert it into a file format that can be distributed and viewed by your intended audience. For more information on the process and intricacies of Publishing, check out Chapter 30.

One of the great things about working with a Flash Project is that you can establish a default Publish setting for the FLA files in your Project and then publish your entire Project in one fell swoop.

Before you actually Publish, you need to set up a default Publishing Profile for your Project's FLAs; let's take a look at how.

Why do you need to set a Publishing Profile only for the FLAs in your Project? Well, the FLA files are the only files that can be added to a Project that are not in their final state. All other files in a Project, such as SWFs, FLVs (Flash video files), and external digital video files (such as QuickTime MOV files), are already in their final format and therefore don't need any kind of export.

1. Make sure you have a Flash Project file open in the Project panel (Window → Project).

2. Select the Flash Project file.

3. From here, you've got two ways to launch the Settings dialog box:

   • Ctrl+click (Mac) or right-click (Win) on the Project file and choose Settings from the context menu.

   • Click the Project button 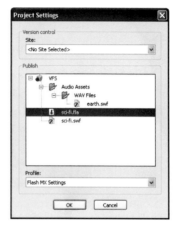 in the top-left corner of the Project panel and select Settings from the subsequent pop-up menu.

Figure 9.9

The Project Settings dialog box

4. When the Project Settings dialog box opens (see Figure 9.9), select the FLA whose Publish properties you want to set.

5. Choose one of the Publish Profiles from the Profile drop-down menu. If you haven't set up any Publish Profiles, the only option available will be Flash MX Settings.

6. If you have additional FLA files in your Project whose publishing properties you want to set, repeat steps 4 and 5.

For more information on how to create Publish Profiles, check out Chapter 30.

Now that you've set the Publish Profile for the FLA file(s) in your Project, you can go ahead and publish your grand interactive creation.

1. Make sure the Project that you want to publish is open in the Project panel (Window → Project).

2. Select the Project file you want to publish.

3. From here, you've got a couple of ways of to publish:

   • Ctrl+click (Mac) or right-click (Win) on the Project file and choose Publish from the context menu.

   • Click the Project button 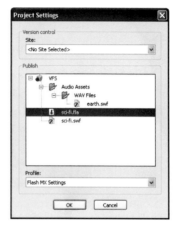 in the top-left corner of the Project panel and select Publish Project from the subsequent pop-up menu.

Working Collaboratively on a Flash Project

One of the greatest strengths of a Flash Project is the fact that multiple authors can work on the same Project at the same time. Further, in this kind of situation, you can establish version control to make sure that each author who is working on a Project file is always using the latest version of a file and that multiple authors on a Project do not overwrite each other's work. This is how it works: Everybody who is working on the Project connects to the remote location where the Project itself is stored. When one author wants to work on one of the files in the Project, they check it out from the remote site. When they are finished, they check the file back in.

The great thing is that when one of the authors checks a file out from the remote location, it is locked until they check it back in, so authors do not overwrite each other's work.

In this section, you'll learn what it takes to work collaboratively on a Flash project. You'll explore how to set up the site where the Flash Project will be located, learn how to set version control for that site, find out how to edit a Project located on a site with version control, and how to open a Project's file directly from a remote site.

Defining a Site for Your Flash Project

One of the key concepts in collaboratively working on a Flash Project is a Site. Essentially, a

Site is a set of rules that defines where the Project is located (either on a LAN or a remote server accessed through FTP) and how you access it, where your local version of the Project sits on your hard drive, and what information is visible regarding the status of a given file in the Project. Without a Site, it is nearly impossible to collaboratively work on a Project. So the bottom line is that if you want to work on a Project with a series of other authors, you must set up a Site.

To set up a Site for your Flash Project, first create the project using the procedures outlined earlier in this section. Then take the following steps:

1. Open the Edit Sites dialog box in either one of two ways:

   • Choose File → Edit Sites.

   • With the Project panel open (Window → Project), click the Version Control button 🔃 and select Edit Sites from the subsequent pop-up menu.

2. When the Edit Sites dialog box opens (see Figure 9.10), click the New button ⟨ New... ⟩.

3. When the Site Definition dialog box opens (see Figure 9.11), enter a name for your Site in the Site Name field.

The name you give to your Site isn't a filename; it's just an arbitrary name that Flash uses to reference the specific Site associated with a specific Project.

Figure 9.11

The Site Definition dialog box

4. From here, you need to tell Flash where the local version of the Project resides on your hard drive. Click the Browse for Folder icon to the right of the Site Root field.

5. When the Browse for Folder dialog box opens (see Figure 9.12), navigate to the location on your hard drive where the local copy of your Project resides, select the folder, and click OK.

   While it's not completely required, it's *very* advisable that *all* the files in your Project are located in the folder on your hard drive that you define as your Site Root.

6. Enter your e-mail address in the E-mail field.

7. Enter your name in the Check Out Name field.

What you enter in the E-mail and the Check Out Name fields is important because if anyone tries to check out a file that has already been checked out, that information appears in a dialog box indicating who currently has the file checked out.

Figure 9.11

The Site Definition dialog box

8. Then you need to tell Flash how you access the remote location where the Project is located. Select one of the options from the Connection drop-down menu:

   - If the Project file is located on a remote computer (server) that you don't have direct access to, select FTP.

   - If you have direct access to the computer that the Project is located on, select Local/Network.

Figure 9.12

The Browse for Folder dialog box

If only for the sake of organization, it's wise to make sure the Project occupies its own folder/directory regardless of whether it's on a remote server or a local machine.

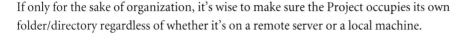

The options that appear next in the Connection section of the Site Definition dialog box depend on the Connection type that you chose in step 8. If you've selected the Local/Network option, the options of which are illustrated in Figure 9.13, then you need to follow these steps:

1. Click the Browse for Folder icon to the right of the Remote Directory field.

2. When the Browse for Folder dialog box opens, navigate to the location where the remote copy of your Project resides, select the folder, and click OK.

If your Project resides on a server to which you don't have direct access, and you've selected FTP from the Connection drop-down menu, there are additional properties you need to set, all of which are accessible in the Site Definition dialog box (see Figure 9.14).

1. Enter the name of the FTP host in the FTP Host field.

2. If the folder that the Project resides in is not in the root directory of the FTP host, you need to input the exact path to the correct folder in the FTP Directory field.

3. Enter your login name in the Login Name field.

4. Enter the password you use to access the remote server in the Login Password field.

5. If you want the password to be saved, click the Save check box. If you leave it unchecked, you will have to manually enter your password every time you connect to the remote server.

6. If you want to check if all the information you've entered is correct, you can test the connection by clicking the Test button.

7. When you've finished entering all the necessary information in the Site Definition dialog box, click OK.

Uploading the Project to the Remote Location

After you've set up a Site, you are just about ready to work collaboratively on your Project. There is, however, one last thing you must do. If you are the primary author (in other words, you are the person who originally created the Project file), you need to move a copy of the Project to the remote location where it will reside. If you don't do this, none of the other authors will be able to access the Project files, which pretty much defeats the whole point of the process.

To move a copy of the Project to its intended remote location, follow these steps:

1. Make sure you've set up a Site for your Project following the steps outlined in the previous section.

2. From the Project panel (Window → Project), open the Project Settings dialog box.

Figure 9.13

The Site Definition dialog box with the Local/Network connection option selected

Figure 9.14

The Site Definition dialog box with the FTP connection option selected

For how to open the Project Settings dialog box, refer to the section "Publishing your Flash Project" earlier in this chapter.

3. When the Project Settings dialog box opens, select the specific Site from the Site drop-down menu and click OK.

4. Now, with the Project panel open, select the Project file.

5. From here, you've got a couple ways of checking in the Project file:

    • Ctrl+click (Mac) or right-click (Win) on the Project file and choose Check In from the context menu.

    • Click the Version Control button ⇅ in the top-left corner of the Project panel and select Check In from the subsequent pop-up menu, shown here.

Figure 9.15

When a Project file has been checked into a Site, a padlock icon appears to the left of its name in the Project panel.

Several things will happen. First, Flash connects with your Site's remote location. If you're using FTP, the negotiation that happens between Flash and the remote computer might take some time (depending on the speed of your connection and the speed of the remote server). You will then get a pop-up message indicating whether or not the connection was made successfully.

6. Once the Project file has been checked in, a padlock icon will be displayed to the left of its name in the Project panel (see Figure 9.15). This means that the Project file has been checked into the remote location and is locked. It cannot be edited until it's been checked out of the remote location (something we'll talk about next).

7. Once you've checked in the Project file, you need to check in all the other files in the Project. If you don't, they won't be available to the other authors. To do this, first select the additional file(s) you want to check in and follow the instructions outlined in step 5.

8. As with the Project file, a padlock icon appears next to the name of the other checked-in files. You won't be able to edit them unless you check them out from the Site.

Editing a File Located on a Site

Once you've established a Site and checked all the files within your project into that Site (as was described in the previous section), you can then check files out and edit them. This process ensures that all the authors working on the Project have access to the most recent versions of the files. Remember, when a file is checked out, it is locked until it is checked back in.

To edit a file located on a Site, follow these steps:

1. Make sure you've got the correct Project open in the Project panel (Window → Project), and then open the Project Settings dialog box.

   For how to open the Project Settings dialog box, refer to the section "Publishing your Flash Project" earlier in this chapter.

2. When the Project Settings dialog box opens, select the specific Site you want to connect to from the Site drop-down menu.

   If the Site you want to connect to is accessible though FTP, you need to have an active connection to the Internet.

3. Click OK to close the Project Settings dialog box. Flash will connect to the selected Site.

Once you connect with a Site, the Project panel displays all the files in that Project as well as any new files that were added by other options.

4. Select the file that you want to check out from the Site.

5. From here, you've got two ways of checking out a Project file:

   - Ctrl+click (Mac) or right-click (Win) on the file you want to edit and choose Check Out from the context menu.

   - Click the Version Control button ⬆️⬇️ in the top-left corner of the Project panel and select Check Out from the subsequent pop-up menu.

6. Once a file is checked out, a green check mark icon will appear to the left of its name.

7. Now you can open the file and make any changes you want. Once finished, save the file, close it, and then check it back in to the Site.

Remember, if you don't check a file back in to the Site, any other authors working on it won't have access to it.

Opening a File Located on a Site

When multiple authors are working on a project, the check-in/check-out feature is a valuable safeguard for maintaining version control and avoiding files being overwritten. However, what if you wanted to bypass all the checking-in/checking-out shenanigans, and simply open a file that is located in a Site? Well, Macromedia has predicted this possibility and included a handy little Open From Site option; this is how it works:

1. Choose File → Open From Site.

2. When the Open From Site dialog box opens, select the site from which you want to open the file from the Site drop-down menu. Flash will connect with the chosen Site and then display its contents (see Figure 9.16).

3. Double-click the file you want to edit and it will open.

Figure 9.16

The contents of the Site are displayed in the Open From Site dialog box.

The Open From Site option does *not* include any way to copy the edited file back to the Site.

Using the Movie Explorer to Manage and Manipulate Movie-Wide Assets

In earlier versions of Flash, it was quite difficult to keep track of the structure of your Flash creation, especially if you were using ActionScripts, nested symbols, or complex Movie Clips. Then, in Flash MX, much to the joy of the Flash community, along came the Movie Explorer (see Figure 9.17).

Essentially, the Movie Explorer displays the contents of your movie hierarchically. The Movie Explorer lets you search your entire movie for any symbol or symbol instance. In addition, you can replace text and fonts with a few easy steps. You can also copy the contents of the Movie Explorer as text to the Clipboard or print the display list in the Movie Explorer. To activate the Movie Explorer, choose Window → Other Panels → Movie Explorer (or use the shortcut Option/Alt+F3).

In the next sections, you'll explore the various Movie Explorer options. You'll also look at how you filter the categories displayed in the Movie Explorer and how you search for items with the Find field. Finally, you'll learn how to edit symbol properties and replace fonts from within the Movie Explorer.

Understanding the Movie Explorer Options

As with many of Flash's panels, the Movie Explorer has an Options drop-down menu (accessible by clicking the icon in the panel's right corner). A quick survey of these options will give you an idea of what you can accomplish working in this panel:

Go to Location Jumps to the selected layer, scene, or frame in the movie. You can accomplish the same thing by simply double-clicking the item in the Movie Explorer.

Go to Symbol Definition Automatically selects all items in the Symbol Definitions section of the Movie Explorer associated with the selected symbol. If the Symbol Definitions section is not visible in the display list, you can enable it by selecting Show Symbol Definitions from the Options drop-down menu. The Go to Symbol Definition option works only if you have the Show Buttons, Movie Clips, and Graphics button toggled, and it's active only when you're working in the Movie Elements section of the display list.

Select Symbol Instances Automatically jumps to the scene in the Movie Elements section of the display list that contains the selected symbol's instance. This option is accessible only when the Show Buttons, Movie Clips, and Graphics button is toggled. In addition, the feature is active only when you're working in the Symbol Definitions section of the display list.

Find in Library Opens the Library (if it is not already open) and jumps to the selected symbol.

Rename Lets you rename the currently selected symbol.

Edit in Place Allows you to edit the currently selected symbol on the Stage without entering Symbol Editing mode.

Edit in New Window Opens up a new window in which you can make changes to the selected symbol.

Show Movie Elements Automatically displays all elements in the Flash movie, organized by scene.

Show Symbol Definitions Displays all the files associated with the currently selected element (by toggling on and off).

Show All Scenes Displays all the scenes in your movie (by toggling on and off).

Copy All Text to Clipboard Copies selected text to your Clipboard so that you can paste it into another program (a word processor, for example).

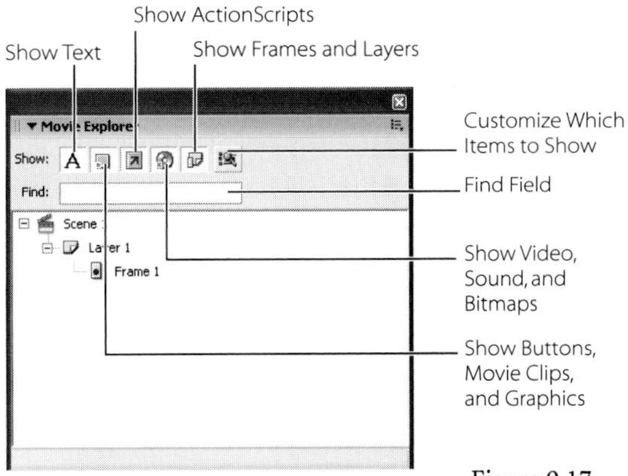

Show ActionScripts

Show Text

Show Frames and Layers

Customize Which Items to Show

Find Field

Show Video, Sound, and Bitmaps

Show Buttons, Movie Clips, and Graphics

Figure 9.17

The Movie Explorer

Cut Cuts selected text.

Copy Copies selected text (but does not place it in the Clipboard as the Copy All Text to Clipboard option does).

Paste Allows you to paste text that has been copied from within Flash or from another application.

Clear Clears selected text. It's important to remember that when you use the Clear option, you are performing the operation on the on-stage instance of the test that you've selected in the Movie Explorer.

Expand Branch Expands the currently selected branch of the hierarchical tree. You can accomplish the same result by clicking the plus (+) sign to the right of any given section of the hierarchy.

Collapse Branch Collapses the currently selected branch of the hierarchy. You can accomplish the same effect by clicking the minus (–) symbol to the right of any given section of the hierarchy. This is the opposite of the Expand Branch option.

Collapse Others Automatically collapses all sections of the hierarchy except for the one currently selected.

Print Automatically prints all the contents of the Movie Explorer (with all sections of the hierarchy expanded). This is a good way to create a hard-copy version of your Flash movie's structure.

Exploiting the Power of the Movie Explorer

Now that you've investigated the Movie Explorer options, you can learn how to manipulate the way your Flash movie's content is displayed and how you can manipulate that content.

Filtering the Displayed Categories

At the top of the Movie Explorer (shown earlier in Figure 9.17), the Show buttons allow you to choose the category or categories of items displayed in the Movie Explorer. When you

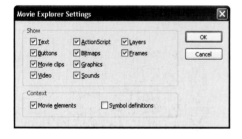

click any of the buttons (or a combination thereof), the Movie Explorer displays only those elements in your file.

From left to right, the buttons are Show Text; Show Buttons, Movie Clips, and Graphics; Show ActionScripts; Show Video, Sounds, and Bitmaps; and Show Frames and Layers. The final button, Customize Which Items to Show, brings up the Movie Explorer Settings dialog box (shown here), which allows you to set the items you want visible, giving you slightly more control over the display.

Searching for Items

When you are working with a particularly large movie with many discrete elements, it can take a long time to locate a given symbol or instance. In that case, the Movie Explorer provides you with a search tool. All you have to do is enter the name of a symbol, instance, font, ActionScript string, or frame number in the Find field, and the Movie Explorer automatically jumps to the location in the hierarchy where the item is located.

If you can't recall the exact name of the element you're looking for, you can enter any part of the name and the Movie Explorer will display any items whose names contain the string you specified.

Editing Symbols

Symbols are the focus of Chapter 7. As discussed there, these reusable elements are an essential tool for streamlining your Flash development.

You will probably find yourself in the situation where you want to alter a given symbol instance from within the Movie Explorer. Here's how:

1. Make sure the Movie Explorer is open (Window → Other Panels → Movie Explorer).

2. Locate the symbol instance you want to edit. You can either navigate to its location in the hierarchy manually or use the Movie Explorer's search tool to find it.

3. Ctrl+click (Mac) or right-click (Win) and choose Edit In Place or Edit In New Window from the pop-up menu. Alternatively, you can choose either of these options from the Movie Explorer's option menu (accessible by clicking the right-pointing arrow in the top-right corner of the Movie Explorer).

> You can also double-click the symbol instance in the Movie Explorer to enter into Symbol Editing mode.

4. Make any changes you want to the symbol instance and then return to working on your movie.

Replacing Fonts

The Movie Explorer lets you search for and replace any specific font you've used in your movie. This is particularly useful if you have many different instances of a given font that you want to change and don't want to change each by hand:

1. Make sure the Movie Explorer is open (Window → Other Panels → Movie Explorer).

2. Type the name of the font in the Find field.

3. After the Movie Explorer has gone to the location in the hierarchy where the font in question resides, select it. As illustrated here, if you've used the same font more than once, it will display all occurrences. To select them all, use Cmd/Ctrl+click.

4. Open the Property Inspector (Window → Properties).

5. Make any changes you want—font, style, color, size, and so on.

6. When you make your changes, your movie is automatically updated.

Using the Find and Replace Function

Arguably one of the most useful, and underrated, new tools in both Flash MX 2004 and Flash MX Pro 2004 is the Find and Replace function. With it, you can search the current document or the current scene for a string of text, a specific font, a color, a symbol, a sound file, a video file, or an imported bitmap. You can then replace the item with another item of the same type. Further, you can search for the next occurrence or all occurrences of an element, and replace the current occurrence or all occurrences.

When you're working on a screen-based movie in Flash MX Pro 2004 (a feature that is not available in Flash MX 2004), you can find and replace elements in the current document or screen, but not in the current scene, because screen-based documents don't use scenes. For more information on screen-based authoring, check out Chapter 13.

To use the Find and Replace function, just follow these steps:

1. Choose Edit → Find And Replace to open the Find And Replace dialog box (see Figure 9.18).

2. Select the scope of your search from the Search In drop-down menu.

From here, depending on what you're searching for, you have a bevy of options, each of which will be outlined in the following sections (all of which assume that you know how to open the Find And Replace dialog box and set the scope of your search).

Finding and Replacing Text

If you want to find and replace text, follow these steps:

1. Make sure that you've opened the Find And Replace dialog box (Edit → Find And Replace) and you've set the scope of the search by selecting one of the options from the Search In drop-down menu.

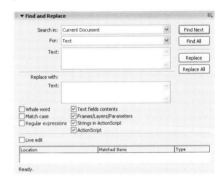

2. Select Text from the For drop-down menu to display the text-specific options:

3. Enter the text you want to search for in the Text box.

4. Enter the text you want to replace it with in the Replace With Text box.

5. From here, you can select any of the following options:

   - Whole Word searches for the text string as a whole word only, bounded on both sides by spaces or punctuation. When Whole Word is not selected, the text can be part of a larger word. For example, when Whole Word is deselected, the word **sin** can be searched as part of the word **single**.

   - Text Fields Contents searches only the contents of your movie's Text fields.

   - Match Case searches for text that exactly matches the case (upper or lower) of the specified text.

- Frames/Layers/Parameters searches only frame labels, layer names, scene names, and component parameters.

- Regular Expressions searches only for text in regular expressions in your movie's ActionScript.

- Strings In ActionScript searches any strings in your movie's ActionScript.

- ActionScript searches all of your movie's ActionScript. When you choose any of the ActionScript options, external ActionScript files (AS) are not included in the search.

6. Select the Live Edit check box if you want to be able to edit the specific element directly on the Stage.

7. To find text, you've got a couple of options:

- Click the Find Next button [Find Next] to locate the next occurrence of the specified text.

- Click the Find All button [Find All] to locate all occurrences of the specified text.

8. To replace text, you've got a couple of options:

- Click the Replace button [Replace] to replace the currently selected occurrence of the specified text.

- Click the Replace All button [Replace All] to replace all the occurrences of the specified text

Whether you're just finding text or finding and replacing it, the results are displayed in the list box at the bottom of the Find And Replace dialog box (as illustrated here). If you've just searched for text and have selected the Live Edit option, you can double-click any of the individual results to jump to the specific string of text in your movie, which you can then edit.

Figure 9.18

The Find And Replace dialog box

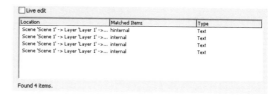

Finding and Replacing Fonts

If you want to find and replace fonts, just follow these steps:

1. Make sure that you've opened the Find And Replace dialog box (Edit → Find And Replace) and you've set the scope of the search by selecting one of the options from the Search In drop-down menu.

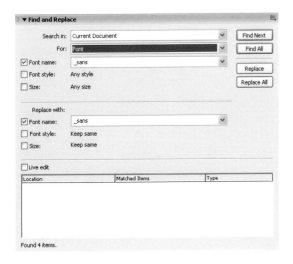

2. Select Font in the For drop-down menu to display font-specific options.

3. If you want to search for a font by name, select the Font Name check box. Then, when the Font drop-down menu is displayed, select the specific font for which you want to search.

4. If you want to search for a specific font style (bold, italic, underline, and so on), select the Font Style check box. Then, when the Style drop-down menu is displayed, select the specific style you want to search for.

5. If you want to search for a specific font size, select the Font Size check box. When the Min and Max fields are displayed, enter a minimum (Min) and maximum (Max) size range for the font you are searching for.

6. To replace the specified font with a different font entirely, select the Font Name check box in the Replace With section of the Find And Replace dialog box. When the Font drop-down menu is displayed, select the font you want to use instead of the font you're searching for.

When the Font Name check box in the Replace With section is deselected, the current font name remains unchanged.

7. To replace the specified font style with a different font style, select the Font Style check box in the Replace With section. When the Font Style drop-down menu is displayed, select the style you want to use instead of the style you're searching for.

When the Font Style check box in the Replace With section is deselected, the current style of the specified font remains unchanged.

8. To replace the specified font size with a new font size, select the Font Size check box in the Replace With section. When the Size field is displayed, enter the value of the replacement size.

9. Select the Live Edit check box if you want to be able to edit the specific font directly on the Stage.

10. To find a font, use the Find Next button Find Next or the Find All button Find All to locate the next occurrence or all occurrences of the specified font.

11. To replace a font, use the Replace button [Replace] or the Replace All button [Replace All] to replace the currently selected occurrence or all occurrences of the specified font.

Whether you're just searching for a font or searching and replacing a font, the results are displayed in the list box at the bottom of the Find And Replace dialog box. If you've just searched for a font and have selected the Live Edit option, you can double-click any of the individual results to jump to the specific font in your movie, which you can then edit.

Finding and Replacing Colors

Any Flash movie, large or small, is composed of many different colors, all of which were most likely chosen very carefully. So what happens if you decide that instead of a color you initially chose, you want to use another? Well, you could go through your entire movie, carefully selecting the unwanted color, and then replacing it with a new color. However, this can be a lengthy process. Instead, you can use the Find and Replace function to search for a specific color and then automatically replace it with another.

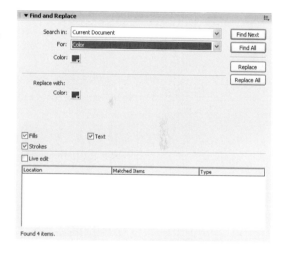

To find and replace a color, follow these steps:

1. Make sure that you've opened the Find And Replace dialog box (Edit → Find And Replace) and you've set the scope of the search by selecting one of the options from the Search In drop-down menu.

2. Select Color in the For drop-down menu to display color options:

3. To select the specific color you want to search for, click the Color swatch and choose that color from the pop-up color palette.

> If the color you want to search for isn't in the pop-up color palette, you can enter an exact Hexadecimal code in the pop-up color palette's Hex Edit text box, click the Color Picker button ⚫ , or specify your own custom color using RGB or HSL. Alternatively, if you move your mouse cursor outside the palette, it will change into an eyedropper, allowing you to select any color visible inside the Flash application's window by clicking it.

4. To select a color to replace the color you're searching for, click the Color swatch in the Replace With section of the Find And Replace dialog box.

5. Select the Fills, Strokes, or Text option (or any combination of the three) to choose the occurrence of the specified color that you're searching and replacing.

6. Select the Live Edit check box if you want to be able to edit the specific color directly on the Stage.

7. To find a color, you've got a couple of options:

   - Click the Find Next button [Find Next] to locate the next occurrence of the specified color.

   - Click the Find All button [Find All] to locate all occurrences of the specified color.

8. To replace a color, you've got a couple of options:

   - Click the Replace button [Replace] to replace the currently selected occurrence of the specified color.

   - Click the Replace All button [Replace All] to replace all the occurrences of the specified color.

Whether you're just searching for a color or searching and replacing a color, the results are displayed in the list box at the bottom of the Find And Replace dialog box. If you've just searched for a color and have selected the Live Edit option, you can double-click any of the individual results to jump to the specific color in your movie, which you can then edit.

Finding and Replacing Symbols

If you want to find and replace symbols instance, follow these steps:

1. Make sure that you've opened the Find And Replace dialog box (Edit → Find And Replace) and you've set the scope of the search by selecting one of the options from the Search In drop-down menu.

2. Select Symbols in the For drop-down menu to display symbol options.

3. Select the symbol instance that you want to replace from the Name drop-down menu.

4. Now you need to select the symbol to replace the symbol you're searching for. Select the symbol instance in the Name drop-down menu located in the Replace With section of the Find And Replace dialog box.

5. Select the Live Edit check box if you want to be able to edit the specific symbol instance directly on the Stage.

If you use Live Edit when searching for a symbol instance, Flash opens the symbol in Edit In Place mode.

6. To find a symbol instance, you've got a couple of options:

   • Click the Find Next button [Find Next] to locate the next occurrence of the specified symbol instance.

   • Click the Find All button [Find All] to locate all occurrences of the specified symbol instance.

7. To replace a symbol instance, you've got a couple of options:

   • Click the Replace button [Replace] to replace the currently selected occurrence of the specified symbol instance.

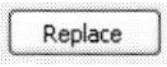

   • Click the Replace All button [Replace All] to replace all the occurrences of the specified symbol instance.

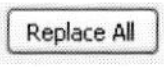

Whether you're just searching for a symbol instance or searching and replacing a symbol instance, the results are displayed in the list box down at the bottom of the Find And Replace dialog box. If you've just searched for a symbol instance and have selected the Live Edit option, you can double-click any of the individual results to jump to the specific symbol instance in your movie, which you can then edit.

Finding and Replacing Audio Files, Video Files, and Bitmaps

If you want to find and replace audio files, video files, or imported bitmaps, follow these steps:

1. Make sure that you've opened the Find And Replace dialog box (Edit → Find And Replace) and you've set the scope of the search by selecting one of the options from the Search In drop-down menu.

2. Select the Sound or Video or Bitmap option in the For drop-down menu to display the specific options (see Figure 9.19).

3. Depending on the option you selected in the For drop-down menu, select the audio file or video file or imported bitmap that you want to replace from the Name drop-down menu.

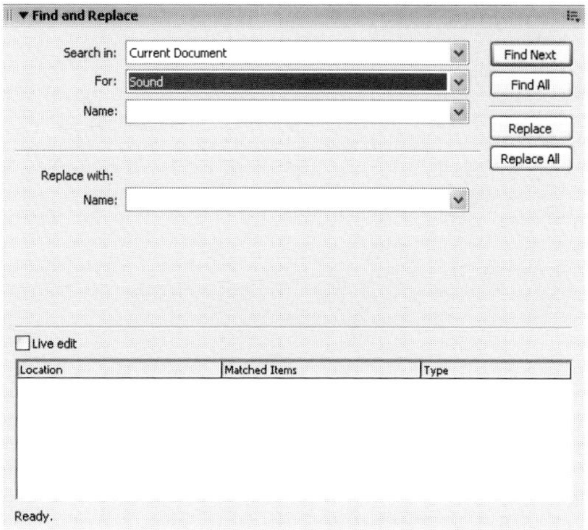

Figure 9.19

The Find And Replace dialog box's audio-specific options. The options for video and bitmaps are exactly the same.

4. Now you need to select the file to replace the file you're searching for. Select the specific file from the Name drop-down menu located in the Replace With section of the Find And Replace dialog box.

5. To find the audio file, video file, or imported bitmap, you've got a couple of options:

    • Click the Find Next button [Find Next] to locate the next occurrence of the specified file.

    • Click the Find All button [Find All] to locate all occurrences of the specified file.

6. To replace the audio file, video file, or imported bitmap, you've got a couple of options:

    • Click the Replace button [Replace] to replace the currently selected occurrence of the specified file.

    • Click the Replace All button [Replace All] to replace all the occurrences of the specified file.

Whether you're searching for an audio file, a video file, or a bitmap, or finding and replacing it, the results are displayed in the list box at the bottom of the Find And Replace dialog box.

Automating Tasks with Commands

During the process of creating a Flash movie, however big or small, you'll be doing a lot of tasks over and over again. What if you could record tasks that have many steps and then replay them whenever you wanted? In Flash MX 2004 and Flash MX Pro 2004, this isn't just a pipe dream, it's a reality. With the help of the new History panel, you can choose any of the steps that you've carried out since you started a new document and compile them into a command that can be saved and run anytime you please. The commands themselves, which are something like macros, are retained permanently (regardless of whether or not you're working in the document they were created in) and become accessible through the program's Commands menu. To actually run a command, all you need to do is select it from Flash's Commands menu.

> The History panel displays a list of the steps you've performed in the currently active document since you opened it. The History panel does not show steps you've performed in other documents. The slider in the History panel initially points to the last step that you performed. Beyond creating commands, you can use the History panel to undo or redo individual steps or multiple steps at once. You can apply steps from the History panel to the same object or to a different object in the document. However, you cannot rearrange the order of steps in the History panel.

In this section, you'll explore how to create and manage commands.

Creating a Command

The process by which you create a command is quite easy; all you need to do is follow these steps:

1. Manually carry out a series of steps that you want to turn into a command.

2. Open the History panel by choosing Window → Other Panels → History. You'll notice that the steps you've taken in the currently active document are listed in the panel. The earliest steps are listed at the top of the panel, while the most recent are listed at the bottom (see Figure 9.20).

Figure 9.20

The History panel. Note the list of steps carried out.

3. Select the steps that you want included in the command. To select multiple steps, hold down the Shift key.

> You might have noticed that some of the steps' associated icons have a small red *x* in their lower-right corner. This means that that specific step, because of its nature, can't be made into a command. If you try to include one of these kinds of steps in a command, the command won't be saved.

4. Click the Save As Command button 💾 located in the lower-right corner of the History panel.

5. When the Save As Command dialog box opens (see Figure 9.21), enter a name for the command in the Command Name field.

Figure 9.21

The Save As Command dialog box

> It's a really good idea to give your command a descriptive name. By doing this, you'll be able to distinguish the purpose of each specific command when you view them in the Commands menu.

6. When you're finished, click OK.

> After you've converted a series of steps into a command, the command is displayed in Flash's Commands menu.

Managing Commands

After you've created a series of commands, you need to be able to manage them. Flash lets you change a command's name as well as delete a command—processes that we'll look at here.

Changing a Command's Name

While you give a command a name when you initially create it, you might find yourself wanting to change its name during the course of your work. Here's how:

1. Choose Commands → Manage Saved Commands.

2. When the Manage Saved Commands dialog box opens (see Figure 9.22), select the command whose name you want to change and click the Rename button .

3. When the Rename Command dialog box opens (Figure 9.23), enter a new name in the Command Name field and click OK.

Deleting a Command

As you work more and more with Flash, you'll begin to accumulate more and more commands, which will inevitably clog up Flash's Commands menu. So it's a good idea to remove commands that you no longer use. Here's how:

1. Choose Commands → Manage Saved Commands.

2. When the Manage Saved Commands dialog box opens (see Figure 9.22), select the command that you want to delete and click the Delete button.

3. When the pop-up alert is displayed, depending on whether or not you want to delete the command, click OK or Cancel.

Figure 9.22

The Manage Saved Commands dialog box

Figure 9.23

The Rename Command dialog box

Inspirational Design Model

Based in the great city of Vancouver, in the wonderful province of British Columbia, in the beautiful country of Canada, Atomic Cartoons (www.atomiccartoons.com) specializes in creating offbeat and hilarious Flash-animated shorts for distribution over the Web. Entertaining the masses, the Atomic Cartoons website features incredibly well-engineered graphics with stylish simplicity that scream creative talent (see Figure 9.24).

Figure 9.24

Atomic Cartoons

© Atomic Cartoons, Inc.

Creating an Illustrated Ocean Scene with Layers and Objects

Throughout Part II, you explored the painting, drawing, and object manipulation tools available to you in Flash MX 2004 and Flash MX Professional 2004. In this tutorial, you'll put all your hard-earned knowledge to work by creating an illustrated ocean scene. As we have yet to cover how to animate objects Flash, the ocean scene itself will be static.

The tutorial's files are on this book's companion CD. Look for ocean_scene.fla in the Hands On 2 folder. In this file, you'll find a copy of the finished ocean scene. You'll also find an additional file, titled undersea_creatures.fla, which you'll need to complete the tutorial.

Creating the Water

Before you start adding the undersea elements to your ocean scene, you'll need to add the backdrop—the water.

1. If you haven't already, create a new document by choosing File → New (or by using the shortcut Cmd/Ctrl+**N**).

2. When the New Document dialog box opens, under the General tab, in the Type list box, select the Flash Document option.

3. Choose Modify → Document (or use the shortcut Cmd/Ctrl+**J**) to open the Document Properties dialog box.

4. Click the Background color swatch and choose a light blue color from the Color Picker. This will act as the color of the sky, which will be visible above the rolling waves of the ocean.

5. When you are finished setting the color of the sky, click OK.

6. Because this scene will have a number of different elements (each occupying a different layer), you need to name the layer whose color you just changed. To do this, double-click the layer's name. When it becomes editable, enter **Sky**.

7. Now, you need to create the water. To start, create a new layer by clicking the New Layer button 🔁 in the bottom-left corner of the Timeline or by choosing Insert → Timeline → Layer.

8. When the new layer is displayed (above the sky layer), double-click the layer name and, once it becomes editable, enter **Water**.

9. To create the water, choose Insert → New Symbol (or use the shortcut Cmd/Ctrl+F8).

10. When the New Symbol dialog box opens, make sure the Graphic radio button is selected and enter **Water** in the Name field.

11. When you enter Symbol Editing mode, select the Rectangle Tool 🔲 from the Toolbox.

12. Before you draw anything, open the Property Inspector (which you access by choosing Window → Properties) and change both the Stroke color and the Fill color to a darker blue than that of the Sky layer.

> By default, any rectangle you draw will have a stroke. This is why you are making the stroke color and the fill color the same—so that it doesn't look as if our Water symbol has a different-colored border around it. Alternatively, you could simply select and delete the shape's stroke after you've drawn it.

13. Now, draw a rectangle that is roughly the width and height of the Stage. Don't worry too much that the dimensions are not completely accurate; you'll fine-tune it shortly.

> At this point, you can also select and delete the rectangle's stroke if you want.

14. Select the rectangle using the Arrow tool ➤ .

15. In the Property Inspector (Window → Properties), enter **550** in the Width (W) field and **370** in the Height (H) field.

16. Now select the Free Transform tool from the Toolbox and click the selected rectangle.

17. When the transform handles appear around the rectangle, click the Envelope button 🖾 (which is located in the Options section of the Toolbox when the Free Transform tool is selected).

18. From here, manipulate any of the handles along the top of the rectangle to create the appearance of rolling waves. When you are finished, depending on the changes you made, your rectangle should look something like this:

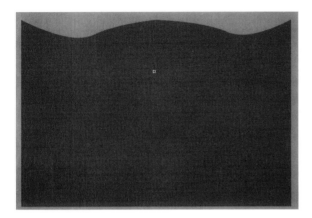

19. Now you need to insert the water into your main scene. Click the Scene link in the Edit toolbar to return to the main Timeline.

20. Select the first blank keyframe in the water layer.

21. Open the Library by choosing Window → Library (or by using the shortcut Cmd/Ctrl+**L**).

22. Drag the Water symbol from the Library onto the Stage. Make sure the bottom of the symbol lines up with the bottom of the Stage. Also, make sure the left and right edges of the symbol line up with the Stage.

Adding Some Bubbles

Now that we've created the oceanic backdrop, we can start adding some elements. We'll start off by adding some floating bubbles.

1. You'll begin by creating a single Bubble symbol that that you'll use in multiple places throughout the scene. To do this, choose Insert → New Symbol.

2. When the New Symbol dialog box opens, make sure the Graphic radio button is selected, enter **Bubble** into the Name field, and click OK.

3. When you enter Symbol Editing mode, select the Oval tool ○ from the Toolbox.

4. Before you draw anything, open the Property Inspector (if it isn't already open), make the Fill either a very light gray or white, make the Stroke color a darker gray, and change the Stroke Height to 2.

5. Now, in the middle of the Symbol Editor (directly over the registration point crosshairs), draw a perfect circle (by holding down the Shift key) about 1 centimeter (or half an inch) in diameter.

6. At this point, your bubble should look something like this. (*top right*)

7. Now you'll add a little more detail to the bubble by adding a cartoon-like feature that will make it look rounded instead of flat. Zoom in on the bubble until it takes up the majority of the workspace. With any of the drawing tools (pencil, pen, paintbrush, and so on), draw a small, skewed rectangle in the top-left quarter of the bubble. This gives the illusion that light is reflecting off the rounded surface of the bubble and should look something like this. (*bottom right*)

You can also fill the little "reflection" you drew with a lighter color than the fill of the bubble itself; this goes a little further toward giving the impression of light bouncing off the surface.

8. Now that you've created the bubble, you can add it to the scene. Click the Scene link in the Edit bar to return to the main Timeline.

9. You'll start off by adding some random bubbles that will add ambiance to the scene. Create a new layer by clicking the New Layer button ⬚ in the bottom-left corner of the Timeline or by choosing Insert → Timeline → Layer.

10. Double-click the layer's name, and when it becomes editable, enter **bubbles**.

11. From here, select the first keyframe in the new bubbles layer and drag the Bubble symbol from the Library (Window → Library) to the Stage.

12. With the Bubble symbol still selected, enter **95** in the X field and **336** in the Y field.

13. Drag a second instance of the Bubble symbol onto the Stage and position it slightly above and to the right of the first Bubble symbol.

14. With the second Bubble symbol still selected and the Property Inspector open, enter **25** in the Width (W) field and **25** in the Height (H) field.

15. Now, with the Property Inspector still open and the second Bubble symbol still selected, select Alpha from the Property Inspector's Color drop-down menu.

16. When the Alpha Amount field is displayed to the right of the Color field, enter **80**.

17. Drag a third instance of the Bubble symbol from the Library onto the Stage and position it above and slightly to the left of the second Bubble symbol.

18. With the third bubble still selected, enter **20** in the Property Inspector's Width (W) field and **20** in the Height (H) field.

19. With the third Bubble symbol still selected, choose Alpha from the Property Inspector's Color drop-down menu and enter **75** in the Alpha Amount field.

20. Drag a fourth instance of the Bubble symbol from the Library onto the Stage, and position it slightly to the top and to the right of the previous bubble.

21. With the fourth bubble still selected, enter **15** in the Property Inspector's Width (W) field and **15** in the Height (H) field.

22. With the fourth Bubble symbol still selected, choose Alpha from the Property Inspector's Color drop-down menu.

23. Enter **65** in the Alpha Amount field.

24. Drag a fifth, and final, instance of the Bubble symbol from the Library onto the Stage, and position it slightly above and to the right of previous (fourth) bubble.

25. With the final bubble still selected and the Property Inspector open, enter **10** in the Width (W) field and **10** in the Height (H) field.

26. With the final bubble still selected, choose Alpha from the Color drop-down menu and enter **50** into the Alpha Mount field.

By this point, you've created a nice little bubble trail that looks something like this:

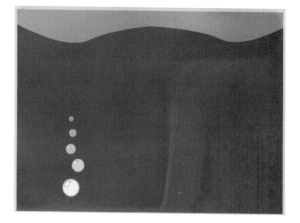

You can certainly add more bubbles to make a longer trail or even create a second trail elsewhere in the scene; it's completely up to you.

Adding Some Sea Life

Now that you've created the backdrop for the scene, it's time to start adding some sea life. However, instead of drawing each undersea creature, you'll take advantage of Flash's ability to use artwork created elsewhere, importing what you need to keep working on the scene. In addition, instead of importing each new element (which will be in SWF format) individually, you'll open an external Library that has all the elements you'll use.

1. Start by choosing File → Import → Open External Library.

2. When the Open As Library dialog box opens, navigate to the Hands On 2 folder in this book's accompanying CD, select the `undersea_creatures.fla` file, and click Open. You'll notice that an additional Library will open with four files (`fish1.swf`, `fish2.swf`, `jellyfish.swf`, and `seahorse.swf`).

3. Select the Bubbles layer and create a new layer by clicking the New Layer button in the bottom-left corner of the Timeline or by choosing Insert → Timeline → Layer.

4. Double-click the new layer's name, and when it becomes editable, enter **Big Fish**.

5. Select the first keyframe in the Big Fish layer, and drag the fish1 symbol from the newly opened external Library onto the bottom-right section of the Stage.

6. Because the fish1 symbol is fairly big, we need to reduce its size slightly so that it fits in better with the overall scene. To do this, select the fish 1 symbol, open the Property Inspector (Window → Properties), and enter **200** in the Width (W) field and **200** in the Height (H) field.

7. When the symbol resizes, you'll notice that it moves slightly. Use the Arrow tool to reposition it in the bottom-right corner of the scene. At this point, your scene should look something like this:

8. Now you'll add a school of fish to the scene. To start, select the water layer and add a new layer by clicking the Insert Layer button  in the bottom-left corner of the Timeline or by choosing Insert → Timeline → Layer.

> Why would you want to create a new layer above the water layer, but below the bubbles layer? Well, by doing this, any objects that you add to the new layer will appear to be behind the floating bubbles you created earlier, giving the illusion of depth to your scene.

9. Double-click the new layer's name, and when it becomes editable, enter **Fish School**.

10. Now select the first keyframe in the fish school layer and drag the fish2 symbol from the external Library you opened earlier onto the Stage. Don't worry too much where you put it because you'll move it into position shortly.

11. As with the first Fish symbol, this new fish is far too big for the scene. Select it, and in the Property Inspector (Window → Properties), click the small padlock icon to the left of the Width (W) and Height (H) fields. By doing this, you guarantee that any change you make to either of the dimension properties will change the other accordingly so that the symbol's aspect ratio is maintained.

12. Enter **50** in the Property Inspector's Width (W) field.

13. Type **196** in the X field and **316** in the Y field.

14. Now drag a second instance of the fish2 symbol from the external Library onto the Stage. Using the Property Inspector, change the second Fish symbol's Width (W) to **30**—remember to click the padlock icon to ensure that the symbol's aspect ratio remains the same.

15. Use the Arrow tool to move the second small fish so that it is slightly above and to the left of the first fish2 symbol.

16. Repeat steps 14 and 15 to add more fish to the school. With each successive fish, vary its position and size slightly (using the Property Inspector) to add more detail to the scene.

17. At this point, your scene should look something like the image to the right.

Finishing the Scene

Now you can complete the scene by adding a few more sea creatures.

1. Select the big fish layer and create a new layer by clicking the New Layer button , located in the bottom-left corner of the Timeline, or by choosing Insert → Timeline → Layer.

2. Double-click the new layer's name. When it becomes editable, enter **jellyfish** in the field.

3. Make sure the first keyframe of the jellyfish layer is selected and drag the Jellyfish symbol from the external Library onto the Stage. As with many of the previous symbols, it doesn't really matter where you stick the jellyfish as you'll fine tune its position in a bit.

4. With the Jellyfish symbol still selected, and the Property Inspector open, enter **75** in the Width (W) field—remember to select the padlock icon to ensure that the symbol's aspect ratio remains the same.

5. From here, enter **100** in the Property Inspector's X field and **88** in its Y field.

6. Now drag a second instance of the Jellyfish symbol onto the Stage.

7. Using the Property Inspector, change the new Jellyfish symbol's Width (W) to **50**, its X value to **170**, and its Y value to **113**.

8. Now drag a third instance of the Jellyfish symbol from the external Library onto the Stage. Make its Width (W) **25**, its X value **185**, and its Y value **80**.

9. At this point, your scene should look something like this:

10. Now for one last element—a lone seahorse. Select the jellyfish layer, and create a new layer by clicking the New Layer button  in the bottom-left corner of the Timeline, or by choosing Insert → Timeline → Layer.

11. Double-click the layer's name. When it becomes editable, enter **seahorse** in the field.

12. Select the first keyframe in the seahorse layer and drag an instance of the Seahorse symbol from the external Library onto the Stage.

13. Using the Property Inspector, change the Width (W) of the seahorse to **30**, its X value to **295**, and its Y value to **130**.

Congratulations, your glorious ocean scene is now finished! Unless you have added your own details or elements, the finished product should look something like this:

PART III

Animating with Flash

While *Flash MX 2004 and Flash MX Professional 2004 have evolved into full-fledged interactive design tools suitable for creating a whole range of groovy media, Flash is, at its heart, still an animation program. Flash's core feature, vector-based graphics, really shines when it comes to animation. As a result, it behooves you to become intimately familiar with all the ways you can infuse your beautiful Flash creation with movement.*

In this part of the book, you'll learn almost everything you need to know about the fundamentals of animating in Flash. You'll start by looking at how to use the Timeline to make your creation zip, bounce, zing, and jump. From there, you'll explore one of the most important aspects of animating in Flash: Movie Clips (a topic that is vital to your future adventures in ActionScripting). You'll then explore one of the most useful tools you can use to control, manage, and manipulate your animation: Scenes. You'll finish Part III by exploring a new feature in Flash MX Pro 2004 that allows you to create Flash movies using a slide metaphor.

CHAPTER 10

Animating with the Timeline

FutureSplash (later to become Flash) was a simple vector-animation program when Macromedia acquired it from FutureWave back in 1997. Though the most recent version of Flash has about 100 times the bells and whistles that FutureSplash did, it is still, at its core, an animation program. Although you can do much more than animate objects, much of the power of Flash MX 2004 and Flash MX Pro 2004 lies in the ability to create movies with content that changes over time.

Until this point, you haven't created anything that *moves* (unless you've shaken your computer monitor around). If you had wanted to create only static images, you could have easily turned to Macromedia Fireworks or Adobe Photoshop. But, no, you want to make things that move and spin and bounce! Whether it's a character that walks across the screen and promptly gets hit by a falling anvil or a button that spins around when users move their cursors over it, you want to create animations. In this chapter, you'll explore the primary tool you use to construct and manipulate animations in Flash MX 2004 and Flash MX Pro 2004: the Timeline.

Topics include the following:

- **Understanding the subtle art of animation**
- **Creating frame-by-frame animations**
- **Creating tweened animations**
- **Animating a mask**
- **Extending a still image through time**
- **Animating a Symbol Instance's Visual Properties with the Property Inspector**
- **Animating with Timeline Effects**

Understanding the Subtle Art of Animation

Animation is the process by which an object's size, position, color, or shape changes over time. In Flash, you have three animation methods, each with their own unique development process and strengths: frame by frame, tweening, and Timeline Effects. Before you start learning about using these methods to infuse your static creations with movement, you need to grasp some fundamental animation concepts, including frames, keyframes, and frame rate.

Getting to Know Frames and Keyframes

Any animation, whether the latest Hollywood 3D animated blockbuster, Walt Disney's original *Fantasia*, or your humble Flash creation, contains *frames*. Each frame contains one static image that, when displayed in succession with other images in other frames, creates the illusion of movement. In Flash MX 2004 and Flash MX Pro 2004, frames are displayed as small boxes horizontally in the Timeline.

> The small boxes in the Timeline are called *cells*. Unfortunately, this term is rarely used, so don't worry if you don't see it in the Flash literature. You can convert any cell into a frame, a keyframe, or an empty keyframe by using the options in the Insert menu.

Each frame's content is displayed as the playhead passes through it, thereby creating something of a digital "flipbook."

In Flash, any frame populated by content that you've directly manipulated (as opposed to, for example, placed by Flash in a tweened animation) is represented in the Timeline by a small black circle called a *keyframe*. A keyframe represents a point on the Timeline where a change occurs in the animation that the animator has directly created or caused. For the time being, know that any time you want to change your animation in any way (add content, subtract content, start the motion of an object, and so on), you'll use a keyframe.

So what exactly is the difference between content in regular frames and content in keyframes? It's pretty simple: Although a keyframe and a frame can have exactly the same content, you can directly manipulate that content only if it resides in a keyframe. If it resides within a frame, there is no way, short of turning the frame into a keyframe (which is a perfectly functional solution), to directly manipulate its content.

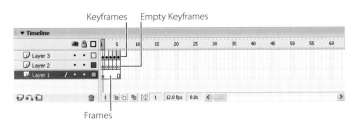

Keyframes Empty Keyframes

Frames

Beyond frames and keyframes, there is a third type of frame you should be aware of. Somewhere between an ordinary frame and a keyframe, an *empty keyframe* is essentially a keyframe that has yet to be "filled" with content. An outline of a small circle represents an empty keyframe.

> By default, Flash designates the first frame of any animation as an empty keyframe. The remaining frames in any given layer are little more than placeholders for future empty keyframes or keyframes (which you need to create).

Understanding Frame Rate

Frame rate determines the rate at which an animation plays. Represented in frames per second (fps), an animation's frame rate is related both to the speed the animation plays at and its overall quality. Think of it this way: If you have a high frame rate, more frames are displayed per second, increasing the animation's quality. The lower your frame rate, the fewer frames displayed per second, increasing the animation's choppiness and decreasing its quality.

You're probably thinking, that's all great, but if a higher frame rate means a better quality animation, then why would anyone ever set a low frame rate? The most important reason you shouldn't always set a high frame rate concerns memory and bandwidth. When you set a high frame rate, you force the user's computer to display more information per second. A higher frame rate might cause some slower computers or slower Internet connections to "choke" on the higher rate of information, causing the animation to hang, skip, or crash entirely.

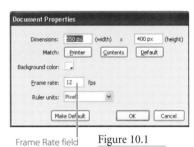

Frame Rate field

Figure 10.1

The Document Properties dialog box

To set your animation's frame rate:

1. Choose Modify → Document or use Cmd/Ctrl+**J** to open the Document Properties dialog box (see Figure 10.1). Alternatively, you can double-click the frame-rate indicator at the bottom of the Timeline.

2. Enter a value in the Frame Rate field.

> Although 12fps is Flash's default frame rate, you're certainly safe if you use a higher frame rate. However, unless you are absolutely confident your users' systems can cope with more information, it's wise to set a frame rate no higher than 20.

How Flash Represents Animation in the Timeline

The Timeline represents the various kinds of animation (and Timeline elements) differently. As a result, it's in your best interest to become familiar with each so that when you get into animating with the Timeline, you won't be caught off guard by the way an animation looks.

- A frame-by-frame animation is usually represented by a layer with a series of sequential keyframes.

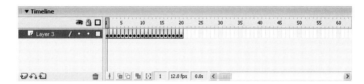

- A motion tween is denoted by a keyframe at the beginning and end, between which a black arrow (representing the actual tween) runs. In addition, a motion tween has a light-blue background.

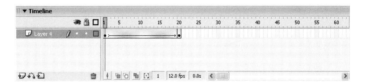

- Like a motion tween, a shape tween is denoted by a keyframe at the beginning and end, between which a black arrow (representing the actual tween) runs. The difference is that the intervening frames are light green instead of light blue.

- When a keyframe is followed by a dashed line, motion tween is incomplete (usually the result of the final keyframe being removed or not added).

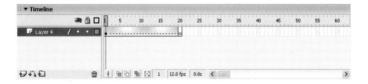

- When a series of gray frames begins with a keyframe and ends with a hollow rectangle, all frames after the keyframe have exactly the same content.

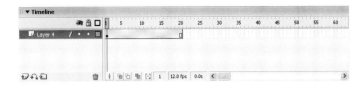

- A frame or keyframe with a lowercase *a* represents a point in the animation where a frame action (global function) has been added. (For more information on actions and ActionScripting, see Parts IV and V of this book.)

In Flash MX 2004 and Flash MX Pro 2004, Actions are now referred to as Global Functions.

Frame Action (Global Function)

- A frame or keyframe with a red flag indicates the presence of a frame label.

Frame labels are extremely useful for identifying and targeting specific frames when you're using actions. You can also use them in the development process to add comments or notes to specific frames. To insert a frame label, select the frame, open the Property Inspector, and enter the label in the Frame Label field.

Changing the Appearance of Frames in the Timeline

Until now, the only way you could actually change the appearance of a frame was to change the height of an entire layer (discussed in Chapter 8). The problem with this was that you weren't really changing the appearance of the frames themselves, but the layer itself. And besides, as you've already discovered, there are only three options for layer height, making it a pretty limited solution.

However, in Flash MX 2004 and Flash MX Pro 2004, you can change the appearance of the frames themselves by using the Frame View button, located in the top-right corner of the Timeline. When clicked, the Frame View button opens a drop-down menu.

Frame View button

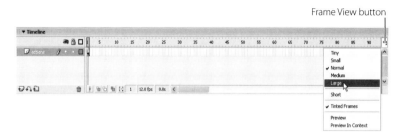

Unfortunately, the option you choose applies to all layers within the Timeline. You can't change the frame appearance for a single layer.

When clicked, the Frame View button opens a drop-down menu containing the following options:

- **Tiny** makes the frames extremely small, allowing more frames to be displayed at any given time in the Timeline.

- **Small** changes the size of the frames so that they are between the Tiny option and the default, Normal.

- **Normal** is the default frame size.

- **Medium** changes the size of the frames so that they are slightly larger than the default Normal size.

- **Large** increases the Timeline's frames to their maximum sizes.

- **Short** reduces the height of the frames in the Timeline.

- The **Tinted Frames** option, which can be toggled on and off, controls whether or not frames with content are shaded or not.

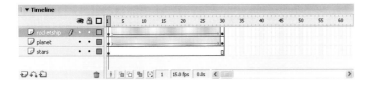

- By selecting **Preview in Context**, Flash creates a thumbnail of each keyframe's contents that is a direct proportional reflection of what is on the Stage, including all the empty space.

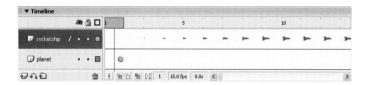

- When you choose **Preview**, you get a thumbnail of each keyframe's contents that fills the entire cell (as opposed to being a proportional representation of the entire Stage). Don't be fooled: Even though the results of Preview and Preview in Context might be similar, the difference usually asserts itself in the amount of white space displayed.

> Displaying extra information in the Timeline, using either Preview or Preview in Context, consumes more processing power, possibly causing your computer to slow down.

Creating a Frame-by-Frame Animation

Way back in the dark ages of animation (*before* computers), animators had to painstakingly create the individual images in each frame, varying each slightly to get the illusion of movement.

In Flash, the most basic form of animation, *frame-by-frame animation,* works the same way. Essentially, frame-by-frame animation works by creating a unique image in each frame. Each frame then becomes a keyframe (because it has content that alters the animation). As the playhead passes through each of the frames, the frame's content displays, creating the illusion of change over time. Frame-by-frame animations are great if you want to exert direct control over the details in your animation.

There is, however, one problem with creating a frame-by-frame animation. Because each frame needs to be "filled" with content unique from the previous frame, you end up creating a *lot* of static material. Imagine if your movie contained an animation that was 300-frames long. You would have to create at least 300 static images—a laborious undertaking. Granted, using the Library, symbols, and symbol instances to recycle some of your material could help reduce the workload. However, whichever way you look at it, you'd be spending a great deal of time creating art assets for your animation.

Having said this, let's look at how you actually create a frame-by-frame animation. You'll start with something particularly mundane, a sphere moving across the Stage, to help you grasp the basics of frame-by-frame animation:

1. Start with a new file (File → New or Cmd/Ctrl+**N**).

2. When the New Document dialog box opens, select the Flash Document option and click OK.

3. Choose Insert → New Symbol. When the Create New Symbol dialog box opens, enter **sphere** in the Name field, make sure the Graphic radio button is selected, and click OK.

4. When the Symbol Editor opens, draw a sphere about 3 centimeters (1 inch) in diameter. When you're finished, return to the Stage by clicking the Scene 1 link in the Edit bar. (See Chapter 7 for how to work with symbols.)

5. Now that you have a sphere in the Library, click the first frame of the Timeline's single layer (which, if you remember, is an empty keyframe by default), open the Library (Window → Library), and drag the sphere onto the left side of the Stage. Notice that the first frame automatically becomes a keyframe (denoted by the small black circle).

> Remember, Flash automatically designates the first frame of any layer as an empty keyframe. As a result, you don't have to go through the process of inserting a keyframe. However, for the remainder of the layer, you'll have to insert each keyframe yourself.

6. Now that you've populated the first keyframe with content, you can create the remainder of the sequence. Click the second frame in the Timeline (just to the right of the keyframe you created) and choose Insert → Timeline → Keyframe (or press F6). This inserts a second keyframe. You'll notice that Flash has automatically populated the keyframe with the content of the previous keyframe. You could keep on adding successive keyframes, and Flash would continue to populate them with the contents of the first one.

> If, for some reason, you don't want the same content in the second frame, just insert a blank keyframe (Insert → Timeline → Blank Keyframe). To add content to the blank keyframe, select it and then add something to the Stage. When you do this, the blank keyframe becomes a keyframe.

7. Make sure you have the second keyframe selected. Select the sphere with the Arrow tool and move it to the right slightly.

8. Select the third frame in the Timeline, and insert a new keyframe (Insert → Timeline → Keyframe).

9. Make sure you have the third keyframe selected. From here, select the sphere and move it slightly to the right.

10. Continue adding successive keyframes and moving the sphere to the right in each one until it has reached the right side of the Stage. Depending on how much you moved the sphere each time (the less you moved it, the more keyframes it will take to move it to the right side of the screen), your Timeline should be filled with a number of keyframes.

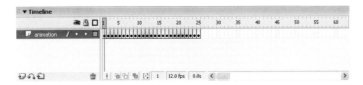

Congratulations, you've created your first frame-by-frame animation. To test it, you can do any of the following:

- Drag the playhead through the Timeline to view the animation.
- Choose Control → Play or hit Return/Enter.
- Choose Control → Test Scene or Control → Test Movie (which opens a new window where the animation will continue to loop).

Working with the Onion Skinning Option

When you were creating a frame-by-frame animation in the previous section, you moved the sphere in each successive keyframe without having a real reference as to its position in the preceding frame. This probably proved to be a little frustrating because, without a way to get the sphere exactly in line with the one in the previous frame, your animation looked a little jumpy. Granted, you could simply click the previous frame, check the position of the sphere, and then click back and adjust the position of the next one. However, this process is a little time consuming and frustrating. This is where *onion skinning* comes in.

Onion skinning lets you see the contents of frames preceding and following the currently selected frame. The concept comes from the traditional pen-and-paper animation technique of using tracing paper to view a sequence of animation frames. With onion skinning, you can do away with all the guesswork inherent in flipping back and forth to see the contents of previous frames and smoothly animate a moving object.

You have several options when using onion skinning:

Turning onion skinning on To turn onion skinning on, click the Onion Skin button  located at the bottom of the Timeline. By doing this, two things happen: First, the Onion Skin marker is displayed in the Timeline header. The Onion Skin marker displays the range of frames included in the onion skinning. To increase, decrease, or change the number of frames included, click one of the handles on either side of the Onion Skin marker and drag it accordingly.

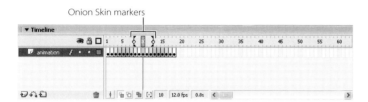

Onion Skin markers

Second, the frames' content within the Onion Skin marker displays as partially transparent. In addition, the contents of the currently selected frame display normally.

If you've got any locked layers in your animation, they won't be displayed when you have onion skinning turned on.

Turning onion skinning outlines on By clicking the Onion Skin Outlines button, which is located at the bottom of the Timeline, you can display the content of multiple frames as outlines (instead of transparent). Note that the currently selected frame appears normally when Onion Skin Outlines is activated.

The particular layer's outline color determines the color of the onion skin outlines.

Editing multiple frames When you have onion skinning turned on, you can't actually edit the contents of a frame unless you've selected it in the Timeline. This can prove a little frustrating, as you will constantly have to switch to a given frame to edit its content. One of the great things about onion skinning is the Edit Multiple Frames button.

Located to the right of the Onion Skin Outlines button, the Edit Multiple Frames button ▣ lets you edit the contents of all frames without having to move from frame to frame. Unlike with simple onion skinning, the Edit Multiple Frames button displays all the contents without any transparency.

Modifying onion markers The Modify Onion Markers drop-down menu is accessible by clicking the Modify Onion Markers button ▣, which is located to the right of the Edit Multiple Frames button at the bottom of the Timeline. Each of the options contained in the menu affect the position of the Onion Skin marker and therefore the frames that are displayed:

- Always Show Markers displays the Onion Skin markers in the Timeline header regardless of whether onion skinning is turned on.
- Under normal circumstances, the Onion Skin range is relative to the current frame pointer and the Onion Skin markers. By selecting Anchor Onion, you lock the Onion Skin markers to their current position in the Timeline header.
- Onion 2 displays two frames on either side of the currently selected frame.
- Onion 5 displays five frames on either side of the currently selected frame.
- Onion All displays all the frames on either side of the currently selected frame.

Understanding Tweening

Now that you've created a frame-by-frame animation, let's take the next step and look at a far more efficient and less time-consuming way to create an animation: *tweening*. Essentially, tweening is the process by which you define a starting point/form and ending point/form for an object and then tell Flash to fill in all the in-be*tween* frames, hence the name.

Two types of tweening are available depending on what you want your animation to do. The first, *motion tweening,* is covered next. The second, *shape tweening,* is covered in the section "Creating a Shape-Tweened Animation" later in this chapter. After looking at motion- and shape-tweened animation, you'll see how you create a motion-tweened animation that follows a path.

Creating a Motion-Tweened Animation

In the previous section, you learned how to create a frame-by-frame animation by filling each frame with content. All in all, the process is pretty clunky. This is where *motion tweening* comes in. Motion tweening is a quantum leap beyond frame-by-frame animation—no more working with frame after frame, painstakingly crafting each image in your animation so it is just right. With motion tweening, you merely create the first and last keyframes in your animation; from there, Flash completes the in-between frames. And because Flash has to save the contents of only the first and last keyframes (along with numerical values concerning how the object changes), tweened animations generally result in smaller file sizes than frame-by-frame animations.

Although you use tweening primarily for animating motion, you can also animate size, color, and orientation. In short, any transformation that can be applied to an object can be animated with tweening.

> You can use motion tweening on text as well as groups of objects.

In this section, you're going to create the same sort of animation you created using the frame-by-frame technique (a square moving across the Stage), but you'll use tweening instead:

1. Start with a new file (File → New or Cmd/Ctrl+**N**).

2. When the New File dialog box opens, choose the Flash Document options and click OK.

3. Choose Insert → New Symbol. When the Create New Symbol dialog box opens, enter **square** in the Name field, make sure the Graphic radio button is selected, and click OK.

4. When the Symbol Editor opens, draw a square about 3 centimeters (about 1 inch) in diameter. When you're finished, return to the Stage by clicking the link in the Edit bar.

5. Now that you have a square ready and waiting in the Library, click the first frame of the Timeline's single layer, open the Library (Window → Library), and drag the square onto the left side of the Stage. Notice that the default blank keyframe automatically becomes a keyframe (denoted by the small black circle).

6. Now that you've created the first keyframe in the animation, you can create the last one. Click frame 25, and insert a keyframe by choosing Insert → Timeline → Keyframe. At this point, your Timeline should look like this:

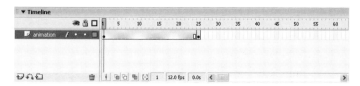

The frames between the two keyframes are just that: frames. They really don't do much except contain the content that is automatically generated by Flash. If you want them to become more, you must insert a keyframe.

Much as in the case of frame-by-frame animation, Flash populated the second keyframe you created with the content of the first. As a result, you are going to want to move the square in the last keyframe to the location on the Stage where you want it to be at the end of the animation:

1. Select the final keyframe.

2. Using the Arrow Tool, click and drag the square to the right side of the Stage. By doing this, you tell Flash that in the first keyframe the square is at the left side of the Stage, and in the last keyframe it's in the right side of the Stage.

3. Now comes the tweening. Select the first keyframe.

4. Choose Insert → Timeline → Create Motion Tween. Alternatively, you can select the first keyframe, open the Property Inspector (Window → Properties), and select Motion from the Tween drop-down menu.

5. Flash fills all the in-between frames, thereby creating the animation. You'll also notice that the Timeline itself changes. The change in the frames' colors as well as an addition of an arrow indicate the presence of a tween.

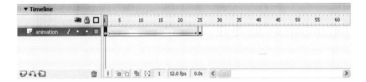

Congratulations, you've created your first tweened animation. To test it, do one of the following:

- Drag the playhead through the Timeline to view the animation.

- Choose Control → Play or hit Return/Enter.

- Select Control → Test Scene/Test Movie to open a new window in which the animation will continue to loop.

Even though the motion tween that you've just created is quite simple, don't think that motion tweening creates only simple animations. You can create some amazingly complex and varied animation with tweening. As an experiment, take the animation you just created, insert a keyframe in the middle, and alter the square's location. When you play the animation, Flash moves the square to the new location defined in the keyframe that you just added and then to the position that you set in the final keyframe.

You also don't have to merely move your square across the Stage. Try increasing the object's size in the final keyframe using the Transform panel (Window → Design Panels → Transform) or the Free Transform tool. When played, the square slowly grows until it reaches the defined size in the final keyframe.

You can also change the visual properties of a tweened symbol using the Property Inspector—something you'll learn how to do in the section "Animating a Symbol Instance's Visual Properties with the Property Inspector" later in this chapter.

Editing a Tweened Animation

Although you can create a motion-tweened animation with Flash's drop-down menu, you can't do much to edit the animation's characteristics this way. Instead, you use the Property Inspector (Window → Properties or Cmd/Ctrl+F3) to manipulate all manner of the tweened animation's characteristics, including those specific to motion tweening.

Some of the options in the Property Inspector apply to other types of tweening, such as shape and motion-path tweening. You'll get to them in the sections "Creating a Shape-Tweening Animation" and "Creating an Animation That Follows a Path," respectively; for now, let's look at the motion-tweening options.

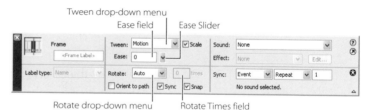

Tween drop-down menu

Ease field   Ease Slider

Rotate drop-down menu   Rotate Times field

Easing a Motion Tween Animation

You probably noticed that your tweened square traveled at a constant rate across the Stage. If you want, you can use the Property Inspector to ease the object in or out of the animation. In other words, it starts off more slowly, gaining speed through the process of the animation. On the other hand, if you ease the object out of the animation, it slows down near the end.

To ease your motion tween, follow these steps:

1. Select the first frame in the motion tween.

2. Open the Property Inspector by choosing Window → Properties or by using Cmd/Ctrl+F3.

3. Enter a value into the Ease field. A positive number eases the object out of the animation, and a negative eases it in. A higher value (either negative or positive) increases the effect. Alternatively, you can use the Ease slider to adjust the value.

You can enter values from –100 to 100 in the Easing field.

Rotating a Motion-Tweened Object

Follow these steps to get an object to rotate through the tweening:

1. Select the first frame in the motion tween.

2. Open the Property Inspector by choosing Window → Properties or by using the shortcut Cmd/Ctrl+F3.

3. Choose one of the options from the Rotate drop-down menu.

   None Applies no rotation to the object.

   Auto Rotates the object once in the direction that requires the least amount of movement.

   CW Rotates the object clockwise. You define the number of rotations by entering a value into the Times field (which is to the right of the Rotate drop-down menu).

   CCW Rotates the object counterclockwise. You define the number of rotations by entering a value into the Times field (which is to the right of the Rotate drop-down menu).

Creating a Motion-Tweened Animation That Follows a Path

When it comes to motion tweening, you've explored how to move an object along a straight line. Granted, you can vary the course of the object's motion by adding more keyframes to the animation (as discussed earlier), creating a zigzag pattern. However, what if you want to make an object move along a circle? *Motion paths* let you move objects along a specific path (see Figure 10.2).

You learned how to create motion guide layers in Chapter 8; in this section, you'll take what you learned in Chapter 8 and combine it with what you've learned about motion tweening in this chapter to craft an animation that has an object traveling along a complex path.

To create an animation that follows a path, use these steps:

1. Create a simple motion-tweened animation with two keyframes, one at the beginning and one at the end. (If you want, you can use the square animation you created earlier in this chapter.) To learn how to create a simple motion tween, see the section "Creating a Motion-Tweened Animation" earlier in this chapter.

2. Select the layer with the tweened animation and choose Insert → Timeline → Motion Guide. Alternatively, you can Ctrl+click (Mac) or right-click (Win) the layer's name and choose Add Motion Guide from the pop-up context menu or click the Add Motion Guide button in the bottom-left corner of the Timeline. This creates a motion guide layer just above the layer containing the animation.

Figure 10.2

The motion path can take any form you desire. This one was drawn with the Pen tool.

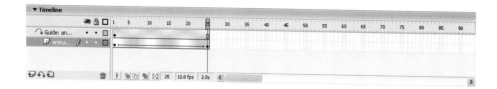

3. Now, with the first frame (the empty keyframe) in the motion guide layer selected, draw the path you want the object to follow (as illustrated back in Figure 10.2). You can use any of these tools: Pencil, Oval, Rectangle, Brush, Pen, or Line.

4. Now it's now time to attach your object to the motion path that you've created. Select the first keyframe of your tweened animation, choose Window → Properties, and make sure the Snap check box is selected so your object's registration point will snap to the motion path.

Snap check box

5. Click and drag the object so the registration point snaps onto the beginning of the path you've drawn.

If the registration point doesn't appear when you click the object, release it, click the central portion of the object (represented by a set of crosshairs), hold your mouse button down for a few seconds, and then drag it to the beginning of the path.

6. Now, click the final keyframe in the animation, and click and drag the object so the registration point snaps onto the end of the path you've drawn.

7. If you want the object to point in the direction of the path that it's moving along, make sure the Orient to Path check box is selected in the Property Inspector.

Orient to Path check box

8. From here, test your animation by hitting Return/Enter, choosing Control → Play, or selecting Control → Test Scene/Test Movie.

You can "unlink" a layer from a motion guide by selecting the layer and either clicking and dragging the layer above the motion guide layer in the Timeline or choosing Modify → Timeline → Layer Properties → Normal.

Creating a Shape-Tweened Animation

While motion tweening moves an object from one point of the Stage to another (or changes its characteristics, such as size or orientation), *shape tweening* morphs an object from one shape to another. You can create some decidedly interesting effects by using shape tweening.

One of the most fundamental things you need to remember about shape tweening is that it works only on shapes drawn on the Stage. You can't shape tween symbol instances, bitmaps, text, or groups of objects. You must break apart these elements (Modify → Break Apart) before you can shape tween them.

To create a shape tween:

1. Create a new document.

2. Select the first frame, which is a blank keyframe by default.

3. Use the drawing tools to create the image you want to start with. Notice that the first frame automatically becomes a filled keyframe (denoted by the small black circle).

4. Click the frame where you want the shape tween to end, and insert a keyframe. As usual, Flash populates the last keyframe with the first keyframe's contents.

5. Manipulate the object (using one of the various transform tools) so it looks like what you want for the final shape tween. (Alternatively, delete the image and create an entirely new one.)

If you place the last keyframe's shape in another location, Flash automatically motion tweens the animation as well. Not only will your object "morph," but it will do so as it moves from one location to another on the Stage.

6. Now select the first frame and open the Property Inspector (Window → Properties).

7. Choose Shape from the Tweening drop-down menu.

8. From here, you can set the shape tween's characteristics:

   • Enter a value into the Ease field to ease the tween in or out. Remember, a positive number makes the tween faster at the beginning, and a negative number makes it faster at the end. Alternatively, use the Ease slider to adjust the value.

   • Choose a blend option from the Blend drop-down menu. Choosing Distributive creates an animation in which the edges of the intermediate shapes are smoother. Alternatively, choosing Angular creates an animation in which straight edges are preserved in the intervening frames.

Blend drop-down menu

9. When you've finished, test your animation by moving the playhead, hitting Return/Enter, and selecting Control → Play or choosing Control → Test Scene/ Test Movie.

Animating a Mask

As explained in Chapter 8, mask layers create a hole through which the contents of one layer are visible. The cool thing about masks is that you can animate them to create any number of interesting effects—from the view through a telescope to the view through a keyhole. In this section, you'll look at how to create a spotlight effect that moves across the Stage, revealing a stationary object as it passes over it:

1. First, create a new document.

2. Choose File → Import → Import to Stage. When the Import dialog box opens, navigate to the Chapter 10 directory on this book's companion CD, choose All Files from the Import dialog box's Files of Type drop-down menu, select the `alien.swf` file, and click OK.

3. Now click frame 25 and choose Insert → Timeline → Frame. This populates the frames from 2 to 25 with the content of the first keyframe.

4. From here, you're going to create the object that will serve as the mask. Select Insert → New Symbol. When the Create New Symbol dialog box opens, make sure the Graphic radio button is checked and enter **circle** into the Name field.

5. When the Symbol Editor opens, draw a single sphere of about 3 centimeters (1 inch) in diameter. Remember, the circle needs to be filled for the mask to work. Beyond that, the color of the fill makes no difference whatsoever.

6. Exit the Symbol Editor by clicking the Scene 1 link in the Edit bar.

7. Now create a new layer by clicking the Insert Layer button in the Timeline. Alternatively, you can Ctrl+click (Mac) or right-click (Win) on the Timeline's existing layer, and choose Insert Layer from the pop-up context menu. You can also choose Insert → Timeline → Layer. This layer will ultimately be converted into the mask layer.

8. Select the first blank keyframe in the new layer and drag the Circle symbol from the Library (Window → Library) to the left part of the Stage.

9. Click frame 25 (in the newly created layer) and choose Insert → Timeline → Keyframe. With the last keyframe selected (the one you just created), click and drag the circle to the right side of the Stage.

10. Select the first keyframe and choose Insert → Timeline → Create Motion Tween. This animates the sphere so that it moves across the Stage and passes over the flying saucer image that you imported earlier.

11. Now it's time to turn the tweened circle into a mask. Ctrl+click (Mac) or right-click (Win) the layer with the circle symbol, and choose Mask from the pop-up context menu. By doing this, you turn the layer with the circle into a mask layer. Notice that the appearance of both layers changes to reflect the relationship. Also, this process locks both the mask and masked layers. They must remain locked for the animation to work.

Don't worry if the flying saucer disappears from the Stage; this is supposed to happen. If you want to view both the flying saucer image and the circle symbol, unlock all the layers.

12. From here, test your animation by hitting Return/Enter and choosing Control → Play or selecting Control → Test Scene/Test Movie.

Extending a Still Image Through Time

So far, you've explored how to do all sorts of cool animations with the Timeline. There is, however, an additional animation trick that, although straightforward, is incredibly useful. Specifically, you can integrate an image into your Flash movie that occupies a span of time (a series of frames) but doesn't actually move. Here's how you do it:

1. Create a new document.

2. Select the first blank keyframe in the single layer.

3. Place the desired image onto the Stage.

4. Click the last keyframe that you would like the image to be visible on.

5. Choose Insert → Timeline → Frame or use the shortcut F5. Alternatively, you can Ctrl+click (Mac) or right-click (Win) and choose Insert Frame from the pop-up context menu.

6. Notice that all the intermediate frames are gray, and a small outline of a rectangle is placed in the final frame. This means that the content from the first keyframe has been carried over to all the frames.

Animating a Symbol Instance's Visual Properties with the Property Inspector

One of the great things about tweening is that you are not limited to position, size, and shape. You can also tween more complicated changes to an object's appearance. You can animate a fade-in/fade-out or color change by taking what you've learned about tweening thus far and combining it with the tools in the Property Inspector (Window → Properties). Back in Chapter 6, you manipulated a symbol's visual properties with the Property Inspector, so its options should be familiar to you. In the following sections, you'll now learn how to animate changes in an object's transparency, brightness, and tint.

> You can carry out the following processes only on symbols, not on shapes or groups of shapes created with Flash's painting and drawing tools directly on the Stage.

Animating a Symbol's Transparency

By animating an object's Alpha effect (or transparency), you can create the illusion of a fade-in/fade-out:

1. Create a new document.

2. Create a tweened animation of some sort using symbols.

3. Now click the first keyframe in the animation and select the object that you want to fade in with the Arrow tool.

4. If it isn't open already, open the Property Inspector by choosing Window → Properties.

5. Choose Alpha from the Color drop-down menu.

6. Enter **0** into the Alpha Value field. By doing this, you are making the object in the first keyframe transparent.

7. Click the last keyframe in the animation, and select the object that you're working on with the Arrow tool.

8. With the Property Inspector open and Alpha selected from the Color drop-down menu, enter **100** into the Alpha Value field. This makes the object opaque (solid) in the final keyframe.

9. Now, test your animation by hitting Return/Enter and going to Control → Play, or select Control → Test Scene/Test Movie. Your object will now fade in.

> To have an item fade out, do the opposite. Set the Alpha Value in the first keyframe to 100 and that of the last keyframe to 0.

Animating an Object's Brightness

Animating an object's brightness is almost identical to the process of animating an object's transparency:

1. Create a new document.

2. Create a tweened animation using a symbol.

3. Now click the first keyframe in the animation and select the object whose brightness you want to change.

4. If it isn't open already, open the Property Inspector by choosing Window → Properties.

5. Choose Brightness from the Color drop-down menu.

6. Enter a value into the Brightness Value field (or use the Brightness slider).

7. Click the last keyframe in the animation, and select the object that you're working with.

8. With the Property Inspector open, enter a different value into the Brightness Value field.

9. Now test your animation by hitting Return/Enter and choosing Control → Play, or selecting Control → Test Scene/Test Movie.

> Because you can't simulate the same sort of brightness experienced in the real world, altering the brightness of an object actually does more to change the intensity of its color.

Animating Color Change

Like the previous two procedures, animating a color change is just a matter of using a different area of the Property Inspector:

1. Create a new document.

2. Create a tweened animation of some sort using a symbol.

3. Now click the first keyframe in the animation and select the object whose color you want to change.

4. If it isn't open already, open the Property Inspector by choosing Window → Properties.

5. Choose Tint from the Color drop-down menu.

6. From here, click the Tint color swatch to open up the Color Picker. From here, choose one of the colors. Alternatively, you can mix a custom RGB color by inputting values into the R, G, and B fields.

7. Click the last keyframe in the animation, and select the object that you're working with.

8. With the Property Inspector open, choose another color.

9. Now test your animation by hitting Return/Enter and going to Control → Play, or selecting Control → Test Scene/Test Movie. Your object will change from the color set in the first keyframe to the color set in the last keyframe.

Using Timeline Effects

So far, you've explored two ways you can add animation to your Flash movie: tweening and frame-by-frame animation. These two methods have been around since the dawn of Flash, and are very tried and true. However, in Flash MX 2004 and Flash MX Pro 2004, Macromedia has introduced a third way of adding animation to your movie: Timeline Effects.

To be completely honest, Timeline Effects are not really a new kind of animation; they are simply a new way of created tweened animation. Timeline Effects were originally created in recognition of the fact that tweening, though easily learned, can take a fair amount of time. Look at it this way: If your movie is fairly animation intense, you can spend a lot of time repeating the tweening process over and over. This is where Timeline Effects come in. They are basically a series of preset (though very editable) animations that you can apply to just about any element in your movie. In total, there are eight Timeline Effects: Blur, Copy To Grid, Distributed Duplicate, Drop Shadow, Expand, Explode, Transform, and Transition.

Not all Timeline Effects are animation-specific. Drop Shadow, Copy to Grid, and Distributed Duplicate don't result in any kind of motion; they simply change the appearance of the selected symbol. Timeline Effects that don't produce an animation are included here so that all Timeline Effects are covered together.

In this section, you'll explore how to apply a Timeline Effect to an Object, edit a Timeline Effect, and remove a Timeline Effect from an object. From there, you'll explore each of the Timeline Effects available in Flash MX 2004 and Flash MX Pro 2004.

You might notice that, when you apply a Timeline Effect, a new folder (complete with any number of different symbols) is added to your Library. You also might notice that, if it isn't already, the symbol you attached the Timeline Effect to is converted into a Movie Clip. Don't worry, this is supposed to happen. When you add a Timeline Effect, Flash generates the additional visual assets that make the effect possible and adds them to your Library. While you can actually go into these folders and manually edit the effect's assets (altering how the effect appears in your movie), I would not advise it.

Applying a Timeline Effect

The Process by which you apply a Timeline Effect to an object is actually quite easy. All you need to do is follow these steps:

Timeline Effects can be applied to text, bitmaps, graphic symbols, button symbols, shapes, grouped objects, and Movie Clips.

1. Select the object you want to apply the Timeline Effect to.
2. From here, you have two options:
   - Choose Insert → Timeline Effects and select one of the effects in the list.
   - Ctrl+click (Mac) or right-click (Win) the object that you're attaching the Timeline Effect to. When the context menu opens, select Timeline Effects and choose an effect from the list.
3. Based on the specific Timeline Effect that you selected, a different dialog box will open, allowing you to edit the properties of the effect.

For the specifics on each Timeline Effect, see the section "Working with Flash's Standard Timeline Effects" later in this chapter.

Editing a Timeline Effect

Once you've added a Timeline Effect, it's just as easy to go back and edit it. Here's how:

1. Select the object you attached the Timeline Effect to that you want to edit.

2. From here, you have a few choices:

   - If it isn't already, open the Property Inspector (Window → Properties) and click the Edit button. The specific Timeline Effects dialog box will open, allowing you to make any changes you want.

   - Ctrl+click (Mac) or right-click (Win) the object to which you attached the Timeline Effect, and choose Timeline Effects → Edit Effect from the pop-up context menu. When the effect-specific dialog box opens, make any changes you want.

   - Choose Modify → Timeline Effects → Edit Effect. When the Timeline Effects dialog box opens, you can change the effect's properties as you see fit.

Removing a Timeline Effect

What if you decide that you would like to remove a Timeline Effect that you had applied to an object within your movie? It's easy as pie; just follow these steps:

1. Select the object you attached the Timeline Effect to that you would like to remove.

2. From here, you have a couple of options:

   - Ctrl+click (Mac) or right-click (Win) the object to which you attached the Timeline Effect and choose Timeline Effects → Remove Effect from the pop-up context menu.

   - Choose Modify → Timeline Effects → Remove Effect.

Working with Flash's Standard Timeline Effects

As mentioned previously, Flash MX 2004 and Flash MX Pro 2004 ship with eight Timeline Effects (not all of which create animation). In this section, you'll explore the intricacies of each.

> One of the coolest things about this new generation of Flash is the JavaScript Application Programming Interface (JSAPI), which allows users to access and extend Flash's program architecture. The JSAPI allows the creation of new behaviors, components, interface elements, and most importantly to this section, Timeline Effects. As a result, as Flash MX 2004 and Flash MX Pro 2004 gain steam, you'll probably see new Timeline Effects become available (either distributed freely or as purchasable add-ons).

Copy To Grid

As with a number of the Timeline Effects, Copy To Grid really doesn't have anything to do with animation. Instead, when applied, it takes the object to which you applied the effect and creates a repeating pattern (laid out along a grid). To use the Copy To Grid Timeline Effect, just follow these steps:

1. With the Arrow tool, select the object to which you want to apply the Copy To Grid effect.

2. From here, you have a few options:

    - Choose Insert → Timeline Effects → Assistants → Copy To Grid.

    - Ctrl+click (Mac) or right-click (Win) the object you're attaching the Timeline Effect to. When the context menu opens, select Timeline Effects → Assistants → Copy To Grid.

3. When the Copy To Grid dialog box opens (see Figure 10.3), enter the number of rows of objects in the Rows field (the default is 2).

4. Enter the number of columns that you want in the grid in Columns field (the default is 2).

5. Now you need to define the distance between the objects in the grid. First, enter a value (in pixels) in the Rows field of the Grid Spacing section to set the distance between the rows in the grid.

Figure 10.3

The Copy To Grid dialog box

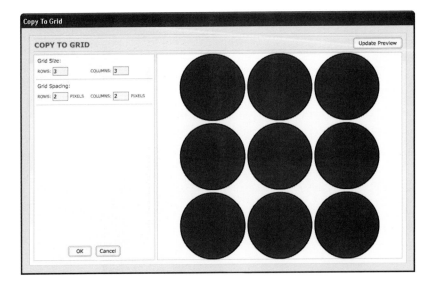

6. Enter a value (in pixels) in the Columns field of the Grid Spacing section to determine the distance between the columns in the grid.

7. To preview how the Timeline Effect will look, click the Update button in the upper-right corner of the Copy To Grid dialog box.

8. When you're finished, click OK.

Distributed Duplicate

Like the Copy To Grid Timeline Effect, the Distributed Duplicate effect really isn't geared toward creating an animation (though you can create an animation with it if you want). Instead, the effect takes the object to which it was applied and creates a number of copies (or clones) whose distance, angle, rotation, scaling, color, and opacity from the original can be fully controlled.

To use the Distributed Duplicate Timeline Effect, follow these steps:

1. With the Arrow tool, select the object to which you want to apply the Distributed Duplicate Timeline effect.

2. From here, you have a few options:

   • Choose Insert → Timeline Effects → Assistants → Distributed Duplicate.

   • Ctrl+click (Mac) or right-click (Win) the object you're attaching the Timeline Effect to. When the context menu opens, select Timeline Effects → Assistants → Distributed Duplicate.

3. When the Distributed Duplicate dialog box opens (see Figure 10.4), enter the number of clones you want to create in the Number Of Copies field (the default is 5).

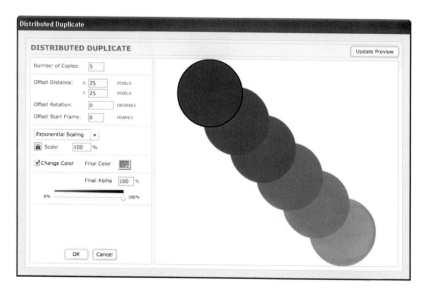

Figure 10.4

The Distributed Duplicate dialog box

4. Now you need to set how far the successive copies are offset from the copy before them. To do this, enter a value (in pixels) in the X field to determine the distance along the vertical axis.

5. Enter a value (in pixels) into the Y field to set the amount of distance along the horizontal axis.

6. Enter a value (in degrees) that you want each successive clone to rotate in the Offset Rotation field. A positive number rotates the object clockwise, while a negative number rotates it counterclockwise.

7. If you want the effect to be animated, enter a value in the Offset Start Frame field. The value represents the delay in frames between the drawing of each successive duplicate. If you enter a value of 0, the effect will not animate.

8. From here, you need to set how (and if) the successive clones are scaled. First, select one of the options—Exponential Scaling or Linear Scaling—from the Scaling drop-down menu.

9. Now enter a value (in percent) in the Scale field. The lower the number, the smaller each object will be each successive step. If you want to control both the X and Y scale values independently, click the Padlock icon to the right of the Scale field and enter a value into the X and Y fields when they appear.

10. If you want the object to change color from its first step to its last, select the Change Color check box. Then, click the Final Color swatch and choose one of the colors from the Color Picker.

11. If you want the transparency of the object to change between its first step and its last, enter a value (between 0 and 100) in the Final Alpha field. Alternatively, you can use the slider below the Final Alpha field to adjust the alpha value of the final step.

12. To preview how the Timeline Effect will look, click the Update button in the upper-right corner of the Distributed Duplicate dialog box.

13. When you're finished, click OK.

Blur

As its name suggests, the blur effect creates the appearance that an object is out of focus. Let's take a look at how the Blur effect works:

1. With the Arrow tool, select the object that you want to apply the Blur effect to.

2. From here, you have a few options:

   • Choose Insert → Timeline Effects → Effects → Blur.

   • Ctrl+click (Mac) or right-click (Win) the object you're attaching the Timeline Effect to. When the context menu opens, select Timeline Effects → Effects → Blur.

3. When the Blur dialog box opens (see Figure 10.5), enter the number of frames that you would like the blur to last in the Effect Duration field.

4. Set the visual quality of the blur effect by entering a value in the Resolution field. A higher resolution means a higher quality blur—but it also means that your final Flash movie will have a larger file size. Likewise, a lower resolution results in low visual quality, but a smaller file size.

5. To set the degree to which the blur increases outward beyond the bounds of the original object, enter a value in the Scale field. The higher the number, the more the blur will expand.

6. From here, you need to determine which direction the blur expands. If you want it to expand horizontally, click the Allow Horizontal Blur check box. If you want the blur to expand vertically, click the Allow Vertical Blur check box.

7. If you want more control of which direction the blur expands, click one of the Direction of Movement arrows (the central arrow expands the blur in all directions).

8. To preview how the Timeline Effect will look, click the Update button in the upper-right corner of the Blur dialog box.

9. When you're finished, click OK.

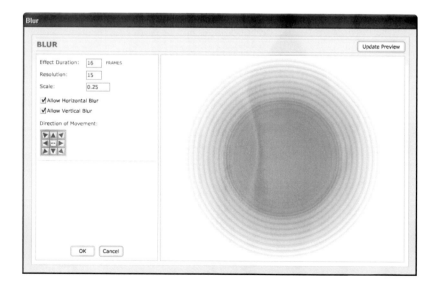

Figure 10.5

The Blur dialog box

Drop Shadow

Like many of the Timeline Effects, Drop Shadow doesn't actually create an animation. However, as drop shadows have become fairly ubiquitous in the world of interactive media, it's a handy effect to have in your quiver. To use the Drop Shadow Timeline Effect, follow these steps:

1. With the Arrow tool, select the object that you want to apply the Drop Shadow effect to.

2. From here, you have a few options:
   - Choose Insert → Timeline Effects → Effects → Drop Shadow.
   - Ctrl+click (Mac) or right-click (Win) the object you're attaching the Timeline Effect to. When the context menu opens, select Timeline Effects → Effects → Drop Shadow.

3. When the Drop Shadow dialog box opens (see Figure 10.6), click the Color swatch and choose a color from the Color Picker to set the color of the shadow.

4. Set the transparency of the shadow by entering a value (in percent) in the Alpha Transparency field. Alternatively, you can adjust the Alpha Transparency slider.

5. Set the distance that the shadow is offset from the actual object by entering a value (in pixels) in the X field (which sets the horizontal distance) and the Y field (which sets the vertical distance).

6. To preview how the Timeline Effect will look, click the Update button in the upper-right corner of the Drop Shadow dialog box.

7. When you're finished, click OK.

Figure 10.6

The Drop Shadow dialog box

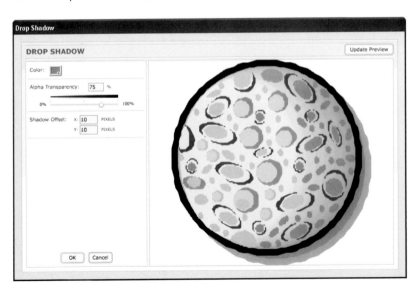

Expand

The Expand Timeline Effect lets you take an object and either blow it up (expand) or shrink it down (squeeze) based on a series of different properties. The Expand Timeline Effect can also be used to scatter a group of objects. To apply the Expand Timeline Effect to an object, follow these steps:

1. With the Arrow tool, select the object that you want to apply the Expand effect to.

2. From here, you have a few options:

    • Choose Insert → Timeline Effects → Effects → Expand.

    • Ctrl+click (Mac) or right-click (Win) the object you're attaching the Timeline Effect to. When the context menu appears, select Timeline Effects → Effects → Expand.

3. When the Expand dialog box opens (Figure 10.7), enter the number of frames you want the animation to take into the Effect Duration field.

4. If you want the object to increase in size, click the Expand radio button. If you want the object to shrink, click the Squeeze radio button. If you want the object to both expand and shrink, click the Both radio button.

How can the object both expand and shrink? Technically, it can't. Instead, when you select the Both radio button, Flash splits the number of frames you designated into two animations: one of the object expanding and one of the object shrinking. Once applied, the animation expands and then shrinks in size.

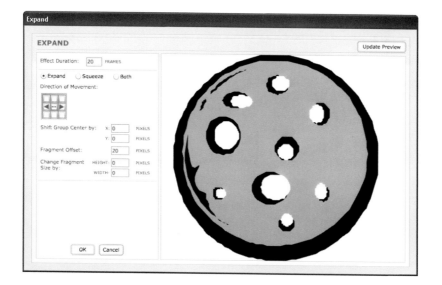

Figure 10.7

The Expand dialog box

5. Click one of the Direction Of Movement arrows to determine which direction the object will expand or contract.

6. If you are working with a group of objects (as opposed to just one), enter a value in the Shift Group Center By X field to shift the center of the group a certain number of pixels along the X axis from where it currently is.

If you are working with a group of objects, Flash automatically determines the center of the group.

7. If you are working with a group of objects, enter a value in the Shift Group By Y field to shift the center of the group to a position a certain number of pixels along the Y axis from its current position.

8. If you are working with a group of objects, enter a value in the Fragment Offset field to determine the distance from each object's original position that they travel away from the center of the group.

9. Now you need to set how much the object expands or contracts. First, enter a value (in pixels) in the Change Fragment Size By Height field to set the object's vertical size change.

10. Next enter a value (in pixels) in the Change Fragment Size By Width field to set the object's horizontal size change.

11. To preview how the Timeline Effect will look, click the Update button in the upper-right corner of the Expand dialog box.

12. When you're finished, click OK.

Explode

As its name suggests, the Explode Timeline Effect lets you shove a stick of digital dynamite under your object, blow it up, and then control how the pieces react afterward. While Explode certainly isn't as complex as some of the exploding-particle effects you see in many upper-level 3D modeling programs, it's still quite fun to play with.

To use the Explode Timeline Effects, follow these steps:

1. With the Arrow tool, select the object to which you want to apply the Explode effect.

2. From here, you have a few options:

    • Choose Insert → Timeline Effects → Effects → Explode.

    • Ctrl+click (Mac) or right-click (Win) the object you're attaching the Timeline Effect to. When the context menu opens, select Timeline Effects → Effects → Explode.

3. When the Explode dialog box opens (see Figure 10.8), enter the number of frames you want the explosion to last in the Effect Duration field.

4. Click one of the Direction Of Explosion arrows to determine which direction the pieces of the exploded object will fly.

5. Now you need to define the characteristics of the arc of the exploding pieces. First, enter a value (in pixels) in the Arc Size X field to set the horizontal distance of the arc, then enter a value (in pixels) in the Arc Size Y field to set the height.

6. Enter a value (in degrees) into the Rotate Fragments By field to determine how much the pieces will rotate as they fly away. A positive number rotates the pieces clockwise, while a negative number rotates them counterclockwise.

7. Now you need to set the size change (if any) of the pieces as they fly away. First, enter a value (in pixels) in the Change Fragments Size By X field to expand the size of the pieces horizontally. A positive number expands the pieces, while a negative number makes them smaller.

8. Enter a value (in pixels) in the Change Fragments Size By Y field to increase (or decrease) the size of the pieces vertically.

9. Enter a value (from 0–100) in the Final Alpha field to set the transparency of the pieces at the end of their arc. Alternatively, you can use the Final Alpha slider.

10. To preview how the Timeline Effect will look, click the Update button in the upper-right corner of the Explode dialog box.

11. When you're finished, click OK.

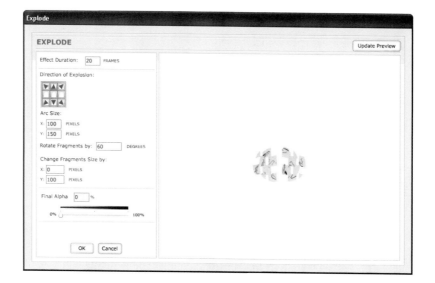

Figure 10.8

The Explode dialog box

Transform

The Transform Timeline Effect is easily one of the most powerful of the Timeline Effects. With it, you can move, scale, fade, rotate, ease, and change the color of an object. Basically, the Transform effect lets you carry out almost all the things you could do if you were using tweening—except you can do it all from a single dialog box.

To work with the Transform effect, just follow these steps:

1. With the Arrow tool, select the object to which you want to apply the Transform effect.

2. From here, you have a few options:

    • Choose Insert → Timeline Effects → Transform/Transition → Transform.

    • Ctrl+click (Mac) or right-click (Win) the object you're attaching the Timeline Effect to. When the context menu opens, select Timeline Effects → Transform/Transition → Transform.

3. When the Transform dialog box opens (see Figure 10.9), enter the number of frames that you want the Transform to last in the Effect Duration field.

4. If you want the object to move to a specific point on the Stage, select Move to Position from the drop-down menu at the top of the dialog box, and then enter the exact coordinates in the X and Y fields.

You can use the Info panel (Window → Design Panels → Info) to get the exact X/Y coordinates of any position on your Stage.

Figure 10.9

The Transform dialog box

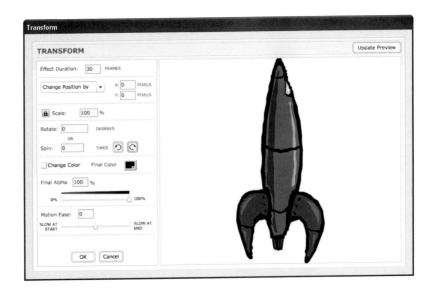

5. If you want to change the object's position by a certain number of pixels (as opposed to moving it to a specific X/Y coordinate on the Stage), select Change Position By from the drop-down menu at the top of the dialog box and enter (in pixels) the horizontal distance in the X field and the vertical distance in the Y field.

6. If you want the object to expand or contract, enter a value (in percent) in the Scale field. If you want to control the horizontal and vertical scale independently, click the Padlock icon 🔒 to the left of the Scale field. Then, when the X and Y fields are displayed, you can enter different values in each.

7. If you want the object to rotate, you have two options:

   • Enter a value (in degrees) into the Rotate field.

   • Enter a value into the Spin field. Click the clockwise button ↻ or the counter-clockwise button ↺ to determine which direction the object spins.

8. If you want the object to change color during the transform, check the Change Color check box. Then click the color swatch and select the final color of the object from the Color Picker.

9. Enter a value (0–100) into the Final Alpha field. This determines the transparency of the object at the end of its transform. Alternatively, you can use the Final Alpha slider.

10. Enter a value into the Ease field (between –100 and 100). This value controls whether the transform starts out quickly and slows near the end or starts out slowly and gains speed. Alternatively, use the Ease slider.

11. To preview how the Timeline Effect will look, click the Update button in the upper-right corner of the Transform dialog box.

12. When you're finished, click OK.

Transition

The Transition Timeline Effect lets you apply a wipe or dissolve to a selected object; let's take a look at how:

1. With the Arrow tool, select the object to which you want to apply the Transition effect.

2. From here, you have a few options:

   • Choose Insert → Timeline Effects → Transform/Transition → Transition.

   • Ctrl+click (Mac) or right-click (Win) the object you're attaching the Timeline Effect to. When the context menu openss, select Timeline Effects → Transform/Transition → Transition.

3. When the Transform dialog box opens (see Figure 10.10), enter the number of frames you want the Transition to last in the Effect Duration field.

Figure 10.10

**The Transition
dialog box**

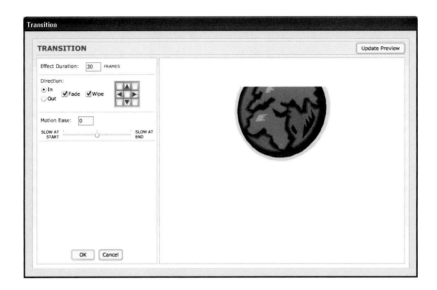

4. Select whether you want the object to Wipe, Dissolve, or Wipe and Dissolve by click-ing the appropriate check box.

5. From there, you need to determine if the object wipes or fades (depending on your choice) in or out. To do so, select the appropriate radio button in the Direction sec-tion of the Transition dialog box.

6. Now, click on one of the Direction arrows to determine in which direction the wipe or dissolve takes place.

7. Enter a value into the Ease field (between –100 and 100). This value controls whether the transform starts out quickly and slows near the end or starts out slowly and gains speed. Alternatively, use the Ease slider.

8. To preview how the Timeline Effect will look, click the Update button in the upper-right corner of the Transition dialog box.

9. When you're finished, click OK.

Inspirational Design Model

Designed by Djojo Studios (whose site appears in this book's color section), Langlevelater (`www.langlevelater.nl/en`) is easily one of the most innovative learning environments on the Web today. Built entirely with Flash and Dreamweaver, the site (see Figure 10.11) was designed for the Floriade Dutch Horticultural Exhibition to teach kids about environmen-tal issues.

Melding Djojo Studios easily recognizable, stylish illustration with an incredibly immersive Flash-based environment, Langlevelater lets kids navigate through a series of virtual pavilions, each mirroring an actual pavilion at the horticultural exhibition. Each pavilion contains topical quizzes, the successful completion of which awards kids with tiles to build their own interactive urban landscapes.

Figure 10.11

Djojo Studios' Langlevelator

CHAPTER 11

Working with Movie Clips

One of the types of symbols discussed in Chapter 7 (but not focused on) was Movie Clips. Probably one of the most fundamentally important aspects of Flash, Movie Clips are fully functional, self-contained movies that can be placed on the Stage and run independently of the Timeline. In addition, you can control Movie Clips using ActionScript, which makes them incredibly powerful.

Because you've already mastered the basic skills necessary to create animations with the Timeline, you'll start off this chapter by exploring the nature of Movie Clips. You'll then learn how to create Movie Clips from scratch as well as from existing animations. Finally, you'll learn how to insert Movie Clips into the main Timeline.

Topics in this chapter include the following:

- **Understanding and exploiting the power of Movie Clips**

- **Creating a Movie Clip from scratch**

- **Converting an existing Timeline animation into a Movie Clip**

- **Inserting Movie Clips into the main Timeline**

- **Manipulating Movie Clips with the Property Inspector**

- **Seeing Movie Clips in action**

Understanding and Exploiting the Power of Movie Clips

It wouldn't be an exaggeration to say that Movie Clips are probably one of the most useful elements in Flash. However, unlike Button and Graphic symbols, Movie Clips are far better discussed in conjunction with animation. Why? Well, Movie Clips are essentially self-contained movies that you can nest within your primary movie. Because they are self-contained, their Timelines run independently of the main Timeline. In other words, you can think of a Movie Clip as a movie within a movie.

You can use Movie Clips in conjunction with other symbols or alone on the Stage. For instance, you could place a Movie Clip in one of the states of a Button symbol to create an animated button—a process discussed in Chapter 15. One of the great things about Movie Clips is that, unlike regular Timeline animations that use a great deal of frames and keyframes, Movie Clips need only one keyframe in the main Timeline to run.

Because Movie Clips run independently of the main Timeline, they can be quite detached from your main movie. Say, for instance, you've got an animation in which several birds (each of which is a Movie Clip) fly across the sky. Under normal circumstances, the Movie Clips will either loop or play once and stop—both of which are pretty limiting when it comes to intricate animations. This, however, is where ActionScript comes into the picture.

Flash's scripting language, ActionScript, allows you to exert a great deal of control over how a given Movie Clip behaves within the main Timeline. Essentially, you can write simple (or complex) scripts that control the behavior of an individual Movie Clip. For example, going back to the "flock" of birds example, you could write a script that would make sure none of the Movie Clips ever come in contact with one another. If you were really ambitious, you could write a script that would force the bird Movie Clips to emulate flocking behavior.

See Chapters 19 and 20 for more information on controlling Movie Clips with ActionScript.

Creating a Movie Clip from Scratch

Creating a Movie Clip from scratch builds on the skills that you've already mastered in Chapters 7 and 9:

1. Open a new document by choosing File → New.

2. When the New Document dialog box opens, select the Flash Document option under the General tab, and then click OK.

3. Choose Insert → New Symbol.

4. When the Create New Symbol dialog box opens, make sure the Movie Clip radio button is selected, enter a name into the Name field, and click OK. (If you're having trouble remembering your way around the Create New Symbol dialog box, refer to Chapter 7.)

5. This opens the Symbol Editor. From here, use the Timeline in the Symbol Editor to create an animation. Remember, a Movie Clip is exactly the same as a regular Timeline animation. You can use any of the Timeline animation techniques (tweening, frame by frame, special effects, Timeline Effects, and so on) that you've already learned. You also aren't limited to a single animated object in a single layer—you could have multiple layers with multiple animated objects.

> Because Movie Clips can contain complex animations, you will probably need to use Graphic symbols. You can create them directly from within the Movie Clip much as you would from the main Timeline, and they're automatically placed in the main movie's Library for future use.

6. When you've finished crafting the animation in your Movie Clip, click the scene link in the Edit bar to return to the main Timeline.

7. Once you've returned to the main Timeline, you can view and test your Movie Clip by opening the Library (Window → Library), selecting the Movie Clip, and clicking the Play button in the preview window's top-right corner.

> You can also test the Movie Clip's animation directly from within Symbol Editing mode—just hit the Return/Enter button.

Converting an Existing Animation into a Movie Clip

It's more than likely that the majority of Movie Clips you create will be produced from scratch. However, you'll probably find yourself in the situation where you'll want to turn an existing animation into a Movie Clip. In that case, follow these steps:

1. In the main Timeline, select every frame in every layer that you want to turn into a Movie Clip.

2. Copy the frames you've selected by choosing Edit → Timeline → Copy Frames or by Ctrl+clicking (Mac) or right-clicking (Win) on the selected frames, and choosing Copy Frames from the pop-up context menu.

3. Select Insert → New Symbol or use Cmd/Ctrl+F8.

> Make sure nothing on the Stage is selected before you insert a new symbol.

4. When the Create New Symbol dialog box opens, enter a name into the Name field, select the Movie Clip radio button, and click OK.

5. When the Symbol Editor opens, select the first frame in the Timeline and choose Edit → Timeline → Paste Frames or Ctrl+click (Mac) or right-click (Win) on the selected frames, and choose Paste Frames from the pop-up context menu. This pastes all the copied frames into the Movie Clip.

6. To return to the main Timeline, click the scene link in the Edit bar.

7. Now that you've returned to the main movie, you can remove the animation you copied to create the Movie Clip (if you so desire). Just reselect all the frames that you previously selected and then delete them by choosing Edit → Timeline → Cut Frames. Alternatively, you can Ctrl+click (Mac) or right-click (Win) and choose Cut Frames from the pop-up context menu.

Inserting Movie Clips into the Main Timeline

Now that you've learned how to create Movie Clips, either from scratch or an existing animation, let's take a look at how to insert them into your main Timeline:

1. If it isn't already, open the Library by going to Window → Library.

2. Click the exact location in the Timeline where you want to insert the Movie Clip. Remember, you'll need to insert a keyframe if one hasn't already been inserted.

3. Click and drag the Movie Clip from the Library onto the Stage. Even though a Movie Clip might be composed of a hundred frames' worth of animated goodness, when it's inserted into the main Timeline, it occupies only a single keyframe.

4. To see how your Movie Clip runs within your main movie, choose Control → Test Movie or Control → Test Scene.

> Movie Clips can't play within the Flash authoring environment. As a result, hitting Return/Enter won't play the Movie Clip. To view how your Movie Clip actually looks within your movie, you'll need to test it in the player by using the Test Movie or Test Scene commands in the Control menu.

Manipulating Movie Clips

Once you have inserted a Movie Clip into the main Timeline, you can manipulate it—as you can all symbols—by using the Property Inspector (Window → Properties). You can also accomplish a series of important operations by using the Library. You'll learn about each option in the next several sections.

Naming a Movie Clip Instance

As you learned in Chapter 7, when you drag a symbol from the Library onto the Stage, you are creating a symbol instance—a copy of the parent symbol in the Library. This is no difference when creating Movie Clips (they are symbols, after all). What you haven't learned, however, is that you can easily assign a unique name to a symbol instance using the Property Inspector. So, the big question becomes, why exactly would you want to assign a name to a symbol instance? Well, as we've already discussed, you can use Action-Script to control and manipulate Movie Clips that reside on the main Timeline. To do this, however, you need to identify each Movie Clip symbol instance with a unique name so that you can appropriately target the ActionScript. So, although the process by which you name a Movie Clip symbol instance is really quite easy (as you'll find out shortly), it is absolutely vital to the creation of any moderately complex Flash creation that fully leverages the phenomenal power of Movie Clips.

To name a Movie Clip symbol instance, follow these steps:

1. With a new document open, drag a Movie Clip from the Library onto the Stage.

2. Select the Movie Clip symbol instance using the Arrow tool.

3. If it isn't already open, open the Property Inspector by choosing Window → Properties.

4. Enter a unique name in the Instance Name field.

Instance Name Field

When entering a name into the Instance Name field, avoid using spaces. If you want a two-word name, use a hyphen (-) or an underscore (_).

Swapping One Movie Clip for Another

You might find yourself in a situation where you want to swap one instance for another. To do this, you use the Swap symbol in the Property Inspector:

1. In the main Timeline, select the Movie Clip you want to swap out.

2. If it isn't already open, open the Property Inspector by choosing Window → Properties.

3. Click the Swap button `Swap…`.

Figure 11.1

**The Swap Symbol
dialog box**

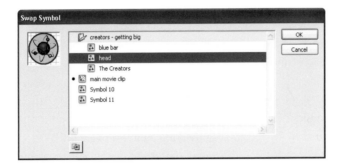

4. When the Swap Symbol dialog box opens (see Figure 11.1), select the symbol you want to swap in and click OK.

> You don't have to swap a Movie Clip for a Movie Clip. You could easily swap a Movie Clip for a Graphic symbol, for example. However, the swapped symbol will retain the behavior (Movie Clip, Button, Graphic) of the symbol it's replacing.

Editing a Movie Clip

If you want to edit the parent symbol of a given Movie Clip, you can open the Library, select the Movie Clip, and choose Edit from the Library Options menu. Alternatively, you can double-click the Movie Clip instance on the Stage and then make any changes you want. Remember, when you've finished up in the Symbol Editor, just click the scene link in the Edit bar to return to the main Timeline.

Duplicating a Movie Clip

You can use the Library to duplicate a Movie Clip, which is useful if you want to replace a symbol with an altered version of itself and don't want to have to go through the trouble of re-creating the symbol from scratch. You just duplicate the symbol, edit it using the Edit command in the Library's Options drop-down menu, and then use it to replace the target symbol instance on the Stage. Let's take a look at the process for duplicating:

1. Open the Flash movie that contains the Movie Clip you want to duplicate.

2. If it isn't already open, open the Library by choosing Window → Library.

3. Select the Movie Clip that you want to duplicate.

4. Select Duplicate from the Library's Options drop-down menu.

5. When the Duplicate Symbol dialog box opens, enter the name for the duplicated symbol into the Name field, make sure the Movie Clip radio button is selected, and click OK.

The duplicate Movie Clip is automatically added to the Library, and you can then manipulate it however you want.

Seeing Movie Clips in Action

Now that you've explored the basics of creating and manipulating Movie Clips, you can put all of your hard-earned knowledge to work. Even though you've yet to explore the ActionScript-related aspects of Movie Clips (discussed in Chapters 19 and 20), there is no better way to experiment with their power and versatility than by using them to create a scene that, under normal circumstances, would prove complex enough to be somewhat overwhelming if it were constructed using the main Timeline alone. Remember that back in the Hands On 1 exercise earlier in this book, you created a static seascape scene? Well, you're going to take this idea one step further and create an animated seascape in which a single fish swims by the camera.

All of the images (in SWF format) in this tutorial are located in the Chapter 11 folder of this book's companion CD-ROM. In addition, the files `seascape.swf` and `seascape.fla` provide an example of how the final product might look.

Creating the Water

To start off, you'll need to create the water in which our marvelous seascape will take place:

1. Create a new document by choosing File → New.

2. When the New Document dialog box opens, select the Flash Document option and click OK.

3. Choose Modify → Document. When the Document Properties dialog box opens, change the Width to **550** and the Height to **400**.

4. Choose a light blue for the document's background color.

5. Click OK to exit the Document Properties dialog box.

6. Now choose File → Import → Import to Stage.

7. When the Import dialog box opens, navigate to the Chapter 11 directory on this book's CD-ROM, locate the `water.swf` file, and click Open. This imports the premade water (complete with gentle rolling waves) onto the Stage and into your Library. The file is nothing spectacular, so you might want to create your own.

> If you can't locate the file, you might have to select the All Files option from the Import dialog box's Files of Type drop-down menu.

8. Position the water so that it lines up with the edges of the movie. At this point, the Stage should look like this:

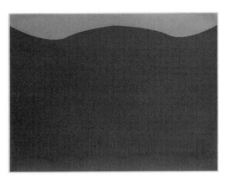

9. Because you are going to have a number of different layers in your scene, it's wise to name each. Double-click on your only layer's icon. When the Layer Properties dialog box opens, enter **Water** into the Name field. Click OK.

Adding the Fish

Now that you've got the ocean occupying a single keyframe of a single layer, it's time to create some fish:

1. Choose Insert → New Symbol (or use the shortcut Cmd/Ctrl+F8).

2. When the Create New Symbol dialog box opens, click the Movie Clip radio button, enter **fish1** into the name field, and click OK.

3. When the Symbol Editor opens, choose File → Import → Import to Stage, navigate to the Chapter 11 directory on this book's CD-ROM, select the `fish1.swf`, `fish2.swf`, or `fish3.swf` files (there are three different fish), and click Open. This imports the image that you'll use to create your fish Movie Clip.

> If the image doesn't appear, it's possible that Flash placed it out of view. Scroll down until it's visible, and drag it up. Remember, the crosshairs represent the symbol's registration point.

4. Now it's time to create the animation where the fish "swims" horizontally from the right to the left. Select the fish with the Arrow tool.

> Whichever fish file you decide to use will be composed of a bunch of different groups. As a result, you'll need to group all the groups together. To do this, just select all the parts of the fish, and choose Modify → Group.

5. If it isn't already, open the Property Inspector by choosing Window → Properties.

6. Enter **470** into the X field and **–78.5** into the Y field.

> You might want to zoom out so that you can see the entire area that the fish will transverse.

7. Click frame 90, and choose Insert → Timeline → Keyframe.

8. With the newly created keyframe selected, select the fish with the Arrow tool.

9. Enter **–470** into the X field and **–78.5** into the Y field.

10. Select the first keyframe, and choose Insert → Timeline → Create Motion Tween.

> The whole point of creating an animation that covers this amount of distance is to ensure that you can place the Movie Clip on one side of the Stage in the work area, have it pass through the ocean scene, and then have it pass into the work area on the other side of the Stage before it loops. This gives the illusion that the fish is simply passing by your line of sight.

11. If you want to add a little more life to your scene, you can have the fish follow a wavy path—opposed to the straight one it currently follows. To add a motion guide, follow the steps described in Chapter 10.

12. Now that you've created the Movie Clip of the fish, you can insert it into the water. Return to the main scene by choosing Edit → Document or by clicking the scene link in the Edit bar.

13. Create a new layer by choosing Insert → Timeline → Layer or clicking the Insert Layer button in the bottom-left corner of the Timeline.

14. Rename the new layer **fish.**

15. If it isn't already, make sure the fish layer is above the ocean layer in the Timeline.

16. Select the first keyframe of the fish layer.

17. Open the Library (Window → Library) and click and drag the fish Movie Clip onto the Stage. You should position the Movie Clip in the work area to the right of the Stage. So far, your scene should look like this.

Now that you've created a basic ocean scene, you can test it—choose Control → Test Movie or Control → Test Scene.

Adding Bubbles to the Seascape

You'll finish off this tutorial by adding some floating bubbles to the ocean:

1. Choose Insert → New Symbol.

2. When the Create New Symbol dialog box opens, click the Graphic radio button, type **bubble template** into the Name field, and click OK.

3. When the Symbol Editor opens, click the first keyframe of the only layer in the Timeline and draw a small circle with the Oval tool in the lower portion of the screen. As this will be the template for your floating bubbles, you should choose a sufficiently bubble-like color for the stroke and fill.

4. You are going to want to take the bubble template Graphic symbol that you created and use it in a Movie Clip to create an animation of a rising bubble. Choose Insert → New Symbol.

5. When the Create New Symbol dialog box opens, enter **bubble** animation into the Name field, select the Movie Clip radio button, and click OK.

6. When you enter the Symbol Editor, select the first blank keyframe in the only layer, and drag the bubble template graphic symbol from the Library onto the Stage.

7. With the bubble template still selected, open the Info panel. Change the X value to **−20** and the Y value to **70**.

8. Click frame 30 and choose Insert → Timeline → Keyframe.

9. With the second keyframe selected, change the bubble template's X value to **−19** and its Y value to **−292**.

10. Reselect the first keyframe in the layer and choose Insert → Timeline → Create Motion Tween. This creates the animation of the rising bubble.

11. To add a little character to the rising bubble, click somewhere in the middle of the tween (say, frame 15 or so).

Even though the entire tween gets selected, don't be fooled into believing that you aren't selecting a specific frame. The playhead indicates the actual frame you've selected.

12. Choose Insert → Timeline Keyframe. By doing this, you've added another keyframe to the middle of the tween you created. Your Timeline should look like this:

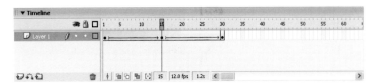

13. With the newly created middle keyframe selected, use either the Transform panel (Window → Design Panels → Transform) or the Scale tool (located in the Toolbox's Options section when the Free Transform tool is selected) to increase the size of the bubble slightly. By doing this, you've created a tween in which the bubble starts off small, gradually gets bigger, and then goes back to its previous size. All of this happens when the bubble is moving.

14. Now you're going to add a little more subtlety to your rising bubble by making it disappear as it nears the top of its tween. First, select the final keyframe in the tween.

15. Using the Arrow tool, select the bubble.

16. If it isn't already open, open the Property Inspector by choosing Window → Properties.

17. Choose Alpha from the Color drop-down menu and enter **0** into the Alpha Value field. This makes the bubble appear transparent by the end of the tween.

Adding More Bubbles

Now that you've created the animation of one rising bubble, you can then add several more that rise at staggered intervals:

1. With the bubble Movie Clip still open in the Symbol Editor, add an additional layer (give it a unique name if you want) by choosing Insert → Timeline → Layer or by clicking the Insert Layer button in the bottom-left corner of the Timeline.

2. Click frame 5 and choose Insert → Timeline → Keyframe or use the shortcut F6. This guarantees that the second bubble won't appear and start rising until the playhead reaches frame 5. As a result, the two bubbles will be staggered.

3. Drag the bubble template Graphic symbol from the Library onto the Stage. With the Info panel, set the new bubble's X value to **–64** and its Y value to **104.**

4. Click frame 35 and choose Insert → Timeline → Keyframe.

5. Repeat the process described in the previous section—the only difference is that you set the bubble's X value to **–60** and its Y value to **–245** using the Info panel to create the second rising bubble.

6. Now that you've created two rising bubbles, you can continue adding rising bubbles. The only thing you have to vary is the frame at which the specific animation starts. You can also vary the size of each bubble instance to add variety.

Adding the Bubbles to the Main Scene

Now you can add your rising bubble Movie Clip to the main scene:

1. Return to the main scene by choosing Edit → Document or by clicking the Scene button in Edit bar.

2. Create a new layer by choosing Insert → Timeline → Layer or by clicking the Insert Layer button in the bottom-left corner of the Timeline.

3. Now, rename the new layer as **bubbles**.

4. Select the first keyframe of the bubbles layer.

5. Open the Library (Window → Library) and click and drag the bubbles Movie Clip onto the Stage. You should position the Movie Clip in the work area just below the Stage. By doing this, you'll get the illusion that the bubbles are passing into view from the bottom of the scene. Your scene should look like this:

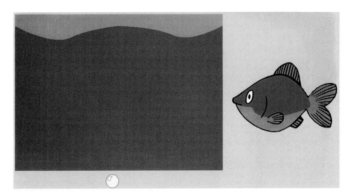

6. Now that you've created a basic ocean scene, you can test it. Choose Control → Test Movie or Control → Test Scene.

Congratulations, you've created your first scene using Movie Clips. Experiment with them by adding more objects to the scene. For example, try adding other fish or swaying sea plants.

Inspirational Design Model

Any good Flash creation will leverage Movie Clips to enhance the user experience. However, because of their sheer power and versatility, there exists an obvious gap between those who simply use Movie Clips and those who exploit Movie Clips to their maximum potential. A great example of an incredible use of Movie Clips is Neostream (www.neostream.com).

Based in Sydney, Australia, Neostream is a top-notch multimedia company that specializes in CD-ROMs, the Web, and corporate identity. Its website is a fast-paced, beautiful example of unbelievable Flash animation and design (see Figure 11.2). The animation is extremely smooth, employing Movie Clips for all manner of elements—including its preloader screen and interface elements. Log on and prepare to be dazzled with some serious animation.

Figure 11.2

Neostream

CHAPTER 12

Using Scenes to Organize Your Flash Movie

By now you've probably figured out that Flash movies can be quite complex. A movie of even moderate size and intricacy can contain many discreet areas of action (interactivity, animation, and so on). As a result, it's fairly easy to create a Flash movie that, although compelling and beautiful, is an unorganized, chaotic nightmare. Whether you are creating a stand-alone animation, a web-based animated short, or a complete Flash site, you're going to have to develop and maintain a method of keeping your Flash creation well organized.

Now, imagine being able to break your creation into any number of manageable chunks, each containing a specific series of events (such as an animation, an interface, or some interactivity)—this is where Flash *scenes* come in. As in theater, you can think of scenes as self-contained chunks that logically break up your movie's content. Each scene is something akin to a mini-movie that is strung together with other mini-movies to create an overall Flash movie. When it comes to movies of any significant complexity, scenes save you a great deal of time and trouble.

In this chapter, you'll explore the following topics:

- **Understanding the power and possibilities of scenes**
- **Creating and crafting scenes**
- **Moving between scenes**
- **Testing scenes**
- **ActionScripting and scenes**

Understanding the Power and Possibilities of Scenes

Scenes are wondrous little tools that segment the overall content in your movie into self-contained, manageable chunks. Each scene acts as a mini-movie that plays one after the other. Although they appear to be somewhat separated from one another within the Flash authoring environment, they really aren't. When you play the overall movie (either from within Flash or after it has been published), the scenes string together as if they were one movie and play according to the sequence listed in the Scene panel. There is never any perceivable lag or flicker between scenes.

Figure 12.1

The Scene Panel

The number of scenes you can have is limited only by the amount of memory in your computer.

The possibilities for scenes are literally endless. Say, for instance, you are creating an entire Flash site. You could use a scene for each individual section and subsection of the site. Another possibility is along the lines of traditional film or theater. Web-based Flash animated shorts are becoming increasingly popular these days. You could use scenes to partition a Flash animated short you created into…well, scenes!

Introducing the Scene Panel

For the most part, you access the majority of scene functionality through the Scene panel (Figure 12.1), which you open by choosing Window → Design Panels → Scene. The Scene panel displays the number and organization of your movie's scenes. In addition, it lets you duplicate, add, delete, and move scenes.

Unlike many other Flash panels, the Scene panel doesn't have any additional options beyond the default Maximize Panel, Close Panel, and Help options.

Introducing the Edit Bar

Nestled above the Timeline and below the main program menu is the Edit bar (see Figure 12.2). You open and close the Edit bar by choosing Window → Toolbars → Edit Bar.

You used the Edit bar in Chapter 7 when you were working with the Symbol Editor (more specifically, moving back to the main Timeline from the Symbol Editor). However, you didn't get a chance to explore its functionality in relation to scenes.

Essentially, Edit bar displays the current scene. When you move to another scene, the Edit bar changes its display accordingly. Also, as illustrated in Figure 12.2, the Edit Scene button in the right portion of the Edit bar displays a drop-down list that lets you switch the currently displayed scene. (For more information about this button, see the "Moving Between Scenes" section, later in this chapter.)

Creating and Crafting Scenes

As mentioned previously, you'll use the Scene panel (Window → Design Panels → Scene) to work with scenes. In this section of the chapter, you're going to explore how to use the Scene panel to add, duplicate, rename, and rearrange scenes.

Adding a Scene

As your movie increases in size and complexity, you are going to want to add more scenes to keep a firm grip on its organization. By using the Scene panel, you can add as many scenes as you want by following these steps:

1. Make sure you have a document open.

2. Choose Window → Design Panels → Scene to open the Scene panel.

3. Click the Add Scene button ➕ located in the bottom-right corner of the Scene panel. Alternatively, besides using the Scene panel to add a new scene, you can also select Insert → Scene.

4. You'll notice that Flash has added an additional scene to the movie. By default, Flash always adds the new scene below the currently selected one. The default naming convention for a new scene is numerical—for instance, Scene 1, Scene 2, and so on.

5. Now all you have to do is select the newly added scene in the Scene panel and start creating.

When you create a new scene, Flash automatically switches to the newly created scene.

Deleting a Scene

If you want to delete a scene, follow these steps:

1. Open the Scene panel by choosing Window → Design Panels → Scene.

2. Select the scene you want to delete.

3. Click the Delete Scene button 🗑 located in the bottom-right corner of the Scene panel.

4. When the prompt appears, click OK. As indicated in the prompt, you cannot undo a scene deletion.

Duplicating a Scene

In previous chapters, you looked at how to copy and duplicate various elements such as objects and animations (mostly for the purpose of converting them to symbols). The process, especially when it comes to copying entire animations, is fairly unwieldy. Imagine, then, having to duplicate an entire scene! The prospect is pretty daunting, especially if your movie (and its respective scenes) has become fairly complicated.

Macromedia has integrated a simple duplicate function that lets you create exact copies of any given scene with a click of a button:

1. With the Scene panel open (Window → Design Panels → Scene), select the scene you want to duplicate.

2. Click the Duplicate Scene button 🔲 in the bottom-right section of the Scene panel.

3. You'll notice that a duplicate of your selected scene, with the word *copy* tagged onto the original name, appears in the Scene panel.

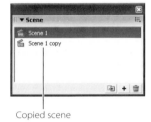

Copied scene

Renaming a Scene

The default name that Flash assigns to a new or duplicate scene is not very original. Although logically numbered, the names aren't particularly useful when it comes to identifying the content of individual scenes in a large movie. To rename a scene, follow these steps:

Figure 12.3

Scene panel with editable scene name

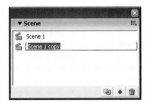

1. With the Scene panel open, double-click the scene whose name you want to change. By doing this, as illustrated in Figure 12.3, the scene's name becomes editable.

2. Type a new name and press Return/Enter (or click anywhere off the Scene panel).

Rearranging Scenes

As mentioned, scenes play sequentially based on their positions in the Scene panel. But you certainly aren't stuck with the order in which the scenes were created (and therefore the sequence that they play). To change the arrangement of scenes, follow these steps:

1. Open the Scene panel (Window → Design Panels → Scene).

2. Click and drag the scene to the location you want (see Figure 12.4). You'll notice that as long as you keep your mouse button down, your cursor changes and a blue line appears in the scene's projected location.

3. To move the scene, just release the mouse button.

Figure 12.4

Scene panel with scene being moved

Moving Between Scenes

Because you are going to want to switch back and forth between various scenes as you work on them, Flash has provided several scene navigation tools:

Scene panel To navigate between the various scenes in your movie, all you need to do is click the desired scene in the Scene panel. Remember, your current scene is displayed in the Edit bar.

Edit Scene button Two buttons dominate the right portion of the Edit bar. The leftmost one, when clicked (as illustrated earlier in Figure 12.2), provides a menu of all the current scenes in your movie. All you need to do is select one and Flash automatically switches to that scene.

Figure 12.5

Movie Explorer with scenes listed

Movie Explorer As discussed in Chapter 9, the Movie Explorer (Window → Other Panels → Movie Explorer) displays the contents of your movie hierarchically, lets you search your entire movie for any symbol or symbol instance, and replaces text and fonts (see Figure 12.5).

Because scenes are part of the overall movie, they are displayed in the Movie Explorer as top-level items in the organizational hierarchy. Simply locate the scene by its name, and click it. Flash automatically switches you to the selected scene.

> Under normal circumstances, the Movie Explorer displays the contents only of the currently selected scene. To display all scenes (and their content), choose Show All Scenes from the Movie Explorer's drop-down Options menu.

Testing Scenes

So far, you've looked at a couple of different ways to test the movie that you've created. When it comes to scenes, you should be aware that if you were to simply hit Return/Enter to play your movie within the Flash authoring environment, you would be able to preview only the currently active scene. Although, when exported, the movie plays all the scenes sequentially, it does not do so from within Flash. As a result, you need to do one of the following:

- To test a scene other than the current one, use the Scene panel to select it, and then hit Return/Enter. Alternatively, you can choose Control → Test Scene.

- Now, if you want to test the movie in its entirety, select Control → Test Movie or use the shortcut Cmd/Ctrl+Return/Enter. This opens the movie in a Flash Player and plays all the scenes according to their sequence within the Scene panel.

You can also play all the scenes in your movie by choosing Control → Play All Scenes.

ActionScripting and Scenes

Although scenes are great for organizing animated content, they do tend to create a fairly linear product. Granted, there isn't much you can do about the linearity of scenes; you certainly can't have two scenes playing at the same time. However, what if you wanted to play your first scene, followed by your third scene, your second scene, and finally your fourth scene? Alternatively, what if you wanted your scenes to play from last to first, instead of first to last? Under normal circumstances, this defies the natural laws of Flash. However, with the use of ActionScript (specifically frame actions), you can be your own Einstein, shattering the conventions of the known Flash universe! But seriously, as is the case in many aspects of Flash, ActionScripting greatly extends scene functionality.

However, at this point it would be a little premature to get into ActionScript. Instead, this section will focus on what is *possible* when you use ActionScript to extend the usability of scenes. For now, all you need to know is that these built-in functions can increase the versatility of scenes:

- `gotoAndPlay()` determines the specific scene and frame that the playhead jumps to when it evokes the action.

- `gotoAndStop()` goes to a specific scene or frame and stops the movie. This is a variation of the `gotoAndPlay()` action that you set by deselecting the GotoAndPlay check box at the bottom of the Actions panel.

- `play()` restarts a movie that has been previously stopped.

- `stop()` ends the movie from playing any further.

If you want to explore the specifics of these very useful built-in functions, check out the ActionScript Reference located on this book's accompanying CD.

Inspirational Design Model

Based in Austin Texas, Terra Incognita is arguably one of the most talented and respected interactive design studios around today. With talented designers (all of whom have a strong background in the social sciences and humanities), Terra Incognita doesn't just design websites, kiosks, or collections databases, they develop innovative and intelligent products that spark the imagination, engage the mind, and lead users on experiences to discover the nature of the human experience.

Their company website (`www.terraincognita.com`) is a phenomenal expression of their dedication to amazingly creative (and technically mind-blowing) digital storytelling (see Figure 12.6).

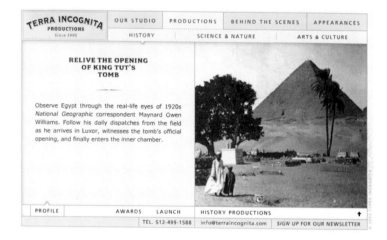

Figure 12.6

Terra Incognita

CHAPTER 13

Creating Interactive Presentations with Slides in Flash MX Professional 2004

As Flash matures, the program is being used for far more than it was ever intended. Not only are designers and content developers using Flash to create exciting new interactive products (mobile applications, kiosks, and even content for console games), but everyday people are using Flash to create content for rather ordinary, non-web-based situations. Take presentations, for example. Businesspeople, students, and teachers, just to name a few, all create computer-based presentations. For the most part, they've relied on Microsoft PowerPoint for their presentation authoring needs. However, a small and growing group of forward-thinking people have turned to Flash as their application of choice for authoring slide shows and multimedia presentations.

In Flash MX Professional 2004, Macromedia has upped the ante by including a whole new authoring paradigm, which is partly designed to allow people to create presentations in a far easier and streamlined method than was available in earlier versions of Flash: Slides. (It's really important to note, right off the bat, that Slides are a feature available only in Flash MX Pro 2004.)

In this chapter, you'll explore the ins and outs of creating Slides-based interactive presentations. The following topics will be covered:

- Introduction to Slides- and Screens-based authoring
- Working with Slides
- Adding content to Slides

Introduction to Slides- and Screens-Based Authoring

In previous versions of Flash, everything was created using the Timeline. This interface uses an authoring paradigm in which all your content is strung together in a linear manner. While (as you saw in Chapter 11) it certainly wasn't impossible to create Flash content that required a more modular approach, it was difficult and time-consuming.

This was especially true in the case of presentations, which require you to be able to author relatively stand-alone chunks (the slides in the presentation), which are then strung together to form the overall presentation. This all changed in Flash MX Pro 2004 when Macromedia introduced Screens-based authoring.

It's important to note that the term *Screens* refers both to Slides and Forms. This chapter shows how to create interactive presentations with Slides. To learn about creating interactive applications with Forms, check out Flash's stellar help feature and documentation.

In Flash MX Pro 2004, when you're working with Screens in general, and a Slides-based document in particular, you are provided with an authoring paradigm in which documents are composed of building blocks that make it easy for you to create complex, hierarchical Flash-based presentations. The cool thing about this is that you can create the individual components of your presentation (each slide) one by one in a very controlled, modular, and accessible manner.

Each slide can be as rich as any Flash movie, complete with animation, interactivity, and even rich media such as digital video or sound.

In the case of a regular, non-Screens-based Flash movie, the movement of the Playhead through the Timeline (in addition to any ActionScript present in the movie) controls the manner in which the movie plays. Now, in the case of a Slides-based document, you don't have the presence of a single, unifying Timeline that runs through all the content. So, how exactly do you control the transition from slide to slide in a Slides-based document? Well, by default, the spacebar and left and right arrow keys function as the control by which someone moves through the slides in your movie. The good thing is that, if you don't want to rely on this default method, you can also use behaviors to create interactive features to control movement through your Screens-based movie.

Beyond creating interactive controls for the navigation of your Slides-based presentation, behaviors also allow you to create animated transitions between slides in the presentation. So, you don't have to settle for a Plain Jane change from one slide to another. Instead, you can fade a slide in or out, rotate a slide as it appears or disappears, have a slide fly in from the edge of a document, or create any number of other transitional effects.

A Screens-based document can be published only for Flash Player 6 format or later, with ActionScript 2. Unfortunately, you cannot save a Screens-based document in any earlier Flash Player format.

Understanding Slide Hierarchy

When you work with a Screens-based document, the Screen Outline pane (which you access by choosing Window → Screens when working on a Screens-based document) at the left of the Document window displays thumbnails of each screen in the current document in a collapsible tree view that represents the hierarchy of the presentation (see Figure 13.1).

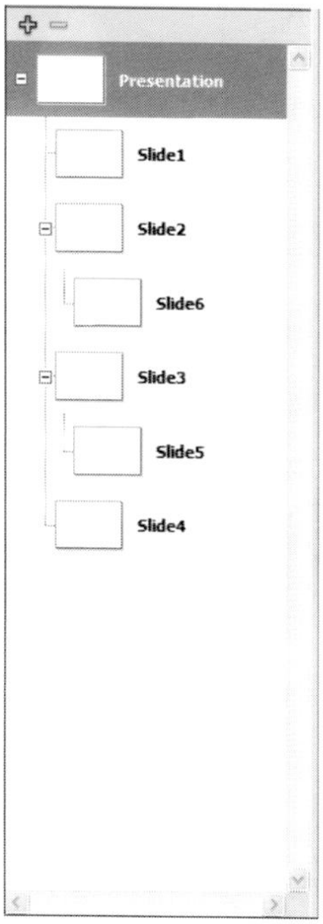

Each Slides-based document has a master slide at the top level, which, by default, is called *Presentation*. This top-level slide acts as the container for everything that you add to the presentation, including other slides. While content can be placed in this top-level slide, you can neither move nor delete the master slide itself.

Not only can you add multiple slides to the document's master slide (a process you'll explore later), you can nest slides within other slides. The relationship between screens within the presentation are described by a family metaphor. A slide that is nested inside another slide is the child of that slide. A slide that contains another slide is the parent of that slide. If a slide is nested several layers deep, all the slides above that slide are its ancestors. Slides that are at the same level are sibling slides. All slides nested in another slide are its descendants. A child slide contains all the content of its ancestor slides. Whew! Make sense? While the terminology of the relationship between slides can seem initially confusing, it's an important thing to become familiar with, especially if your presentation features lots of content.

In many ways, Screens in general, and Slides in particular, are much like nested Movie Clips. First, child slides inherit the behavior of their parent slides. Second, target paths are used to send ActionScript from one slide to another. It's important to note, however, that unlike nested Movie Clips, neither do slides appear in the Library nor can you create multiple instances of them.

Figure 13.1

The Screen Outline pane displays each of the slides in your movie in a hierarchical manner.

Working with Slides

Now that you've had a good introduction to the whole idea of Slides, it's time to actually go through the steps necessary to create an interactive presentation with Slides. In this section, you'll start by looking at how to create a Slides document, add additional slides to the document, and manipulate the properties of the slides. From there, you'll explore how you can use behaviors to create both navigation elements and animated transitions.

Creating a New Slides Document

The process by which you create a Slides document is quite easy. All you need to do is follow these steps:

1. Choose File → New. The New Document dialog box opens.

2. In the New Document dialog box, select Flash Slide Presentation from the Type list box (located under the General tab).

3. Click OK.

In addition to using the New Document dialog box to create a new Slides-based document, you can also select Create New: Flash Slide Presentation from the Start Page.

Adding Slides to Your Document

Once you've created a new Slides document, you'll want to add slides to your presentation. Here's how:

1. With the Screen Outline pane open (Window → Screens), select the slide you want to add the new slide after.

By default, when you add a new slide to your document, Flash places it at the same level after the currently selected slide. If the document contains nested slides below the currently selected slide, the new slide is added after the nested slide, at the same level as the selected slide.

2. From here, you have a couple of ways to insert a screen:

   - Click the Insert Screen button ⊕ located along the top of the Screen Outline pane.
   - Choose Insert → Screen.
   - Ctrl+click (Mac) or right-click (Win) and select Insert Screen from the pop-up context menu.

You can just as easily insert a nested slide. Here's how:

1. With the Screen Outline pane open (Window → Screens), select the slide you wish to nest the new slide below.

> Flash inserts a new nested slide directly after the currently selected slide, and nested one level down. If the document already contains a nested slide or slides below the currently selected slide, the new slide is inserted after the last nested slide below the selected slide.

2. From here, you have a couple of ways to insert a nested screen:

   - Choose Insert → Nested Screen.
   - Ctrl+click (Mac) or right-click (Win), and select Insert Nested Screen from the pop-up context menu.

> It's worth noting that when you insert a nested slide, it acquires its parent's content. This is useful when creating a sequence of slides that share a large number of common elements as it saves you from having to place the same content in each slide separately.

Manipulating the Properties of Slides

Like many elements in Flash, slides have a set of properties that you can manipulate to fine-tune how your interactive presentation looks and acts. While you can set the document properties (Stage Color, frame rate, etc.) of your presentation using the Document Properties dialog box (Modify → Document), slide properties are unique to each slide in your presentation.

To set the properties of a slide within your presentation, just follow these steps:

1. With the Screen Outline pane open (Window → Screens), select the slide whose properties you want to set.

2. Open the Property Inspector (Window → Properties). You'll notice that the Property Inspector displays the properties of that slide.

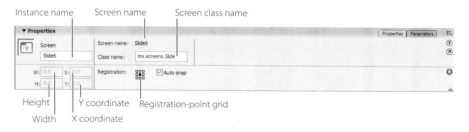

3. From here, you can set any of the following properties:

Instance Name The slide's instance name is a unique identifier used when you target that slide with ActionScript. By default, each slide is assigned a default instance name when it's inserted into the presentation. The instance name is also used as the slide name in the Screen Outline pane. To change the slide's default instance name, simply type a new name into the Instance Name field.

When you change the instance name, not only does the slide's name change in the Screen Outline pane, but it also changes in the Property Inspector as well.

Width and Height The width (W) and height (H) properties are read-only. This means that because they are actually determined by the contents in the selected slide, you can't change them.

X and Y Coordinates The X and Y coordinate fields set the position of the slide's registration point (in pixels). You can also set the slide's registration point using the Registration Point Grid or the Auto Snap option.

Class Name The class name specifies the ActionScript class that slide belongs to. The class itself determines what ActionScript methods and properties are available for the screen. By default, slides are assigned to the `mx.screens.Slide` class. If you want to assign a different class to the selected slide, simply enter a new class name into the Class Name field.

Class names are quite similar to Objects in ActionScript. To learn more about classes in ActionScript, see Chapter 17.

Registration Point Grid The Registration Point Grid provides you with another method to change the slide's registration point. By default, the slide's registration point is in the center of the document. To change the slide's registration point using the Registration Point Grid, simply click one of the small squares within the grid.

Auto Snap The Auto Snap option keeps the slide's registration point in the same position in relation to screen contents regardless of whether you add, remove, or move the slide's contents.

Changing the Slide's Parameters

Unlike the slide's properties, which affect how the slide's content behaves, the parameters of a slide affect how the slide itself behaves and plays.

To set the properties of a slide within your presentation, just follow these steps:

1. With the Screen Outline pane open (Window → Screens), select the slide whose properties you want to set.

2. Open the Property Inspector (Window → Properties). You'll notice that the Property Inspector displays the properties of that slide.

3. Click the Parameters tab located in the top-right corner of the Property Inspector to get access to the slide's parameters.

When the Property Inspector is undocked, the Parameters tab can be found in the lower-right corner.

4. From here, all you need to do is click the value to the right of the specific property, and then choose one of the options from the pop-up menu that opens (which you access by clicking the down arrow that is displayed when you click the value).

   autoKeyNav The autoKeyNav parameter determines whether or not the default keyboard setup is used for navigating through the slides. If True is selected, the right arrow key (or the Spacebar) moves to the next slide and the left arrow moves to the previous slide. If False is selected, there is no default keyboard setup for navigation.

It's important to note that the autoKeyNav parameter can be different for each slide.

   If Inherit is selected, the slide will have the same autoKeyNav value as its parent.

If, for some reason, a slide's parent's autoKeyNav parameter has also been set to Inherit, Flash will search all the parent slide's ancestors for an autoKeyNav that has not been set to Inherit, and then use that for the child slide. However, if the child slide's parent is the root (master) slide in the document, the Inherit value will automatically be changed to True.

   autoLoad The parameter autoLoad indicates whether the content should load automatically (when the value is set to True), or wait to load until the Loader.load() method is called (when the value is set to False).

contentPath If you want to load an external SWF file into a slide's loader component, all you need to do is enter an absolute or relative path for the `contentPath` value.

overlayChildren The `overlayChildren` parameter determines whether the content from a previous slide is visible when you move to the next slide in the sequence. If the value is set to True, the content is visible. If you set the value to False, the previous slide disappears when the next slide is displayed.

playHidden Given that any slide can have animation as well as static content, you need to determine if the animation continues to play if the user moves past the slide with the animation to the next slide in the sequence. This is where the `playHidden` parameter comes in. When the `playHidden` parameter is set to True (which is the default setting), the slide continues to play when it's hidden after being shown. When `playHidden` is set to False, however, the slide stops playing if it is hidden and resumes playing at Frame 1 if it is shown again.

Organizing a Slides Document

As your Slides document increases in complexity, you need to exert maximum control over its organization to preserve both your workflow and your sanity. There are several basic (though extremely useful) skills you'll want to master. This section shows how to delete slides from your presentation, move slides, and rename a slide.

Deleting a Slide from Your Presentation

During the process of creating your interactive presentation, you might find yourself in a situation where you would like to remove one of the slides from the sequence. To do so, just follow these steps:

1. With the Screen Outline pane open (Window → Screen), select the slide you want to remove from the sequence.

2. Cmd+click (Mac) or right-click (Win) the slide, and select Cut or Delete Screen from the drop-down context menu. Alternatively, you can click the Delete Screen button in the Screen Outline pane.

Moving a Slide

As you've already learned, the sequence of the slides within the Screen Outline pane (partially) determines the sequence that your presentation plays. As a result, it's a good idea to become familiar with how you can reorder the slides within your presentation. Let's take a look at how:

1. With the Screen Outline pane open (Window → Screens), select the slide that you want to move.

2. Drag the slide to the location in the hierarchy where you want it moved. You'll notice that a blue bar appears in the current location of your mouse. This indicates the projected position of the slide (see Figure 13.2). You'll also notice that the horizontal position of the blue preview line also moves depending on where you drag your cursor. By dragging the cursor right or left of a slide within the hierarchy, you can move the slide relative to other slides (in other words, nest).

3. When the blue preview bar is in the desired location, release your mouse button, and the slide will move.

Renaming a Slide

When you add slides, they are automatically given a default name. To get a better idea of any given slide's contents at a glance, you might want to change this default name to something more descriptive. Let's take a look at how:

1. With the Screen Outline panel open, select the slide whose name you want to change.

2. From here, you've got a couple of ways to rename the slide:

   • Double-click the slide's name. When the field becomes editable, simply type a new name.

   • Open the Property Inspector (Window → Properties) and enter a new name into the Instance Name field, which is located on the left side of the Property Inspector.

Navigating Between Slides with Behaviors

Earlier in this chapter, you learned that, by default, the arrow keys and the spacebar control movement through the presentation. However, with the use of behaviors, you can exert far more control over how your presentation can be moved through. The great thing about Slide Navigation behaviors is that you can apply them to a button, Movie Clip, or even the screen itself.

To add a Slide Navigation behavior to your presentation, just follow these steps:

1. Select the button, Movie Clip, or slide that you want to trigger the behavior.

2. Open the Behaviors panel by choosing Window → Development Panels → Behaviors.

3. Click the Add Behavior button  in the upper-left corner of the Behavior panel.

4. When the pop-up menu opens, go to Screen, and then make a selection from one of the options in the subsequent submenu.

   • Go to First Slide jumps you to the first slide in the document.

   • Go to Last Slide jumps you to the final slide in the document.

   • Go to Next Slide moves you to the next slide in the sequence.

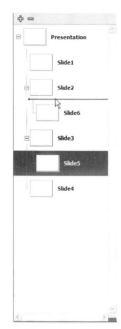

Figure 13.2

The blue preview bar that is displayed when you are moving a slide gives you an indication of the slides projected position within the document's hierarchy.

- Go to Previous Slide moves you to the previous slide in the sequence.
- Go to Slide lets you choose a specific slide to which the presentation jumps.

5. If the behavior requires that you select a target screen (Go To Slide), the Select Screen dialog box opens (see Figure 13.3). Select the target slide in the hierarchical tree.

6. Click the Relative radio button to use a relative target path or the Absolute radio button to use an absolute target path. When you are finished setting the target slide, click OK.

For more information on absolute and relative target paths, check out Chapter 20.

7. If you want to change the default Event that triggers the behavior, click the event for the newly inserted behavior and select a new event from the drop-down menu.

It's important to remember that the available Events will depend on the specific item (button, Movie Clip, or slide) to which you attached the behavior. See Chapter 14 to learn more about Events.

Creating Slide Transitions with Behaviors

A little earlier in this chapter, you learned that you don't have to settle for the default Plain Jane transitions you get when working with a Slides document. With the help of behaviors, you can add some cool slide transitions that add spice and visual interest to your presentation. Let's take a look at how:

1. With the Screen Outline pane open (Window → Screens), select the slide you want to add the transition to.

2. Open the Behaviors panel by choosing Window → Development Panels → Behaviors.

3. Click the Add Behavior button ⚛ in the upper-left corner of the Behavior panel.

4. When the pop-up menu opens, select Screen → Transition to open the Transitions dialog box.

5. Select a specific transition from the Transitions list box on the left side of the Transitions dialog box. Notice that an animated preview of the selected transition is displayed just below the Transitions list box.

6. From here, you need to determine whether the transition is applied when the slide appears or when it disappears. Click the In radio button to play the transition as the slide appears or the Out radio button to play the transition as the slide disappears.

7. Enter a value (in seconds) into the Duration field to determine how long the transition lasts.

8. Select an option from the Easing drop-down menu—remember, you can see a preview of your transition just below the Transitions list box.

9. At this point, depending on the particular transition you selected, you might have to set additional parameters, all of which will appear in the lower-left corner of the Transitions dialog box.

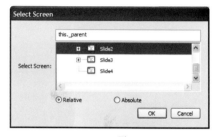

10. When you're finished setting the properties of your transition, click OK.

11. If you want to change the default Event that triggers the transition, click the event for the newly inserted behavior and select a new event from the drop-down menu.

Figure 13.3

The Select Screen dialog box allows you to set the target screen of a behavior.

Adding Content to Slides

Now that you've seen how to work with slides, how do you add content to them? It's simple: You just click a slide and add content as you would in a regular Flash movie. Animation, audio, symbols, buttons, Movie Clips, text, bitmaps. Anything you can add to a regular Flash movie, you can add to a Slides-based movie.

> While you can add lots of animation to any of your slides just as you would with a regular Flash movie, you'll need to expand the Timeline (which, by default, gets collapsed when you create a new Slides document) before you begin animating.

If it helps, think of each slide as a mini Flash movie that is separate from all the other slides.

Inspirational Design Model

Founded in August 2000, Titoonic (`www.titoonic.dk`) is a creative web-production company located in Copenhagen, Denmark. Although the company specializes in all manner of web-based multimedia, it is best known for its 3D character animation and design. It has been responsible for the design and implementation of numerous 3D Flash characters whose implementation includes visual guides on websites, character-based Flash games, greeting cards, and "webisodes."

Founded by a group of highly creative individuals whose backgrounds include classical animation and graphical storytelling, Titoonic is pushing the boundaries of cutting-edge 3D Flash development with their extremely stylish and compelling 3D character design. Titoonic's website (see Figure 13.4) is incredibly well designed and features a healthy dose of zany charm—making a definite source of inspiration.

Figure 13.4

Titoonic

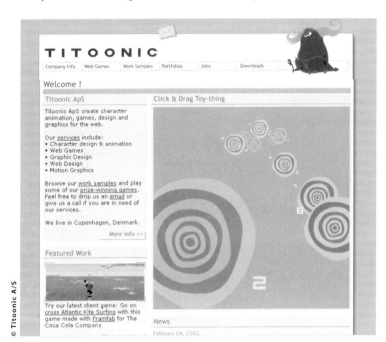

© Titoonic A/S

Animating a Sci-Fi Spectacular Space Scene

In this tutorial, you'll take all that knowledge you've amassed about animating in Flash and put it to good use.

Ever wanted to travel into space? Well, with the mighty power of Flash at your disposal, you'll create the next best thing: a sci-fi animated voyage through the cosmos. The animation will draw on all the techniques you've learned throughout Part III, including Timeline animations, Movie Clips, and scenes. The project itself will be broken up into six scenes. The first will be an animation of a rocket taking off from Earth. From there, you'll create four outer space scenes with the rocket blasting away from Earth, traveling through deep space, heading toward a planet, and landing on a mysterious planet. The last scene you create will add a little "Hollywood" to the animation.

 You can find all the images and files used in this tutorial in the Hands On 3 directory on this book's accompanying CD. You will also find a copy of the finished movie (`sci-fi.swf` and `sci-fi.fla`), so you can get an idea of what it might look like. However, as with all the tutorials in this book, the process is far more important than the final product.

Creating the Rocket Ship

Start off this tutorial by creating the first scene in the animation—your rocket ship blasting off from Earth:

1. Create a new file (File → New).

2. When the New Document dialog box opens, choose Flash Document from the Type list box.

3. Open the Document Properties dialog box (Modify → Document). Change the frame rate to **15** and make the document's background color black.

4. Click OK.

5. Now, double-click the existing layer's name. When it becomes editable, enter **sky**.

6. Select the Rectangle tool ⬜.

7. If it isn't open already, open the Property Inspector (Window → Properties) and set the Stroke Color to No Color by clicking the box with the red line through it just to the left of the color wheel in the Color Picker.

8. Set the Fill Color to a light blue (suitable for the sky).

9. Once you've set the Rectangle tool's fill and stroke, select the first keyframe of the sky layer and drag a rectangle that is either the exact same size as the Stage or slightly larger.

Why are we creating a blue rectangle? Why don't we just make the background of the movie the necessary light blue? Well, for any given movie, Flash applies the background color across all scenes. Because the majority of our scenes will take place in space (and therefore require a black background), we're using the rectangle tool to create a "false" background with the color we require for the intro scene.

10. Create a new layer by clicking the Add Layer button located in the lower-left corner of the Timeline or choosing Insert → Timeline → Layer.

11. Rename this newly created layer **ground**.

12. Once again, select the Rectangle tool from the Toolbox.

13. Click the Stroke Color swatch in the Toolbox and hit the No Color button, which is the box with a red line through it just to the left of the color wheel. This guarantees that the shape you draw won't have any stroke.

14. Now click the Fill Color swatch and choose a brown or green color (the rectangle will serve as the ground, so pick an appropriate color).

15. Select the first keyframe in the ground layer, and draw a rectangle that occupies about one-third of the bottom of the Stage. So far, things should look something like this.

As you can see, the landscape that we've created is not very interesting. To spruce up your movie, you might want to add additional elements (buildings and so on); it's up to you.

16. To keep things tidy, you need to name your scene. Open the Scene panel (Window → Design Panels → Scene), double-click Scene 1 (the only scene in your movie thus far), and type the name **takeoff**.

17. Now you need to import all the graphics you'll use in the scene. Choose Insert → New Symbol. When the Create New Symbol dialog box opens, make sure the Graphic radio button is selected, type **rocket ship** into the Name field, and click OK.

18. When the Symbol Editor opens, choose File → Import → Import to Stage. When the Import dialog box opens, navigate to the Hands On 3 folder on this book's accompanying CD, select `rocketship.swf`, and click Open. By doing this, you'll place the rocket ship graphic into the Symbol Editor. (Sometimes, when you import complex graphics, they'll appear as discrete parts as opposed to one graphic. As a result, you'll need to group all its elements. However, in the case of the rocket ship graphic, everything has already been grouped.)

If you don't see the image in the Symbol Editor, scroll down. Sometimes Flash doesn't place the imported graphic in the center of the Symbol Editor. All you need to do is click and drag the rocket ship to the center of the Symbol Editor. Remember, where you put the image in relation to the small crosshairs determines where its registration point is.

19. From here, you'll turn the static rocket ship graphic into a Movie Clip where flames shoot from its exhaust ports. First, select the rocket ship graphic in the Library and choose Properties from the Library Options pop-up menu. Alternatively, you can click the Properties icon at the bottom of the Library.

20. When the Symbol Properties dialog box opens, select the Movie Clip radio button and click OK. Now the static rocket ship graphic is a Movie Clip.

21. Now it's time to add some flames. Name the existing layer **rocket ship** (remember, you're still working on the Movie Clip within the Symbol Editor).

22. Create a new layer and call it **flames**.

23. Move the flames layer so that it is below the rocket ship layer.

24. Select frame 5 in the rocket ship layer and choose Insert → Timeline → Frame.

25. Select the second frame in the flames layer and choose Insert → Timeline → Keyframe.

The first keyframe will be left blank to simulate the rocket ship without any flames. The reason for this will become apparent when you put the scene together.

26. With the second keyframe selected (the one you just added), draw some flames coming from the exhaust of the rocket ship with the Pen tool. Use the Paint Bucket tool to fill the outline you've created with a red color. So far, your flames should look something like the image to the left.

27. Now click the third frame in the flames layer and choose Insert → Timeline → Keyframe.

28. Click the fourth frame in the flames layer and choose Insert → Timeline → Blank Keyframe.

For how to use the Pen tool or the Paint Bucket, see Chapter 4.

29. With the newly created blank keyframe selected, draw another set of flames coming from the rocket ship's exhaust. Make sure they are similar, but not identical, to the first set of the flames you drew, and fill them with an orange color using the Paint Bucket. They should look something like the image to the left.

30. Click the fifth frame in the flames layer and choose Insert → Timeline → Keyframe. By doing this, you've created a Movie Clip in which the flames you've drawn will alternate. Because the Movie Clip will loop indefinitely when it's used in the main Timeline, you'll get a simple (but effective) moving flame effect.

31. Now it's time to insert the rocket ship Movie Clip into the launch scene. If you are still in the Symbol Editor, switch back to the main Timeline by clicking the takeoff link in the Edit bar.

32. Insert a new layer and call it **rocket ship**.

33. With the first keyframe of the rocket ship layer selected, click and drag the rocket ship Movie Clip from the Library onto the Stage. Position it so that it is in the middle of the scene. So far, the scene should look something like this.

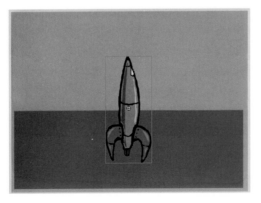

34. Now it's time to do some animating. Select frame 30 in the rocket ship layer and choose Insert → Timeline → Keyframe.

Remember you left the first keyframe in the flames layer blank when you were creating the rocket ship Movie Clip? Well, here is where that amazing foresight comes in. If you hadn't left that first keyframe blank, you would have had flames coming out of the rocket ship while it was simply sitting there. The blank keyframe gives the illusion of the rocket ship starting up.

35. Select frame 30 in the ground layer and choose Insert → Timeline → Frame or use the shortcut F5.

36. Select frame 30 in the rocket ship layer and choose Insert → Timeline → Keyframe.

37. Select frame 30 of the sky layer and choose Insert → Timeline → Frame.

38. With frame 30 in the rocket ship layer selected, move the rocket ship Movie Clip up until it's outside the Stage.

39. Select the first keyframe in the rocket ship layer and choose Insert → Timeline → Create Motion Tween. This creates a tweened animation in which the rocket ship flies up into the sky.

Instead of using the Create Motion Tween command, you could use the Transform Timeline Effect to move the rocket ship's position.

40. To add a little more detail, select the first keyframe in the rocket ship tween, open the Property Inspector (Window → Properties), and set the Ease to **–100**. This gives the illusion that the rocket ship starts off slowly but then picks up speed as it rises.

41. Now, save the file by choosing File → Save. When the Save dialog box opens, navigate to the location on your hard drive where you want save the file, enter **sci-fi** into the File Name field, and click Save.

You can test your movie by hitting Return/Enter. If you want the rocket ship Movie Clip to play, select Control → Test Movie.

Speeding Away from Earth

Now that you've created the first scene in your animation, you can create the second one. You'll be continuing your space voyage by creating a scene in which the rocket ship speeds into space with Earth receding in the background. As it will add another dimension to the scene, you'll engineer a little visual trickery to simulate the illusion of depth and distance:

1. Make sure you have the sci-fi file open.

2. Open the Scene panel (Window → Design Panels → Scene) and add a second scene by clicking the Add Scene button (at the bottom of the Scene panel) or choosing Insert → Scene.

3. Double-click the name of the scene you've just created and enter **departure** in the field.

4. If it isn't selected already, select the departure scene.

5. Now you'll create the stars that will be scattered throughout the space portions of your animation. Choose Insert → New Symbol.

6. When the Create New Symbol dialog box opens, enter **star** in the Name field, select the Graphic radio button, and click OK.

7. When the Symbol Editor opens, use the Ellipse tool to draw a small yellow circle. Make sure the circle's stroke is also yellow. As with much of this tutorial, you are certainly welcome to create something a little fancier for your stars. However, because the stars are meant to be in the background, it might be wise to rely on something understated.

8. When you've finished creating your star (which you'll use repeatedly in the space scene), return to the main Timeline by clicking the departure link in the Edit bar.

9. Now import the graphic you'll be using for Earth. Choose Insert → New Symbol. When the Create New Symbol dialog box opens, enter **earth** in the Name field, select the Graphic radio button, and click OK.

10. When the Symbol Editor opens, choose File → Import → Import to Stage.

11. When the Import dialog box opens, navigate to the Hands On 3 directory on this book's accompanying CD, locate the earth.swf file, and click Open.

12. Now you're set to start adding assets to your scene. Use the Edit Scene button (in the right portion of the Edit bar) to switch the departure scene.

13. Change the single existing layer's name to **stars**.

14. Open the Library (Window → Library), select the first keyframe in the stars layer, and repeatedly drag the Star symbol onto the Stage. The number of stars you place on the Stage is totally up to you.

15. Now add an additional layer to the main Timeline by choosing Insert → Layer or clicking the Insert Layer button in the bottom-right corner of the Timeline.

16. Double-click the layer's name and type **earth**. Alternatively, you can double-click the layer's icon (just to the left of the name itself) to open the Layer Properties dialog box and enter **earth** in the Name field.

17. With the Library open (Window → Library), drag the Earth symbol onto the Stage. Position it so that it's located in the bottom-left corner of the Stage. So far, your scene should look something like the image to the right.

18. Now create a third layer and call it **rocket ship**.

19. Select the first keyframe in the rocket ship layer, open the Library (Window → Library), and drag the rocket ship Movie Clip (which you created in the previous section of this tutorial) onto the Stage.

20. The rocket ship Movie Clip's current size and orientation isn't appropriate for the current scene. As a result, you'll have to fiddle with it a bit. First, select it and choose Modify → Transform → Flip Horizontal.

21. Select the Free Transform tool ⊡ from the Toolbox, click the rocket ship Movie Clip, and select the Rotate and Skew button in the Options section of the Toolbox.

22. Rotate the rocket ship Movie Clip roughly 45° clockwise. This gives your rocket ship a decent trajectory as it speeds away from Earth.

> Alternatively, you can simply use the Transform panel (Window → Design Panels → Transform). Just click the Rotate radio button and enter **45** in the Rotate Value field.

23. Now, with the first keyframe still selected, use either the Free Transform tool or the Transform panel to shrink the Rocket Ship symbol so it's small. By doing this, you create the illusion that the rocket ship is far away at the start of the animation. Later, you'll add to the illusion of depth and distance by having the rocket ship "fly toward" the viewer.

24. Select the Rocket Ship symbol with the Arrow tool and position it so that it's somewhere over the middle of the Earth symbol. So far, your scene should look something like the image to the right (note the *very* small Rocket Ship symbol in the middle of the Earth symbol).

25. Now that you've placed all the elements you'll use in the scene, it's time to do some animating. Select frame 35 in the stars layer and choose Insert → Timeline → Frame.

26. Select frame 35 in the earth layer and choose Insert → Timeline → Frame.

27. Select frame 35 in the rocket ship layer and choose Insert → Timeline → Keyframe.

28. Select the keyframe that you just created in the rocket ship layer. Click and drag the Rocket Ship symbol to a location just outside the top-right corner of the Stage.

29. With the Free Transform tool or the Transform panel, increase the Rocket Ship symbol to larger than its original size. Once you've scaled the symbol, make sure that all of it is off the Stage. Once animated, this will create the illusion that the rocket ship flies from Earth past your point of view. At this point, frame 35 should look something like this.

30. Select the first keyframe in the rocket ship layer, and choose Insert → Timeline → Create Motion Tween. This creates a tweened animation of the rocket ship increasing in size as it "flies" past the camera. However, depending on where the rocket ship is in the final keyframe, the animation could look a little bit funny, as if the rocket ship were flying without its nose pointed exactly forward. You'll remedy this by adding a straight path that the rocket ship will move along.

31. Select the first keyframe in the rocket ship layer and click the Add Motion Guide button ✦ at the bottom-left corner of the main Timeline.

32. Select the first keyframe in the motion guide layer (which appears directly above the rocket ship layer) and use the Line tool to draw a trajectory from the middle of the Earth symbol to a few centimeters past where your rocket ship ends up in the final keyframe.

> Because the scene's background is black, you will have some problems with the line (whose default color is also black) getting lost. To avoid this, either change the stroke color before you draw the line (by using the Stroke Color Picker in the Toolbox's Colors section) or change the background color of your movie temporarily by choosing Modify → Document and clicking the Background Color swatch.

33. With the first keyframe in the rocket ship layer selected, click and drag the small Rocket Ship symbol so that it snaps to the start of the linear motion path. Because the Rocket Ship symbol is small, you might want to use the Zoom tool 🔍 to get a better look at the area you're working with.

34. Now click the last keyframe in the layer and click and drag the larger Rocket Ship symbol so that it snaps onto the end of the motion path.

> If you have trouble snapping the rocket ship's registration point to the path, make sure Snap to Objects is turned on (View → Snapping → Snap to Objects). Also, you might have to click the registration point and then hold your mouse down for a second before dragging to make the snapping registration point appear.

35. Select the first keyframe in the layer and open the Property Inspector (Window → Properties).

36. Click the Orient to Path check box and set Easing to **-100**. By doing this, the rocket ship will always point in the direction of the path. By changing the Easing, the rocket ship will start off slowly and gain speed as it travels along the path, furthering the illusion of depth and distance.

37. It's time to animate Earth receding into the distance. Click keyframe 35 in the earth layer and choose Insert → Timeline → Keyframe.

38. With the newly created keyframe selected, click and drag the Earth symbol into the work area, just outside the bottom-left corner of the Stage. With keyframe 35 still selected, use the Free Transform tool or the Transform panel to shrink the Earth symbol to about 25 percent of its former size. When animated, this creates the impression that Earth is moving off into the distance.

39. With the first keyframe of the earth layer selected, choose Insert → Timeline → Create Motion Tween.

You've just finished the second scene in the animation! To test it, simply hit Return/ Enter. If you want the rocket ship Movie Clip to work properly, select Control → Test Scene. If you want to view the entire animation thus far (including Scene 1), go to Control → Test Movie.

Zipping through Space

Now that you've created the scene in which the rocket ship zips away from Earth, you can start on the third scene in the animation, the rocket ship careening through space:

1. Make sure you have the sci-fi file open.

2. Open the Scene panel (Window → Design Panels → Scene), and add a third scene by clicking the Add Scene button **+** (at the bottom of the Scene panel) or by choosing Insert → Scene.

3. Double-click the name of the scene that you've just created, and enter **travel** in the field.

4. Select the single layer in the Timeline, and change its name to **stars**.

5. Now, with the stars layer still selected, click frame 30 and choose Insert → Timeline → Frame.

6. Select the first blank keyframe in the stars layer, open the Library, and click and drag as many instances of the Star symbol as you want onto the Stage.

7. From here, you'll need to add some "texture" to the scene by including a planet for the rocket ship to pass by. Choose Insert → New Symbol.

8. When the Create New Symbol dialog box opens, enter **planet1** in the Name field, click the Graphic radio button, and click OK.

9. When the Symbol Editor opens, choose File → Import → Import to Stage.

10. When the Import dialog box opens, navigate to the Hands On 3 directory on this book's accompanying CD and select `planet1.swf`.

11. Remember to click and drag the graphic to the registration point marker in the middle of the Symbol Editor.

12. Return to the main Timeline. From there, create a new layer by clicking the Insert Layer button in the bottom-left corner of the Timeline or by choosing Insert → Timeline → Layer, and name it **planet**.

13. With the first keyframe of the planet layer selected, click and drag the planet1 symbol from the Library onto the right portion of the Stage. At this point, your scene should look something like the image to the left.

14. Now you can add some movement to the planet. With the planet layer selected, click frame 30 and choose Insert → Timeline → Keyframe.

15. Select the final keyframe in the planet layer (the one you just created), and click and drag the planet1 symbol about four centimeters (1.5 inches) to the left.

16. Now, select the first keyframe in the planet layer and choose Insert → Timeline → Create Motion Tween. By adding a little motion to the planet, you'll create the illusion that the rocket ship is traveling at high speed.

17. Now for the actual rocket ship. Create a new layer in the main Timeline and call it **rocket ship**.

18. Select the first keyframe in the rocket ship layer and drag the rocket ship Movie Clip from the Library into the work area just to the left of the Stage.

19. Use the Free Transform tool or the Transform panel to orient the rocket ship horizontally. So far, your scene should look something like this.

20. Now, with the rocket ship layer selected, click frame 30 and choose Insert → Timeline → Keyframe.

21. Click the final keyframe in the rocket ship layer (the one you just created) and click and drag the rocket ship Movie Clip to the other side of the Stage into the work area.

22. Select the first keyframe in the rocket ship layer and choose Insert → Timeline → Create Motion Tween.

You've just completed the animation of the rocket ship hurtling though space. To test it, simply hit Return/Enter. If you want the rocket ship Movie Clip to work properly, you'll have to select Control → Test Scene. If you want to view the entire animation thus far (including Scene 1 and 2), choose Control → Test Movie.

Approaching Planet X

Now it's time to create the sequence in the animation in which your little rocket ship flies toward its intended destination, the mysterious Planet X:

1. Make sure you have the sci-fi file open.

2. If it isn't open already, open the Scene panel (Window → Design Panels → Scene) and add a fourth scene by clicking the Add Scene button **+** (at the bottom of the Scene panel) or by choosing Insert → Scene.

3. Double-click the name of the scene that you just created and enter **descent** in the field.

4. Select the single layer in the Timeline and change its name to **stars**. Now, with the stars layer still selected, click frame 30 and choose Insert → Timeline Frame.

5. Select the first blank keyframe in the stars layer, open the Library, and click and drag as many instances of the Star symbol as you want onto the Stage.

6. From here, you'll need to add the planet to the scene. Choose Insert → New Symbol.

7. When the Create New Symbol dialog box opens, enter **planet2** in the Name field, click the Graphic radio button, and click OK.

8. When the Symbol Editor opens, choose File → Import → Import to Stage.

9. When the Import dialog box opens, navigate to the Hands On 3 directory on this book's accompanying CD and select `planet2.swf`.

10. Remember to click and drag the graphic to the registration point marker in the middle of the Symbol Editor.

11. Return to the main Timeline. From there, create a new layer by clicking the Insert Layer button in the bottom-right corner of the Timeline or by choosing Insert → Layer, and name it **planet x**.

12. With the first keyframe of the planet x layer selected, drag the planet2 symbol from the Library to the lower-right portion of the Stage. As the symbol is fairly large, use the Free Transform tool or the Transform panel to shrink it to about 3 centimeters (1 inch) across, or about 123×123 pixels. So far, your scene should look something like this.

13. Select frame 30 in the stars layer and choose Insert → Timeline → Frame or use the shortcut F5.

14. Now click frame 30 in the planet x layer and choose Insert → Timeline → Keyframe.

15. With the last keyframe selected in the planet x layer, select the planet2 symbol and increase its size (with either the Free Transform tool or the Transform panel) to the point where it dominates much of the Stage. At this point, the scene should look something like this. (*top right*)

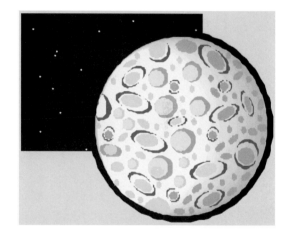

16. Now, with the first keyframe in the planet x layer selected, choose Insert → Timeline → Create Motion Tween.

17. At this point, you can start working on the rocket ship itself. Create a new layer and call it **rocket ship**.

18. Select the first keyframe in the rocket ship layer and drag the rocket ship Movie Clip from the Library onto the Stage. Position it so that it's in the work area just outside the top-left corner of the Stage.

19. Use either the Rotate tool or the Transform panel to rotate the rocket ship Movie Clip so that it's pointing toward the planet2 symbol. The result should be something like this. (*center right*)

20. Now, with the rocket ship layer still selected, click frame 30 and choose Insert → Timeline → Keyframe.

21. Select the keyframe that you just created and move the rocket ship Movie Clip over the middle of the planet. Then, use the Scale tool or the Transform panel to reduce its size substantially. The result should be something like this (note the *very* small rocket ship symbol). (*bottom right*)

22. Select the first frame in the rocket ship layer and choose Insert → Timeline → Create Motion Tween.

23. Much as in the case when you created the first scene, your rocket ship's movement might look a little off. To correct this, you'll create a straight motion path for it to follow. Select the first keyframe in the rocket ship layer and click the Add Motion Guide button ✦ at the bottom-left of the main Timeline.

24. Select the first keyframe in the motion guide layer (which appears directly above the rocket ship layer) and use the Line tool to draw a trajectory from where the rocket ship starts to where it ends in the final keyframe. Remember, you could run into problems if the Line tool draws a black line along the black background.

25. With the first keyframe in the rocket ship layer selected, click and drag the large Rocket Ship symbol so that it snaps to the start of the linear motion path.

26. Now click the last keyframe in the layer and click and drag the smaller Rocket Ship symbol so that it snaps onto the end of the motion path. You'll probably need to zoom in because the rocket ship is so small.

27. Select the first keyframe in the layer and open the Property Inspector (Window → Properties).

28. Click the Orient to Path check box and set Easing to **100**. By doing this, the rocket ship always points in the direction of the path. By changing the Easing, the rocket ship starts off fast and slows down as it travels along the path, furthering the illusion of depth and distance.

You've just finished the animation in which your rocket ship approaches Planet X. To test it, hit Return/Enter. If you want the rocket ship Movie Clip to work properly, choose Control → Test Scene. If you want to view the entire animation thus far (including the other scenes), select Control → Test Movie.

Landing on Planet X

Now that you've animated your rocket ship approaching the mysterious Planet X, you need to animate the scene in which your intrepid explorer actually lands.

1. Make sure you have the sci-fi file open.

2. If it isn't open already, open the Scene panel (Window → Design Panels → Scene) and add a fourth scene by clicking the Add Scene button **+** or by choosing Insert → Scene.

3. Double-click the name of the scene that you just created and enter **landing** in the field.

4. Rename the existing layer **alien landscape**.

5. Select the first keyframe of the alien landscape layer and choose File → Import → Import to Stage.

6. When the Import dialog box opens, navigate to the Hands On 3 directory on this book's accompanying CD, and select alien_landscape.swf.

The imported alien landscape background is premade so that you don't have to go through the fuss and muss of creating it yourself. However, if you want to see something else on the surface of the mysterious Planet X, feel free to create it yourself.

7. Position the imported background so that it overlaps the Stage exactly. At this point, your scene should look something like this. (*top right*)

8. Insert a new layer and call it **rocket ship**.

9. With the first keyframe of the rocket ship layer selected, click and drag the rocket ship Movie Clip from the Library (Window → Library) onto the Stage. Position it so that it is in the Workspace just above the top of the Stage. At this point, the scene should look something like this. (*bottom right*)

10. Now it's time to do some animating. Select frame 30 in the rocket ship layer and choose Insert → Timeline → Keyframe.

11. Select frame 30 in the alien landscape layer and choose Insert → Timeline → Frame or use the shortcut F5.

12. With frame 30 in the rocket ship layer selected, move the rocket ship Movie Clip up until it's "sitting" on the ground of the alien landscape.

13. Select the first keyframe in the rocket ship layer and choose Insert → Timeline → Create Motion Tween. This creates a tweened animation in which the rocket ship lands on Planet X.

14. To add a little more detail, select the first keyframe in the rocket ship tween, open the Property Inspector (Window → Properties), and set the Ease to **100**. This gives the illusion that the rocket ship starts off fast, but then slows down as it lands.

Adding Some Hollywood Glamour

You're just about there! You've finished the first five scenes in your animation. In the final scene, you'll add a bit of cheesy Hollywood to cap it all off:

1. Make sure you have the `sci-fi` movie open.

2. If it isn't open already, open the Scene panel (Window → Design Panels → Scene) and add a sixth scene by clicking the Add Scene button or by choosing Insert → Scene.

3. Double-click the name of the scene that you just created and enter **finale** in the field.

4. Choose Insert → New Symbol.

5. When the Create New Symbol dialog box opens, type **To Be Continued** in the Name field, click the Graphic radio button, and click OK.

6. Select the Text tool from the Toolbox.

7. *Before* you add any text, open the Property Inspector (Window → Properties).

8. When the Property Inspector opens, choose a font from the Font drop-down menu. (To preserve the effect, choose something big and blocky.) Then enter a size (make it large) in the Size field.

9. Because the background of your movie is black, choose a light color for the text such as white.

10. Now, without clicking your cursor anywhere else, type **To Be Continued…** in the text box.

11. When you're finished, click your cursor anywhere outside the text box. Click and drag the text to the center of the Symbol Editor.

> If the edges of your text are jaggy, select the text and choose View → Preview Mode → Anti-alias Text.

12. To create a dramatic fade-in text effect, switch back to the main Timeline by clicking the finale link in the Edit bar and select the first keyframe in the scene's single layer. (If you want, you can name the layer something distinct. However, because it will be the only one in the scene, it's not necessary.)

13. Drag the To Be Continued symbol from the Library onto the middle of the Stage.

14. Click frame 15 and choose Insert → Timeline → Keyframe.

15. Select the first keyframe in the layer and then select the actual text symbol itself. From there, if it isn't open already, open the Property Inspector (Window → Properties).

16. Choose Alpha from the Color drop-down menu and enter **0** in the Alpha Value field.

17. Now click the first keyframe in the layer and choose Insert → Timeline → Create Motion Tween. This creates the fade-in text effect.

Congratulations, you've completed the final scene in the animation! To view the entire animation, select Control → Test Movie.

> If you want to have the animation stop at the end (instead of simply looping over and over), add a stop( ) frame action. To learn more about adding frame actions, see Chapter 14.

PART IV

Adding Basic Interactivity

One *of the more elusive terms we hear as developers of digital media is* interactivity. *This word appears frequently in books, tutorials, and articles, and is usually used to qualify or categorize the media we produce. It has become a sort of buzzword, such that in many circles,* interactive *equals* cool. *In its defense, though, many things (digital and otherwise) are interactive and require this cyber-savvy stamp of approval. One fear, however, is that the word is used so often that either it has lost its meaning or its meaning has been diluted.*

So what exactly is interactivity? *Merriam-Webster's Collegiate Dictionary defines* interactive *as "of, relating to, or being a two-way electronic communication system…that involves a user's orders (as for information or merchandise) or responses…." Well, that gets us started—a two-way communication between a person and a machine, but how does this relate to Flash? That's where you come in. As a developer of Flash movies, you are the "ghost in the machine," the person responsible for determining the nature of communication between your movies and your audience. Flash movies can respond to audience input in whatever manner you define; your task is to decide how that response will be delivered. This part of the book opens the floodgates to the vast world of interactivity. You will begin to understand the techniques that afford communication between your audience and your Flash creations.*

CHAPTER 14

Adding Interactivity with ActionScript Behaviors

Up to this point, you have used Flash as a tool for creating low-bandwidth graphics and animation. But you can also use Flash to transform these elements into dynamic components of learning applications, nonlinear stories, and interactive interfaces. It's not difficult to add this kind of functionality to your Flash movie, and it's all done with the help of behaviors.

Behaviors are one of the many new features added to the release of Flash MX 2004 and MX Professional 2004. Behaviors are ready-made sets of commands written in Action-Script, Flash's object-oriented programming language. In the most basic sense, behaviors tell a Flash movie how to perform. With a few simple menu selections, you can use behaviors to control many aspects of your Flash movies, including Timeline navigation, linking to URLs on the Web, loading and managing media assets and more. Behaviors are especially helpful to new Flash users as they provide a "hands-off" means of adding interactivity and enhancing the functionality of your movies.

This chapter focuses on using ActionScript behaviors and includes these topics:

- **What ActionScript is**

- **The role of ActionScript behaviors**

- **Object and frame behaviors**

- **Mouse events**

- **Behaviors for interactivity and navigation**

Understanding ActionScript

ActionScript is one of the more dynamic features that Flash offers its users; it allows you to add interactivity to your Flash movie. ActionScript can enable your audience to control the playback of your movie with mouse clicks, keystrokes, and custom menus. It also allows you as the designer to build a movie that plays in precisely the manner you desire.

To use ActionScript in Flash, you don't have to be a programmer. If you plan to get into intermediate or advanced scripting, understanding programming can help, but it's not essential. For more advanced users, Flash MX 2004 and MX Pro 2004 provides a comprehensive, intuitive interface called the Actions panel, which allows you to compose ActionScripts and place them in your movie. If you prefer not to write ActionScript on your own, behaviors can automate the process.

So, what is ActionScript? It's an object-oriented programming language that is native to the Flash environment. *Object-oriented* means that scripts are attached to "objects" or elements of your movie. When those objects encounter a particular event while the movie is running, their script is executed. For example:

```
on(press){
    gotoAndPlay("nextStop");
}
```

In this script, the press mouse event will cause the movie to jump ahead to a frame label named "nextStop" and continue playing from that position. Or, in more general terms, the event cues an action that changes the playback of the movie.

The relationship between events and actions is a fundamental concept of object-oriented programming. If you are new to scripting languages or have never seen any kind of programming, this might look a little weird, but don't be discouraged. As you become more familiar with ActionScript, its syntax and structure will seem less cryptic.

To write Actionscripts for your Flash movie, you must first become familiar with the Actions panel. See Chapter 17 to learn more about the details of hand-coding in your Flash movies. If you prefer to let Flash handle the scripting workload for you, then you must first be introduced to behaviors.

What Behaviors Are

In previous Flash versions 5 and MX (or Flash 6), users who didn't want to hand-code ActionScript were able to work with the Actions panel in what was called Normal mode. Normal mode provided a means to write ActionScript through a series of menus, check boxes, and text fields. It was a kind of form for ActionScript: fill it out and your script would be assembled. With the latest release of Flash, this is no longer the case.

Flash MX 2004 and MX Pro 2004 facilitate easy, hands-off ActionScripting through behaviors. Like Normal mode in Flash 5 and MX, behaviors allow users to control their movies with ActionScript with a minimal amount of typing. Just as ActionScript has the Actions panel, behaviors have the Behaviors panel (see Figure 14.1). You select a behavior from a menu, choose your options, and click OK; the behavior does the rest. Whereas Normal mode required much more attention and time in creating a script, behaviors have already been written. They simply rewrite themselves to fit your particular needs and are added to your movie as a block of ActionScript.

Navigating the Behaviors Panel

The Behaviors panel is your interface for adding ActionScript to a Flash movie without the hassles of typing everything by hand. Through a series of cascading menus and dialog boxes, you can select a behavior, define any required parameters, and add it to your movie.

To display the Behaviors panel, select Window → Development Panels → Behaviors or press Shift+F3.

The Behaviors panel is a completely new feature of Flash MX 2004 and MX Pro 2004. If you have any experience with Macromedia Dreamweaver MX, you will be right at home, for their design and functionality are very similar. The anatomy of the Behaviors panel can be seen in Figure 14.1.

Following are descriptions of the Behaviors panel's features:

Behaviors panel pop-up menu This menu provides access to options that change the display of the Behaviors panel.

Add Behavior button Click this button to choose from the cascading menu of available behaviors.

Delete Behavior button Click this button to remove a behavior.

Current Selection field This area will display the name of the currently selected symbol or frame.

Move behaviors up or down These buttons allow you to reorder behaviors within the panel.

Behaviors pane Behaviors and related events are displayed in this area of the panel. This area is divided into two columns: Events and Actions.

Events Lists the handler that will initiate each behavior.

Actions Describes the task the behavior will perform.

Figure 14.1

The Behaviors panel provides an interface for selecting and customizing behaviors.

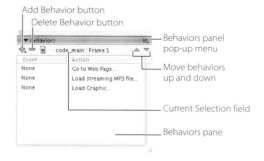

Working with Object Behaviors

Behaviors can be attached to two kinds of objects in Flash: buttons and Movie Clips. The attached behavior is executed when the object receives an event message. These messages generally come in the form of mouse interactions or other kinds of user input directed at the button or Movie Clip. When you attach a behavior, you specify the event trigger for each object.

Behaviors are attached to buttons and Movie Clips because they are the interactive components of your Flash movie. As objects, they can receive mouse clicks, data, and other kinds of information while the movie is running. The structure that you create with objects and their attached behaviors determines the way your audience interacts with your movie.

In Flash, it's important to remember that button and Movie Clip objects are stored in the Library as *symbols*. Symbols are a special part of any Flash movie. Each time they are used, they stand alone as an individual unique occurrence, or *instance,* of the symbol. (For details about symbols and instances, see Chapter 7.)

You can think of an instance as a copy of a symbol. Any changes made to an instance will not affect the original symbol or any other instances of that symbol. This characteristic remains true when you attach behaviors to a symbol instance. Any behaviors applied to an instance are available only at the time the instance occurs in a movie. This means that behaviors remain exclusive to the instance where they are attached.

For behaviors to be executed, however, they must first be triggered by some kind of event in the movie. In ActionScript (and many other object-oriented languages), these trigger events are monitored by *event handlers.* Because behaviors are prewritten Action-Script statements, they must follow the same guidelines and use handlers to help watch for the events that trigger them.

Event Handlers

Object-oriented languages work in a cause-and-effect manner. Where an ActionScript command produces the "effect" or the result of a script, an event handler identifies the "cause" (a mouse click, for instance) that pulls the trigger. For example, consider the following script:

```
on(thisEvent){
    doAnAction;
}
```

Of course, this code is only fictional ActionScript. The handler, on, *is* part of Action-Script. However, there is no event named thisEvent, and there is no such statement as doAnAction. This bit of imaginary code provides a simple model for the sequence of events and ActionScript statements. The event handler is almost always the first statement. The handler on is followed in parentheses by the name of the event that will set the script into motion. This can be interpreted as "when the following event occurs…". The handler creates the first part of a sentence that will tell your Flash movie to do something. That "something" is filled in by an ActionScript statement. The entire script can be better understood in sentence form: "When the following event occurs, doAnAction." Action-Script provides handlers for many different kinds of events. For example, each operation your audience can perform with a mouse is an event, and ActionScript provides event handlers for press, release, rollOver, and so on. We will discuss the specifics of each handler later in this chapter.

As a designer or developer of interactive media, you need to understand when and how each event occurs in the context of the movie and how each handler will affect the way your audience will experience your movie. If you were creating an interactive music mixer in Flash, what mouse-event handler would you want to use for buttons to turn the tracks off and on: a mouse button press or a mouse button release? Our vote would be for a press event because when you deal with a music mixer, you want to be sure that the person playing it can sync the audio tracks and maintain a steady beat the entire time. The press event is easier to time rhythmically because it's similar to hitting a drum. The press event is more like actually playing an instrument. Similarly, if you want something to appear when a person's mouse touches a particular button, you would use a rollOver event. To enable drag-and-drop functionality, you can use press to pick up something and drag it and release to put it down.

There are many situations where you will find that some event handlers are more appropriate than others. With thoughtful planning and consideration, it's simple to choose the event handlers that allow your behaviors to execute in the best way possible.

Working with Frame Behaviors

As you've probably guessed, frame behaviors are ActionScript statements that are attached to a frame in your Flash movie. Specifically, behaviors must be attached to a special kind of frame called a *keyframe*. Keyframes are used to signify important changes in the Flash movie for both animation and ActionScript. (To read more about keyframe concepts and animation, see Chapter 10.)

When a behavior is attached to a keyframe, the frame shows a small letter *a* in the Timeline (see Figure 14.2).

You attach behaviors to frames to cause your movie to play back in a particular manner. Take, for example, the Go To and Play behavior. It tells the Timeline to skip to a frame number or label and play from that point. The ActionScript for the behavior reads as follows:

Figure 14.2

Frame behavior in the Timeline

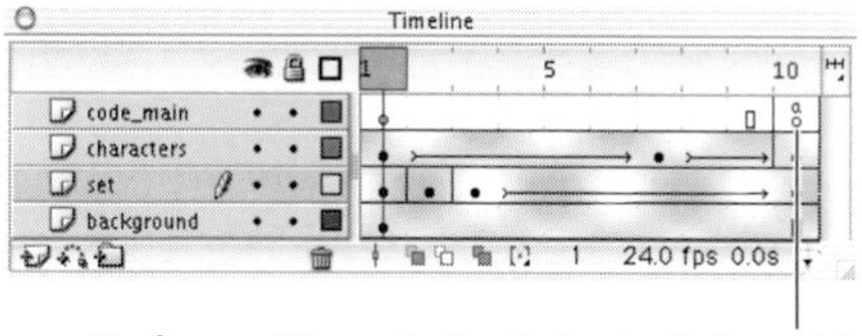

Keyframe with an attached behavior in frame 10

```
this.gotoAndPlay(1);
```

If you attached this behavior to frame 10 of a Flash movie, it would create a playback loop. When the movie reached frame 10, it would immediately be sent back to frame 1 and told to continue playing. The cycle would persist until another behavior told the movie to either stop playing or do something else.

The greatest difference you will notice between behaviors attached to objects and behaviors attached to frames is the absence of an event handler. The Behaviors panel will reflect this and display "None" in the Events column. Frame behaviors require no specific handler because they are executed when the frame is played in the Flash movie.

Using ActionScript Behaviors

Now that we have discussed the basic concepts involving behaviors, we can move on to the good part: implementing them in your Flash movie. To use behaviors in your movie, you must attach them to either an object or a frame. This is done through a simple process of selecting the object or frame, choosing the behavior you want to use, and then defining any parameters that the behavior requires.

You use behaviors to control your movie so that it behaves exactly as you want. Behaviors can be used to control interactivity, to "listen" for user input, to cue or load media assets, and to control the flow and direction of movie playback—just about anything that affects the way your movie is presented to the audience. Behaviors make Flash less of an animation program and more of an authoring environment for interactive media applications. Here are just a few possibilities that behaviors can offer your Flash movie:

- Create interactive navigation.
- Control sound and video.
- Load external JPEG images.
- Link to HTML pages on the Internet or send e-mail.
- Communicate with host applications or other Flash movies.

Attaching Object Behaviors

Attaching a behavior to either a button object or a Movie Clip object is a fairly simple and straightforward process. Here are just a few things to keep in mind along the way:

- You must first select an object in the Timeline (or on the Stage) before you can attach a behavior to it. If you call upon the Behaviors panel and have no object selected, the behavior will be attached to a frame.
- Behaviors are attached to an instance of a button or Movie Clip symbol; all other instances of the object will be left untouched.

It's important to test a behavior after it has been attached. In Editing mode, only simple navigational behaviors such as Go To and Play work properly. To test a behavior, you must test your movie. Select Control → Test Movie and try out the newly applied behavior. Here are the basic steps for attaching a behavior:

1. Select the object in the Timeline or on the Stage.

2. To open the Behaviors panel, choose Window → Development Panels → Behaviors from the menu bar or press Shift+F3.

3. The Behaviors panel appears. Select the following:

   A behavior Choose from the list of behaviors in the Add Behavior menu.

   Behavior parameters Many behaviors require specific parameters so that they function correctly. If
   you choose a behavior of this sort, a dialog box
   (such as Rewind Video) will open and prompt you
   for further information.

   An event handler Object behaviors (attached to
   buttons and Movie Clips) will have a default handler. If necessary, you can change it in the Events
   column of the Behaviors pane.

> You can attach multiple behaviors to a single object. To do this, repeat steps 1–3 for each new behavior.

To learn how to attach specific behaviors and define their parameters, see the section "Using Behaviors for Basic Movie Navigation and Interactivity" later in this chapter.

Mouse Events

When you attach a behavior to a button or Movie Clip object, Flash automatically assigns a mouse-event handler. This handler determines what event within the movie will execute the statements(s) contained in the script. In most cases, the default handler provided by Flash will do the trick, but there might be times when you must change the mouse event to accommodate a particular kind of interaction.

Figure 14.3

Event handlers are listed in the Behaviors panel.

To change the mouse-event handler for a behavior:

1. Select the object with the event handler that needs to be changed.

2. Open the Behaviors panel and locate the event you want to change.

3. Click the name of the event. A small drop-down menu opens beside the name. Click the menu's triangle to reveal its contents (see Figure 14.3).

4. Choose a new event from the menu by clicking its name.

Following are the names and descriptions of the ActionScript event handlers for behaviors:

Press Cues an object's script when the mouse button is pressed while the cursor is over the object.

Release Cues an object's script when the mouse button is released while the cursor is over the object. `Release` is the default mouse event.

Release Outside Cues an object's script when the mouse button is released and the cursor is *not* over an object.

Key Press Doesn't involve the mouse at all. Executed when the key listed in the adjacent field is pressed.

Roll Over Cues an object's script when the cursor moves over (or within) the object.

Roll Out The `rollOut` event cues an object's script when the cursor moves away from (or leaves) the bounds of the object.

Drag Over Involves a combination of two different mouse behaviors: a drag and a rollover. The mouse is pressed over an object, the mouse is dragged outside the object, and the script is finally cued when the mouse is dragged back over the object.

Drag Out The `dragOut` event cues an object's script when the mouse is pressed over the object and dragged outside its bounds.

Remember that any of these event handlers can be used to cue multiple behaviors for a single object. This means that any one object can have more than one behavior attached to it. For example, if you were to attach two Go To and Play behaviors, the ActionScript would look something like this:

```
on(press){
    this.gotoAndStop(2);
}
on(release){
    this.gotoAndStop(3);
}
```

In this script, a button tells a movie to stop at frame 2 when the mouse is pressed, and then go to frame 3 when the mouse is released.

For a sample movie that demonstrates each handler in context, see the movies `Handler-Man.swf` and `HandlerMan.fla` on this book's companion CD.

Attaching Frame Behaviors

Frame behaviors provide another kind of ActionScript that you can use in a Flash movie to control the way it plays back. When a keyframe with an attached behavior is encountered in the Timeline, that behavior is executed and the movie reacts accordingly. For more specifics on frame behaviors, refer to the section "Working with Frame Behaviors" earlier in this chapter.

Frame behaviors can be used within Movie Clips as well as in the main Timeline. They are especially useful for creating internal Movie Clip loops.

To attach a frame behavior:

1. Select a keyframe where you wish to attach the behavior. If no keyframe is available, Flash will automatically attach the behavior to the first available keyframe to the left (earlier) in the Timeline. If you need to insert a keyframe, choose Insert → Timeline → Keyframe.

2. With a keyframe selected, choose Window → Development Panels → Behaviors or press Shift+F3 to display the Behaviors panel.

3. The Behaviors panel opens. Select a behavior and if required, its parameters (see the section "Attaching Object Behaviors" earlier in this chapter).

4. Click OK in the dialog box.

5. If necessary, repeat steps 3 and 4 to attach additional behaviors.

6. Frame behaviors require no event handler, because each behavior is executed when the frame is played in the Timeline. The Behaviors panel reflects this by stating "None" in the panel's Events column. To test your behavior, select Control → Test Movie.

Setting a Target Path in Behavior Dialog Boxes

Many behaviors control the playback and attributes of Movie Clips. For a behavior to generate the ActionScript, it needs to have the correct Target Path. A Target Path is equivalent to a Movie Clip's "address" in your Flash movie. It allows ActionScript commands to locate a Movie Clip Timeline and send commands to it.

Target Paths are one of the more important aspects of Flash development. To learn more about them, see Chapter 19.

1. If you plan to control the main Timeline, click _root at the top of the hierarchy and move on to step 2. If you need to control a different Timeline, select from the list of Movie Clips and click the clip instance you want to use (see Figure 14.4). If your Movie Clip does not have an instance name, you can give it one. Click the name of the clip, and when prompted, click Rename. Give the clip a unique name that you will remember and click OK.

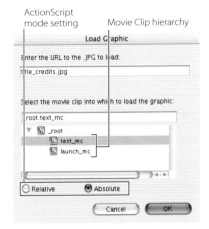

ActionScript mode setting   Movie Clip hierarchy

Figure 14.4

The Load Graphic dialog box allows you to specify a Target Path to the Movie Clip where you will load an external JPEG.

2. The Mode setting allows you to choose how Movie Clips are targeted by ActionScript:

   - *Relative* shows you only Movie Clips that are in the current scene. At the top of the outline, this refers to the current Timeline or Movie Clip.

   - *Absolute* shows every clip in the entire movie. In this mode, _root (at the top of the outline) shows the path to the clip from the main Timeline.

   Although either mode will work, you might find that relative paths are more concise and can sometimes be easier to understand.

3. Click OK to complete the Target Path and finalize the behavior.

Changing a Behavior's Action

When you attach a behavior to a button or Movie Clip object, you often have to define parameters that determine how the behavior affects your movie. If you make a mistake or change your mind after attaching the behavior, it's easy to go back and fix the problem.

To change the action performed by a behavior:

1. Select the object with the event handler that needs to be changed.

2. Open the Behaviors panel and locate the behavior you want to change.

3. Double-click the behavior in the Actions column of the Behaviors pane. The behavior's dialog box opens.

4. Make any additions or changes to the behavior in the dialog box and click OK.

Viewing the ActionScript Behind Behaviors

After attaching a behavior, you might want to see the ActionScript that it generated. This is a good idea because you get a sense of what the code controlling your movie looks like "under the hood." It allows you to learn ActionScript syntax, and you can check to see that the script was generated correctly.

To view the ActionScript that constitutes a behavior:

1. Select the object or frame to which you attached the behavior.

2. Select Window → Actions from the main menu or press F9.

3. The Actions panel opens. Here you can see the script that makes up the behavior you attached (see Figure 14.5).

To learn more about ActionScript and the Actions panel, see Chapter 17 and other related topics covered in Part V of this book.

Using Behaviors for Basic Movie Navigation and Interactivity

Behaviors represent the next step of evolution in the basic scripting functionality provided by Flash. While behaviors are very easy to understand and use, unfortunately they do not provide the kind of depth that was available in previous releases of Flash. If you compare the variety of options offered in behaviors with the functionality found in Flash MX's Normal Scripting mode, you'll find that behaviors are limited. They still provide access to high-quality ActionScript, but the *scope* of behaviors' ActionScript coverage is very limited. This is lamentable; however, third-party developers might fill in the gaps and provide the behaviors that Macromedia has neglected in this release. To learn more about third-party behaviors, see the section "Installing Additional Third-Party Behaviors" later in this chapter.

Figure 14.5

The ActionScript that makes up a behavior can be viewed in the Actions panel.

Flash MX 2004 and MX Pro 2004 Behaviors

In spite of the fact that the variety of behaviors that ship with Flash MX 2004 and MX Pro 2004 is limited, they are still very useful. You will find that attaching them to objects and frames in your movie is relatively simple and provides a quick way to add ActionScript functionality without the hassle of hand-coding. This section walks you through the steps involved in attaching many of the behaviors found in Flash MX 2004 and MX Pro 2004.

Data

The Data category has one behavior offering: Trigger Data Source. This behavior is used in tandem with either the WebServiceConnector component or the XMLConnector component. Because the topic of data binding is beyond the scope of this book, this behavior will not be covered here. For additional information, see the DataBinding Quickstart files that ship with Flash MX Pro 2004.

Media

Media behaviors are available in both versions of Flash MX 2004. However, due to the fact that they work only with Components that are available in the Pro version, they are useful only in that context. To summarize, these behaviors enable you to associate cue points in a streaming video or MP3 with frame labels on the main timeline or in a Movie Clip timeline. This creates a relationship between the video cue points and frame labels, and provides tight synchronization between the two elements. To learn how you can use behaviors to sync streaming media with text and animation in a Flash movie, see Hands On 8.

Embedded Video

Flash MX was the first version of Flash that made it possible to include high-quality digital video footage in a Flash movie. With the release of Flash MX 2004 and MX Pro 2004, video is supported in an additional way through behaviors. The Behaviors panel gives you access to many different options that enable you to quickly and easily control the playback of video that is embedded within a Flash movie.

The Embedded Video behaviors are as follows:

Play Starts the playback of a video instance.

Pause Interrupts the playback of a video instance.

Stop Ends the playback of a video instance.

Fast Forward Advances the video by the specified number of frames.

Rewind Rewinds the video by the specified number of frames.

Hide Causes a video instance to disappear from the Stage.

Show Causes a video instance to appear on the Stage.

Many of these behaviors are interrelated and will be discussed according to the functions they perform and how they can work together.

USING BEHAVIORS TO CREATE VIDEO PLAYBACK CONTROLS

Video is a linear medium: It starts, plays the duration of the program, and is finished. In Flash, this can be changed. The Embedded Video behaviors allow you to control video playback and make it feel less linear. You can skip around within a video, pause it, resume playback, and watch it as many times as you like. It's like using Flash to build your very own remote control.

To control playback of a video in Flash:

1. Click the button where you plan to attach the behavior.

2. Select Window → Development Panels → Behaviors or press Shift+F3 to open the Behaviors panel.

3. Click the Add Behavior button ⊹ and depending on what you want to do, choose from the options in the Embedded Video category, listed in the previous section.

After you've made your choice, the behavior's dialog box opens (see Figure 14.6).

4. In the Target Video field, navigate to the video instance you want to control and select it.

5. If you are attaching a Fast Forward or Rewind behavior, enter a value in the Number of Frames field. This field determines how many frames are skipped when rewinding or fast forwarding.

6. When finished, click OK. The behavior is now complete. If necessary, return to the Behaviors panel and change the behavior's event handler. Then, save your movie and select Control → Test Movie to see how the behavior works.

USING BEHAVIORS TO CONTROL THE DISPLAY OF EMBEDDED VIDEO

In addition to controlling all the playback attributes of embedded video, behaviors allow you to toggle the video on and off or make it visible or invisible. This can be useful in certain situations where you want to step away from a video presentation and focus your audience's attention on graphic or audio elements. By making the video disappear, you can free some screen real estate for other elements within your movie or application.

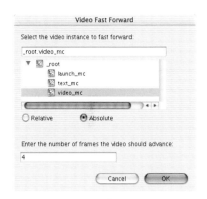

Figure 14.6

The Video Fast For-ward dialog box

To show or hide a video instance:

1. Click the button where you plan to attach the behavior.

2. Select Window → Development Panels → Behaviors or press Shift+F3 to open the Behaviors panel.

3. Click the Add Behavior button ⊕ and depending on what you want to do, choose from the Hide and Show options in the Embedded Video category. After you've made your choice, the behavior's dialog box opens.

4. In the Target Video field, navigate to the video instance you want to show or hide and select it.

5. Click OK. The behavior is now complete. If necessary, return to the Behaviors panel and change the behavior's event handler. Then, save your movie and select Control → Test Movie to see how the behavior works.

Graphics

There is a graphics-oriented behavior: Load Graphic. You can use this behavior to load an external JPEG image into your movie. External JPEGs cannot be loaded onto your movie's Stage directly. Rather, they must be loaded into a Movie Clip. This Movie Clip acts as a kind of frame or "shell" that contains the JPEG you load. Because the JPEG graphic is loaded into a Movie Clip, this behavior is in the Movie Clip category of the Behaviors panel.

To load an external JPEG using the Load Graphic behavior:

1. Choose Insert → New Symbol (Cmd/Ctrl+F8) and create a new Movie Clip named **shell**. (The name is actually not important. *Shell* is used here only for the purposes of example).

2. Open your movie's Library (Window → Library) and double-click the shell Movie Clip symbol. Flash opens the clip in Symbol Editing mode.

3. Select the empty keyframe in the main Timeline.

4. Choose Window → Development Panels → Behaviors or press Shift+F3 to open the Behaviors panel.

5. Click the Add Behavior button ⚓ and choose Movieclip → Load Graphic. The Load Graphic dialog box opens (see Figure 14.7).

6. If the image you wish to load is in the same folder or directory as your movie, replace `*.jpg` in the image field with the name of the image, for example, `title_image.jpg`. If the image is in another location, such as a different folder on a CD-ROM or your web server, you need to enter either the relative or absolute path to the image. An absolute path includes the entire URL, such as `http://www.myflashsite.com/images/myfile.jpg`. A relative path tells the movie to link within the file structure starting from where the Flash movie is saved, for example, `currentfolder/media/images/myFile.jpg`.

7. If you're attaching this behavior to a button or a frame that is on a different Timeline from the one you wish to control or affect, follow the guidelines described in the section "Setting a Target Path" earlier in this chapter and target the Movie Clip into which you want to load the JPEG.

8. Click OK to finalize the behavior. Then, drag an instance of the shell Movie Clip and position it in your movie. The upper-left corner of the graphic will be aligned at the registration point of the Movie Clip. If, for example, the clip is at X-Y coordinates (20, 30), the graphic's upper-left corner will be at this position as well. If the graphic is 300×100 pixels, the lower-right corner will be at (320, 130).

9. Save your movie. If you specified a relative path to the JPEG, be sure to save it where it will be able to find and load the graphic. If you attached the behavior to a button, you might want to change the behavior's event handler. Select Control → Test Movie to see how the behavior works.

Movie Clip

The Movie Clip category of behaviors allows you to control many different aspects of your movie. Because Movie Clips are so integral to Flash development, they cover a broad range of topics and can be used to perform a wide variety of functions in your movie.

The Movie Clip behaviors are as follows:

Bring Forward　Places a Movie Clip in front of objects on the next Timeline layer.

Bring to Front　Places a Movie Clip in front of all objects in your movie.

Send Backward　Places a Movie Clip behind objects on the next Timeline layer.

Send to Back　Places a Movie Clip behind all objects in your movie.

Duplicate Movie Clip Makes a copy of a Movie Clip.

Go to and Play at Frame or Label Sends a Timeline to play at a specific location.

Go to and Stop at Frame or Label Causes a Timeline to stop at a specific location.

Load External Movie Clip Loads an external Flash movie.

Unload Movie Clip Removes an external Flash movie.

Start Dragging Movie Clip Allows your audience to drag a Movie Clip across the Stage.

Stop Dragging Movie Clip Locks a Movie Clip in place so that it can't be dragged.

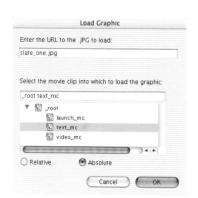

Figure 14.7

The Load Graphic dialog box

Many of these behaviors are interrelated and will be discussed according to the functions they perform and how they can work together.

CHANGING THE STACKING ORDER OF MOVIE CLIP OBJECTS

The Behaviors panel provides you with four behaviors for changing the stacking order of Movie clips: Bring Forward, Bring to Front, Send Backward, and Send to Back. When Flash changes the stacking order of a Movie clip, it simply puts the targeted clip in front of or behind one or more elements in your movie. If a clip is hidden or obscured and you need to show it, or vice versa, these behaviors help you get the job done.

To change the stacking order of Movie Clips:

1. Click the button or Movie Clip instance where you plan to attach the behavior. These behaviors cannot be attached to frames.

2. Select Window → Development Panels → Behaviors or press Shift+F3 to open the Behaviors panel.

3. Click the Add Behavior button ⊕ and depending on what you want to do, choose from the options in the Movie Clip category:

   Bring Forward Places the specified clip above the object that is immediately above it in your movie's Timeline.

   Bring to Front Places the specified clip on top of every other object in your movie.

   Send Backward Places the specified clip beneath the object that is immediately below it in your movie's Timeline.

   Send to Back Places the specified clip beneath every other object in your movie.

   After you've made your choice, the behavior's dialog box opens.

4. If the clip you want to manipulate happens to be the clip to which you've attached the behavior, click OK and the behavior will be attached to the current clip. If you plan to

change the stacking of a different clip, select the name of the Movie Clip instance you want to affect from the Target MC field and click OK.

5. The behavior is now complete. If necessary, return to the Behaviors panel and change the behavior's event handler. Then, save your movie and select Control → Test Movie to see how the behavior works.

CREATING TIMELINE NAVIGATION

Navigation is one of the most important aspects of an interactive Flash production. By directing the playback of different Timelines, you can present and refresh your movie's content any way you see fit.

To direct the playback of Timelines in your Flash movie:

1. Click the button, frame, or Movie Clip instance where you plan to attach the behavior.

2. Select Window → Development Panels → Behaviors or press Shift+F3 to open the Behaviors panel.

3. Click the Add Behavior button ⬇ and depending on what you want to do, choose from the options in the Movie Clip category:

   • Go To and Play at Frame or Label sends the targeted Timeline to play at a specific frame or frame label.

   • Go To and Stop at Frame or Label stops the targeted Timeline at a specific frame or frame label.

   After you've made your choice, the behavior's dialog box opens.

4. Select the Movie Clip you want to target in the Target MC field. If you want to control playback of the main Timeline, select _root at the top of the hierarchy.

5. In the Frame (label) field, enter the frame number or frame label name where you want to send the Movie Clip.

6. Click OK. If necessary, return to the Behaviors panel and change the behavior's event handler. Then, save your movie and select Control → Test Movie to see how the behavior works.

BEHAVIORS TO MANAGE MULTIPLE MOVIES

As a theater production brings different cast members onto the stage, you can call additional movies to play in a Flash production. Rather than have one gigantic movie that contains all the elements you need, you can have a single main "host" movie that loads additional small SWF files as needed. This modular approach can be a very effective way to develop in Flash. To learn more about it, see Chapter 19 and Hands On 5.

To call additional movies, you can use two behaviors: Load External Movie Clip and Unload Movie Clip. Through the process of loading and unloading movies, Flash can string together a series of movies or layer one on top of another to create different playback permutations. Additionally, it allows you to play several movies in a single browser window. Rather than reload the browser when you need to link to a different movie, you can simply replace one movie with another. This technique produces a much smoother presentation of the content.

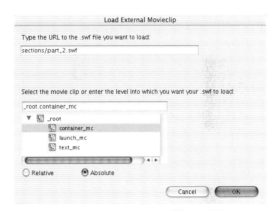

Figure 14.8

The Load External Movie Clip dialog box

To load additional movies in the Flash Player:

1. Click the button, frame, or Movie Clip instance where you plan to attach the behavior.

2. Select Window → Development Panels → Behaviors or press Shift+F3 to open the Behaviors panel.

3. Click the Add Behavior button ⬚ and choose Movie Clip → Load External Movie Clip. The Load External Movie Clip dialog box opens (see Figure 14.8).

4. Loading external Movie Clips really means loading separate SWF, or final, published Flash files. If the SWF you wish to load is in the same folder or directory as your movie, replace `*.swf` in the Movie Name field with the name of the file, for example, `intro.swf`. If the file is in another location, such as a different folder on a CD-ROM or your web server, you need to enter either the relative or absolute path to the image. An absolute path includes the entire URL, such as `http://www.myflashsite.com/movies/myfile.swf`. A relative path tells the movie to link within the file structure starting from where the Flash movie is saved, for example, `currentfolder/movies/myFile.swf`.

5. If you're attaching this behavior to a button or a frame that is on a different Timeline from the one you wish to control or affect, follow the guidelines described in the section "Setting a Target Path" earlier in this chapter and target the Movie Clip into which you want to load the SWF. The loaded file will have its own upper-left corner aligned with the registration point of the clip it is loaded into (see Figure 14.9). If you would like to load a movie so that its left corner is at X-Y coordinates (50, 50), load the SWF into a Movie Clip with a registration point at (50, 50).

6. Click OK to finalize the behavior. Then save your movie and select Control → Test Movie to see how the behavior works. When an SWF file is loaded into a Movie Clip instance, the contents of the instance (graphics, sounds, scripts, and so on) are removed and replaced by the newly loaded clip.

Figure 14.9

When an external SWF is loaded into a Movie Clip, the external file's upper-left corner is aligned with the registration point of the "host" Movie Clip.

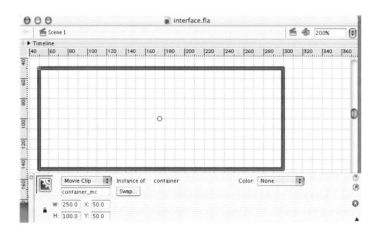

Once an SWF has been loaded into a clip, it will be part of the host movie until you specifically remove or replace it with another loaded SWF. You remove loaded clips using the Unload Movie Clip behavior.

To unload a movie in the Flash Player:

1. Click the button or Movie Clip instance where you plan to attach the behavior. This behavior cannot be attached to a frame.

2. Select Window → Development Panels → Behaviors or press Shift+F3 to open the Behaviors panel.

3. Click the Add Behavior button ⊹ and choose Movie Clip → Unload Movie Clip. The Unload Movie Clip dialog box opens.

4. Choose the Movie Clip instance that holds the SWF you want to unload from the Target MC or level field.

5. Click OK to finalize the behavior. Then save your movie and select Control → Test Movie to see how the behavior works. When an SWF file is unloaded from a Movie Clip instance, the contents of the instance are completely emptied. The instance is still on your movie's Stage but it will not be visible until another SWF is loaded into it.

MAKING MOVEABLE INTERFACE ELEMENTS

One of the best aspects of interactive media is that viewers can rearrange and customize your content to fit their own needs. Not only can they make selections by clicking buttons and menus, they can "grab" something with the mouse and "drag" it around to reorder and move parts of the interactive interface. To provide this option, your moveable items must be Movie Clips and they must be draggable. This is where behaviors can help you out.

To make a Movie Clip draggable:

1. Click the Movie Clip instance where you plan to attach the behavior.

2. Select Window → Development Panels → Behaviors or press Shift+F3 to open the Behaviors panel.

3. Click the Add Behavior button ⊹ and choose Movie Clip → Start Dragging Movie Clip. The Start Dragging Movie Clip dialog box opens.

4. Choose the Movie Clip instance you want to make draggable from the Target MC field.

5. Click OK to finalize the behavior. Then return to the Behaviors panel and change the event handler from On Release (the default) to On Press. While this step was optional with other behaviors, it is a necessity here. The reason is that to get an authentic drag, the action must begin when the draggable object is first grabbed. In ActionScript and behaviors terms, this happens with the On Press event.

6. When finished, save your movie and select Control → Test Movie to see how the behavior works. At this point, you might feel a bit like Spiderman: The draggable Movie Clip sticks to your "hand" and you can't get it off. To learn how to stop dragging, see the next series of steps.

Don't accidentally attach this behavior to a button on your main Timeline. If you do, it will force the entire movie to be draggable or you will be made to drag something other than what you clicked. Ultimately, the results will be very confusing to your audience.

What goes up, must come down. What can be dragged, must be dropped. If you add a behavior that allows your audience to drag a Movie Clip about the Stage, you must also allow them to drop it.

To stop dragging a Movie Clip:

1. Click the Movie Clip instance where you plan to attach the behavior. Ultimately, this should be a Movie clip that has a Start Dragging Movie Clip behavior already attached.

2. Select Window → Development Panels → Behaviors or press Shift+F3 to open the Behaviors panel.

3. Click the Add Behavior button ⊹ and choose Movie Clip → Stop Dragging Movie Clip. The Stop Dragging Movie Clip dialog box opens.

4. Click OK to finalize the behavior, because it takes no parameters. The Behaviors panel will show an On Release handler for the behavior. This is the best choice, as it complements the On Press event that facilitated dragging in the first place.

5. Save your movie and select Control → Test Movie to see how the behavior works.

DUPLICATING A MOVIE CLIP

Duplicating, or copying, Movie Clips can be an interesting way to generate graphic and animated patterns in your movie. For examples of interesting ways that duplicated clips can be used to meet artistic ambitions or design goals, see the Flash work of Joshua Davis (www.joshuadavis.com) and Erik Natzke (www.natzke.com). Duplicated clips can be repositioned to create a variety of surprising patterns and juxtapositions.

With the help of behaviors, you can make copies of Movie Clips and offset the position of each new copy.

To copy a Movie Clip instance:

1. Click the button or Movie Clip instance where you plan to attach the behavior. This behavior can't be attached to a frame.

2. Select Window → Development Panels → Behaviors or press Shift+F3 to open the Behaviors panel.

3. Click the Add Behavior button ⊹ and choose Movie Clip → Duplicate Movie Clip. The Duplicate Movie Clip dialog box opens (see Figure 14.10).

4. Choose the Movie Clip instance that you want to copy from the Target MC field.

5. Enter the offset values. These numbers determine how far the duplicate(s) will be placed from the original clip.

   - X-offset positions the copied clip on the horizontal axis. Use positive integers to place it to the right of the original and negative integers to place it to the left.

   - Y-offset positions the copied clip on the vertical axis. Use positive integers to place it below the original and negative integers to place it above.

6. Click OK to finalize the behavior. If necessary, return to the Behaviors panel and change the behavior's event handler. Then save your movie and select Control → Test Movie to see how the behavior works.

Sound

The Sound category offers a reasonable selection of behaviors. Unfortunately, these behaviors are not very flexible and allow you to exercise only a limited amount of control over the sound playback in your movies. Although we are describing these behaviors and their functionality for the sake of completeness, we strongly recommend that you explore composing the ActionScript on your own. Ultimately this means more work, but provides greater flexibility. See Chapter 25 for further details.

The Sound behaviors are as follows:

Load Sound from Library Accesses a sound that is saved in your movie's Library.

Load Streaming MP3 File Enables you to call upon an external MP3 file and play it in your movie.

Play Sound Plays a specified Library sound once.

Stop Sound Stops a specific sound that was cued from the Library.

Stop All Sounds Stops all sounds playing in your movie.

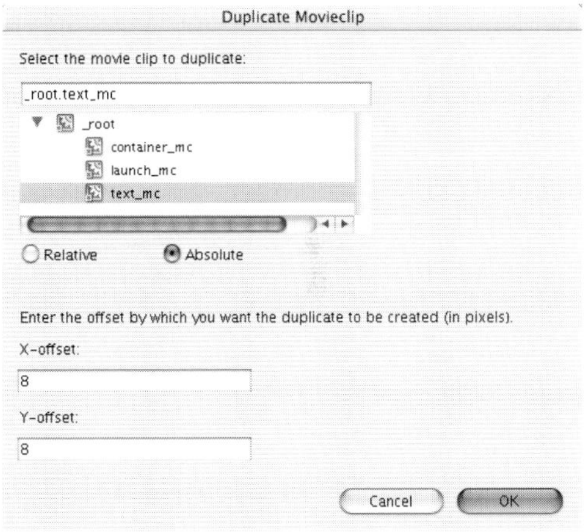

LOADING SOUND FROM THE LIBRARY

This behavior allows you to gain control over a sound stored in your movie's Library. To do this, the sound must first have a Linkage ID, which is a unique name that allows the behavior to recognize which sound it should load. To learn how to do this, see the section "Attaching Sounds with Linkage Identifiers" in Chapter 25.

To load a sound from the Library:

1. Click the button, frame, or Movie Clip instance where you plan to attach the behavior.

2. Select Window → Development Panels → Behaviors or press Shift+F3 to open the Behaviors panel.

3. Click the Add Behavior button 🔧 and choose Sound → Load Sound from Library. The Load Sound From Library dialog box opens (see Figure 14.11).

4. Type the Linkage ID for the sound you want to load.

5. Type a unique name for the loaded sound in the Instance field. Whereas the Linkage ID was a name that allowed Flash to find the right sound to load, an instance is a new name for the sound once it has been loaded.

6. If you want the sound to play after it has been loaded, check the Play This Sound When Loaded box. When checked, the sound plays only once. If this box is unchecked, the sound does not play when this behavior is executed.

7. Click OK to finalize the behavior. If necessary, return to the Behaviors panel and change the behavior's event handler. Then save your movie and select Control → Test Movie to hear how the behavior works.

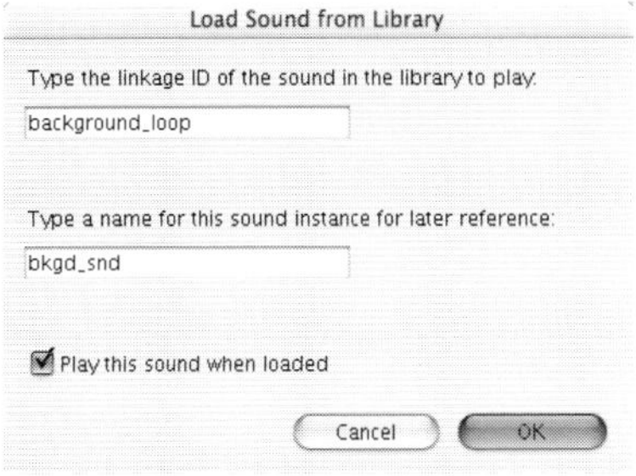

PLAYING SOUND

This behavior allows you to cue (play) a sound that has been loaded into your movie from the Library. It is useful when you want the sound to load and play at different times. For example, you can load the sound in frame 1 of your movie, and use this behavior on a button to cue the sound with a mouse click.

Figure 14.10

The Duplicate Movie Clip dialog box

Figure 14.11

The Load Sound from Library dialog box

To play a sound from the Library:

1. Attach a Load Sound From Library behavior to an object or frame in your movie. If you omit this step, the sound will not be able to play.

2. Click the button, frame, or Movie Clip instance where you plan to attach the behavior.

3. Select Window → Development Panels → Behaviors or press Shift+F3 to open the Behaviors panel.

4. Click the Add Behavior button 🔁 and choose Sound → Play Sound. The Play Sound dialog box opens.

5. Type the instance name for the sound you want to play in the Sound ID field.

6. Click OK to finalize the behavior. If necessary, return to the Behaviors panel and change the behavior's event handler. Then save your movie and select Control → Test Movie to hear how the behavior works.

STOPPING SOUND

This behavior allows you to stop the playback of a sound that has been loaded into your movie from the Library. Once the loaded sound has been cued, this behavior will stop it.

To stop a sound from the Library:

1. Click the button, frame, or Movie Clip instance where you plan to attach the behavior.

2. Select Window → Development Panels → Behaviors or press Shift+F3 to open the Behaviors panel.

3. Click the Add Behavior button 🔁 and choose Sound → Stop Sound. The Stop Sound dialog box opens.

4. Type the instance name for the sound you want to stop in the Sound ID field.

5. Click OK to finalize the behavior. If necessary, return to the Behaviors panel and change the behavior's event handler. Then save your movie and select Control → Test Movie to hear how the behavior works.

STOPPING ALL SOUNDS

This behavior allows you to turn off the audio elements of your movie and leave any active Timeline animations untouched. When executed, it terminates the playback of all audible sounds. Looping event sounds and sounds attached from the Library won't be heard until they are cued again. Stream sounds will play when they are encountered again in the Timeline. (For more information on cueing sounds, see Chapter 24.)

To silence all sounds in your movie:

1. Click the button, frame, or Movie Clip instance where you plan to attach the behavior.

2. Select Window → Development Panels → Behaviors or press Shift+F3 to open the Behaviors panel.

3. Click the Add Behavior button ⊹ and choose Sound → Stop All Sounds. The Stop All Sounds dialog box opens. Click OK; the behavior requires no parameters.

4. If necessary, return to the Behaviors panel and change the behavior's event handler. Then save your movie and select Control → Test Movie to hear how the behavior works.

LOADING STREAMING MP3 FILE

This behavior allows you to load an external MP3 file and stream it into your movie. *Stream* means that the movie will load a portion of the sound and then start to play it back. This behavior is useful for large MP3 sounds because they can be kept outside your movie and it isn't necessary to load the entire sound before it can start to play. Using some additional features of ActionScript you can do much more with external MP3 files than this behavior provides. To learn more about these possibilities, see Chapter 25.

Figure 14.12

The Load Streaming MP3 File dialog box

To load and stream an external MP3 file:

1. Click the button, frame, or Movie Clip instance where you plan to attach the behavior.

2. Select Window → Development Panels → Behaviors or press Shift+F3 to open the Behaviors panel.

3. Click the Add Behavior button ⊹ and choose Sound → Load Streaming MP3 File. The Load Streaming MP3 File dialog box opens (see Figure 14.12).

4. Enter the path that will locate the MP3 file you wish to play. You can enter either a relative path or an absolute path to the link. An absolute path includes the entire URL, such as `http://www.vonflashenstein.com/sound.mp3`. A relative path tells the movie to link within the file structure where the Flash movie is saved, for example, `currentfolder/audio/sound.mp3`.

5. Type an identifier name for the sound you want to stream in the Instance field.

6. Click OK to finalize the behavior. If necessary, return to the Behaviors panel and change the behavior's event handler. Then save your movie and select Control → Test Movie to hear how the behavior works.

Because your sound is a streaming MP3, playback will be delayed to allow a portion of the file to load. If your MP3 is saved on a local hard drive or CD-ROM, the delay will be minimal. If your MP3 is on the Web, the speed of your connection, network traffic, and the size of the MP3 will all be factors in the time it takes the sound to stream.

Projector

Projector behaviors control Flash movies that are playing as stand-alone files, usually called *projectors*. This behavior category has one offering: Toggle Full Screen mode. This allows you to alternate between allowing your projector to play back in a window that fits the size of your movie or a window that fills the entire screen.

To attach a Toggle Full Screen behavior:

1. Click the button or Movie Clip instance where you plan to attach the behavior. Because this behavior allows you to toggle, you have to attach it to an object that can receive mouse or keyboard input.

2. Select Window → Development Panels → Behaviors or press Shift+F3 to open the Behaviors panel.

3. Click the Add Behavior button 🔧 and choose Projector → Toggle Full Screen Mode. A dialog box opens with a message explaining what the behavior will do.

4. Click OK. If necessary, return to the Behaviors panel and change the event handler. To test this behavior, you need to publish your movie as a projector. See Chapters 30 and 32 to read more about this.

> This behavior is the perfect candidate for an On Key Press event. By setting the event trigger to, for example the *F* key, your audience can press *F* on their keyboard to switch between regular and full screen.

Web

The Web category of behaviors is limited to one choice: Go to Web Page. This behavior can be used to open a URL in the browser window or a frame of the current HTML document or to send e-mail to a specified address. If a browser isn't running when the behavior is called, the URL is opened in the system default browser.

To link to a Web page using behaviors:

1. Click the button, frame, or Movie Clip instance where you plan to attach the behavior.

2. Select Window → Development Panels → Behaviors or press Shift+F3 to open the Behaviors panel.

3. Click the Add Behavior button 🔧 and choose Web → Go to Web Page. The Go to URL dialog box opens (see Figure 14.13).

4. The URL field is a parameter that defines the URL to which you will link. You can enter either a relative path or an absolute path to the link. An absolute path includes the entire URL, such as `http://www.vonflashenstein.com/file.html`. A relative path

tells the movie to link within the file structure where the Flash movie is saved, for example, `currentfolder/folder0/file.html`.

If you would like to send e-mail, type **mailto:** followed by the e-mail address you want to receive the message, for example, `mailto:dr@vonflashenstein.com`.

Figure 14.13

The Go to URL dialog box

5. The Open In drop-down menu tells the web browser in which frame to load the URL. Choose a default from the menu:

   - `_self` targets the window and frame where the movie is currently sitting.

   - `_blank` targets a new browser window.

   - `_parent` targets the current window and replaces only the frameset where the movie is currently sitting. This option is best if you have nested framesets and you want to retain that structure.

   - `_top` targets the current window and replaces all framesets with the new URL. Use `_top` if your movie is in a frame and you want the new URL to fill the entire browser window.

6. Click OK to finalize the behavior. Then save your movie and select Control → Test Movie to see how the behavior works.

Removing Behaviors

After attaching a behavior, you might find that you have to remove it. After all, mistakes happen to all of us. This is why it is equally important to be sure that there are no mistakes when you remove a behavior. If a behavior isn't removed properly, it can create all sorts of problems that can be both frustrating and confusing.

To remove a behavior:

1. Select the object or frame that is attached to the behavior you want to remove.

2. To open the Behaviors panel, choose Window → Development Panels → Behaviors or press Shift+F3.

3. Locate the behavior in the Behaviors pane. Click to highlight it.

4. Click the Remove Behavior button and the behavior will disappear.

As an added precaution, we recommend double-checking the Actions panel to be sure that the entirety of the behavior's ActionScript has been removed. With the frame or object still selected, choose Window → Actions to display the Actions panel. Check to see that all the ActionScript created by the behavior has been deleted. If there are some remaining bits and pieces of the old behavior, click and drag to select the old script and press Delete.

Installing Additional Third-Party Behaviors

One of the best aspects of behaviors, new to Flash MX 2004 and MX Pro 2004, is the ability for users to adopt third-party behaviors. This presents a very interesting development not only for Flash as an application, but for the Flash community as well.

This kind of third-party relationship was first established when Flash MX announced Components: ready-made widgets that do everything in your movies from scrolling text to creating complex menus. Components are unique in that they can be developed by one Flash user and shared with many others. While behaviors provide your movies with a different kind of functionality from Components, they do share a common characteristic: They can be created by an individual (or company) and shared with (or sold to) other users. Behaviors can be written in XML (Extensible Markup Language) and saved as files with an `.xml` suffix.

If you find that the behaviors that ship with Flash MX 2004 and MX Pro 2004 don't quite fulfill all your needs and you want to avoid hand-coded scripting, third-party behaviors could be a good solution. At the time of printing, we were unable to produce a sufficient list of third-party behavior developers, so please consult our website, `www.vonflashenstein.com`, to get the latest information.

Once you have acquired third-party behaviors, you will need to install them so that they're available in your Behaviors panel. If the developer of the behaviors you want to install has not provided you with instructions on how to complete the installation, follow these steps:

To install third-party behaviors in Windows:

1. Quit Flash MX 2004 or MX Pro 2004 if it is currently running. New behaviors won't be available until the program is restarted.

2. From your computer's hard drive, choose Program Files → Macromedia → Flash MX 2004 → en → First Run → Behaviors. Open the Behaviors folder.

3. Follow steps 4–5 (see below).

To install third-party behaviors in Macintosh:

1. Quit Flash MX 2004 or MX Pro 2004 if it is currently running. New behaviors won't be available until the program is restarted.

2. In the Finder, select Go → Applications. Next navigate through the following folders: Macromedia Flash MX 2004 → First Run → Behaviors. Open the Behaviors folder.

3. Follow steps 4–5.

4. The Behaviors folder contains many XML documents and a few other miscellaneous files. To be safe, don't remove anything you encounter here! Drag the behavior XML file(s) into the Behaviors folder and close it.

5. Launch Flash MX 2004 or MX Pro 2004. The next time you open the Behaviors panel, the new behavior(s) will be available.

> Due to the fact that behaviors could come from an enormous variety of sources, we can't guarantee that these installation instructions will work for all behaviors. If you encounter problems, contact the developer of the behaviors you wish to install.

Inspirational Design Model

Behaviors allow you to transform static graphics and animations into functional applications and engaging interactive experiences for your audience. Flash makes it possible to create truly unique presentations of information, stories, and entertainment because it offers its users the ability to extend choices and share a degree of control with their audience.

A wonderful example of this can be found with Scott McCloud's digital comic, *The Right Number* (www.scottmccloud.com/comics/trn/intro.html). Scott more aptly describes this as an "online graphic novella about math, sex, obsession, and phone numbers." However you want to say it, the work is ingenious. For *The Right Number,* Scott has extended his concept of Sequential Art in an entirely new way. The story unfolds as a kind of "comic tunnel," where each story cell doubles as a container that holds the next cell in the sequence (see Figure 14.14). Whereas traditional comics demand that you follow the flow from left-to-right across the page, *The Right Number* allows you to journey down the story tunnel in a kind of telescopic fashion.

© Scott McCloud

Figure 14.14

Scott McCloud's *The Right Number* is a Flash-based online graphic novella. It costs 25 cents to see the full story, but it's well worth the small investment.

Scott McCloud's work in exploring the art and style of comics is known throughout the United States (and possibly the world). To learn more about Scott and his books and see many other online comics, visit his website at `www.scottmccloud.com`.

CHAPTER 15

Creating Interactive Controls

At this point, you should know what behaviors are and should understand some of the basic components of the ActionScript language. What is missing is something to put all of this knowledge to use. Behaviors allow your audience to control the movie—but control it with what? Your movie needs some kind of switch or button to unlock its interactive potential.

Building controls in Flash is an essential step toward creating a movie that is both great to look at and easy to experience or play. At the most basic level, you can create simple buttons to turn a movie on or off and to skip to different sections. Flash controls can be as simple as those found on a VCR. They can also become an integral part of the overall design of your movie. As you progress to a more advanced stage, you will be able to create robust interfaces with flexible navigation options and a savvy look and feel.

In this chapter, you will learn about:

- Button controls that are built into Flash

- Creating your own button controls

- Multilayered controllers

- Animated controllers

- Flash interfaces with multiple navigation buttons

- Scalable/flexible interactive controllers

- Integrated design and navigational elements

Adding Interactivity with Simple Buttons

Flash is capable of managing complex and dynamic interactivity, but it's not always necessary to pull out all the stops for your movie. Sometimes you might find that simple elements are just as effective as complex ones. Designing a movie for interactivity is no exception. For Flash developers or designers who are just learning the program or want to keep things easy, there are many options for adding interactive controls. The good news is that these options don't demand a lot of work or experience, and the results can be very satisfying.

Selecting Buttons from the Flash Common Library

Flash has several Common Libraries to offer its users. These Libraries include things such as sounds, Movie Clips, and, yes, buttons. They are resources that are linked to the program and thus will be available every time you use Flash.

Figure 15.1

The Common Library for buttons

The buttons in the Common Library are great for quick mock-ups or tests. Although some of the buttons in the Library might not fit your personal standards or design goals, all of them are very functional and can prove to be valuable assets in the Flash environment.

To open the button Library, select Window → Other Panels → Common Libraries → Buttons (see Figure 15.1). This Library looks like any other in Flash. The only exception is its contents. It contains a wide assortment of buttons that are designed and ready for use in a movie.

For more information about working with Libraries and shared assets in Flash, see Chapter 7.

The Library is organized with a series of individual folders that contain button *families*. Each family of buttons contains a group of graphics that originate from a common background and have a similar look and feel. This allows you to use the family as a set and maintain a consistent look for all navigational or interactive elements.

To use a Common Library button in your movie:

1. Select Window → Other Panels → Common Libraries → Buttons to display the Library if it's not open already.

2. Open the folders within the Common Library panel to find the button you want. Folders in the panel can be opened and closed by double-clicking the folder icon (see Figure 15.2).

3. Do either of the following:

- Drag a button from the Common Library to the main Library for your movie. If your movie Library isn't visible, you can display it by selecting Window → Library or pressing F11.

- Drag a button from the Common Library directly to the Stage. It will automatically appear in your main movie Library.

At this point, the button is a symbol in your movie, either on the Stage or in your main Library, waiting to take the Stage.

From here, there are many different options for your button. If you put it directly onto the Stage, it becomes an instance in your movie and can have ActionScript or behaviors attached to it. To learn more about attaching ActionScript and behaviors to a button, see Chapter 14. If you would like to change the color, size, or any other attributes of the button and customize it to better fit your movie, see the section "Editing Buttons in Your Movie" later in this chapter.

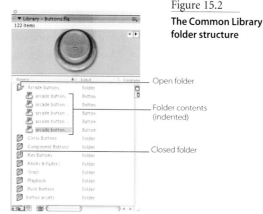

Figure 15.2

The Common Library folder structure

Open folder

Folder contents (indented)

Closed folder

Creating Your Own Buttons

Although using buttons in the Common Library is convenient, you will likely want to create some of your own. After all, this is why we're here; working in Flash is fun! But beyond the fun factor, the process of creating your own buttons has some specific advantages as well. The greatest of these, of course, is that with some effort, you will get exactly what you want. A custom button can be built to your exact specifications so that it fits the specific design goals of your movie. Interactive controls are a big part of a Flash movie, and it's important to get them right.

So, in Flash, what exactly is a button? It is a short, interactive movie with only four frames. Each of the frames represents a different appearance, or "state," of the button that reflects user interaction. These different states are saved as separate images in keyframes along the Timeline of the button movie. As you move the mouse over the button and click it, it changes states accordingly by displaying the correct keyframe image.

By making a button change appearance while it's being manipulated, you show your audience that it is more than just a graphic. The simple animation lets them know that the button is "active" in the movie and that clicking it will produce a change in your movie.

Like Movie Clips, buttons are another kind of symbol. You can create a single button and use it repeatedly. Every instance of a button will be treated independently throughout an animation or interactive movie.

The four states of a button are as follows:

Up This first state represents the appearance of the button when the cursor is not over it. This can also be considered the "inactive" state.

Over The second keyframe of the button Timeline represents the Over state. This creates the appearance of the button when the cursor is positioned over it. Note also that when the cursor is moved over a button, the Flash Player changes it from the standard arrow-pointer to a hand with a finger-pointer.

Down The third keyframe of the button Timeline shows the button graphic when it is clicked and held.

Hit The fourth and final keyframe defines the area of the button that will respond to a mouse click. Think of the Hit state as the button's hot spot. It defines the area that must be clicked for the button to execute any scripts or behaviors attached to it.

Table 13.1 contains illustrations and descriptions of the four states of a typical button.

Table 13.1

**The Four States
of a Button**

STATE	ILLUSTRATION	DESCRIPTION
Up		Appearance when the cursor is not over the button
Over		Appearance when the cursor is over the button
Down		Appearance when the mouse clicks the button
Hit		Defines the button area that can respond to a click

Now that you know a bit more about what goes into a button, you are ready to create your own. Just follow these steps:

1. Select Insert → New Symbol (Cmd/Ctrl+F8) to display the Create New Symbol dialog box.

2. Choose Button as your behavior and enter a name for the button in the Name field.

3. Click OK, and you are switched to Symbol Editing mode (see Figure 15.3). Notice that there are several changes to the appearance of Flash in this mode. The title of your symbol appears beside a button icon in the Scene and Symbol bar. The frames of the main Timeline disappear and are replaced by the new frames of your button. Also, the frames of the new Timeline are labeled to show the four states of your new button. The first frame for the Up state contains a blank keyframe.

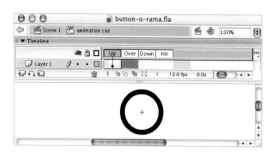

Figure 15.3

The Timeline in Symbol Editing mode

4. Create an Up state for the button by doing any one of the following:

   • Use the Flash drawing tools to create a graphic.

   • Import a graphic file and drag it onto the button's Stage.

   • Drag an instance of another graphic or Movie Clip symbol to the Stage to create an instance within a button.

   The crosshairs in the middle of the Stage represent the registration point of the button.

It's possible to use Movie Clips within Button symbols, but you are not allowed to put a button within a button. Using a Movie Clip as part of a button creates an animated button. For more on this, see the section "Creating Animated Buttons" later in this chapter.

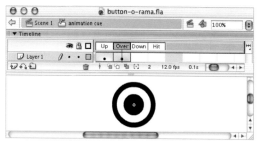

5. To create a new keyframe for the Over state, click the Over state frame and then select Insert → Timeline → Keyframe. Flash automatically duplicates the previous frame in the new keyframe. Alternatively, if you know that the graphic for the Over state is going to be completely different from that of the Up state, select Insert → Timeline → Blank Keyframe.

6. Create or make changes to the graphic in frame 2, or use any of the methods outlined above to alter the appearance of the Over state.

7. Repeat steps 5 and 6 for both the Down and Hit states.

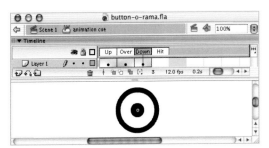 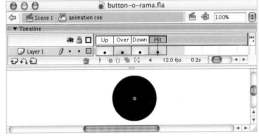

The Hit state is unique and constitutes a very important part of the button. It defines the area that will respond to any mouse clicks on the button. It's important that the Hit state has a solid graphic so that clicks don't "slip through the cracks" in the button. It's also important to be sure that the Hit state is large enough to be clicked. If it's too small, your audience might have a difficult time trying to click the right spot.

If you are creating a button that consists solely of text, the Hit state graphic is extremely important. Letters such as *o* have "holes"; a mouse click in the middle of an *o*-shaped button will not be recognized if the Hit state is also shaped like an *o*. To avoid this potential problem, create a rectangular-shaped Hit state that is approximately the same size as the chunk of text that makes up your button. Because the button Hit state is invisible, this will not have an undesirable effect on the appearance of the button, and will make the button much easier for your audience to use. If you plan to use lots of text buttons, there is an even easier way to approach this. To learn more, see the section "Creating Invisible Buttons" later in this chapter.

8. With graphics for the four states in place, your button is ready to go. To leave Symbol Editing mode, either select Edit → Edit Document (Cmd/Ctrl+**E**) or simply click the Timeline icon for the current scene of your movie.

9. Drag your button from the Library to the Stage to create a button instance in your movie.

10. As needed, attach ActionScript or behaviors to the button so that it can be used to control various elements of your movie. For a discussion of behaviors, see Chapter 14. If you are interested in more advanced button-related ActionScript, refer to Chapter 20.

These are the fundamental steps for creating a simple button for your Flash movie. From this point on, the possibilities are virtually limitless. For a discussion of how to add sound to a button in your movie, see Chapter 23. If you want to continue to work with your movie and explore the potential of buttons as interactive control sources, read on. In the next section, we will discuss the ins and outs of testing your buttons and making any changes or edits to their components.

Previewing, Testing, and Editing Buttons

Once you have created your buttons, it's a good idea to test them to be sure that they work properly and look the way you want. Flash offers two main techniques for testing buttons: You can work in the authoring environment or use the Test Movie option. Depending on your movie project, one technique might suit you better than the other. Whatever the case, it's a good idea to become familiar with both so that you are able to work smoothly and efficiently.

Previewing Buttons in the Flash Authoring Environment

It's possible to preview your buttons while you are working in Flash's authoring environment (also known as authoring mode). By default, Flash keeps all buttons in an inactive state while you are creating your movie. If necessary, you can activate your buttons and test them while you create the rest of the movie.

To test buttons in authoring mode, select Control → Enable Simple Buttons. A check mark appears next to the option, indicating that it is turned on. To turn it off again, simply repeat the process, and buttons will be disabled.

> Working in Flash with buttons activated can sometimes be difficult. For example, it can be tricky to select a button on the Stage when it is enabled. If you need to select an activated button, you can click outside the button and drag a selection around it. Flash highlights the button with a rectangular marquee to let you know it is selected.

Testing Buttons

Previewing buttons in authoring mode gives you a rough idea of what they will look like in your final movie. However, Movie Clips won't be visible when you preview your buttons in authoring mode. Also, most ActionScript and behaviors attached to the button are disabled in this mode. To get a sneak peek at any animated buttons or attached code, you must test your movie or scene. To preview animated buttons, select Control → Test Movie (Cmd/Ctrl+Return/Enter) or Control → Test Scene (Cmd/Ctrl+Option/Alt+Return/Enter). For more specifics on testing and previewing movies, see Chapter 30.

Editing Buttons in Your Movie

If your test or preview shows that a button needs some tweaking or fine-tuning, you will have to go back and edit the button. The good news is that if you have used a single Button symbol over and over (meaning that you used multiple instances of the button), any changes you make to the Button symbol will be updated in every instance. For more details on symbols and instances, see Chapter 7.

There are three ways to edit buttons in your Flash movie: You can edit a button on the Stage ("in place"), in Symbol Editing mode, or in a separate window. These options will achieve the same results, but you might find that one technique works better for you than the others.

To edit a button in place, do either of the following:

- Double-click the button instance.

- Ctrl+click (Mac) or right-click (Win) the instance and select Edit In Place from the context menu.

When you edit a button in place, items on the Stage will fade to the background. The Timeline and Edit bar will change appearance to reveal the button Timeline and keyframes. This option allows you to edit the button and see how it changes in relation to other items around it on the Stage.

You can edit a button in Symbol Editing mode in one of four ways:

- Select the name of the button you want to edit from the Edit Symbols menu ⬛ in the Scene and Symbol bar.

- Ctrl+click (Mac) or right-click (Win) the instance and select Edit from the context menu.

- Select the symbol instance on the Stage and choose Edit → Edit Symbols from the menu bar.

- In the Library panel, either double-click the symbol's button icon or highlight the symbol and choose Edit from the Library options menu.

To edit a button in a separate window, Ctrl+click (Mac) or right-click (Win) the instance and select Edit In New Window from the context menu. The new window will open directly over the window that contains your main Timeline.

All these options reveal basically the same thing: the button's Timeline and access to the four button states and keyframes. When you see this, you are free to make any necessary changes to the button. You can make changes using any of the tools available to you in Flash, by adding Movie Clip instances to the button and by importing bitmap graphics or other external files. Remember that any changes made here will affect all instances of the button in your movie.

When you are finished editing your button, do *one* of the following:

- Select Edit → Edit Document (Cmd/Ctrl+**E**).

- Click either the Scene button or the Back button (see Figure 15.4) in the Scene and Symbol bar between the Stage and the Timeline to return to the main Timeline of a particular scene.

For more information on moving around quickly and efficiently in the main Timeline, see Chapter 3.

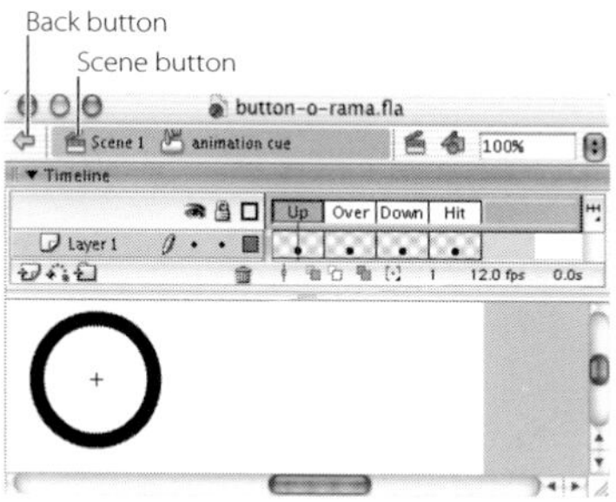

Back button
Scene button

Figure 15.4

In the Scene and Symbol bar, both the Scene and Back buttons take you from Symbol Editing mode to the main Timeline.

Creating Complex Buttons

So far, we have covered all the basic steps for creating buttons and using them in your movie. With these essential skills, you are ready to move on to the next level: creating complex buttons and designing them to support the theme or concept of your movie. These buttons do more than serve as navigational icons. They allow you to give the audience a clear means of moving through your movie while offering visual interest and punch. Once you start to explore the possibilities outlined here, you will see the benefit that these techniques can bring to your Flash productions.

Creating Multilayered Buttons

Buttons are not only controllers in your movie—they are graphics that have an impact on its overall look and feel. This presents you with several choices. On one hand, you can try to make the button as unobtrusive as possible, so that it is transparently woven into the fabric of your movie. On the other hand, you can play it up and allow the button to make a bold visual statement.

In the next example, you will see how to create a graphically dynamic button with components on several different layers. You can find the source files for this example on this book's companion CD. Look for the files named `multilayer.fla` and `multilayer.swf` in the Chapter 15 folder.

To create a multilayered button:

1. Select Insert → New Symbol or press Cmd/Ctrl+F8. The Create New Symbol dialog box opens.

2. In the Create New Symbol dialog box, choose Button as the behavior and give the symbol a name. Then click OK.

3. Flash automatically jumps into Symbol Editing mode. You will see the button Timeline and the Up, Over, Down, and Hit state keyframes.

4. The beauty of the multilayered button is that each graphic layer is independent. One layer can change without affecting the others. To add another layer to the

button Timeline, select Insert → Timeline → Layer or click the Insert Layer button in the Timeline. The new layer appears in the Timeline with an empty keyframe in the Up state frame.

5. Begin by drawing a graphic on Layer 1 to represent the Up state of the button. When you are finished, click Layer 2 and draw an additional portion of the graphic. Because each part is on its own layer, you have more flexibility to change the various states of the button.

6. If necessary, repeat steps 4 and 5 to create additional layers for the button.

7. When the Up state is complete, click Layer 1 and select Insert → Timeline → Keyframe to add a keyframe for the Over state. When you do this, Flash automatically inserts a new frame in Layer 2 and duplicates the Up state graphics in the new frames (below left).

8. Draw a new graphic for the Over state of Layer 1 or make changes to the duplicated frame as needed. Then click frame 2 of Layer 2, insert a new keyframe, and adjust this image as needed.

9. Repeat the process outlined in steps 7 and 8 to create the appearance for the button's Down state (below right).

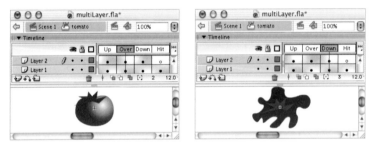

In the example on this book's companion CD, you can see that the button is a tomato. When it's rolled over, both the stem and the fruit change color. Then, when the tomato is clicked, it is squished and changed to a dark color. You can manipulate each element (stem and fruit) separately because each layer is autonomous and will not directly affect the other.

10. Insert a new keyframe in Layer 1 to complete the button and give it a Hit state. Remember, the Hit state isn't visible; it's what enables the button to respond to mouse interaction. Even though the button has several layers, it's acceptable to put a Hit state keyframe in only one layer.

11. When you have finished creating the button, select Edit → Edit Document to return to the main Timeline. To preview your button, choose Control → Enable Simple Buttons. This option allows you to see how the multilayered button looks when manipulated by the cursor.

Creating Animated Buttons

You have seen how multilayered buttons provide a new graphic dimension to your button controls. With each element on a separate layer, you can edit and control them independently. This technique also opens the door to a variety of additional possibilities that can add yet another layer of interest to your Button symbols.

Buttons are by default a kind of animation. When you roll over them, there is a graphic change. When you click them, there is another change. It's not a linear animation but rather one that demonstrates that the graphic is somehow significant; the animation begs you to click it. We can take this idea a step further by creating animated buttons. Such buttons use a Movie Clip or small animation to represent one of their states. Generally, this is done at the Over state, although it is certainly not a requirement. If a Movie Clip were used for the Up state, the animation could be distracting. If it were used as the Down state, there is a chance that the Movie Clip animation wouldn't be seen at the instant the button is clicked. The Over state presents the animation when the button is active (rolled over). It grabs your attention and adds more to the rollover effect than just a change of graphic.

In the next example, you will see how to create an animated button by using a Movie Clip. You can find this example on this book's companion CD. Look for the files named `animated_button.fla` and `animated_button.swf` in the Chapter 15 folder.

To create an animated button:

1. Create a graphic on the Stage to use as your button. When it is complete, drag around it to select the entire graphic, and either choose Insert → Convert to Symbol or press F8. In the Create New Symbol dialog box, select the Graphic behavior and give the symbol a name in the Name field. Click OK.

2. The symbol appears in the Library. Delete the symbol from the main Timeline Stage.

   This graphic symbol will be used as the starting point for each component of our button. We use a symbol so that instances of the symbol can be used repeatedly in the button animation.

3. Select Insert → New Symbol or press Cmd/Ctrl+F8. This time, choose the Movie Clip behavior, give the clip a name, and click OK when you are finished. Flash takes you immediately to Movie Clip Editing mode.

4. You can now create the animation that will be used as the Over state of your button. Drag the graphic symbol from the Library to the Stage while you are in Movie Clip mode. Use the arrow keys to nudge the symbol so that its registration point lines up with the registration point of the new Movie Clip. To help with this, you can monitor the position of the graphic by looking at the X and Y coordinate fields in the Property Inspector.

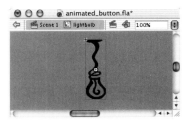

Lining up the registration points is a good idea because you will use the graphic symbol several times in this process. This ensures that that each instance of the symbol is positioned in exactly the same place. Alternatively, you can use the Align panel (Cmd/Ctrl+**K**) and have Flash handle the registration for you automatically. To learn more about working with the Align panel, see Chapter 6.

5. Create the animation using keyframes, tweening, and any other techniques that are available to you in Flash (see Figure 15.5). If you want the animation to play only once, is a good idea to add a `stop()` statement to the last frame of the Movie Clip's timeline. Otherwise, it will loop continuously (which might be desirable in certain situations). If you need to change the symbol, you can select Modify → Break Apart (Cmd/Ctrl+**B**) and edit its characteristics directly. For more information on keyframes and animation concepts, see Chapter 10.

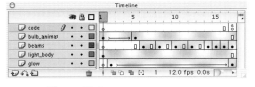

Figure 15.5

The Timeline for the Movie Clip in the file `animated_button.fla`**. Notice that there are instances of both tweened and frame-by-frame animation in the timeline.**

6. When you have finished creating your Movie Clip, select Edit → Edit Document and return to the main Timeline.

7. At this point, you are ready to create the button. You have a graphic and you have a Movie Clip; now is the time to bring it all together. Choose Insert → New Symbol, and the Create New Symbol dialog box opens again. This time, choose the Button behavior and enter a name in the Name field.

8. Click OK, and Flash jumps into Button Editing mode.

9. Drag the graphic symbol to the Stage and use the arrow keys or Align panel to move it into place so that the registration points line up.

10. After the Up state graphic is in place, you can move on to the Over state. Select Insert → Timeline → Keyframe to insert a new keyframe. The keyframe appears in frame 2 as the Over state graphic. Flash automatically copies the Up state graphic into the new keyframe. You will need to swap this with the Movie Clip you created in step 5. Select

the graphic in the Over state frame and then click the Swap Symbols button on the Property Inspector.

The Swap Symbol dialog box opens and allows you to exchange graphics for the Movie Clip symbol. Be sure that the Property Inspector displays Movie Clip in the Symbol Behavior menu after you have swapped symbols; otherwise, the clip will not animate. For specifics on swapping symbols, see Chapter 7.

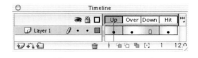

11. The bulk of the work is now over. You have an Up state and an animated Over state. The next step presents a choice depending upon your intentions for this button:

    - If the animation is all you need to complete the button, click in frame 3 of the button Timeline and choose Insert → Timeline → Frame. This will extend the Movie Clip instance one frame and allow it to serve as the Down state as well. This will not cause the animation to replay.

    - If you want an additional change to the button when it is clicked, you need to create a keyframe for the Down state in frame 3 of the button Timeline. Flash will duplicate the contents of the previous keyframe in the new frame. Using any of the previously described techniques, insert a graphic for the Down state in this keyframe.

The example on this book's accompanying CD, `animated_button.fla`, demonstrates the results of the first choice. However, you can experiment with this file using the techniques described in the second. Look for the graphic symbol named `light_down` in the movie's Library. This graphic could work well as a Down state graphic for this particular animated button. Try it and see what you think.

12. Click frame 4 of the Button Timeline and choose Insert → Timeline → Blank Keyframe. Use any of Flash's painting or drawing tools to create a Hit state that is appropriate to the shape and size of your animated button. With keyframes and graphics for each of the four states, your animated button is now ready to go.

13. Select Edit → Edit Document (Cmd/Ctrl+**E**) to return to the main Timeline and save your movie. Because we used a Movie Clip, Flash won't give us a true preview of our animated button in authoring mode. To see the button in action, add an instance of the animated button to the movie; then select Control → Test Movie and give it a spin.

An animated button is a button like any other. Once it's in your Library as a Button symbol, you are free to use it throughout your movie. You can attach actions or behaviors to instances of the animated button and use it as a means of controlling other movie elements and playback.

Creating a Multiple-Button Interface

A multiple-button interface is somewhat self-explanatory: There are several buttons that compose a navigational scheme. This is useful in situations where you want to put all navigational elements in a single location, such as a menu bar running along the top or bottom of your movie. The cool thing about navigation bars is that the buttons can double as bookmarks, so that when you click one, it changes appearance and tells your audience "you are here."

In the next example, you will learn how to create a navigation bar with two buttons. Although it's a simple task, the concepts presented here can be used to build larger and more complicated interfaces. You can find the finished files for this example on this book's accompanying CD. Look for the file named navBar.fla in the Chapter 15 folder.

> Although this is a simple task, there are many steps to ensure consistency in the navigation bar. Be sure to follow the steps carefully!

To create a navigation bar with multiple buttons:

1. Open nav_lesson.fla and save it to your computer's desktop. This file is also located in the Chapter 15 folder of this book's accompanying CD. This file contains a button that you will use to build the navigation bar.

2. Use the Rectangle tool to draw a box that fills the width of your movie, making sure that the box is tall enough to accommodate your button.

3. You are ready to add your button now. Select Insert → Timeline → Layer to add a layer to your movie Timeline. It isn't necessary to put items on different layers, but it can be helpful in keeping your movie organized. Name the new layer **buttons**. For more details on organizing and working with layers, see Chapter 8.

4. Select the buttons layer in the Timeline. Drag the button from the Library to the left corner of the navigation bar graphic. Because you started this step by selecting the buttons layer, it will be the layer where the Button symbol is kept.

5. Repeat step 4 to create a second instance of the button, only this time, drop the button farther to the right of the first button instance. These two buttons will serve as the controls for the navigation bar.

6. Next you need to enter some text so that you can distinguish which button will connect with which part of the movie. Create a new layer (Insert → Timeline → Layer) and name it **text**. Then use the Text tool to enter text as follows (below right):

    ·   Beside the first button, create a text box and enter **Page 1** in a small point size.

    ·   Enter **Page 2** in a separate text box beside the second button.

    ·   In a large point size, type **Page 1** somewhere near the middle of the Stage. This will serve as a temporary marker to help you when testing the navigation bar buttons.

    For more details about using the Text tool, see Chapter 5.

7. Select Insert → Timeline → Layer and name the new layer **markers**. Enter **page1** in the Frame Label field of the Property Inspector. The frame label will help with the ActionScript behaviors for the navigation.

8. The final step in setting up the navigation bar involves adding a frame action so that the movie will play correctly. Choose Insert → Timeline → Layer and name the new layer **actions**. Click the keyframe in this new layer and select Window → Development Panels → Actions (F9) to display the Actions panel. Drag a `stop()`function from the Global Functions → Timeline Control category to the Actions panel text box. If you are not yet acquainted with the Actions panel, see Figure 15.8 and Chapter 17.

9. All the basic elements for our movie and navigation bar are now set. Stop and save your movie (File → Save). With these in place, we can create an additional section for the movie.

10. Now you can add some additional content to the movie. Go to the main Timeline and click frame 10 of Layer 1. Hold down the Shift key and click frame 10 of your topmost layer (it should be named *actions*). This makes a multiple selection across all layers.

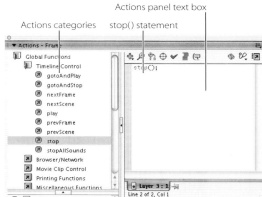

Figure 15.6

The Actions panel

11. With a range of empty frames selected, you can create new frames. Choose Insert → Timeline → Keyframe. Because all layers were selected, all layers get new keyframes. Notice that layers that contain objects have a new instance of that object in the new keyframe. The frames between keyframes fill in accordingly.

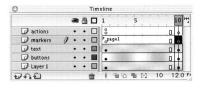

12. Use the Text tool A to change the large text at frame 10 so that it reads **Page 2**. We need to see some sort of contrast between one scene and the next so that we can test the movie later and determine whether or not it is working.

13. Select the empty keyframe in the markers layer at frame 10. Enter **page2** in the Frame Label field of the Property Inspector.

14. You are now ready to make your navigation bar jump to a new location in the movie. Make sure that you are working with the main Timeline on frame 10. If it isn't open already, open the Behaviors panel (Window → Development Panels → Behaviors) and select the button on the left.

15. Attach a behavior that will control the navigation of the main Timeline. In the Behaviors panel, click the Add Behavior button and choose Movie Clip → Go To And Stop At Frame Or Label, and make the behavior go to the frame label **page1**.

For specifics on attaching behaviors to button objects, see Chapter 14.

16. Move the playback head of the main Timeline back to frame 1. Select the button on the right and attach a Go To And Stop At Frame Or Label behavior. Make this behavior go to the frame label **page2** (see Figure 15.7).

Figure 15.7

Whereas the right button in frame 1 has a behavior that jumps to frame label "page2," the left button at frame 10 has a behavior that jumps to frame label "page1."

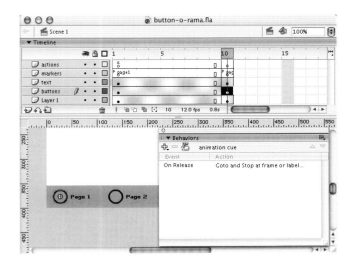

17. Your movie should now have buttons that will take you from one scene to another. To test that everything is working correctly, select Control → Test Movie.

18. Provided that there are no problems with your movie, you should be ready to finish the last feature of the navigation bar. One of the best qualities of a navigation bar is that it can serve as a kind of bookmark to let your audience know where they are in your movie at all times. To create this feature, all you need to do is manipulate a few of the graphics in your movie. Choose Window → Library to display the Library.

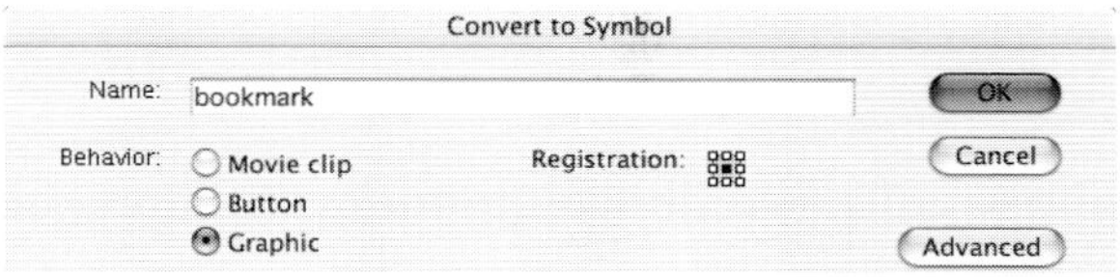

Figure 15.8

When you create the graphic symbol from the button's Down state, be sure that the registration point is set to be in the middle. The button's registration point is also in the middle, so the two will line up exactly.

19. Double-click the button icon in the Library to open the button in Symbol Editing mode. Click the third keyframe in the Timeline (the Down state) to select that portion of the button only.

20. Choose Insert → Convert to Symbol (F8) to display the Create New Symbol dialog box. Choose the Graphic behavior and name the new symbol **bookmark**. Be sure that the registration point is set to be in the middle of the symbol (see Figure 15.8). Click OK to return to Symbol Editing mode and select Edit → Edit Document to return to the main Timeline.

21. With the new graphic in the Library, you are ready to add the bookmark feature to your navigation bar. Move the playback head to frame 1 in the main Timeline; then select the leftmost button on the navigation bar.

22. Click the Swap Symbol button on the Property Inspector to display the Swap Symbol dialog box. Switch the Button symbol with the Bookmark symbol you just created. This puts the graphic symbol in place of the button and creates the effect of a bookmark in frame 1 of your movie. To read more about swapping symbols with the Property Inspector, see Chapter 7.

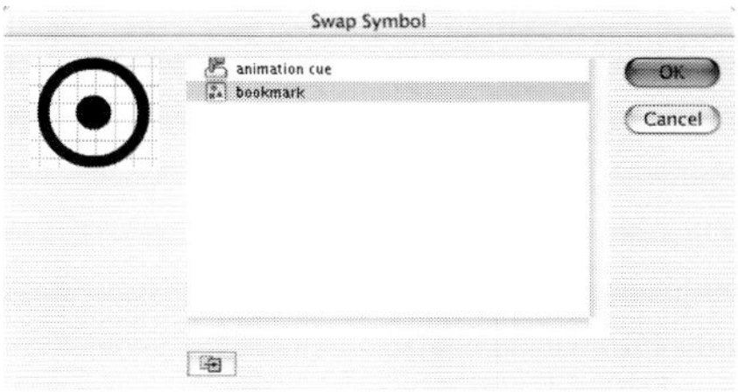

23. Advance the main Timeline to frame 10 and repeat the previous step. Be sure to select the button on the right before you swap symbols.

24. Your movie is complete! Or at least the navigation bar portion of it is. Select Control → Test Movie to give your navigation bar a test drive. Notice how the Bookmark symbol acts like a real bookmark. When you click a button to move to a particular scene, the graphic doesn't change after it has been clicked. This is like a "permanent Down state" to signify which section of the movie is currently playing.

Although the steps outlined here are for a movie with only two locations, it's possible to use this technique to build a navigation bar for an entire Flash website. Using these ideas, and with the help of additional graphics, scenes, and behaviors, you will be able to create a navigational tool that meets the demands of any Flash movie.

Creating Invisible Buttons

The term *invisible button* probably sounds a little suspicious to you. After all, what's the use of a button if someone can't see it to click it? Good question; let's explain further.

An invisible button is transparent. It has no physical/onscreen attributes to speak of. It is purely functional. It lacks Up, Over, and Down states and has only a Hit state. This might seem to contradict any previous discussion of buttons, but it doesn't. Remember, the Hit state is the state that defines the active area of the button, the "hot spot," or the area that responds to mouse interaction. This characteristic makes it, in many ways, the most important state of a button. Invisible buttons use it exclusively to their advantage.

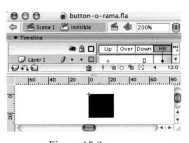

Figure 15.9

The invisible button has only a Hit state graphic that is registered at coordinates (0,0).

Put another way, an invisible button is a button that has only a Hit state and will respond to mouse interaction. When creating a movie in Flash MX 2004 and Flash MX Pro 2004, invisible buttons will not appear in your final, published SWF movie. However, they will be present as functional buttons that your audience can click to make choices and selections while interacting with your movie or application. Because of their uniqueness, invisible buttons are not practical in all situations. They are, however, *extremely* helpful and can save a lot of time under certain circumstances.

An invisible button, because it is transparent, can lie on top of any object in your movie without obscuring or hiding it. And because it is a button positioned over another object, that object seems to act like a button even though it might not be. Invisible buttons give you the flexibility to turn any object into a button by simply placing them over the object.

To create an invisible button:

1. Select Insert → New Symbol or press Cmd/Ctrl+F8. The Create New Symbol dialog box opens.

2. In the Create New Symbol dialog box, choose Button as the behavior and give the symbol a name. Then click OK.

3. Flash automatically switches to Symbol Editing mode. You will see the button Timeline and the Up, Over, Down, and Hit state keyframes.

4. Click the fourth frame (the Hit state), and the frame will be highlighted. Choose Insert → Timeline → Blank Keyframe (or press F7) to create a blank keyframe for the button's Hit state.

5. Use the Rectangle tool to draw a square button or the Oval tool to draw a round button. The size isn't all that important, but something around 25 pixels square or in diameter is a good starting point.

6. Use the Align panel (Window → Design Panels → Align or Cmd/Ctrl+**K**) to position the upper-left corner of the button at the registration point or Stage coordinates (0,0). The Property Inspector can also help with the alignment. For an illustration of the finished invisible button, see Figure 15.9.

7. When your button is aligned and finished, choose Edit → Edit Document to return to the main Timeline Stage and save your movie.

Creating an invisible button is a snap. It's just like creating a regular button, with the exception that there are no Up, Over, or Down states to worry about. After the button has been created, Flash puts it in your movie's Library as a Button symbol for use later on. As a symbol, invisible buttons can turn many different graphic and animated elements of your movie into buttons.

To use an invisible button in your movie:

1. Find the layer in the Timeline that holds the object you want to make work as a button. Create a new layer *above* this layer and name it **buttons**. To learn more about creating layers in the Timeline, see Chapter 8.

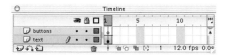

2. Choose Insert → Timeline → Blank Keyframe to create a keyframe for the invisible button in the same frame as the object. If necessary, use the F5 key to extend the number of frames so that the new layer has enough frames to match that of the object.

3. If it isn't open already, open your movie's Library (Window → Library). Click the Invisible Button symbol and drag it into the newly created keyframe in the Buttons layer.

4. Return to your movie's Stage. The invisible button appears as a semi-transparent blue box. Use your mouse and/or the arrow keys to nudge it into place so that it completely covers the object you wish to turn into a button.

5. It is likely that your button does not exactly fit the size and shape of the other object. This is no problem. Use the Free Transform tool (as illustrated in Figure 15.10) to reshape or resize the button as necessary. Remember to make it large enough so that it isn't too difficult for your audience to locate and click it.

6. Now that your button is positioned, you are free to attach behaviors or other Action-Scripts as needed.

In addition to allowing you to turn any object into a button, invisible buttons have a few other benefits as well:

*   Invisible buttons are Button Symbols, meaning that a single button can be reused over and over again in different instances with unique sizes and positions on the Stage.

*   Invisible buttons can make any object act like a button: graphic, Movie Clip, text field, bitmap image, you name it.

*   Making Hit states for text buttons can be tedious. Invisible buttons have a definable shape, making them perfect for text or other objects with irregular or uneven shapes.

Figure 15.10

The Free Transform tool can be used to resize an invisible button. Here, it makes adjustments for a button to fit over the word *home*, **thus making the word a button.**

To try your hand at invisible buttons, check out `invis_buttons.fla` in the Chapter 15 folder of this book's companion CD. This movie has two completed invisible buttons and all the trappings to complete three more. The buttons use behaviors to navigate to different frame markers of a Movie Clip. If you haven't learned how to do this, see Chapter 14.

Inspirational Design Model

Designing interactive media is so much more than just making "cool" stuff. Designers must take their audience into consideration so that their message is accessible and presented in the most effective manner. No matter how cool the animation or presentation of content, if an audience doesn't understand how to play or interact with the movie, you've lost them.

This is why intuitive interactive controls are so crucial to design. A naturally flowing, intuitive design will be much more appealing to your viewers than a confusing display of technical fireworks and animation prowess. Remember, your audience is seeing a movie for the first time. Things that might seem obvious to you as the movie's creator can be potentially confusing if the design isn't easily understood.

This chapter's feature is the Homestar Runner website, found at `www.homestarrunner.com`. The entire site is filled with hilarious games, comics, and animations. Of particular interest is their interface for the "Toons" section of the website (see Figure 15.11). Visitors can navigate through their offering of cartoons by using a *TV Guide*–style menu and a four-button remote control. Not only is this clever, but it presents a very familiar system that their audience will grasp immediately.

Figure 15.11

"Toons" section from the Homestar Runner website

CHAPTER 16

Creating Flash Applications with Components

Upon reading this part of the book, you undoubtedly can see that Flash has a lot to offer when it comes to creating a unique experience for your audience. Behaviors allow you to regulate the flow of your movie, and you can create buttons that provide a way to make choices. These and other interactivity-building characteristics have been part of Flash for years, and as the program has continued to grow, they have become more important. In fact, Flash is used by many developers to create full-featured applications.

Applications? Whoa, wait a second! If you are new to Flash, it is likely you were drawn to the program by its reputation as an animation tool. You probably also heard that it also can work really well for building websites. But applications? Yes. Since the release of Flash MX, Macromedia has been supporting a community of online application developers. These teams create all kinds of applications for the Web; everything from amortization charts to video-conferencing environments. And now that Flash is evolving once again, it contains additional features to support this kind of work. Components are one feature that represent the latest advances in this area.

Components are drag-and-drop building blocks for interactive Flash applications. They provide instant functionality for a wide variety of interface elements that are common to applications: scroll bars, text input fields, list and check boxes, radio buttons, and so on. Components help to make Flash MX 2004 and MX Professional 2004 an environment for the development of applications.

Whether you are developing applications or simply building a personal website, components can help in a variety of ways. This chapter discusses the many facets of components:

- **The nature of components**

- **Version 2 component families**

- **How to implement components in a Flash application**

- **How to customize components**

- **Additional component resources**

What Components Are (and Are Not)

Components are, in a word, "cool." They represent many of the things that are great about Flash, the authoring application, and the Flash community. Components actually got their start in Flash 5, though they weren't called components then; they were called Smart Clips. The idea behind Smart Clips was that on any application development team, you often have two kinds of people: the programmers and the designers.

Designers make pretty things. More specifically, they make pretty things that work well and don't confuse their audience. Programmers write code. Their code makes the pretty, functional things created by the designers actually do something meaningful. In an ideal world, these two groups would exist in a perfect, symbiotic relationship where each benefits from the expertise of the other. The reality is that this is not always the case. Some designers can write code, though according to programmers, it is usually "completely wrong" and "impossible to use if we have to make changes." Programmers can do design, but they tend to make even the most simple, utilitarian interfaces look as if they were designed for a first-person shooter game ("Do we really need that much chrome?"). We hate to stereotype, but this is often the case.

Flash 5's Smart Clips were meant to preserve the ideal harmony between programmers and designers. The designers would create a Movie Clip of, for example, a menu and make it as stylish as they wanted. They would then pass it off to the programmers who would add all the code to make it functional. This was a Smart Clip. It combined good design and solid code to create a reusable Movie Clip symbol.

Figure 16.1

Components can be found in the Components panel (Cmd/Ctrl+F7).

Well, for one reason or another, Smart Clips never really took off, at least not within the Flash community at large. They were a great idea, but something was missing. When Flash MX was released, it was announced that Smart Clips would be replaced by something new that Macromedia called *components*, and they continue to be a part of Flash MX 2004 and MX Pro 2004 (see Figure 16.1).

Components are a lot like Smart Clips. They have good design and can be customized to fit specific needs. The components that ship with Flash MX 2004 and MX Pro 2004 all have the same graphic *theme* known as Halo, which will give your component-based applications a unified look. They are built by programmers and have flexible yet solid code to make them work in a variety of settings. Components deliver what Smart Clips could not: a flexible interface widget that is immediately ready for application development.

As great as components sound, we don't want to give you the impression that they are the answer to all your application-development wishes. Yes, they are useful, and yes, they save time. However, with the release of Version 2 components in Flash MX 2004 and MX Pro 2004, many of the components are targeted to the high-end of the application-development community. To get Version 2 components to deliver their best or most useful functionality, you need to be very comfortable writing ActionScript. For those of you who are not interested in developing applications or ready to leap into advanced ActionScript, this is probably disappointing. We understand these concerns and offer as much guidance about each new component as space allows.

Overview of Flash Components

In Flash MX 2004 and MX Pro 2004, components are divided into three categories: Data, Media, and User Interface (UI). Components in the Data category require advanced ActionScript and will not be covered in this book. To learn more about these components, refer to the Help panel (F1). Media components for streaming audio and video are discussed in Hands On 8. This topic is limited to Flash MX Pro 2004 users. To learn about other ways to incorporate streaming audio and video into a Flash movie, see Chapter 25 (for audio) or Chapter 31 (for video). You will find that you still have loads of options that aren't limited to the Pro version of Flash and often provide much simpler solutions.

UI Components

If you used components in Flash MX, then you should be right at home with many of the new components in Flash MX 2004 and MX Pro 2004. The UI components provide a wide array of options for building interfaces for Flash applications. This set includes most of the widgets you find in any kind of software application, so your audience will be comfortable working with radio buttons, list boxes, text fields, and so on. The UI components are:

- Button
- CheckBox
- ComboBox
- Label
- List
- Loader
- Menu
- NumericStepper
- ProgressBar
- RadioButton
- ScrollPane
- TextArea
- TextInput

The UI components will be covered in the next section of this chapter.

Combining Version 1 and Version 2 Components

If you used components in Flash MX, then you were using Version 1 (v1) components. Flash MX 2004 and MX Pro 2004 ship with Version 2 (v2) components. V2 components represent the next step in Flash components and component architecture. Because they are fundamentally different from a programming perspective, Macromedia strongly discourages you from creating applications that use both v1 and v2 components, claiming that it will lead to "unpredictable behavior."

This means that it is a bad idea to use older Flash MX (or v1) components in an application you build in Flash MX 2004 or MX Pro 2004 where you plan to *also* use v2 components. However, if you have a few v1 components that you just can't live without, you are in luck. You can use them in an application that meets the following criteria:

- the application uses *only* v1 components
- the final SWF is published for Flash Player 6
- the application uses ActionScript 1.0

The application will be able to run correctly if your audience is using Flash Player 6 or 7, and the functionality of your v1 components will remain intact. To learn how to publish movies for Flash Player 6 and ActionScript 1.0, see Chapter 30.

Employing UI Components in Your Flash Applications

The UI components are among those that are most common to all computer software. They will enable the users of your application to make choices, get and provide information, monitor the status of an application as it's loading, and scroll through large text files and graphics.

The process of adding a component to your application is very straightforward:

1. Select the component in the Components panel.
2. Drag the component to the Stage and position it. If necessary, you can use the Free Transform tool to change the size and dimensions of any component (see Figure 16.2).

Figure 16.2

The Free Transform tool can be used to resize a component. Here, you see it adjusting the dimensions of a Button component.

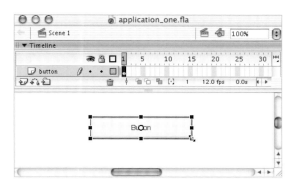

3. Enter any required parameter values that the component might need in the Property Inspector (see Figure 16.3).

Parameter column   Value column

Some components (such as the ComboBox and List) require multiple values for one parameter. It is easy to enter these values using the Values dialog box. To enter multiple values:

1. Click the value column for the parameter you wish to edit.

2. Click the Magnify button at the right side of the column 🔍. The Values dialog box opens (see Figure 16.4).

3. Use the Add button (+) to add a value. Use the Remove button (−) to clear a value. Use the up and down arrow buttons to reorder values in the list.

4. When you're finished, click OK.

4. Attach a behavior or write ActionScript to make the component do something.

5. Save your movie and test it to confirm that the component works.

> Live Preview is a feature that allows you to see the changes made to a component while you are building your application. Not all changes can be reflected in Live Preview, but it gives you an idea of what the component will look like in your published application. Choose Window from the main menu bar and look near the bottom for the Enable Live Preview option. If it is checked, Live Preview is turned on. To change this, select Enable Live Preview and it will be disabled. Live Preview can be helpful; we recommend that you take advantage of it and leave it enabled.

Retrieving Information from Components Using ActionScript

As you will soon discover, it is very easy to add components to your application and customize them to fit your needs. What can be difficult, however, is getting them to do something useful once they have been configured to work in the context of your Flash movie or application. For this task, you have two choices: ActionScript and behaviors.

Behaviors provide the easiest solution. For Button and CheckBox components, behaviors make it easy to navigate to a new frame number or label or open a link on the Web. If your application calls for this kind of functionality, your best choice is to use behaviors. To learn more about behaviors, see Chapter 14.

For more advanced functionality, you will need to use ActionScript. ActionScript is the programming language that developers use to communicate with Flash. It is very powerful and can allow you to do just about anything with your Flash movies and applications. To learn more about ActionScript, see Chapter 17. In the meantime, because you need ActionScript to get your components to do anything useful, it's time for a little Action-Script crash course.

Consider the following statements:

```
listenerObj=new Object();
listenerObj.event = function(eventObj){
    statements;
}
eventSrc.addEventListener("event",listenerObj);
```

This ActionScript will not actually run. This is a kind of "script template" that will allow you to retrieve information from many of the UI components. Here's how it works:

```
listenerObj=new Object();
```

The first line creates a listener object, an element that waits to respond to events that take place in your movie.

```
listenerObj.event = function(eventObj){
    statements;
}
```

The next three lines create a function for the listener object. The function represents what the listener should do when the events it's waiting for actually happen. The tasks the function performs would be written where you see the placeholder, *statements*.

```
eventSrc.addEventListener("event",listenerObj);
```

The last line brings this all together. *eventSrc* is the instance name of a component in your Flash application. When *event* happens to the component (*eventSrc*), the event (such as click or change) is broadcast to the listenerObj, which then performs the function you associated with it.

This basic structure will be used in many of the examples of this chapter. It is by no means the only way to use ActionScript in conjunction with components. It will, however, provide a means for you to retrieve the information selected or entered by the users of your applications.

In many examples, we will use the trace() function in the *statements* line. This causes Flash to print information to the Output panel. It is not especially relevant to the final, published application but it is extremely helpful while you are in the building stage because it allows you to track information that is passed to and from your application in real time. In lieu of `trace()`, a more concrete method would be to assign the output of a component to a variable where it can be stored temporarily and retrieved later. To learn more about variables, see Chapters 17 and 18; to work on a project that incorporates components and real ActionScript, see Hands On 4.

Getting Audience Confirmation with the Button Component

A Button component might come as a bit of a surprise. Why do we need one when buttons can be so easy to create? However, the Button component is a valuable addition to the component set. It provides additional functionality (such as toggle) beyond a regular button symbol. It also was designed with the Halo theme, so it will match the look of other Flash components.

To add a Button component to a Flash application:

1. Choose Window → Development Panels → Components or press Cmd/Ctrl+F7 to open the Components panel.

2. Click the Button component (in the UI Components category) ▭ and drag it to the Stage. Drop the component where you want it to be positioned in your application, and if necessary, align it with the other elements of your application.

3. Choose Window → Properties (Cmd/Ctrl+F3) to open the Property Inspector and go to the Parameters tab.

4. The Button component has the following parameters, which you can define as needed:

   icon You can add a custom icon to the Button component to lend a more stylized look to its default appearance. This icon must be a Movie Clip with a Linkage ID in your movie's Library. Enter the Linkage ID name in the Value field. The icon will not appear in the component until you test your movie. To learn how to assign a Linkage ID to a Movie Clip, see Chapter 19.

   label This parameter determines the name that will appear on the button, such as "OK." Enter a name in the Value field.

   labelPlacement This parameter determines where the label is positioned relative to the button's icon: right, left, top, or bottom. Choose an option from the Value field. If your button doesn't have an icon, this parameter has no effect.

   selected Click the Value field to change the selected option. If this parameter is set to `true`, the button appears in the down position. When set to `false` (default), the button is up.

   toggle When set to `true`, this parameter makes the button function as a toggle switch. The default is `false`.

5. To add functionality to your Button, attach a behavior (as described in Chapter 14) or write ActionScript to make it perform the desired tasks in your application.

6. Save your movie and choose Control → Test Movie to see how your Button component works.

> You can find additional Button components in the Buttons Common Library. Choose Window → Other Panels → Common Libraries → Buttons, or Window → Other Panels → Common Libraries → PayPal Buttons.

Making Selections with the CheckBox Component

The CheckBox component is common to many kinds of software interfaces; it allows you to present the user with an option they can accept or reject by clicking to check or uncheck the box.

To add a CheckBox component to a Flash application:

1. Choose Window → Development Panels → Components or press Cmd/Ctrl+F7 to open the Components panel.

2. Click the CheckBox component (in the UI Components category) ⊠ and drag it to the Stage. Drop the component where you want it to be positioned in your application, and if necessary, align it with the other elements of your application.

3. Choose Window → Properties (Cmd/Ctrl+F3) to open the Property Inspector. Give the component an instance name and go to the Parameters tab.

4. Edit the CheckBox component's parameters as follows:

   label This parameter determines the name or text that will appear beside the CheckBox. Enter a name in the Value field.

   labelPlacement This parameter determines where the label is positioned relative to the CheckBox: right, left, top, or bottom. Choose an option from the Value field.

   selected Click the Value field to change the selected option. If this parameter is set to `true`, a check mark appears in the box. When set to `false` (default), there is no check mark.

5. Save your movie and choose Control → Test Movie to see how your CheckBox component works.

Here's a simple example to demonstrate how you could use this component in an application. This example is also available in the Chapter 16 folder of this book's accompanying CD. See the file named `checkBox_component.fla`. Let's say you wanted to get confirmation that it was OK for someone to receive e-mail from you. Drag a CheckBox component to the Stage, give it the instance name **contact**, and enter the following ActionScript in the keyframe that holds the component:

```
sendMail=new Object();
sendMail.click = function(eventObj){
    var mail=eventObj.target.selected;
    trace(mail);
}
contact.addEventListener("click",sendMail);
```

This script uses the Event Listener function that was described earlier in this chapter. Place this component beside a text field that reads "Send me e-mail" and you can use the value of the *mail* variable to track whether or not it's OK to send e-mail to a user.

Providing Multiple Choices with the ComboBox Component

A ComboBox is another standard GUI element, a drop-down menu that allows users to choose from a list of predefined options. For example, it's a good way to let site visitors identify postal codes and states or provinces.

To add a ComboBox component to a Flash application:

1. Choose Window → Development Panels → Components or press Cmd/Ctrl+F7 to open the Components panel.

2. Click the ComboBox component (in the UI Components category) and drag it to the Stage. Drop the component where you want it to be positioned in your application, and if necessary, align it with the other elements of your application.

3. Choose Window → Properties (Cmd/Ctrl+F3) to open the Property Inspector.

4. Edit the ComboBox component's parameters as follows:

    editable This parameter determines if the items in the ComboBox can be changed by the user. False (uneditable) is the default.

    labels This parameter gives each item in the ComboBox a name. Click the Magnify button and open the Values dialog box to add, remove, or reorder labels.

    data This parameter gives each labeled item in the ComboBox a specific numeric or text value. Click the Magnify button and open the Values dialog box to add, remove, or reorder data. Be sure that each data value correctly corresponds to a label.

    rowCount This parameter determines how many items will be visible in the Combo-Box. If the component contains more items than the value of *rowCount*, a scroll bar is automatically added.

5. Save your movie and choose Control → Test Movie to see how your ComboBox component works.

Here's a simple example to demonstrate how you could use this component in the context of an application. This example is also available in the Chapter 16 folder of this book's accompanying CD. See the file named `comboBox_component.fla`. Let's say you wanted to provide a set of ZIP codes for your users to choose from. Drag a ComboBox component to the Stage, give it the instance name **codes**, enter a few local ZIP codes for both the `labels` and `data` parameters, and enter the following ActionScript in the keyframe that holds the component:

```
form=new Object();
form.change = function(eventObj){
    var zip=eventObj.target.selectedItem.label;
    trace(zip);
}
codes.addEventListener("change",form);
```

Here is the Event Listener function once again. This is slightly different from the function you used for the CheckBox. For a ComboBox component, the `change` event works best to cue the function. You can use the value of the *zip* variable to store a user's ZIP code information.

Displaying Text with the Label Component

The Label component provides a consistent means of formatting text elements of an application. It can be used as a label for ComboBoxes, NumericSteppers, and other components that don't have any sort of label built in.

To add a Label component to a Flash application:

1. Choose Window → Development Panels → Components, or press Cmd/Ctrl+F7 to open the Components panel.

2. Click the Label component (in the UI Components category) **A** and drag it to the Stage. Drop the component where you want it to be positioned, and if necessary, align it with the other elements of your application.

3. Choose Window → Properties (Cmd/Ctrl+F3) to open the Property Inspector.

4. Edit the Label component's parameters as follows:

   autoSize This parameter determines how the Label component resizes to fit the text it contains. The parameter can be any one of the following values:

   - `none`: The label doesn't resize.
   - `left`: The right and bottom of the label resize.
   - `center`: The bottom of the label resizes.
   - `right`: The left and bottom of the label resize.

html This parameter determines if the label can have its text formatted in HTML. Set the parameter to `true` if you want to take advantage of HTML formatting.

text This parameter assigns text to the label. If you want to format the text in HTML, you need to use ActionScript.

5. Save your movie and choose Control → Test Movie to see how your Label component works.

Here's a simple example to demonstrate how you could use this component in an application. This example is also available in the Chapter 16 folder of this book's accompanying CD. See the file named `label_component.fla`. Drag a Label component to the Stage, give it the instance name **title**, set the `html` parameter to `true`, and enter the following ActionScript in the keyframe that holds the component:

```
title.text="This is your <b>last shot!</b>";
```

This script uses the *text* property to assign text to the label. And, because the `html` parameter is `true`, the bold tag (`<b>`) will make the last few words have a bold weight. Be sure that your component is long enough to accommodate the length of the phrase.

Organizing Information with the List Component

The List component is one of the most useful in the entire UI components set. It provides a scrollable list where you can present choices or information. When a user makes a selection, their choice can be used to affect other elements of your application.

To add a List component to a Flash application:

1. Choose Window → Development Panels → Components or press Cmd/Ctrl+F7 to open the Components panel.

2. Click the List component (in the UI Components category) 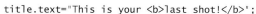 and drag it to the Stage. Drop the component where you want it to be positioned, and if necessary, align it with the other elements of your application.

3. Choose Window → Properties (Cmd/Ctrl+F3) to open the Property Inspector.

4. Edit the List component's parameters as follows:

labels This parameter gives each item in the list a name. Click the Magnify button and open the Values dialog box to add, remove, or reorder labels.

data This parameter gives each labeled item in the list a specific numeric or text value. Click the Magnify button and open the Values dialog box to add, remove, or reorder data. Be sure that each data value correctly corresponds to a label.

multipleSelection This parameter determines if a user is able to select more than one item in the list. When set to `true`, they can; when set to `false` (the default), only one selection is permitted. Users can press Cmd/Ctrl+click to make multiple selections.

rowHeight This parameter sets the height, in pixels, for a row in the list. The default is 20. Setting `rowHeight` to higher values increases the space between items in the list.

5. Save your movie and choose Control → Test Movie to see how your Label component works.

To see an example of the List component in action, see Hands On 4 after this chapter.

Accessing External Resources with the Loader Component

The Loader component allows you to load outside resources into your application. Outside resources available to you via this component are SWF files and JPEG images. This component is advantageous because it allows you to keep SWF and JPEG elements separate, reducing the file size of the final, published application.

To add a Loader component to a Flash application:

1. Choose Window → Development Panels → Components or press Cmd/Ctrl+F7 to open the Components panel.

2. Click the Loader component (in the UI Components category) and drag it to the Stage. Drop the component where you want it to be positioned, and if necessary, align it with the other elements of your application.

3. Choose Window → Properties (Cmd/Ctrl+F3) to open the Property Inspector.

4. Edit the Loader component's parameters as follows:

autoLoad This parameter determines if loading begins immediately (`true`) or if it must be initiated through another means (`false`). The default is `true` so that all content is loaded automatically.

contentPath Enter the absolute or relative path to the file you wish to load. A relative path must be relative to your application; an absolute path should contain the full URL to the file. If you are testing the application, be sure that all external SWF files are in the same folder as the application's FLA file. Once the application has been published, you can load SWF files in other folders. You can enter the absolute path for JPEG graphics anytime. If you have an Internet connection and Live Preview is enabled, you will be able to see the graphic while building your application.

scaleContent This parameter determines how the loaded content is resized. When `true` (default), loaded content is scaled to fit the dimensions of the Loader. When `false`, the Loader is scaled to fit the dimensions of the content.

5. Be sure that your external file(s) are in the correct location according to what you specified for the `contentPath` parameter.

6. Save your movie and choose Control → Test Movie to see how your Loader component works.

> Be sure that any JPEG images you want to load are not progressive JPEGs; the Flash Player can't handle them.

Making Numeric Choices with the NumericStepper Component

Use the Numeric Stepper component to allow users of your application to choose from a set of numbers for information such as their date of birth. Simply click one of the Numeric-Stepper's arrow buttons, and the value will increase or decrease.

To add a NumericStepper component to a Flash application:

1. Choose Window → Development Panels → Components or press Cmd/Ctrl+F7 to open the Components panel.

2. Click the NumericStepper component (in the UI Components category) 🔟📋 and drag it to the Stage. Drop the component where you want it to be positioned, and if necessary, align it with the other elements of your application.

3. Choose Window → Properties (Cmd/Ctrl+F3) to open the Property Inspector.

4. Edit the NumericStepper component's parameters as follows:

   maximum This parameter determines the highest value to be displayed in the stepper.

   minimum This parameter determines the lowest value to be displayed in the stepper.

   stepSize This parameter sets the increment by which the values of the stepper will change. For example, a value of 0.25 would produce the values 1.25, 1.5, 1.75, 2, and so on.

   value This parameter sets the initial value to be displayed in the stepper.

5. Save your movie and choose Control → Test Movie to see how your NumericStepper component works.

Here's a simple example to demonstrate how you could use this component in an application. This example is also available in the Chapter 16 folder of this book's accompanying CD. See the file named `numStepper_component.fla`. Drag a NumericStepper component to the Stage and give it the instance name **year**. Set the `maximum` parameter to **1995**, minimum to **1965**, stepSize to **1**, and value to **1972**. Enter the following ActionScript in the keyframe that holds the component:

```
box=new Object();
box.change = function(eventObj){
    var num=eventObj.target.value;
    if(num<1978){
        trace("You're GenX");
    }else{trace("You're Millennial");}
}
year.addEventListener("change",box);
```

This script checks the current value of the NumericStepper instance named year. Each time it is clicked, the Output panel prints the generation name for each year. The *num* variable stores each birth year as it appears in the stepper and can be reused later in the application.

Managing External Resources with the ProgressBar Component

The ProgressBar component allows your users to view the download progress as your application loads or as external resources are loading into the application. The Progress-Bar component can work as a preloader for the entire application or help monitor the progress of SWF and JPEG files loaded via a Loader component.

To add a ProgressBar component to a Flash application:

1. Choose Window → Development Panels → Components or press Cmd/Ctrl+F7 to open the Components panel.

2. Click the ProgressBar component (in the UI Components category) and drag it to the Stage. Drop the component where you want it to be positioned, and if necessary, align it with the other elements of your application.

3. Choose Window → Properties (Cmd/Ctrl+F3) to open the Property Inspector.

4. Edit the ProgressBar component's parameters as follows:

    label The value of this parameter determines the text to be displayed in the Progress-Bar's label. Values should be specified with the following placeholders:

    - %1 is the placeholder for the total number of bytes loaded.

    - %2 is the placeholder for the total number of bytes.

    - %3 is the placeholder for the percentage of bytes loaded.

    - %% is the placeholder for the percent sign (%).

        The expression %3%% Loaded would produce the text "50% Loaded" if you had loaded 300K of a 600K application.

labelPlacement This parameter sets position of the text label in relation to the bar. The values are top, bottom, right, left, and center.

conversion This parameter sets an integer to use for dividing the numbers produced by %1 and %2, or the value of bytes loaded and total bytes, respectively. The default is 1. A value of 1024 is recommended so that you can convert bytes to kilobytes.

direction This parameter determines the direction in which the ProgressBar moves, right or left.

mode The ProgressBar component can work in one of three modes: event, polled, and manual. *Polled* is the recommended mode. It provides instant functionality to monitor the loading of assets in your movie. Use *event* or *manual* in applications that involve more complex ActionScript.

source This parameter determines the instance name of the source you want to monitor as it loads. To monitor the load progress of an entire application, enter _root.

5. Save your movie and choose Control → Test Movie to see how your ProgressBar component works. You might want to use the Simulate Download feature while you are testing your movie. This will give you a better idea of how the component is functioning. To learn how to use this option, see Chapter 30.

Here's an example to demonstrate how you could use this component to make a preloader for an application or other Flash movie. You will need to look in the Chapter 16 folder of this book's accompanying CD for the file named progBar_component.fla.

1. Open the file and save it to your hard disk.

2. Choose Control → Test Movie.

3. Once you are in Test Movie mode, choose View → Download Settings → DSL.

4. Choose View → Simulate Download. You will see the progress bar slowly advance across the screen. When it reaches 100%, you will see a photo of a cat.

Return to Movie Editing mode. Click the ProgressBar component in the middle of the stage and look at its parameters in the Property Inspector. By setting mode to polled and source to _root, you can create a preloader for any Flash movie or application.

Creating Interface Buttons with the RadioButton Component

Radio buttons are a common element of many forms that you fill out on the Web. Whereas check boxes allow users to make multiple choices from a set of options, a radio button set allows only a single selection. The RadioButton component allows you to add this kind of functionality to your Flash applications.

To add a RadioButton component to a Flash application:

1. Choose Window → Development Panels → Components or press Cmd/Ctrl+F7 to open the Components panel.

2. Click the RadioButton component (in the UI Components category) and drag it to the Stage. Drop the component where you want it to be positioned in your application, and if necessary, align it with the other elements of your application.

3. Radio Buttons work only in sets or groups. Choose Window → Library to open the Library. You should see a component icon labeled RadioButton. Drag at least one more instance onto the Stage and position it near the other RadioButton instance(s).

4. Choose Window → Properties (Cmd/Ctrl+F3) to open the Property Inspector.

5. Edit the RadioButton component's parameters as follows:

   label This parameter determines the name that will appear beside the RadioButton. Enter a name in the Value field.

   labelPlacement This parameter determines where the label is positioned relative to the RadioButton: right, left, top, or bottom. Choose an option from the Value field.

   selected Click the Value field to change the selected option. If this parameter is set to `true`, a dot will appear inside the button. When `false` (default), there is no dot.

   data This parameter determines the value that is assigned to the RadioButton. Enter a value (numeric or text) in the Value field.

   groupName This parameter assigns the RadioButton to a group or the set of choices to which it will belong. The default value is `radioGroup`. If you plan to use more than one set of RadioButton components in an application, be sure that each set has a unique value for `groupName`.

6. Save your movie and choose Control → Test Movie to see how your RadioButton component works.

This example demonstrates how you could use this component in an application. The example is also available in the Chapter 16 folder of this book's accompanying CD. See the file named `radioButton_component.fla`. Let's say you needed to get the year your users graduated (or will graduate) from college and you knew that it would be one of four possible dates. Drag four RadioButton components to the Stage. Give each instance a date for the `data` and `label` parameters and keep the default value `radioGroup` for the `groupName` parameter. For one instance, set the `selected` parameter to `true`. Enter the following ActionScript in the keyframe that holds the component:

```
rButton=new Object();
rButton.click = function(eventObj){
```

```
        var grad=eventObj.target.selection.data;
        trace(grad);
    }
    radioGroup.addEventListener("click",rButton);
```

Here, once again, is the famous Event Listener function that was described earlier in this chapter. The *grad* variable stores a user's graduation year based on which button they click.

Managing Large Objects with the ScrollPane Component

The ScrollPane component is an excellent addition to the Flash MX 2004 and MX Pro 2004 component set. Unfortunately, it doesn't take the place of a good old-fashioned scroll bar. The ScrollPane component isn't specifically designed to scroll through text fields, and though it can do it, it involves a few more steps than a simple v1 ScrollBar component. To learn how to scroll large fields of text, see Chapter 20.

The ScrollPane component does have some great features that you might want to take advantage of. It was designed specifically to scroll JPEG images, SWF files, and internal Movie Clips. This makes it ideal if you have to fit large items into small spaces. Users can scroll using horizontal and vertical scroll bars or by clicking and dragging the content within the ScrollPane.

To add a ScrollPane component to a Flash application:

1. Choose Window → Development Panels → Components or press Cmd/Ctrl+F7 to open the Components panel.

2. Click the ScrollPane component (in the UI Components category) ![icon] and drag it to the Stage. Drop the component where you want it to be positioned, and if necessary, align it with the other elements of your application.

3. Choose Window → Properties (Cmd/Ctrl+F3) to open the Property Inspector.

4. Edit the ScrollPane component's parameters as follows:

   contentPath Enter the absolute or relative path to the SWF or JPEG file you wish to display in the ScrollPane. A relative path should be relative to your application; an absolute path should contain the full URL to the file. You can also display a Movie Clip with a Linkage ID saved in your movie's Library. Enter the Linkage ID name in the value field. To learn how to assign a Linkage ID to a Movie Clip, see Chapter 19.

> Be careful with SWF files! They automatically assume the background color of the movie hosting them, so you can't depend upon a file's background color to be visible when it's hosted inside another movie's ScrollPane component. You can remedy the situation by using a graphic to serve as your movie's background. You can see an example of this in dimensions.fla, found with the other example files noted at the end of this section.

scrollDrag When set to `true`, this parameter allows your users to click on the contents of the ScrollPane and drag them with the mouse. A value of `false` (default) disables this feature.

hLineScrollSize This parameter determines the number of horizontal units the Scroll-Pane content moves when the arrow button is clicked.

hPageScrollSize This parameter determines the number of horizontal units the Scroll-Pane content moves when the scroll bar track is clicked.

hScrollPolicy Use this parameter to display horizontal scroll bars. `on` will show scroll bars whether they are needed or not, `off` will hide scroll bars, and `auto` will show scroll bars when they are required.

vLineScrollSize This parameter determines the number of vertical units the ScrollPane content moves when the arrow button is clicked.

vPageScrollSize This parameter determines the number of vertical units the Scroll-Pane content moves when the scroll bar track is clicked.

vScrollPolicy Use this parameter to display vertical scrollbars. `on` will show scrollbars whether they are needed or not, `off` will hide scrollbars, and `auto` will show scroll bars when they are required.

5. Be sure that your external file(s) are in the correct location and that Movie Clips have the correct Linkage ID according to what you specified for the `contentPath` parameter. Save your movie and choose Control → Test Movie to see how your ScrollPane component works.

To see an example of a ScrollPane component in action, see the `scroll_pane` folder inside the Chapter 16 folder of this book's accompanying CD. Be sure that you copy the entire folder to your computer's hard disk before you test it out. The additional files in the folder are required content for the various scroll panes in `scroll_pane.fla`.

Getting Feedback with the TextArea Component

The TextArea component can be used to collect comments for your users. It provides a large field where they can type their thoughts or ask a question. The TextArea component accommodates both multiline text and word wrap, so it is ideally suited to handle large strings of textual information.

To add a TextArea component to a Flash application:

1. Choose Window → Development Panels → Components or press Cmd/Ctrl+F7 to open the Components panel.

2. Click the TextArea component (in the UI Components category)  and drag it to the Stage. Drop the component where you want it to be positioned, and if necessary, align it with the other elements of your application.

3. Choose Window ➔ Properties (Cmd/Ctrl+F3) to open the Property Inspector.

4. Edit the TextArea component's parameters as follows:

   text This parameter assigns content to the TextArea. To assign multiline text content, you can use either ActionScript or an HTML line-break tag (`<br>`). This is because you can't use a carriage return as part of a parameter in the Property Inspector. To enter multiline text in the Property Inspector, type:

   ```
   line 1<br>line 2<br>line x
   ```

   The `<br>` tag inserts a line break between the individual lines. See the example later in this section to learn more about how to enter multiline text with ActionScript.

   html This parameter determines if the TextArea can have its text formatted in HTML. Set the parameter to `true` if you want to take advantage of HTML formatting.

   editable This parameter determines if the TextArea is editable (`true`) or not (`false`).

   wordWrap This parameter determines if the contents of the TextArea will wrap to the next available line (`true`) or not (`false`). When set to `false` and the length of a line of text goes beyond the width of the text area, a horizontal scroll bar is automatically added to the component.

5. Save your movie and choose Control ➔ Test Movie to see how your TextArea component works.

Here's a simple example to demonstrate how you can assign multiline text to a TextArea component. Drag a TextArea component to the Stage and give it the instance name **tome**. Then enter the following ActionScript in the keyframe that holds the component:

```
tome.text="line 1";
tome.text+="\rline 2";
tome.text+="\rline 3";
tome.text+="\rline 4";
```

This script uses the `text` property to assign text to the TextArea. The Addition Assignment Operator (`+=`) adds new text to the TextArea and the escaping character `\r` inserts a carriage return to start a new line. To learn more about working with text strings, see the ActionScript Reference on this book's companion CD.

Collecting Data with the TextInput Component

Whereas the TextArea component was useful for collecting and displaying large amounts of text, the TextInput component is meant only for single-line text. This component is ideal for collecting elements of a mailing address and e-mail contact information and for checking passwords.

To add a TextInput component to a Flash application:

1. Choose Window → Development Panels → Components or press Cmd/Ctrl+F7 to open the Components panel.

2. Click the TextInput component (in the UI Components category) ⟦abl⟧ and drag it to the Stage. Drop the component where you want it to be positioned, and if necessary, align it with the other elements of your application.

3. Choose Window → Properties (Cmd/Ctrl+F3) to open the Property Inspector.

4. Edit the TextInput component's parameters as follows:

   text This parameter assigns a single line of content to the TextInput field.

   editable This parameter determines if the TextInput field is editable (`true`) or not (`false`).

   password Set this parameter to `true` if you want users to enter a password in the TextArea field. As they type, the characters of their password will appear as asterisks (`*`).

5. Save your movie and choose Control → Test Movie to see how your TextInput component works.

To see an example of this in context, see the file `textArea_input_component.fla` in the Chapter 16 folder of this book's accompanying CD. In this sample file, you can see how a simple script can be assigned to a Button component to verify a password and make an adjacent text field editable.

Stepping Beyond Components

It should be clear by now that components allow you to leverage a great deal of control when creating applications in Flash. Through a simple drag-and-drop process, you can quickly and easily add interface elements that bring your applications to life. After using components and putting them to work in your movie, it might seem that you have run the gamut of possibilities, but there is still more you can do with them. In this section, you will learn how to *skin* a component, giving it an entirely new look. You can also learn where to go to get additional component resources and how to install them so that they are available alongside the others in the Components panel.

Skinning Components with Custom Themes

In the computer software world, the terms *skin* refers to a piece (or pieces) of art that can used to change the appearance of an application. A popular example would be skins for MP3 players. By applying different skins to the player, you can get rid of the default appearance (usually bland and monotone) and replace it with something that looks like a furry animal, a brick wall, viscous fluid—just about anything. The skin graphics *become* the appearance of the application and establish an entirely new look and feel. The process of changing an application's appearance in this manner is known as *skinning*.

Since v1 components were released in Flash MX, it has been possible to skin them. Now, with v2 components, it is still possible, though the process has changed a bit. Component skins are called *themes*. Themes reside in the Libraries of FLA files. You can open these files to see all the parts that compose the theme of any given component. The default theme for v2 components is called *Halo*. To skin a component, all you need to do is replace the Halo theme with a new theme. If you don't have a theme, you can create one.

Creating a Custom Theme

The easiest way to create a custom theme is to open an existing theme file, choose File → Save As, and rename the existing file. This way, all the ActionScript required for the component is already part of the theme and your modifications will affect only the graphics.

To create a custom theme:

1. Choose File → Open and navigate to the folder where Flash is stored on your computer's hard disk. On Macintosh systems, go to:

   ```
   Applications/Macromedia Flash MX 2004/First Run/ComponentFLA
   ```

   In Windows, go to:

   ```
   Program Files\Macromedia\Flash MX 2004\en\
     ↳ First Run\ComponentFLA
   ```

2. Choose SampleTheme.fla and click OK.

3. SampleTheme.fla should now be open. Choose File → Save As. Give the file the name **myTheme1.fla** and save it in a location you will remember.

4. Choose Window → Library to open the Library. In the Library panel, double-click the folder icons to navigate through the following folders: Flash UI Components 2 → Themes → MMDefault. The MMDefault folder displays additional subfolders that contain the theme Movie Clips for many of the v2 components (see Figure 16.5).

5. Open the folder that contains the theme of the component you want to change. For the sake of example, let's open the ProgressBar Assets folder. Then, open the Elements folder. You should see seven Movie Clip icons .

6. Open each Movie Clip individually and edit it. The name of the clip should give you an idea of its role in the overall component. For example, ProgTrackRight is the graphic for the right-side edge for the track (or

Figure 16.5

After opening a theme FLA file, the Library panel will allow you to view and edit the Movie Clips that make up a component theme or "skin."

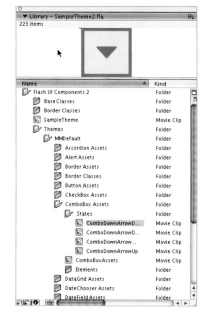

frame) that holds the ProgressBar. You will need to edit these elements carefully so that they line up with the others to create the entire component. For an example, see Figure 16.6. It might also help to zoom in (Cmd/Ctrl+=) or out (Cmd/Ctrl+–) when editing a theme, because many of the graphic elements tend to be small.

7. When editing the Movie Clips, it is vitally important that their graphic elements remain at the (0, 0) registration point. If you move them to another location, the final component will not display properly in your movie. After editing the clips, go back and use the Align panel or Property Inspector to check the registration.

8. Once you've finished editing the Movie Clips, you can edit additional clips for another component or close the FLA file.

These steps apply to any theme file you wish to edit. Of course, there are always subtle differences from one to the next, but the process remains basically the same. You can also edit the Halo theme. If you would like to try to make adjustments to this default theme, you will find it in the same folder as `SampleTheme.fla`. Navigate to the `ComponentFLA` folder (as described earlier) and open the file `HaloTheme.fla`.

Applying a New or Custom Theme

Once you have acquired or created a new theme, you need to apply it to a Flash application that uses components.

To apply a new theme to a component:

1. Open the Flash document that contains the component with the theme you want to change. Open the document's Library (Window → Library).

2. Choose File → Import → Open External Library and select the FLA file that contains the new theme. If you are continuing the process from the previous lesson, open `myTheme1.fla`.

Figure 16.6

ProgTrackLeft, Prog-TrackMiddle, and ProgTrackRight are the Movie Clips that serve as the track or frame of the ProgressBar component. Notice that when editing these theme graphics, a stroke is left off one or more edges so that they line up correctly with the other Movie Clips.

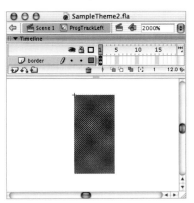
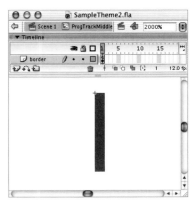
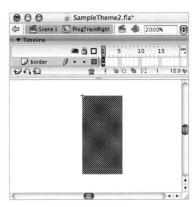

3. The FLA file will open as an additional Library. Navigate through the following folders: `Flash UI Components 2` → `Themes` → `MMDefault` to find the `Assets` folder of the component that you want to change, for example, `ProgressBar Assets`.

4. Drag this folder from the `myTheme1.fla` Library to the Library belonging to the open Flash document. If your open document was named `introApp.fla`, the document's Library would reflect this same name.

5. You're finished, though it doesn't look like it. Live Preview will not display changes to component themes. To see how the theme looks, choose Control → Test Movie. To get a sense of the changes that can be made by skinning a component, see Figure 16.7.

Figure 16.7

Here you see two Button components. The version on the top shows the default component appearance created by the Halo theme. The version on the bottom is a custom theme. Notice that the rounded edges of the Halo-themed button have been replaced by square corners of the custom theme.

Additional Components Resources

The set of v2 components that ship with Flash MX 2004 and MX Pro 2004 are helpful for most general interface needs. However, there are a few important components that are missing (for example, the ScrollBar), or you might find that you have a need beyond the default set of UI components. In either case, there are plenty of resources available for getting additional components. Some of these sites charge a fee for their components; others don't. Visit each site to see their current offerings and pricing information.

Macromedia Flash Exchange   This is the official components source. Macromedia Flash Exchange always has a huge list of downloadable components and other things to extend the abilities and functionality of Flash. Many downloads are free; others cost money. If you are interested in developing your own components and sharing them, Exchange provides a forum for this as well. Visit the Flash Exchange at `www.macromedia.com/exchange/flash`.

Eyeland Studio   Eyeland Studio, Inc., is directed by components guru J. Scott Hamlin. Eyeland has lots of different components to choose from. Many are available via subscription, but there are a few freebies. Pay a visit to `www.eyeland.com` to see what they have to offer.

FlashComponents.net   This site is probably one of the best-known resources for Flash components. FlashComponents.net is an open forum of exchange for components, components discussions, tutorials, and information about Flash development. Visit this great resource at `www.flashcomponents.net`.

Installing Additional Components

Once you have picked up a new component or two, you need to install them to use them in your applications. There are two ways to do this: by importing the component's FLA file as an external Library or by using Macromedia's Extension Manager application.

INSTALLING COMPONENTS AS AN EXTERNAL LIBRARY

You can install Flash components as an External Library when the components are distributed in FLA files. This process is somewhat similar to applying a new theme to an existing component in your movie.

To install a component from an FLA file:

1. Open the Flash document where you want to add the new component. Open the document's Library (Window → Library).

2. Choose File → Import → Open External Library and select the FLA file that contains the new component.

3. The FLA file will open as an additional Library. Click the component's icon ◼ in the external Library and drag it to the Library of the movie you're working with.

4. Click the menu in the title bar of the external Library panel and choose Close Panel.

5. To implement the new component in your movie, drag the component from the Library to the Stage and edit its parameters in either the Property or Component Inspector.

INSTALLING COMPONENTS WITH THE EXTENSION MANAGER

When you install Flash, a little application called the Extension Manager is also installed. This utility allows you to install software that extends the functionality of various Macromedia applications including (of course) Flash MX 2004 and MX Pro 2004. If you get third-party components that are saved as MXP files, the Extension Manager will allow you to install them.

To install components with the Extension Manager:

1. Launch the Extension Manager. If you don't know where this application is stored, do a search for *Extension Manager*. It should be in the folder where you installed Flash. If you are working in Flash MX 2004 or MX Pro 2004, you can also choose Help → Manage Extensions.

2. Choose Flash MX 2004 or Flash MX Professional 2004 from the Product menu (see Figure 16.8).

3. Choose File → Install Extension (Cmd/Ctrl+**O**).

4. Navigate to the component file that you want to install. It should be named with an `.mxp` extension. Select this file and click Choose.

5. As installation starts, you will be presented with a disclaimer. Read it and click Accept if you agree with the message. Installation will then commence.

6. Once installation has finished, click OK to confirm that it has completed. At this point, the Extension Manager will show the name of the component that you just installed in its main window. If you wish to install additional components, repeat steps 3–6.

After installing a component with the Extension Manager, open Flash and choose Window → Development Panels → Components. The newly installed component should be ready to use. If you opened the Extension Manager from within Flash, you will need to restart the application.

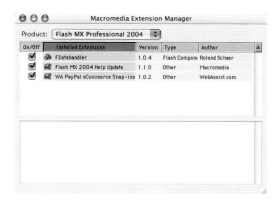

Inspirational Design Model

Coexist, LLP (www.coexistonline.com) was founded behind the concept of the Coexist logo, which combines three monotheistic religious symbols to spell the word *coexist* (see Figure 16.9). Coexist, LLP aims to promote understanding between people throughout the world without regard to religious beliefs and ideologies.

Figure 16.8

The Macromedia Extension Manager application

Figure 16.9

The Coexist logo was the impetus behind Coexist, LLP.

The Launch of the Coexist logo t-shirt "is the building block to a perpetual appreciation for coexistence through the lens of fashion and design." To help sell with the sales aspect of their website, Coexist, LLP uses the WebAssist PayPal eCommerce Snap-in (`www.webassist.com/Products/ProductDetails.asp?PID=24`). This "snap-in" is a Flash component developed specifically to facilitate online payments through PayPal. The WebAssist eCommerce snap-in component is easy to use and configure, and best of all, available for free! Download a copy for your next e-commerce project at the WebAssist website, or look for the version available on this book's accompanying CD.

Creating a Favorites Application with Behaviors and Components

This Hands On tutorial will help you cap off Part IV of this book and put some of your new Flash skills to work. Here we will combine the techniques covered in this part: using behaviors to add navigation and incorporating components for additional interactive functionality.

The first thing you should understand about this favorites application is that it is just that: an application. It is a "unit" of computer software that performs certain tasks. In this case, the application allows you to organize favorite photos and websites and share them with people who visit your website.

This application *is not* an entire website. Though Flash is perfectly capable of creating complete websites, that's not what this application is meant to do. It is a small element that can be added to your website. The application could appear alongside text and graphics, embedded in HTML, or it could exist on its own as one of your links. However you plan to incorporate it, we hope this application will be useful to both you and your audience.

If you like, you can see the finished files before you start creating the application on your own. They might be helpful because they will allow you to see the finished product (see Figure H4.1) and get an idea of what it looks like and how it will work. The finished files are named `favorites_app.fla` and `favorites_app.swf`. You can find them in the Hands On 4 folder on this book's accompanying CD-ROM. Realize that this lesson presents one way that you can design your application. If you would like to change the layout, use different graphics, and so on, feel free to do so. The value of this lesson is based more on the process that is presented than on exactly duplicating each step. If you are ready to begin, keep reading, good luck, and have fun!

Figure H4.1

The finished
~~r~~ites application
look something
~~t~~his. If necessary,
~~y~~ou can use the file
~~favo~~rites_app.fla
as a guide.

Phase 1: Setting the Stage

We can begin by creating a new, empty Flash document and filling it with the assets the application requires.

To start building the favorites application:

1. Launch Flash MX 2004 or MX Professional 2004.

2. Choose File → New and select Flash Document from the New Document dialog box. Click OK. Then choose File → Save As, give your document a name, and click OK to save it to your computer's hard disk.

3. The first order of business is to set the size of the Stage. Choose Modify → Document to display the Document Properties dialog box. Set Width to **470** and Height to **234**; then click OK.

4. Your application needs to have five layers in the main Timeline. Click the Insert Layer button four times to insert four new layers. From top to bottom, name the layers as follows: **code**, **titles**, **buttons**, **components**, and **photos**. Now, with layers in place, you can populate them with various elements of your application.

5. Click the photos layer to select it. Choose Window → Development Panels → Components to open the Components panel. Drag a Loader component from the UI category of the Components panel to the Stage.

6. Use the Property Inspector (Window → Properties or Cmd/Ctrl+F3) to make the dimensions of the component 240 (width) by 180 (height), and position it so that its upper-left corner is at X-Y coordinates (10, 24).

7. Click the components layer to select it. Drag a List component from the UI category of the Components panel to the Stage.

8. Using the Property Inspector, set the List component's dimensions to 200×180. Position it at (260, 24) and give it the instance name **webList**.

9. Click the buttons layer to select it. Drag a Button component (also in the UI category) to the Stage.

10. Once again, use the Property Inspector to set the Button component's dimensions to 20×20. Position it at (205, 209) and give it the instance name **back**.

11. Repeat steps 9 and 10. Place a second Button component at (230, 209) and give it the instance name **forward**.

12. To see what your application should look like at this point, see Figure H4.2.

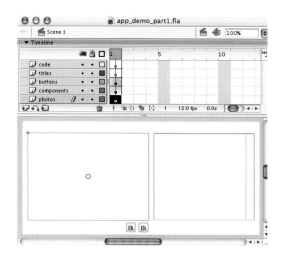

Phase 2: Building the Application

With layers for the various elements of your application and most of these elements in place, you are ready to begin the real work of putting this thing together.

To build your favorites application:

1. It will help your audience if the various parts of your application are labeled. Click to select the titles layer of the main Timeline and select the Text tool from the Tools panel.

2. Click the upper-left corner of the Stage to create a new text box and type **my favorite photos**. Check the Property Inspector to be sure that the text is Static Text, and choose a font, size, and color that you think works well for your application. Position the text at X-Y coordinates (10, 5).

3. Repeat steps 1 and 2. The new text should read **my favorite websites**. Place this line of text at (260, 5).

4. Press Cmd/Ctrl+**S** to save your application.

5. This next series of steps is a bit more complex than what you have done in this lesson so far. You'll turn the Loader component into a Movie Clip so that you can control it with behaviors. Click to select the Loader component on the Stage. Choose Modify → Convert To Symbol or press F8. The Convert To Symbol dialog box opens.

6. In the Convert To Symbol dialog box, enter **photos** in the Name field and select Movie Clip for its behavior. Check the Registration box so that the registration point is set at the upper-left corner of the new symbol. Click OK.

Figure H4.2

After laying out all the elements of your application, it will look like this. The Loader component is visible only when it's selected.

7. The newly converted Movie Clip should be displayed in your movie's Library. Choose Window → Library to open the Library and see the clip.

8. In the Library, double-click the photos Movie Clip icon to open it in Symbol Editing mode.

9. Now you're going to add some features to this clip so that it will work as a kind of "frame" that holds and loads JPEGs into your application. Start by renaming layer 1 of the Movie Clip **loaders**. Click the Add Layer button in the Timeline to create a new layer and name it **code**.

10. Click the first keyframe of the loaders layer to highlight the Loader component, then click the component itself to select it.

11. Open the Property Inspector; it should display parameters for the Loader. Give it the instance name **frame1** and enter parameters for the Loader as follows:

    • Set autoLoad to true.

    • Set scaleContent to false.

12. For the contentPath parameter, enter the name of a JPEG image that you want to show in your favorites application. Be sure that this image is saved in the same folder as the file for your application, and check to see that it is *not* a progressive JPEG. Flash can't handle this kind of JPEG file.

> This lesson assumes that the JPEGs you use are 240x180 pixels. Be sure to resize your images before using them in this application or to set the scaleContent parameter to true so that your images are resized by the Loader.

 If you don't have any JPEG files available, feel free to use the files we've provided on this book's accompanying CD and copy them to the location where you've saved your favorites application. Look for lil_dog.jpg and hanalei.jpg in the Hands On 4 folder.

13. Click frame 2 of the loaders layer in the Timeline. Press F6 to insert a new keyframe. When you do this, Flash duplicates the contents of the previous keyframe in the new keyframe.

14. Click to select the Loader component in the second keyframe. Go to the Property Inspector.

15. Give the component the instance name **frame2** and set the contentPath parameter to the name of another JPEG image you want to show in your application.

16. Because the photos Movie Clip now has two frames, you need to add a bit of Action-Script to prevent it from cycling through these frames continuously. Click the empty keyframe of the code layer. Choose Window → Development Panels → Actions and type the following statement in the Actions panel:

    ```
    stop();
    ```

    The stop() function will prevent the Movie Clip Timeline from playing until you tell it to do so.

17. Choose Edit → Edit Document to return to the main Timeline.

18. Click to select the instance of the photos Movie Clip on the main Timeline. Go to the Property Inspector and enter **photos_mc** as its instance name. This will enable you to control the Movie Clip from the buttons with behaviors.

19. Click the back instance of the Button component on the main Timeline. Go to the Property Inspector and enter <– (Shift+, then a hyphen) for the label parameter.

20. Repeat the previous step for the forward instance, but this time enter –> (a hyphen, then Shift+.) for the label parameter. These labels identify your buttons as forward and back buttons for the photo section of your application.

21. Now that your buttons look as if they should do something, you can make them do something by attaching behaviors. Click the forward instance to select it. Choose Window → Development Panels → Behaviors to open the Behaviors panel (see Figure H4.3).

22. If the Current Selection area of the Behaviors panel reads "unsupported selection," click the Behaviors panel menu in the upper-right corner and choose Reload to refresh the panel.

23. Click the Add Behavior button (+) and choose Movie Clip → Go To And Stop At Frame Or Label. The Go To And Stop At Frame Or Label dialog box opens.

24. Click the Absolute radio button in the dialog box and select photos_mc from the Target MC field.

25. Enter the number **2** in the Frame (Label) field and click OK. This behavior will send the photos_mc clip instance to frame 2 of its timeline, and reveal the image that is loaded into the Loader component at the second frame.

26. Repeat steps 24 and 25 for the back instance; only this time, set the photos_mc clip instance to stop at frame 1 of its timeline.

Figure H4.3

The Behaviors panel allows you to attach behaviors to the Button component and navigate through the photos Movie Clip.

27. Save your work. Then select Control → Test Movie and click the forward and back buttons to navigate through the images.

28. Now it's time to move on to the List component. You will use it to display a list of your favorite websites. Click the List component to select it and look at the Property Inspector.

29. Enter parameters for the List component as follows:

   - Labels: Enter the names of your favorite sites. These are the names that will appear in the application.

   - Data: Enter the full URL for each site, for example, `http://www.vonflashenstein.com`.

   Be sure that the order of labels and data parameters is consistent. Otherwise, clicking a label will take your users to a different site than reflected by the label. If you are unsure how to enter these parameters into the Property Inspector, read more about the List component in Chapter 16.

30. The List component by itself is useful only for holding information. To make it work, you need to add some ActionScript that extends its functionality. Click to select the empty keyframe of the code layer of the main Timeline. Open the Actions panel (F9) and enter the following statements:

```
url=new Object();
url.change = function(evt){
    var link = evt.target.selectedItem.data;
    getURL(link,"_blank");
}
webList.addEventListener("change",url);
```

   These statements use an Event Listener function to open the website that is selected in the List component. When the change event occurs (which happens whenever a user clicks an item in the List), the data value of that item is stored in the variable link. The variable is then plugged into the getURL() function, which opens the value of link in a new browser window.

31. Save your work; the application is now complete!

Phase 3: Testing the Application

An important part of application development is testing. You want to be sure that the application you've created will behave in the ways you and your users expect.

   To test your favorites application:

1. Choose Control → Test Movie from the main menu bar. Flash switches to Test Movie mode and your application is presented in a new window.

2. Click the forward and back buttons. Each should show a different image in your photo gallery.

3. Click each name in the List component and wait for the URL to load. Be sure that each item links to the correct website.

If any aspect of your application behaves incorrectly, go back in the lesson and check that you followed each step carefully. Possible causes for error could be

- Missing instance names for the photos Movie Clip or any of the components

- Incorrect parameters assigned to one or more components

- Wrong parameters assigned for the behaviors attached to buttons

- JPEG images need to be saved in the same location as the file for your application. If you need to keep them in a separate location, be sure to specify the correct path so the Loader component can locate the images.

Phase 4: Steps for the Future

Your favorites application is finished for now. If you are interested in expanding the application or working it into your website, here are a few suggestions.

Add more photos to the gallery. As it stands now, the application has only two photos. You would probably like to expand upon this. Unfortunately, the standard behaviors that ship with Flash MX 2004 and MX Pro 2004 have limitations that make this somewhat awkward. Your best bet is to write the ActionScript yourself. Attach the following Action-Script statements to the forward button instance:

```
on(click){
    _root.photos_mc.nextFrame();
}
```

Attach similar ActionScript statements to the back button instance:

```
on(click){
    _root.photos_mc.prevFrame();
}
```

Notice that the handler uses the click event to trigger these scripts. This is an event that is unique to the Button component; it has no effect when used with Button symbols in Flash.

These scripts use the nextFrame() and prevFrame() functions to advance the timeline of the photos_mc clip instance one frame at a time. You can fill the photos timeline with as many Loader components as you like and the buttons will allow your audience to browse through them all.

Use Dreamweaver to embed this application in the HTML of your website. Dreamweaver is a great tool for web development. It allows you to take a hands-off approach when doing HTML markup and makes it very easy to incorporate Flash movies into a web page. To learn more about integrating Dreamweaver and Flash, see Chapter 27.

If you do plan to put your application on the Web, be sure to upload the HTML, the SWF file of the application, and the JPEG images you display in your photo gallery.

PART V

Adding Advanced Interactivity with ActionScript

Up to *this point in the book, you have worked with the elements of Flash that have helped the application build its reputation: clean vector graphics, smooth Timeline animation, and an intuitive user interface that streamlines your work flow. You have also learned how to make your movies interactive by adding behaviors: simple scripts that direct a movie's playback and allow your audience to experience your content on their own terms.*

In recent years, Flash has become much more. Its scripting capabilities have grown considerably. ActionScript, once a simple "traffic cop" that controlled the flow of Timelines, has become the "governor" of your Flash movie, with control over nearly every level of the movie. With this increased control comes the increased potential to make a simple Flash animation into an immersive multimedia experience.

In this part of the book, you will begin to dig deeper into the specifics of ActionScript and learn how to use the language as a tool for making your movies play and respond intelligently to the requests of your audience. Part V contains these topics:

CHAPTER 17

Understanding and Using ActionScript

So, you are ready to take the plunge into the world of ActionScript. Congratulations! You will find that familiarity and competence with ActionScript allows you to do much more with your Flash creations than you could ever do with just behaviors. Where you find yourself hitting a ceiling with behaviors, hand-coded ActionScript offers a new world of possibility. This is one of the most exciting and rewarding aspects of working in Flash—but it can also be the most difficult and demanding.

This is not a warning to scare you off; it is a call to arms. Learning ActionScript and becoming comfortable with the language is a challenge. Getting to the point where you can use the language with fluidity can be even more tenuous. However, none of this is impossible. What is most important is that you practice diligently. Learning ActionScript (or any programming language, for that matter) is similar to learning to speak a foreign language: To use it fluently, you have to practice every day. Practice can be as basic as trying to create simple movies that perform tasks using capabilities of the ActionScript language. Repeated exposure to the language through this kind of routine will give you a good feel for the language in context. The more you practice, the more of the language you learn and the more comfortable you become with its elements.

This chapter covers fundamental ActionScript terms and concepts and gets you started with some advanced scripting techniques. It includes these topics:

- ActionScript as an object-oriented language

- Components of a script in the context of a simple movie

- How scripts flow

- How to plan scripts before you create your movie

- Introduction to ActionScript terms

- The Actions panel: your scripting interface

Knowing and Applying the Anatomy of ActionScript

ActionScript is most similar to the programming language JavaScript. In fact, ActionScript is derived from the JavaScript specifications set forth by the European Computer Manufacturers Association (ECMA).

> For more information about the history, role, and members of the ECMA, go to its website: `www.ecma-international.org`.

As an object-oriented scripting language, ActionScript has components that follow a particular organization. Elements of a movie are organized into *classes*. Classes can then be expressed as individual or independent parts called *objects*. An object is an *instance* of a class.

A class has information that it passes on to each object it creates. This information comes in the form of *properties*, which are the qualities of an object, and *methods*, which are the "tasks" an object can perform. In Flash, there are several predefined classes that create objects, such as Date objects and Sound objects. One of the most common predefined objects, the Movie Clip, has properties such as `_framesloaded` and methods such as `play()`.

It's possible to create your own objects using ActionScript. For example, you could use a *constructor* function to create the class Dogs, with properties such as `_spotted` and `_scruffy`, and the method `fetch`.

Understanding ActionScript 2

One of the most significant changes to Flash with the release of Flash MX 2004 and Flash MX Professional 2004 is the introduction of ActionScript 2, the next big step for ActionScript as a language. ActionScript 2 includes enhancements that lend it greater power and scope than the previous version. These changes make it easier to develop object-oriented applications with Flash and ActionScript. Programmers who have an object-oriented background or currently develop in other object-oriented languages (such as Java) should find the transition to ActionScript a smooth one.

ActionScript 2 marks an interesting change for Flash as a development tool. It allows users to treat Flash less as an authoring tool and more as a development environment. But what does this mean for the average Flash user? Will ActionScript 2 ruin your favorite program? We believe it's safe to say no. Talks with Macromedia suggest that the Flash you've grown to love will maintain the same "personality" as it evolves. The fact that Flash has been split into two releases might seem to suggest otherwise, but if you look at both Flash MX 2004 and Flash MX Pro 2004, you should find that each version has retained the characteristics that have made Flash such a favorite.

While many advancements in the program are exciting, some will not be covered in this book. Writing object-oriented programs with Action-Script goes far beyond the mandate of Flash MX Savvy. What you will find, however, is a solid approach to working with ActionScript that allows you to get great results out of Flash. We have chosen to focus on the various aspects of the application that are most helpful to beginners, intermediates, and intermediates looking to advance their skills. While ActionScript 2 doesn't fit this rubric, the nuts and bolts of ActionScript as a language certainly do.

Figure 17.1
The coffee break movie

Breaking Down a Script

One way to understand how scripts work is to dissect a script that is functioning in the context of a movie. This approach is helpful because seeing a movie is the proof; you can witness the script running right before you. Once you grasp what is happening on the movie's Stage, you can take a look behind the scenes and see what kind of script is making the movie act a certain way or do a certain thing.

In the following example (`coffee_break.fla` in the Chapter 17 folder on this book's companion CD), the audience's standard pointer cursor is replaced with a jittery, caffeine-deprived custom cursor. When someone clicks to "fill" their coffee mug, the jitters disappear and steam rises as coffee is poured into the mug. This movie (see Figure 17.1) takes place in a single frame, although the jitter and steam animations take around 100 frames. The hand holding the mug is an instance of a Movie Clip; the jitters and steam animations are also Movie Clip instances inside the mug clip.

The only scripts in the movie are a series of statements on the main Timeline directed at the `coffee_mc` Movie Clip instance. These scripts are responsible for attaching the custom cursor, cueing the animations, and playing the sound.

Open and play the movie so that you can see exactly what it does. Also, select the keyframe in the code layer and open the Actions panel (by pressing F9) to see the scripts that control the instance's behavior as a custom cursor. For a specific breakdown of the scripts in this movie, refer to Figure 17.2.

Figure 17.2
The Actions panel with scripts for the `coffee_mc` instance

```
1  Mouse.hide();
2  coffee_mc.startDrag(true);
3  sfx = new Sound();
4  sfx.attachSound("pour");
5
6  coffee_mc.onMouseMove = function() {
7      coffee_mc._x = _root._xmouse;
8      coffee_mc._y = _root._ymouse;
9  }
10 fillerUp_mc.onMouseDown = function() {
11     if (coffee_mc.hitTest(fillerUp_mc)) {
12         coffee_mc.jitters_mc.gotoAndPlay("fade");
13         coffee_mc.steam_mc.gotoAndPlay("fill");
14         _root.sfx.start();
15     }
16 }
```

When the movie loads into the Flash Player, these statements on the main timeline execute:

```
Mouse.hide();
coffee_mc.startDrag(true);
sfx = new Sound();
sfx.attachSound("pour");
```

The Mouse object hides the pointer cursor and the `startDrag()` function makes this coffee mug Movie Clip draggable. These statements make the mug a kind of custom cursor by replacing the pointer with the mug. The next two lines invoke a Sound object using the `new Sound()` constructor function and attach the sound `pour` to a sound instance named `sfx`.

The next function is called whenever the mouse is moved:

```
coffee_mc.onMouseMove = function() {
    coffee_mc._x = _root._xmouse;
    coffee_mc._y = _root._ymouse;
}
```

The statements inside the function lock the horizontal and vertical position of the mouse to the registration point of the `coffee_mc` Movie Clip instance.

Finally, one last function is called when the mouse is clicked, or more specifically, pressed down. The function is called by the `onMouseDown` event and runs through a conditional:

```
fillerUp_mc.onMouseDown = function(){
    if (coffee_mc.hitTest(fillerUp_mc)){
        coffee_mc.jitters_mc.gotoAndPlay("fade");
        coffee_mc.steam_mc.gotoAndPlay("fill");
        _root.sfx.start();
    }
}
```

The conditional `if` statement asks if the `coffee_mc` clip instance has collided with or is over the fillerUp instance. If the instances intersect, the conditional returns a True value, sends the `jitters_mc` instance to play at the frame labeled `fade`, and sends `steam_mc` to play at the label `fill`. After doing this, the script plays the sound object `sfx` that was created when the movie was first loaded. The conditional has no `else`, or alternative statement. This means that if the two clips don't intersect when the mouse is clicked, the `if` statement returns a False value and nothing is done. Without the conditional statement to check whether the hand is over the glass, any `mouseDown` event would cause the animation and the sound to play. Try pulling this script apart and changing different parameters to see what different kinds of behavior you can create.

There are two other scripts in this movie. In the `jitters_mc` and `steam_mc` Movie Clip instances, there is a `stop()`function at frame 1 of each clip's Timeline. This prevents the clip from playing until it receives a message that tells it to jump ahead to a frame label and begin the animation.

How Scripts Flow

What is almost more important than understanding the elements of a language is understanding the *flow* of a language. Flow refers to the way that a script is read and processed while your movie is running. When scripts do not work properly, the cause is often a mistake in the flow, or order of the script, rather than a misuse of terms or incorrect syntax.

As do most programming languages, ActionScript follows a logical, step-by-step flow. This means that lines are executed in sequential order, starting at the top and working their way down through the script.

For example, in the following script, the playback head stops, sets the `_alpha` property, or transparency, of a Movie Clip named `plane` to 50 percent, and then continues playing at frame 11:

```
stop();
_root.plane._alpha=50;
gotoAndPlay(11);
```

The actions are carried out specifically in the order they are listed.

A script can take several diversions as it travels along in your movie. In ActionScript, there are statements known as *conditionals* that will reroute your script flow. This detour in the flow of the script is usually done to test a condition and then do something as a result of the test.

One of the most common conditionals is an `if` statement. Here is its basic structure:

```
if(thisStatementIsTrue){
    do thisStatement
}
```

The `if` statement tests a condition, which can be evaluated as either True or False; and if the evaluation is True, the statements in the body of the `if` statement are executed. The `if` statement can provide an `else` alternative. This way, if the condition tested is False, the script will execute a separate action—the statements in the body of the `else` part of the statement (see Figure 17.3). For example:

```
if(thisStatementIsTrue){
    do thisStatement
}else{
    do aDifferentStatement
}
```

In a script where the `if` statement evaluates False and there is no `else` alternative, the statements in the body of the `if` are skipped entirely.

These structures are very useful for testing different parameters in your movie and telling Flash to act accordingly.

Related to the conditional script structure is the *loop* structure. The loop structure creates a repetition and performs a task or process repeatedly until a value is achieved to satisfy the demands of the loop (see Figure 17.4).

For example:

```
i=0;
while(i<3){
    trace("i is "+i);
    trace(i+" is less than 3");
    i++;
}
trace("loop completed!");
trace("i is "+i);
trace(i+" equals 3");
```

This script is executed in the same step-by-step fashion as the `if` conditional. However, there is a slight delay before the script makes it to the last line. This script uses a `while` loop and detains the script flow while it runs the variable *i* through an increasing series of values. This script methodically increases the value of *i* by 1 as long as it is less than 3 and the `trace()` function prints results to the Output panel. When the script has completed this task, it continues down the line to execute the last statements, and print a final evaluation.

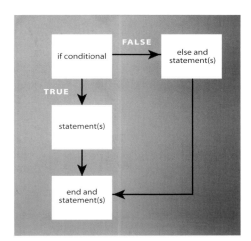

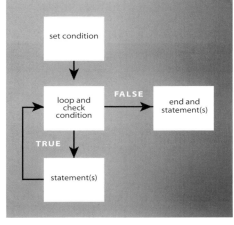

Figure 17.3

The flow of an `if…else` **statement**

Figure 17.4

The flow of a `while` **loop**

The entire loop prints the following:

```
i is 0
0 is less than 3
i is 1
1 is less than 3
i is 2
2 is less than 3
loop completed!
i is 3
3 equals 3
```

Loops such as this are especially helpful for repetitive actions and information processing. For more information on the `trace()` function, loops, and loop syntax, see Chapter 21,
as well as the ActionScript Reference on this book's accompanying CD.

Planning and Assigning Scripts

Every designer or animator knows that one of the most essential parts of the development
process is planning and storyboarding. Planning is crucial. It allows you to think things
through before committing to a final version. It's also an opportunity to look at the big
picture before zeroing in on the details during production. Planning answers the most
important question: What am I creating?

Just as planning is common practice for design and animation, it should be so for
scripting. Before writing a single line of ActionScript, you should know the purpose of
every script and how it will work toward a goal in your movie.

To begin the process, you need to start at the top and decide what you need the movie
to do. Then, break it down to the next level: What movie elements are needed to accomplish this? When the various movie components are clear, you should decide how they
work and whether they interact. Once things have been reduced to this level, you should
have a good start toward defining the purpose of ActionScript in your movie. The next
step is, of course, to start writing scripts.

The best strategy for writing scripts is to start simply. Get one element of the movie
working before you move on to the next one. This technique allows you to isolate problems
as they occur. It's also good to get in the habit of saving your work often and saving multiple
versions of a project. This way, if something goes off track, you can go back to the last
working version and pick up where you left off, rather than build a movie from scratch.

If you are new to ActionScript, you are likely to spend a fair amount of time digging
through ActionScript references or the built-in Help panel (F1) looking for the language
elements you need to build your scripts. Inevitably, you will encounter things that are not
immediately helpful, but might be helpful in the future. In these occasions, it's a good idea
to keep a list or journal of the terms you discover. That way, when the time comes and you
need a term, you can reference your notes rather than dig through a book again.

Getting Familiar with ActionScript Terminology

As a powerful and flexible scripting language, ActionScript has many components within the language itself. It's important to understand these terms and how they fit together in the ActionScript family. The following list, organized alphabetically, is a breakdown of the key ActionScript terms and their general descriptions. For a more detailed account of these terms, see Chapter 20.

Actions is a generic name for a term that tells a movie or one of its components to do something while the movie is running. In previous versions of Flash, ActionScript "commands" were called *actions*. It is more accurate to call them *functions* because they do something, or *statements* because they give your movie instructions. Macromedia and the Flash community seem to agree that the term *actions* is no longer appropriate.

Arguments (or **parameters**) are containers that hold information and pass it on to statements or functions. For example, the custom function `newUser` has two arguments: `userName` and `userID`.

```
function newUser(userName,userID)
```

These arguments are stored and used later in the function. Similarly, ActionScript functions can take arguments. For example:

```
gotoAndStop(5);
```

The `gotoAndStop()` function requires an argument so that it knows where to stop the Timeline.

Classes are categories of information in your movie. Each object belongs to a class and is an individual *instance* of that class. To define a new object, you must create an instance of the object based on its class. This is done with the help of a constructor function.

Constants are script elements that do not change. For example, an integer (whole number) is a constant and can be used to check the value of an expression. The key SPACE is a constant because it always refers to the spacebar.

Constructors are functions that are used to create objects based on classes. The function, in turn, has arguments that can give each object its own set of properties specific to the object's class.

Data types describe the kind of information that a variable or ActionScript element can communicate. In ActionScript, the data types are string, number, Boolean value (True and False), object, Movie Clip, and undefined or null (no data). For more information on data types, see Chapter 18.

Events happen while your movie is running. They are generated by such things as mouse clicks, the loading of Movie Clips, and keystrokes. Events are used to trigger functions and other ActionScript statements.

An **expression** is any chunk of information that can produce a value. For example:

```
on(release){
    gotoAndPlay(_currentframe+1);
}
```

This script sends the movie to the frame number equal to the value of the expression `_currentframe+1`.

Functions are information processors, the "worker bees" of any Flash movie. They can be passed information in the form of arguments and return a value or perform a task. You can also create Custom Functions, which are great if you want to create a unique ActionScript routine or task that will be used repeatedly throughout a movie.

Handlers are used to perform functions in response to events. In ActionScript, there are handlers for both mouse and Movie Clip events.

Identifiers are unique names assigned to functions, methods, objects, properties, or variables. The first character of an identifier must be either a letter, dollar sign ($), or underscore (_). A full identifier name can use these characters as well as numbers. For example, you can have a Movie Clip instance named `code_mc` or a function called `routine1`.

Instances are individual objects that belong to a class. For example, the `today` instance could belong to the `Date` class.

An **instance name** is a unique name used to refer to a specific instance of an object in your movie. This could be an instance of a TextField, Sound, or Array object. Movie Clips are treated like objects but are fundamentally different because we create Movie Clips in Flash and save them as Symbols. However, to control them with ActionScript, Movie Clips (like objects) require an instance name. For example, a Movie Clip symbol named `logoMovie` can be used repeatedly throughout a movie. You must give each instance a unique instance name, such as `logo1` or `logo2`. Each instance in the movie must be referred to by its unique instance name. This distinction allows ActionScript to control each instance of the one Movie Clip symbol independently.

Keywords are words with special meaning in the ActionScript language and are unavailable for use as variables, functions, and so on. Refer to Chapter 18 for a list of ActionScript keywords.

Methods are functions that belong to and can be performed by objects. For custom objects, you can create custom methods. In ActionScript, each predefined object (such as the Sound object or MovieClip object) has its own methods. For a list of object methods, see the ActionScript Reference section on this book's accompanying CD.

Objects are instances of a class. ActionScript has several built-in classes that are called objects; these include the Sound object, the Date object, and the MovieClip object.

Operators are elements that are used to calculate and compare values. For example, the forward-slash (/) operator is used to divide one number by another.

A **property** is any kind of quality that belongs to an object and can define an instance of an object. For example, the _x property determines the X coordinate of a Movie Clip on the Stage.

Target paths are used to pass information along the chain of Movie Clip instance names, variables, and objects in a movie. For example:

```
menuBar.item1.selected
```

This is the target path to the variable `selected`, which is inside the Movie Clip `item1`, which is inside the Movie Clip `menuBar`. For more details on the hierarchy of Movie Clips, see Chapter 20.

Variables are storage locations that hold information and values. Variables can be used for permanent or temporary storage. You can set, modify, and retrieve the value of a variable and use it in scripts while a movie is playing.

Using the Actions Panel for Advanced Scripting

As you learned while working with behaviors, the Actions panel is your interface for adding ActionScript statements to a Flash movie. It provides several window components that allow you to select ActionScript elements, arrange and order them as you see fit, and edit any individual parameters as needed.

In Flash 5 and Flash MX, the Actions panel had two modes of operation: Normal and Expert. Normal mode provided a menu-driven interface that allowed users to create their scripts with a minimum of typing. Flash MX 2004 and MX Pro 2004 have replaced Normal Scripting mode with behaviors, thus making Expert Scripting mode the only means of scripting in Flash MX 2004. You will probably find behaviors much more limiting than Normal mode ever was. However, hand-coding ActionScript in the Actions panel gives you enormous freedom and flexibility, and you'll find it provides several enhancements that make it easy to work with the scripts you create.

Scripting with the Actions Panel

The *Actions panel* (see Figure 17.5) is your interface for creating scripts that will be executed in a Flash movie. It is a window where you can create and modify the interactivity of your movie. To help with this process, the Actions panel provides several tools that can automate different aspects of scripting, provide help when needed, and organize the scripting workspace.

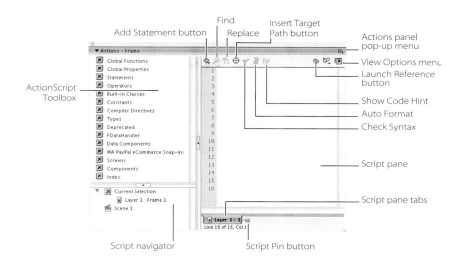

Figure 17.5

The Actions panel contains several unique and useful new features for composing Action-Scripts.

Following are descriptions of some Actions panel features:

ActionScript Toolbox This menu is one location where you can access an ActionScript Library. Actions can be selected in this area of the panel and dragged into the Script pane.

Script Navigator This menu is best described as where the Movie Explorer meets the Actions panel, and it is surely one of the best new enhancements. The Script Navigator allows you to locate a script anywhere in your movie and immediately call it up in the Script pane.

Script pane Scripts are displayed in their entirety here. This is the area where you compose ActionScript.

Add a Statement button Use this button to add an ActionScript statement. The button opens to a cascading series of menus. When an item is selected, it appears in the Action-Script text box.

View Options menu The View Options menu allows you to enable the line-numbering and word-wrap features of the Actions panel.

Launch ActionScript Reference button This handy button gives you access to Flash MX 2004's built-in ActionScript reference. Click it, and the Help panel appears.

Actions Panel pop-up Menu This menu provides access to many additional Actions panel features such as panel preferences and options for script formatting.

Script Pin button The Script Pin button allows you to "stick" a script to the panel. This is the digital equivalent of a pushpin cork board: Once you pin a script to the panel, it stays there. This feature allows you to make one script viewable at all times while selecting other objects in your movie.

Script pane tabs A new feature with this release of Flash is the introduction of Script pane tabs. Once you pin a script in place, it is assigned a tab. The Actions panel can hold many different tabs, enabling you to have instant access to the most important scripts in your movie.

Working with Actions Panel Features

The Actions panel is stocked with lots of tools that will help make writing ActionScript easier. While the panel won't write scripts for you, it can provide assistance with writing and editing, keep your scripts organized, and control the way scripts appear in the panel. You are able to search scripts and perform find-and-replace edits for ActionScript terms that appear more than once. It's also possible to write your scripts outside Flash and include them in your movie from an external location. Additionally, the Actions panel allows you to print scripts and check for errors before testing your movie.

SCRIPT DISPLAY OPTIONS

In Flash MX 2004 and 2004 Pro, there are several new (and very welcome) additions to the Actions panel. Many of these features affect the way a script is displayed in the panel, offering greater control over the display and organization of information.

WORD WRAP

Scripts with long lines of text often go beyond the bounds of the Script pane. In previous versions of Flash, you could view these scripts only by either scrolling the Script pane left and right or increasing the size of the Actions panel. Now in Flash MX 2004 and MX Pro 2004, all you need to do is turn on the Word Wrap feature. Word Wrap forces lines of ActionScript that stretch beyond the bounds of the Script pane to break and continue on the next line when the pane runs out of space. When this option is enabled, long lines of code are visible within a single Actions panel.

To turn on Word Wrap:

1. Choose Window → Development Panels → Actions or press F9 to open the Actions panel.

2. Select the Actions panel pop-up menu and select Word Wrap or press Shift+Cmd+**W** (Mac)/Shift+Ctrl+**W** (Win). A check appears beside the menu option in the menu.

To deactivate Word Wrap, return to the pop-up menu and deselect Word Wrap. The check beside the menu option disappears.

When Word Wrap is on, long lines of ActionScript code break and continue on the next line, much as a web browser does.

SCRIPT NAVIGATOR

The Script Navigator is very similar to the Movie Explorer panel. It uses a hierarchical menu to display the contents of your movie. The difference is that the Script Navigator shows only elements that have scripts attached: frames, buttons, and Movie Clips with attached scripts. This makes it the perfect tool for locating any script in your movie and calling it to the Script pane.

To locate a script with the Script Navigator:

1. Choose Window → Development Panels → Actions or press F9 to open the Actions panel.

2. Click the triangles in the Script Navigator to reveal nested buttons, Movie Clips, and Timeline frames.

3. Click the name of the frame or object that has the script you want to edit. The script appears in the Script pane.

For more details about the hierarchical tree structure, see Chapter 9 for details on the Movie Explorer.

SCRIPT PIN AND SCRIPT PANE TABS

Script pane tabs provide an easy way to organize your scripts. Each pinned script is given its own tab that appears below the Script pane in the Actions panel. You can navigate from one pinned script to the next by simply clicking the tab of the script you want to view or edit.

To pin, unpin, or change tabs for a script:

1. Choose Window → Development Panels → Actions or press F9 to open the Actions panel.

2. Select the script you want to pin. Either click the frame or object that is attached to the script or use the Script Navigator to display the script.

3. Do any of the following:

   - To pin a script in place, click the Pin button ⚲. The script gets a new tab, which is highlighted at the left-hand edge of the Script pane (see Figure 17.6).

   - To unpin a script, click the Unpin button ⚲. The script's tab disappears when a script or different frame or object is selected. Alternatively, Cmd+click (Mac) or right-click (Win) on a tab and choose Close Script to remove a script's tab.

   - To navigate to a new script, click the tab for the script you need to see.

Figure 17.6

When a script is pinned to the Actions panel, a new tab is created and stored in the panel. These tabs can be used to navigate between other pinned scripts in your movie.

This new functionality provides a great way to both organize and edit ActionScripts in your movie.

LINE NUMBERING

The Actions panel's line-numbering feature allows you to better manage long scripts. Line numbering gives each line in your script an "address" of sorts, so that you can easily refer to each script element by number. To activate or deactivate line numbering:

1. Choose Window → Development Panels →Actions or press F9 to open the Actions panel.

2. Select the View Options menu and do either of the following:

   • To display line numbering, select View Line Numbers or press Shift+Cmd+**L** (Mac)/Shift+Ctrl+**L** (Win). A check appears beside the menu option in the menu.

   • To hide line numbering, select View Line Numbers. The check beside the menu option disappears.

When line numbers are on, they appear in the vertical gray strip between the Actions Toolbox and the text box (see Figure 17.7). When the option is off, the gray strip is empty.

AUTO FORMAT

The ActionScript examples that you read in this book were specially prepared so that they were written as neatly and clearly as possible. In the real world, though, this isn't always the case. If you are "in the trenches" and under a tight deadline for preparing a script-intensive movie, the last thing on your mind is the tidiness of your script. A neat, orderly script isn't a necessity, but often a neat script makes it easier to find syntax errors or other glitches that prohibit a script from running properly or running at all.

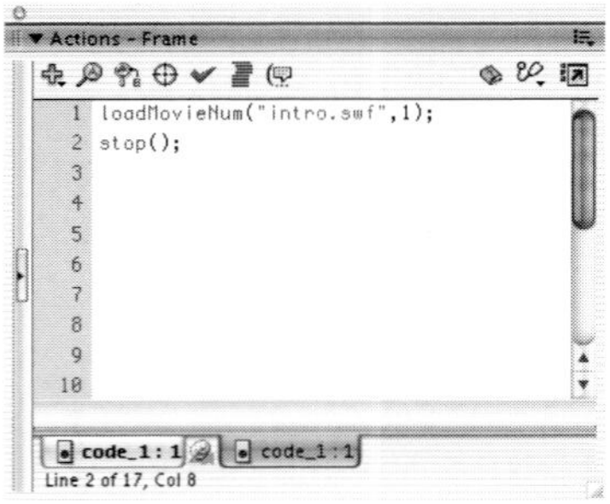

Luckily, the Actions panel offers an auto-format feature that enables you to automatically clean up a messy script by using a single mouse click or keyboard shortcut. To apply auto-formatting to a script:

Figure 17.7

The Actions panel with the line numbering option turned on

1. Select the object or frame that contains the script you wish to format.

2. Choose Window → Development Panels →Actions (F9) to open the Actions panel.

3. Do one of the following:

   • Press Shift+Cmd+**F** (Mac)/Shift+Ctrl+**F** (Win).

   • Choose Auto Format from the Actions panel pop-up menu.

   • Click the Auto Format button 🗐.

   Your script is automatically reformatted.

When you are using the auto-format feature, it's possible to control how Flash formats your scripts. To set the parameters for auto-formatting:

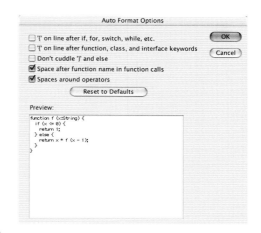

1. Click the Actions panel pop-up menu and select Auto Format Options. The Auto Format Options dialog box opens.

2. In the Auto Format Options dialog box, use the check boxes to turn on or off the various formatting parameters. To see how a particular formatting option affects your script, look at the Preview window at the bottom of the dialog box. When finished, click OK to return to the Actions panel.

Once you have set the formatting options, they will be applied to the current script whenever you use Auto Format.

ACTIONS PANEL TEXT DISPLAY

Flash MX allows you to have complete control over the display of actions in the Actions panel. This includes font, size, text color, and spacing. These options are controlled from the ActionScript Editor tab of the Preferences menu. To open this menu, do either of the following:

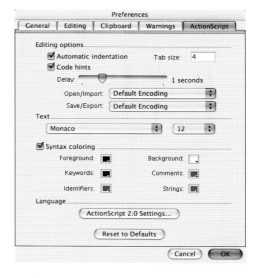

- Select Flash → Preferences (Mac) or Edit → Preferences (Win) and choose the ActionScript tab.

- Click the Actions panel pop-up menu and select Preferences.

You can set several options on the ActionScript tab:

Spacing Check the Automatic Indentation box, and Flash will automatically indent your scripts. To set the amount of indentation, type a number in the Tab Size field.

Imported/Exported Text Encoding Flash MX 2004 and MX Pro 2004 now support Unicode text encoding for ActionScript. This means you can import text in languages other than your system default language. To take advantage of Unicode support, select UTF-8 in the Open/Import and Save/Export drop-down menus. To work only with the system default language, select Default Encoding.

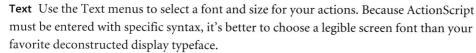

Text Use the Text menus to select a font and size for your actions. Because ActionScript must be entered with specific syntax, it's better to choose a legible screen font than your favorite deconstructed display typeface.

Color Flash allows several options for the display color of actions in your movie. When the Syntax Coloring box is checked, you can set a specific color for the following Action-Script elements: Foreground (text), Background (window color), Keywords, Comments, Identifiers, and Strings. Syntax coloring can make it easier to visually organize your scripts based on the color of individual script entries. Use the color swatch next to each element to choose a display color. If you prefer to view your scripts without the syntax coloration, deselect the Syntax Coloring option and choose appropriate foreground and background colors.

SYNTAX VERSION TRACKING

Although you're working in Flash MX 2004 and MX Pro 2004, you can still publish your movie for older versions of the Flash Player. Previous releases of Flash were made to publish movies for Flash Player 6 (and below) and ActionScript 1. As a result, you cannot use certain terms when publishing for older versions. It can be hard to keep track of which terms are available in which versions, so the Actions panel makes it easy for you. Any terms that are unavailable in the version for which you are publishing will be highlighted in a bright yellow color. You cannot use these terms unless you switch your publish settings to a higher version number. You can read more about publishing movies in Chapter 30.

Inserting a Target Path

If you want to direct ActionScript statements to affect a specific Movie Clip instance or other object in your movie, use a target path. A *target path* is the specific address for a Movie clip or other object. Without target paths, your scripts cannot locate the objects you want to control. Target paths were required for behaviors and they are equally important when you write ActionScript by hand. To learn more about target paths, see Chapter 20.

Often, target paths can be long and complex, and if you make a mistake when you type one, your movie will not perform properly. Luckily, the Actions panel provides an additional tool to help you avoid errors.

To enter a target path using the Actions panel:

1. Click the Insert Target Path button ⊕. The Insert Target Path dialog box opens and displays an outline of the Movie Clips in your movie.

2. Select the clip you wish to target, and the instance name appears in the Target field.

3. The Mode setting allows you to choose how the path is composed:

   - *Relative* writes the path starting from the current timeline.

   - *Absolute* writes the path starting from _root (at the top of the outline), and shows the path to the clip from the main Timeline.

   Although either mode works, you will find that relative paths are more concise and can sometimes be easier to understand. Click OK to return to the Actions panel. Your target path is added to the Script pane.

   The Insert Target Path dialog box shows you only Movie Clip timelines. If you need to insert a target path to a different kind of object (such as an Array or Sound), you can still use the dialog box. Simply follow the previous steps, locate the timeline where the object resides, and following the target path that was generated in the Script pane, type a period (.) followed by the name of the object you wish to target. For more details about the specifics of target paths, see Chapter 20.

Automatic ActionScript Input Using Code Hints

Code hints are intended to provide you with menu options so that rather than type an entire script, you can select pieces of it from a menu. Because code hints appear in the Actions panel alongside your script, it's easy to choose from the menu and build your script in a somewhat systematic fashion. You can use code hints to insert handler events, actions, and action parameters into a script. You can choose to have code hints displayed automatically or to call upon them as needed. When they are set to be automatic, Flash detects when you need a code hint and displays it in the Actions panel. Although the feature stems from a good idea, its actual implementation is a little cumbersome.

   To enable automatic code hints:

1. Choose Edit → Preferences and select the ActionScript tab, or click the Actions panel pop-up menu and choose Preferences. The Preferences dialog box opens.

2. Check the Code Hints box to turn on automatic display of code hints. You can also use the Delay slider set the period of delay before a code hint appears; the minimum period is 0 seconds (no delay), and the maximum is 4 seconds.

3. Click OK to leave Preferences and return to your movie.

WRITING SCRIPTS WITH CODE HINTS

As mentioned earlier, code hints can be used for three ActionScript elements: event handlers, actions, and action parameters. In the steps that follow, you will learn how to use code hints to build a script with a minimum amount of typing.

   Say, for example, you wanted to enter the following script:

```
on(press){
    menu.gotoAndPlay(5);
}
```

This button script will send the Movie Clip instance menu to play at frame 5. To enter this script using code hints:

1. Select a button object in your movie.

2. Choose Window → Actions (F9) to open the Actions panel.

3. Type **on(** in the Actions panel text box. If automatic code hints are enabled, a code hints menu of event handlers is displayed beside your script (see Figure 17.8).

   If code hints are disabled, do one of the following to display the code hints menu:

   - Press Ctrl+spacebar.
   - Click the Show Code Hint button 🖳.
   - Select Show Code Hint from the Actions panel pop-up menu.

4. Because you are writing a handler, the code hints menu knows to give you a list of handler events. Now you must choose the handler you want to use from the menu. There are two ways to do this:

   - Use the arrow keys to navigate to the handler event, and press Return/Enter to make your selection.
   - Choose and double-click an event from the menu.

   Use either technique to select the press event. Flash enters the event into your script. Type **)(** and press Return/Enter to start a new line. Your incomplete script should now look like this:

   ```
   on(press){
   ```

5. Start the second line of your script by typing **menu**. This is the instance name of the Movie Clip you are scripting for in this example. If you are scripting for a clip with a different instance name or target path, insert that information here at the beginning of line two.

6. With the instance name (or target path) in place, you can use a code hint to enter an action. Flash doesn't always understand what action to display when you ask for a code hint. Here you are scripting to control a Movie Clip, but what if the menu instance were a Sound object or an Array? Flash has no way of knowing this. You must provide some additional information to give the code hint a little clue about your script. Type **_mc** after the word menu. Your script should now read like this:

   ```
   on(press){
       menu_mc
   ```

   The _mc class suffix lets Flash know that the menu instance is a Movie Clip. For a complete list of class suffixes, see Table 17.1 at the end of this section.

Figure 17.8

Code hints appear in the Actions panel text box along with your scripts.

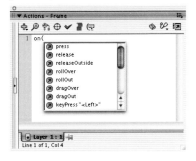

Using suffixes such as _mc is one of the "gotcha" features of code hints in Flash MX. By changing the script from *instanceName* to *instanceName*_mc, you are telling Flash to look for a completely different Movie Clip instance. The _mc suffix is interpreted as part of the full instance name. If you plan to use code hints when writing scripts for your movies, you will need to find a work-around solution. The best way to manage this situation is to name all of your instances with the appropriate code hint suffix. That way, there will be no confusion in your scripts.

7. After the _mc class suffix, type a period (.). If code hints are enabled, the code hints menu should appear. If not, use one of the techniques described in step 3 to display the menu.

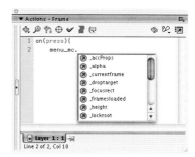

8. Using one of the code hint selection techniques described in step 4, choose the gotoAndPlay() action from the code hints menu. Your incomplete script should now look like this:

```
on(press){
    menu_mc.gotoAndPlay(
```

9. This next step might come as a bit of a surprise! After entering the gotoAndPlay() function via the code hints menu, you are automatically faced with another code hint choice—only this one is different from the others you have seen. This code hint appears in a yellow box and is called a tooltip-style code hint. Tooltip code hints are used to enter parameters for actions. The gotoAndPlay() action requires one parameter, a frame number. When the yellow tooltip code hint appears, you can type a value, and it will be inserted as the parameter for the current function. Type 5; then type a closing parenthesis ()). This will hide the code hint. End the line with a semicolon (;).

Some actions require more than one parameter. To enter multiple parameters when using code hints, simply type the parameters in the proper order, separating them with commas. Don't rely on Flash's tooltip-style code hints to give you the correct number or order of the parameters. To learn the correct parameter syntax for an action, see the ActionScript Reference on this book's accompanying CD-ROM.

10. Press Return/Enter to start a new line, and type the closing curly-brace character (}) to end your script. The finished script should now read like this:

```
on(press){
    menu_mc.gotoAndPlay(5);
}
```

Table 17.1

Code Hint Class Suffixes

SUFFIX	OBJECT CLASS	SUFFIX	OBJECT CLASS
_array	Array	_so	SharedObject
_btn	Button	_sound	Sound
_camera	Camera	_str	String
_color	Color	_stream	NetStream
_connection	NetConnection	_txt	TextField
_date	Date	_video	Video
_fmt	TextFormat	_xml	XML
_mc	MovieClip	_xmlsocket	XMLSocket
_mic	Microphone		

To use code hints, enter the appropriate suffix after the name of the object you wish to control.

Remember to update all your instance names in the Property Inspector so that your code hint suffixes will reference the correct instance names. In this example, you would need to change the instance menu to menu_mc.

Code hints are designed to make scripting a little less keyboard intensive. You should be the judge of whether or not they are helpful. One of the beauties of Flash MX 2004 and MX Pro 2004 is that the interface is completely customizable. Use the features you like, and ignore those you don't.

Navigating, Searching, and Replacing ActionScripts

To look for portions of an ActionScript, click the Actions panel to give it focus, and use the pop-up menu in the upper-right corner of the Actions panel:

Select **Go to Line** (**Cmd**+, (Mac), Ctrl+**G** (Win)) to skip to a particular line in a long script.

Select **Find** (Cmd/Ctrl+**F**) or click the Find button 🔍 to locate a particular word or phrase. **Find Again** (Cmd+**G** (Mac), F3 (Win)) will locate the next occurrence of that text.

Select **Replace** (Cmd/Ctrl+Shift+**H**, (Mac), Cmd/Ctrl+**H** (Win)) or click the Replace button 🔁 to find one set of text and replace it with another.

When using these features of the Actions panel, Find and Replace searches the entire script body, but only in the immediate script window. To do a movie-wide search, go to the main menu bar and choose Edit → Find and Replace. (For more information about this feature, see Chapter 9.)

Getting Files in and out of the Actions Panel

There are several ways to move data in and out of the Actions panel. Use the pop-up menu in the upper-right corner of the panel to handle these tasks:

Import text This option is particularly useful if you prefer to write scripts in a text- or script-editing program and want to integrate them directly into your movie.

To import an external ActionScript (.as) file:

1. Click the Script pane where you want the imported file to begin.

2. Select Import from File or press Shift+Cmd+**I** (Mac)/Shift+Ctrl+**I** (Win), and browse to a text file composed of ActionScript (see Figure 17.9).

3. Click OK. Flash drops the imported file into the Actions panel starting from the position of the cursor.

Export your script Select Export as File or press Shift+Cmd+**X** (Mac)/Shift+Ctrl+**X** (Win), give the file a name with the extension .as, and click Save. Flash exports a text file containing your script.

Print Select Print, pick your print options, and click Print.

> When you print scripts from the Actions panel, Flash doesn't include any information about the file that contains the script or the script's location in the movie. If you plan to print several scripts, it can be helpful to include comments that note where each script resides in your movie. (To learn more about working with comments, see Chapter 18.)

Figure 17.9

This ActionScript file (composed in the text editor BBEdit) can be imported directly into the Actions panel.

Checking for Syntax Errors

Unlike scripting with behaviors, the Actions panel gives you complete control over what is entered in the text box. The downside of this feature is that there is no way to check automatically for errors as you input the statements. To ensure that your scripts are syntactically correct before testing your movie, you can check the syntax in the Actions panel by doing one of the following:

- Click the Check Syntax button ☑ near the top of the Actions panel. This button looks like a check mark.

- In the pop-up menu in the upper-right corner of the Actions panel, select Check Syntax.

- Press Cmd/Ctrl+**T** while the Actions panel is active.

```
//////////////////////////////////////////////////
//////////// SHUFFLE FUNCTION ////////////////////
//parameter: an array; shuffle its contents /////
function shuffle(deck) {
    var list = deck.concat();
    var sorted = new Array();
    for (var i = 1; i<=list.length; i++) {
        var r = Math.floor(Math.random()*list.length);
        if (list[r] != undefined) {
            sorted.push(list[r]);
            delete list[r];
        } else {
            i--;
        }
    }
    return sorted;
}
//////////// end shuffle function ////////////////////
```

Whichever option you choose, if the script is free of syntax mistakes, you will get a message that asks you to acknowledge this. If there are errors, you will be alerted, and any errors are printed in the Output panel. (For more specifics on using the Output panel, see Chapter 21.)

This script contains errors. The errors encountered are listed in the Output Panel.

OK

Working with an External Script Editor

Although the Actions panel gives you total control, you might find it helpful to take advantage of an external editor and do your scripting outside Flash. If this is the case, all you need to do is replace any chunks of ActionScript with this line:

```
#include "actionScriptFile.as"
```

Here, `actionScriptFile.as` is a text file that contains all of the necessary code for the frame or object where `#include` is attached. The `#include` directive imports the lines of ActionScript from the external AS file and runs it in the movie as though it were written directly in the Actions panel. To use this technique to import ActionScript from an external file:

1. Write your script in an external editor and save it with the `.as` extension.

2. Type `#include` in the text box.

3. After the `#include` directive, enter the path to the external script file. Use the forward-slash character (/) to delimit the path. For example, if `movie.fla` and `extScript.as` were in the same folder, the path would be `extScript.as`. If the script file were in a subfolder named scripts, the entire statement would be:

```
#include "scripts/extScript.as"
```

Once you publish a movie that uses external scripts, those scripts become a permanent part of the movie. To make any changes to the script, you will have to change the Action-Script in the `.as` file and republish your movie.

External ActionScript files (`.as`) can be written in the Script Editor window if you use Flash MX Pro 2004 (see Figure 17.10). The Script Editor is simply an oversized version of the Actions panel that is used solely to compose external files. To open the Script Editor, choose File → New and select ActionScript file from the column of choices. This window allows you to write scripts and save them as `.as` files. Later, you can import these scripts directly into the Actions panel.

Attaching ActionScripts with the Actions Panel

The greatest difference between attaching simple behaviors and complex scripts is that most complex scripts are composed with the Actions panel. This is primarily because the Actions panel offers more flexibility for creating scripts on your own terms, in the order you prefer.

```
// get items for menu //

menu = new Array();

menu[0] = "item1.swf";
menu[1] = "item2.swf";
menu[2] = "item3.swf";
menu[3] = "item4.swf";
menu[4] = "item5.swf";
menu[5] = "item6.swf";
menu[6] = "item7.swf";
menu[7] = "item8.swf";
menu[8] = "item9.swf";
```

Figure 17.10

The Script editor window is similar to the Actions panel and allows you to compose Action-Script that will be kept outside your Flash movies.

When you attach behaviors, you have to go through the process of choosing the behaviors from a panel and configuring both their parameters and (if necessary) their event. This is very convenient for small or simple tasks, but for long, complex scripts, attaching behaviors can become tedious. Moreover, behaviors don't really provide a wide array of functionality, so what you can do with them is fairly limited. This means that you have access to your script only through the options that a behavior's dialog box provides. In many cases, this is sufficient, but with the Actions panel, it's never an obstacle; every element of your script is available for changes or modification.

Attaching Scripts to Frames, Buttons, and Movie Clips

The objects in Flash that can have scripts attached to them are buttons and Movie Clips. With the right kind of script, buttons will respond to many kinds of mouse interaction, including clicks, rollovers, and drags. Movie Clips can also respond to events such as loading into memory or playing through a frame. Additionally, both kinds of objects can monitor and record user keystrokes while a movie is running. In order to execute the attached script, buttons and Movie Clips require an event handler. When you worked with behaviors, handlers were automatically included. In the Actions panel, this isn't the case, so be sure to remember a handler. It assigns a trigger event that will set your script in motion. Without it, a script attached to an object will never execute. For a review of ActionScript event handlers, see Chapter 14.

Frame scripts are a close relative of object scripts. The biggest difference is that no handler is required. By default, when the movie playback head reaches a frame containing a script, that script is executed.

To use the Actions panel and attach an object or frame script:

1. Select a frame, button, or MovieClip object and then either choose Window → Development Panels → Actions or press F9.

2. Enter an ActionScript statement by doing one of the following:

   • Select a statement from a category of the ActionScript Toolbox and either double-click it or drag it to the text box.

   • Use the Add Actions button (+) and select an action from the pop-up menu.

   • Type ActionScript directly into the text box window.

When you attach a script to an object be sure to include a handler.

3. When you are finished, it's a good idea to check the syntax of your script. Either select Check Syntax from the Actions panel pop-up menu, click the Check Syntax button, or press Cmd/Ctrl+T.

4. If the script is free of errors, select Control → Test Movie to see how it works in your movie.

To keep the script displayed in the Actions panel at all times, click the Script Pin button, and the script will remain in a tabbed window of the text box. Even if you select other objects or frames in your movie, the "pinned" script won't disappear.

Inspirational Design Model

ActionScript opens Flash to an enormous world of possibilities. With the help of Action-Script, Flash is no longer just a vector animation tool; it can be used to create rich multi-media websites, interactive forms, cartoon serials, and games.

"Houdini—Master of the Extraordinary" is a combination game and cartoon developed by Sarbakan of Quebec, Canada (see Figure 17.11). It chronicles the many fictional adventures of Harry Houdini in his struggle against dark agents of long forgotten cults, discredited mediums, and scheming spiritualists who would like nothing better than to see him disappear for good. Visit www.sarbakan.com/images/portfolio/houdini/gameEn/houdini.html to discover Houdini's story and guide him on an adventure. This delightful game allows you

Figure 17.11

Houdini—Master of the Extraordinary **by Sarbakan**

to play the role of Houdini, and use the arrow keys and space bar to help this master magician uncover evil plots and rescue antiquities.

Sarbakan has a knack for striking a perfect balance of ActionScript programming, animation, storytelling, and fun. To experience other Sarbakan examples like Houdini, see the entry for "Arcane" in this book's Color Gallery.

CHAPTER 18

Writing ActionScript

The previous chapter introduced the fundamental ActionScript terms and some of the concepts of using the ActionScript language. In this chapter, you will peel back another layer and delve deeper into the world of Flash-based scripting.

So far, you have seen the possibilities that ActionScript can offer to your movies: It transforms them from simple linear animations to complex interactive applications and experiences. What is missing right now is a framework for you to use when constructing your scripts. You need to learn the conventions and rules of the language. Without these, it's impossible to use ActionScript to communicate intelligently. This chapter covers these topics:

- **Elements of ActionScript syntax**

- **Key components of the ActionScript language**

- **The kind of information ActionScript handles**

- **Storing script elements for reuse**

- **Performing computations in ActionScript**

- **ActionScript commands**

- **Setting conditions for scripts**

- **Using functions and predefined objects**

Learning ActionScript Syntax

Like all spoken languages, computer languages such as ActionScript follow a particular set of rules, or *syntax*. It's crucial to understand the syntax of the language so that you can use it to say something meaningful. After all, the purpose of a language is to communicate, and ActionScript provides you with a communication link to Flash.

Knowing all of the ActionScript terms in this book can be helpful if you want to become an expert "ActionScripter." But it is even more important to know the rules that define how all the terms are used and how they work together as a language. Once you have grasped the rules of ActionScript syntax, you are well on your way to becoming a fluent "speaker" or scriptwriter, and an excellent communicator with your Flash movies.

Punctuation Marks in ActionScript

You will use several different punctuation marks when writing an ActionScript. You can use punctuation to issue a command or track the path to a movie or variable. It is also there to help annotate your scripts and provide both explanation and instruction. Mainly, the purpose of punctuation is to bring order to your scripts and organize their contents so that Flash can understand how the scripts should be executed.

ActionScript Dot Syntax

The ActionScript dot syntax was introduced when Flash evolved to version 5. The dot syntax makes ActionScript look similar to JavaScript. If you are comfortable with JavaScript, learning ActionScript will put you in familiar territory. The construction for the dot syntax is as follows:

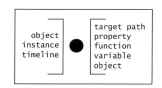

The left side of the dot can refer to an object, instance, or Timeline in your movie. The right side of the dot can be a property, target path, variable, function, or even another object that is directed at or found within the element on the left side. Here are three examples:

```
myClip._visible=0;
menuBar.menu1.item3=152;
_root.gotoAndPlay(5);
```

In the first example, a Movie Clip named `myClip` is made invisible by setting the `_visible` property to `0` with the dot syntax. The second example shows the path to the variable `item3` through `menu1`, a nested Movie Clip in the Movie Clip named `menuBar`. The variable is assigned a value of 152. The third example uses the `_root` reference to command the main Timeline to jump to frame 5 and play. In each example, you can see how the left side of the dot names or references an object, while the right side contains either a new object, or some kind of instruction or parameter that defines or manipulates the first object to the left of the dot.

> The dot is also known as the *dot operator* because it can be used to issue commands and modify properties. For more information on other ActionScript operators, see the "Operators" section later in this chapter.

ActionScript Slash Syntax

The slash syntax was used in Flash 4 and has since been replaced by the dot syntax. Although slash syntax is still supported in Flash MX 2004 and MX Pro 2004, it is deprecated, or no longer preferred. This syntax was used primarily in Flash 4 to delimit target paths. For example, the path to the nested Movie Clip `leg` through the clips `spider` and `body` was expressed like this:

```
"/spider/body/leg";
```

Now, using the dot syntax, the same path is written this way:

```
spider.body.leg;
```

The slash syntax was used to access variables belonging to other Timelines and was also used with the `tellTarget` function to target Movie Clips. Now that the `tellTarget` action has been deprecated, it's better to use the dot syntax and the `with` statement.

Comments

It is a good idea to make notes as you write your scripts. Notes can provide guidance or instructions to someone who has to edit your scripts. They can also be helpful if you are forced to abandon a project for a period of time; when you come back to the code, your notes will remind you what each part of the script was doing.

To make notes in ActionScript, you have to insert them as *comments*. To insert comments, type two forward slashes (//) and enter your notes after them. For example:

```
// checks to see if all movie frames are loaded
if(_framesLoaded >=_totalFrames){
// if TRUE, then it starts the move at frame 6
   gotoAndPlay(6);
}else{
// if FALSE, it loops back to frame 1
   gotoAndPlay(1);
}
```

In ActionScript, anything on the same line that follows the double slash will be ignored by Flash. This means that you can type anything you like after the slashes because Flash will not interpret comments as ActionScript. Comments also allow you to "turn off" parts of a script. If there are one or more lines that are causing problems, you can comment them out and run the script without those lines. Flash will ignore the commented lines and run everything else in the script. To learn more about this technique, see Chapter 21.

> To insert large notes or blocks of text within your scripts, you can use multiline comments (/*). This handy tool makes it easy to write long messages or explanations within the body of your ActionScripts. Simply begin the note with the opening character sequence (/*) and end with the closing sequence(*/). All statements that are written between these markers will be ignored by the Flash Player.

When the ActionScript Editor Preferences are set to default, comments appear in the script window in a light gray color so that you can distinguish them from other parts of your script. To change this, select Flash → Preferences (Mac) or Edit → Preferences (Win) or choose Preferences from the Actions panel pop-up menu. Go to the ActionScript Editor tab and select a new color from the swatch menu next to the word *Comments*.

Curly Braces

ActionScript organizes the elements of a script by using the curly brace characters ({}). (These characters are also called *curly brackets*.) In the following script, all the statements between the pair of curly braces will be executed when the mouse is pressed:

```
on(press){
    gotoAndStop(50);
}
```

A script can also include multiple sets of curly braces:

```
on(press){
    with(fishClip){
        gotoAndStop(50);
    }
}
```

In this example, the curly braces organize the script into two parts. The on(press) handler executes the with statement, then with targets the instance fishClip, sends it to frame 50, and stops it.

> Statements within curly braces are often referred to as *blocks* of a script. This often makes it easier to refer to a specific portion of the script, for example "the with block."

Parentheses

Parentheses are used in ActionScript to assign arguments for functions or to set the order of operations in an expression. For example, the duplicateMovieClip() function has three arguments: *target, instance,* and *depth*. Here you use the parentheses to list the arguments after calling the action:

```
duplicateMovieClip("alien","alien_copy",1);
```

This statement duplicates (makes a copy of) the clip `alien`, names the duplicate `alien_copy`, and sets it at a depth of 1 above the original.

You can also use parentheses to alter the order of operations. The expression 2 + 3 * 4 evaluates to 14, whereas the expression (2 + 3) * 4 evaluates to 20 because the parentheses force you to do the addition first.

Semicolon

In ActionScript, the semicolon (;) is used to mark the end of a statement. For example:

```
on(release){
    introClip._visible=0;
}
```

Here, the statement that makes the instance `introClip` invisible is terminated with a semicolon. If you forget to use the semicolon, Flash will still compile the script correctly. However, it is good practice to follow correct syntax conventions and always terminate statements with the semicolon character.

Semicolons are also used to separate the parameters in a `for` loop structure. To learn more about this ActionScript convention, see the "Conditionals" section later in this chapter.

Other ActionScript Syntax Conventions

Aside from the mechanics of ActionScript, there are a few other conventions that are important to understand so that you can work flexibly with the language. Certain terms in the language are "protected" or reserved because they have a specific meaning in Action-Script. Other terms must follow a specific upper- or lowercase structure so that Flash will know how to interpret them.

Constants

Constants are terms or properties that retain a specific and unchanging value in ActionScript. In a script, they are written in all-capital letters. Constants are part of three ActionScript objects: the Key object, the Math object, and the Number object.

The following script uses the Key object to test whether the spacebar has been pressed:

```
if(Key.isdown(Key.SPACE)){
    laser.shoot(1);
}
```

The spacebar has a constant value, and it is a property of the Key object. When it is pressed, the statements below it execute.

In the next example, the Math object uses the constant value of `PI` to evaluate the area of a circle:

```
area=Math.PI*(radius*radius);
```

In the following example, the `MAX_VALUE` constant is used to set the variable `duration` to the highest possible value in ActionScript:

```
duration=Number.MAX_VALUE;
```

Keywords

Keywords are ActionScript terms that are reserved and have a specific purpose in the language. These terms are used only in a specific context and are not available as names of variables, functions, objects, or instances. See the following for a list of ActionScript keywords.

break	case	class	continue	default	delete
do	dynamic	else	extends	for	function
get	if	implements	import	in	instanceof
interface	intrinsic	new	on	onClipEvent	private
public	return	set	static	switch	super
this	typeof	var	void	while	with

ActionScript Case Sensitivity

For the most part, ActionScript is fairly forgiving when it comes to upper- and lowercase letters. If you are scripting in Expert mode, you will notice that the color for a term will change if it isn't entered in the preferred upper- or lowercase syntax. For example, `stop()` is usually colored blue. If you were to enter it as `Stop()` (note the capital S), it would change to black. However, in most cases, Flash would still be able to interpret your script without error. To be safe, it is best to follow proper ActionScript syntax at all times; capitalize anything that should appear in uppercase, and keep all lowercase terms free of capital letters.

The release of ActionScript 2 and Flash Player 7 slightly changes the rules of case sensitivity for programs written in ActionScript. Now, movies published for Flash 7 Player will implement case sensitivity. This means that names of functions, keywords, variables, objects, and so on will be held to strict case sensitivity. For example:

```
var count=0;
var Count=0;
```

Here, a Flash 7 movie would consider these to be two different variables: `count` (with a lowercase first letter) and `Count`. Similarly, the following statement, which would cause errors in Flash 6 and below, is acceptable in Flash 7:

```
sound = new Sound();
```

Correct syntax demands that the constructor function for a Sound object use a capital *S* for the word *sound*. In Flash 6, where case sensitivity was looser, `sound` and `Sound` were interpreted as the same thing, so this statement produces an error. However, because Flash 7 uses strict case sensitivity, sound and Sound are considered to be different and there is no error. While this technique will work in Flash 7 movies, it is strongly discouraged because it can lead to a world of confusion. The following statement exemplifies a better way to create a Sound object:

```
mySound = new Sound();
```

This is probably somewhat confusing if you are new to ActionScript and programming in general, so the bottom line is this: Follow good practices and use the correct syntax at all times. If you are consistent and adhere to the rules, these issues can be avoided. Keep reading to explore these practices further.

Learning ActionScript Language Elements

So far, you have learned the conventions of ActionScript and how the pieces of the lan-

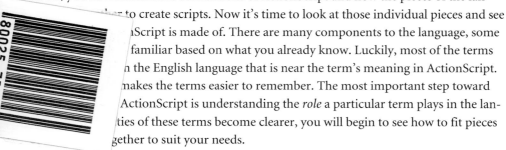

 to create scripts. Now it's time to look at those individual pieces and see

Script is made of. There are many components to the language, some familiar based on what you already know. Luckily, most of the terms n the English language that is near the term's meaning in ActionScript. makes the terms easier to remember. The most important step toward ActionScript is understanding the *role* a particular term plays in the lan-ties of these terms become clearer, you will begin to see how to fit pieces gether to suit your needs.

Data Types

As you learned earlier, data types define the kind of information that can be represented by elements of ActionScript. There are six types of information used in a script: string, number, Boolean, object, Movie Clip, and undefined. We will discuss the specifics of each type.

Strings

Strings are literal chunks of information that hold a textual value. They are composed of any combination of letters, punctuation, and numbers. String data is enclosed in quotes (" " or ' ') and treated as a single piece of information. Because strings are literal, they are case sensitive, so for instance, the strings "one" and "One" are different. In the following example, Joe is a string stored in myName:

```
myName="Joe";
```

Strings can be combined, or *concatenated*, to link string information together. For example:

```
fullName=myName+" Smith";
```

The addition operator (+) is used to concatenate string data. Note that in the preceding example, the string " Smith" contains a space. This is to prevent the two string elements from getting closed up when they are concatenated. When the strings are combined, full-Name will contain the string 'Joe Smith'.

Strings can also be organized alphabetically by using the comparison operators: <, >, =<, and >=. Flash uses the Latin 1 character set. When evaluating strings alphabetically, the letter *z* holds the highest value, while *A* holds the lowest. Note the following expression:

```
"alligator"<"zebra"==true
"alligator">"Zebra"==true
```

Here you can see how lowercase letters hold a higher value than uppercase ones. For more information on operators and comparisons, see the "Operators" section later in this chapter.

Numbers

Numbers are characters that hold a specific numeric value. In ActionScript, number values can be manipulated in expressions using mathematical operators such as addition (+), subtraction (–), multiplication (*), division (/), modulo (%), increment (++), and decrement (– –). You can also use ActionScript's predefined Math object to evaluate numbers and expressions. For more information on this, see the "Operators" section later in this chapter or the ActionScript Reference on this book's accompanying CD.

Booleans

A *Boolean* is a value that is either True or False. Booleans are used in conditional statements to evaluate script elements and see if values have been met or initialized. The following statements evaluate whether or not all of a movie's frames have been loaded into memory:

```
if(_framesloaded==_totalframes){
    introMovie.gotoAndPlay(2);
}
```

If the current number of loaded frames (_framesloaded) is equal to the total number of frames (_totalframes), the statement inside the parentheses returns a Boolean value of True. If not, it returns False. In most conditional statements, the Boolean value is returned by an expression and not tested explicitly in the if statement. For more specifics on this, see the "Conditionals" section later in this chapter.

Objects

An *object* is a collection of information organized into properties. These properties have names and values that can be accessed in a Flash movie. The object data type allows you to manipulate the properties assigned to a particular object. In the following statement, the object money has a property named myAccount, which is assigned the value 5000:

```
money.myAccount=5000;
```

Flash allows you to create your own objects or use one of the built-in objects such as Date, Array, and Color.

Movie Clips

Movie Clips are self-contained animations that run independently in a Flash movie. They are self-contained because they have their own Timeline. Movie Clips have properties such as _alpha or _rotation that can be assigned values in ActionScript. Here, a Movie Clip instance is rotated to 180 degrees:

```
spinClip._rotation=180;
```

Movie Clips also have methods that you can use to control them. In this example, a clip is instructed to stop on the first frame of its Timeline:

```
audioClip.gotoAndStop(1);
```

Movie Clips are one of the most interesting, complex, and useful data types in a Flash movie. In fact, they're so important, we've dedicated an entire chapter to them. See Chapter 19 for more details on Movie Clips and their role in Flash.

Undefined

Undefined exists to represent a lack of data, or no data. A variable that has no value returns undefined. A variable with no value cannot be considered an "empty" variable. Without a value, it does not exist and is therefore undefined. For example, the following statement returns nothing; as a nonexistent container, the variable is declared but has no value:

```
var one;
```

Here, one is undefined and is relatively useless to you. On a related note, if you want to create an empty variable, you can set the value of the variable to be null. Rather than not existing at all (undefined), the variable exists but has an "empty," or null value.

The next statement returns null; the variable is an empty but *existing* container:

```
var two=null;
```

If you want to erase a variable's value, or create a variable and make it empty, null is a very helpful term. To learn more about variables, see the next section.

Variables

Variables serve as storage locations for information that you need in a script. Variables are like pockets where you can put something, keep it there for a while, and then retrieve it when it's needed again later in your movie. To use a variable, you have to first *declare*, or state, the variable. Then you must *initialize* the variable to let Flash know that you are going to store something in it. Once you have initialized the variable with a starting value, it will hold that value until it is changed. To change the value of a variable, all you have to do is add to it, subtract from it, or reinitialize it.

Variables can be used to hold any type of data: string, number, Boolean, object, or Movie Clip. For example, the variable x can be initialized to either a numeric value or a set of string data:

```
x=24;
x="myName";
```

Variables can also be used in conditional loops to serve as the loop counter. For example:

```
j=2;
while(j>0){
    duplicateMovieClip(_root.ship,"ship"+j,j);
    _root["ship"+j]._y=_root.ship._y+50*j;
    trace("duplicated"+j);
    j-;
}
```

In this example, the variable j is initialized to 2. Every time it passes through the `while` loop, it is reduced by 1, or reinitialized until it no longer meets the conditions of the loop. The variable j is also used to help name the duplicated Movie Clips and assign the level of each new clip in the `duplicateMovieClip` statement. In the next statement, j is used in an expression to position the new Movie Clips at a location that is $50*j$ pixels away from the original clip. That's a lot of work for one variable! The important thing to realize is that you can use a variable over and over again in your scripts to help perform a variety of tasks.

When you use a variable, it's important to give it an appropriate name. There are a few rules concerning this. First, a variable must be an identifier—a combination of letters, numbers, underscore (_), or dollar sign character ($). See Chapter 17 for specifics on identifiers. Second, a variable cannot be an ActionScript keyword, and it must be unique within the timeline where the variable was created. It's good practice to name a variable something meaningful that relates to the job it will perform in your movie. If you use a variable to store the name of a visitor to your website, name the variable something like *siteVisitor* to keep things simple. For example, if visitors enter their names in an input text field, give the field the variable name *siteVisitor*. This way, any time you want to use a visitor's name, you can just call on the variable, and the name will be available immediately. If you wanted to print a farewell message in the text field goodbye, you would write:

```
goodbye.text="Thanks for visiting "+siteVisitor;
```

We already mentioned that movies published for Flash Player 7 implement strict case sensitivity. This is especially important to consider when naming variables. Here are a few additional naming strategies you can employ to help ensure consistency:

Lowercase, uppercase Multi-word names can be more descriptive, but of course a space is not allowed in the names of ActionScript objects and variables. You can work around this by using an uppercase first letter for the any additional words in the name. For example:

```
firstSecondThird=0;
```

Underscore character Use the underscore character (_) to separate individual words written in all lowercase, for example:

```
first_second_third=0;
```

Alphanumeric Use a combination of letters and numbers to give similar or related variables unique names. For example:

```
item1=0;
item2=1;
```

Whatever method you choose to use, be consistent! It will save you headaches and frustration.

Using the *trace()* Function with Variables

In the previous conditional loop script example, you might have noted the line that reads trace("duplicated"+j);. trace is a special function of ActionScript that allows you to monitor different elements of your script. In this line, the script will trace the word *duplicated* and concatenate it with the current value of *j*. It can be very helpful to use this function because it allows you to track the value of your variables as they change while your script executes.

To use the trace()function, all you have to do is enter the information you want to monitor in the parentheses following trace. When you test your movie, Flash will print all the information you asked it to trace in the Output panel. Anything entered within quotes will be treated as a literal string and appear in the Output window exactly as it was entered. This can be helpful because it allows you to make a label for each item you need to trace. For the example trace("duplicated"+j);, the Output window will print:

```
duplicated2
duplicated1
```

This printout reflects the value of the variable *j* as it goes through the while loop twice, each time decreasing its value.

Variable Scope

One of the most important aspects of variables is their availability, or *scope*. A variable's scope determines how it is available to other portions of your movie. Because you use variables to store and retrieve information, having them available is very important. In ActionScript, variables have a scope that is global, timeline-specific, or local.

If a variable is global, it is shared by all Timelines in your movie and is available at any time. Any script in any part of your movie can access or change the value of a global variable. You declare a global variable by using the reference _global. For example, this statement will create a global variable named *store1* and initialize its value to 1:

```
_global.store1=1;
```

The value of *store1* can be retrieved at any point in your movie with this statement:

```
trace(store1);
```

Because the variable is global, it is always available, by name.

A Timeline-specific variable is also available throughout your movie. However, you must always use a target path when working with the variable; otherwise, Flash won't know where to find the information the variable is storing. Declare a Timeline variable by giving it a name and assigning it a value. For example, to create a Timeline-specific variable named *store2*, you would enter the following statement on any Timeline (Movie Clip, main Timeline, and so on):

```
store2=2;
```

If you created this variable on the main Timeline, its value could be retrieved at any point in your movie with this statement:

```
value=_root.store2;
```

If you created *store2* on the Timeline of the Movie Clip instance sprocket, you would access it by using this target path:

```
value=_root.sprocket.store2;
```

Because the variable is scoped to a particular Timeline, you must refer to it using a target path, or the "address" of the variable in your movie.

A local variable is different. Local variables are scoped to functions and can be changed only within the block of script or function where they reside. This can be helpful if you have a value that needs to exist for only a very brief period of time. To make a variable local, you must use the var action when you declare and initialize the variable. For example:

```
function init3(){
    var store3=3;
}
```

This script declares the variable *store3* as a local variable and initializes its value to 3. As a local variable, *store3* is available only within the curly braces ({}) of the function where it resides, and it will be "alive" (contain a value) only while the function is executing. To summarize:

- To create a global variable, type **__global.name**= and assign a name and value.
- To create a Timeline-specific variable, type the name of the variable and use the assignment operator (=) to assign a value.
- To create a local variable inside a function, type **var**, followed by the variable name, and use the assignment operator (=) to assign a value.

Operators

Operators are used to produce values. They are characters that instruct ActionScript how to combine, remove, or compare the values in an expression. On both sides of the operator, you have the values, known as the *operands*. The operator takes the operands, performs its function on them, and leaves a final value for the expression.

If there is more than one operator in an expression, they are executed in a specific order, which Macromedia calls *precedence*. Operators with the highest precedence are executed first, followed by others in order of highest to lowest precedence. For example:

```
total = 3 + 4 * 5
total = 23
```

According to the rules of precedence, the 4 and 5 are multiplied first, and then the 3 is added. Tables 18.1–18.4 list some of the ActionScript operators in order of precedence, from highest to lowest. Where operator precedence is equal, operations are performed from the left to right.

Numeric Operators

Numeric operators are used to add, subtract, multiply, and divide the operands of an expression. Table 18.1 lists the ActionScript numeric operators. Operators with the highest precedence are listed first; precedence decreases as you move down the table.

OPERATOR	OPERATION
++	Increment by one
– –	Decrement by one
*	Multiplication
/	Division
%	Modulo
+	Addition
–	Subtraction

Table 18.1

The Numeric Operators

Comparison Operators

The comparison operators are used to compare the value of two operands and return a Boolean (True or False) value based on the comparison. Table 18.2 lists the ActionScript comparison operators. Comparison operators have equal precedence and are read from left to right.

OPERATOR	OPERATION
<	Less than
<=	Less than or equal to
>	Greater than
>=	Greater than or equal to

Table 18.2

The Comparison Operators

Logical Operators

Logical operators are used to compare two Boolean values and return a third Boolean value. LogicalAND will evaluate to `true` if all conditions are true. LogicalOR will evaluate to `true` if one of the conditions is True and `false` if all conditions are False. LogicalNOT inverts the value of an expression—for example, `!false==true`. Table 18.3 lists the ActionScript logical operators. Operators with the highest precedence are listed first; precedence decreases as you move down the table.

OPERATOR	OPERATION
!	LogicalNOT
&&	LogicalAND
||	LogicalOR

Equality and Assignment Operators

The equality operators are used to test for equality between two operands. The operation will return a Boolean value based on the operands. The assignment operators make assignments and initialize variables. Table 18.4 lists the equality and assignment operators. Operators with the highest precedence are listed first; precedence decreases as you move down the table. All compound assignment operators (+=, −=, *=, and so on) have equal precedence and are read from left to right.

OPERATOR	OPERATION
==	Equality
===	Strict equality
!=	Inequality
!==	Strict inequality
=	Assignment
+=	Addition and assignment
−=	Subtraction and assignment
*=	Multiplication and assignment
/=	Division and assignment
%=	Modulo and assignment

> ActionScript's bitwise operators, which are used to set and evaluate values at the bit level, are beyond the scope of this book and will not be covered. To learn more about them, refer to the documentation that ships with Flash.

ActionScript's Global Functions

The ActionScript language incorporates many built-in, or global, functions. These functions are part of the language and are used to perform many of the more common, frequently needed tasks in a Flash production. In the past, Macromedia referred to these global functions as *actions*. This term seems to have gone out of favor. Ultimately, this is good, as the term *actions* was not really appropriate in a computer language such as ActionScript. Whatever you prefer to call them, the global functions are statements in ActionScript that issue commands to a movie or one of its components, telling it to do something. For example:

```
gotoAndPlay(5);
```

The `gotoAndPlay()`function tells the current timeline to go to frame 5 and continue playing when it gets there.

Here's another example:

```
duplicateMovieClip("myClip","myOtherClip",1);
```

This action makes a copy of the Movie Clip `myClip`, names the copy `myOtherClip`, and sets it at stacking level 1 above the original clip.

Global functions are one of the largest portions of the ActionScript language. They can be found in the ActionScript Toolbox section of the Actions panel. Click the Global Functions icon to display a list of categories. Each contains a set of functions that are available to you.

Conditionals

In the preceding chapter, you learned about the flow of scripts. *Conditionals* are used to direct this flow. Conditionals are statements that present a script with a condition to be tested. The test returns a Boolean value, either `true` or `false`. Depending on this outcome, the script is routed in the appropriate direction by the conditional structure. In Action-Script, the main conditionals are `if`, `if...else`, `switch`, `while`, `do...while`, and `for`.

"if" and *"if...else"* Statements

Statements that test whether a condition evaluates to either `true` or `false` use the `if` statement. ActionScript evaluates the condition in the first line of the script and then proceeds to execute the appropriate statements that follow, based on the condition's evaluation. For example:

```
if(y<_currentframe){
    move=Math.PI*y;
    saucerClip._x=saucerClip._x+move;
}
```

In this script, if the statement `y<_currentFrame` evaluates to `true`, the following statements within the curly braces are executed. If it evaluates to `false`, the code in the `if` block is skipped and execution of the script skips to the first statement after the closing curly brace of the `if` block. `if` conditionals can have alternative statements as well. The preceding example could be expanded as follows:

```
if(y<_currentFrame){
    move=Math.PI*y;
    saucerClip._x=saucerClip._x+move;
}else{
    gotoAndPlay(1);
    y++;
}
```

This second script has an `else` block. This means that if the `y<_currentFrame` statement evaluates to `false`, the statements following `}else{` are executed as an alternative.

Simplifying *if...else* with the *switch* Statement

The `switch` statement is a newer conditional structure that provides an alternative to `if...else` statements. This conditional structure presents a script with a series of cases, each of which will be executed depending on the value of the condition to be tested. Consider the following statements:

```
num=1;
switch(num){
    case 1:
        trace("case 1 was true");
        break;
    case 2:
        trace("case 2 was true");
        break;
    case 3:
        trace("case 3 was true");
        break;
    default:
        trace("no case was true")
}
```

In the preceding `switch` statement, the value of `num` is tested over several conditions, or cases. If a case returns `true`, meaning that the value of the case equals that of the variable running through the conditional, its statements are executed. In this example, the Output panel would print "case 1 was true" because the value of `num` happens to be 1. If the first line read `num=3`, you would see "case 3 was true" in the Output panel. If no cases evaluated as `true`, the `default` case's statement(s) would be executed.

Notice that within each case statement, there is a `break` action. This ensures that only a single condition's statements are executed. If you ran this script but removed `break`, it would print the following:

```
case 1 was true
case 2 was true
case 3 was true
no case was true
```

`break` causes a script to quit executing statements in the current block. This is defined by the pair of curly braces (`{}`) that contain the `switch` statement's case conditions. Without the `break` statement, the remaining conditions in the body of the `switch` statement will be evaluated as `true`.

Looping Scripts with Conditional Statements

ActionScript conditionals can also be used to loop repetitive tasks that perform an action or actions a certain number of times. A loop is created with either the `while`, `do...while`, or `for` action. Each of these loop structures has some kind of *counter* that monitors the number of times the loop should be executed. Generally, the counter is initialized as a variable at the outset of the loop and is either decremented or incremented (decreased or increased by one) with every loop cycle. The function of each loop structure is identical, but the way each performs its function is unique.

The `while` loop establishes a condition and then executes statements within the curly braces until the condition is no longer true. In the next example, the variable *k* is used as the loop counter and is decremented each time the loop statements are executed. This loop will execute three times:

```
k=3;
while(k>0){
    duplicateMovieClip("spotClip","spot"+k,k+1);
    k--;
}
```

The `do...while` loop executes its statements first and then tests the condition to see whether the loop should continue. If the condition evaluates to `true`, the loop continues. With this kind of loop, the statements are always executed at least once, even if the condition is `false`. For example:

```
k=3;
do{
    duplicateMovieClip("spotClip","spot"+k,k+1);
    k--;
} while(k>0);
```

The `for` loop puts all of the necessary loop information in the first statement: the counter initialization, the condition, and the count expression. For example:

```
for(k=3;k>0;k--;){
    duplicateMovieClip("spotClip","spot"+k,k+1);
}
```

Here you can see that the loop conditions and the count are the same as in the `while` and `do...while` examples. However, all of the information to establish and control the loop has been economically placed in the first line of the loop.

Another loop structure, `for...in`, is used to loop through the properties or nested objects of an object. This action can modify properties or use methods to control multiple nested Movie Clips or multiple objects. To learn more about `for...in` loops, see Hands On 5 and the ActionScript Reference on this book's accompanying CD.

Custom Functions

In the preceding chapter, functions were presented as doers and information processors. You call them or give them a set of arguments, and they perform a specific task using those arguments. ActionScript's global functions are powerful, but limited to an array of prescribed routines for common tasks. You can exercise this same kind of power for tasks of your own. ActionScript allows you to create custom functions. These can be very useful if you have a series of tasks or operations that have to be performed over and over again in your movie. For example, if you need to frequently scale a Movie Clip to 50 percent of its original size, you can write a function. Rather than having to use both the _xscale and _yscale properties every time you want to scale a clip, you can call on the function and it will do all the work for you.

First, you must define the function. The syntax for defining a function is as follows:

```
function functionName(arguments){
    statement(s);
}
```

Here is a function named Half that reduces the horizontal and vertical scale of a Movie Clip by 50 percent and moves it 100 pixels up and to the left:

```
function Half(myClip) {

    myClip._x-=100;
    myClip._y-=100;
  myClip._xscale=50;
    myClip._yscale=50;
}
```

In this function, the term myClip is used as an argument. When the function is called, the Movie Clip listed within the parentheses (an argument to the function) will be scaled down accordingly. When you create a function, it's best to put the script that declares the function in a frame at the beginning of your movie. If ActionScript hasn't read your function, it won't know what to do when you call it later.

When creating a function, it is essential to give it a unique name within your movie so that there is no confusion between functions, variables, and instances. For example, if you had a function named Half and a variable named Half, you would open the door to possible error and confusion with the ActionScript in your movie. If you can't use any other name, append the name with a prefix such as funHalf for the function and varHalf for the variable.

Once you've created the function, you are free to call it whenever you need it in your movie. A function can be called in any script or in any handler, and from any level or Timeline of your movie. Here is an example where the Half function is called when a button is clicked and released:

```
on(release){
    _root.Half(invaders.rogue_1);
}
```

In this script, the clip rogue_1 (nested inside the clip invaders) is moved and sized down by 50 percent using the Half function. The target path to rogue_1 is passed as an argument to the function, and the clip is scaled. Because the Half function was created on the main Timeline, it is necessary to include the target reference _root when the function is called from a different Timeline.

Objects

Objects are one of the many data types in Flash, and as such, they can be referred to directly in an ActionScript statement. They are also an important element of the language because they hold chunks of information that affect different elements of your movie. Objects have properties that can be set and reset as needed within a movie. They also have methods, which are built-in functions specific to each object, and can be used to produce values or perform tasks.

For a list of the predefined objects in ActionScript, consult the Actions panel (F9). Look for the category named Built-in Classes in the ActionScript toolbox (see Figure 18.1). You can double-click the icon beside each Object to reveal the properties and methods that belong to it. For specifics on each class, chooose Help panel (F1) → ActionScript Reference Guide → Using the Built-in Classes → Overview of Built-in Classes.

Figure 18.1

The names, properties, and methods of ActionScript's predefined objects are in the Built-in Classes category of the Actions panel.

Inspirational Design Model

For an example of the kind of interactive depth and interest that Flash can create, take a look at Andy Foulds Design: www.foulds2000.freeserve.co.uk/index_v2.html (see Figure 18.2). This site features an interesting blend of text, imagery, animation, and interactivity, much of which takes place in three dimensions. Follow the links Web

Design → Samples to see his work. In addition to Andy's professional work, check out his Flash samples. These "studies" present all kinds of interesting menu designs and compelling imagery.

Figure 18.2

Andy Foulds is a photographer and web designer.

CHAPTER 19

Writing ActionScript for Multiple Timeline Movies

One of the most important aspects of using ActionScript to create Flash content is to understand how Flash movies are constructed. In this case, *constructed* is not used in the hands-on sense, but the compositional. It is essential to know what Flash movies are made of and how their components are put together.

As an animation tool, Flash creates motion sequences using pictures and text. If this were all it could do, by today's standards, the application would be simple indeed. However, Flash can layer and combine multiple animations. Additionally, you can use ActionScript to tell Flash how to assemble these animations and make them "talk" to one another. The simple behaviors and functions of individual animations can be used together in the same space, and as they interact with each other through ActionScript, rich and complex behaviors emerge.

To truly maximize the interactive potential of your movies, you must understand how to use Flash as a container or arena for animated content, and how many simple movies can synergize to create an interactive experience with great depth and potential. This chapter will cover:

- Concepts of a multi-timeline Flash movie
- Absolute and relative target paths
- Timeline scope
- How to control specific Timeline instances
- Using Movie Clips as internal Timeline resources

How Flash Manages Multiple Movie Timelines

When a Flash movie plays, all its elements are seen or heard on the movie Stage. This creates the illusion that all the movie components exist on an even playing field and share the same space within the Flash environment. Although they do share the common space of the Stage and its boundaries, there is a hierarchy to this space and to the elements that inhabit it.

Every Flash movie you create has a particular organization based on the animations it contains. This rule applies to animations in the form of both Movie Clips and additional Flash movies, or SWF files, that are loaded into a host Flash movie. When additional movies are loaded into a Flash movie, they are placed in a hierarchy and loaded onto a new movie level. In Flash, the main Timeline is the absolute bottom and is referred to as _level0 or _root. Subsequent movies that are loaded are stacked on top of it in succession: _level1, _level2, _level3, and so on. As each movie is loaded onto its own level, it maintains its autonomy and plays its Timeline independently of the other level Timelines.

Movie Clips also exhibit a similar kind of hierarchical relationship. One Movie Clip can contain another clip or clips. These, in turn, can contain additional Movie Clips. The stacking can go on and on. This stacking process is known as *nesting* Movie Clips. In the same way that movies can contain multiple independent Timelines on various levels, Movie Clips can hold other clips, and each clip can behave independently, though the Movie Clip hierarchy has a different set of terms used to describe this relationship. A nested clip is known as a *child,* and the clip hosting it is referred to as the *parent.* A clip can be both a child and a parent. If clip A contains clip B, and clip B contains clip C, then B is both a parent of C and a child of A. Ultimately, all Movie Clips are children of the Timeline where they are playing. In the preceding example, if clips A, B, and C all exist in the movie on _level2, then level 2 is the parent, and A, B, and C are all children. For an illustration of this, see Figure 19.1.

So, how would all this apply in a Flash movie? Take, for example, a movie that contains an animated character named BubbleBody, or BB for short. If you wanted to create an animation of BB jumping straight up in the air, you would need to consider several things. As BB prepares for the jump, he crouches down, his head sinks a bit, and his arms widen. As he springs upward, he shoots his arms up over his head, and his fingers stretch to the sky. While this is happening, his legs push up, leaving the crouch stance and coming together as he rises above the ground.

Many things are going on in this animation. One of the greatest challenges is trying to make each event happen, and happen together, so that the animation looks as natural as possible. By making each part of BB's body a Movie Clip and nesting these clips inside a single BB clip, you can achieve this kind of synchronization and control. As the main BB clip rises, all the others (arms, legs, hands, and so on) rise with it. As the arm Movie

Clips stretch to the sky, the hand instances are carried with it. This is accomplished because a nested clip sits on the Timeline of another clip. As the host clip is changed or moved, the nested clip is carried along with it.

In addition to keeping all the elements together, nested clips allow you to control each element independently. To create a "wave hello" animation with ActionScript, you would have to script the forearm Movie Clip to rotate 120 degrees, and also to tell the hand clip to rotate in some fashion. Creating the rotation with ActionScript is simple, and with independent control over each body part, you are able to manipulate the parts individually. In this case, because the hand clip is a child of the arm, the hand moves with the arm as it is raised. Then, because the arm is the parent clip, it is unaffected when the hand clip executes its "wave" rotation.

Writing Target Paths

To create this kind of animation, or to get the kind of control described in the preceding example, you need to send ActionScript commands from one Timeline to another. In this case, a button or other control element has to send the commands along the hierarchy to tell the arm and hand clips to execute the appropriate actions.

The process of passing ActionScript commands and information to a Movie Clip is known as *targeting*. When you target a clip, you send a command through the Timeline chain so that it reaches the specific clip. This process can be compared to sending mail. To send a message to someone, you need their address. Targeting a Movie Clip in ActionScript works the same way. If you don't enter the correct target path (or address) for the clip, the clip won't receive the message. In ActionScript, there are two ways to refer to a clip's target path: absolute and relative.

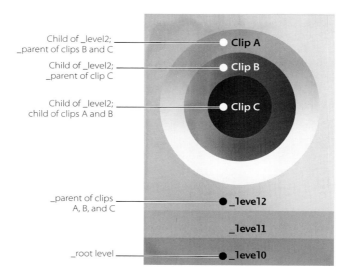

Figure 19.1

The hierarchical relationship of movie levels and Movie Clip parents and children. Here, the movie has three levels: 0, 1, and 2. Movie Clips A, B, and C exist on level 2 and are nested inside one another. Clip A is a parent of B and C, and B is a parent of C.

Child of _level2;
_parent of clips B and C ———— ● Clip A

Child of _level2;
_parent of clip C ———— ● Clip B

Child of _level2;
child of clips A and B ———— ● Clip C

_parent of clips
A, B, and C ———— ● _level2

● _level1

_root level ———— ● _level0

Using _root and _level to Create Absolute Target Paths

An *absolute path* is the ActionScript equivalent of a postal address for a Movie Clip instance. In the same way that your mailing address specifies country, state or province, postal code, street, building number, and so on, an absolute target path describes the location of the clip instance relative to the main Timeline. Going back to the BB animation presented earlier, the absolute path to BB's hand Movie Clip would be

```
_root.BB.upperBody.armL.handL
```

This script example uses the _root reference to access the main Timeline. If, however, BB were in a movie on level 2, the target path to the hand would be

```
_level2.BB.upperBody.armL.handL
```

You can use absolute target paths to send commands, retrieve variable values, and call functions. Target paths allow you to communicate any ActionScript information to Movie Clip instances and Timelines from any other location in your movie. Absolute paths are always a safe choice when the levels and nests of a movie start to get complex. To get an idea of clip instances that make up BB, see Figure 19.2.

Figure 19.2

The BubbleBody Movie Clip is created from nine separate, nested Movie Clips. Notice how the Insert Target Path dialog box shows the hierarchical breakdown and structure of clip instances.

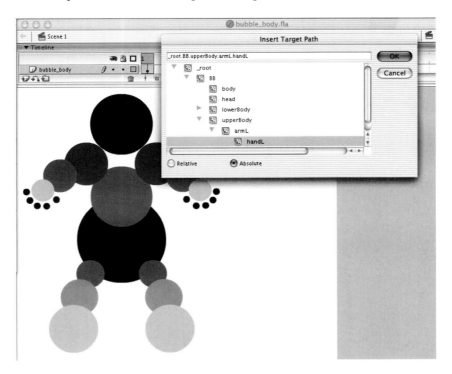

Using _parent and this to Create Relative Paths

You can also target clips with *relative paths*. These paths don't refer directly to the main Timeline, but rather the location of the clip you want to target relative to the location of the script that makes the call. Going back to the BB example, if you wanted to send a command from the handL clip to the armL clip, you could use the absolute target path

```
_root.BB.upperBody.armL._rotation=0;
```

Or you could use the relative path

```
_parent._rotation=0;
```

As you can see, in this case, the relative path is much shorter. Relative paths can use a different reference: _parent. This reference translates to "go back one nest level." Because the handL clip is a child nested inside armL, a script on the armL Timeline needs to go back only a single nest level. If you needed to go back farther, you could use the reference twice:

```
_parent._parent._visible=false;
```

This statement, if made in the handL clip, would make BB's upper body disappear.

There is an additional relative target path reference called this, which refers to the current Timeline or the Timeline where the script using the target path resides. this is a convenient term because it allows you to access a clip directly from its own Timeline rather than enter a long, specific target path to the clip. To send a message to armR directly from the upperBody Timeline, you can use the this reference:

```
this.armR._rotation=-120;
```

The preceding script would rotate the armR instance to −120°. The this reference works to keep script actions relative to the Timeline where they are called: a child clip instance, a movie level number, or even the main Timeline (although the need for this is rare).

> You can write target paths in two different ways: typing them by hand or using the Target Path button in the Actions panel. To learn about this feature of the Actions panel, see Chapter 17.

Controlling Multiple Movie Timelines with ActionScript

Now that you know how to properly refer to the various Timelines in your Flash movie, you will apply what you know about ActionScript to control their playback and attributes. There are four main ActionScript components that you can use to do this:

Global functions are ActionScript's built-in commands used to control Timeline playback. These include statements such as gotoAndPlay(), stop(), and nextFrame().

Methods that are specific to the MovieClip object can also be used in this context. There are several global functions that can be used as MovieClip methods. Others are unique to the MovieClip object, such as getBounds() and hitTest().

Properties, or the attributes of a Movie Clip, can be altered when you target a clip. Many of the Movie Clip properties are discussed in Chapter 20 and the ActionScript Reference on this book's accompanying CD.

Timeline references are generic terms used to identify and target a particular timeline.

Depending on the type of Timeline that you have to control with ActionScript, you will use a different set of ActionScript statements and syntax to achieve the desired effect.

Using Timeline References

Timeline references allow you to identify a specific Timeline by using a generic, or non-specific, name. Whereas Movie Clip instances require unique identifiers to complete their target paths and gain control via ActionScript, other Timelines can be identified more easily. Timeline references are a vital part of writing target paths in ActionScript. They allow you to control the elements that reside on various Timelines, as well as gain access to a Timeline's variables and functions.

_root

This is the most fundamental reference in all of ActionScript. _root refers to the main Timeline, the mother of any Flash movie. _root (also known as _level0) is the foundation to which all other content is either saved or loaded. Calls to any custom function or variable created on the main Timeline should always be preceded with a _root reference.

_lockroot

_lockroot is a new reference introduced in Flash MX 2004 and MX Pro 2004. As developers continue to make their Flash movies more and more modular, the _lockroot reference fulfills a much-needed role in ActionScript. If you create a movie and include a line of ActionScript that refers to the variable _root.count, that code will look on the main Timeline for the value of count. However, what if that movie needs to be loaded into _level4 at some point? Once it is loaded into a new document level, the value of _root changes to the movie Timeline that is hosting your original movie at _level4. Your variable doesn't reside there!

_lockroot helps alleviate this potential problem. To ensure that your movie can always locate values and functions on its own main Timeline, enter the following statement:

```
this._lockroot=true;
```

By defining _lockroot as true, a movie knows that all references to _root really mean its own main Timeline rather than the Timeline of a movie it's loaded into.

This reference can be used only for movies that are published for the Flash Player 7. If you don't have access to the source file of the movie you want to load, you can use this workaround. Load the SWF into a Movie Clip instance on the main Timeline:

```
loadMovie("loader.swf","container_mc")
```

When the clip is loaded, attach a script to the clip instance that sets _lockroot to true:

```
onClipEvent(load){
    this._lockroot=true;
}
```

This tells the clip instance to keep all references to _root on its own Timeline rather than the main Timeline of the movie to which it belongs.

_level

This reference identifies layers of content that have been loaded into the Flash Player as additional SWF files. _level0 is synonymous with _root. All subsequent levels are _level1, _level2..._leveln. When loading additional files into the Flash Player or sending Action-Script commands to files that have been loaded, you need to use a _level reference. Look back at Figure 19.1 for an illustration of a movie with various content levels.

_parent

A Timeline that contains another Timeline is considered a _parent. Because it can contain individual Movie Clip Timelines, the main Timeline is a _parent. Similarly, any Movie Clip that contains nested clips is also a _parent. This reference identifies the Timeline or instance that *contains* the Timeline or Movie Clip instance where an ActionScript call is made.

Timeline references are used throughout this book. You can also check their individual listings in the ActionScript Reference section.

Loading Movie Levels

To load additional movies, use the loadMovieNum() function. The syntax for load-MovieNum() is as follows:

```
loadMovieNum("URL",level)
```

This function has two main arguments:

URL is the argument that specifies the location and name of the movie (SWF) file to be loaded. This URL can be either absolute or relative to the file loading the movie and should be specified as a string (in quotes).

`level` is an integer argument used to specify where the new movie will be loaded. To load the movie on a new level, specify that level in this argument, for example, `1`. This would cause Flash to load the movie into _level1.

The following statement loads the movie `levelTwo.swf` into movie level 2:

```
loadMovieNum("levelTwo.swf",2);
```

Alternatively, you can use the `unloadMovieNum()` function to reverse the process. The main difference with this function is that it takes only one argument—an integer that identifies the level to be unloaded:

```
unloadMovieNum(1);
```

This script removes the movie currently playing on level 1.

Related to loadMovieNum() and unloadMovieNum() are the functions loadMovie() and unloadMovie(). Although the two sets of functions have very similar purposes, each set takes a slightly different syntax. Depending on the application, you might find one set better than the other. For example, this next statement loads the movie `begin.swf` into a clip instance named `intro`, which is located on the main Timeline:

```
loadMovie("begin.swf","_root.intro");
```

loadMovie() uses a string to identify the location where a movie will be loaded. This provides the added flexibility to load movies into Movie Clip instances as well as movie levels. The upper-left corner of the loaded movie is aligned with the registration point of the host Movie Clip. loadMovieNum() has a more compact syntax, but is unable to load movies into clip instances. A good rule of thumb is this: Use loadMovieNum() to load movies into levels, and loadMovie() to load movies into Movie Clips. For specifics, see the ActionScript Reference on this book's CD.

Attaching Movie Clip Instances

To *attach* a Movie Clip means to call a clip from your movie's Library and put it on the Stage in place of another clip. You can attach clips using the attachMovie() method of the MovieClip object. The syntax for attachMovie() is as follows:

```
clipInstance.attachMovie("id","name",depth)
```

This method has three main arguments:

id is the Linkage ID name you use to export the clip from the Library. A clip cannot be attached until it has a Linkage ID. To understand this process further, see the next section of this chapter.

name is the instance name you want to assign to the attached clip.

depth is the position the new clip will take in internal clip stacking level. Your first attached clip can have a depth of 0, the second a depth of 1, and so on. Clips with higher depths cover those with lower depth values. If you want to stack the clips in reverse order, you can specify a depth of 8 for the first clip, 7 for the second, and so on.

For example:

```
enemy_1.attachMovie("explode","explode_1",1);
```

In this sample script, a clip with the Linkage ID `explode` is attached to `enemy_1`. It is given the instance name `explode_1` and assigned a depth of `1`.

Attaching Movie Clips is useful in certain specific contexts. For example, you could do this in a game where you want an enemy ship to explode, as demonstrated in the previous script. Components use attached Movie Clips whenever you assign an icon graphic to a Component instance. To attach any kind of Movie Clip, it must first be exported from your movie's Library.

Exporting Movie Clips and Linkage Identifiers

Exporting Movie Clips from the Library is a simple but necessary step to dynamically gain access to a Movie Clip as a resource. Every exported clip is given a unique name, called its Linkage ID. This name is what allows you to refer to the clip specifically. Once a clip has been exported, it is available to be shared with other Flash movies, attached to Movie Clip instances, and used as a graphic icon in Flash v2 Components.

To export a clip and assign a Linkage ID:

1. Open your movie's Library (F11) and select the clip that you need to export.

2. Select Linkage from the pop-up menu in the upper-right corner of your movie's Library. The Linkage Properties dialog box opens.

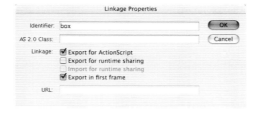

3. Click the box that reads Export for ActionScript. A name automatically appears in the Identifier field. This is the name that will be used as the clip's Linkage ID. You may change it if necessary. Exported clips can be used in a variety of ways:

   • If you plan to attach the exported clip using `attachMovie()`, uncheck the Export in First Frame box. This will allow your movie to load more quickly, but it involves a small additional step. See the note at the end of this section.

   • If you are planning to use the clip as an icon for a Component, be sure Export in First Frame is checked.

4. Click OK.

Once the clip has been exported with a Linkage ID, it is available to be called by Action-Script later in your movie.

Because they are not selected to export in the first frame, exported clips that you want to use via `attachMovie()` need to be made available in the frame(s) of your movie by another means. Drag an instance of the clip to the keyframe where you plan to attach it, but position it *outside* the bounds of the stage. It will not appear until you need it. When it is attached, it will move from that location to the location where you attach it.

Targeting Movie Clip Timelines to Control Playback

You can use the following global functions to control timelines in your Flash movie:

gotoAndPlay() Skips to a frame, frame label, or scene and plays from that location.

gotoAndStop() Skips to a frame, frame label, or scene and stops at that location.

play() Plays through the frames of a Timeline.

stop() Stops playback of a Timeline.

To target the timeline for a Movie Clip instance, you must use either a relative or absolute path to the clip you wish to target. After you specify that clip, you can use the dot operator to state the function you would like to use to manipulate the instance. For example:

```
_root.upperBody.armL.handL.gotoAndPlay("peace");
```

This starts at the main Timeline, goes up a chain of nested instances, and tells the instance `handL` to start playing at a frame label named `peace`. It might help to think of targeting with the dot operator as moving from the general to the specific.

The following script stops the parent of a nested Movie Clip at frame 1 on the parent's Timeline. When executed, the child clip that called this script would be able to continue playing independently.

```
_parent.gotoAndStop(1);
```

Here is one of the most useful functions of all:

```
stop();
```

A lone `stop()` function in frame 1 is all it takes to prevent a Movie Clip instance from playing before you want it to begin. These simple playback functions are some of the most important in all of Flash, even for complex movies and applications. You will find examples in a variety of contexts throughout this book. Also, to learn the proper syntax for these functions, see the ActionScript Reference on this book's CD.

Understanding Movie Clips beyond Animation

When you first learned to use Flash, if you thought of Movie Clips as "animation containers," you were right. However, as your skills with the program evolve, it can help to broaden your view and start to approach the all-mighty Movie Clip from a different perspective.

From this day forward, we'd like you to think of Movie Clips as "information containers." This means, of course, that they are animation containers—but they are also text containers, sound containers, graphics containers, and ActionScript containers. When you think about it, there's really no difference between the main Timeline and a Movie Clip Timeline. The only distinction is that one has been designated as the parent of all others. This is an important difference, but only in the sense that it describes the hierarchy of a Flash movie. The important point is that all Timelines in a movie can be used to hold a variety of media. The better you understand this, and the sooner you start to think this way, the easier it will be to gain creative flexibility within Flash.

There are probably a zillion different ways to demonstrate this, but we'll start with something that is both familiar and fun: a cartoon thought bubble. First of all, go to the Chapter 19 folder on this book's CD and open the file named good_thoughts.swf. Roll your mouse over the character and see what happens. You should see a thought bubble appear and reveal what this little guy is thinking (see Figure 19.3). This example is a perfect illustration of what a Movie Clip can do beyond simple animated routines. By looking at the way the FLA file is put together, you will get a sense of how Movie Clips can be used as containers.

To examine the Movie Clip structure of this example:

1. Open good_thoughts.fla in the Chapter 19 folder on this book's CD.

2. Click to select the code layer of the main Timeline, then press F9 to open the Actions panel. You should see the following statements:

```
idea_button.onRollOver=function(){
    _root.bubble_mc.gotoAndPlay(2);
}
idea_button.onRollOut=function(){
    _root.bubble_mc.gotoAndStop(1);
}
```

Figure 19.3

This simple movie uses a series of Movie Clips to make the character communicate his cartoonish thoughts through a thought bubble.

There is an invisible button placed over the character with the instance name idea_button. These statements tell a clip instance named bubble_mc to play at frame 2 when you roll over the button.

3. Let's see what happens on frame 2 of this clip. If you look at the contents of the thoughts layer, you should see a small white dot. This is actually the bubble_mc Movie Clip instance. When a Movie Clip has an empty first frame, it is represented on the stage as a white dot with a black stroke. Click to select the clip instance, and then double-click to edit the clip in Symbol Editing mode.

4. Now that you're in Symbol Editing mode, you should be able to see the contents of the clip's Timeline. The first frame is empty except for

a `stop()` function in the code layer. This is there to prevent the clip from playing until it's cued. This creates the impression that there is nothing on the stage when the clip is actually available and ready to go.

The next six frames are occupied with the animation of the thought bubble popping out. When it is told to play at frame 2, this animation is what you see.

5. In frame 8 of the code layer, you should see the following statements:

    ```
    thought_mc.gotoAndPlay(2);
    stop();
    ```

    These statements work in a similar fashion to what you've seen already. When this frame is played, a separate clip instance named `thought_mc` (on the thoughts layer) is told to go play at frame 2, and the current Timeline is halted.

6. Click the white dot for the `thought_mc` instance. Similar to the `bubble_mc` instance that we saw earlier, this clip also has an empty first frame except for the `stop()` function in the code layer. Double-click to edit this clip in Symbol Editing mode. You will see that it has a long Timeline where the thoughts that fill the bubble are allowed to play.

So why is this simple thought bubble constructed of a series of nested Movie Clips? Because the nested elements make them easy to control. You can send one `gotoAndPlay()` call that cues another. This "chain reaction" cues all the necessary components of the animation. The modular design also makes it easier to edit and change the clips. If you wanted to introduce a larger bubble or a bubble with a different shape, it would be easy to put it in a new keyframe on the thought bubble Movie Clip Timeline. Then, when you wanted to show that bubble, you would send the clip to play at frame 9 (for example) rather than frame 2.

In this same manner, you could also give the character different thoughts. In this file, frame 2 shows a thought about Movie Clips. You could easily expand this so that frame 43 talked about ActionScript, frame 84 said something about Components, and so on. The concept of "Timeline" is a fundamental aspect of the program, and Flash is very adept at managing multiple Timelines. By creating your Flash movies as a series of nested and interrelated Movie Clips, you can stretch the possibilities of the program.

Inspirational Design Model

In this chapter, we would like to feature a website that is near and dear to our hearts, the site that has been a tireless champion for *Flash MX Savvy*: the von Flashenstein website (`www.vonflashenstein.com`).

This choice was not made to serve as a shameless self-promotional plug. Rather, it is an appropriate choice based on the way the site was constructed in Flash (see Figure 19.4). Every element from the weird-o lab equipment to the specific content areas to the characters themselves is built out of Movie Clips and external Timelines. When you roll over an object that prompts a character to "think," you are triggering a Movie Clip animation. When you click to go to the Dungeon for downloadable files or the Lab Equipment for script samples, you are loading a new SWF into _level2.

Once you start the development of Flash movies in this modular fashion, you will find that even large movies with lots of assets are manageable. Everything can be discreetly contained in its own independent timeline. This allows you to work on your movie in little chunks: while you are developing it in the formative stages, and when you are editing or updating it in the future.

Figure 19.4

The von Flashen-stein website is the home of *Flash MX Savvy* and the lair of Dr. von Flashenstein and his precociously appalling assistant, Müvie Klip.

Flash MX 2004 Color Gallery

This section includes some of the best and brightest creations in the world of Flash. As a source of inspiration, we've brought together a wealth of examples from the most creative, cutting-edge Flash designers around. What you will see here is just a glimpse of the masterful work exhibited by these select individuals and organizations. If you like what you see, visit the websites to experience these pieces firsthand.

ABOVE: Looking to kill some time? The entertainment portal Heavy (www.heavy.com) has just about everything you need to while away your workday afternoon. Count on the Heavy Pop-Up Radio to have the grittiest hip-hop, alternative, punk, and funk cued in the playlist. You can use Heavy free of charge, or once you're really addicted, subscribe for premium services. **BELOW**: Check out Heavy Games for original titles such as *Iron Stomach* and old-school arcade favorites such as *Spy Hunter*, *Joust*, and *Defender*.

ABOVE: Heavy has a lot of music to offer—we mean a lot. Visit the Insound section for a sampling of the latest picks at the underground music mecca, Insound (www.insound.com). You can sample the artists at Heavy, then follow the links for more info at the Insound site. **BELOW:** VH-1 fan? You might enjoy the Heavy parody "Behind the Music That Sucks." Also be sure to check out these other music-related sections: Sumosonic, Heavy Grooves, and Heavy Music. Keep your eyes peeled for freebie MP3 giveaways!

ABOVE: Soontira Sutanont, or "Goi," earned her MFA in graphic design from Indiana University, Bloomington, in the spring of 2003. Her thesis project, "Life, Land, & the Road" focused on the much-debated Highway I-69 project in south-central Indiana. Her intent was to explore the different meanings of "quality of life" as perceived by Indiana residents on both sides of the issue. **BELOW:** This exhibit is a work in mixed media. A Flash animation plays continuously to display text with facts, figures, maps, and quotes surrounding the I-69 project. The animation is projected onto a poster that mixes photography and letter-pressed text.

ABOVE: Arcane by Sarbakan (www.sarbakan.com) is a horror/mystery adventure inspired by the pulp serials of the early 20th century. Arcane is written for teenagers and adults and follows two parallel storylines. Though they follow a traditional serial structure, the Arcane stories are interactive games. Each episode requires you to help the characters explore their environment and solve the mystery. **BELOW:** Prescott, Ophelia, and Gregor (left-to-right around the table) work to unravel yet another enigma surrounding the Elder Star Society. In each episode, you must master the characters' abilities to make it to the story's end and win the game.

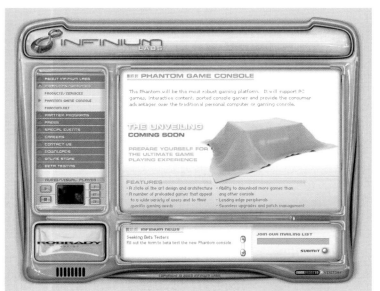

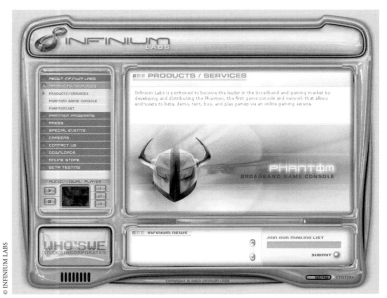

ABOVE: Infinium Labs (www.infiniumlabs.com/intro.html) is a global game development and entertainment company. They are the designers and manufacturers of the Phantom, a high-performance game console that aims to deliver interactive content to a broad audience. The Infinium Labs website has a sophisticated, 3D, "techie" look that will make any gamer foam at the mouth. **BELOW:** The Infinium Labs site uses ActionScript in a variety of ways to offer textual information, three different audio tracks, news, downloadable files, and a subscription to their mailing list. If you like interface design that is driven by a technological look and feel, you will love this site.

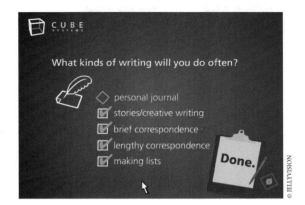

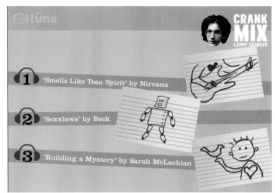

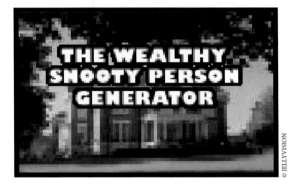

ABOVE: Jellyvision (www.jellyvision.com), the company that created the irreverent interactive trivia game *You Don't Know Jack*, is hard at work developing products to remind us that interacting with a computer doesn't have to be a drag. First, there was the GUI ("gooey"); now there's iCi ("icky"). iCi, or the Interactive Conversation Interface, is brilliantly simple: It uses clever dialog to facilitate the exchange of information (a *conversation*) between a user and a machine. Visit the Demos section to see and hear what iCi is all about. **BELOW**: Jellyvision's award-winning *You Don't Know Jack* is back. With more than 5 million copies sold in the series, Jellyvision plans to release the 11th version, *You Don't Know Jack* Gold in early 2004. The latest Jack installment is unique in that it is the first U.S. release developed entirely in Flash. If you've had doubts about Flash as a tool for developing CD-ROM content, think again. Jellyvision used Flash because it was able to manage the fast-paced delivery of audio and animation they require for the game. Plus, as a Flash-based application, it gives them the option to distribute *You Don't Know Jack Gold* via the Internet.

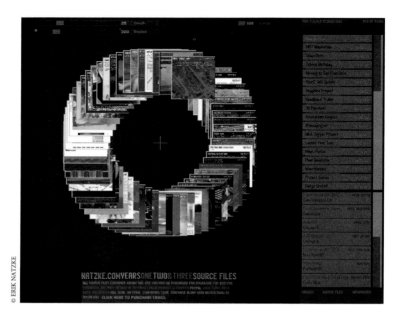

© ERIK NATZKE

© ERIK NATZKE

ABOVE: Erik Natzke (www.natzke.com) is a true Flash artist. This latest version of his site is filled with sketches and musings, links to Flash resources, and other information about the man himself. Natzke considers the site to be an "online journal" where he can freely explore ideas and experiment without external pressures and expectations. **BELOW:** *Click and Drag* is a moveable image gallery. Click the images and watch them go! The blend of motion and gritty urban photography is nice contrast to the clean digital lines created by Flash.

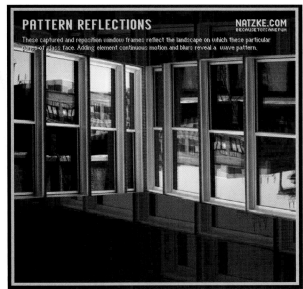

PATTERN REFLECTIONS   NATZKE.COM
                                       BECAUSE TOYS ARE FUN
These captured and reposition window frames reflect the landscape on which these particular
panes of glass face. Adding element continuous motion and blurs reveal a wave pattern.

© ERIK NATZKE

MOUSE TOY   NATZKE.COM
                                       BECAUSE TOYS ARE FUN
The patterns in nature lend inspiration to artificial growth structures.

© ERIK NATZKE

ABOVE: *Pattern Reflections* is another interesting study in motion. Move your mouse in all four directions to get different variations in the scale, speed, and direction of the window-pane graphics. Watch for the gorgeous contrast created as the image transitions from crisp to blurry. **BELOW:** Not only can this guy create fantastic art with Flash, he's a talented photographer. *Mouse Toy* uses programmatic growth and motion to replicate organic, natural patterns. The animation in this piece is wonderful. What is especially evocative is the choice of color. Notice how the color of the swirling circles complements the background imagery.

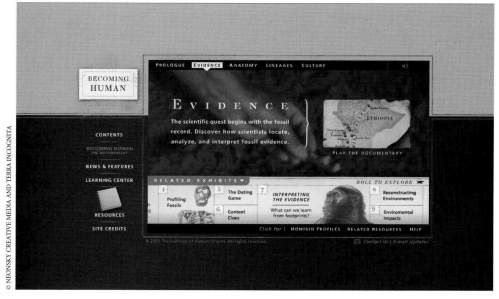

ABOVE: Developed jointly by NeonSky Creative Media (www.neonsky.com) and Terra Incognita (www.terraincognita.com) for the Arizona State Institute for Human Origins, *Becoming Human* (www.becominghuman.org) is an original interactive Flash documentary that explores human evolution from our earliest ancestors to the emergence of *Homo sapiens.* **BELOW:** *Becoming Human* features a host of innovative and interactive tools (such as interactive exhibits) that allow you to go beyond the Flash documentary itself and pursue your personal exploration into the fascinating world of human evolution.

ABOVE: *Becoming Human* is partitioned into several sections that allow you to explore questions about culture, hominid anatomy, archaeological evidence, and lineage. Each section features not only a spectacular linear Flash documentary narrated by the prestigious paleoanthropologist Dr. Donald Johanson, but also topical discussions by many other prominent scholars in the field of human evolution. **BELOW:** The combination of the linear documentary and interactive exploratory tools (both of which were created totally in Flash) makes *Becoming Human* one of the most interesting, innovative, and cutting-edge Flash creations out there.

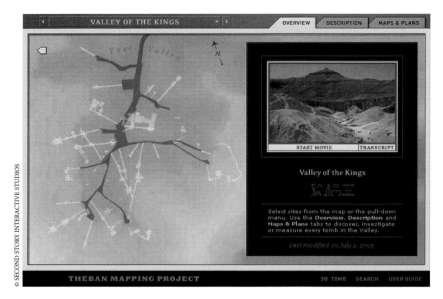

ABOVE: Created by Second Story Interactive (www.secondstory.com), the Theban Mapping Project site (www.thebanmappingproject.com) features *The Atlas of the Valley of the Kings*, an incredible example of interactive Flash edutainment that lets people explore the valley, where from 1500 B.C. to 1000 B.C., ancient Egyptian pharaohs were buried in expansive underground complexes. **BELOW**: From professional Egyptologists to school children, this site serves the needs of a wide and diverse audience. Visitors unfamiliar with the valley can go on a virtual tour of a 3D tomb or watch narrated movies. For experienced academics, the site offers the opportunity to research the architecture and decoration of every chamber in every tomb in the valley.

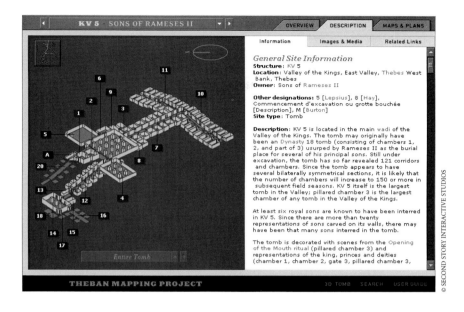

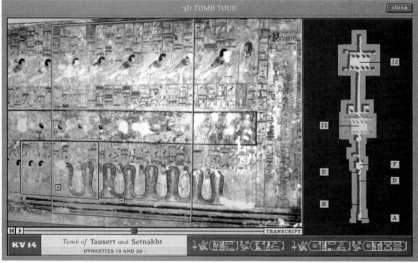

ABOVE: The *Interactive Atlas*, which is a stand-alone multimedia experience, displays compelling movies, dynamic information, and gripping images in context with detailed maps and measured drawings of the tombs within the Valley of the Kings. **BELOW:** The information and media delivered in the Interactive Atlas is made possible by the efforts of the Theban Mapping Project, an Egyptological expedition (based at the American University in Cairo) dedicated to preparing a comprehensive archaeological database of Thebes (an area which the Valley of the Kings is a part of) and conserve and preserve the incredible archaeological resource for study by future generations.

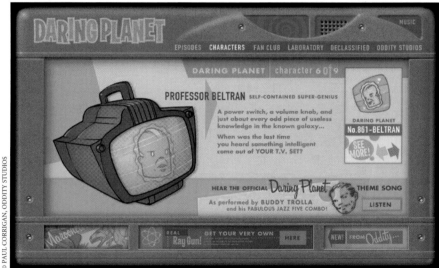

ABOVE: Woohoo, more fun than a barrel of psychic monkey girls! Created by the insanely talented Paul Corrigan, Daring Planet (www.daringplanet.com) is easily one of the most creative and entertaining uses of Flash in the universe. Designed as a promotional site (and future platform) for a campy retro sci-fi serialized Flash-animated toon, Daring Planet is an interactive (and outright enjoyable) feast for the eyes. **BELOW:** Drawing inspiration from old B-movie sci-fi/horror posters from the '50s and '60s and pop-culture/subculture advertising and references from the '40s, '50s, and '60s, Daring Planet's design features an authentic retro look reminiscent of period comic books and magazines. If you look closely at the site's design, you'll notice subtle visual touches such as cheap paper, bad registration, subpar printing procedures, and colors that bleed that give it a true retro style.

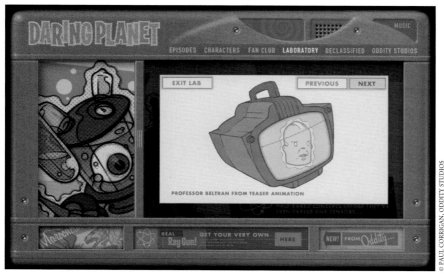

ABOVE: One of the goals of the Daring Planet project is to create an immersive online environment for fans and casual visitors alike. Complete with a developer's journal, animation samples, tutorials, and regular character-specific features, Daring Planet provides much more than the anticipated episodes and storylines. It's also a destination that combines expert illustration, copywriting, storytelling, and design in a way that both surprises and delights. **BELOW:** The individual Daring Planet episodes (which are currently in production) will be serialized, self-contained plots that fit within a larger, continually evolving saga. They will include components of sequential, frame-based art that is punctuated with animated sequences, sound effects, and a background musical score. Ultimately, the storytelling mechanism will be designed to make the most of traditional comic-book pacing, animated embellishments, and online interactivity.

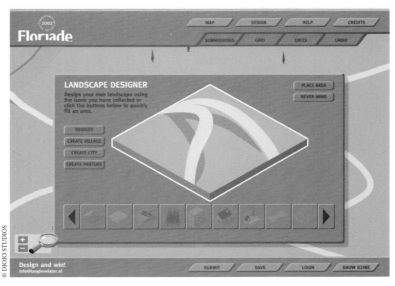

ABOVE: Designed by Djojo Studios (www.djojostudios.com), Langlevelater (www.langleve-later.nl/en) is easily one of the most innovative, immersive learning environments on the Web today. Built entirely in Flash, the site was created for the Floriade Dutch Horticultural Exhibition to teach kids about environmental issues. **BELOW**: Melding Djojo Studios' easily recognizable stylish illustration with an incredibly immersive Flash-based environment, Langlevelater lets kids navigate through a series of virtual pavilions, each of which mirrors an actual pavilion at the horticultural exhibition. Each pavilion contains topical quizzes, the successful completion of which awards kids with tiles to build their own interactive (and environmentally sustainable) urban landscape.

CHAPTER 20

Creating Advanced Interaction

Okay, you can admit it: Learning all the technical ins and outs of ActionScript isn't a picnic. The language has many layers of detail, and understanding the relationships between them is a tough thing to wrap your brain around. If you are like most people, it will take months of mental pain and frustration to get a handle on how it all comes together. But be patient. As you progress, you will find that the moments of ActionScript success far outnumber the periods of frustration.

You have tackled the technical side of ActionScript, and you are now ready to put your newly acquired skills to use. As you can imagine, the possibilities that ActionScript offers are virtually unbounded; it can sometimes be stifling just trying to think about what you want to do with a particular movie, let alone how you will actually accomplish the task. The best approach to take is this: Think about *what* you would like to create rather than *how* you will create it. Let your artistic or design goals provide direction first; then figure out how they will be accomplished.

This chapter should provide the materials you need to help get you started. It would be impossible to cover all the features of both Flash and ActionScript in a single book. Here you will find examples that cover many of the Flash and ActionScript essentials. Think of these lessons as starter kits for your movies. Just add your own ideas, and you will be up and running in no time. As always, remember to work in small chunks, save often, and test your movie each time you add a new feature or change a script. If you follow this process, it will be much easier to pinpoint an error or problem if and when one occurs. Good luck, and have fun!

This chapter covers the following topics:

- **Techniques to organize your code**
- **Button and Movie Clip scripting beyond the basics**
- **Creating a slider to control movie elements**
- **How ActionScript watches and records keystrokes**
- **Scripting randomness and animation**
- **Using ActionScript to manipulate graphic elements of your movie**
- **Managing data with Arrays**
- **Working with text fields and the Date object**

Centralizing and Organizing Your Code

As your Flash creations grow in complexity, it is important to keep them organized. FLA files that have advanced functionality often require more ActionScript that enables them to perform. This code can be attached in a variety of places: frames, buttons, and Movie Clip instances. This isn't necessarily hard to keep track of, but once you start nesting Movie Clips and buttons within other clips, things can start to get out of hand. You might find that you have to go to frame 1 of a clip that's inside a clip that's inside another clip that's part of a separate SWF file that gets loaded into another clip. Whew! Confused? We are.

The key to preventing this scenario is to keep your code organized and, as much as possible, centralize your ActionScript in one location. There are several recommendations we can make to help you keep things neat and tidy:

- All custom or user-created functions should go in frame 1 of your movie's main Timeline. This way, all functions are loaded right away and available to be called later on. Also, you know where their code is saved *and* you know to call them from the `_root` level. This habit will make your custom functions much easier to manage.

- Create objects (such as Sound objects or Arrays) in the first frame of the main Timeline, the first frame of a Movie Clip, or in an `onClipEvent(load)` handler attached to a Movie Clip instance.

- Timeline variables can be treated similarly to objects. Initialize them in the first frame of the main Timeline, the first frame of a Movie Clip, or in an `onClipEvent(load)` handler attached to a Movie Clip instance. They will be scoped to the Timeline on which they were created.

- Scripts that control the behavior of buttons and Movie Clips can be written using event handler method syntax:

```
object.eventHandlerMethod=function(){
    statements;
}
```

These are functions that should go in a frame on the main Timeline or in a Movie Clip instance. Event handler methods provide an alternative to the syntax you use to attach a script directly to a button or Movie Clip:

```
on(event){
    statements;
}
```

While each will yield similar results, because event method handlers can be attached to a frame on a Timeline, it's often easier to locate and edit these scripts. To learn more about event handler methods, see the next section of this chapter.

These suggestions and techniques will be put into practice in the examples in this chapter and throughout this book. They will help you keep your movies organized. Once this becomes a habit, you'll find that it can be a time saver in many ways. Your scripts will be much easier to locate and you will know when and from where statements get executed.

Button Scripting: Revisited and Expanded

Buttons are one of the most basic and intuitive kinds of interactive controls. Their role in an interactive movie is straightforward: You click them and something happens. Like a Movie Clip, a button can have a script attached to it. When the button is clicked, any attached ActionScript statements are executed in accordance with the handler that is managing them. To learn more about buttons and handlers, see Chapter 15.

At the most basic level, a button will have a single on() handler with an event and a single statement. For example:

```
on(release){
    gotoAndPlay(15);
}
```

When the mouse button is released, the action that sends the movie to play at frame 15 is executed. The handler event (release) sets the action in motion. For many buttons, this is all the complexity you will need, especially in the case of basic movie navigation. However, button scripts are capable of much more.

The event handlers used with button scripts can support multiple statements within a single handler, as can any of the other handlers in ActionScript. This means that you can make a button do all sorts of things when it is clicked: control the main Timeline, control other Timelines, play and stop sounds, perform functions or other computations, and send or modify variables—anything that is possible within ActionScript. When the handler's event occurs, all statements within it are executed from top to bottom and your movie is updated accordingly.

It's also possible to attach multiple handlers to a single button. This technique multiplies the performance of the button because it is no longer executing statements at the occurrence of a single event. For example:

```
on(rollOver){
    swish.start();
}
on(press){
    click.start();
}
on(release){
    ring.start();
}
```

This script sample plays three different sounds—swish, click, and ring—when you interact with the button. Swish is played when the mouse moves over the button, click is played when the mouse is pressed, and ring is heard when the mouse is released. All of this scripting creates a very musical and interactive button!

Event Handler Methods

Event handler methods were first introduced in Flash MX. Like regular event handlers, they provide a means to attach scripts to objects such as buttons and Movie Clips. The difference is that event handler methods don't have to be attached to the object itself. Rather, they can be assigned from a separate location. This makes it easy to centralize all your button- and Movie Clip–related ActionScript in one location.

An event handler method is easy to understand if you examine each word in the name:

event An occurrence; something that takes place while a movie is playing. The most familiar example of an event that can occur to an object is a button being clicked.

handler Executes statements (in this case, a function) when the handler's event occurs.

method A function associated with an object.

Now let's put it all together. An event handler method is ActionScript code associated with an object that performs a function when the prescribed event occurs to that object. They allow you to define specific kinds of object interaction that will set a function into motion and effect changes in your movie. You can use event handler methods to control several of the various objects in a Flash movie, including text fields, Movie Clips, and buttons.

Assigning Functions to Buttons with Event Handler Methods

Buttons have always been objects of a Flash movie, but when Flash MX was introduced, they were given their own object class. As a result, it's now possible to assign a unique instance name to a button and to control its behavior and properties via ActionScript. This feature will not significantly change the way you create Flash movies. It will, however, expand the possibilities of what you can do with a button in your interactive movies.

The Button object has its own set of event handler methods. These are used like the events for the on() handler: They determine which button event must occur for the assigned function to be called.

Like regular buttons, Button objects can be used as interactive controllers in your movie. The only difference is that the Button object must have a unique instance name assigned to it. This way the assigned function "belongs" to the Button. The function contains a statement (or statements) that is (are) executed when the event handler method occurs and calls the function. The basic syntax looks like this:

```
buttonInstance.eventHandlerMethod=function(){
    statements to be executed when eventHandlerMethod occurs
}
```

The Button object events and their descriptions are as follows:

Button.onDragOut Occurs when the cursor is pressed over the button and dragged outside its bounds.

Button.onDragOver Occurs when the cursor is pressed over the button, dragged outside its bounds, and then dragged back inside.

Button.onKillFocus Occurs when the button loses keyboard focus.

Button.onPress Occurs when the cursor is pressed over the button.

Button.onRelease Occurs when the cursor is first pressed, then released over the button.

Button.onReleaseOutside Occurs when the cursor is first pressed over the button and then released outside the button's bounds.

Button.onRollOut Occurs when the cursor is moved outside the bounds of the button.

Button.onRollOver Occurs when the cursor is moved within the bounds of the button.

Button.onSetFocus Occurs when the button is given keyboard focus.

As you can see, there are many similarities between the Button object's event handler methods and regular button event handlers.

Now that you are acquainted with the Button object and its associated events, you are ready to learn how to assign a function to a Button object. First, open a new Flash document and create a Button symbol. For specifics on creating buttons, see Chapter 15. To use an event handler method and assign a function to a Button object:

1. Select the button on the Stage. Choose Window → Properties or press Cmd/Ctrl+F3 to open the Property Inspector.

2. In the instance name field, type an instance name for the button. For the sake of this example, use the name `clicker`.

3. Insert a new layer in the Timeline and call it **code**. Select the first keyframe of the code layer and choose Window → Actions (F9) to open the Actions panel.

4. Enter the following statements:

```
clicker.onRelease=function(){
    trace("clicked");
}
```

This script assigns a function to your `clicker` button instance. The function will print the phrase *clicked* in the Output panel and will execute when the mouse is pressed and released over the `clicker` button instance.

5. Select Control → Test Movie to give your new function a try. When you click the button, the Output panel should appear with the message *clicked*.

One advantage of this new scripting technique is that rather than having to attach scripts to each button individually, you can assign them to each button from one location in your movie. If you have many buttons and button scripts, this can centralize the task of scripting for all of these elements. Be sure that for every Button object script you write, the object's corresponding button instance is on the Timeline at the same frame number. If a script is read on frame 1 but the button isn't encountered until frame 2, Flash won't know where to assign the function, and it will fail.

Assigning Functions to Movie Clips with Event Handler Methods

Movie Clip objects can also take advantage of the flexibility and tidiness afforded by event handler methods. In the same fashion, you can write ActionScript for all your Movie Clips and use event handler methods and keep your code in a single location.

Movie Clips have their own set of event handler methods. If you are familiar with Flash 5 syntax, they are similar to the events for the `onClipEvent()` Movie Clip handler: They determine which event must occur for the assigned function to be called. Like the Button object, Movie Clips must have a unique instance name assigned to them. This way the function "belongs" to the clip. The function contains a statement (or statements) that is (are) executed when the event handler method occurs and calls the assigned function. The basic syntax looks like this:

```
clipInstance.eventHandlerMethod=function(){
    statements to be executed when eventHandlerMethod occurs
}
```

This syntax is identical to that you would use for Buttons. The only difference is in the various events associated with Movie Clip objects. The Movie Clip events and their descriptions are as follows:

MovieClip.onEnterFrame Occurs each time a new frame is played. The rate of this event is governed by a movie's frame rate.

MovieClip.onKeyDown When a clip is on the Stage and has focus, this event occurs when a key is pressed.

MovieClip.onKeyUp When a clip is on the Stage and has focus, this event occurs when a pressed key is released.

MovieClip.onLoad This event occurs when a clip is first loaded onto the Stage. However, due to the order in which Flash executes handlers, this event is useful only when used to create custom classes. To initialize variables on a Movie Clip Timeline or define the parameters of a clip instance when it loads, use the older `onClipEvent(load)` syntax as an alternative, and attach it to the clip instance directly.

MovieClip.onMouseDown Occurs each time the mouse is pressed while the clip is on the Stage.

MovieClip.onMouseMove Occurs each time the mouse is moved while the clip is on the Stage.

MovieClip.onMouseUp Occurs each time the mouse is pressed and then released while the clip is on the Stage.

MovieClip.onUnload Occurs when a clip is removed from the Stage.

These events will respond while the prescribed clip instance is on the Stage. Note that the mouse does not have to be over the instance for the event to occur. For example:

```
start.onMouseDown=function(){
    trace("mouse was pressed");
}
```

When the `start` clip instance is on the Stage, this event handler method's function responds to all mouse clicks: those over the clip and those in other locations. To be more specific, and demand that the function respond only when the mouse clicks on the `start` clip instance, you can use the following:

```
start.onPress=function(){
    trace("mouse was pressed");
}
```

`onPress` has been discussed as an event for Button objects. However, it's perfectly legal to use this and other button-related events for Movie Clip instances. This is a great advantage because you can force mouse interaction to occur over a specific clip instance. Ultimately, this allows you to make Movie Clips work and behave a little like buttons. For a complete list, see the events associated with the Button object earlier in this chapter.

Using the Movie Clip *onClipEvent()* Handlers

In Flash 5, if you wanted to monitor the events that occurred to a clip instance, the Action-Script had to be assigned with an `onClipEvent()` Movie Clip handler. This handler waited for the prescribed event and cued the script statements at the appropriate time. For example:

```
onClipEvent(event){
    statements;
}
```

This syntax has been set aside in favor of the event handler methods described earlier. However, it is still supported, and in the case of `onClipEvent(load)`, it is necessary. Consider the following:

```
onClipEvent(load){
    range = 100;
}
```

The `load` event happens only once, when a clip is first loaded onto the Stage. This event is easiest to capture when called from an `onClipEvent()` handler. Imagine this script was on frame 1 of the main Timeline:

```
firstClip.onLoad=function(){
    stop();
}
```

The `firstClip` instance would never stop. Why? Because the clip doesn't exist on the Stage when `onLoad` happens. The Timeline ActionScript is executed first, before `firstClip` is "born," or loaded. The order ActionScript is read and executed makes it necessary to cue scripts from the `load` event in the older syntax.

Use `onClipEvent(load)` to initialize any variables on the Timeline where the handler is attached. In the previous example, *range* is set to 100. Because the variables are created when the clip first loads, they will be ready for other scripts that might execute on that Timeline in the future. Similarly, this event is also good for setting the position of a clip when it loads or executing functions that prepare it for the rest of its "life" in the movie.

Other Movie Clip handler events are identical to those found in the event handler methods. The syntax to employ the events is the only real difference. See Table 20.1 to see the equivalent events in each syntax.

Table 20.1

Flash MX Event Handler Methods and Equivalent Flash 5 Movie Clip Handlers

EVENT HANDLER METHOD (FLASH MX+)	MOVIE CLIP HANDLER (FLASH 5)
MovieClip.onEnterFrame	onClipEvent(enterFrame)
MovieClip.onKeyDown	onClipEvent(keyDown)
MovieClip.onKeyUp	onClipEvent(keyUp)
MovieClip.onLoad	onClipEvent(load)
MovieClip.onMouseDown	onClipEvent(mouseDown)
MovieClip.onMouseMove	onClipEvent(mouseMove)
MovieClip.onMouseUp	onClipEvent(mouseUp)
MovieClip.onUnload	onClipEvent(unload)

Scripting for User Input and Interactivity

Flash is a great application for creating vector animations, and with the help of Action-Script, it is also great for creating interactive games, interfaces, presentations, music players—the list goes on and on. When you are creating an interactive application, it helps to be able to monitor how your audience is interacting with your movie. That way, the movie can react appropriately and respond to the wishes and intentions of the audience. After all, this is what makes something interactive to begin with.

At the time of this writing, the main ways to communicate or interact with a computer program are through mouse and keyboard input. Someday (probably closer than we think), the mouse and keyboard will be under glass in museums around the world and everyone will marvel that we actually used to *use* these things. Well, until that day comes, everyone is stuck in the Stone Age with these two basic input devices. In keeping with the times, ActionScript provides a series of functions, properties, and methods that allow you to create your movies with mouse and keyboard input in mind.

Scripting for Custom Controllers

What is a *custom controller*? You can describe it as any kind of movie element, other than a button, that you create to direct the playback and display of your movie. As with most things you do in Flash, there is virtually no limit to the variety of controllers you can create: knobs that turn, rotary menus, virtual joysticks, and so on. The main thing that most custom controllers have in common is that you manipulate them with the mouse as though you were able to physically touch the controller. Even though actual contact is impossible in Flash, these objects attempt to simulate the experience. Custom controllers present the illusion that you can tweak some sort of physical object in your movie.

To create this illusion, it's necessary to be able to drag or move items around on the movie Stage. ActionScript allows you to create this kind of interaction with Movie Clips by providing two built-in functions: `startDrag()` and `stopDrag()`. These terms are fairly self-explanatory; `startDrag()` makes a specified clip draggable, while `stopDrag()` ends the drag and keeps the clip locked in a stationary position. Each function has its own syntax. Whereas the `stopDrag()` function can be used on its own, the `startDrag()` function takes arguments, as shown in its syntax:

```
startDrag("target",lock,left,top,right,bottom)
```

The arguments of this action are as follows:

target represents the instance or path to the instance you wish to make draggable. If this argument is left blank (as an empty string ""), or provided as `this`, it refers to the clip or current Timeline that has the function attached.

`lock` is a Boolean value: `true` if the clip's registration point should lock to the mouse position, or `false` if the clip is locked to wherever it is first clicked. `lock` is an optional argument.

`left`, `top`, `right`, and `bottom` are optional arguments used to define the coordinate boundaries for the drag. All coordinates are relative to the Timeline where the clip resides. If you plan to use these arguments, be sure to also enter a value for `lock` to ensure proper syntax.

Creating a Slider to Scroll a Timeline

One of the most common and useful kinds of custom controllers is the *slider.* A slider is simply a knob or lever that can be moved along a horizontal or vertical path. As the slider is moved, it changes some element or parameter in your movie within a range of values you've defined. Sliders (also known as faders) are most often used as sound volume controllers, but they can also be used to create color changes, to position and scale objects on the Stage, to load additional Movie Clips, to navigate, and so on. When you create a slider, you start by creating the slider knob. Then you define the slider's bounds and put it on the Stage. Once it is in the movie, you can attach all kinds of ActionScript to make it perform the way you desire.

Here is a step-by-step example that shows you how to create a slider that scrolls a Timeline. You will find the file, named `slider.fla`, in the Chapter 20 folder on this book's companion CD. This example would be useful if you wanted your movie to present information from various periods of history. The process outlined here is fairly general, so any of the ideas presented should transfer to different kinds of sliders that you might need to create for your own movies.

To create a slider:

1. Create a button or Movie Clip to use as the slider knob. It does not have to be anything special, just something that works well in a draggable context. Give the symbol the name **knob_button**. Buttons can work particularly well because they will respond to interaction with their Up, Over, and Down states.

2. Use the Align panel (Cmd/Ctrl+**K**) and center the graphics of the button or Movie Clip horizontally and vertically (see Figure 20.1).

3. When you are finished, select Edit → Edit Document or click the Back button to return to the main Timeline.

4. Select Insert → New Symbol (Cmd/Ctrl+F8) to display the Create New Symbol dialog box.

5. Enter the name `slider knob` and choose the Movie Clip behavior. Click OK, and Flash will jump into Symbol Editing mode.

6. Drag the button or Movie Clip you created in step 1 to the Stage of the slider knob Movie Clip. Use the Property Inspector to give it the instance name **knob**, and use the Align panel to center it on the Stage.

7. Insert a new layer in the clip's Timeline and name it **code**.

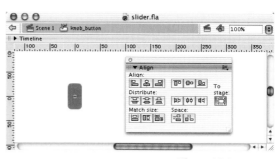

8. Click the empty keyframe in the code layer and choose Window → Actions (F9) to display the Actions panel. By attaching code to the Movie Clip Timeline, the scripts will be available for every instance where the slider knob is used.

9. Enter the following statements:

```
knob.onPress = function() {
    startDrag("knob", false, left, top, right, bottom);
    dragging = true;
}
knob.onRelease = function() {
    stopDrag();
    dragging = false;
}
knob.onReleaseOutside = function() {
    stopDrag();
    dragging = false;
}
```

Figure 20.1

When creating a button or Movie Clip to manipulate as a slider, it helps to align the graphics so that they are centered horizontally and vertically on the Stage.

These statements turn on or off the ability to drag the slider knob when the clip or button is pressed and released, respectively. Note that there are no specific values assigned to the startDrag() function that set the bounds for the drag. Instead, you use a set of variables that will be initialized later.

Why two handlers for the release event, you ask? You never know if someone's mouse will have a "firm grasp" on the thing they are dragging. By using the additional onReleaseOutside event, it is possible to stop dragging the knob even if the mouse is no longer over it.

10. Close the Actions panel and return to your main movie Timeline.

11. When working with a slider, it can help to have some kind of graphic that shows its path. Use one of the painting tools to draw a line across the bottom of the Stage, leaving enough room for the slider knob.

12. Then use the Oval tool to create a series of five dots along the line. Position each dot on the Stage at the X (horizontal) values 100, 200, 300, 400, and 500.

13. To line these graphics up properly, use the Info panel (Cmd/Ctrl+**I**) and check the middle square of the Symbol Position option . This allows you to monitor the position of all graphics from their center.

14. Drag an instance of the `slider knob` Movie Clip to the Stage and position it directly over the first dot at X coordinate 100. It might help to select the symbol and type **100** into the X field of the Property Inspector.

15. Now that the clip is in your movie, you can assign the remaining statements that are needed to make the slider. Choose Window → Library to open the Library. Double-click the `slider knob` clip icon in the Library to open it in Symbol Editing mode.

16. Select frame 1 of the code layer and choose Window → Actions (F9). Add the following statements to the beginning of the script you entered in Step 9:

    ```
    top = knob._y;
    left = knob._x;
    right = knob._x+400;
    bottom = knob._y;
    ```

    When the clip first appears on the Stage, these statements are executed. They initialize the variables that are used to set the boundaries for the drag. According to these actions, the drag is locked to the current vertical value of the `knob` instance (`knob._y`) and is allowed to move 400 pixels to the right of the current horizontal value (`knob._x`). Because these variables are initialized only once (when the clip plays its first frame), the position of the slider knob is stored when the movie starts playing, and its drag boundaries are created relative to that position.

17. Save your movie and select Control → Test Movie to see how it works. At this point, your slider should be able to move around freely on the Stage and remain confined within 400 pixels of its initial horizontal location. However, the slider should not be able to move up or down.

18. Next, you need something to control with the slider. Create a new Movie Clip symbol and name it `screen`.

19. Make the `screen` Movie Clip a rectangle that is 1000×100 pixels. Be sure that the rectangle is positioned exactly in the center of the Stage. To do this, use the Align panel (Window → Align, or Cmd/Ctrl+**K**).

20. The rectangle graphic should stretch 500 pixels to the left and right of the Movie Clip registration point. Create some kind of graphic or text element that appears within

the rectangle every 200 pixels. Because the `slider.fla` example is a Timeline, there are dates located at regular increments along the graphic.

21. When you have finished with the `screen` Movie Clip, return to the main Timeline. Create a new layer and name it **screen**.

22. Drag an instance of the clip onto the Stage so that it is above the slider and its left edge is at 175 pixels. This should put the clip's registration point at 675 pixels. Choose Window → Properties (Cmd/Ctrl+F3) to open the Property Inspector and confirm this.

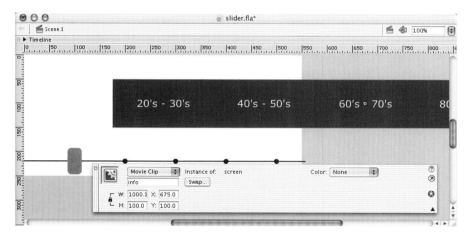

23. After the clip is positioned correctly, use the Property Inspector and enter the name **info** in the instance field to create a unique instance of the `screen` Movie Clip.

24. Now you can compose the ActionScript that is needed to make the slider control the position of the `info` instance. Return to the Timeline of the `slider knob` clip. Select the keyframe of the code layer and open the Actions panel.

25. Add these additional statements to the end of the script in the window:

```
this.onMouseMove=function(){
    if (dragging){
        _root.info._x = 675-(knob._x*2);
        updateAfterEvent();
    }
}
```

These actions will control the _x position of the `info` instance relative to the _x position of the `knob` instance. Here is how it works: 675 is the total distance from the left edge of the Stage to the registration point of the `info` instance. As `knob` moves to the right 100 pixels, `info` should move left by 200 pixels, covering twice as much ground as knob. The expression `knob._x` returns the current horizontal position of the `knob` instance. Then, as it moves to the right, its _x location value is doubled and subtracted from 675. As knob moves farther from 0, `info` moves farther from 675, in the opposite direction, at twice the rate. The final value produced by this expression is used to set the _x position of the `info` instance. For a comparison of the values, see Table 20.2.

So why are they moved at different "rates"? Both `slider` and `knob` have five different sections of information to present. However, whereas knob has to move only 100 pixels to get to a new section, `info` has to move 200 pixels. As knob moves right in increments of 100 pixels, the value is doubled and subtracted from 675. This new value is assigned to the _x property of `info`, which moves `info` across the Stage to the left.

Table 20.2

_x Values for slider.fla Movie Clips

KNOB._X	INFO._X
0	675
100	475
200	275
300	75
400	−125

The completed script for the slider should look like this. The comments have been added to clarify what each section of code accomplishes.

```
// timeline variables needed to set bounds
top = knob._y;
left = knob._x;
right = knob._x+400;
bottom = knob._y;
// turns dragging on/off
knob.onPress = function() {
    startDrag("knob", false, left, top, right, bottom);
    dragging = true;
}
knob.onRelease = function() {
    stopDrag();
    dragging = false;
}
knob.onReleaseOutside = function() {
    stopDrag();
    dragging = false;
}
// manages scroll movement
this.onMouseMove=function(){
    if (dragging){
        _root.info._x = 675-(knob._x*2);
        updateAfterEvent();
    }
}
```

Your Timeline slider is now ready to go. Select Control →
Test Movie to try it out. See Figure 20.2 for an illustration
of the finished product.

The slider.fla movie has some additional features not
covered in this example. There are a few text enhancements that help clarify the information it presents. Also,
there is a layer mask that creates a window through which
you can view the contents of the Timeline. To learn more
about creating layer masks, see Chapter 8.

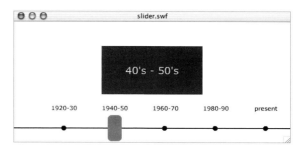

Figure 20.2
The final
slider.fla
Timeline

Recording and Monitoring Keystrokes

In addition to monitoring mouse-type interactions, ActionScript can be used to track keyboard input and interaction. This functionality enables you to create interactive controls,
which in turn allows your audience to use their keyboard to interact with your movie. This
kind of interaction can be particularly useful for creating games, interactive animators,
quizzes, and easy-to-use presentations.

To take advantage of this feature, you can use one of ActionScript's predefined objects
known as the Key object. The Key object and its methods allow you to track and set all
parameters concerning keyboard input in your movie. Here is a partial list of Key object
methods:

isDown(keyCode) Used to return a Boolean value: true if the key in the keyCode argument
is pressed, and false if it is not.

getCode() Returns the key code of the last key pressed while the movie was running.

getAscii() Similar to getCode(), returns the ASCII value of the last key pressed.

addListener() Use addListener() to tell the Key object when onKeyUp() and onKeyDown()
events occur.

In the preceding examples, the term keyCode was used as a placeholder for the argument where you would normally enter an ActionScript key code value. Key code values
are ActionScript constants. They are numbers used to represent the keys on a standard
keyboard. For example, the key code for the letter *A* is 65. For a complete listing of Action-
Script key codes, see the Key Code Values table in the ActionScript Reference on this
book's companion CD.

> You might remember the on(keyPress) handler that is associated with behaviors. This han-
> dler, when attached to a button, will also track keystrokes that occur while the movie is play-
> ing. To read more about on(keyPress), see Chapter 14.

Using Keystrokes and Event Listeners to Track Answers in a Quiz

The keyboard can be a very useful alternative to the mouse when it comes to interacting with your movie. More than 90 different key codes are used to represent the keys on a standard keyboard. Not only does this present you with a lot of options for interaction, but it opens the door to creating movies that can be used by more than one person at a time. Use the Key object both to record keys that are pressed while the movie plays and to assign specific keys as hot keys or interactive controls.

One thing to keep in mind when building interactive movies that use the keyboard is that a few keys have specific functions in Flash's Test Movie mode. These keys are Return/Enter, the comma (,) key, and the period (.) key. Try to avoid using these keys if possible. If you must use them, select Control → Disable Keyboard Shortcuts while you are in Test Movie mode. This will void their functions while working in Flash.

In the next example, you will learn how to set up a basic keyboard interface that serves as the input device for a Flash-based quiz. Open the file named keyPress.fla in the Chapter 20 folder on this book's companion CD to see these scripts in their specific context. You will find that this process is very simple once you become comfortable with the ActionScript terms used to create this kind of interaction.

To monitor keystrokes in your movie:

1. Create a new layer in your movie's main Timeline and name it **code**.

2. Select Window → Actions (F9) to display the Actions panel and then enter these statements:

```
keyChecker=new Object();
keyChecker.onKeyDown = function(){
   trace("the key was: " + Key.getCode());
}
Key.addListener(keyChecker);
```

3. Select Control → Test Movie and try your movie by typing with the keyboard. When you type, you initiate an onKeyDown event that executes the statements in the script. The Output panel returns the message you specified with the trace() function and gives you the key code for each key you press.

   This works because you created an event listener. An event listener is an object; in this example, it is the Generic object named keyChecker. The object is paired with an event handler method using the onKeyDown event. When a key is pressed, the Key object (Key) is notified. Then, because the listener keyChecker was added to Key, Key tells keyChecker what event just happened. If it was an onKeyDown event, the function for keyChecker's event handler method is executed.

The key code is provided by the Key object, using the `getCode()` method. This method retrieves the code, which is then concatenated in a string and printed in the Output panel. If you don't have the ActionScript Reference available, you can use this technique to get any key code values that you need.

4. Return to Movie Editing mode and open the Actions panel to display the script you just entered. Delete or comment out (//) the line that starts with `trace` and enter the following statements within the curly braces, after the commented line:

```
if(Key.isDown(32)) {
    trace("SPACE is key code " + Key.getCode());
    quiz.gotoAndStop(1);
}
if(Key.isDown(65)) {
    trace("A is key code " + Key.getCode());
    quiz.gotoAndStop(3);
}
if(Key.isDown(66)) {
    trace("B is key code " + Key.getCode());
    quiz.gotoAndStop(2);
}
if(Key.isDown(67)) {
    trace("C is key code " + Key.getCode());
    quiz.gotoAndStop(3);
}
```

These statements monitor which keys have been pressed and then send the movie to a new location accordingly. Specifically, the script checks the answer to the first quiz question and sends the `quiz` clip instance to a specific frame based on whether the answer is right or wrong. It also provides the opportunity to try the question again. If the spacebar is pressed (key code 32), the instance returns to frame 1. The other key codes are as follows: 65 = A, 66 = B, and 67 = C.

The Key object is not case sensitive. When using it to track keystrokes, there is no difference between *a* and *A*.

5. To make the quiz, choose Insert → New Symbol (Cmd/Ctrl+F8). Name the symbol **questions** and select Movie Clip as its behavior. Click OK. Flash switches to Symbol Editing mode.

6. Press F5 twice to add two additional frames to layer 1 of the Movie Clip. Rename this layer **code**.

7. Insert a new layer and name it **text**. Click to select frame 2 of this layer and press F7 to add an empty keyframe.

8. Repeat this process to add a third keyframe in frame 3. When finished, the text layer should have three empty keyframes and the code layer should have one.

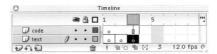

9. Click to select the first frame of the code layer. Open the Actions panel (F9) and type the following statement:

   ```
   stop();
   ```

   This function prevents the Timeline from playing before it should.

10. Then return to the text layer. Use the Text tool to type the word **CORRECT!!** in the second keyframe and **SORRY, NO.** in the third keyframe.

11. Now you must write a multiple-choice question. It doesn't matter what it is, but it has to have three possible answers: A, B, and C. Based on the script you attached to frame 1 of the main Timeline, make answer B the correct choice. Use the Text tool to write your question and put it in the first keyframe of the text layer.

12. Choose Edit → Edit Document to return to the main Timeline. Then grab the clip you just created and drag it to the Stage.

13. Use the Property Inspector (Cmd/Ctrl+F3) to give the clip the instance name **quiz**. Then, if necessary, use the Align panel (Cmd/Ctrl+**K**) to align the quiz instance to other elements on the Stage.

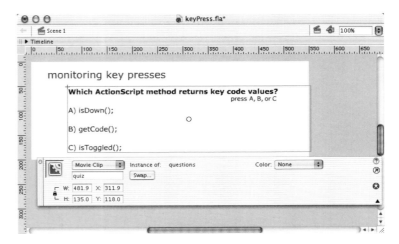

14. Select Control → Test Movie and give your quiz a try. If you wrote your question correctly, pressing B should render a "CORRECT!!" answer, while A and C are incorrect. If this isn't working properly, you can either change the script or reorder the answers to your question.

ActionScripting to Control Graphic Elements

One of the most important aspects of Movie Clips is that you can modify their appearance via ActionScript. This is an extremely important factor when it comes to creating interactive movies. In addition to navigational features in your movie, any kind of interactive control element can be scripted to move, scale, stretch, hide, spin, or perform any combination of these actions on a Movie Clip instance. Ultimately, this enables you to create interactive animation in your movie because you have access to all the parameters that affect the way graphics are positioned and displayed.

ActionScript provides a healthy dose of commands to manipulate visual content. Listed below are the properties you can use to alter the appearance of Movie Clip instances. You can find specifics of each in the ActionScript Reference on this book's companion CD.

_alpha is used to change the transparency of a Movie Clip instance.

_height sets and returns the height, in pixels, of a Movie Clip instance.

_rotation sets the rotation, in degrees, of a Movie Clip.

_visible takes a Boolean argument. `true` makes a Movie Clip visible, while `false` hides the clip. Hidden clips remain active (continue to play, run scripts, and so on) in your movie.

_width sets and returns the width, in pixels, of a Movie Clip instance.

_x and **_y** are two properties that set and return the X and Y coordinates of a Movie Clip. If a clip is on the main Timeline, its coordinates are relative to the point (0, 0) in the upper-left corner of the Stage. If a Movie Clip is nested inside another clip, its coordinates are relative to the registration point of the `_parent` clip.

_xscale and **_yscale** are two properties that set and return a percentage value that specifies the scaling of a Movie Clip instance. For example, setting `_xscale=200` would double a clip's width.

In addition to these properties, there is a collection of methods associated with the predefined Color object. Using a small collection of methods, the Color object allows you to set and return RGB color values of a Movie Clip. To learn more about these methods, refer to the "Scripting Color Changes" section later in this chapter, or see the entry for the Color object in the ActionScript Reference on this book's companion CD.

Scripting Animation

Many of the properties associated with Movie Clip appearance deal with the position of Movie Clips. By rapidly changing the position of a clip, you can create the illusion of smooth motion, or animation. ActionScript can also be used to modify the size or scale of a Movie Clip instance. Again, when done over a period of time, this creates an animated effect.

You can change these ActionScript properties in combination with one another to produce interesting graphic results. The results are not much different than those you get when creating a tweened animation. The main difference is that with ActionScript, the changes can be dynamically modified with scripting. And when you combine them with other ActionScript components, you are able to interactively control the appearance and movement of Movie Clips.

In the following examples, you will learn how to control and animate a Movie Clip using ActionScript. Two of the most basic graphic parameters are presented here: position and size. With the help of additional ActionScript statements, you will be able to take a simple Movie Clip instance and either set it in motion or cause it to grow and expand.

Animating Graphic Elements with Motion and Custom Cursors

This lesson, like the slider controller discussed previously, also deals with the _x and _y properties for a Movie Clip. As mentioned earlier, these properties are used to monitor and set the X and Y coordinates of a Movie Clip instance, either on the Stage or within another clip instance. With the help of a few variables and some ActionScript number crunching, you will see how to create an ever-changing, organic animation. Also, you will learn how to take this animation and lock its position to that of the mouse cursor, providing an additional layer of animation.

The scripts presented here are in the flyCursor.fla file inside the Chapter 20 folder on this book's companion CD. You can also look at the finished version, flyCursor.swf, to get an idea of how the final animation looks and behaves.

To create a dynamic animation with ActionScript and attach it to a custom cursor:

1. Create a Movie Clip that you want to use for your animation. This example uses a Movie Clip of a fly because the animation will randomly flutter around a single position on the Stage.

2. Drag this Movie Clip to the Stage to create an instance and use the Property Inspector to name it **fly_mc**.

3. Insert a new layer in the main Timeline and name it **code**. Select the first frame of the code layer and choose Window → Actions to open the Actions panel.

4. Enter the following statements in the window:

```
moveValue=8;
fly_mc.onEnterFrame=function(){
    v=fly_mc._x;
    h=fly_mc._y;
    buzzV=Math.random()*moveValue-moveValue/2;
    buzzH=Math.random()*moveValue-moveValue/2;
    fly_mc._x=v+buzzV;
    fly_mc._y=h+buzzH;
}
```

To put it simply, this script does three things: It stores the current position of the instance, generates a random number between –4 and 3.99, and adds it to the original instance location, jumping it to a new position on the Stage.

In more specific terms, this is what is happening:

- The variables *v* and *h* are used to store the position of the instance on the enterFrame event.

- The Math object is used to randomly generate values stored in the variables *buzzV* and *buzzH*. The random() method produces a value between 0.0 and 0.999.... This value is then multiplied by moveValue (8) to render a value between 0 and 7.99. Then it subtracts half of moveValue (moveValue/2) or 4. If the first random value is 1 and you subtract 4, you get –3. By subtracting half of the total possible value, both negative and positive numbers are produced. Ultimately, this expression yields numbers in the range of –4 and 3.99.

> It's necessary to use negative numbers to keep the clip from slowly drifting off to the lower-right corner of the Stage. If both the x and y values are always increasing positively, the clip will always move away (down and right) from the (0, 0) origin in the upper-left corner of the Stage.

- *buzzV* and *buzzH* are added to the original position variables (*v* and *h*), and the sum is used to set the _x and _y properties of the Movie Clip instance. Because this script is rapidly executed on each onenterFrame event, it creates the animated illusion of hovering.

5. Select Control → Test Movie to see the script in context and watch the fly buzz around the Stage.

It's pretty cool to watch the fly buzz around on its own, but there are other things you can do with this to make it even more entertaining. ActionScript provides a set of properties that allow you to track the position of the mouse cursor in your movie. Using X and Y coordinates, ActionScript will return the position of the cursor on the movie Stage. The properties are as follows:

_xmouse returns the X (horizontal) coordinate position of the mouse cursor.

_ymouse returns the Y (vertical) coordinate position of the mouse cursor.

All coordinates are returned relative to the movie origin, or coordinates (0, 0), located at the upper-left corner of the Stage. When you use these properties to get the mouse position, it's good practice to specify the Timeline you want to track. For example, to track the mouse on the main Timeline, you would write:

```
hPos=_root._xmouse;
vPos=_root._ymouse;
```

In this example, *hPos* and *vPos* are variables that store the current X and Y mouse coordinates. Using these properties, you can replace the standard pointer cursor with the fly. Not only will it keep its frenetic buzzing, but you'll be able to move it across the screen with the mouse.

To turn the fly into a cursor:

1. Select the first frame of the code layer and choose Window → Actions to open the Actions panel. You should see the script you wrote in the previous steps. Add the following statement above the first line of code:

    ```
    Mouse.hide();
    ```

    This method of the Mouse object hides the pointer cursor. The cursor is still there; you just can't see it.

2. Now enter another series of statements below the `Mouse.hide()` line:

    ```
    fly_mc.onMouseMove=function(){
        fly_mc._x=_root._xmouse;
        fly_mc._y=_root._ymouse;
    }
    ```

    This block is responsible for turning the Movie Clip instance into a cursor. It uses the _xmouse and _ymouse properties to lock the clip to the position of the cursor. This works because the horizontal and vertical positions of the clip (_x and _y properties) are set to the mouse cursor position relative to its coordinates on the main Timeline Stage (_root).

The completed script should look like this; the comments have been added to clarify what each section of code accomplishes:

```
// hide the mouse
Mouse.hide();
// lock clip instance to mouse position
fly_mc.onMouseMove=function(){
    fly_mc._x = _root._xmouse;
    fly_mc._y = _root._ymouse;
}
// set a value to determine range of movement
moveValue=8;
// randomize the movement of the clip on every frame
fly_mc.onEnterFrame=function(){
    v=fly_mc._x;
    h=fly_mc._y;
    buzzV=Math.random()*moveValue-moveValue/2;
    buzzH=Math.random()*moveValue-moveValue/2;
    fly_mc._x=v+buzzV;
    fly_mc._y=h+buzzH;
}
```

3. Close the Actions panel and test your movie. The results are quite surprising! Not only does the fly buzz around on its own, but your cursor controls where it goes when it's buzzing. Your fly has two different sources controlling the animation: its own randomized-motion script and the position of the mouse cursor. This produces a "layered" animated effect that is much more interesting than what you can achieve by tweening on the Timeline.

Here are a couple more techniques you might want to try in addition to this script:

- In this script example, the hover range was set to a maximum of about 4. You can change this to create a more subtle or abrupt hover effect.

- Try creating tweened animations using this animated clip. Or use this technique to create dynamic, ever-changing background graphics that are constantly in motion.

Resizing and Duplicating Graphic Elements

Everyone knows the saying "there is always a bigger fish," which refers to the fact that everything is relative. Just when you think you have found something that is the absolute biggest or best, something better comes along. In Flash, you can use the _xscale and _yscale properties to create a bigger fish. And in the next example, that is exactly what you will do.

These properties are used to both set and retrieve the horizontal and vertical scale of a Movie Clip. Each property is entered and returned a percentage value. With the help of a few ActionScript functions, you can use scripting to change the size of an object by stretching its length and width to a percentage of the original size. The scripts in this example can be found on this book's companion CD in a file named `fishScaler.fla` inside the Chapter 20 folder.

To script changes to the scaling of a Movie Clip instance:

1. Open a new file and select Modify → Document to set the Stage dimensions to 400×400 pixels. Be sure the frame rate is at least 12 frames per second. Click OK.

2. Create a new Movie Clip symbol of a fish. Make it an animated clip that moves from right to left. Be sure that the clip both starts and ends slightly more than 200 pixels from its registration point (see Figure 20.3).

3. Return to the main Timeline and drag your fish Movie Clip to the center of the Stage; put its registration point at the coordinates (200, 200). Give it the instance name `fishy` in the Property Inspector.

4. Test your movie to see the `fishy` instance in action.

5. Return to Movie Editing mode, select Insert → New Symbol, and create a new Button symbol. The design of the button is left in your capable hands. The button in the `fishScaler.fla` example is made to look as though it is underwater.

6. When you have finished with the button, return to the main Timeline and drag your button onto the Stage. Position it either above or below the fish Movie Clip animation.

7. You are now ready to enter the ActionScript that will scale (resize, not prepare for cooking) the `fishy` Movie Clip instance. Create a new layer in the main Timeline and name it **code**. Enter the statement:

```
count=0;
```

Figure 20.3

The fish Movie Clip starts at an _x value of 240 and ends at _x = –235.

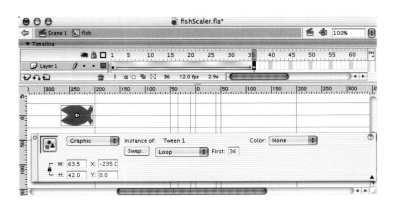

8. Next click the button and open the Actions panel once again. Enter the following statements in the window:

```
on(release){
    count+=1;
    _root.fishy.duplicateMovieClip("fishy"+count,count);
    _root["fishy"+count]._xscale=count*200;
    _root["fishy"+count]._yscale=count*200;
}
```

9. Close the Actions panel and select Test → Movie. Each time you click the button, you will see a larger fish appear as it moves across the Stage. This effect is created through the combination of the duplicateMovieclip function and the _xscale and _yscale properties. The preceding script executes each time the button is clicked. When this happens, the *count* variable (initialized on the main Timeline) is incremented and used to perform two tasks. The fishy instance, or *parent*, is duplicated. And each duplicate, or *child*, has the value of *count* appended to its name and is placed at the stacking level of *count* relative to its parent clip.

Each duplicate is still on the _root or _level0 Timeline, but it occupies a new "virtual" layer above the _root. Duplicates are placed in an internal hierarchy called a *stacking level*. When a clip is duplicated, its duplicates are placed in a stacking level above its parent Timeline. Stacking levels work like layers in the Timeline, but they are generated via ActionScript when a clip is duplicated. Because a duplicate clip cannot exist in the same space as the original, each is placed in a unique location, or stacking level, above the last duplicate or source. In this example, fishy is duplicated and placed at stacking level *count*. The variable *count* is incremented each time the button is clicked, and the clips continue to stack above the original fishy instance.

Then, the _xscale and _yscale properties are used to scale each child to a value of *count*200. Because *count* is incremented with each button click, the child clips are gradually scaled by increasing values, creating bigger and bigger fish.

You might notice that each duplicate seems to move faster than those that came before it. This is because, as the duplicate clip is scaled, it has twice as far to travel as the clip that preceded it. All properties of the clip are scaled, including the width of the area it must travel. However, it must travel the new distance in the same number of frames. A clip that moves 400 frames in 3 seconds is not as fast as a clip that must move 1,600 frames in that same time span.

This example shows how the properties _xscale and _yscale can be used to dynamically change the size of a Movie Clip. You will also find that the _height and _width properties produce similar results when used in this fashion. To learn more about these properties, see their listings in the ActionScript Reference on this book's companion CD.

Writing a Function to Scale Graphic Elements

Everything that you just accomplished with the fishScaler.fla file will allow you to scale a single clip instance. However, what if you wanted to scale several clip instances in your movie? You could write a different block of code for each instance, but that would be a real pain. The best solution in this case is to write a custom function. A custom function is a block of code that you create to do something specific in your movie. In this case, you can write a function to scale and duplicate a graphic. This will save you the time and hassle of having to write individual scripts for every clip that you might need to modify.

The basic syntax of functions was discussed in Chapter 18. It might help to briefly revisit the section on functions so that the steps in this lesson aren't confusing. To start, open fishScaler.fla in the Chapter 20 folder on this book's companion CD. Or, if you are continuing from the previous lesson, you can work from the same file. If you would like to see the final version of the movie with a working function, open fishScaler_function.fla, which is also in the Chapter 20 folder.

To write the function:

1. The first order of business is to get rid of the old code. Select the first keyframe of the code layer in the main Timeline. Delete any ActionScript statements that you see there.

2. Then select the button you created to do the duplication work and delete all the ActionScript attached to it.

3. Out with the old; in with the new. Choose File → Save As, enter a new name for the file, and save it to your computer's hard disk. A new file will allow you to return to your original work if you ever have to.

4. Click to select the fishy clip instance. Press F9 to open the Actions panel and enter the following statements:

```
onClipEvent(load){
    count = 0;
}
```

This creates a Timeline variable for the instance. By scoping the variable to the Timeline, it is independent of any other clips and their Timeline variables. This will allow you to scale each clip instance individually, since each will have its own count value.

5. Now you can write the function. Click the first keyframe of the code layer in the main Timeline. Press F9 to open the Actions panel and enter the following statements:

```
function scale(clip){


}
```

This is the basic syntax for your function. You use the `function` statement to declare your function and give it the name `scale`. The `scale` function will need one parameter: It will need to know which clip instance you want it to scale. Use the variable *clip* to store this parameter. The `clip` instance name will be passed to the function as this parameter when it's called.

6. With the skeleton of your function in place, you can now fill in its statements:

```
function scale(clip){
    var newCount = clip.count+=1;
    clip._xscale=newCount*200;
    clip._yscale=newCount*200;
}
```

The statements of the function work as follows:

```
var newCount = clip.count+=1;
```

This line creates a variable to store the value of *count* that resides on the Timeline of `clip`, or the instance that the function will scale. Because it was initialized with the statement `var`, this variable will be "alive" only while the function executes its statements.

```
clip._xscale=newCount*200;
clip._yscale=newCount*200;
```

The next two lines manage the resizing of the clip by multiplying the value of *count* by 200 to double the current horizontal and vertical size.

7. Now that you have a function, you need to call it. Click to select the `button` instance in the movie. Press F9 to open the Actions panel and enter the following statements:

```
on (release){
    _root.scale(_root.fishy);
}
```

This button script calls the function. Because the function was created on the main Timeline, you call it with the `_root` reference. And, because `fishy` is also on the main Timeline, it is targeted in the same manner.

8. Choose Control → Test Movie to try out the function. As before, when you click the button, the fish will double in size.

To see the real benefit of functions, create a few more clip instances similar to `fishy`. For each, use a different button to call the `scale` function, for example:

```
on (release){
    _root.scale(_root.squiddy);
}
```

This script calls the function to scale an instance named `squiddy`. Because your function was defined in frame 1, it is available throughout your movie. In this example, you call the function but pass it a different instance as its parameter. The function uses the parameter to determine which clip it will affect, so in this case, `squiddy` is the clip that gets scaled.

In the previous examples, _root wasn't absolutely necessary. However, it was included to demonstrate the importance of defining the correct scope when calling functions and passing parameters to them.

This example should help clarify the steps involved in writing functions. You can use these techniques to write many different kinds of functions, not just ones that manipulate graphics. Experiment with the basic syntax presented here to create functions that crunch numbers, control navigation, manipulate text, and so on.

Managing Text, Numbers, and Complex Data

Though Flash was created foremost as an animation program, it should be clear that it can do much more than make things zoom around the screen. As Flash has developed, it has become an authoring tool capable of building complex multimedia. Flash can be used to create everything from online applications to games to interactive art installations. One of the qualities that enables the program (and its users) to produce such a diverse body of work is its ability to manage information in the form of text and data. ActionScript has many different built-in functions and objects that you can use to control the flow of information in your Flash movies—something as simple as a text field or as complex as a series of responses to a question. In this section, you will explore several facets of the Action-Script language and learn how you can compose scripts to manage the flow of information in your movies and applications.

Scrolling Text in Text Fields

Text fields are ubiquitous in contemporary multimedia. They are used to display current events and news, provide instruction, tell stories, and so on. Even though the word *multimedia* suggests that text could be replaced with narration, it is often desirable to provide information that can be read rather than heard.

In Chapter 5, you learned how to create text and text boxes in a Flash movie. In this lesson, you will take the next step and learn how to scroll that text. First we should clarify what it means to *scroll*. When a text field contains more text than it can display, it is necessary to scroll the text, or move it up and down incrementally so that it's possible to read the entire block of text displayed in the text field.

ActionScript makes it possible to create a scrolling text field. This is basically a series of buttons that allow you and your audience to browse a column of text by clicking buttons that move the text up and down in the field. To do this, of course, you need some buttons to serve as your scrollers. You also need to use two properties of the Text object that deal specifically with the text field: `scroll` and `maxscroll`. The role of these properties is as follows:

TextField.scroll both sets and returns the number of the topmost line in a text field. As you scroll through a text field and the number of the top line either increases or decreases, Flash updates the scroll property accordingly.

TextField.maxscroll returns the number of the top line in a text field when the bottommost line is visible. Use this property to retrieve the value to display the end of a text field. `maxscroll` can be checked but not set by ActionScript.

Here is a simple lesson covering the steps for creating a scrolling text field. To see all this in context, refer to the files `scroll_text.fla` and `scroll_text.swf` in the Chapter 20 folder on this book's companion CD.

To create a scrolling text field:

1. Create a Dynamic Text field on the Stage of your movie using the Text tool.

2. Select Window → Properties (Cmd/Ctrl+F3) and give the field the following attributes:

   · Multiline

   · Show border around text.

   · Type the name **poetry_txt** in the instance field.

   · If desired, use the Character panel to define a default font, size, and color for the text in the field. To learn more about text field attributes, see Chapter 5.

Steps 3 and 4 are optional. If you don't want to use ActionScript to enter the text for your text field, you can type it into the field directly.

3. Create a new layer in the main Timeline and call it **code**. Click the first keyframe of the code layer and select Window → Actions to display the Actions panel.

4. Enter the following statements:

```
poetry_txt.text="line 1 goes here\r";
poetry_txt.text+="and line 2 here\r";
```

Enter the text for your field where it reads `line 1 goes here`…and `line 2 here`. This initializes the text for your text field to the information that you enter. With this syntax, you are initializing `text` property of the `poetry_txt` instance as a string that contains the text you wish to display. Note that you use the addition operator (+) to concatenate (or join) the information and add to the contents of the field. Also, the escaping character \r is used to put a "carriage return" in the string. This starts a new line of text. Refer to Figure 20.4 to see this in context.

If you elect not to enter the text with ActionScript, simply type your text into the field. To do this, you must first set the Dynamic text box to handle scrolling text. Otherwise, it will just expand to accommodate the text you enter. Choose Text → Scrollable. Notice how the handle in the lower-right corner of the text field changes from an open square to a closed square. Now when you type in the field, it will remain the same size.

_____
Figure 20.4

You can set the text for a Dynamic text field by concatenating strings of text in ActionScript.

5. Now that the text is in place, you can add the buttons that will scroll it up and down. Create a new layer in the main Timeline and call it **buttons**. Create a button (or borrow one from Window → Other Panels → Common Libraries → Buttons) and drag it onto the buttons layer.

6. Then open the Property Inspector and give the button the instance name `txt_down`.

7. You also need a second button to scroll the text up. You can do this easily if you duplicate the `txt_down` button and give it a new instance name. Click to select the `txt_down` instance. Press Cmd/Ctrl+**C** to copy it.

8. Then press Cmd/Ctrl+Shift+**V** to paste the button in place (over the instance you just copied). Use the arrow keys to nudge the duplicate button into place and give it the instance name `txt_up`. Your buttons are now ready to go.

9. Now it's time for the ActionScript that will manage the scroll functionality. Select the first keyframe of the code layer and open the Actions panel. Enter the following statements:

```
txt_down.onPress = function(){
    if (poetry_txt.scroll<poetry_txt.maxscroll){
        poetry_txt.scroll++;
    }
}
```

These statements assign a function to the onPress event for your down button. When the button is clicked, it checks to see if the top line of the text field (determined by *scroll*) is less than the value of maxscroll. If it is, the text field's top line is not yet at the point where the field's last line will be visible. If this is true, then the *scroll* property is incremented and the text field moves up one line. If it is false, then nothing happens and the text field holds its position.

10. You must also add a complimentary script to manage upward scrolling:

```
txt_up.onPress = function() {
    if (poetry_txt.scroll>1) {
        poetry_txt.scroll–;
    }
}
```

These statements assign a function to the onPress event for your up button. When the button is clicked, it checks to see if the top line of the text field (determined by *scroll*) is greater than 1. If it is, the field is scrolled upward by decrementing the value of *scroll*. If *scroll* is not greater than 1, it must be equal to 1. This tells Flash that the top line of the text field is visible and no scrolling is required.

11. Select Control → Test Movie to test your movie and see how the scroll buttons work.

As you click, the text field should move up or down in increments of one line.

Scrolling by clicking buttons can be a pain, especially when there is a long block of text you are trying to get through. Flash MX 2004 and MX Pro 2004 have made this easier by introducing the ability to scroll through text fields using the mouse wheel. Unfortunately, this feature is available only on Windows computers. However, you can still implement mouse-wheel scrolling if you are authoring on a Macintosh. You just won't be able to test it in your movies or take advantage of mouse-wheel scrolling in movies that use it. Macromedia hopes to resolve this issue with Flash Player 7 in the future.

To add mouse-wheel scrolling functionality to your text field:

1. Return to frame 1 of the code layer in your movie. Enter the following statements:

```
poetry_txt.mouseWheelEnabled=true;
mouseEars=new Object();
mouseEars.onMouseWheel=function(value) {
    poetry_txt.scroll+=value;
}
Mouse.addListener(mouseEars);
```

The first line enables mouse-wheel scrolling. It is true by default, but it doesn't hurt to turn it on explicitly. Setting the parameter to false will disable mouse-wheel scrolling.

The next series of statements create an event listener called mouseEars and add it to the Mouse object. When the Mouse object is notified that the mouse wheel is being manipulated, it tells mouseEars to execute its assigned function for the onMouseWheel event. The function in turn moves the contents of the text field up or down in line increments of 1.

2. Select Control → Test Movie to test your movie and see how the scroll wheel functionality works. Remember, you have to test this on a computer running Windows. If you try on a Mac, you won't get any results no matter how accurately you wrote your script!

To learn more about other Text Field properties that can control scrolling, including horizontal scrolling, see the ActionScript Reference on this book's accompanying CD.

Using an Array to Create a Dynamic Greeting Message

One of the most useful aspects of ActionScript is that you can use it to make your movie less predictable. Rather than have text and graphics appear in the same place, at the same time, and in the same color with each repeated visit to your website, you can pleasantly surprise your audience with something that has more variety. In this lesson, you will learn how to use ActionScript to create a simple Array and use it to print a different greeting each time someone navigates to the home page of a website or interactive interface.

First of all, it would be good to clarify what an *Array* is. An Array is an informational structure that is organized into multiple containers, with each container holding a piece (or pieces) of information. An Array is like a dresser (bureau, wardrobe, chest-of-drawers, and so on). It is one large structure that holds containers that in turn hold different items. A dresser has drawers for socks, underwear, T-shirts, and sweaters. Each drawer is a discrete location for each article of clothing. An Array works in much the same way. Where a dresser has drawers, an Array has *elements*; each element can contain a piece of information: a string, a number, a variable, or even another Array. And because an Array is a single item, wherever it goes, it carries with it all the information it contains. This makes it much easier to move information around as a group rather than as individual pieces. So in a nutshell, Arrays make it easier to store and work with collections of information because they keep their contents neat and organized.

The variety of applications for Arrays is almost dizzying. In fact, the usefulness of Arrays could fill not one but several books alone! Here you will learn how to create an Array in ActionScript and use it to effect some interesting and dynamic changes in a Flash movie.

To complete this exercise, you need to retrieve some files from this book's accompanying CD. Go to the Chapter 20 folder and copy the entire folder named Array to your computer's Desktop. This project requires several SWF files. It simulates the interactive interface or website for an international organization. You will make changes to this project so that every time a visitor goes to the first section of the movie, a new translation of "hello" is printed in the upper-left corner of the movie. Open the file `international_club.fla` and select Control → Test Movie. As you click the buttons that line the bottom of the movie, you will notice that different words appear at the top. However, when you click the yellow button to return to the first section, *Greeting*, you see no text at all. This is where you will create your Array.

To create an Array that displays a greeting:

1. Open `banner.fla`, which is also in the Array folder. At this point, the entire Array folder should be saved on your computer.

2. Click the middle of the Stage. If it is not open already, press Cmd/Ctrl+F3 to open the Property Inspector. You will notice that what you clicked is not the Stage, but a Movie Clip instance named **text_clip**. You will create your Array in a script that is attached to this clip.

3. With the clip still selected, choose Window → Actions or press F9 to open the Actions panel.

4. Enter the following statements:

```
onClipEvent(load){
    greeting=new Array();
}
```

This script creates a new Array named `greeting` when the Movie Clip is loaded onto the Stage.

5. Click after the semicolon character to start a new line and type **`greeting[0]="Hello!";`**. The script should now read:

```
onClipEvent(load){
    greeting=new Array();
    greeting[0]="Hello!";
}
```

This line is very important. It creates the first element in your Array and stores in it the string *Hello!* Arrays identify their elements with numbers and start counting at 0.

6. You can now add a few more elements to your Array and fill each with another new string:

```
onClipEvent(load){
    greeting=new Array();
    greeting[0]="Hello!";
    greeting[1]="Bonjour!";
    greeting[2]="Hola!";
}
```

7. The `greeting` Array has a more international flavor now. By adding strings in elements 1 and 2, the Array now contains a grand total of 3 elements: 0, 1, and 2.

8. Now that the Array has a few items, you can put them to use. Click after the last semicolon, press Return/Enter, and add the following statements:

```
choice=Math.floor(Math.random()*greeting.length);
hello_txt.text=greeting[choice];
```

These lines should fall between the line that contains *Hola!* and the last curly brace.

So what do these statements do? Good question; actually they are some of the most important in the entire movie:

- *choice* is a variable. It stores a random number that is generated by the expression on the other side of the assignment operator (=). The random number will always be between 0 and the last position number in the Array.

- The `length` method (part of ActionScript's Array object) retrieves the length of, or number of items in, an Array. This number is multiplied by a random number in the range of 0 to 0.999… and then rounded down to the next-lower integer. Given the current length of the Array, this will always be an integer between 0 and 2. That information is used in the next line.

- With the help of the Array Access Operator ([]), the Array item stored in element *choice* is retrieved from the greeting Array and assigned to the text property of the Text Field instance hello_txt. For example, if *choice* is 2, the text property will be set to the value of the greeting Array's element 2, or *Hola!*

- Of course, hello_txt is the Text Field instance inside the banner Movie Clip. Whatever value is assigned to hello_txt.text will appear in the text field—in this case, *Hola!*

9. Take the opportunity to test this out. Select Control → Test Movie. The movie will appear on your screen and display one of the three greetings in the Array.

10. Close the movie and test it again. You have a 1 in 3 chance of seeing the same thing, though hopefully you read a different greeting. If you don't believe it, test your movie over and over. Each time you are likely to see a new greeting appear on your screen.

11. Add a few more lines to your script. The final script should look like Figure 20.5. Feel free to ignore the lines with comments (//). These have been added only to identify which language is used for each greeting.

12. Save your movie and test it again. If you repeat the testing process several times, you will see a greater variety of greetings. This script still works even though the size of the Array has more than doubled. Why? Because you are using the number of items or length property of the Array to set the bounds for your selection. As the elements in the Array increase, so does the range of items it has to choose from when this script makes its random selection.

13. To test this movie in context, close the banner.fla file and open international_club.swf.

14. Click the first keyframe of the code layer. Press F9 to open the Actions panel. You should see the following statements:

```
loadMovieNum("banner.swf",1);
loadMovieNum("greeting.swf",2);
```

These lines reveal something interesting about this movie: Its contents are not really part of the main movie, but separate SWF files that are loaded into _level1 and _level2, respectively, using the loadMovieNum() function. _level1 is set to hold banner.swf, which has Arrays you created and a text field to print your greeting. _level2 will hold greeting.swf, one of the graphics files that occupy the middle area of the movie.

Figure 20.5

The final script increases the number of international greetings to 10.

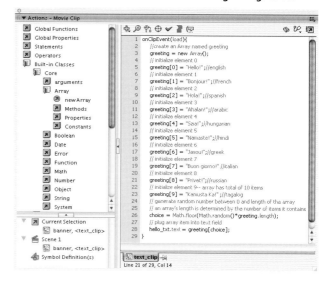

15. Select Control → Test Movie and navigate to the various sections of this movie. Be sure to click the yellow *greeting* button frequently. Notice that each time this button is clicked, a new greeting appears. This works because `banner.swf` is being loaded at `_level1` of the Flash Player. Each time the movie is loaded, the Movie Clip with your Array script is also loaded, creating the Array, making a greeting choice, and printing it to the text field.

16. To see some of the other little scripting tricks going on with this movie, look at the scripts attached to the brown, red, and green buttons on the main Timeline of the `international_club.fla` file. The movie at `_level2` is reloaded with every button-click to refresh the screen with an image that fits the theme of a particular section.

Watching the Clock with the Date Object

If your Flash movie has to work with elements of time, you need look no further than the Date object. The Date object is a part of ActionScript that allows you to set and retrieve the current date and time and format that information to fit your particular needs. It can tell you the current year, month, day, minute, second, and millisecond. All times are retrieved from the system clock of the host computer playing a Flash movie. So while the Date object might be able to handle precise measurements of time, it is only as accurate as the clock where it gets its information.

The Date object has a wide variety of methods to help you work with time measurements. For a complete list, see the Date object's entry in the ActionScript Reference on this book's companion CD. The Date object terms used in this lesson are as follows:

Date.getTime() This method returns the date, in milliseconds, for a Date object. The milliseconds are calculated by determining the time elapsed between `Date` and midnight of January 1, 1970.

new Date() This is the constructor function for a Date object. You can create an object for the current day and time or for a specific date either in the past or future. Specific dates can be created using the following syntax:

```
new Date(year, month, day, hours, minutes, seconds, milliseconds)
```

For details on the proper formatting for a Date object, see the ActionScript Reference on this book's accompanying CD.

In this lesson, you will create a Date object for some event in the future (such as your birthday or the beginning of a vacation) and use the Date object to construct a countdown timer. This will be a fun ActionScript exercise and help build anticipation for the big day!

 If you want, you can open the finished file to get a feel for what it does. Open `countdown.fla`, which is saved in the Chapter 20 folder of this book's accompanying CD. Copy the movie to your hard disk, then open it and choose Control → Test Movie. This file is set to count down to an important birthday on March 3, 2004. If you want to create this file on your own, open countdownCD.fla and follow the steps of the lesson.

To create a countdown timer:

1. First let's get acquainted with the elements of the movie. Many components of count-downCD.fla have been completed for you so that you can get down to business with the ActionScript. There are two layers in the movie: code and text. Code has three keyframes and will be reserved for ActionScript. In the text layer, there are four text fields for days, hours, minutes, and seconds. Each field has an instance name so that you can assign a value to it via ActionScript. The instance names are, from left-to-right: days_txt, hours_txt, min_txt, and sec_txt.

2. Click to select the first keyframe of the code layer and press F9 to open the Actions panel. Enter the following statement:

   ```
   launch=new Date(2004, 2, 3);
   ```

   This statement uses the Date object constructor function to create a Date object named launch. The date is set for March 3, 2004. The year is entered as a four-digit integer. The month is also an integer; however, ActionScript starts counting months at 0. In this case, January = 0, February = 1, and March = 2. The day is specified as an integer from 1 to 31. If you like, you can create a different date for something you look forward to in the future. The key is that it must be a *future* date; the script you will write here is not meant to track the time that has passed since an event.

3. Now that you have a date set, you will write a function that counts down to that date. Start a new line in the Actions panel and enter the following statements:

   ```
   function updateClock(){


   }
   ```

   This gives you the skeleton for a function named updateClock().

4. Now, in the space between the curly braces ({}), enter the following lines of code:

```
var today=new Date();
var wait=launch.getTime()-today.getTime();
```

The first statement creates the local variable *today*. When the Date object constructor function is invoked this way, the new object is set to the current date and time that it was created. The second statement creates another local variable. *wait* stores the number of elapsed milliseconds between *launch* (the "big future event") and *today* (the current time). This is possible because the getTime() method is able to retrieve the number of milliseconds for any given date.

5. Now that the function can determine the number of milliseconds until the date you are counting down, that period of time can be broken down into more manageable units. Add the following statements to your script:

```
var daysUntil = Math.floor(wait/86400000);
days_txt.text = daysUntil;
```

You divide the time you have to wait by 86,400,000 (the number of milliseconds in a day) and round down to the next-lower integer. This value is stored in *daysUntil* and assigned to the days_txt Text Field instance.

6. Continue to format the remaining time with the following statements:

```
var hoursUntil=(wait%86400000);
hours_txt.text=Math.floor(hoursUntil/3600000);
```

To get the remaining number of hours, you can use the Modulo operator (%). It returns the remainder of the expression *wait*/86400000. Whatever number of days does not divide evenly into *wait* are leftover milliseconds that must be accounted for another way. These leftovers are divided by 3,600,000, or the number of milliseconds in an hour. This value is rounded down and displayed in the hours_txt Text Field instance.

7. You have a few more values to format. Enter the remaining statements:

```
var minUntil = (hoursUntil%3600000);
min_txt.text = Math.floor(minUntil/60000);
var secUntil = (minUntil%60000);
sec_txt.text = Math.ceil(secUntil/1000);
```

These remaining statements work in an almost identical fashion. The only difference is with the values they use. hoursUntil%3600000 returns the remaining minutes in milliseconds, then divides by 60,000 as there are 60,000 milliseconds in a minute. minUntil%60000 returns the remaining seconds (again in milliseconds), then divides by 1,000 as there are 1,000 milliseconds in a second. This last value is rounded up

rather than down. We don't need to worry about the remainder of milliseconds.
After all, we're not *that* anxious! The final function should look like this:

```
function updateClock(){
    var today=new Date();
    var wait=launch.getTime()-today.getTime();
    var daysUntil=Math.floor(wait/86400000);
    days_txt.text=daysUntil;
    var hoursUntil=(wait%86400000);
    hours_txt.text=Math.floor(hoursUntil/3600000);
    var minUntil=(hoursUntil%3600000);
    min_txt.text=Math.floor(minUntil/60000);
    var secUntil=(minUntil%60000);
    sec_txt.text=Math.ceil(secUntil/1000);
}
```

8. Now that the function is complete, you need to do two additional things: Call the
    function and make sure that it is called at regular intervals during your movie. To call
    the function, click to select the second keyframe of the code layer. Enter the following
    statement in the Actions panel:

    ```
    updateClock();
    ```

    That's it! Because there is no `stop()` function in frame 1, the movie will continue to
    play after it has digested the code in that frame. When the movie arrives at frame 2,
    the function will fire.

9. Add one more statement to be sure that the function is called regularly. Click to select
    the third keyframe of the code layer and enter the following statement in the Actions
    panel:

    ```
    gotoAndPlay(2);
    ```

    When the movie plays frame 3, it encounters this statement and is promptly sent
    back to frame 2. The function is executed again and then on to frame 3, and so on,
    and so on. The statements in frames 2 and 3 create a loop that calls the
    updateClock() function every other frame. Because your movie is set to 30 frames per
    second, that means the countdown clock is updated 15 times every second.

10. Choose Control → Test Movie to test your countdown
    timer. If possible, watch your system clock and countdown
    timer simultaneously so that you can see how one reads
    from the other (see Figure 20.6).

Figure 20.6

**The countdown
timer uses Action-
Script's Date object,
which gets the cur-
rent time from the
host computer's
system clock.**

Inspirational Design Model

For an interesting blend of design, illustration, digital art, and programming, point your browser to Presstube (www.presstube.com). You'll find everything from 2D pen-on-paper sketches to very complex animations generated by ActionScript. Go to the Archive section and check out the "Programmatic + Misc." link (see Figure 20.7). Here you will see some truly gorgeous Flash pieces that draw themselves and/or react to audience input. Presstube is a site where the artists who run it can freely express themselves; it's not a recommended experience for readers with more conservative sensibilities.

Figure 20.7

Presstube is filled with interesting, hand-drawn illustrations and Flash animation very heavy on the ActionScript.

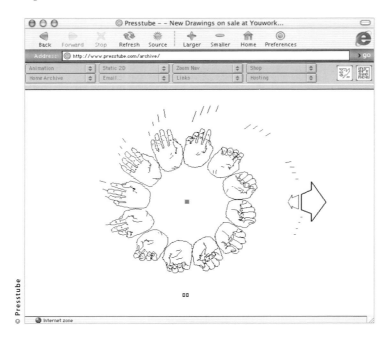

CHAPTER 21

Troubleshooting ActionScript

In previous chapters, you have run the gamut as far as ActionScript is concerned. You have been bombarded with the terms, elements, techniques, concepts, technical and syntactical conventions, properties, methods, and commands of the language. You have probably been working and experimenting with ActionScript in your movies and run into a problem here and there.

Sometimes problems arise from unfamiliarity with the material you are using; other times they are caused by a simple typing error or misplaced character in your script. And, of course, there are times when an error or problem occurs and you have no idea whatsoever why something has gone wrong. These kinds of situations can be frustrating and sometimes even a little scary. The purpose of this chapter is to present a set of tools that you can use when the problems with the ActionScript in your movie are not immediately recognizable. The chapter covers these topics:

- Authoring techniques to help avoid problems before they arise
- ActionScript conventions to aid in the troubleshooting process
- Using the Flash Debugger window
- Tracking script elements in the Output panel

Scripting and Working Smart: Some Suggestions

Even the most proficient and knowledgeable ActionScript gurus get stuck in technical ruts. One thing that separates them, though, is their ability to get out of these ruts. Experience has taught them how to step away from the problem, evaluate the situation, and dive in again with an appropriate solution. Often, technical problems are easily solved not through scripting wizardry but through a logical and methodical reevaluation of your code. Moreover, by practicing good, consistent habits while planning and writing your scripts, many problems can be avoided altogether. This section provides a set of useful tips and recommendations that should help you practice good scripting form and avoid many common technical stumbling blocks.

Although good *physical* form while typing (keeping your back straight, putting your feet on the floor, and so on) is critical in preventing repetitive stress injuries, good *scripting* form means good habits that minimize the possibility of errors. Good form ultimately means working smarter. It can also help you flush out problems and find their solutions when they do pop up. Following is a list of things you can do to help avoid problems while working on your Flash projects and writing ActionScript.

Use appropriate variable names. Variables are storage locations for many different kinds of information: values, properties, Movie Clip instances, frame labels—just about anything in a movie. When you initialize a variable, try to select a name that is meaningful—ideally a name that makes reference to the role or purpose of the variable. A variable name must also be an identifier. For more on identifiers, variables, and variable naming suggestions, see Chapter 18.

Use ActionScript terms correctly. Some elements of ActionScript are read-only, which means that they can be checked but not set. Many terms use a specific configuration or upper- and lowercase letters and punctuation. When in doubt about a particular term, consult this book's ActionScript Reference (on the accompanying CD-ROM) or the ActionScript Dictionary section of the Help panel (F1).

Work deliberately; test movies and scripts often. While you are creating a Flash movie, it's easy to be swept away by the pure joy of creativity and forget about the technical feasibility of what you are doing. Without compromising your work style, try to approach the creative process by taking small steps. With every little accomplishment or scripting victory, test the movie to ensure that *every* element is still working properly.

Save multiple versions, and back up your files. Everyone knows about frequent saves; but everyone forgets occasionally, too. Backup files are essential to ensure against disk errors, hard-drive crashes, and other anomalies that can plague the citizens of a digital world. Saving multiple versions of a file helps protect against major mistakes, lost data, corrupted files, and so on. If a newer version has problems or is altered beyond repair, it can be helpful to return to a previous version and start afresh.

Use the *trace* function to track variables and properties. The trace function is one of the most helpful parts of ActionScript. It allows you to get feedback from the Flash Player and tells you what is *really* going on in your movie with variables, loops, and other script elements. To learn more about this, see the section "Using trace" later in this chapter.

Use comments to mark up your code. Comments, created by typing a double forward slash (//), tell Flash to ignore whatever is written after the slashes. Use comments to leave notes to yourself or another member of your team, to make citations about the portions that work and the portions that don't, and so on. Comments can also help to keep script sections organized.

> For blocking out large chunks of code, see also the multiline comment characters (/* and */) in Chapter 18.

Storyboard a script to check the logic and flow. If you are going to tackle a large project involving a lot of ActionScript, it can be helpful to start by working on paper. You can plan and conceptualize your script outside of Flash, and then step into the program once you are ready to begin development. It can also be helpful to plan complex loop structures on paper, where you can do all the computations and logic in a medium that shows the flow of information.

Build your movie in small chunks. It can be advantageous to break a project into sections and tackle them one by one, a kind of divide-and-conquer approach. Get one portion of your movie working before moving on to the next.

Identify problems as they arise. If something seems to be amiss, chances are it is. It's always better to deal with problems right away than to let them linger. Also, as you troubleshoot and try different solutions, think about how temporary fixes might negatively impact other movie elements in the future.

It's often better the second time around. If you have the time, try re-creating a project you just finished. In other words, develop the movie or application, then build it again. You might find that in the second round, you are intuitively led to more elegant solutions to problems that were frustrating in the first round of development.

This list of recommendations is not ActionScript dogma. Everyone has their own work style and must approach their projects in a way that encourages both creativity and productivity. The hope is that some of these techniques will help you avoid errors and focus on the more important aspects of a project.

Troubleshooting Tips

Try as you might, some problems simply cannot be avoided. When they occur, they are like sand in the gears of your scripting machine. Technical scripting errors can bring your productivity to a screeching halt and create frustration in the ranks of your development team. The good thing about technical errors is that you can overcome them. They are *errors,* and all you have to do is set things straight; change them and make them the way they ought to be.

Sound too easy to be true? Well, probably, but it surely does feel good to think about problems so confidently. Attitude can be a great asset when it comes to overcoming technical problems and errors. When you are calm and collected, it is easier to think with perspective and to examine the situation at hand logically. To do this, you must look at your scripts from every possible angle to try and discover what portion or component is causing the problem, and why.

Self-Help: Queries for Troubleshooting Common Mistakes

Following is a series of questions you can ask to get to the bottom of an ActionScript-related problem with your movie.

Is the syntax correct? There are many different ActionScript elements: functions, properties, methods, statements, and so on. It can be very easy to confuse one syntax for another, so be sure that you are using each term properly.

Make sure that you correctly spell each term and use the right upper- and lowercase characters where they are needed (for example, onMouseUp, not onmouseup).

Be sure to include a semicolon (;) at the end of statements, and be sure to use curly braces ({}) to enclose the block statements of handlers and loops. ActionScript is often forgiving when it comes to missing semicolons, but a misplaced or forgotten curly brace will stop the Flash Player dead in its tracks when it is trying to read and process your scripts.

> If you're not sure of your syntax, Flash will tell you! While working in the Actions panel, simply click the Check Syntax button or press Cmd/Ctrl+**T** to verify the "correctness" of your Action-Script statements.

Watch your operators carefully! When evaluating a condition, 10<=10 evaluates as True because 10 is equal to 10, whereas 10<10 evaluates False (10 is not less than 10). Similarly, the assignment operator (=) and equality operator (==) have very different uses. The assignment operator is used to *assign* a value:

```
var i=0;
```

The equality operator is used to test whether two expressions are equal and will return a Boolean value:

```
if(this._x==bounds._x){
    //statement(s) if expressions are equal (returns True)
}
```

The Check Syntax feature of the Actions panel won't catch these kinds of mistakes, so it's extra-important to confirm that you have specified the correct operators for loops and conditional statements.

Did you specify the arguments correctly? On a related note, many ActionScript elements (functions and methods, in particular) can take arguments. Check to be sure that all arguments are entered properly. For example, if you entered a variable or identifier where there should be a string, your script will not run properly. The following statement will not execute properly because the gotoAndPlay() function dictates that the name of a target frame label must be specified as a string:

```
gotoAndPlay(intro);
```

The correct syntax is:

```
gotoAndPlay("intro");
```

Here, using the right syntax, the frame label "intro" is specified as a string and the statement will execute properly. Without the quotes however, intro is interpreted as a variable that contains value. If there's no such variable, the statement won't execute properly because it has no value to use for the target argument of the gotoAndPlay() function.

Is the handler getting executed? Every script is called from some kind of handler. However, if a handler does not get executed, the scripts it contains will not be called. Use the trace function to test for handler activity. For example, to test and see if a Movie Clip is responding to a mouse click event, you could write:

```
block_mc.onPress=function(){
    trace("clicked");
    //other statements...
}
```

Did you use the correct target path? When you are creating a movie with multiple Movie Clip instances and Timelines, it can be easy to get confused and forget which clips and movies reside where. Check to see that you have correctly specified all of your target paths to functions, objects, Movie Clips, and their properties. For more specifics on this, see the section "Monitoring Scripts with the Output Panel" later in this chapter.

What's the scope? While global (_global) variables are available at any time throughout an entire movie, others are not. Timeline-specific variables must be recalled using a target path to the Timeline where they were created. To read more about variables and their scope, see Chapter 18.

Does your math check out? How many expressions are you using in a script? Do they add up correctly to achieve the results you desire? If it is helpful, you can use the trace function to help with some in-context number crunching.

Are loops and conditionals executing properly? When you use a loop or conditional, you set the parameters to test a condition and then have ActionScript do something as a result of that condition. If a script is not behaving properly, check to see that its loops and conditional statements are being executed correctly.

Are all Movie Clips and Button objects instances? Unless a Movie Clip or Button object is an instance, you will not be able to target (control) it with ActionScript. Consult the Property Inspector (choose Window → Properties or press Cmd/Ctrl+F3) to be sure that each Movie Clip or Button object you wish to target has a unique instance name.

Do all variables and functions have unique names? It is essential that all variables and functions are identifiers. They must have unique names so that they won't be confused with other elements in your movie.

Flash Troubleshooting Tools

Beyond the mental analysis of a technical problem, it's good to have additional resources that can help dig you out of trouble when problems do occur. It's good to be able to look at a script, walk through it slowly, step by step, and uncover the statements that are problematic. However, sometimes this can prove to be an enormous task! In the same way that it is helpful to create a movie in small, deliberate steps, it can be equally beneficial to troubleshoot in the same manner. You hunt for problems carefully, and make sure that one area of the movie is trouble free before moving on to the next area.

Flash provides a set of tools that can make this process easier. Using these as part of your troubleshooting strategy can help you break a problem down by isolating different parts of a script and testing them individually. Some of these tools are formalized; others are more like scripting techniques. All the tools will help you work through ActionScript problems and get your scripts running smoothly.

Comments were discussed earlier as a means of leaving notes and reminders within the body of a script. You are able to do this because Flash ignores anything that follows the double slash (//). This feature makes comments the perfect tool for turning certain parts of a script on and off. For example, in the following script, part of the conditional statement is turned off so that the script will execute but not run the statements within the conditional.

```
onClipEvent(enterFrame){
    _root.Bbi._y-=j;
    i+=1;
    if(i>20){
        //_root.gotoAndPlay(1);
    }
}
```

By "turning off" a portion of a script that works correctly, you can isolate script elements that are problematic or force the script to not run particular statements.

The Debugger was introduced with Flash 5 and has been a valuable asset ever since. It offers a series of menus that allow you to monitor Movie Clip instances, variables, properties, and in general, all of the technical happenings of your movie. To learn more about the Debugger, see the next section of this chapter.

The Output panel can be used several different ways in your movie. It is involved any time you use the `trace` function. All items that you ask to trace will be printed in the Output panel. Additionally, it can be used to provide information about any objects and variables that are active in your movie. To learn how to use this tool, see the section "Monitoring Scripts with the Output Panel" later in this chapter.

Using the Debugger

The Debugger is your window to all the inner workings of your movie. It displays all the Movie Clip instances and levels in your movie, as well as the properties of each. The Debugger will also track all the variables that are active within a given Timeline in your movie. It is an extremely useful and efficient tool because it presents all of the technical elements you need to monitor a movie within a single window. Use the Debugger to isolate errors in your scripts and look "under the hood." A close examination of your scripts and how they are executing can be invaluable when your movie isn't running properly.

To run, the Debugger requires additional software known as the Flash Debug Player. This is a special version of the Flash Player that automatically installs with the main Flash authoring application. The additional software is what allows Flash to load information about your movie into the Debugger window as you test a movie.

Activating the Debugger

In Test Movie mode, when you select Window → Debugger or press Shift+F4, the Debugger window opens. However, it is in an inactive state and is nothing more than a shell waiting to receive information. To initiate debugging in your movie, you must *activate* the

Debugger. This launches the Debug Player component and allows the Debug window to receive information.

To activate debugging in your movie, choose Control → Debug Movie (Shift+Cmd/Ctrl+Return/Enter). Flash automatically jumps into Test Movie mode. The Debugger window opens and displays the contents of your movie. The Debugger is paused by default. To initiate debugging, click the green Continue button in the Code View menu.

Debugger Elements

While activated and running in Test Movie mode, the Debugger no longer looks like a dead window. It has several components, all of which are helpful in giving insight into the workings of your movie. Figure 21.1 shows the Debugger in an active state.

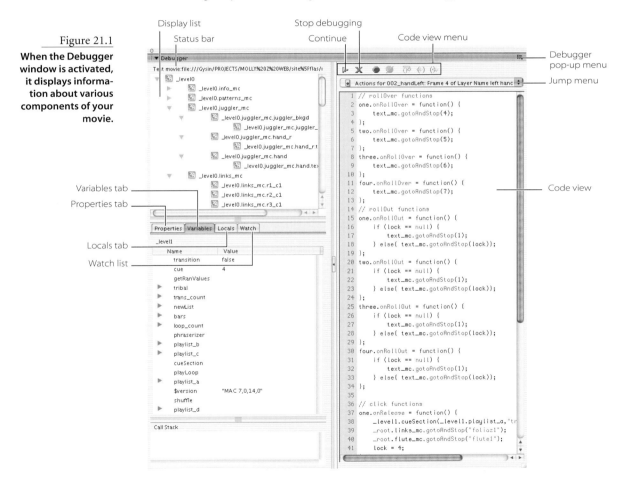

Figure 21.1

When the Debugger window is activated, it displays information about various components of your movie.

Status Bar

At the very top of the Debugger window is the status bar. It shows the following information:

- Debugging status—whether you're working in Test Movie mode from your local computer, or in Remote Flash Player while debugging from a remote location

- The movie's local file path or URL

Display List

When the Debugger is activated, the Display List shows you a breakdown of each movie level and Movie Clip instance, including a separate clip level for global variables (_global). This list is updated as movies are duplicated, removed, loaded, or unloaded from the main Timeline. The Display List shows these items in a format similar to the Movie Explorer so that you can see the hierarchical relationship between clip instances. If your movie contains lots of clips, you can resize the dimensions of the Display List so that it is taller, to show more information.

Properties Tab

The Properties tab is used to monitor and change properties of a given Movie Clip instance. You can monitor a clip's properties while you test a movie and change them directly from the Debugger window. Any changes made in the Properties tab will not permanently affect your movie. They can only temporarily alter clip parameters while you test the movie.

To display the properties for a Movie Clip, select the clip in the Display List and then click the Properties tab. The tab will show a long list of clip properties. Depending on the clip and the way you use it in your movie, some properties might be constantly updating and changing in the Properties tab window.

To change the values for a property, select the clip instance you would like to modify from the Display List. Double-click the property value and then enter a new value in the field. Press Return/Enter, and your movie will update itself accordingly.

Variables Tab

The Variables tab gives you access to a live display of all the variables currently active on a given Timeline. You can select a Movie Clip instance in the Display List, and the Variables tab will list the current values of the variables that the instance contains. Selecting the _global clip in the Display List will show any global variables that your movie contains.

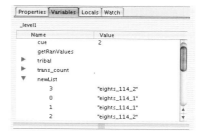

It is also possible to change variable values as you are testing your movie. Simply select the variable in the list, double-click its value, and enter a new value. Press Return/Enter, and your movie will respond accordingly.

Watch List Tab

The Watch List provides an easy way to monitor a set of variables from one location. For example, if you wanted to simultaneously monitor the variables in two different Movie Clips, you would have to jump back and forth between them in the Display List while watching the Variables tab. The Watch List allows you to select these variables and put them in one location so that they can be monitored easily within a single window. To do this, you must add the variables to the Watch List.

To create a Watch List, you can do one of three things:

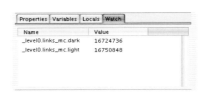

- Select a variable in the Variables tab. Ctrl+click (Mac) or right-click (Win), and select Watch from the context menu. Alternatively, you can select the variable and choose Add Watch from the Debugger pop-up menu. Any variables selected for a watch will be marked with a blue dot in the Variables tab.

- Ctrl+click (Mac) or right-click (Win) in the Watch List window.

- Double-click on a new line and enter the target path to the variable you wish to watch.

It is not possible to directly assign an item from the Properties tab (such as _alpha or _currentframe) to the Watch List. Flash allows you to watch variables only. As a workaround, initialize a variable to the property you want to watch and then use the Debugger to set a watch for that variable. For example, if you need to constantly monitor the horizontal position of a Movie Clip, create a variable for the _x property:

```
block_mc.onEnterFrame=function(){
    block_hPos=block_mc._x;
}
```

Then use the Variables tab to set a watch for the variable block_hPos.

You can remove an item from the Watch List by Ctrl+clicking (Mac) or right-clicking (Win) the item and then deselecting Watch in the context menu. You can also highlight the item and select Remove Watch from the Debugger pop-up menu.

Breakpoints

In Flash MX 2004 and MX Pro 2004, you can now set and remove breakpoints in your script. Breakpoints allow you to pause scripts and user-defined (custom) functions in your movie. You can then walk through them step by step to more closely examine how and when each line effects changes in your movie.

To set and remove breakpoints in the Actions panel:

1. In the Actions panel text box, click the line where you would like to set your breakpoint.

2. Do one of the following:

   - Choose Set (or Remove) Breakpoint ✎ from the Debug Options button menu.

   - Control+click (Mac) or right-click (Win) and choose Set (or Remove) Breakpoint from the context menu.

   - Type Cmd/Ctrl+Shift+**B**.

   - Click in the area where the Actions panel displays line numbers to insert or remove a breakpoint. If line numbers aren't visible, choose View Line Numbers from the View Options menu in the Actions panel.

To set and remove breakpoints in the Debugger:

1. Use the Debugger's Jump menu to find the script where you want to insert the breakpoint.

2. In the Code View box, click the line where you would like to set your breakpoint.

3. Do one of the following:

   - Choose Toggle Breakpoint or Remove All Breakpoints from the Code View menu (see Figure 21.2).

   - Control+click (Mac) or right-click (Win) and choose Set Breakpoint, Remove Breakpoint, or Remove All Breakpoints from the context menu.

   - Type Cmd/Ctrl+Shift+**B**.

   - Click the line numbers in the Code View area to insert or remove a breakpoint.

Once you have set breakpoints, it's possible to move through your script line by line. This is done by using the Step In, Step Over, and Step Out buttons (see Figure 21.3).

Step Over causes your script to skip a statement. If you place a breakpoint at the line where the function is called, the function will be ignored.

Step In advances your script to the next line within a function.

Step Out forces the debugger out of a user-defined (custom) function.

Figure 21.2

The Code View menu includes two options to set and remove breakpoints.

Figure 21.3

The controls for moving through a script line by line are Step Over, Step In, and Step Out.

> Step In, Step Over, and Step Out work only within user-created functions. Set your breakpoint where the function is called and these options will allow you to navigate through its statements.

For troubleshooting custom functions, this feature cannot be beat. And as you become more proficient with ActionScript, using Step In, Step Over, and Step Out is a topic you should be sure to investigate further. For more details on how to monitor the flow of your scripts, choose Help → Help (F1). Then navigate to ActionScript Reference Guide → Writing and Debugging Scripts → Debugging Your Scripts → Stepping Through Lines of Code.

Remote Debugging

Sometimes you might find it helpful to examine your scripts and do your debugging while your movie is running "live." For example, if you are working on a movie that involves heavy communication of variables to and from a server, it's essential to know that all the information is being exchanged properly. To activate remote debugging of a Flash movie, two steps are required: enable remote debugging for your movie, and activate the Debugger from a remote location.

ENABLING REMOTE DEBUGGING

To enable remote debugging for your movie:

1. Choose File → Publish Settings. The Publish Settings dialog box opens.

2. Select the Flash tab in the Publish Settings dialog box and check the Debugging Permitted option.

3. If you want to password-protect your movie so that only a select few can access the movie for debugging, enter a password in the Password box. If you don't enter a password, no password will be required to debug your movie. When you're finished setting these options, click OK.

4. When ready, publish your movie. Choose File → Publish or press Shift+F12. In addition to the SWF file, Flash will also create a file with the .swd extension. This file is necessary for remote debugging. Upload it to the server along with your SWF file(s), HTML, and so on. Be sure that the SWD and SWF files are in the same directory on the server.

5. To prepare your movie for remote debugging, Flash must be ready to receive information from the remote files. Choose Window → Debugger (Shift+F4) to open the Debugger. Click the Debugger pop-up menu and select Enable Remote Debugging.

   Your movie is now ready for remote debugging.

ACTIVATING REMOTE DEBUGGING

Once you have made all the necessary settings in Flash, you are ready to do some remote debugging. To activate the remote debugger:

1. Launch Flash MX 2004 or MX Pro 2004.

2. Use either a web browser or the stand-alone Flash Player to open your finished movie from its remote location, by entering the movie's URL. The Remote Debug dialog box opens.

3. Choose either Localhost or Other Machine. Select Localhost if the Debug Player and Flash MX 2004 or MX Pro 2004 are on the same computer. Select Other Machine if they are on different computers and enter the IP address of the computer running Flash. If you are unsure which option to use, choose Localhost. Click OK.

4. If you published your movie so that it requires a debugging password, you'll be asked to enter it. After doing so, click OK.

Your computer switches to the Flash authoring application, and the Debugger is activated. You can use any of the techniques described to debug your movie from its location on the server.

To read the latest information on debugging movies in Flash MX, consult the Macromedia website, `www.macromedia.com/support/flash`.

Monitoring Scripts with the Output Panel

The Output panel adds a much-needed element to the ActionScript equation. An essential part of building any movie that uses ActionScript, the Output panel allows you to ask specific questions of the Flash Player and get feedback.

What kinds of questions can you ask it? Anything that pertains to your movie. Unfortunately, you can't ask, "Why isn't this @#$%&!! thing working!" but you can ask for things such as the values of variables and properties, the location of objects on the Stage, the path to a Movie Clip instance, or the current frame number of a Movie Clip instance. The Output panel will answer questions about any of the properties or parameters known in ActionScript. Additionally, the window is there to display any scripting errors as they arise. If you script something that Flash doesn't understand, it will tell you where the problem lies by printing a message in the Output panel.

In some cases, it's possible to get the Output panel to give you information without asking it a question directly. The List Objects and List Variables functions allow you to get information about the objects and variables in your movie by using simple menu options.

In movie editing mode, the Output panel is usually hidden and unnecessary. That's because its role deals more with the testing of movies than creating them. As you compose ActionScript and check its syntax, the window might pop open if there is an error to report.

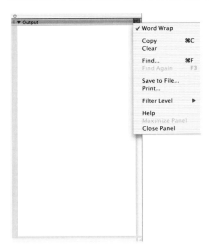

Figure 21.4

The Options menu of the Output panel

When you're working in Test Movie mode, Flash will open the Output panel whenever it has something to tell you; it will either report an error or respond to a question that you had asked it directly while using the trace function. (To learn more about trace, see its description later in this chapter.)

To open the Output panel on your own, select Window → Development Panels → Output or press F2. The Output panel will be displayed, and its contents will be blank. The Output panel offers the following in its Options menu (see Figure 21.4):

Word Wrap Finally! If you used the Output *window* in Flash 5 and MX, you probably had to struggle with resizing it to fit the message it displayed. Now in Flash MX 2004 and MX Pro 2004, the message will wrap to fit the size of the Output panel. Word wrap is enabled when this option is checked (default).

Copy (Cmd/Ctrl+C) Copies the contents of the Output panel to your computer's Clipboard.

Clear Erases the contents of the Output panel.

Find (Cmd/Ctrl+F) Searches the contents of the Output panel.

Find Again (F3) Repeats the preceding search.

Save to File Saves all information in the panel to a text file.

Print Prints all contents in the Output panel.

Filter Level Sets the level of detail for information printed in the Output panel.

List Objects Function

While working in Test Movie mode, you can call upon the Output panel to give you specific information about all the objects in your movie. This information is delivered in a cascading, outline form to give you an idea of the hierarchy of objects as well. List Objects will tell you the level number, frame number, type of object (MovieClip, Button, or shape), and absolute target path to each Movie Clip instance. This feature can be especially handy when taking stock of a movie's "cast" or tracking down an errant target path.

To list the objects in a Flash movie:

1. Save your movie and then select Control → Test Movie to jump into Test Movie mode. (The List Objects feature isn't available in regular movie editing mode.)

2. Choose Debug → List Objects (Cmd/Ctrl+**L**). The Output panel opens and prints the information for all movie objects in the window. For an example, see Figure 21.5.

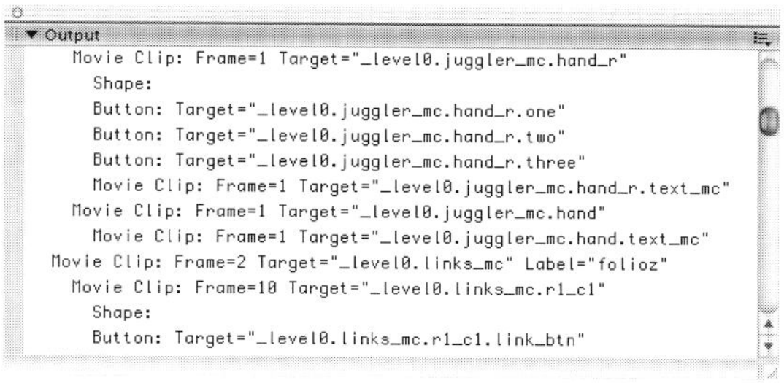

```
▼ Output
    Movie Clip: Frame=1 Target="_level0.juggler_mc.hand_r"
        Shape:
        Button: Target="_level0.juggler_mc.hand_r.one"
        Button: Target="_level0.juggler_mc.hand_r.two"
        Button: Target="_level0.juggler_mc.hand_r.three"
        Movie Clip: Frame=1 Target="_level0.juggler_mc.hand_r.text_mc"
    Movie Clip: Frame=1 Target="_level0.juggler_mc.hand"
        Movie Clip: Frame=1 Target="_level0.juggler_mc.hand.text_mc"
Movie Clip: Frame=2 Target="_level0.links_mc" Label="folioz"
    Movie Clip: Frame=10 Target="_level0.links_mc.r1_c1"
        Shape:
        Button: Target="_level0.links_mc.r1_c1.link_btn"
```

Figure 21.5

The Output panel can list all the objects in a movie while Flash is running in Test Movie mode.

List Variables Function

List Variables is another function that is available only while Flash is running in Test Movie mode. Its purpose is somewhat self-explanatory. When selected, List Variables causes the Output panel to print all the variables in a movie, the target path to their location, and their value when the function is called.

To list the variables in a Flash movie:

1. Save your movie and then select Control → Test Movie to jump into Test Movie mode. (The List Variables feature isn't available in regular movie editing mode.)

2. Choose Debug → List Variables (Cmd+Option+**V** [Mac]/Ctrl+Alt+**V** [Win]). The Output panel immediately prints all the variables in your movie, their target path, and their value at the time they are printed.

Variables and objects are not tracked dynamically when you use the List Variables or List Objects option. Rather, when you select either List Variables or List Objects, the Output panel prints the specified information at the instant it receives the command. To continuously monitor variables or objects in your movie, it's best to use either the Display List in the Debugger's Variables tab, or the trace function.

Using *trace*

The trace function is every ActionScripter's best friend. It enables you to ask Flash to report specific bits of information about your movie. Flash answers your queries by printing information to the Output panel each time you ask for it. This question-and-answer routine can allow you to gather all kinds of information about your movie and to track things such as dead handlers, Movie Clip parameters, target paths, variable values, results of functions, and so on. Once you get started using trace, you will wonder how you ever created scripts without it.

Because it is a function, `trace` is entered in the Actions panel alongside all your other script statements. The syntax is as follows:

```
trace("literal info in quotes"+variablesOrProperties);
```

You can see that `trace` will accept several different kinds of information. It can be helpful to use literal statements when you use `trace`, especially if you are tracking multiple parameters, for example:

```
trace("loopcount: "+i);
trace("horizLoc: "+_root.ball._x);
trace("vertLoc: "+_root.ball._y);
trace("instance: "+_root.ball.newBall+i);
```

This example demonstrates the fundamental techniques involved in using `trace`. Place quotes around all information that you want to appear in the Output panel exactly as it appears in the `trace` statement (such as the name of the thing you want to trace). Flash interprets this as a literal string and prints it verbatim. This is extremely useful for creating labels for your information. For an illustration of this, see the preceding script example. The labels `loopcount:`, `horizLoc:`, `vertLoc:`, and `instance:` will appear in the Output panel exactly as they appear in the `trace` statement because they were entered as strings.

Another common feature is the addition operator (+). This character concatenates information so that it appears as one "thought" in the Output panel. For example,

```
trace(":"+"-"+")");
```

would print to the Output panel as simply

```
:-)
```

You can enter `trace` anywhere within a script, although you might find that some locations are better than others. For instance, to track a variable that increments while a loop is executed, you want to put the `trace` statement inside the loop so that it monitors the loop value each time it cycles through.

Inspirational Design Model

When we decided to present an inspirational example for each chapter, the idea was that each artist/site/game/movie/etc. we presented would be a shining example of the material covered in the chapter. This chapter is an exception. No one wants their work to be remembered as an example of debugging and troubleshooting! However, these tasks are something that everyone has to do at one point or another during the development process.

The example presented for this chapter is the Macromedia website or, more specifically, the Flash resources found at `www.macromedia.com/software/flash/`. This is an invaluable resource for Flash users and has many things to offer developers of all abilities. Here is a partial list of the Flash offerings at the Macromedia site:

- Training and tutorials
- Galleries of professional Flash work
- Application documentation and downloads
- Related software and products
- User forums, discussion groups, feature requests, and TechNotes

The Macromedia TechNotes and Flash Support Center user forums are particularly helpful and can be a great source of information if you are stuck figuring something out. Remember, nothing is created in a bubble, and it can be good to get outside input. These resources are there to help members of the Flash community, so take advantage of them. Remember to use proper "netiquette" when interacting with any kind of user group, and be sure to read the FAQ sheet before posting any messages.

Do you have an idea for improving Flash? Submit a feature request to Macromedia to let them know what you think of the product.

Creating a Modular Flash Website with Movable Pop-Up Windows

This part of the book has provided an introduction to the ActionScript language and walked you through various examples. You learned ActionScript vocabulary and syntax and how to put it together in ways that allow you to "say" something to Flash. Some of the things you did were very simple; others explored more advanced topics. In this section, you will combine much of what you have learned to see how the elements of ActionScript can come together to create a complete system of interaction.

This lesson shows you how to create a website interface that uses pop-up windows. It would be accurate to say that the term "pop-up window" has developed a stigma in recent years. Many advertisers on the Internet use pop-up windows to bombard users with unsolicited offers and "special deals." Pop-ups are great for delivering digital junk mail.

In spite of this stigma, they also have good uses. Pop-ups, by nature, get our attention. When something springs onto the screen, it's hard for people to ignore it. It also sends a message: "Here's something new," or "We're moving on to something different." The pop-up clearly conveys a change of content to your audience, and provides a way of differentiating one section of a Flash movie or application from another.

Additionally, from a development point of view, pop-ups allow you to develop content modularly. Rather than make an audience wait to download the entirety of your Flash movie when all they need to see is one section, pop-ups allow you to separate your content into smaller pieces so your audience can load only the sections that interest them.

To complete this lesson, you will need a few files. Go to the Hands On 5 folder on this book's companion CD and copy the following files to your computer's hard disk: `main.swf`, `main.fla`, `main_cd.fla`, `popUp.swf`, `popUp.fla`, and `popUp_cd.fla`. To see what this lesson is all about, double-click `main.swf` to open it. Once the file is open, click the word *history* in the interface; a pop-up window will spring onto the screen (see Figure H5.1). Click the pop-up window's gray title bar ad drag it. You can move it across the bounds of the screen. Finally, click the Close button in the upper-right corner of the pop-up. The window disappears. This is what you are about to create.

Figure H5.1
**The history button
of the interface (top)
opens a pop-up win-
dow (bottom) when
you click it.**

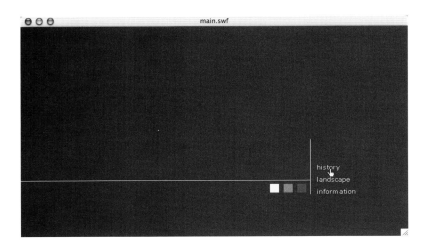

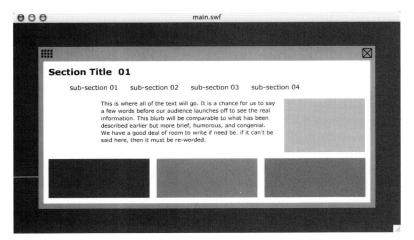

If you get lost or confused, you have a safety net of sorts. The files main.fla and popUp.fla are the finished files. They contain all the scripts you will write and all the art you will place. Use them whenever you want to peek under the hood of this movie. To start the lesson, you will use the files main_cd.fla and popUp_cd.fla. These documents contain all the symbols and graphics that are required. If you prefer to use your own artwork, you may.

To create an interface that triggers pop-up windows:

1. Open main_cd.fla and popUp_cd.fla. You will work on each movie, so it's helpful to have each file open. To switch from one document to another, use the Window menu and select the name of the file you want to edit.

2. Choose Window → Library (F11) to open the Library for each movie. Keep the Libraries open throughout this lesson.

3. Choose Window → Actions (F9) to open the Actions panel and Window → Properties to open the Property Inspector (Cmd/Ctrl+F3). You will also want to have these available at all times. If your screen is looking a little cluttered, you can try docking or minimizing some of the panels. To learn more about these procedures and how to customize Flash's workspace, see Chapter 3.

   Once the necessary files and panels are open, you can begin.

Phase 1: Designing the Main Interface

The first task is to get your main interface in shape to trigger the pop-up windows. Make main_cd.fla the active document. As the name suggests, this is the file that will serve as the core of your interface. To create the interface:

1. First and foremost, let's discuss what's already in this file and its reason for being there. The Stage size is 768×432. This allows the interface to occupy the entire browser window when a browser has been maximized at a screen resolution of 800×600. This is a good size to use if you are targeting a general web audience. If you aim for a more tech-savvy crowd, you could go up in size to accommodate a higher screen resolution.

   The design of the interface is minimal. All that is required for the lesson is some text that serves to identify the different links. Feel free to expand the design to fit your particular needs and taste. Remember, this lesson is meant to demonstrate a *process,* not "The Only Way to Do Something."

2. To trigger the pop-ups, you need to have some buttons. This example is the perfect candidate to use invisible buttons, as discussed in Chapter 15. Click the buttons layer in the Timeline to select it. Then drag the button button from the Library to the Stage. Position it over the word *history.*

3. Use the Free Transform tool to resize the button so that it completely covers the word and give it the instance name **history** in the Property Inspector.

4. Repeat this process for the words *landscape* and *information*, resizing the buttons and assigning the instance names **landscape** and **information**, respectively. The invisible buttons will cover the text with a semi-transparent blue box. This is there to show you where the buttons are positioned, but it will not appear in your final movie.

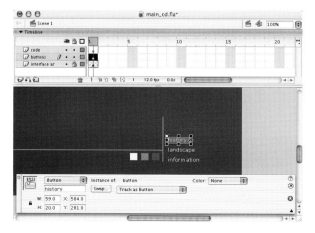

5. Now let's assign some functions to the buttons. This will not be a final script, just something to test that everything is working properly. Click the empty keyframe of the code layer to select it and enter the following statements in the Actions panel:

```
history.onRelease=function(){
    trace("clicked");
}
landscape.onRelease=function(){
    trace("clicked");
}
information.onRelease=function(){
    trace("clicked");
}
```

These statements allow you to check that the button is working by printing the word *clicked* to the Output panel. Save your movie, then choose Control → Test Movie.

6. Click each chunk of text. For each click, you should see a message appear in the Output panel.

Eventually, these buttons will be used to trigger the pop-up window and load it into your Flash movie at _level1. However, before you can do that, you need to create the pop-up window file so that you have something to load. That's your next step.

Phase 2: Creating the Pop-Up Window and Scripting Its Behavior

Now that the main interface is in shape, you can move on to create the pop-up window movie. Make popUp_cd.fla the active document and you are ready to continue.

1. The first thing you will notice about this file is that it appears to be empty, and it is! Don't worry, filling it with content is our focus here. Go to the movie's Library and double-click the icon for the window Movie Clip. This opens the clip in Symbol Editing mode.

If you can't find the symbol in the Library, be sure you're looking in the right place. Remember, you have two Libraries open right now. The Library panel's title bar will let you know which is which.

2. This is the clip you'll use for the pop-up window. The first order of business is to add a button that will allow you to drag the pop-up window. Click the empty keyframe in the bar button layer of the Movie Clip's Timeline. Drag the button button to the Stage and drop it near the upper-left corner of the gray box.

3. Use the Property Inspector to position it at X-Y coordinates (0, 0). Give it a width of **668**, a height of **30**, and assign the instance name **bar_btn**. When you're finished, the blue invisible button should cover the top "frame" of the pop-up window (see Figure H5.2).

4. Your audience needs to know that the pop-up window is draggable. To make this clear, you can put a "handle" graphic on the window's title bar. Click the empty keyframe in the bar graphics layer of the Movie Clip's Timeline. Drag the graphic symbol grab_handle to the Stage and drop it near the upper-left corner of the gray box.

5. Use the Property Inspector to position it at X-Y coordinates (6, 6).

6. Finally, you need to provide a way for your audience to close the pop-up window. With the bar graphics layer still selected, drag the button close to the Stage and drop it near the upper-right corner of the gray box.

7. Use the Property Inspector to position it at X-Y coordinates (643, 6) and give it the instance name **close_btn**.

This step completes the mechanics for the pop-window. As for content, we will leave that aspect of development in your able hands.

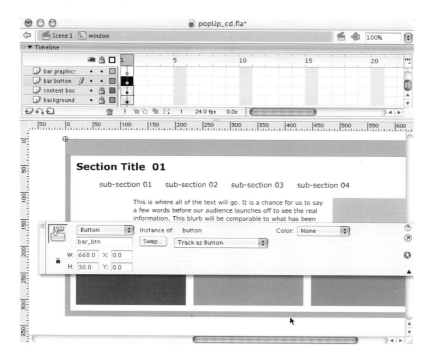

Figure H5.2

The pop-up window has an invisible button that covers its top so that you can click and drag it across the screen.

8. The pop-up window is complete within itself as a Movie Clip symbol; now you must bring it to the Stage so that it is part of the actual movie. Choose Edit → Edit Document to return to the main Timeline.

9. Drag the `window` Movie Clip from the Library to the window layer of the Timeline. Position it at X-Y coordinates (50, 50) and assign the instance name `window_mc`. When this movie is loaded into `_level1` of the main movie, the clip will appear in this position. Because both movies have identical stage sizes, and loaded movies are always registered at the (0, 0) origin in the upper-left corner, the pop-up window will appear in the middle of the Stage.

10. Now it's time to add the ActionScript that will make your pop-up window draggable. Click to select the empty keyframe of the code layer and enter the following statements in the Actions panel:

```
window_mc.bar_btn.useHandCursor=false;
top=_x;
left=_y-window_mc._width+30;
right=Stage.width-30;
bottom=Stage.height-30;
```

The first line is optional. It prevents the hand cursor from appearing when the mouse moves over the `bar_btn` button instance. The remaining four lines are vital: They set the bounds in which someone can drag the pop-up window. If these were not included, it would be possible to drag the window off the screen and not be able to get it back.

- `top=_x;` sets the top boundary to the top of the Stage.

- `left=_y-window_mc._width+30;` sets the left boundary at the width of the pop-up window minus 30 pixels. This ensures that at least 30 pixels (the height of the title bar) will always be visible when the pop-up window is dragged off the left edge of the screen.

- `right=Stage.width-30;` sets the right boundary similar to the left boundary. It prevents the left edge of the pop-up from going beyond the value that is 30 less than the edge of the Stage. Because the Stage is 768 pixels wide, the right boundary is 738.

- `bottom=Stage.height-30;` sets the parameter so it's identical to the right boundary, except it sets the value based on height so that the clip can't be dragged below the bounds of the Stage.

11. Start a new line in the Actions panel and enter these additional statements:

```
window_mc.bar_btn.onPress=function(){
    window_mc.startDrag(false,left,top,right,bottom);
    window_mc.bar_btn.onMouseMove=function(){
        window_mc._x=_xmouse;
        window_mc._y=_ymouse;
        updateAfterEvent();
    }
}
```

If you worked with the examples in Chapter 20, this code should be familiar. It is essentially the same code that was used to create slider controllers. This function targets the bar_btn instance and makes window_mc a moveable Movie Clip. There is one subtle difference between this script and the examples presented earlier:

```
window_mc.bar_btn.onMouseMove=function(){
    window_mc._x=_xmouse;
    window_mc._y=_ymouse;
    updateAfterEvent();
}
```

This function is embedded inside the main function. After the onPress event, while onMouseMove executes, this function makes the position of the Movie Clip (window_mc) lock to the position of the mouse. updateAfterEvent() enables these statements to execute independently of the movie's frame rate, and facilitates a smoother dragging motion.

12. The previous statements initiated dragging; now you must add something to stop it when the mouse is released. Add these additional statements to the Actions panel:

```
window_mc.bar_btn.onRelease=function(){
    stopDrag();
}
window_mc.bar_btn.onReleaseOutside=function(){
    stopDrag();
}
```

It helps to initiate a stopDrag() from both events because you never know if someone's mouse will be over the button or not when they stop dragging. Select Control → Test Movie and try dragging the window around the screen.

This ActionScript can also be written as:

```
window_mc.bar_btn.onRelease=window_mc.bar_btn.on
    ➥ReleaseOutside=function(){
    stopDrag();
}
```

This alternative syntax allows you to combine both handlers so they execute identical statements.

13. Your pop-up window is nearly complete. All you need now is a script that will close the window when you click the Close button. Enter this last set of statements in the Actions panel:

```
window_mc.close_btn.onRelease=function(){
    _level0.popUpClose();
}
```

This calls the function popUpclose() at the _level0 (_root level) when someone clicks close_btn. If this seems incorrect, then you've been paying attention so far! There is no such thing as popUpclose(). It's neither a built-in ActionScript function nor have we created it—yet. We will create this and other functions when we go back to the main movie. It's best for the functions to reside there so that they are always available. However, we will eventually need to call the function from this movie, so it's OK to add a script now even though it won't work until later. See the finished script in Figure H5.3.

14. The pop-up window is now complete! Save your work and choose Control → Test Movie to temporarily publish your movie as an SWF file. You will need the SWF for the next set of steps.

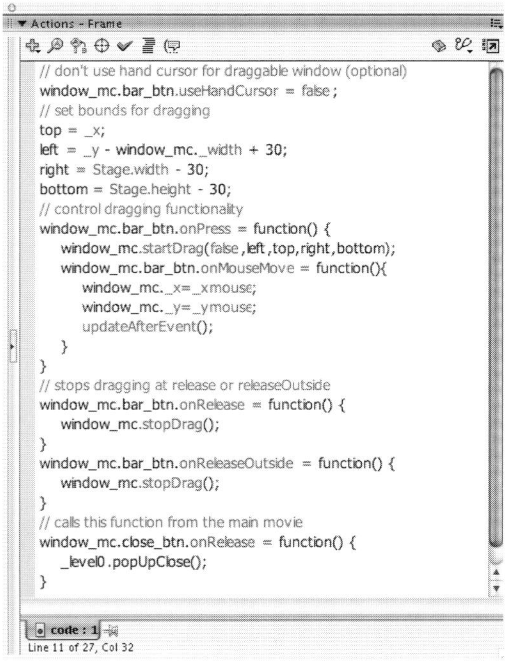

Figure H5.3

The finished script to make the pop-up window draggable should look like this. Comments have been added to help clarify the role of each set of statements.

Phase 3: Writing Functions to Make the Pop-Ups Pop

The majority of our work is done. The tasks that remain will allow the movie to manage the pop-up window and bring all the elements together. Make main_cd.fla the active document and you are ready to complete the lesson.

1. From here, everything that you do will be based in ActionScript. Click the code layer to select the script you already entered, open the Actions panel, and enter the following statements:

```
function popUpOpen(window){
    loadMovieNum(window, 1);
}
```

This will be the function to open the pop-up window. You create the function so that it takes one parameter: the name of the SWF file you wish to use as the pop-up. That parameter is passed to ActionScript's built-in loadMovieNum() function, which loads the SWF at _level1.

2. Now you need to reverse the process and create a function that unloads the SWF to close the pop-up. Enter these additional statements:

```
function popUpClose(){
    unloadMovieNum(1);
}
```

This will be the function that closes the pop-up window. Now when the pop-up's Close button gets clicked, it is able to call a valid function.

3. With functions in place, you can finally add the code to open the pop-up. Change the function for the history button to read like this:

```
history.onRelease = function() {
    popUpOpen("popUp_cd.swf");
}
```

Now when history is clicked, rather than printing a message to the Output panel, it will open the pop-up window. Select Control → Test Movie and try it out.

4. Once you're in Test Movie mode, click history to open the pop-up and click the Close button to make it go away. Great, it works! However, there is a slight bug. While the pop-up window is open, move your mouse over the area where the buttons are positioned in the main movie. You should see the cursor change to the hand pointer (see Figure H5.4). This situation will be confusing to your audience. They don't see anything that looks clickable yet they get a cursor that tells them they can click. This is because the buttons at _level0 are still active. If you click, you will either reload the pop-up window or get a message in the Output panel. This situation has the distinct possibility to cause problems in the future, so it's best to make sure it never happens. You can do this by disabling the buttons when a pop-up window is loaded.

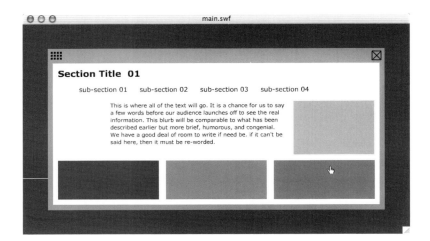

5. To disable the buttons, start by putting them in an Array. This allows you to manage them as a set. Create the array with the following statement:

```
buttons=new Array("history","landscape","information");
```

Type this line of code at the top of the Actions panel script pane above the functions that you created in steps 1–3. It creates an Array named `buttons` and assigns the three buttons in your movie to elements 0 through 2.

6. Now you will write a loop that puts the Array to good use. Update the `popUpOpen()` function as shown in the following statements:

```
function popUpOpen(window){
    loadMovieNum(window, 1);
    for (var item in buttons){
        eval(buttons[item]).enabled=false;
    }
}
```

The statements that you've added create a `for…in` loop. This loop structure is used expressly to cycle through the properties of objects. In this case, you're looping through the contents of the Array `buttons`. For every `item` in `buttons`, you will perform a task. That task is to set the `enabled` property of each `item` to `false`. The `enabled` property determines if a button is functional (`true`) or not (`false`). By cycling through the array of buttons, this loop disables each one, rendering it inactive in your movie.

One last technical note: When you created `buttons`, each button was added to the array as a string. The `eval()` function is needed here to convert the name of the button from a string to an identifier. Buttons (and Movie Clips) *must* be targeted as identifiers if you want to control any of their properties. To learn more about eval(), see the ActionScript Reference on this book's companion CD.

7. You've probably guessed the last step: If you disable the buttons with one function, you have to re-enable them with another. This is exactly right, and you'll do it with the popUpclose() function. Change the function to read:

```
function popUpClose(){
    unloadMovieNum(1);
    for (var item in buttons){
        eval(buttons[item]).enabled=true;
    }
}
```

There should be no mystery here. This function uses the same looping syntax, only it does the reverse and enables all of the buttons in the array. Cool!

8. Select Control → Test Movie. Click all the buttons. Then try to click them again when the pop-up window is open. You should find that the hand cursor is now absent in the presence of the pop-up window.

9. Close the pop-up window. The hand cursor should be back and the buttons should be active once again.

10. Your movies are finally finished. Congratulations! If you want to prepare these for delivery on the Web or CD-ROM, you should publish each file before delivery in its final medium. See Chapter 30 for details on publishing final SWF files.

Phase 4: Moving On—Next Steps and Ideas for the Future

Most people in creative fields would probably agree that nothing is ever really finished. This lesson certainly subscribes to that school of thought. It's done but not finished; there's a lot that you could do to push this further. Here are a few suggestions:

- Add more pop-up windows—you have the functions to do it! Create additional SWF movies such as popUp.swf and use the popUpOpen() function to cue them from the other buttons. Each pop-up will be loaded into _level1.

- Expand the flexibility of the function. Consider:

```
function popUpOpen(window,location){
    loadMovieNum(window, location);
    for (var item in buttons){
        eval(buttons[item]).enabled=false;
    }
}
```

Here the parameter `location` has been added. You could specify different values for this to load movies at _level1, _level2, and so on.

- Rather than loading document levels, try creating the pop-ups by loading the SWF files into Movie Clip instances on the Stage. This will allow you to use the `getDepth()` and `swapDepths()` methods of the MovieClip object to change the stacking order (layering) of clips.

Whatever creative decisions you make, good luck and have fun working with this idea.

Working with Audio

Part VI begins one of the most interesting, important, and, we daresay, fun aspects of working with Flash—sound. Sound means all sorts of things: sound effects (Bang! Ka-pow! Crunch!), music, dialog, and any other audible elements of your Flash production. Sound adds life to your movies and animations. It provides extra impact for scenes that are funny or scary, gives your characters voices, and allows your audience to take a break from reading and to listen to your story or presentation.

Sound effects can offer feedback to your audience. For every button click or other interaction with your Flash application, sound can let your audience know that their request was received. And music…there are so many possibilities! Use music for theme songs, background ambience, and dramatic flair. Or harness the power of ActionScript to create interactive audio environments in which your movie's sound is dictated solely by the whims of the folks who are experiencing it. Whatever the audio demands and goals of your Flash movie, this part of the book will surely set you on the right path.

CHAPTER 22

Understanding Digital Audio in the Flash Environment

Sound is one of the most neglected yet potent components of contemporary multimedia. In this context, the word *sound* means many things: sound effects, music, narration, and dialog. Although all of these elements can lift a work of multimedia to new heights, designers rarely take full advantage of the possibilities afforded by sound in their Flash productions. Sound in and of itself is a powerful medium; it communicates through channels that are unavailable to imagery and text. This characteristic doesn't make sound superior, but rather makes it uniquely suited to capturing and holding the attention of an audience through their sense of hearing.

There are many reasons why sound hasn't been a major player in the multimedia arena, particularly with web-based multimedia applications. Most of these are not germane to the topics surrounding Flash and will be saved for another time. What is very relevant, though, is the fact that Flash works well with audio components. It provides several options that allow you to include both sound and music in your movies. Every developer who opens or downloads a copy of the software should take advantage of the richness it can bring to their projects.

This chapter will introduce you to some of the possibilities that audio adds to the Flash equation. If you are new to working with sound on your computer, you will also learn some of the basic technical terms and theory surrounding digital audio. The topics in this chapter are as follows:

- **Digital audio sample rate and bit depth**
- **Stereo and mono sound**
- **Flash-compatible digital audio file types**
- **How and where to acquire sounds for your work**
- **Preparing audio for the Flash environment**
- **Planning a movie with sound in mind**
- **Working with looped sounds**

Digital Audio, Technically Speaking

To a Flash designer or developer, the technical specifics of digital audio might seem remote, abstract, and insignificant to the overall production of a Flash movie. Nothing could be further from the truth. In fact, the technical specifics of digital audio have a very important impact on your project, especially when it comes to publishing and delivering your final movie. A developer who knows the ins and outs of digital audio will be able to prepare and plan for a project while keeping sound in mind from the very beginning. Technical knowledge not only allows you to select the right options for your movie at the outset of a project, it enables you to troubleshoot problems when they arise. Plus, with a good understanding of how digital sound files work, it's much easier to bend them to your creative will in the context of your Flash projects and movies.

Sample Rate

It's likely that most of you reading this book have had some sound-recording experience using some form of magnetic tape. Whether it was with a toy tape recorder, Dictaphone, open-reel tape deck, or other recording device, magnetic tape has been accessible to people for both professional and hobbyist recording for many years. In this medium, sound waves are converted to magnetic impulses and stored on long strands of tape. When played back, these impulses are able to re-create sounds by imitating the pulsation of the original sound waves.

If you have worked with sound in this way, you have experience with *analog* sound recording. It's called analog because the magnetic information tries as closely as possible to remain true, or *analogous*, to the shape and amplitude of the original sound wave. Positive and negative curves in a sound wave are mimicked by the positive and negative magnetic charges on the recorded audio tape. For an illustration of this, see Figure 22.1.

In the world of interactive multimedia, analog recording has been supplanted by *digital* sound recording. In digital recording, positive and negative magnetic impulses have been replaced by the 1s and 0s of binary code. When making a digital recording, the digital recording device (a computer, for instance) examines the sound wave and takes snapshots of its amplitude. These snapshots are called *samples,* and the speed at which the snapshots are taken is called the *sample rate.* See Figure 22.2 for an illustration of sample rate.

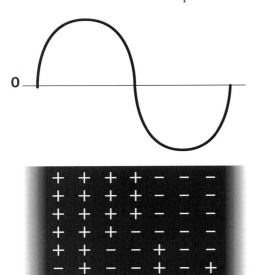

Figure 22.1

Magnetic tape is used in analog sound recording. Charged particles are scattered on the tape to exactly represent the shape of the original sound wave.

For most consumer digital audio, the sampling rate is 44.1kHz, or 44,100 samples per second. This means that for every second of audio you wish to store digitally, there are over 44,000 pieces of information to represent that single second of sound. If you were to drop the sampling rate by half (22.05kHz), you would still be able to represent the original wave. However, because you would be trying to do it with half the amount of information, the quality of the sound would suffer. As samples are removed from a digital sound, it has fewer and fewer snapshots to re-create the original source sound.

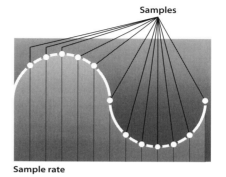

Figure 22.2

A digital recording device takes samples, or snapshots, of a sound wave. These are interpreted by the playback device and used to re-create the original sound using the digital information.

Bit-Depth Resolution

Bit depth is another important term in the world of digital sound recording. It is the number of values available to describe the amplitude of the wave for a given sample. Where sample rate is used to describe a sound along the X axis, bit depth is a measurement along the Y axis. For an illustration of this, see Figure 22.3.

DIGITAL SAMPLING RATE AND THE NYQUIST THEOREM

The sample rate of 44.1kHz was neither selected whimsically nor plucked from a hat. It's actually rooted in scientific study into the transmission of data signals.

In the 1920s, Harry Nyquist developed many theories surrounding sound recording. One of these had an important impact on digital audio recording technology. The Nyquist theorem states that to accurately represent a sound, the sample rate must be at least twice the value of the highest frequency you wish to record. The reason for this is simple. A wave has two portions: positive and negative. To represent this accurately, you must have at least one snapshot from each of the extremes. Because human hearing tops out at around 20kHz, the Nyquist theorem proposes that the sample rate for recording should be at least 40kHz. This figure is twice as high, and can capture samples quickly enough to represent both the positive and negative slopes of a sound wave within the range of human hearing.

The sampling rate for a standard audio CD is 44.1kHz, which is 4,100Hz over the minimum value. This allows plenty of room to capture all the important frequencies and allows some extra room for others that make their way into the sound recording.

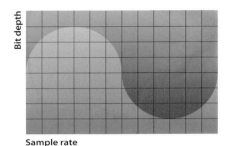

Bit depth

Sample rate

Figure 22.3

Bit depth measures the amplitude (Y axis value) of a wave for each sample (X axis) in the sound file.

Bit depth, like sample rate, has finite resolution. While most recording devices can sample sounds at 44.1kHz, 48kHz, or 96 kHz, they are also generally limited to a bit depth of 8, 16, or 24. Bit depth is represented by binary numbers. In an 8-bit system, there are 256 possible values ($2^8 = 256$), ranging from 00000000 to 11111111. With 16 bits, the values increase to a possible 65,536 ($2^{16} = 65,536$): 0000000000000000 to 1111111111111111. Clearly, you can see that 16-bit quality offers a much broader spectrum of values. At this resolution, it's less likely for samples to be rounded off to the nearest binary value. They will generally remain more true to the original wave shape than an 8-bit sound. To see the difference between the two possibilities, see Figure 22.4.

High-resolution recording settings (namely 24-bit and 96kHz) are becoming more common in both amateur- and professional-quality recording equipment; however, these settings cannot be used for playback. The audio needs to be "sampled down" to consumer-quality levels before you bring it into Flash. This means that the audio you want to use in your Flash productions should be limited to a maximum sample rate of 44.1 kHz and a maximum bit-depth of 16.

Figure 22.4

Eight-bit sounds have fewer values for each sample. Consequently, many samples are rounded to the nearest value, and the original wave shape is compromised in the digital recording. Because 16-bit sound offers a higher resolution with greater accuracy, there is less rounding, and a wave remains more true to the original (although still far from perfect).

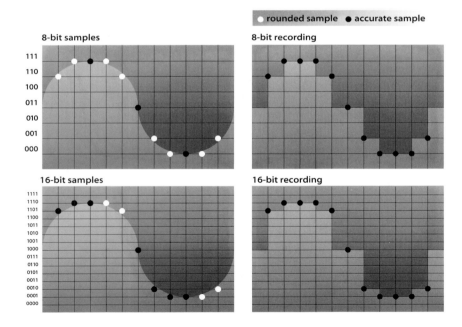

Stereo vs. Mono

If you have purchased any electronics during the last few decades, you have undoubtedly heard the term *stereo*. Whether or not you know it, you have probably been enjoying stereo sound recordings throughout most of your life. But what does it mean exactly? Most people usually answer that question by saying, "It sounds better!" Sure, in many cases, it does sound better, but that's not much of an answer. Stereo means that a sound is played through two simultaneous channels: left and right. As their names suggest, each channel has a unique position. A sound can be played back entirely in the right speaker channel, entirely in the left speaker channel, or any combination in between. This creates the aural illusion of space and position in an audio recording.

The process (and for many, the art) of assigning left and right channel information to a sound is known as *panning*. In a stereo sound recording, each element can have its own unique pan information. For instance, in a rock 'n' roll recording, you might hear drums and bass share the right and left channels equally, while the lead guitar is panned to the left and the rhythm guitar is panned to the right. There are no rules when it comes to stereo sounds; the best judge is your ears. Later in this chapter, you will learn about some of the considerations in using stereo sound from a sound design point of view.

The alternative to stereo sound is *monaural*, or mono, sound. The name is a bit of a giveaway. Monaural sounds have only a single channel and can be played through a single speaker. In the case of a two-speaker setup, mono sounds are shared equally between the left and right speakers. Because they contain no positional information, mono sounds are great for dialog, sound effects, and other elements in which position isn't crucial to the success of a sound, or in which the sound's position can be assigned later through another means, such as an ActionScript command.

> Flash has several options that allow you to control stereo and mono parameters for a sound in your movie. To learn about the basic control options, see Chapter 23. To see some of the more advanced options provided by ActionScript, see Chapter 25.

Storing Sound: Digital Audio File Types

All of the technical specifics surrounding a sound have to be stored somewhere so that a sound can be played back and used in a Flash movie. As you can imagine, quite a lot of room is required to store a sound file. For a CD-quality sound recording, you have 44,100 sound samples per second, each with a 65,536-digit binary number to describe the sample value. If the sound is stereo, and thus has information for two channels, you have to double all of the sample and bit-depth information. For a 10-second, CD-quality, stereo sound, you need 1.7MB to store all of the necessary information. That amounts to around 30MB for your average 3-minute song!

If you are scared off by this, don't be. There are many techniques that you will learn to curb the size of sound in your Flash movies. At this point, your major concern should be the *kinds* of sounds that you can use in the Flash authoring environment. You know that digital audio information is based on three things: sample rate, bit depth, and channel composition (stereo/mono). All of this information is organized and packaged as a digital sound file that can be read by software on your computer, including Flash.

Flash is capable of handling most of the contemporary sound file formats that you will encounter. Each file format has its own particular idiosyncrasies. However, once the sound is in the Flash environment, it's available for use in your movie in a variety of ways. Following is a list of the different kinds of digital sound files that you can use with Flash. To learn more about how you can incorporate these files in your Flash movie, see Chapter 23.

AIFF: Audio Interchange File Format (.aif) This format is for Macintosh import only, although most Windows-based computers should be able to read and play AIFF files with the help of QuickTime 4 or higher.

WAV: Windows Audio File Format (.wav) This format is primarily for Windows, although Macintosh computers can import WAV files into Flash if QuickTime 4 or higher is present.

MP3: MPEG Layer 3 (.mp3) This format can be imported on both the Macintosh and Windows platforms. This is the only compressed audio format that can be imported into Flash. To learn more about MP3 compression, see Chapter 23.

The following sound types require QuickTime 4 or higher:

Sound Designer II Although Digidesign no longer manufactures the software, the Sound Designer II format (Macintosh only) is still used with Pro Tools audio-editing and audio-mixing software.

QuickTime movies (sound only) QuickTime movies don't have to contain video information. These video-less files are called *sound-only* movies and can be used in Flash on either the Windows or Macintosh platform.

AU: Sun AU (.au) This format is used primarily with Sun or Unix computers and can be used in Flash on either the Windows or Macintosh platform.

System 7 Sound This is a Macintosh-only sound format that is used for the general system sounds of the Macintosh operating system.

Preparing Audio for Flash

Sound and music can add another dimension to your Flash movies. They can add the finishing touches to your animations and graphics by communicating tone. With the right sound components, a scene can be truly funny, dramatic, scary—whatever you like. Selecting or producing the right sound can make a huge difference in the success of a Flash production.

You are probably excited about getting some sounds into your movie so that you can see how all this works. However, it's important to be sure that your sounds are ready to be a part of a Flash movie before they hit the vector stage. After you have either created or found the right sounds, it's essential that you edit and prepare the files to fit your needs. This process demands an extra step before a sound is used in your movie, but it ensures that the sound is ready for the task.

Sound Resources

There are many, many sources where you can acquire audio for a Flash production. The first (and best) resource might be yourself. If you sing, play an instrument, or beat on pots and pans, you can create audio for a Flash production. Be creative! In many creative endeavors, the sincerity and originality of a work can far outshine its technical attributes. Something doesn't have to be "polished" to be good: It simply has to *work*. It must work in the context of your movie and fit the mood or message you wish to convey.

So, to all of you closet minstrels out there who are working with Flash, get offline for a few minutes and write some songs. Take a portable recording device outdoors someday and see what sounds you can record in your neighborhood. Are you doing a movie about the outdoors? Go for a hike and record everything: footsteps, birds, trees, water, and so on. You will be amazed at how the audio experience of the hike translates to your sound recordings. Do you need a sound effect of someone falling down? Record the sound of yourself kicking a cardboard box. Professional Foley artists and sound designers (people who create sound effects for a living) don't always use a recording of an actual object or event to serve as the sound for that specific object or event. Do you think that's actually fire you hear? No, it's the sound of someone crumpling cellophane or a plastic shopping bag. The possibilities are vast when it comes to producing your own sound effects and music (see Figure 22.5). Use your resources, be creative, and above all, follow your instincts over what you think is "right" or "expected."

As far as the technical side goes, when it comes to getting this done, you are on your own. The technical considerations of audio production are beyond the scope of this book. At the very least, you will need some kind of recording device, a cable to connect it to the computer, a sound card or audio input jack on the computer, and some audio software to record the sounds as digital files. If you have a laptop computer or a long audio cable, you can experiment with recording directly into the computer. For details on this, consult your owner's manual and the documentation for your sound card and audio software.

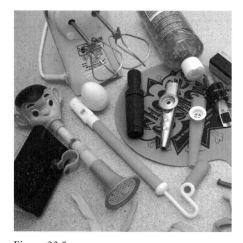

Figure 22.5

Some of the best sound effects can be produced with toys, old electronics, and other noisemakers you find around the house. Yes, that *is* a Whoopie Cushion.

If you have tried and tried with no luck, or you simply don't have the time or resources, there are alternatives to creating your own sounds and music for a Flash movie. Here is a brief list of your options:

Sound effect CDs Sound effect libraries can be purchased for use in multimedia productions. Generally, you have to buy them from a company that distributes licensed music products and audio-sample libraries. A few examples include:

Sound Ideas (www.sound-ideas.com) has an enormous variety of sounds to choose from, including many that have been licensed from companies such as Hanna-Barbera and Lucasfilm.

Sound Effects Library (www.sound-effects-library.com) offers vast online resources for finding sound effects. It also has many commercial libraries available including sound effects from the BBC.

Hollywood Edge (www.hollywoodedge.com) produces a wide variety of sound effects libraries—everything from animals and automobiles to drones and dark ambience.

This is just a small sample of what is available. Be sure to read and obey the licensing agreement for any library of this kind.

Royalty-free music and loop CDs These are also a fine source of music and loop material for your projects. The sound effect resources listed previously have plenty to offer in this category. In addition, you can try:

Primesounds (www.primesounds.com) has just about anything you need to whet your audio appetite. Check out this site for sound effects, samples, music tracks, loops, and grooves.

Propellerhead (www.propellerheads.se) is the Swedish software company that manufactures Reason, ReBirth, and Recycle. Not only is their software great for creating music, they have a lot to offer to those looking for musical "starter recipes."

As always, watch the licensing agreement to be sure that you use the product legally. When appropriate, give credit to the composer whose work you are using.

Flash and sound-effect resource websites. Websites such as www.sounddogs.com, www.sonify.org, and www.flashkit.com offer links to many different sound resources where you can go to find sound effects, music, and audio loops for your movies. Always be sure to read the legal agreement before using anything you get on the Web. Just because you downloaded something doesn't mean that you can use it any way you'd like.

Editing Sound Files

No matter where or how you acquire your sound files, it's important to edit them and make sure that they are ready for the Flash environment. Editing can accomplish several things. Because sound files demand a fair amount of storage space and add to the final size of a Flash production, it's important to make sure that any unneeded material is stripped from the sound file. Also, you want to ensure that the file is free of clicks, pops, and other strange noises that might have made their way into your recording.

If you can't hear a sound file, it is virtually useless unless you are going for an effect that requires an especially low sound volume. Before you bring any sounds into a Flash movie, you want to be sure that their output level is as healthy as possible. Once a sound is in Flash, you can always turn it down, but you can never turn it up.

The next two sections cover the most important and essential audio editing techniques for preparing a sound for a career in your Flash movie. While there are *many* other things you might want to do to ready a sound, these techniques are considered to be the most important and should be done to every single sound file before implementing it in a Flash movie.

Trimming and Cutting Sound Files

The name of this editing technique says it all, but why is it so important to trim your sound files? Well, because an extra second of CD-quality, mono sound can add between 80 and 90 kilobytes to your final movie before it is published. If you have lots of sound files with lots of extra space in them, this figure will really start to add up. The difference in file size between a 3-second drumbeat and 3 seconds of silence is … nothing. It takes exactly the same amount of space to store silence as it does a full symphony orchestra, so make your files count!

Any time you open a recorded sound file or music file, you are bound to have some dead space at the beginning and end of the sound. Your task is to make sure that this empty space is eliminated. Not only does this help keep your movie file size down, but it helps the file to play more quickly. If a sound has a quarter-second pause before anything is heard, it will always sound as though it is starting late—not because Flash is running slowly, but because it has to play through the silence or other junk before it gets to what is important (see Figure 22.6). Trimming sound files takes away the parts that are unnecessary and helps optimize their performance in a movie.

To trim a sound file, follow these steps:

1. Open the sound in your audio editor of choice. In a Windows environment, Sound Forge or Adobe Audition are great choices. If you use a Mac, you can choose between Spark and Peak. To read more about specific audio applications, see Chapter 28.

2. Navigate to the beginning of the sound file. Depending on the instrument or object that makes the sound, the wave will look very different. Play the sound and watch the playback head as you listen. You should be able to see and hear the point in the wave where the significant part of the sound begins. You might need to do this several times to pinpoint the spot.

3. Once you have found the "real" beginning of the sound, click that spot and drag a selection to the beginning of the sound file. You should see something like the picture in Figure 22.7.

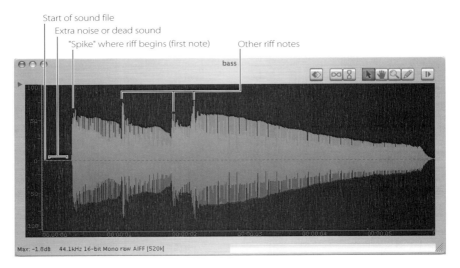

Figure 22.6

This sound file of a bass riff has unnecessary information at the beginning. Of course, listening is the key, but here you can tell where the musical information begins by the "spike" in the waveform. The wave is most active (tallest) where notes and other sounds are heard in the recording.

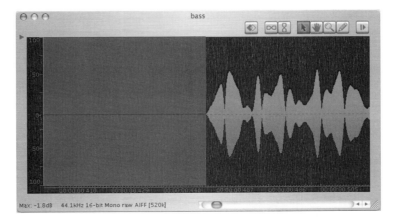

Figure 22.7

To trim a sound file, you start by making a selection of the unneeded material at the beginning of the file.

4. Play back the selection and listen. Do you hear anything important to the sound? You shouldn't. Remember, you are trimming the *unwanted* material out of the file. When you play back the selection, you should be listening to all of the dead space that you want to trim off the file. If your audio editor supports this function, play back the unselected portion of the sound file. In this case, playing the unselected portion should allow you to hear exactly what you want with no extra space or silence.

5. If your selection is correct and all of the extra material is selected, clear the unwanted material by either pressing Delete or selecting Delete from the Edit menu in your audio editor. If your selection is not quite right, you can always delete the unwanted material and go back for another pass to get the remaining portion of the wave. Or choose Edit → Undo and start the process again.

6. Remember that a sound file has two parts, a head and a tail. You just learned how to trim the head. To trim the tail, the steps are the same. The only exception, of course, is that you will make changes to the end of the file rather than the beginning.

There are a few other considerations when it comes to trimming files. You should try as much as possible to trim them at points where the wave crosses the zero-amplitude center axis. There are many crossings in a single sound file, because a wave is constantly in flux between negative and positive amplitudes. By trimming at an axis point, you eliminate the possibility of a pop or click when the file plays back, because the wave is starting at a point of silence (see Figure 22.8). Alternately, after making your edit, you can fade out a tiny portion (a few samples or milliseconds) at the beginning of the sound to bring the wave down to zero amplitude.

It can also be helpful to use fade-outs when trimming files, especially if you have a sound that sustains. If you select the beginning or end portion of a waveform and apply the fade-out effect, your audio editor will gradually decrease the sound's current volume to silence over the portion of the wave you selected (see Figure 22.9). A fade-out allows you to shorten the length of a sound that decays over a long time, such as that of a gong or cymbal crash.

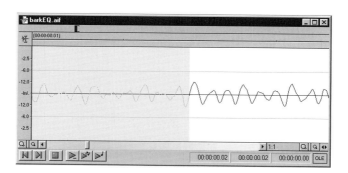

Figure 22.8

When the selection is deleted, the wave will be trimmed at a zero point (shown here in Sound Forge as Infinity) to ensure a smooth start.

Before fade-out

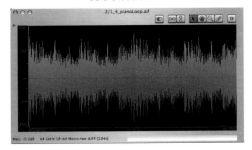

After fade-out

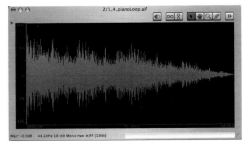

Figure 22.9

Here you can see the difference in a sound file before and after a fade-out effect was applied.

Normalizing Audio Files

Volume is one of the most important aspects of sound. If a file doesn't have a strong volume, you will be unable to hear it. In general, it's better to have to turn something down because it's too loud than to crank it up because it's not loud enough. As the chief audio engineer for your Flash movie, you have the responsibility for ensuring that all your sounds are heard, and heard at the correct volume.

While assembling your audio, it can be difficult (if not impossible) to tell how loud a sound should be out of context. The good news is that with Flash, you can bring all your sounds into the program and then tweak the volume as you create your movie. This provides a great deal of flexibility and takes much of the pressure and guesswork out of the audio production.

Because Flash allows you to manipulate volume from within your movie, you want to be sure that all your sounds come into the movie at the strongest possible volume. Your audio editor can help you do this with a command called *Normalize*. Normalize looks at an entire waveform and boosts it proportionately within a volume range that you specify without clipping or distorting the sound. Basically, it ensures that a sound is as loud as it can be without going over its limit.

Clipping and/or distortion is what happens when a sound's level is set too high and pushed beyond the capabilities of the digital recording or playback device. Although in some analog applications, distortion is an interesting effect, digital audio distortion is especially harsh. Avoid it at all costs. To learn more about ways to avoid clipping, see Chapter 28.

To normalize audio for your Flash movie:

1. Open the sound file you wish to normalize. Then choose Edit → Select All.

2. Depending on which editor you use, the Normalize command could be in a variety of locations. Generally, it's on a menu named something like Effects or Process. Choose Normalize from the menu where you find it.

3. A dialog box should open, asking what settings you want to use for normalizing. For most multimedia work, a good rule of thumb is to normalize between 96% and 98%. This boosts the entire file proportionately to 96–98% of its maximum volume. If your audio application measures normalize levels in decibels (or dB), normalize between −1 and −0.04dB. After Normalize has been executed, save the sound file.

You can see the difference between files that have normalized and those that have not. In Figure 22.10, note the difference in the amplitudes of the various waveforms.

Planning for Audio Interactivity

When it comes to audio, sound, and music, one of the most common flaws in contemporary Flash work is a lack of planning and vision for the role of sound in the production. While developers spend more and more time pushing the visual and interactive envelopes with stunning graphics and ActionScript magic, there is a shortage of truly creative audio work. If you want to have an engaging Flash website or interactive animation, you should look beyond the visual possibilities Flash offers and explore some of its nonvisual aspects.

Sound is one of the keys to creating *immersion,* a sense of bathing in the content of a story or production. To make an audience feel as though they cannot leave your movie or website, you need to achieve this feeling of immersion. Sound helps create immersion because it draws an audience into an image, feeds them additional information about the image, and allows them to interpret its meaning within your story. Sound provides subtext to the dramatic flow and helps communicate a message that is left incomplete or vague by the visual elements alone. Sound can also create a sense of mood, and help to guide the audience on an emotional journey.

You can take advantage of these characteristics by adding sound and music to your Flash movies. This is not an "add audio and stir" recipe, however. To use audio to its fullest, you must plan how it will be used and decide which portions of your movie are best suited to audio components. You must select where sound will be used, and what sounds or music best convey the message that you want to communicate.

Figure 22.10

The sound on the left has been normalized, while the sound on the right has not.

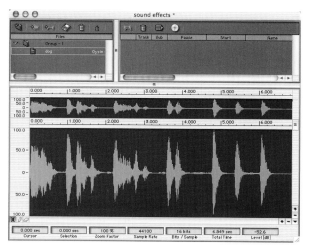
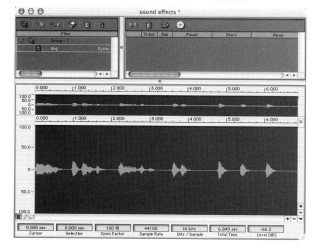

Let's say, for example, that you are creating a movie that is like a fairy tale storybook—something that contains a collection of short stories and nursery rhymes. What kinds of sounds would you want to use, and what portions of the movie should use those sounds? There are no right or wrong answers to these questions. The important thing is that the sounds support the movie and make it a better, more immersive experience. You could consider using chimes, soft bells, mystical hums, and twinkle sounds for buttons or navigational elements. You could use soft classical music behind story narration and insert story-specific sound effects (such as knocks at the door) where appropriate. You could even add specific sounds to elements when they are clicked or moused over, such as comments from Snow White's magic mirror.

The options for something like this go on forever; your creativity is the only limit. The important thing to remember is to *plan* for this. In the same way that you will choose color palettes, fonts, and other visual parameters, you will need to make some decisions about the content and use of audio in your movie. Not only does such planning provide you with direction, but it allows you to create the movie while knowing that sound will be a part of the final production. Your movie can be designed and scripted so that the audio is included and tested with all the other elements, rather than tacked on at the end.

Working with Sound Loops

Sound loops can be one of the most useful tools to a Flash developer. They can also be one of the most dreaded aspects of Flash content for your audience. Sound loops are musical phrases or rhythmic patterns that are played over and over and over ad nauseum. Sound loops often get a bad (and generally well-deserved) rap simply because they are not used well. Granted, listening to the same riff played repeatedly can grate on one's ears. However, there are different techniques that you can employ to create more musical interest with your loops and to get more mileage from them in a Flash movie.

First of all, loops are especially easy to use within Flash. The software supports looped sounds very well and does a good job of keeping the loop going without dropping beats or losing time. Because sound loops are somewhat "native" to the Flash environment, they can offer a certain amount of reliability over other kinds of sounds. Another advantage of loops is that they are compact. A loop might be only a few kilobytes large, but when it's played continuously over a long period of time, it can span the duration of an infinitely large sound file. This is a definite advantage, and it can significantly affect the final size of your Flash movie.

One of the reasons that loops get a bad name is that they are too simple. The shorter the loop, the less it contains, and consequently, less musical contrast occurs within the looped phrase. Ultimately, this means that the loop sounds boring after a short listen because there is not as much music to hold your interest. Drum loops are probably the greatest offender in this case. This situation can be remedied, however: Simply use longer loops. The longer the loop sound file, the more you get to hear before it repeats itself. This helps make the loop less obvious and adds more contrast within the looped phrase.

You can take this technique a step further. Most loops tend to be broken into even chunks. Musically speaking, this means that the loops are in even bar or beat phrases: 4 beats, 8 beats, 2 bars, 4 bars, and so on. How you count the bars and beats is irrelevant. What is important, though, is that they are all *even*. The symmetrical structure makes it easy for your ears to organize the sound and detect the loop. The remedy is to create uneven loops: 7 beats, 3 bars, 5 bars, and so forth. Although this doesn't eliminate the loop altogether, it does help to mask the loop by placing the repeat point in an unexpected location within the musical phrase.

On the companion CD, open the file `loops.swf`, which is in the Chapter 22 folder. It contains buttons that loop the playback of three sound files: `oneBar`, `fourBar`, and `fiveBar`. Click the green Play buttons and listen to these files carefully. You should be able to hear a distinct difference in the looped quality of these. Note how the one-bar phrase has an immediately detectable loop, while the longer, four-bar phrase holds your interest and is harder to spot. At the extreme end of things, there is a five-bar looping phrase. Hopefully, you can hear how it is the least easy to identify as a loop. It still repeats, but with less frequency and in an uneven pattern.

Creating sound loops can be simple, but it requires some time and patience if you really want to do it well. To create loops, all you really need is a digital audio editor that supports looped playback of a sound file. Software currently available that will allow you to create loops from pre-recorded audio include Sound Forge and Audition for Windows computers, or Spark and Peak for the Mac. Most of these applications have a loop utility or feature that allows you to ensure a smooth loop that's free of clicks, pops, and other editing glitches. Additionally, on the Windows side, Sonic Foundry manufactures a program called Acid, which is used specifically for creating sound loops and loop-based music. Mac users can check out one of Apple's latest applications, Soundtrack. Like Acid, Soundtrack enables users to produce original music from pre-recorded loops and riffs. To learn more about working with these applications and preparing audio content for your Flash movie, see Chapter 28.

Inspirational Design Model

Nineteen Point Five Collective, at www.npfc.org, is a group of artists who focus their efforts on all forms of multimedia expression: sound, video, 3D imagery, and web/interactive media development. Their music is *transmedia*—it sounds at home whether heard on the Internet, in a multimedia application, or in a live-performance venue.

The NPFC website is designed entirely in Flash and does an excellent job of presenting the group's music in an accessible, easy-to-use fashion (see Figure 22.11). The digital audio waveform doubles as a progress bar for the current music track as it streams into the player. Note especially how their eclectic blend of musical sensibility meshes with the look and feel of their site to create a seamless, distinct impression of the group.

Figure 22.11

Nineteen Point Five Collective can be heard via Flash at www.npfc.org.

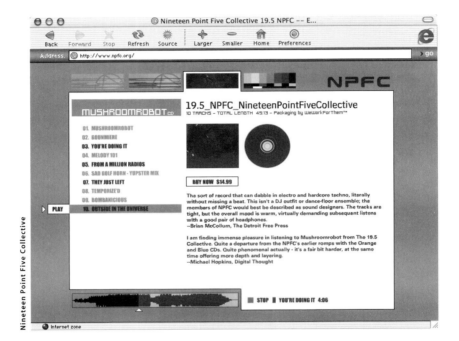

Nineteen Point Five Collective

CHAPTER 23

Flash Audio Basics

Audio elements such as music, sound effects, and narration can add greatly to the depth and interest of your Flash productions. Because sound is a unique, nonvisual medium, it can push your animations and interactive movies to a whole new level of creativity, expression, and fun. Now that you've read Chapter 22's general introduction to digital audio, you're ready to approach it specifically in the Flash environment.

As do most other interactive authoring applications, Flash has its own set of rules governing the way it handles audio. These rules are what you are about to learn. When approaching them, however, try not to think of them as rules, because *rules* carry a bad connotation. When you think of rules, it's too easy to focus on the limitations of what can and cannot be done. Think of this chapter's topic as a set of techniques that you must implement to work with audio in Flash.

More specifically, the rules are a set of techniques that can be mastered. And when you are completely comfortable with them, your potential is limited only by the ability to use the techniques creatively to achieve your goals. Not only can Flash be a tool for dynamic animations and interactivity, but you can use it to deliver great audio as well.

This chapter covers the following topics:

- **Bringing sounds into the Flash environment and implementing them in your movies**
- **Attaching sounds to buttons**
- **Controlling sound playback**
- **Using sound effects**
- **Understanding sound export options and compression**

Importing Sound Files

To begin using audio in the Flash environment, you must first get the audio files into your movie Library. You do this by importing a sound or sounds. Your computer's operating system determines what kinds of sounds you can import. In general, Flash can import WAV files with Windows, AIFF files with Macintosh, and MP3 files with both platforms.

For more details on all the sound file types that are available to Flash, see Chapter 21.

To import sound files in Flash:

1. Select File → Import to Library. The Import dialog box opens.

2. From the Show drop-down menu, choose the All Sound Formats option. This causes the Import dialog box to render anything that is not a sound file unavailable. This can make it easier to find the files you need. Locate the folder containing the file(s) you wish to import. If you need to select multiple files, use Shift+click (Mac) or Ctrl+click (Win).

> Sounds can be imported as a group (as discussed here) or individually, depending on your needs and work flow.

3. When you're finished selecting all your sound files, click Import to Library. All the selected files will be imported into your movie's Library. You can confirm this by checking the contents of the Library. Select Window → Library (F11) to display the Library panel. All the sounds you just imported should appear there with the speaker icon beside the filenames (see Figure 23.1). When a sound is selected in the Library, its waveform appears in the top of the Library window. You can audition the sound by pressing the Play button in the upper-right corner of the panel.

4. Once the sound files are in your movie's Library, they will be available for unlimited use within your movie. Sounds can also be part of Libraries that are shared among several movies. To read more about Shared Libraries, see Chapter 7.

Adding Sound to a Movie

Importing sounds is the first part of the process. Once you have sounds in your Library, you must then place them in the movie Timeline so that they become a part of a movie's playback. To add sounds to a Timeline, you use the Property Inspector (see Figure 23.2).

This multifaceted interface element is your window to many of the parameters affecting sound behavior in your movie.

To add a sound to your movie:

1. Create a new layer and name it something like **sound**. This isn't an essential step, but it can help keep individual sounds on their own separate layers in your movie. Each layer can be named with a title that describes the sound it contains (`introRiff`, for example). And it's easier to manipulate the positioning of sounds when they are independent of other movie elements.

Figure 23.1

The Library panel displays sound files with a speaker icon beside the filenames.

> Although Flash can play only eight sounds simultaneously, there is virtually no limit to the number of sound layers you can have in a movie. On a *very* basic level, this feature makes Flash behave like a multi-track audio application, where you can stack many sounds on top of one another.

2. Click the frame where you would like the sound to start playing and then select Insert → Timeline → Keyframe to insert a new keyframe.

3. Select Window → Properties (Cmd/Ctrl+F3) to display the Property Inspector.

   At this point, you should already have imported sounds into your movie. If you haven't, see the preceding section to learn how this is done.

4. Choose a sound from the Sound drop-down menu. The Property Inspector will display the attributes of the file you select: its sample rate, bit depth, length in seconds, and file size. The sound you select will be the sound that is cued when Flash plays the current selected keyframe.

5. If desired, select an option from the Effect drop-down menu. To learn more about Effect options, see the section "Working with Audio Effects" later in this chapter.

6. Select an option from the Sync drop-down menu:

   - In general, use Event for shorter sounds that you wish to be played in time with a visual event in your movie, for example, a "thud" sound of a cartoon character falling down. Event sounds will play in their entirety until they are stopped or the sound is over.

   - Use the Stream sync if you want Flash to force the movie animation to lock playback with a sound file. To learn more about the various sync modes in Flash, see Chapter 24.

Figure 23.2

The Property Inspector serves as the interface for sound control in your movie.

Unlike event sounds, stream sounds will play only through the number of frames they occupy in the Timeline. You must add extra frames to accommodate the length of a stream sound. Also, if you plan to use an MP3 file as a stream sound, you must recompress the file within Flash before publishing your movie. To learn more about this, see the section "Exporting and Compressing Audio Files" later in this chapter.

7. Select a repeat option for the sound. This is a new feature to Flash MX 2004 and MX Professional 2004. Previously, you had to enter a very high number if you wanted the sound to loop continuously. Now, you have a few more specific options:

   - Select Repeat and enter 1 in the adjacent field (or leave the field blank). This will play the sound only once.

   - Select Repeat and enter a number between 0 and 65,535 in the adjacent field. The sound will repeat the number of times that you specify.

   - Select Loop. The sound will repeat continuously until it is stopped at a different keyframe or silenced via ActionScript.

   When you are finished, you should have something that looks like Figure 23.3.

Stopping Sounds

Once a sound starts playing in Flash, there are few things to interrupt it. In most cases, a sound will continue to play until either it runs out of frames (if it is a stream sound), it is

Figure 23.3

Here the sound transition.aif is cued as an event sound with no effect and will be looped continuously.

finished, or it runs out of loops. These events depend largely on the length of the sound file and the parameters you assign the sound when it is first played in your movie. There are times, though, when it might be necessary for you to intervene and stop a sound or series of sounds explicitly.

To stop a specific sound from playing:

1. Click the frame in the sound layer where you would like to stop the sound.

2. Select Insert → Timeline → Keyframe to insert a new keyframe.

3. Select Window → Properties to display the Property Inspector if it is not already visible.

4. In the Sound drop-down menu, select the name of the sound file you want to stop playing. Choose the Stop option from the Sync drop-down menu. When the new keyframe is reached, the specified sound will stop playing.

To stop all sounds from playing:

1. Choose the frame where you want to stop the playback of every sound in your movie. It is also common to have a button that can be used to stop your movie's sounds.

2. Open the Actions panel and enter the following statement:

```
stopAllSounds();
```

   If you want to use a button to stop the sounds in your movie, write the following function:

```
sound_ctrl.onRelease=function(){
    stopAllSounds();
}
```

   This function is specific to the button instance `sound_ctrl`. You can replace that name with a button or Movie Clip instance name in your own projects.

3. Depending on where you attach this function, when the frame is played or the button clicked, every sound that is currently playing in your movie will stop. Playback cannot resume until each sound is explicitly started once again.

This technique of stopping all sounds is particularly useful if you need to stop several sound files simultaneously to sync with an animation, or to create a "sound off" button for your movie.

Attaching Sound to a Button

It is common to use sounds in conjunction with a button. In the same way that the various button states offer visual indications of interaction, sounds can help add to the interactive experience by offering audible feedback. For example, if you wanted to create a button that looked and sounded like the door to a haunted house, you could add the sound of a low "creeeeak!" to the button's Over state. Then you could use the sound of a rusty latch or doorknob for the Down state. Ultimately, both of these sounds would make the door button much more interesting (and scary) in the context of your movie.

Adding sound(s) to a button is a very simple and effective way to add some audio interest to your Flash production. Here's how you do it:

1. Import into your movie any sounds you need for the button. To learn how to do this, see the section "Importing Sound Files" earlier in this chapter.

Flash's built-in sound Library has a decent offering of general-purpose button sounds. Select Window → Other Panels → Common Libraries → Sounds to display this Library. Grab any of the sounds you find there and drag them into the Library panel for your movie.

2. Select the button on the Stage where you would like to attach the sound and choose Edit → Edit Symbols. Flash jumps into Symbol Editing mode for the button you selected. In this mode, you should be able to see the button's Timeline with the Up, Over, Down, and Hit keyframe states. To learn more about the various states of a button, see Chapter 15.

3. Insert a new layer in the button Timeline and name it **sounds**.

4. Click the Over state frame in the new layer and then select Insert → Timeline → Keyframe to insert a new keyframe.

5. Select Window → Properties to display the Property Inspector if it isn't already visible. In the same way that you added a sound to the main Timeline, you will add a sound to the button's Timeline (see Figure 23.4). Select a sound file from the panel's Sound drop-down menu. Assign any effect you want to use, and set the sync to Start. To learn more about Start sync and the other sound sync options, see Chapter 24.

6. Select Edit → Edit Document to return to the main Timeline. You can test the button sound in Movie Editing mode by selecting Control → Enable Simple Buttons. If you would like to test the sound in the context of the entire movie, select Control → Test Movie. Roll your mouse cursor over the button to hear the sound you just attached.

Figure 23.4

A button Timeline with a sound attached to the Over state keyframe

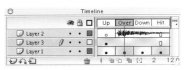

In the same way that you attached a sound to the Over state of a button, you can attach a sound the Down state. This helps to create a more realistic "click" effect. Simply follow the steps previously outlined in this section. Create a new keyframe for the Down state and attach the sound you wish to use. Because the two keyframes represent different button events, they will be cued separately—one when the cursor rolls over the button, and another when the button is clicked.

When working with button sounds, it is important that the waveform is trimmed so that there is no dead space at the start of the audio file. If your sound has dead space, there will be a lag between when the sound is cued and when you actually hear it.

Working with Audio Effects

One of the most overlooked aspects of audio production and design in interactive media is the use of audio effects. Audio effects are accomplished by altering the volume level and pan position of a sound's playback. Dramatic or even subtle changes of volume and position can add a new dimension to even the most ordinary sounds. You can use audio effects to give a sound a particular kind of character; for example, make it sound near or far, or make it sound as if it's moving from one side to another. Audio effects add depth to a sound by creating a sense of space and presence.

Using your audio editor, you can apply audio effects to a sound before you import it into the Flash environment. However, Flash allows you to set the audio effects for the sounds in your movies, and there are several advantages to this feature. First of all, effects are applied to a sound when it is placed in the Timeline, so each individual instance of a sound can have its own effect. This keeps you from having to import multiple versions of the same sound, each with a different effect. The other advantage of the Flash sound effects feature is that it helps minimize the file size for sounds that require pan effects. If you remember from Chapter 22, sounds that contain stereo information (left and right channels) require twice as much space in your movie's Library. But by using the Flash audio effects, you can apply panning to a mono sound and get the same results for half the number of audio file kilobytes. Not a bad deal!

Pan effects are best for mono sound effects. For example, if you wanted a "swoooosh!" sound to start in the left speaker and end in the right one, you could use a mono file and have Flash take care of panning it for you. The alternative would be to create the pan effect in your audio editor. While it would sound the same, the stereo "swoooosh!" sound would be twice as large because it would contain the stereo information for left and right speaker channels.

To apply audio effects to a sound in your movie Timeline:

1. Click the sound's starting keyframe and then select Window → Properties to display the Property Inspector if it isn't already visible.

2. The Property Inspector will show you the name of the sound, its sync setting, and the number of repetitions. There is also an Effect drop-down menu that contains several effects options:

   - **Left/Right Channel** plays the sound in only the left or right speaker.
   - **Fade Left to Right** and **Fade Right to Left** pan a sound from one speaker to the other over the duration of the sound file.
   - **Fade In** starts a sound at silence and gradually increases it to full volume.
   - **Fade Out** starts a sound at full volume and gradually decreases it to silence.
   - **Custom** opens the Edit Envelope dialog box, which can be used to create custom audio effects. To learn more about this, see the next section of this chapter.

If you apply effects to looped sounds, you might experience some inconsistencies in their playback. For instance, a Fade Left to Right effect will work for only the first iteration of the sound. All subsequent loops will play in the right channel because that is where this effect "leaves" the sound. To work around this, you can create a custom effect to control the entire looped sequence. You can learn more about this in the next section as well.

3. After you have applied an effect, select Control → Test Movie to listen to the effect in the context of your movie.

If your movie is a linear animation in the Timeline and doesn't require any special ActionScript to play properly, or if you are working with your sounds in a Movie Clip Timeline, you can listen to audio effects in Movie Editing mode. Select Control → Play (or press Return/Enter) to play the sounds in the Timeline.

Creating Custom Effects with Sound Envelopes

Depending on your audio design intentions, there are situations in which you will need to have precise control over the effects applied to a sound. This can be done by creating custom audio effects. Flash allows you to do this by manipulating the *envelope:* changes in volume over time. By creating different envelope combinations in the left and right channels, you can produce many different and interesting audio effects.

To create a custom audio effect:

1. Click the starting keyframe of the sound whose effect you want to edit and then select Window → Properties to display the Property Inspector if it isn't already visible.

2. In the Property Inspector, either choose Custom from the Effect drop-down menu or click the Edit button. The Edit Envelope dialog box opens (see Figure 23.5).

Figure 23.5

The Edit Envelope dialog box offers many options for changing various sound parameters to create an audio effect.

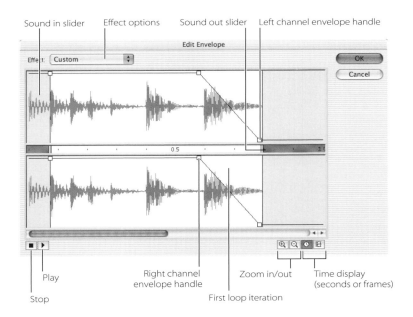

3. The most important thing to understand about this editing tool is that it is controlling the envelope (again, think volume) of each channel. Even if the sound is mono, you are still able to manipulate it to create stereo effects because it will be routed to both the left and right channels, as defined by the envelope edits you make. By changing the envelope of each channel, you put more or less of the sound in a particular channel.

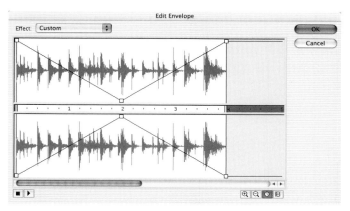

Click and drag the envelope handle for each channel to adjust the volume of the sound to be played in each channel. For example, to create an effect that pans from left to right and back again, click the left channel envelope line to create a new handle at the end of the sound's waveform.

4. Click in the middle of the envelope line to create another handle, and drag it to the bottom of the envelope. Do this for the right channel, but make it a mirror image of the left envelope (see Figure 23.6). This way, whatever is happening in one channel, the opposite will take place in the other. As the left channel's envelope fades, the right channel becomes louder, and vice versa. When opposite channels carry different amounts of the sound, a pan effect is created.

Figure 23.6

This envelope configuration will create a pan effect from left to right and then back again.

5. After you finish tweaking the envelope, click OK to return to the main Timeline.

The Edit Envelope dialog box has a few other features that can help you create effects and edit a sound:

- Use the Play and Stop buttons to audition an effect.

- Use the Zoom buttons to see more or less of the sound wave. This is helpful if you are trying to create very precise envelope changes.

- Use the Sound In or Sound Out slider to trim the beginning or end of a sound file. This can be useful for last-minute tweaks to button sounds.

- If you apply an effect to a looped sound, the subsequent loops will be displayed in a hazy, gray color. You can use the envelope handles to create effects for the remaining cycles of the sound loop.

- An envelope can have only seven handles per channel. If this is too limiting, you should consider using ActionScript to control volume and panning. See Chapter 25 for specifics on audio-related ActionScript.

Exporting and Compressing Audio Files

When you finish creating a Flash movie, you must go through the process of *publishing* your movie, or finalizing it for presentation to your audience. When you publish a Flash movie, all of your audio content is *exported,* and included in the final movie. When a sound is exported, it is often changed from its original format to something that is more manageable in a bandwidth-sensitive environment. Because audio can greatly add to the size of a movie file, the process of exporting sounds generally involves *compression.*

Compression comes in many different forms and is used to shrink, or compress, the final size of a sound file. Compression takes the original file and squeezes it down to a more portable, compact file that is easier to use in situations where file size is a crucial part of development. Sound great? Not always. Compression can have an adverse affect on sound files. In general, file size and sound quality are directly related. As you add more compression, the file size drops, but so does the sound quality.

As a sound file is compressed, certain parts of the sound (usually those deemed least important by the compression codec) are removed. Although this works to create a more compact sound, it also takes away certain elements of the original. The more this is done, the fewer original elements remain, which can leave you with a sound of very marginal quality. Don't be too discouraged, though. Flash offers several different compression and resampling options that allow you to strike a happy balance between file size and sound quality.

Adjusting Individual Export Settings

You have a great deal of control when it comes to exporting sounds in Flash. In general, it is best to use individual settings for each sound in your movie, for a couple of reasons.

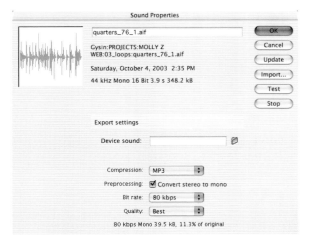

First, all sounds are different. Some sounds might sound fine at a low quality level or under high levels of compression. Second, sounds that are short or not as important in your movie can be squeezed down even further with high-compression, minimum-quality settings.

To set the export settings for a sound in your movie:

1. Select Window → Library to display the Library panel.

2. Highlight the sound name in the Library and then select Properties from the Options drop-down menu in the Library panel. Alternatively, you can double-click the sound's speaker icon. The Sound Properties dialog box opens.

3. If the sound has been changed outside of Flash since it was imported, click the Update button. This retrieves the most recent version of the file.

4. Choose an option from the Compression drop-down menu and select the settings you want to use. To learn more about your options, see the next section of this chapter.

5. Click the Test button to audition the sound and re-adjust the compression settings as needed. When you are finished, click OK to return to your movie. Each sound you adjust in this fashion will be exported with the settings you specify.

Selecting a Compression Option

Flash offers several compression choices, which are suited to different applications depending on your needs. When you select one of these from the Compression drop-down menu, its options (sample rate, bit depth, and so on) appear at the bottom of the Sound Properties dialog box. Note that as you change these options, the dialog box updates information about the size of the compressed sound.

Default Compression

To use the Default compression options, leave the menu selection as Default. This will apply whatever options are set in the Publish Settings dialog box to the sound. To check the publish settings for your movie, select File → Publish Settings (see Figure 23.7). Here you can set the compression options for both stream and event sounds in your movie.

> To learn more about the export settings in the Publish Settings dialog box, see their individual listings later in this section.

If the Override Sound Settings box is checked, Flash will export all sounds, regardless of their settings in the Library, with the parameters defined in the Publish Settings dialog box. This produces the same results as setting all sounds to Default compression in the Library.

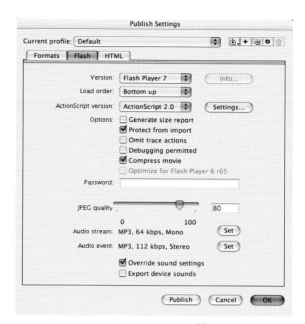

Figure 23.7

The Publish Settings dialog box enables you to define the default sound compression parameters for sounds in your movie.

ADPCM Compression

ADPCM, which stands for adaptive differential pulse-code modulation, is best for short sounds that can work well at lower quality settings.

To use ADPCM compression:

1. Select ADPCM from the Compression drop-down menu.

2. Check the Convert Stereo to Mono box if you want to mix your stereo sounds into a single channel.

3. Select a sample rate between 44kHz and 5kHz. In general, the higher the sample rate, the better the sound quality you can expect.

4. Select ADPCM bits between 5 and 2. Again, a higher number of bits equals better quality.

MP3 Compression

MP3 compression is very popular for distributing CD-quality or near-CD-quality audio in a compact digital format. MP3 compression is probably the best choice for music, some dialog, longer sound effects, and any kind of stream sync sound in your movie. It yields great results in terms of both final file size and sound quality.

To export with MP3 compression:

1. Select MP3 from the Compression drop-down menu.

2. Choose a bit rate between 160Kbps and 8Kbps (kilobits per second). You should get good results with MP3 settings at just about any quality; however, the general rule that higher settings equal better quality still applies. When in doubt, produce multiple versions and weigh the aesthetics of exported sound quality versus file size. Your ears should be the final judge. A setting of 56Kbps yields a happy medium between acceptable quality and manageable size; use 112Kbps or higher to achieve near-CD-quality sound.

3. If you select a bit rate of 20 or above, you have the option to mix stereo channels to a single mono channel by checking the Convert Stereo to Mono box. As expected, this will decrease file size by half.

4. Select a Quality setting:

   - **Fast** compresses files quickly but has the poorest quality. This option is not recommended for sounds that are predominant or significant in your movie.

   - **Medium** takes longer to compress but renders the files at a better quality than Fast.

- **Best** is your best choice for music or files where quality is important. Although it takes longer to compress the files, it renders the highest quality MP3s for your movie.

These quality settings have no effect on the final size of a compressed MP3 file.

Raw Compression

This option translates to no compression. Rather, the sound is either mixed to a single channel and/or sampled down to a lower sampling rate.

To use the Raw settings:

1. Select Raw from the Compression drop-down menu.

2. Check Convert Stereo to Mono if you want to mix your stereo sounds into a single channel.

3. Select a sample rate between 44kHz and 5kHz. In general, the higher the sample rate, the better the sound quality you can expect.

Speech Compression

The Speech compression option is designed specifically for spoken sounds. When used on narration and dialog, it produces decent-sounding results while maintaining a small file size.

To use Speech compression:

1. Select Speech from the Compression drop-down menu.

2. Select a sample rate between 44kHz and 5kHz. In general, the higher the sample rate, the better the sound quality you can expect. Be sure to test each sound before settling on a compression setting.

> Speech compression doesn't support stereo sounds. All sounds are automatically converted to mono.

QuickTime Compression Options

Flash allows you to publish your movie as a QuickTime Flash movie rather than Shockwave Flash. With this publish option, there are additional sound options that affect the quality of sound in the QuickTime movie. Note that the compression options presented here are available *only* if you plan to publish your movie as a QuickTime Flash movie.

QuickTime compression settings are applied only to the *streaming* sounds of a Flash movie published in QuickTime format. Event sounds will not be published with the Quick-Time settings. If you are using event sounds in your movie, use the Property Inspector and change their sync to Stream before publishing the final movie file.

When working with Flash movies that will be published as QuickTime, you have a good deal of flexibility in terms of what you can do with audio. There is no limit to the number of tracks, so feel free to use as much audio as you deem necessary. And, because QuickTime files are linear, all the sounds will be mixed to a single audio track (or a pair of tracks if you use stereo sounds).

To set QuickTime compression settings:

1. Select File → Publish Settings. In the Formats tab, check the box for QuickTime. A QuickTime tab is displayed; select it.

2. Check the box for Streaming Sound that reads "Use QuickTime Compression." This activates the Settings button.

3. Click the Settings button, and the Sound Settings dialog box opens. (There are several different dialog boxes that carry the name *Sound Settings*. In this step, the Sound Settings dialog box will affect QuickTime streaming sounds.)

Here you can choose from a variety of QuickTime sound settings, each of which has its own individual options. See Table 23.1 for a complete list. Because some compression schemes are better suited to certain tasks than others, try to find a codec that fits your specific needs. It might help to experiment with several different options and test them back to back on several systems before making a final compression decision.

Table 23.1	COMPRESSION CODEC	DESCRIPTION/APPLICATION
Compression Options	24-bit Integer, 32-bit Integer	Increases bit depth (sample size) to 24 and 32.
	32-bit Floating Point, 64-bit Floating Point	Increases bit depth (sample size) to 32 and 64. Most computers are incapable of playing sounds at this high bit depth and will convert back to 8- or 16-bit.
	ALaw 2:1	Poor-quality compression; not recommended.
	IMA 4:1	Decent compression ratios; must be 16-bit; fine for CD-ROM delivery.
	MACE 3:1, MACE 6:1	Dated codecs; not worth the trouble.
	Q Design Music 2	Superb compression ratios; great for streaming music.
	Qualcomm PureVoice	Superb compression ratios; preferred format for streamed dialog and narration.
	uLaw 2:1	Old codec; not worth the trouble.

4. After you have selected the right compression options, click OK in the Sound Settings dialog box, and then select the Flash tab in the Publish Settings dialog box.

5. It's necessary to disable Stream and Event sound options in the Flash tab when exporting a QuickTime Flash movie; otherwise, sounds are doubled in the final QuickTime file. Click the Set button next to the Audio Stream label. The Sound Settings dialog box opens again, this time for Flash streaming sounds.

6. Choose Disable from the Compression drop-down menu. This prevents extra streaming sound instances from getting into your final movie. Click OK.

   Repeat this process with the Set button beside the Audio Event label. This disables Event sound compression in your Flash movie. Click OK in the Publish Settings dialog box when you have finished. Even though the compression options in the Flash tab have been disabled, your movie's Stream sounds will be published with the settings you specified in the QuickTime tab.

Here's a time-saving tip: Some of the compression options in Flash (MP3 in particular) work slowly to compress the sounds in your movie. Publishing a movie with lots of sounds can take a *really* long time. This is fine for the final round of publishing, but when you're testing your movie, it can bring your development process to a screeching halt. One way to work around this is to *not* compress sounds while testing your movie. This way, there's no extra time involved and the sounds are added to the temporary SWF file as is. To do this, check the Override Sound Settings box. Then set the compression settings for Event and Stream sounds (as appropriate) to Raw. Deselect Convert Stereo to Mono, and set Sample Rate to match the sample rate of the sounds you imported. The sounds will still be added to your movie, but with no compression. This process is great during development, but be sure to compress when you publish your final version. Uncheck the Override Sound Settings box, and you're ready to publish a final file using the setting you specified for each individual sound.

Inspirational Design Model

Paul D. Miller, aka DJ Spooky That Subliminal Kid, is a New York City–based writer, musician, and conceptual artist. You can check out some of his recent work at the Museum of Contemporary Art website: `www.moca.org/museum/digital_gallery/pmiller` (see Figure 23.8).

Errata Erratum was created by DJ Spooky, with the technical assistance of Andrew Enoch. It features the rotoreliefs of Marcel Duchamp and allows you to "create your own 'remix' of sounds" by both artists. Use the interface to explore different combinations of grooves, musical textures, and animated imagery. You can find instructions for *Errata Erratum* and an essay by discussing the inspiration and motivation behind the work at `www.moca.org/museum/dg_detail.php?dgDetail=pmiller`. For more information about Paul D. Miller/DJ Spooky That Subliminal Kid, please visit `www.dj_spooky.com`.

Figure 23.8

Paul D. Miller, aka DJ Spooky That Subliminal Kid, is the creator of *Errata Erratum,* a Flash work of audio and visual elements prepared by DJ Spooky and Marcel Duchamp.

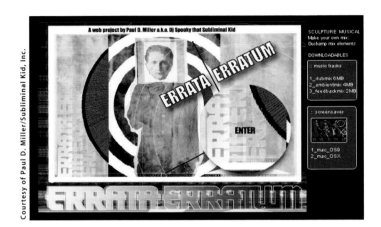

CHAPTER 24

Synchronizing Audio with Animations

When one thinks of animation, it is hard not to be reminded of the classic Warner Brothers cartoons starring Bugs Bunny, Daffy Duck, the Road Runner, Wile E. Coyote, Elmer Fudd, and Marvin the Martian. And, when you think about these animated cartoons, it's impossible not to remember all the crazy sounds that were so much a part of the show: anvils clanking on heads, *zips, swooshes,* and nimble violin strings plucking out the sound of a character's tiptoe entrance onto the screen. All these sounds were crucial to the success of the animation; they communicated the things left unsaid by the visual track.

As you know by now, Flash is much more than an animation program. It can be used to create interactive menu systems, games, websites, and more. Are these animations? No, not really, but in the Flash environment, you have to think about everything as if it were an animation. Flash's Timeline structure applies to just about every element of the program, including buttons, Movie Clips, and scenes; even graphics are affected by this structure because they are *used* in Timelines. Whatever your design goals might be, try to think of every project as a kind of animation.

As in the classic Warner Brothers cartoons, you will get more out of your Flash movies through the creative use of sound, and one of the keys to this is synchronization. This chapter discusses how Flash deals with sound in the context of animations, and how you can get the best results through synchronization of audio and visual events. The chapter covers these topics:

- Specifics of the Flash synchronization options: Event, Stream, Start, and Stop

- Lip-syncing and forcing the animation frame rate

- Creating complex animation and button sound events

- Syncing audio with Movie Clips

Synchronization Options in Flash

Any time you attach a sound to a frame in the Timeline, you must assign a sync option in the Property Inspector (see Figure 24.1). The *sync options* (short for *synchronization*)—Event, Stream, Start, and Stop—tell Flash how to play a sound when it is encountered in your movie. Synchronization determines the relationship between the sound (music, sound effects, dialog, and so on) and animated components of your movie.

In Flash, a sound can be made to play and loop independently of the animation in the Timeline, resulting in loose synchronization. Or you can have the sound lock the movie's frame rate to keep tight sync between audio and visual tracks. Flash also considers the act of stopping a sound to be a kind of sync, and will allow you to halt playback to match a visual event. Learning how these choices affect your movie is an important part of fine-tuning an animation and getting the most out of your movie's sounds.

Using Event Sync

Event sync is one of the most commonly used means of audio synchronization in Flash. Its name is fairly self-explanatory; this option creates a sound event by responding to an animation event in your movie. When Flash plays a frame that contains an event-synced sound, that sound is cued to play in its entirety, independently of the Timeline. If the Timeline stops playing frames, an event sound will continue to play until it has finished or has run out of loops. Think of an event sound as a kind of cue that you can attach to a Timeline frame.

Event sounds offer a lot of flexibility with your movie because all you have to do is set them in motion and let the sound take it from there. Because event sounds play independently of your animation, you don't have to worry about having enough frames to accommodate the length of the sound. These characteristics make event sounds ideally suited to various applications in a Flash movie:

Buttons *Button sounds* are usually attached to the Over and Down states of a button animation. When the mouse cursor is moused over a button, a sound is played; when the button is clicked, another sound is played. Because these button events (Over and Down) can happen quickly, it is important to use a sync option that will respond quickly. If a button is moused over or clicked more than once, the Event sync option will cue the sound each time and will mix multiple instances of the sound together. Consequently, this allows you to create interesting layered sound or musical effects with multiple button sounds. To learn more about the specifics of this technique, see the section "Working with Event Sound Effects and Music" later in this chapter.

Figure 24.1

The Property Inspector has a pop-up menu where you can assign the type of sync you wish to use for each sound. Here the sync option is set to Event.

If you are adding sound to a button and you specifically *don't* want sounds to layer and overlap, see the explanation of Start sync at the end of this section.

Sound effects If your movie calls for sound effects, the Event option is definitely the one to use. It allows you to perfectly sync an animation event, such as a basketball going through the hoop, with the sound *swish!!* Create a new keyframe with an event sound on one of your movie's sound layers. The frame should line up with the correct moment in the animation. When your movie plays back, you will see the ball go through the hoop and hear a gratifying *swish!!* to make the animation complete. To learn more about the specifics of this technique, see "Working with Event Sound Effects and Music" later in this chapter.

Stingers In film scoring, sudden musical stabs that are played to add dramatic punch are called *stingers.* For instance, a woman is peacefully sleeping in her bed when the French doors to her chamber mysteriously open…you hear nothing. Then suddenly, as the vampire's face appears, you hear a high violin tremolo, and the hairs on the back of your neck stand up straight! This device has been used for years to enhance the dramatic tension of cinematic and cartoon scenes. In the same way that you add sound effects, you can use the Event sync option to cue dramatic musical stingers in your movie.

Using Stream Sync

Stream sync is quite a bit different than the other sync options available to you in Flash. Stream sync locks the movie's frame rate to the playback of the sound and will skip (or "drop") frames if the

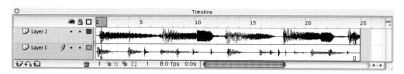

Figure 24.2

The top sound (Layer 2) does not have enough frames to play the entire file. You can tell because the waveform is cut off at the last frame. Notice that the bottom sound (Layer 1) *does* have enough frames. The waveform ends as a straight, horizontal line similar to what you would see in a digital audio editor.

animation cannot keep the pace. This option makes Flash more like a video-editing application, where the audio and video tracks are locked together to preserve their synchronization. The opposite of event sounds, stream sounds will play only if they have enough frames to accommodate their length. In many cases, you will have to add frames to enable long sounds to play completely. For an illustration of this, see Figure 24.2.

Due to the nature of the Stream sync option, we recommend that you avoid looping stream sounds if possible. Audio data cannot be reused as efficiently when sounds are set to stream. Flash will add unnecessary extra information to your final movie and create a larger SWF file. The Stream sync option does, however, have some excellent uses:

Scored music If you have long sections of music that are supposed to sync precisely with an animation, the Stream sync option is your best bet. The Stream audio will force Flash to maintain a consistent frame rate and keep tight synchronization between audio and animation events.

Lip sync To create tightly synchronized talking or singing animations, use Stream sync. It allows Flash to maintain a consistent pace and keep the dialog or music in sync with the mouth animation. To learn more about the specifics of this technique, see the section "Creating Lip Sync Animations" later in this chapter.

Multitrack audio All sync options in Flash allow you to play up to eight different sounds simultaneously. If you place each sound on its own layer, you can create a multitrack sound movie. Using the Stream sync option, it is possible to do this in a way that keeps all the tracks (individual sound layers) synchronized perfectly.

Using Start Sync

The *Start sync* option is very similar to Event sync. When the sound's frame is played, the Start option cues the sound and plays it in its entirety. The only difference is that if another instance of the sound is already playing, the new instance will not be heard. You can use Start sync as a kind of filter to prevent too many occurrences of a single sound.

Start sync is the best choice for buttons in situations where you do not want a button's sound to play more than once. For example, if you attach a sound to the button's Over state frame and use Event sync, the sound will be heard each time your mouse moves over the button. If the mouse crosses over the button frequently, this can cause too many simultaneous instances of the sound. Start sync prevents this because only one instance of the sound is allowed to play at a time.

For an example of Event sync versus Start sync with buttons, open the file button-Sync.swf in the Chapter 24 folder of this book's companion CD-ROM. Quickly move your mouse over the "Event" button several times. You will hear the sound repeated each time your mouse crosses over the button. (This particular sound is Visor Hum Loop from Window → Other Panels → Common Libraries → Sounds.) The more you do this, the more confusing things can start to sound. Next, do the same with the "Start" button. This time, no matter how often your mouse crosses over the button, you will hear only one instance of the sound. Start sync helps to keep your button sounds tidy.

Syncing Sounds to Stop

The final sync option Flash offers is Stop, and, as you probably guessed, this is what you use to silence a sound's playback. *Stop sync* is used specifically to silence sounds that were cued via Event or Start sync. To sync the end of a sound:

1. Insert a new keyframe where you would like the sound to end. The keyframe should be positioned so that the sound will stop in sync with an animation event.

2. Select Window → Properties to display the Property Inspector. From the Sound pop-up menu, choose the name of the sound you wish to stop from the Sound pop-up

menu and then select the Stop sync option. When the Timeline reaches this frame, the sound you have specified will stop.

The Stop sync option works for event and start sounds, but stream sounds must be handled differently. You must make the last frame of the stream sound exactly match the animation event. To stop a stream sound:

1. Find the animation event in the Timeline you wish to sync with the end of a stream sound. The event is usually represented by a keyframe. Remember the frame number where the event takes place.

2. Stream sounds will play only through the number of frames they occupy, so to stop a stream sound, you must determine the number of extra frames and clear them from the Timeline. Find the last frame of the stream sound you wish to stop.

3. Click the last frame of the stream sound, then Shift+click to extend your selection backwards to the frame *immediately following* the frame that contains the event where you want to stop the sound. For

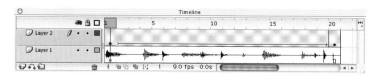

Figure 24.3

In this Timeline, the stream sound that starts at frame 1 is stopped to sync with an event in the animation at frame 20.

example, if you want to sync the sound to stop at keyframe 20, you would extend the selection to frame 21. Press Shift+F5 and the range of selected frames will disappear from the Timeline. The frames that remain should end at the same frame number as the event to which you synced the sound. The results in the Timeline should look something like Figure 24.3.

4. After you have cleared the unnecessary frames, select Control → Test Movie to see and hear how the sync works. You can add or subtract additional frames to the sound if the sync needs some tweaking.

Flash Synchronization Techniques

Now that you know how Flash handles animation/sound synchronization, you are ready to dig deeper into the subject and see how these techniques work in the context of your movie. As with many things in Flash, the techniques are simple; the real magic comes through your ability to use them creatively and move beyond the capabilities of the software. The examples presented here should not be seen as absolute answers, but as points of departure for your own wild and creative uses of sound synchronization.

Creating Lip Sync Animations

Many different options are available to you for creating lip sync animations. Depending on the kind of animation you wish to create, Flash allows you to animate with either loose, stylish synchronization or with lifelike accuracy, or with anything in between. A good lip sync animation can make animated characters come to life in your movie.

This technique uses the Stream sync option to force the animation to keep pace with the audio track. Another advantage of this option is that with stream sounds, you can *scrub* the audio track. When you scrub a track, you use the mouse to move the playback head over the audio waveform and hear what part is synchronized with a particular frame. Scrubbing allows you to test certain sections manually to see how the audio and animation line up.

To create a lip sync animation, it is assumed that you have drawn a character, recorded some dialog, and imported it into your movie. The only quirk to this technique is that your character's mouth has to be on its own layer. The reason is that when you animate a lip sync, you don't use just one mouth graphic. Rather, you use several mouth graphics that have different shapes representing the different mouth positions for the various words and letters in your character's language. The various mouth positions occupy their own keyframes on their own layer, and change to match the character's speech. The character's face and body can be left unchanged.

In this lesson, all of the media has been created for you. On this book's companion CD-ROM, open the file named lipSync.fla inside the Chapter 24 folder and save it to your hard drive. If you would like to see what you are getting yourself into, open lipSync.swf to see and hear the finished file.

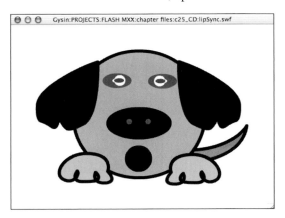

To create a lip sync animation:

1. Using the lipSync.fla file, insert two new layers; name one dialog and the other mouth.

2. Insert a new keyframe (select Insert → Timeline → Keyframe) in the second frame of the dialog layer. Select Window → Properties and choose woofwoofbark.aif from the Sound pop-up menu. Select the Stream sync option. You want to use stream so that the animation will be forced to keep pace with the audio and maintain a tight synchronization.

3. You are now ready to create the animation for the phrase "woof woof, bark." Notice that the waveform looks chunky in some places and flat in others. The dense, chunky areas are where the sound is loudest (see Figure 24.4). If you click the playback head and drag it across the Timeline (scrub the sound), you will hear the audio track play back slowly. This should give you an idea of what "words" fall on which frames in the Timeline.

Figure 24.4

The peaks of the audio waveform show you which places are the loudest, and the valleys represent the quiet sections.

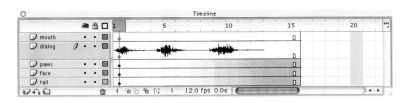

4   Select keyframe 1 of the mouth layer. Drag the closed graphic symbol from the Library to the Stage and place it where the mouth should be. This will start the mouth animation in a closed position. Use the Info panel (Cmd/Ctrl+Opt/Alt+I) to help position the different mouth graphics. Click the middle square marker in the Info panel's Symbol position option. This tells Flash to determine a symbol's X-Y coordinates from the vertical and horizontal center of the symbol.

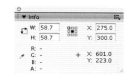

5. Create a blank keyframe (press F7) in frame 2 of the mouth layer and drag the W graphic symbol to the Stage, placing it where the mouth should be (roughly X = 275, Y = 300). To be sure your alignment is consistent, use either the Align panel or Info panel. The W graphic symbol creates a mouth position to say the letter *w* and starts the first part of your animation.

6. Create another blank keyframe in frame 3 of the mouth layer and drag the F graphic symbol to the Stage. Add another blank keyframe to frame 4 and drag the closed graphic symbol to the Stage. This completes the first word, "woof."

7. Continue adding blank keyframes and placing symbols on the Stage until the entire phrase is paired with mouth position graphics. It can be fun to experiment with this on your own, but if it becomes frustrating, you can refer to Table 24.1 for a listing of which symbols go in which frames.

8. When you have finished, select Control → Test Movie to hear and see what the dog has to say! This dialog is short, so the synchronization is not a great issue here. However, when you select the Stream sync option, you can start to work with longer lines of dialog, and the animation will keep the sync.

FRAME	GRAPHIC SYMBOL (MOUTH POSITION)
1	Closed
2	W
3	F
4	Closed
5	W
6	F
7, 8	Closed
9	B
10	A
11	K
12	Closed

Table 24.1

Frame and Graphic Symbol Combinations for the *lipSync.fla* Movie

Lip sync animation is a topic that can grow extremely complex. Although this simple example is just a glimpse of the big picture, all of the important concepts are addressed here. There are several additional steps you can take to become more proficient with this technique:

•   Keep a hand mirror with you when you work so that you can speak the words and watch the position of your mouth as you speak.

•   Don't lose sight of the entire phrase. Some letters and words don't always match with the mouth shapes you think they should.

- Use temporary gotoAndPlay() statements to isolate and loop specific parts where you need to focus on a word or words.

- Drawing good mouth shapes is critical! You can read about the art of drawing animation in *The Animator's Workbook* by Tony White (Watson-Guptill Publications, 1988) or *The Animation Book: A Complete Guide to Animated Filmmaking—From Flip-Books to Sound Cartoons to 3-D Animation* by Kit Laybourne (Three Rivers Press, 1998).

- See the following article at the Gamasutra website to learn about animation from artistic and scientific perspectives: `www.gamasutra.com/features/20000406/lander_01.htm`.

Working with Event Sound Effects and Music

Event sounds offer you the greatest amount of freedom and flexibility when cueing your sounds. As a result, it is also the loosest of all the sync options in Flash. This is not necessarily a bad thing. Even though "loose sync" might sound negative, there are actually times when it is especially useful.

Event sync is appropriately named because you pair the sound (music, effect, and so on) with an *event* in your movie or animation. When the visual event occurs, the sound is triggered. This is, of course, a very tight kind of sync, where both a visual event and a sound happen at exactly the same moment. However, after the initial sound cue, the sync becomes much less clear. Event sounds will play independently of the Timeline and continue to be heard until the entire sound has finished playing or has been stopped explicitly. For example, if you wanted to use the sound of a cymbal crash for a "falling down" animation, the cymbal would continue to ring long after the character's rear end hit the pavement.

Because Event sync sounds will continue to sustain depending on their specific length, you can achieve all sorts of interesting layering effects with multiple sounds in your movie. For example, if a waiter drops a tray full of dishes and glasses, you would hear not one *crash!* but a flurry of *cracks, shatters,* and *smashes!* Depending on how the scene is animated, you can pair a specific sound effect to each event where a bowl, plate, or glass hits the floor. All you need to do is create a separate sound layer for each effect you wish to use. Then, insert a new keyframe that lines up with the animated event you wish to sync, and attach a sound with the Event sync option. As the Timeline plays through the series of animated events, each sound will be cued at the appropriate time. See Figure 24.5 for an example of this in your movie's Timeline. Because each sound is left to play independently, each will continue to ring until the sound is over, creating a great, layered sound effect to enhance your animation. The advantage of this technique is this: Rather than have to create a long sound effect and guess when each element falls into place, you can build the entire effect in Flash and get much better synchronized results.

Figure 24.5

This Timeline shows how event sounds can be paired with animation keyframes to create a layered sound effect.

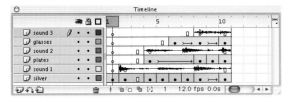

There are a few things to keep in mind when working with Event sound effects:

- Event sounds are heard when they are first encountered in the Timeline. To prevent latency, be sure that the sound is trimmed and has no dead space or silence at the start of the sound file. To learn more about trimming audio files, see Chapter 22.

- If you are layering several loud sounds, you might need to adjust their envelopes so that the sounds aren't distorted when played in your movie. To learn more about working with sound envelopes in Flash, see Chapter 23.

- Flash can play only eight sounds simultaneously. Look at your Timeline to see if there are any spots where eight different audio layers have active sounds at the same time. If you encounter this in your Timeline, try some re-adjustments to prevent too many overlaps.

- In the same way that this technique works for sound effects, it can also work for music, particularly sweeping flourishes, melismatic vocal cues, horn and guitar riffs, and so on. Experiment with this technique to see what kinds of interesting musical effects you can create with event sounds.

Syncing Audio with Movie Clips

Movie clips are one of the most important elements in any Flash movie. They can perform their own independent animations, apart from the activity taking place on the main Timeline. Consequently, Movie Clips can be a great asset to the synchronization of sound in your movies. In Chapter 19, you learned about the autonomy of Movie Clips. This is especially relevant when it comes to the playback control and synchronization of sound files. You can create Movie Clips that contain sound files attached to their various frames. Then, by targeting a clip, you are able to control the sound or sounds it holds in its frames. This technique takes you one step beyond playing sounds from your main Timeline and affords a great deal of audio playback control.

In this example, you will learn how to use Movie Clips to control sound playback. You can take a look at the finished files, which are in the Chapter 24 folder on this book's companion CD-ROM: audioMC.fla and audioMC.swf. To use Movie Clips to sync sounds, there are two steps you must take: create the sound Movie Clip and set up a means of controlling the clip.

To create a Movie Clip that can sync sounds:

1. If you have not done so already, import a sound into your movie. Then select Insert → New Symbol, assign the name **audio**, and check the Movie Clip radio button.

2. Click frame 2 of the audio Timeline and insert a new keyframe; then press F5 to insert an additional frame.

3. Create another new keyframe at frame 4 and add one new frame after it. Finally, add one last keyframe at frame 6. The finished frame construction should look like Figure 24.6.

4. Now that the clip has its basic structure, you can start to fill in its elements. Attach the following statement to keyframe 1:

```
stop();
```

This stops the clip from playing any farther in the Timeline; it is ready and waiting at frame 1.

5. Enter another ActionScript statement in keyframe 2:

```
stopAllSounds();
```

This will silence all sounds in the movie when this Timeline reaches frame 2.

6. Attach your sound to keyframe 4 and assign the Start sync option. Enter the number of repeats or set the sound to loop. Here you use the Start sync option so that if the sound is already playing, it will not be interrupted or overlapped.

7. Attach the following ActionScript statement to keyframe 6:

```
stop();
```

This line is an important part of the Movie Clip because it completes the "cycle" of statements contained in the clip. The clip cues the sound at frame 4; then, as it continues through the Timeline, it reaches the stop() statement at frame 6. The clip's playback halts, but the sound continues. Because the sound was cued with Start sync, it will play independently of any Timeline until it has either finished playing or exhausted its repetitions. If the sound was set to loop continuously, it will play until it is explicitly stopped.

Now that you have completed the Movie Clip, you can create a means to control it in your movie. There are many different ways to do this. Here you will learn both how to make the controls part of the clip itself and how to control the clip from the main Timeline.

To put controls in the clip itself:

1. If you are not already in Symbol Editing mode, select the audio Movie Clip from the Edit Symbols menu ⊞ or double-click the clip's icon in the Library.

2. Insert a new layer in the clip and drag a button onto its Stage. This will serve as your Play button. Attach the following ActionScript statements to the button:

```
on(release){
    this.gotoAndPlay(4);
}
```

These statements should make perfect sense: Because the sound file is cued at frame 4, you have to send the Movie Clip to play at frame 4 to start the sound.

3. Drag a new button to the Movie Clip's Stage once again to serve as your Stop button and attach the following statements:

```
on(release){
    this.gotoAndStop(2);
}
```

> The term this is not absolutely necessary in these examples. It is used to make an explicit reference to the current Timeline. A simple gotoAndPlay(4) or gotoAndStop(2) would work just as well.

This script sends the Movie Clip back to frame 2. When it gets there, it will encounter the stopAllSounds() function. This will halt the clip's playback at frame 2 and stop any currently active sounds in the movie.

Let's recap what is happening in the clip. When it is first loaded into the movie, it is stopped at frame 1 and no sound is heard (remember, the sound is at frame 4). When it receives a message to go to frame 4, the sound is cued and the clip is told to stop at frame 6. The sound continues to play independently of the Timeline. Then, when you wish to stop the sound, the Stop button sends the clip to halt at frame 2, where it encounters the stopAllSounds() function. This quiets the clip and prevents it from playing any further.

4. These statements complete the controls for your Movie Clip. Exit Symbol Editing mode and return to the main Timeline. Drag an instance of the audio Movie Clip to the Stage of the main Timeline. Select Control → Test Movie and experiment with switching the sound on and off.

It's great to be able to toggle the sounds on and off from the clip itself, but it's equally important to be able to control the clip from the main Timeline. To do this, you will need to target the clip specifically so that you can send it to play at the correct frames:

1. Give your audio Movie Clip the instance name **soundMC** in the Property Inspector. Then, drag two buttons to the Stage of the main Timeline (if there are no buttons in your movie's Library, you'll need to create some). Use one for Play, and the other for Stop.

2. Attach the following statements to the Play button:

```
on(release){
    soundMC.gotoAndPlay(4);
}
```

3. Attach the following statements to the Stop button:

```
on(release){
    soundMC.gotoAndStop(2);
}
```

Both sets of statements target the soundMC instance with an absolute target path.

4. Select Control → Test Movie. You should now be able to toggle the sound with both sets of buttons—those in the Movie Clip and those on the main Timeline.

When you control a clip from the main Timeline, it's not necessary to have buttons built into the clip itself. If you want, take the buttons out of the clip and leave it in your movie as a sound-only Movie Clip. A Movie Clip does not have to have graphics to work, only frames. In this case, the clip's frames are filled with nothing but actions, keyframes, and a sound cue.

There are a few additional features in the demo file for this exercise. Check out audioMC.fla in the Chapter 24 folder on this book's companion CD-ROM. Here, the Movie Clip Timeline has frame labels. The ActionScript that controls the audio playback uses these rather than frame numbers. This technique can be helpful if you have a hard time remembering what happens at which frame number. Additionally, the buttons on the main Timeline have their ActionScript assigned via Event Method Handlers. You may find this to be an easier way to keep all the sound-control code in a single location.

Inspirational Design Model

Looking for something to say that would have been really mean and nasty a few hundred years ago? Then pointeth thine browser, fair lads and lasses, to www.wraevn.com/insult. Here thoust can partaketh of Bill Shakespeare's Insult Factory of Fun (see Figure 24.7).

This time-killer was created by composer and sound designer Brandon E.B. Ward. It uses Flash to compose insults in Elizabethan English. After you write an insult on the "parchment," click Shakespeare's head to hear him speak the insult. Note the synchronization of animation and sound effects when the quill is writing. Visit at thine own risk, thou fawning, flap-mouthed puttock!

Figure 24.7

Bill Shakespeare's Insult Factory of Fun uses Flash to compose random insults in Old English.

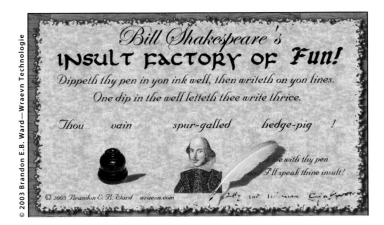

CHAPTER 25

Controlling Audio with ActionScript

Up to this point, your exposure to audio in the Flash environment has consisted mainly of sounds that are attached to your movie's Timeline and cued when their host frames are played. This technique works well for cueing music, sound effects, and dialog in such a way that they line up in sync with an animation. The only disadvantage to this approach is that all sounds are bound to frames, within either a Movie Clip or your main Timeline. As a result, if a Timeline has sounds you need but is not currently loaded, you are forced to call it to the Stage, adding an extra and often unwanted step to the process. Flash changes all of this with ActionScript.

When Flash evolved to version 5, it introduced the Sound object. The Sound object is an element of ActionScript that allows you to have complete control over every sound in your movie, whether the sound is in a Timeline or not. Flash MX has continued the tradition with terms that allow you to load external sounds, manage sound playback, and track sound-related events. The Sound object opens the possibilities for interactive audio in Flash, and allows you to change every sound parameter dynamically through scripting rather than with keyframes and sync options. This chapter will show you how to:

- **Create Sound objects**
- **Play and stop sounds with ActionScript commands**
- **Set and dynamically change a sound's volume**
- **Set and dynamically change a sound's pan position**
- **Apply stereo effects to sounds**
- **Use interactive controls to manipulate sound in your movies**
- **Load external MP3 sound files into a movie**

Working with the Sound Object

The Sound object is one of ActionScript's predefined objects. You use it to control the playback parameters of sounds in your movie. The Sound object allows you to play and stop sounds, set their volume level, and change their position and volume in the left and right speakers. The Sound object also makes it possible for you to monitor the volume, panning, and effects applied to a particular sound. To use this object, it's important to understand what it is and how it works as part of the ActionScript language.

Understanding the Sound Object

As do all objects in ActionScript, the Sound object holds information about various components of your movie. Just as the MovieClip object holds information about the properties of a particular clip, and the Math object stores specifics of arithmetic, this Sound object stores information about a movie's sounds and their properties. More specifically, it stores information as to whether a sound is currently playing and, if so, how loud, in what speaker(s), and so on. To monitor or control a sound via ActionScript, you must create a new Sound object. Once a sound has an object associated with it, the object allows you to pass information to and from the sound.

Objects can encapsulate the specific attributes of an element in your movie and allow you to control them. They also serve as a medium of exchange. In the exchange, you must have currency—something common that can be understood and used by both your movie and its objects. ActionScript refers to this kind of currency as *methods*. Methods are used to send and retrieve information between your movie and its objects. Every object has a particular set of methods that it implements. The Sound object has methods that check and set volume and panning, play (start), and stop active sounds in your movie. When you need to communicate with an object, you must use its methods.

Using the Sound Object

The first step toward working with the Sound object is knowing how to create a Sound object instance. Without it, you will have no means of communicating with a particular sound. When you create a new Sound object, it can be used to control:

- All sounds currently available in the Flash Player (all SWF files loaded in at various levels)
- All sounds currently available in the movie
- The sounds in a specified Movie Clip instance
- A sound you specifically attach to the object

Depending on how you create the object, you will be able to use it for any of these applications. The generic constructor for a Sound object is as follows:

```
soundObjectName=new Sound("targetInstance");
```

Here, soundObjectName is a placeholder for whatever you wish to call the object. *target-Instance* is an optional argument (enclosed in quotes) for the function. If you plan to control the sounds in a particular Movie Clip, you must target the clip specifically.

To create an object for every movie currently available in the Flash Player, no target argument is necessary. Use this constructor:

```
globalMovieSound=new Sound();
```

Here, *globalMovieSound* is the name of a new object to control the sounds on all Timelines.

To create an object for all sounds in a Movie Clip or on a specific Timeline, you must create the object and specify a target argument as a string (in quotes):

```
monkeyClipSound=new Sound("bananas");
loadedSound=new Sound("_level1");
```

In the first example, an object named monkeyClipSound is created to control the attributes of sounds in the Movie Clip named bananas. The second statement creates an object named loadedSound for all sounds on the Timeline of the movie loaded at _level1.

When a Sound object targets a sound in another Timeline, the object can be used only to control the volume and panning of the sound. Play and stop don't work because the sound is bound to the frames of the Timeline where it resides. However, Sound objects can control individual sounds that reside in a movie's Library. To facilitate this, you must attach the sound directly to the object. To learn how to do this, see the section "Attaching Sounds with Linkage Identifiers" later in this chapter.

Controlling Sound Playback

Creating a Sound object is an essential step to controlling your sounds dynamically with ActionScript. Without the object, you have no means of issuing commands to the sound. After you construct an object for a specific sound, you are free to invoke the methods of the Sound object to control their playback.

Controlling a sound via ActionScript offers several advantages over the conventional frame-based sound cues. First of all, if you want to cue only a particular sound, you don't have to target a Movie Clip or Timeline to play a specific frame. In many cases, the Sound object allows you to refer to a sound specifically, and you can cue it without having to play the frame where it resides in your movie. Conventional ActionScript has provisions for you to stop all sounds in your movie. In addition to providing this same stop feature, the Sound object allows you to start all the sounds in your movie with a single set of script commands.

The other advantage of controlling a sound through ActionScript is greater flexibility. Any element of your movie that uses scripting represents an opportunity to control sound playback. As graphic elements of your movie are dynamically manipulated or moved, you can echo these changes in your sound scripting.

Here are some of the Sound object methods used to control sound playback:

start(secondsOffset,loops) Used to cue sounds. start() can take two optional arguments. The *secondsOffset* argument can be used to start a sound from any point within the sound file. To start a 10-second sound at its halfway point, you would specify an offset of 5. The *loops* argument establishes the number of times a sound will play. If no loop is specified, the sound will play once (the default). To play it twice, enter a value of 2; enter 3 to play it three times, and so on.

> To cue a sound using the start() method of the Sound object, the sound must first be exported from the Library using the Linkage option. To learn more about this, see the section "Attaching Sounds with Linkage Identifiers" later in this chapter.

stop("soundID") Used to stop sounds. stop() will silence all sounds in the object that it is used to control. The optional argument *soundID* is used to stop sounds that were attached to the Sound object directly with symbol linkage.

To see specific examples using these methods, see the section "Playing and Stopping Sounds" later in this chapter.

Setting Volume and Pan Parameters Dynamically

Without the help of ActionScript and the Sound object, you are forced to cue sounds by placing them in frames of your main Timeline or a Movie Clip. The same is true for the parameters that affect a sound's volume and panning. To change this kind of information for a sound placed in a keyframe, you must use the Edit Envelope dialog box and drag the envelope handles into position (see Figure 25.1). Although this technique does give you a convenient graphical representation of the changes affecting a sound's envelope, the changes are permanent and cannot be altered after the movie is published. To make changes to an envelope effect, you have to go back to the keyframe where the sound is cued, open the Sound panel, and enter a new envelope shape.

ActionScript expands the possibilities tremendously by providing four methods for setting and monitoring the volume and pan parameters of a sound. And because this can all be accomplished via scripting, you have the potential to dynamically change volume and pan information at any time and from any location in your movie. Here are the methods:

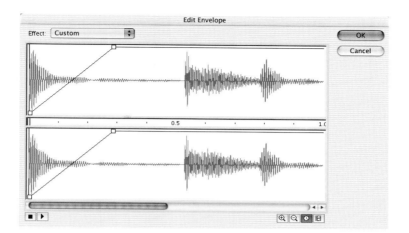

Figure 25.1

The Edit Envelope dialog box

setVolume(**volume**) Controls the volume of a sound's playback. Specify the argument *volume* between 0 (muted) and 100 (full volume). The default volume setting is 100.

getVolume() Monitors the volume of a Sound object. This method returns a value between 0 and 100, representing the current volume of the object.

setPan(**pan**) Sets the pan position for a Sound object. The argument *pan* determines where the sound is positioned. A value of 100 indicates that the sound is panned hard right (panned completely to the right speaker); –100 indicates that the sound is panned hard left (panned completely to the left speaker); and 0 indicates that the sound is centered (the default pan position). Once an object's panning has been set, it will remain in that position until it is changed.

getPan() Monitors the pan position of a Sound object. This method returns values ranging between –100 (hard left) and 100 (hard right), which represent the pan position of the object. The value 0 (the default) means that a sound is shared equally between the two speakers.

To see specific examples using these methods, see the section "Setting Volume and Pan Levels" later in this chapter.

Creating Special Stereo Effects

ActionScript provides a special Sound object method that allows you to create unique effects with stereo sounds in your movie; it is called setTransform(). While the effects it creates are similar to those accomplished with panning, there is a bit more to this method. You might remember from Chapter 22 that stereo sounds are sounds that have been mixed with different components in the left and right speaker channels. For instance, a barbershop quartet might have the bass and lead voices mixed more heavily in the left channel, while the baritone and tenor voices are mixed more to the right. If you were to listen to only one channel of a stereo mix, you would hear an incomplete rendition of the audio because it would be missing about half of its components.

The setTransform() method doesn't affect sounds directly. To use it, you must create a generic object that applies the transform information to the sound object you wish to alter. The generic object (call it a *transformer*) allows you control each channel of a stereo mix and assign output values for each as percentages. For each channel of stereo sound, the transformer object has two properties, one that controls a channel's left output, and one for the right. This gives you a total of four properties that can be used to alter the stereo composition of a sound. See Table 25.1 for a rundown of the generic object (transformer) properties.

Confused? Take a look at two examples of property settings to see how they would work in context. The following properties play a stereo sound as true stereo; all of the left information is played in the left speaker, and all right information is played in the right speaker:

```
ll = 100
lr = 0
rr = 100
rl = 0
```

These next property settings swap the left and right channel information to create a reverse stereo effect; all left information is played right, and all right information is played left:

```
ll = 0
lr = 100
rr = 0
rl = 100
```

Of course, by changing the values assigned to each property, you can create many different kinds of interesting stereo effects.

Once the properties have been stored in the generic transformer object, it is passed to the sound object via the setTransform() method. Here is a breakdown of the method's syntax:

***setTransform*(transformer)** Applies the properties stored in the *transformer* object to a sound object.

***getTransform*()** Retrieves the properties applied to a sound object in the last setTransform command.

For an example of using the setTransform() method and creating a generic transformer object, see setTransformer.fla in the Chapter 25 folder of this book's companion CD.

PROPERTY	VALUE	DESCRIPTION
ll	0–100	Percentage of left channel sound to play in the left speaker
lr	0–100	Percentage of right channel sound to play in the left speaker
rr	0–100	Percentage of right channel sound to play in the right speaker
rl	0–100	Percentage of left channel sound to play in the right speaker

Table 25.1

Properties for the `transformer` **Used with** `setTransform()`

Cueing Sounds with the Sound Object

The Sound object provides you with a great deal of flexibility in controlling sound playback. You will find that it offers substantial advantages over conventional frame-based sound cues because you can cue sounds at any time and manipulate their attributes dynamically. Now that you know what the Sound object is and how it works, you're ready to put it to use in the context of your Flash projects. This section shows you how to use the Sound object to export and attach a sound from your movie's Library and then cue it in your movie.

Attaching Sounds with Linkage Identifiers

One of the most useful functions of the Sound object is that it allows you to play sounds that are not directly inserted in a Timeline keyframe. However, before you can do this, you must attach the sound to the object you are using to cue the sound and control it. By attaching a sound, you are adding it to your movie while it is running. In some ways, this is the ActionScript equivalent of cueing a sound from a frame. The main difference is that when a sound is attached, it is done with ActionScript. Consequently, it can be paired with button clicks, keystrokes, and other types of user interaction.

To attach a sound to a Sound object, you must first export the sound from your movie's Library. Here are the steps:

1. In your movie's Library, highlight the name of the sound you wish to export.

2. In the Options pop-up menu, select Linkage. You can also Ctrl+click (Mac) or right-click (Win) and select Linkage from the context menu. The Linkage Properties dialog box opens (see Figure 25.2).

3. Check the button next to Export for ActionScript and give it a unique name in the Identifier box. The Identifier is the name you will use to attach the sound to a Sound object. In Figure 25.2, the exported sound will be attached to an object as `libSound`.

   Notice that the option labeled Export in First Frame is checked by default. This means that the sound will be

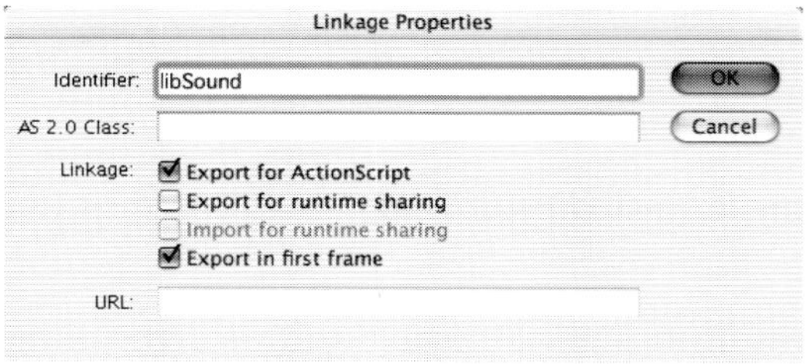

Figure 25.2

The Linkage Properties dialog box is used to export a sound from the Library so that it can be attached to a Sound object.

added to the first frame of your movie when it is loaded into the Flash Player. If you are using large audio files, this puts a heavy burden on the first frame, because the sounds and other elements in frame 1 must be loaded before any other content. Ultimately, this can result in a very long initial download that must take place *before* a preloader is encountered. To learn how this can be avoided, see "Adding the Audio Files" in Hands On 6.

4. Click OK when you are finished. The sound is now ready to be attached to a Sound object.

> The Linkage Properties dialog box is also used to include sounds as a Shared Library asset. Shared Libraries allow you to exchange common files between several different Flash movies. To learn more about creating and working with Shared Libraries, see Chapter 7.

After you export the sound from the Library, you are able to attach it to a Sound object. This step officially associates the sound with an object, which in turn can be used to control the various parameters of the sound's playback. An object can have only one sound attached at a time. Attaching a new sound to an object will replace any sounds the object previously contained. To attach a sound, you use the attachSound method, which has this syntax:

```
sndObj.attachSound("idName")
```

Here, *sndObj* is a placeholder for the name of the object to which you will attach the sound. The argument *idName* (a string, entered in quotes) is used to declare the name of the identifier associated with the exported sound you wish to attach.

The following example creates a new Sound object called movAudio and attaches the sound exported from the Library as libSound:

```
movAudio=new Sound();
movAudio.attachSound("libSound");
```

After completing these steps, any methods applied to the movAudio object will affect the playback of the sound file exported as libSound.

Playing and Stopping Sounds

Two of the most important methods of the Sound object are those used to play and silence sounds. After all, a sound has to be cued (or stopped and recued) before you can make any audible changes to its panning, volume, or stereo composition. To cue a sound from scratch:

1. Go through the steps of exporting the sound from the Library and assigning it an identifier. To learn more about this, see the preceding section.

2. Once you have exported the sound, you can add the following script statements to the script of a button, frame, or other movie element:

```
mySound=new Sound();
mySound.attachSound("bkgdLoop");
mySound.start(0,999);
```

This script example does three things:

- It creates a new Sound object named mySound.

- It attaches the sound exported as bkgdLoop to the object.

- It cues the sound from its beginning and loops it 999 times.

Assume for the moment that this object controls a sound that is 4 seconds long. To loop the sound 999 times from its halfway point, you would enter:

```
mySound.start(2,999);
```

This statement uses the *secondsOffset* argument to start the 4-second sound 2 seconds (or halfway) into the file. This becomes the new "beginning" of the audio file. Each new loop will start from this point.

Another variation on this would be to use a variable to set the number of loops for a particular sound. For example:

```
loop=4
mySound.start(0,loop);
```

In this example, the variable *loop* is initialized to 4 and will cause the mySound object to loop four times. However, because *loop* is a variable, you are able to manipulate its value with ActionScript in other portions of your movie. You can create some sort of interactive controller (slider, button, keystroke, and so on) that will increase or decrease the number of times a sound will loop when it is cued.

When playing sounds via the Sound object, you'll find that you can also exert a fair amount of control in stopping sounds. Consider the following statements:

```
addASound=new Sound();
addASound.attachSound("ambient");
addASound.start();
addASound.stop();
```

This script example does the following:

- It creates a new global Sound object named addASound.

- It attaches the linked sound ambient to the object.

- It cues the sound.

- It stops all sounds in the movie (because the object is global). If the addASound object were targeted to a specific level or Movie Clip, this final statement would stop only the sounds in that target clip.

The `stop()` method will also accept an argument in its parentheses; this argument is known as `soundID`. The argument is available so that you can silence a specific sound by referring to its symbol identifier. Consider the following examples:

These statements are on the main timeline:

```
sound1=new Sound();
sound1.attachSound("ambient");
sound1.start();
sound1.stop("ambient");
```

These statements are attached to a Movie Clip called `effect_mc`:

```
onClipEvent (load){
    sound2 = new Sound(this);
    sound2.attachSound("effect");
    sound2.start();
}
```

Here you see the same set of commands as before. The main difference is that the `stop` method uses an argument in its parentheses. In this case, even though `sound1` is a global Sound object, the only sound that will be stopped is `ambient`. Because `ambient` is an attached sound, and because it is stopped explicitly, it will cease to play. Other sounds, such as `effect`, will continue playing. If the line read

```
sound1.stop()
```

then all sounds would cease playing. If the line read

```
effect_mc.sound2.stop()
```

then `effect` would cease, but others would continue. This is because `sound2` was created on the `effect_mc` Movie Clip Timeline. Its sounds belong to (or are "scoped") to that Timeline because the Sound object was created using `this`.

Scripting to Control Volume and Panning

At this point, you have learned about the Sound object, how it is used, and how to cue sounds in your movie using ActionScript and the Sound object methods. The Sound object allows you to control all parameters of sound playback through scripting; this includes ActionScript techniques that can dynamically set the volume level and pan position of a sound in your movie. Using ActionScript to create different kinds of controllers or script calls, you are able to make changes to a movie's audio based on user interaction and various movie events. The best thing about this is that the changes can take place at runtime and be continually updated to match the interactive structure of your movie.

This section presents several key concepts that show you how to set volume and pan levels using ActionScript. Related to this, there are also techniques for creating audio fades and stereo effects. As are many of the examples presented in this book, these are *germ* ideas. The intention is that you grasp the basic concepts here and then take them to new heights in movies of your own. Dig in and, most of all, have fun! With the precise audio control that ActionScript adds to your movies, you will find an entirely new level of sound possibilities in Flash.

Setting Volume and Pan Levels

Volume and panning are two of the most important considerations when it comes to putting together an audio mix. By assigning each sound its proper level, you are able to create an ideal balance among all audio components of a movie: sound effects, music, dialog, and narration. Positioning a sound in the stereo field helps create an audio environment where each element has its own niche in the overall sound composition of your movie. With the help of ActionScript, this can all be done using a few simple lines of code that set the audio changes in motion.

When you manipulate volume and pan data in Flash, it is assumed that the sound you wish to affect is already playing. If a particular sound associated with the Sound object has not yet been cued, Flash will have nothing to control. However, once a sound *is* playing, you are free to use the methods of the Sound object to change its pan and volume attributes.

To set the volume level of a sound, you must use the setVolume() method. This method uses the dot operator to apply the volume information to the Sound object that you specify in your script. For example, to set the level of a sound to full volume, enter the following statement:

```
myObject.setVolume(100);
```

In this example, myObject is the name of the Sound object you will affect. This script example is often preceded by statements that create the Sound object myObject, attach a sound from the Library, and cue the sound using the start() method. Of course, these elements don't have to appear in the same script window as the setVolume() call, but they are usually executed in the movie before you can manipulate the sound's volume.

The setVolume() method can also be used to control a frame-based sound in your movie once it has started playing. Sounds attached to the frames of Movie Clips or to loaded SWF files can have their volume manipulated by the Sound object as well. Consider the following example:

```
loaded=new Sound("_level1");
loaded.setVolume(50);
```

In this script, a new Sound object named loaded is created for the sound(s) of the SWF file playing on level 1. The setVolume() method lowers the level of these sounds to 50 percent of their total volume. Using this same syntax, the method can also target the volume of sounds in Movie Clip instances:

```
sound3=new Sound("_root.intro.part2");
sound3.setVolume(80);
```

When you create a Sound object and enter the target path to a specific Movie Clip, the object can manipulate the volume (and pan) of any sounds that belong to its Timeline.

Controlling panning with ActionScript is very similar. The main difference is that the setPan() method takes both positive and negative numbers as arguments: −100 to pan hard left, and 100 to pan hard right. Consider the following script:

```
bass=new Sound("bass_mc");
bass.attachSound("fenderjazz");
guitar = new Sound("guitar_mc");
guitar.attachSound ("strat");
bass.start(0,100);
bass.setPan(-75);
guitar.start(0,50);
guitar.setPan(75);
```

This example cues two sounds after creating objects for each and attaching sound files from the Library. After each cue, the setPan() method is invoked to position each sound in an individual location: bass is panned mostly to the left, and guitar mostly to the right. I say *mostly* because each statement pans 75 percent of the sound to one speaker but leaves the remaining 25 percent in the opposite speaker. This pan configuration creates a fair amount of stereo separation for the sounds but still allows them to mingle and blend a bit.

> You can also use setPan() to manipulate the panning of sounds in a Movie Clip or loaded SWF file. Simply enter a target argument in the parentheses when you create the Sound object. Any methods that manipulate that Sound object will apply to the targeted Timeline.

When setting the pan position of sounds, there is no "golden rule" to follow. Your best bet is to use your ears and develop a scheme that sounds good and fits your sound design goals. Remember, to correctly hear the panned sound, you must have a two-speaker stereo setup for your computer. If you don't have access to a set of speakers, headphones are always a good way to hear the subtle details of an audio mix.

Scripting Volume Controls

Once you have mastered the basics of manipulating volume settings, it's possible to combine that knowledge with what you already know about ActionScript, and create controls for changing the volume of various sounds in a movie. In previous chapters of this book, you used ActionScript to control many different parameters of graphic elements in your movie. The only difference here is that rather than use ActionScript to change the visual properties of Movie Clips, you will use it with the Sound object methods to change the properties of audio playback.

You already know that the setVolume() method is the part of ActionScript used to create changes in audio level. Here you will incorporate that technique with a few basic statements inside a Movie Clip to create a simple, yet flexible and powerful, volume controller.

To get an idea of what you will be creating, open the volumePanner.swf file found in the Chapter 25 folder of this book's companion CD. Although this example doesn't cover the specifics of creating this movie's graphic component, you can take a look at the finished Timeline in the volumePanner.fla file to get an idea of how it was constructed.

To create a set of volume control buttons, follow these steps:

1. Prepare a couple of items before you begin working on this exercise:

   - First, you need a sound to control. Import a sound to your movie's Library and export the sound symbol using the Linkage Properties dialog box. To learn more about linking sounds, see the section "Attaching Sounds and Symbol Linkage" earlier in this chapter.

   - You also need at least one button to serve as part of your volume controller. One is sufficient because it can be used several times in the same Timeline. However, if you want to create two buttons, you can. To learn more about creating buttons, see Chapter 15.

2. After you've set up your sound and button in step 1, begin by selecting Insert → New Symbol. Name the symbol **volume** and select Movie Clip as its behavior. Click OK, and Flash jumps into Symbol Editing mode.

3. Rename the first layer **code** and press F7 six times to create six empty keyframes in the layer.

4. Click the first keyframe and press F9 to open the Actions panel. Enter the following statements:

```
cue=new Sound();
cue.attachSound("yourLinkedSound");
cue.start(0,100);
```

In this example, the reference yourLinkedSound is a placeholder based on whatever name you assigned to the sound you exported using Linkage Properties. Also, the name of the Sound object cue is arbitrary and can be changed if you want; just be sure to use the new name consistently throughout your scripts.

5. Click the second keyframe and display the Actions panel once again. Enter these statements:

```
cue.setVolume(100);
stop();
```

These statements set the initial volume and stop the playback head at frame 2.

6. In the remaining five keyframes, you will enter similar lines of ActionScript. See Table 25.2 for a listing of scripts and the keyframes they go in. When you've finished entering all the statements in their various frames, close the Actions panel and return to the `volume` Movie Clip Timeline. The role of these statements will be explained shortly.

7. Insert a new Layer and name it **buttons**. The frames in this layer should span all seven frames of the code layer. Grab a button from your movie's Library and drag it to the Stage of the `volume` Movie Clip. Drag another button to the Stage and position it near the first button. If you use different buttons, you don't need to change them once they're on the Stage. The buttons used in `volumePanner.fla` are identical, but one has been rotated 180° to help show which one raises the volume and which one lowers it.

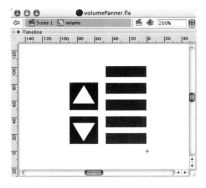

8. Click the button you wish to use as the "Lower Volume" button and open the Actions panel. Enter the following statements:

```
on(release){
    if(_currentframe<7){
        nextFrame();
    }
}
```

When this button is clicked, the script checks to see the position of the playback head in the Movie Clip. If it's at a frame number less than 7, the clip is told to advance a frame using the `nextFrame()` function. Your `volume` Movie Clip has seven frames. Once the clip is in frame 7, it doesn't advance if the button is clicked. Also, because the script uses `nextFrame()`, it advances the Timeline only one frame at a time. In the Timeline, each frame contains a statement that sets a new volume level. With each new frame, the clip stops and updates the volume level of the Sound object.

9. Click the button you wish to use as the "Raise Volume" button and open the Actions panel. Enter the following statements:

```
on(release){
    if(_currentframe>2){
        prevFrame();
    }
}
```

This button works similarly to the Lower Volume button. Each time the button is clicked, the script checks the current frame where the clip is stopped. If the frame is greater than 2, the playback head moves to the preceding frame number, or to the left across the Timeline. Because the `setVolume` statements increase in value from right to left, the Sound object volume gradually raises as the head moves closer to frame 2.

10. Close the Actions panel and return to your movie's main Timeline. Grab an instance of the `volume` Movie Clip and drag it from the Library to the Stage. At this point, you don't need to assign an instance name to the clip. Select Control → Test Movie to give this controller a spin. As you click the Lower Volume button, you should hear the sound level drop; conversely, the Raise Volume button should increase the volume of the sound.

KEYFRAME	ACTIONSCRIPT
3	`cue.setVolume(80);`
4	`cue.setVolume(60);`
5	`cue.setVolume(40);`
6	`cue.setVolume(20);`
7	`cue.setVolume(0);`

Table 25.2

Keyframe Statements for the Volume Movie Clip

Creating Audio Fade-Ins and Fade-Outs

What exactly is a *fade-in* or *fade-out*? It's an audio effect that gradually raises or lowers the volume of a sound to either ease it up to full volume or taper it off to silence. As you've probably already guessed, fade-ins and -outs require you to manipulate the volume of a sound as you did to create a volume controller. This is true, but with one exception: Fades are gradual effects; once you set them in motion, they happen slowly over time. To create a fade, you must design a Movie Clip structure that can gradually take a sound from one volume extreme to another in a single step, rather than with the individual mouse clicks you used to create volume controls.

Open the file `fadeInOut.swf` or `fadeInOut.fla` from the Chapter 25 folder on this book's companion CD. Play around with the fade-in and fade-out buttons to see and hear exactly what happens with a fade controller. The process of creating a fade is simple, and based on what you already know about volume controls, you should easily grasp the concepts behind a fade controller.

To create controls that fade a sound in and out, follow these steps:

1. Prepare a couple of items before you begin working on this exercise:

   - Here again, you need a sound to control. Import a sound to your movie's Library and export the sound symbol using the Linkage Properties dialog box. To learn more about linking sounds, see the section "Attaching Sounds with Linkage Identifiers" earlier in this chapter.

   - You need at least one button to serve as part of your fade controller. One is sufficient because it can be used several times in the same Timeline. However, if you want to create two buttons, you can. To learn more about creating buttons, see Chapter 15.

2. Begin by selecting Insert → New Symbol. Name the symbol **fader** and select Movie Clip as its behavior. Click OK, and Flash jumps into Symbol Editing mode.

3. Rename the first layer **code** and enter 13 empty keyframes in the layer (you should have a total of 14 in the entire clip). Click the first keyframe and press F9 to display the Actions panel. Enter the following statements:

```
cue=new Sound();
cue.attachSound("yourLinkedSound");
cue.start(0,100);
cue.setVolume(100);
```

In this example, the reference yourLinkedSound is a placeholder based on whatever name you assigned to the sound you exported using Linkage Properties. Also, the name of the Sound object cue is arbitrary and can be changed if you want; just be sure to use the new name consistently throughout your scripts.

4. Click the keyframe at frame 2 and enter a stop() function in the Actions panel. The remaining 12 keyframes will need fairly repetitive and similar statements. See Table 25.3 for a listing of each keyframe and its corresponding script.

This step completes your work for the fader Movie Clip. If you looked at the fadeInOut.fla file on the CD, you'll notice that there some graphic enhancements to the clip. These are optional and won't influence the functionality of the Movie Clip in your movie.

5. Close the Actions panel and switch back to Movie Editing mode and your main Timeline.

6. Drag the fader Movie Clip to your Stage and assign it the instance name fade in the Property Inspector.

As it appears on the CD, fadeInOut.swf has a simple graphic element that represents an LED volume meter. Add this option if you want. If you followed the preceding step, the clip won't have any sort of significant graphical representation—only a hollow circle to serve as a placeholder for the clip. The fade instance (as described in this lesson) is what you call a *sound-only Movie Clip*, meaning that the clip has sound(s), frame(s), and, in most cases, some ActionScript. Sound-only clips are ideal for holding and controlling audio. They can be targeted just as any other clip can; the only difference is that they don't have any kind of visual animated components.

7. Create a new layer in the main Timeline and name it **buttons**. Drag two buttons to this layer of the Stage to serve as your fade-in and fade-out controls. If necessary,

change one of the two buttons graphically so that it is distinguishable from the other. It should be clear which one will perform the fade-in and which one will perform the fade-out.

8. Select the fade-out button and open the Actions panel. Enter the following statements:

```
on(release){
    _root.fade.gotoAndPlay(3);
}
```

This script targets the clip instance `fade` when the button is clicked and sends it to play at frame 3. The clip is sent to frame 3 because this is the button used to fade a sound out. Frame 3 is the frame where the volume begins to decrease (see Table 25.3). Notice, however, that there is no `stop()` function until the clip reaches frame 8. Between frames 3 and 8, the `setVolume()` method gradually decreases the volume of the sound. Then, once it has been set to a level of 0, the clip is stopped.

9. Select the fade-in button and open the Actions panel. Enter the following statements:

```
on(release){
    _root.fade.gotoAndPlay(9);
}
```

KEYFRAME	ACTIONSCRIPT
3	cue.setVolume(80);
4	cue.setVolume(60);
5	cue.setVolume(40);
6	cue.setVolume(20);
7	cue.setVolume(0);
8	stop();
9	cue.setVolume(10);
10	cue.setVolume(20);
11	cue.setVolume(40);
12	cue.setVolume(60);
13	cue.setVolume(80);
14	cue.setVolume(100); gotoAndStop(2);

Table 25.3

Keyframe Statements for the Fader Movie Clip

This script targets the clip instance `fade` when the button is clicked and sends it to play at frame 9. The reason should be clear. At frame 9, the volume is set to a level of 10; at frame 10, a level of 20; and so on. When the volume finally reaches a level of 100 at frame 14, the clip is sent to frame 2 and told to stop. It will sit there until another button click executes a script that runs it through the fade-in or fade-out animation once again.

10. Select Control → Test Movie and give your fade controller a try.

After testing this Movie Clip, you might find that the fade is either too short or too long for your purposes. You can fix this easily because there are a couple of strategies for tweaking the length of a fade.

If your fade is too short, do one of the following:

- Create a longer animation. If you put a greater distance between the keyframes that set volume levels, it will take Flash longer to execute the animation.

- Adjust your volume levels in smaller increments. In this exercise, you adjusted the sound in increments of 20 percent. Adjusting the volume in chunks of 5 percent or 2 percent will create a longer, more gradual fade effect.

- Lower the frame rate of your movie. The more slowly a movie's frames are played, the slower the individual `setVolume()` scripts are executed. Realize, however, that this will affect the speed of animated elements in your movie.

If you wish to *shorten* a fade (that is, decrease its length), simply reverse either of the techniques for lengthening the fade.

Scripting Pan Controls

Another important element of audio control is *panning*. By placing sounds in the stereo field, you can create a sense of space in the "world" of your movie. Panning assigns a source location to ambient sound effects and allows you to balance the positioning of multiple music tracks. And with the help of some additional ActionScript, the Sound object can be used to create controllers that dynamically adjust the pan position of a particular sound.

The finished file described in this exercise is the same that you used if you worked with the volume control buttons. If you haven't yet seen and heard this movie, open the `volumePanner.swf` or `volumePanner.fla` file found in the Chapter 25 folder of this book's companion CD. In addition to the volume button controls, there is a slider that, when moved left or right, adjusts the panning of the movie's sound accordingly. This exercise assumes that you are already familiar with the basics of creating a slider type of controller. If you would like to learn more about this topic, see Chapter 20.

To create a stereo pan controller:

1. Prepare a couple of items before you begin working on this exercise:

   - You need a sound to control; for this exercise, either a mono or stereo sound will do. However, because you will be manipulating the pan position, a mono sound really makes the most sense. Import a sound to your movie's Library and export the sound symbol using the Linkage Properties dialog box. To learn more about linking sounds, see the section "Attaching Sounds with Linkage Identifiers" earlier in this chapter.

   - You will need one button to serve as the knob of your slider. To learn more about creating buttons, see Chapter 15.

2. You can begin with the sound elements of this movie. You will create a new Movie Clip that is a sound-only clip. It will have one purpose: to cue a sound to play in this movie.

3. Select Insert → New Symbol. Give the symbol a name and set its behavior to Movie Clip.

4. In this new Movie Clip, insert one empty keyframe in the first layer. In frame 1, enter the following statements:

```
cue=new Sound();
cue.attachSound("yourLinkedSound");
cue.start(0, 100);
```

If you are looking at the volumePanner.fla file found on this book's companion CD, the Sound object is created in the Movie Clip labeled *volume*, which has the instance name audio.

Again, "yourLinkedSound" is a placeholder for the sound you exported from your movie's Library.

5. In the second keyframe, attach a stop() function. This series of ActionScript commands creates a Sound object, attaches a sound from the Library, and plays the sound (all in frame 1). When the clip finishes executing these statements and moves to frame 2, the Movie Clip will stop, but the sound will continue to play.

6. Return to Movie Editing mode and drag the clip onto the Stage of the main Timeline.

7. Press Cmd/Crtl+F3 to open the Property Inspector and assign the instance name **audio** for the clip. This will allow you to target the clip so that you can control the panning of the Sound object you created in frame 1.

8. With a Sound object in place, you can create the pan controller. Select Insert → New Symbol. Name the symbol **slider** and select Movie Clip as its behavior. Click OK, and Flash jumps into Symbol Editing mode.

9. Drag the button to the Stage of the slider Movie Clip and use the Align panel to position it in the exact middle of the Stage. Click the button to be sure it's selected. Use the Property Inspector to give it the instance name **pan_button**.

10. Return to the Movie Clip's Timeline and rename the layer that contains the button **controller**. Then, add a new layer to the Timeline and name it **code**.

11. Select the first empty keyframe of the code layer and press F9 to open the Actions panel. Enter the following statements:

```
L=pan_button._x-50;
T=pan_button._y;
R=pan_button._x+50;
B=pan_button._y;
mid=pan_button._x;
```

These statements help define the bounds of the slider. With these variables in place, you can complete the code for the pan controller:

```
pan_button.onPress=function(){
    startDrag(this,false,L,T,R,B);
    dragging=true;
}
pan_button.onRelease=function(){
    stopDrag();
    dragging=false;
}
```

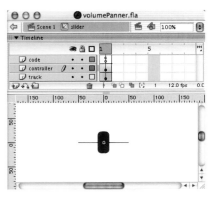

Figure 25.3

The pan slider button (inside the slider Movie Clip) should have its guide line positioned behind it with the centers aligned.

```
pan_button.onReleaseOutside=function(){
    stopDrag();
    dragging=false;
}
this.onMouseMove=function(){
    if (dragging){
        _root.audio.cue.setPan((pan_button._x-mid)*2);
        updateAfterEvent();
    }
}
```

These statements are nearly identical to those used in the slider example in Chapter 20. The main difference is the addition of the variable *mid*. If the clip is being dragged, it executes the following statement:

```
_root.audio.cue.setPan((pan_button._x-mid)*2);
```

This pans the sound in your movie. This line targets the sound using an absolute path from the main Timeline and uses the setPan method to control the sound's left or right speaker position. The expression ((pan_button._x-mid)*2) returns a value between −100 and 100 based on pan_button's current horizontal position. It subtracts the starting position (mid) from the current position (_x) and multiplies that by 2. Because the value for _x lies between −50 and 50, the expression always returns −100 to 100.

12. Now you are ready to assemble the final component of the slider controller. Create a new layer in the Timeline and name it **track**. Position this layer *below* the controller layer in the Movie clip Timeline.

13. Draw a horizontal line 100 pixels long on the track layer. (You can use the Property Inspector to confirm the length.) This guideline is the other graphic component of the slider. Position it so that it is directly behind the button (pan_button), making sure that the two elements have their centers aligned (see Figure 25.3). Pan information in Flash can have a maximum value of 100 and a minimum of −100. By using a line graphic that is 100 pixels long, it will always appear that the slider button is "locked" to the line because pan_button starts in the middle of the line and can move 50 pixels left or right. When the values in this range are multiplied by 2, the pan values are updated accurately.

14. Return to Movie Editing mode and drag the slider Movie Clip onto the Stage of the main Timeline. The pan slider is now complete! Select Control → Test Movie to give it a try. As the sound plays, you should be able to drag the slider left and right, affecting the position of the sound in your stereo speakers or headphones.

If you like using sliders to control audio parameters, see Hands On 6 to learn how to create a mixing board application that uses slider controls for both volume and pan.

Loading External Sounds with ActionScript

One of the most compelling audio-related features of Flash is its ability to load external MP3 sound files. Rather than include a sound or group of sounds in your movie, you may now leave them outside your movie and call them in as needed.

This approach presents several advantages. First, sounds always add to the size of your final SWF file. So keeping sounds outside the final movie allows it to be smaller and might help it load more quickly. Additionally, because using external files cuts down significantly on movie file size, you'll be able to use a Library of sounds from which your audience can pick and choose. If they want to browse your movie while listening to classical music, reggae, western swing, or whatever, you can give them a host of files to choose from and then load the appropriate soundtrack for each visitor. External sounds can be loaded into a Flash movie from any location on the Internet. This means it's also possible to use Flash to create a forum for MP3 playback. Your audience can share the URLs of sounds that they want you and others to hear, making your movie a sort of MP3 jukebox.

The list of other possibilities goes on and on. As always, Flash is limited only by your time, budget, and creativity. The capability to load external MP3 files was originally introduced with Flash MX, so your movie must be published for Flash Player 6 or higher to take advantage of it. The required ActionScript terms are as follows:

Sound.loadSound("url",stream) Used to load external MP3s into the specified Sound object. `loadSound()` takes two arguments. Enter the externalMP3's URL as a string, and enter a Boolean value for *stream*. A setting of `false` means that the sound must load entirely before it can begin playback; `true` makes the sound a streaming sound, and it will begin to play once a sufficient amount has been downloaded.

Sound.getBytesLoaded() Used to monitor the number of bytes in an external sound that have been loaded into the specified Sound object.

Sound.getBytesTotal() Returns the total number of bytes for the specified Sound object. You can use the methods `getBytesLoaded()` and `getBytesTotal()` to create preloaders for external sound files.

Now that you are familiar with some of the new Sound object terms, you can get down to business. To make the following introductory procedure as simple as possible, we have prepared a starter file for you on this book's companion CD. Go to the Chapter 25 folder and open the file loadMP3.fla; copy it to your computer's desktop. Several additional steps have already been completed so that you can focus on the most important aspects of this technique.

To load an external sound, follow these steps:

1. First, you must have a remote MP3 file that you can load. We recommend that you start with a small file so that while you're testing this procedure, you don't waste time waiting for a large file to load. Upload an MP3 file to your web server and write down the file's URL.

> If you don't have a web server or an MP3 file to use, we've provided one for you. Use the following URL to link to the file savvySound.mp3: http://www.vonflashenstein.com/resources/savvySound.mp3.

2. In the loadMP3.fla file, select the first (and only) keyframe of Layer 1. Press F9 to open the Actions panel. You'll see something that resembles Figure 25.4.

3. In line 2, notice the phrase "enterYourURLHere." Replace that phrase with the absolute URL of the MP3 file that you want to load into your movie. An absolute URL is written as http://www.myDomain.com/file.mp3, where *myDomain.com* is the name of your domain and *file.mp3* is the name of your MP3 file.

Line 1 creates the Sound object loaded. Line 2 uses the loadSound() method to load the external file that you just specified. false, an argument to loadSound(), determines that the loaded sound will behave like an event sound and must be completely loaded into memory before it can begin its playback.

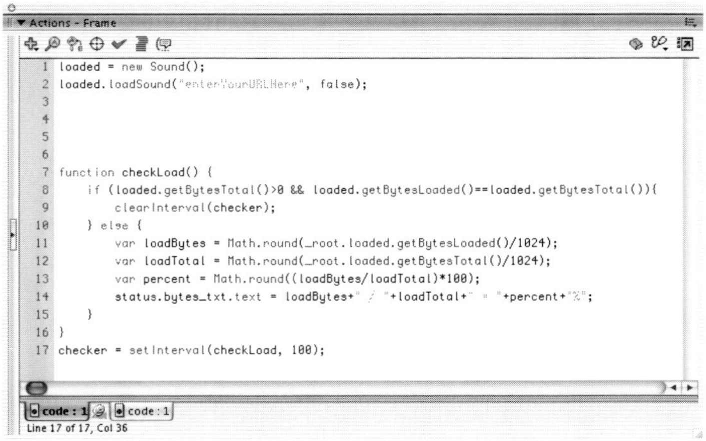

Figure 25.4

The ActionScript for the first keyframe of the loadMP3.fla file. You'll enter the URL for your external sound within the quotes of the load-Sound statement.

```
   1  loaded = new Sound();
   2  loaded.loadSound("enterYourURLHere", false);
   3
   4
   5
   6
   7  function checkLoad() {
   8      if (loaded.getBytesTotal()>0 && loaded.getBytesLoaded()==loaded.getBytesTotal()){
   9          clearInterval(checker);
  10      } else {
  11          var loadBytes = Math.round(_root.loaded.getBytesLoaded()/1024);
  12          var loadTotal = Math.round(_root.loaded.getBytesTotal()/1024);
  13          var percent = Math.round((loadBytes/loadTotal)*100);
  14          status.bytes_txt.text = loadBytes+" / "+loadTotal+" = "+percent+"%";
  15      }
  16  }
  17  checker = setInterval(checkLoad, 100);
```

Line 17 of 17, Col 36

4. You'll notice that lines 3–6 are blank. This is where you write a function that cues the sound once it has loaded. Enter the following statements starting at line 3:

```
loaded.onLoad=function(){
    loaded.start(0, 100);
    status.gotoAndStop(7);
}
```

When the Sound object `loaded` has completely loaded into the Flash player, its `onLoad` event occurs. This event executes the statements within the function: The sound is cued using `start()`, and a Movie Clip named `status` is skipped to frame 7 of its timeline. If you look at the Timeline of the status clip (see Figure 25.5), you can see that in frames 1–6, it plays through an animation loop. This animation loops while the external MP3 is loading. Once the sound has loaded, it's sent to frame 7, where the animation stops.

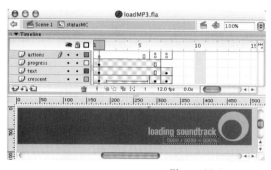

Figure 25.5

The Timeline of the status **Movie Clip instance has an animation loop that plays while the MP3 is loading.**

5. There is a good deal of ActionScript in frame 1 that you don't have to write. Let's examine this script line by line:

Line 7 This creates a custom function named `checkLoad()`.

Line 8 This conditional statement checks the status of the sound while it's loading. It tests two things: whether the total byte count of the sound is greater than 0 and whether the bytes that have been loaded are equal to the total number of bytes. Only when both these statements are True (when the file has completely loaded) will the script execute line 9. Otherwise, when False, it skips ahead to lines 11–14.

It's good to check whether Sound.getBytesTotal() is greater than 0. This helps prevent a sound that's slow to load from jumping the gun. If the sound hasn't loaded at all, it contains 0 bytes. Because it has loaded 0 bytes and contains 0 bytes, the statement 0==0 will obviously return True, and Flash will think that the sound has loaded completely.

Lines 11–14 If the sound hasn't loaded completely into `loader`, a series of alternative statements will execute to show the load progress:

loadBytes is a variable storing the number of loaded bytes.

loadTotal is a variable storing the number of total bytes.

percent stores the percentage of the sound that has loaded.

bytes_txt is a text field in the `status` clip instance. Its contents are set to an expression that shows the number of loaded bytes over the number of total bytes and what percentage of the total sound this represents. This information is concatenated as a string and plugged into the text field.

Lines 11 and 12 use the `Math.round()` method to round the byte count to the nearest integer. Values are divided by 1,024 to give the kilobyte count.

Line 17 This line is probably the most important in the entire script sequence because it is responsible for calling the `checkLoad()` function. It creates the interval `checker` using the `setInterval()` function. This interval calls the `checkLoad()` function every 100 milliseconds. This means that, every one-tenth of a second, `checkLoad()` monitors the download progress of the MP3 and updates the movie accordingly.

Line 9 This statement falls within the block of code that executes when the MP3 has loaded completely. It uses the `clearInterval()` function to cancel the `checker` interval and stop monitoring the download progress of the MP3.

6. Select Control → Test Movie to give the loaded sound a try. As the sound is loading, the gold crescent spins, and the text field prints a numeric display of the loading sound's progress. Once the sound has finished loading, the spinning graphic stops, and the text in the Movie Clip changes to read "Welcome to the site."

If your movie doesn't work properly right away, here are a few things to check:

• Be sure you are connected to the Internet.

• Check the speed of your connection. A busy network will slow the loading process.

• Be certain that your URL to the external sound is correct.

This section has given you just a glimpse of the possibilities offered by external sounds. To learn about additional ActionScript terms that can enhance your movies and their ability to work with external sounds, see the "Sound Object" section of the ActionScript Reference on this book's companion CD.

Inspirational Design Model

Creating a truly interactive audio experience is a very difficult thing to do, not so much from a technical angle but from a point of communication. The designer's greatest task is deciding how to make the sound interactive while ensuring that it still works synergistically with the movie's graphic components.

Illustrator Molly Z's website (`www.mollyz.biz`) is an example of a site where imagery and sound come together to make a complete statement (see Figure 25.6). Each section has a unique color and design scheme. As visitors move from one content area to the next, the visual changes are complemented by variations in the audio: A triangle is added to the mix, a talking drum is removed, descending chords play on piano, and so on. Every musical transition and phrase is locked to an interactive event. When the audience clicks and moves to a new section, they hear as well as see the effects of their choice.

Figure 25.6

`www.mollyz.biz` **is a Flash-based website that makes extensive use of interactive audio.**

Creating a Mixing-Board Application

If you've ever spent time in a recording studio, radio station, or video-production facility, you've probably seen a mixing board. And if you were lucky, you had a chance to play with the mixer's faders and knobs and hear how the changes you made affected the overall sound. What was this experience like? Exhilarating, to be sure. It can be a real rush to move the controls around and change the mix of a song or soundtrack. You imagine yourself in the producer's seat at the recording session for your favorite band. It's fun to be in control and hear how the changes you make are reflected in the music.

By leveraging the power of ActionScript, you can bring this same experience to the visitors and audience of your Flash-based website. In this lesson, you will learn how to create a mixing board using ActionScript, sound files, and a few simple graphics. The steps involved are simple, but the concepts presented here are very important. This lesson will teach you about:

Sound object scope Learn how the Sound object can be used to control individual sounds and sounds on separate Timelines.

Attached sounds and download time By attaching sounds from the Library, you gain a lot of flexibility in controlling individual sound playback. Here you will learn how to work with these kinds of sounds and get them to load quickly in the Flash Player.

These concepts were addressed in Chapters 22–25. Here you will see them presented in a more specific context. The techniques can be applied in a variety of situations. Once these ideas have been mastered, you will find a way to make them work in Flash creations of your own.

 If you would like to see the final mixing board in action, navigate to the Hands On 6 folder of this book's companion CD and open `mixer.swf`. There you can manipulate the faders that control the pan and volume of a four-track drum groove. To see the source for this file, open `mixer.fla`. This is what your file will look like when you complete this lesson.

To begin the lesson, you will need the "starter" file, `mixer_ho6.fla`, which is also in the Hands On 6 folder. It has several components of the mixer in place and allows you to focus on the more important aspects of creating the mixer. Copy `mixer_ho6.fla` to your hard drive, open it with Flash MX 2004 or MX Professional 2004, and you're ready to go.

Phase 1: Creating a Channel Strip Movie Clip

A mixing board consists of several *channel strips*. In audio engineering lingo, a channel strip (as you might have guessed) represents one channel or track of audio. It controls one component of the mix while other channel strips in the mixing board control others. When you create the mixing board in Flash, each channel strip is a Movie Clip. This makes it easy to add extra channels to the mixer: When you need another channel, you simply drag another channel-strip clip instance to the Stage.

To create the channel-strip Movie Clip:

1. The file `mixer_ho6.fla` should be open. Press Cmd/Ctrl+**L** (or F11) to open the Library, press F9 to open the Actions panel, and press Cmd/Ctrl+F3 to open the Property Inspector. You will need these throughout the lesson, so it's good to make them available early on.

2. Double-click the `channel_strip` Movie clip icon in the Library. This opens the clip in Symbol Editing mode. Click the knobs layer to select it, and drag an instance of the `v_knob` Movie Clip to the Stage.

3. Use the Property Inspector to position the clip at X-Y coordinates (23, 206). This is the object you'll use to manipulate volume. Use the Property Inspector to give it the instance name **vol_knob**.

> If the Movie Clip doesn't line up correctly, you can fix its position with the Info panel. Open the Info panel (Cmd/Ctrl+**I**) and click the small square in the upper-left corner of the Symbol position marker. This sets Flash to track the position of Symbols from their upper-left corner rather than their center. This is the default setting. If you had to change it in the past, you'll need to reset the option for this lesson.

4. Now you can add a controller to manipulate the channel's panning. Drag an instance of the `h_knob` Movie Clip to the Stage. Use the Property Inspector to position the clip at X-Y coordinates (39, 53.5).

5. The code that controls the volume and mute is in the first keyframe of the `v_knob` and `h_knob` Movie Clips. You can double-click each clip to open it in Symbol Editing mode and see its script. The ActionScript is almost identical to that which was covered in Chapter 25. There is one small difference. The ActionScript in frame 1 of the `v_knob` Movie Clip is as follows:

```
this.onMouseMove=function(){
    if (dragging&&_parent.mute==false){
        _parent.channel.setVolume(B-vol_button._y);
    }
    updateAfterEvent();
}
```

There is an additional condition that must be met to change the volume. According to these statements, the clip must be in the process of dragging *and* a variable called *mute* must be `false`. The logical AND operator (`&&`) stipulates that both conditions must be met for the enclosed statements to execute. `dragging` is set when the clip is clicked. `mute` is a variable that will be created and discussed later in the lesson.

Figure H6.1

The mute button is used to silence the audio controlled by the channel. It shows each channel's current playing status. Click it to toggle the sound off or on. There's also a label for each channel beside the mute button.

6. One feature that is part of every mixing board is a mute button. It allows you to mute (silence) the audio track that is controlled by the channel strip. The mute button for this mixer also includes a label (see Figure H6.1) so that you know the name of the channel you mute when you press it. In the Library, double-click the `mute_button_label` Movie Clip icon to open the clip in Symbol Editing mode.

7. The text that will serve as the label for each channel will be added later via ActionScript. To facilitate this, the text field inside the mute button needs to have an instance name. Click the text field to select it, and assign the instance name **name** in the Property Inspector.

8. Select frame 1 of the code layer and enter the following statements in the Actions panel:

```
stop();
play_btn.onRelease=function(){
    nextFrame();
}
```

9. Select frame 2 of the code layer and enter these statements in the Actions panel:

```
_parent.channel.setVolume(0);
_parent.mute=true;
stop_btn.onRelease=function(){
    nextFrame();
}
```

10. Select frame 3 of the code layer and enter these final statements in the Actions panel:

```
_parent.channel.setVolume(_parent.vol_knob.B -
    ➡ _parent.vol_knob.vol_button._y);
_parent.mute=false;
play_btn.onRelease=function(){
    prevFrame();
}
```

Each frame has a different set of ActionScript commands, and each is responsible for managing the mute functionality of the mixing board:

• Frame 1 stops the clip to keep it from advancing into the other frames. It also assigns a function to the mute button (`play_btn`) that advances it one frame (to frame 2).

- Frame 2 sets the volume of the Sound object channel to 0, silencing it. It also updates the variable *mute* to true; this tells the host Movie Clip the sound is muted. Note that when the clip is in frame 2, the mute button changes appearance. This is to visually reinforce that the button was pressed.

  - Frame 3 un-mutes the channel. The volume of the Sound object channel is reset. This script evaluates the position of the vol_knob instance and uses this value to set the channel's volume when the mute is turned off. The *mute* variable is updated again to reflect that the mute is off. The button functions in frames 2 and 3 will send the Timeline back and forth. When it reaches frame 2, the sound is muted; when it is sent to frame 3, the volume is turned on again.

At this point, you might ask why you need to have a variable that monitors when a sound is muted and when it isn't. The reason is this: If someone pressed a channel's mute button and then moved the volume slider, the slider's script would overrule the mute and you would hear the channel at the volume level set by the slider. This bug creates unwanted results in the mixer because it is impossible to mute a channel, change the channel's volume, then un-mute it later and be able to hear the new volume level. To work around this, you use the *mute* variable. By tracking when a channel is muted and when it isn't, you can prevent the slider from changing the volume when a channel should be muted. This condition is checked in the code described in step 4.

11. With the code for all three keyframes in place, you can finalize this portion of the channel strip. Double-click the channel_strip Movie clip icon in the Library. This opens the clip in Symbol Editing mode.

12. Click the mute label layer to select it, and drag an instance of the mute_button_label Movie Clip to the Stage.

Figure H6.2

The channel_strip **clip in its final form**

13. Use the Property Inspector to position the clip at X-Y coordinates (6, 12). Use the Property Inspector to give it the instance name **title**. The finished channel_strip Movie Clip should look like Figure H6.2.

Phase 2: Adding the Audio Files

Phase 1 was the hard part and offered little reward: Nothing is working yet! Don't worry, we'll get there. Let's move on to some easier and more fruitful aspects of this lesson. To add the audio files:

1. Because we're such good guys, we've included audio files that you can use for this lesson. If you want to use these, skip ahead to step 2.

   You might prefer to use sounds of your own. If that's the case, you'll need to import four audio files. To make them work in this context, the clips need to have the same tempo so that they can be heard together and make musical sense. To review the steps involved in importing sounds, see Chapter 23.

2. Each sound needs to have a Linkage ID so that it can be exported from the Library and cued via ActionScript when the mixing board is loaded. In the Library, there is a Sounds folder. Inside this folder there are four WAV files: imbira.wav, log.wav, shak.wav, and yang.wav. Ctrl+click (Mac) or right-click (Win) on imbira.wav and select Linkage from the context menu. The Linkage Properties dialog box opens.

3. Check the Export For Actionscript box and uncheck the Export In First Frame box. In the Identifier field, enter **imbira** (see Figure H6.3). Click OK.

Figure H6.3

The option to export in first frame is left unchecked. This allows the non-audio portions of the movie to load first.

4. Repeat steps 2 and 3 for the remaining three sounds and set identifiers as follows: **log**, **shak**, and **yang**. If you're using your own audio files, write down the identifier names so that you can refer to them later.

   When the Export In First Frame box is checked, the sounds are added to frame 1 of your movie and loaded into the Flash Player along with everything else in frame 1. This doesn't add to the download time of a movie, but it prevents your audience from seeing anything in frame 1 until all the sounds have loaded. If you use a lot of sounds, the wait can be considerable before your audience sees or hears something. When this happens, it looks as if your movie doesn't work. One way to overcome this delay is to deselect the Export In First Frame option. However, when you do this, the sounds will not be loaded into your movie at all. You have to incorporate the sounds manually so that they are available when you need them. We'll do this next.

5. Select Edit → Edit Document to return to the Main Timeline. Press Cmd/Ctrl+F8 to create a new symbol. Give it the name **linkage_sounds**, select Movie Clip as its Behavior, and click OK.

6. Flash jumps into Symbol Editing mode. Add four new layers to the Timeline of the linkage_sounds Movie Clip. Name the top layer **code**. Name the remaining four layers as follows: **imbira**, **log**, **shak**, and **yang**.

Figure H6.4

The linkage_sounds Movie Clip Timeline has five layers. Layers imbira–yang require two keyframes.

7. Click frame 2 of the **imbira** layer, then hold down Shift and click frame 2 of the **yang** layer. Press F7 to convert these frames to blank keyframes. The Timeline should look like Figure H6.4.

8. Select the first keyframe of the code layer. Enter the following statement in the Actions panel:

```
stop();
```

9. Select the second keyframe of the imbira layer. Use the Property Inspector to attach the sound imbira.wav to this keyframe. Do the same for the remaining three keyframes and attach log.wav, shak.wav, and yang.wav to the second keyframe of the layer with the same name.

10. For each sound, use the Property Inspector to set the Sync option to Event.

11. Press Cmd/Ctrl+**E** to return to the Main Timeline. Click to select the linkage IDs layer. Drag an instance of the linkage_sounds Movie Clip to the Stage.

Now that the steps involving this clip are complete, we can discuss what it does. Its purpose goes back to the fact that the sounds in the Library were marked to *not* export in the first frame. Because they will not be automatically added to your movie, they have to be included through another means. This Movie Clip does that. The first keyframe has a stop() function, so frame 2 (the frame that holds the sounds) is never reached. However, because frame 2 is part of a Movie Clip Timeline and that clip has been placed on the Stage, the sounds will be loaded into the Flash Player as part of the linkage_sounds Movie Clip. This accomplishes the same task as exporting the sounds in the first frame, it's just done in a different order, which allows the elements in frame 1 to load more quickly.

Phase 3: Finalizing the Mixer with ActionScript

You've done it! All the elements are prepared and it's time to put the finishing touches on your audio mixer. To complete the project:

1. Click to select the channels layer. Drag an instance of the channel_strip Movie Clip to the stage. Position it at X-Y coordinates (0, 0).

2. Drag another instance of the clip and put it at (100, 0). Because the clip is 100 pixels wide, the clips will appear side by side.

3. The movie is 400 pixels wide, which leaves room for three additional clip instances. Position the third at (200, 0), the fourth at (300, 0), and the fifth at (400, 0). The five clips should fill the entire stage.

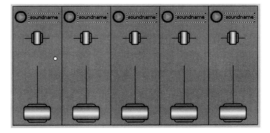

4. The channel_strip instances need to have instance names. From left to right, use the Property Inspector and assign the instance names **one**, **two**, **three**, **four**, and **master**.

5. The final steps of this lesson include adding the ActionScript that will pair a sound with each channel strip. Select instance one and enter the following statements in the Actions panel.

> Don't enter the line numbers into the Actions panel; they are included here only so that you can easily follow the line-by-line explanation.

```
1. onClipEvent(load){
2.    title.name.text="imbira";
3.    channel = new Sound(this);
4.    channel.attachSound("imbira");
5.    channel.setPan(0);
6.    channel.setVolume(0);
7.    channel.start(0,9999);
8.    mute = false;
9. }
```

The code works as follows:

- Line 1 uses the handler onClipEvent() to execute these statements as the clip is loaded onto the Stage.

- Line 2 assigns the name *imbira* to the text field name inside the mute button clip instance (title).

- Line 3 creates a Sound object named channel. This object belongs to, or is "scoped to," the current Timeline. When you use onClipEvent(load), the current Timeline is the Movie Clip where this script is attached.

- Line 4 attaches the sound with the Linkage ID imbira to the object.

- Lines 5–6 set the volume and pan of the sound to 0. This reflects the positions of the volume and pan sliders for each channel.

- Line 7 cues the sound and repeats it 9,999 times.

- Line 8 initializes the *mute* variable to false because the sounds are not muted when the channel strip is loaded. This variable is used to monitor the status of each channel's mute button.

6. Click the text box area of the Actions panel. Select (Cmd/Ctrl+**A**) and copy (Cmd/Ctrl+**C**) these statements.

7. Select the second channel strip (instance two), click the text box area of the Actions panel, and paste (Cmd/Ctrl+**V**) the code you copied from the other instance. For every occurrence of the word *imbira*, substitute the word **log**.

8. Repeat the process described in steps 6 and 7 and replace the word *log* with **shak** for instance three.

9. Do steps 6 and 7 one last time for instance four and replace *shak* with **yang**. You should now have ActionScript statements attached to each channel_strip instance. When each instance loads, it should specify a label for the channel, create a Sound object, attach a sound to it, set pan and volume, and cue the sound.

> In line 2, for instances three and four, you can enter the name label text as *shakere* (instance three) and *yangtze* (instance four). These are the real names of the instruments, which were shortened to accommodate the names of the WAV files.

One thing that might seem strange is that with all four instances, each has an identically named Sound object (channel). At first glance, you might think that this would create conflicts between the various Sound objects in the movie. Up to this point, we've been fairly insistent that all objects and variables have unique names. The reason you can get away with identical names here lies in the way you created each Sound object. When you created the objects, you stated:

```
channel=new Sound (this);
```

By specifying the parameter this, you are telling Flash that the Sound object belongs to (or is "scoped to") the current Timeline. It will therefore control all the sounds that reside on that Timeline. Your mixing-board application recognizes the channel object belonging to instance one as distinctly different from the channel objects that belongs to instances two, three, and four. Though they all have the same names, they belong to different Timelines. This difference of scope maintains their individuality and renders each instance of channel_strip and each channel Sound object contained within as unique. Because each channel strip is treated as an individual instance that contains its own objects, Flash will allow you to have many instances of the channel_strip clip. The only limitation is that up to eight sounds can play simultaneously: one for each channel of audio supported by the Flash Player.

10. Every mixing board also includes a channel known as the Master Fader. This is the master volume control that sets the overall volume output of the mixer. The fifth channel_strip instance will serve as your master fader. Select the master instance and enter the following statements in the Actions panel:

```
onClipEvent(load){
    title.name.text="master";
    channel=new Sound();
    channel.setVolume(0);
    mute=false;
}
```

These statements are nearly identical to those attached to the other channels; however, there is one very important difference. Notice the line that creates the Sound object; it reads `channel=new Sound()`. The parentheses in the Sound object constructor function are empty. This creates a global Sound object, meaning a Sound object that controls *all* the sounds in the *entire* movie. Before, your sound objects were scoped to the Timeline where they were created using `this` inside the parentheses. The empty parentheses give this object reign over every sound in the mixer. No matter what the volume or pan of an individual channel strip, this new master channel strip (Master Fader) will set the overall volume of the mix.

11. The mixing-board application is finally complete. Save your movie and select Control → Test Movie to hear how it works. First move the master fader up so that you have an overall volume level.

12. Move the volume knobs up and down to hear changes of volume, and move the pan sliders left-to-right to hear changes in pan position.

13. Click the mute button to silence a track, then click mute again to bring the track back to its original volume. Mute also works on the master fader to silence the entire mix.

> Flash does a great job of maintaining the synchronization of the audio files. Even with eight sounds playing simultaneously, Flash is able to keep their rhythms locked together.

Phase 4: Moving On—Next Steps and Ideas for the Future

There are so many things that you could do with this mixing-board application. As mentioned earlier, Flash supports up to eight simultaneous sounds, so feel free to add up to four more channels and fill up the components of your mix.

Because Flash does such a good job of maintaining sync with the sound files, this movie could be used as part of a live performance with a DJ, solo performer, or larger ensemble (see Figure H6.5). To do this, we recommend that you publish your mixer as a stand-alone Flash projector. To learn more about stand-alone files, see Chapter 32.

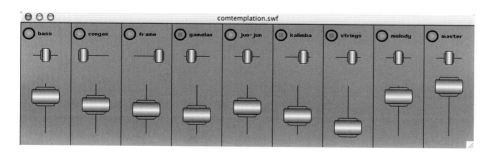

Figure H6.5

This version of the mixer was produced for a live performance. It required eight separate channels for a composition entitled "Contemplation."

PART VII

Integrating Flash with Other Programs

Great *bodies of work—art, music, literature, drama, and so on—are not created in a bubble. It's impossible to accomplish creative goals without some kind of outside input, and creating in Flash is certainly no exception. Up to this point in the book, you have read, studied, and practiced many different aspects of creative work you can do with Flash. Sometimes, however, it's important to step away and consider the bigger picture. Flash is an excellent and versatile application, yes. But it cannot do it all.*

Depending on your creative goals, it's likely that you won't be able to do everything you want to do or dream of doing in Flash alone. The good news is that, as one of the more versatile applications available today, Flash shares common ground with plenty of other kinds of software. Not only can you bring your Flash creations into other authoring environments, but you can bring many foreign file types and media into Flash. This part explores the relationships between Flash and other digital media applications.

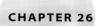

CHAPTER 26

Working with Flash and Director

In spite of the fact that Flash is a great multimedia authoring application, there are times when it might not be able to deliver all the functionality that you require. Even with the flexibility and speed of vector art and animation, and the interactive possibilities offered by ActionScript, neither Flash nor any other application, for that matter, can do it all. *Multimedia* by nature and definition is an enormous vein of expression; it embraces the synergy of various forms and makes them one. When your projects are open to this kind of crossover, you will find an entirely new realm of possibilities to satisfy your goals, whether they be rooted in art, entertainment, business, learning, or another form of communication.

Whereas Flash is uniquely suited for fast delivery on the Internet and in other bandwidth-conscious applications, Macromedia Director shines in the realm of CD and DVD-ROM development, as well as in the creation of Shockwave content for the Web. There is no doubt that Director is the multimedia authoring tool of choice for projects that are large in scope and require many different kinds of media. Director allows you to work with 2D bitmap graphics, 2D vector graphics, digital video, sound, true 3D graphics (introduced in Director 8.5), and most important to this discussion, Flash SWF files. In this chapter, you will learn how Director and Flash can be used together to create interactive movies that possess the best characteristics of each application. The chapter covers these topics:

- **Getting Flash movies into a Director movie**
- **The characteristics of Flash in the Director environment**
- **How Flash movies function as sprites**
- **Communicating with Director via ActionScript**
- **Communicating with Flash via Lingo**

Working with Flash in the Director Environment

Flash movies are supported in Director with the help of the Flash Asset Xtra. Currently, Director MX ships with a Flash Asset Xtra that supports the functionality of Flash Player 6. At the time of this writing, Macromedia had not introduced a new Flash Asset Xtra to support the expanded functionality of Flash MX 2004 and the Flash 7 Player. Until Macromedia releases an updated version of the Flash Asset Xtra, any Flash movies that you wish to run within Director should be targeted to the capabilities of Flash 6. Older versions of Director might support Flash, but often with limitations as to which versions. Table 26.1 provides a guide to Flash and Director version compatibility.

Table 26.1

Director/Flash Asset Xtra Compatibility

FLASH PLAYER VERSION	DIRECTOR VERSION
7 (Flash MX 2004/Flash MX Pro 2004) and earlier	Unknown at time of publication
6 (Flash MX) and earlier	MX (9.0)
5 and earlier	8.5
4 and earlier	8.0, 7.02
3 and earlier	7.0
2	6.5, 6.02

> Movies created in Flash MX 2004 and MX Pro 2004 can always be saved to a lower version if you don't have a version of Director that supports them. To learn how to do this, see Chapter 30. To read the most up-to-date information concerning Flash and Director version compatibility, see www.macromedia.com/support/director/programs_fl.html.

With the help of Lingo, Director's native scripting language, you are able to manipulate many of the parameters that control the playback of a Flash movie while it is contained in a Director movie. There are several advantages that this scheme can offer to your multimedia projects:

Graphics flexibility Director deals primarily with bitmap graphics. As a result, if any stretching or scaling of graphics is required in your movie, Director will probably not be able to do this very well (the graphics will be stretched into gigantic chunky blobs). Vector graphics change this because they can be scaled without losing resolution. Although vector graphics can be created in Director, the vector drawing tool it offers isn't nearly as sophisticated as those found in Flash. Flash is championed as an animation application, but it's also great for creating still images such as titles, credits, and interface elements. If you need to stretch or scale an image or object in Director, use Flash to create it.

Expanded control over animated elements Although Lingo gives you a great deal of control over the elements of a Director movie, there are some tasks that Flash can make easier, simply because of the way the application works. In Flash, the Movie Clip is an essential part of any Flash production. As an independent Timeline, a Movie Clip can maintain animated autonomy and keep an agenda that's separate from other elements of a Flash movie. In Director, this works largely to your advantage. Use Flash to create an SWF marionette, where each of the puppet's limbs is a separate Movie Clip. Then, in Director, you can use Lingo to target each clip individually to make your marionette perform a variety of animated routines. To read more about this technique, see the section "Manipulating Flash Sprites with Lingo" later in this chapter.

Best of both scripting worlds Where Flash has ActionScript, Director has Lingo. Chances are, if you know either of these languages or JavaScript, you have a good footing for picking up the one you don't currently know. Although ActionScript is much closer to JavaScript than Lingo, Lingo has changed over the years and adopted a dot syntax that makes it more like the other languages. When working with both Flash and Director, you can use ActionScript to control elements in Director, and Lingo to control elements of a Flash movie.

Clearly there are many advantages, many of which are bound only by your creative ingenuity for solving problems and combining or layering your work. Director can be used to create something as simple as a gallery of your favorite SWF creations, or something as complicated as a massive multiplayer world where users can create their own characters and interact with other members of the online community. The first step to any of this involves getting Flash into the Director environment and understanding how it behaves once it's there.

Importing Flash Movies

To incorporate Flash movies in your Director projects, you must first bring the Flash file into the Director authoring environment. Similar to Flash, this process is called *importing*. Once a file has been imported into Director, it is stored in the *cast,* and is ready to be used in the Director movie.

Director? Cast? Wait a second… Yes, you see a pattern emerging here. Macromedia uses the analogy of a theater or film production to describe the elements of the software. It is done very well too, and makes learning the software a little easier. Any media elements that can be used in the movie are stored in the cast and called *cast members,* just like actresses and actors sitting in the wings of a theater (this is like the Library in Flash). As you probably guessed, all action in the movie takes place on the *Stage*.

Taking the analogy a step further (and closer to opera), the window that manages the placement of cast members on the Stage is called the *Score*. As soon as a cast member is placed in the Score, it is referred to as a *sprite*. The Score has horizontal rows for sprites (called *channels*), and vertical columns for frames. (This is similar to the Flash Timeline,

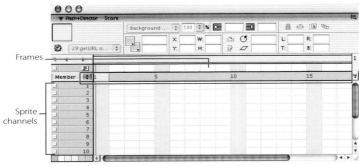

Frames

Sprite
channels

which has layers and frames.) Additionally, the rows for sprite channels are numbered (see Figure 26.1). When you manipulate an element in Director, you often refer to it by its sprite number, such as *sprite(1)* or *sprite(13)*. There are many levels of complexity in the Director environment, depending on how much of the program you need to use. Consult the Director Help files (Help → Director Help) for specifics on the interface and its components.

Figure 26.1

The Score in Director consists of sprite channels (rows) and Timeline frames (columns).

For a Flash movie to be part of a Director production, it has to be a sprite in the Score and on the Stage; for it to be a sprite, it has to be a cast member. And to be a cast member, it must first be imported into a Director movie. Whew! So many steps! It might sound confusing, but once you've grown accustomed to Director, it's very easy to understand how all the elements are interrelated.

To import a Flash movie into your Director project:

1. In Director, select File → Import (Cmd/Ctrl+R). The Import Files dialog box opens. It's similar to the one used in Flash, only larger and more detailed.

2. The window at the top allows you to browse for the files you need. Use the drop-down menu to locate the SWF files that you want to import.

3. After you locate and select the file you need, click the Add button. This will place the file in the lower window, which is like an on-deck circle for files about to be imported. Continue to use the top window to browse for any additional files you need.

4. When you have finished, click the Import button. This will make all of the selected files part of your Director movie cast and a permanent part of the Director file.

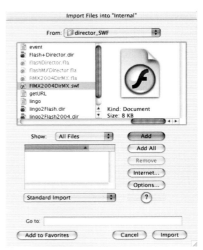

Flash Scenes are supported inside Director movies, and will play back in the order you set in the Scenes panel. However, navigating between Scenes can only be done via ActionScript inside a Flash movie. Lingo syntax does not support Scenes in a Flash cast member.

In addition to the buttons and methods discussed here, Director offers a range of other import options that go beyond the scope of this section. Consult the Director Help files (Help → Director Help) for all the options available to you while importing media.

Understanding Flash Movie Properties

Once you have successfully imported a Flash movie into your Director project, it will appear as a cast member in the Internal Cast window (see Figure 26.2). Director automatically includes for you the Flash Asset Xtra that is needed to support the Flash cast member, so there is no need to retrieve it from your computer's hard drive. However, if you plan to create a stand-alone projector, be sure that the supporting Flash Asset Xtra and any other Xtras you need are available for the final projector file.

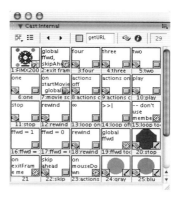

Figure 26.2

Director's Internal Cast window holds Flash movies and many other types of media for use in a Director production.

From here, you are free to use Director to work with the movie in any way you see fit. Flash cast members are somewhat unique in the Director environment because they are interactive multimedia movies *within* an interactive multimedia movie. As a result, there are many parameters that can be assigned to the Flash cast member to determine how it will perform as a cast member in Director. You can set these parameters using the Flash Asset Properties dialog box. In this window, you can control many characteristics of a Flash movie: its playback quality, scaling properties, sound options, and so on. Think of this dialog box as your interface for customizing the technical details of a Flash cast member.

To access the Flash Asset Properties dialog box and edit the parameters of a Flash member:

1. Select the Flash cast member that you want to edit.

2. Click the Property Inspector button in the upper-right corner of Director's Cast panel. This button, noticeable because it is an italic letter *i* within a blue circle, is present in many different locations of the Director interface, but will always launch the Property Inspector.

3. In the Property Inspector, select the Flash tab and click the Options button. The Flash Asset Properties dialog box opens.

The window offers you the following options for editing a Flash cast member:

Media management If you use the Browse button to link to a Flash file, the field at the top of the window will show the path to that file, either on your computer's hard drive or on the Internet.

Flash movies can be either imported or linked. If you check the Linked box, the file will be handled from a remote location. When the movie is used in your Score, Director will go to the remote location and call that member to the Stage. Linked members will stream into memory unless Preload is checked. Preload requires that the entire Flash movie be loaded before playback begins.

Unless you are creating a Shockwave movie that will appear on the Internet, it is recommended that you leave the Linked option deselected so that a Flash member is imported to the cast and saved as a permanent part of your movie.

Playback There are several playback options that control how the Flash movie will be delivered in the Director movie:

   Image Determines whether the image track of a movie is visible. If the box is checked, you will see the Flash movie; if it is unchecked, you will not. Deselect this option for sound-only or script-only SWF files.

   Sound Toggles the audio track of a Flash member. If the box is checked, the movie will play with its sound on; if unchecked, the movie will play silently.

   Paused Determines how the movie will play when it is first encountered in the Score. If Paused is checked, the first frame of the Flash movie is displayed. After that, the movie will have to be prompted either by Lingo or by a control in the Flash movie itself to begin playback. If Paused is unchecked, the movie will play immediately when Director loads the movie onto the Stage.

   Loop An on/off option that determines how a movie will act when it has finished playing. If Loop is turned on (checked), the movie will resume playback at its first frame and first Scene after it finishes playing. If Loop is unchecked, the movie will play once and then stop.

   Direct to Stage Controls the priority that Director assigns to a Flash cast member. If this option is checked, Director will devote resources to making the movie play back as quickly and smoothly as possible. This option disables sprite ink effects and will always place a Flash sprite on top of any others in the movie. We recommend you use this option whenever possible to ensure the best possible performance.

Quality Director has several quality options for Flash cast member playback. These options produce the same results as those found in the HTML tab of Flash's Publish

Settings dialog box. The settings are High, Auto-High, Low, and Auto-Low. Lowering the quality might help to improve performance in some situations. To read more about Quality settings, see Chapter 30.

Scale This field allows you to enter a scale value for the cast member. This value will be used for the Flash movie each time it appears in your Director movie. Settings in this field are directly related to choices made in the Scale Mode drop-down menu.

Scale Mode This menu offers several options concerning the scaling of Flash cast members when they are manipulated either in the Score or by Lingo:

Auto-Size The default setting. This option locks the scaling of the Flash movie to the scaling of a sprite in your Director movie. As a sprite is scaled, so will the Flash movie be scaled. This option defaults the value of the Scale field to 100 percent so that the Flash movie and the sprite maintain the same scale relationship. If you change this number to 50 percent, the Flash movie will retain the new scale value and always be one-half the size of the sprite that holds it. Change it to 200 percent, and the Flash movie will be twice the size of the sprite and appear cropped within its bounding box.

No Scale Retains the size of the Flash cast member as it is set in the Scale field. No matter how a sprite is stretched or shrunk, this option leaves the Flash movie at the size set by the Scale option. If a sprite is scaled to a value less than that specified in the Scale field, the Flash movie will be cropped by the sprite bounding box.

The remaining options—Show All, No Border, and Exact Fit—are identical to those found in the HTML tab of Flash's Publish Settings dialog box. To read more about these options, see Chapter 30.

Rate This option allows you to control the speed of playback (frame rate) of a Flash movie cast member. This functionality is unavailable to you in Flash, and is thus another reason to combine Flash and Director. Rate has three settings:

Normal Retains the original frame rate settings of the SWF file.

Lock-Step Matches the playback of your Director movie with the Flash member, frame for frame. If the Director movie is set to play at 30 frames per second, so will a Flash cast member when Lock-Step is enabled. Lock-Step usually provides the best performance.

Fixed Activates the fps (frames per second) field and allows you to enter a custom value to set the frame rate of a Flash cast member. This setting is unique and will override tempo settings in both the original Flash movie and Director's Score. However, a Flash movie will not play faster than the frame rate that is set in the Director movie.

The frame rate of your Director movie is also a factor here. As the host of your Flash movie, it has dramatic effects on overall performance. In Director, select Window → Control Panel and set the frame rate to 30fps or higher.

Figure 26.3

The Property Inspector provides an alternative means of setting the attributes of a Flash cast member.

Besides the Flash Asset Properties dialog box, there is another means of changing the parameters of a Flash cast member. One of the more important windows in the Director interface is the Property Inspector (see Figure 26.3). It is very similar to the Property Inspector found in Flash's interface and provides a lot of the same kind of functionality. It allows you to access many options and parameters that define a component of your movie: scaling, color, name, and other specifics that are unique to each element or cast member.

To display the Property Inspector for a Flash cast member, highlight that member in the cast window and then click the Property Inspector button ⓘ . It will allow you to change the following attributes of a Flash cast member:

- Member name and path

- Scale mode: Auto-Size, No Scale, and so on

- Quality: High, Auto-High, and so on

- Rate: the Flash member's frame rate

- Playback options: Image, Audio, Loop, DTS (Direct to Stage), Paused, Preload, and Static. Static is an option available only in the Property Inspector. Select this option if the Flash member does not contain any animation; Director will be able to manage it more efficiently.

The Property Inspector is a quick alternative to using the Flash Asset Properties dialog box and provides a way to edit the most common attributes of a Flash cast member.

Getting a Flash cast member to perform smoothly in a Director movie can sometimes be a lot of work. Even though the vector format is lean and flexible, the amount of memory required to display a Flash sprite can often bog Director down. The solution? Unfortunately there are no clear answers. Experiment with different settings for the Flash cast member until you achieve the results you expect, and look for tips and suggestions throughout this chapter that address specific issues that will affect playback performance.

Editing Flash Cast Members

One of the best aspects of working with Macromedia's MX application line is their ability to work together. You can edit a Flash cast member from within Director MX and see the changes immediately reflected in your movie. While working in Director MX, you can take a brief "detour" to Flash, make the necessary tweaks to your movie, and return to Director to see the effects of your changes. You can do all this without the hassle of importing new files, which can really streamline your workflow.

To edit a Flash cast member from within Director, do either of the following:

- Double-click the Flash cast member in the cast or the Flash sprite on the Stage or in the score.

- Select the Member tab of the Property Inspector and click the Edit button.
  From here:

1. Flash MX 2004 or MX Pro 2004 launches and opens the source FLA file associated with the Flash cast member.

2. Make the necessary changes and click the Done button above Flash's Main Timeline.

3. Flash republishes the Flash movie as a SWF and returns to Director MX.

To edit a Flash cast member successfully, Director must be able to locate the member's source FLA file. To specify a source file for a Flash cast member:

1. Select the Flash cast member in the Cast panel.

2. Open the Property Inspector (click the blue *i* button).

3. Select the Flash tab and click the Browse button.

4. Locate the source FLA file and click Choose. The file you select will be the FLA that Director opens when you need to edit a Flash cast member.

If Flash MX 2004 or MX Pro 2004 was installed before Director MX, it should automatically be identified as the default editor for Flash movies. If it is not, you need to set this up manually. Select Help → Director Help and navigate to Media → Using Flash and Other Interactive Media Types → Editing A Flash Cast Member.

Using Flash Movies as Sprites

To make a Flash cast member officially part of your movie, you must place that cast member on the Stage. Unless a cast member is brought to the Stage (either physically or through Lingo), it will not make an appearance in your movie. When you drag a cast member from the cast window to the Stage, it becomes a sprite and is automatically assigned a sprite number based on the next available sprite channel in the Score. For example, if you presently have six sprites in your movie and you drag a Flash member to the Stage, it will be referred to as *sprite(7)* throughout the Director movie. This number is very important, because it is how you identify the Flash member when you want to control it with Lingo scripts. For instance, `sprite(7).visible=0` makes your Flash movie, sprite(7), invisible. You can also create a sprite by dragging a cast member to the Score window directly. This allows you to place it in whichever sprite channel you desire, and automatically centers the sprite on the Stage.

> Confused about the Score and the Stage? One of the greatest challenges in learning Director is understanding the role of each window and how its elements are used in a movie. If a cast member appears on the Stage, it is automatically also in the Score. While the Stage is the window in which your movie takes place, the Score is where all the technical elements of a movie are determined, such as a cast member's time on the Stage, script placement, and overall movie structure (frames, markers, and so on).

Once a Flash cast member has become a sprite in your Director movie, there are several behaviors that you can expect it to exhibit. Listed below are some of the capabilities and limitations of a Flash movie once it's part of a Director project:

Playback A Flash movie will play back in a Director movie as long as the Director movie has enough frames to accommodate its length. For instance, a Flash movie with 100 frames could play only halfway in a Director movie with 50 frames. One workaround for this characteristic is placing the Flash movie in a single Director frame and attaching the following Lingo statements to the frame script channel of the Score:

```
on exitFrame
   go to the frame
end
```

This creates a continuous playback loop and allows the Flash movie to play in its entirety while Director loops in a single frame. Additionally, if the Loop parameter of the Flash cast member is turned on, the movie will loop inside Director continuously. To learn more about working with Flash movies while Director is looping its playback, see the section "Controlling Flash Playback with Lingo" later in this chapter.

Vector format As a vector graphic, your Flash movie is excellent for applications where you need to stretch and resize graphics or text without distortion. With the help of Lingo, Director allows you to do this dynamically, based on audience interactivity in your movie.

Sprite manipulation In addition to its own built-in animated characteristics, a Flash movie member can be moved and repositioned on the Stage as a sprite to create another layer of animated interest. To learn more about this, see the next section of this chapter.

Be careful about using too many Flash sprites in a Director movie. Every Flash sprite requires its own instance of the Flash Asset Xtra. This can chip away at memory and cause slow performance.

Presentation If the Flash movie has Direct to Stage turned on, it will always appear on top of other sprites, and Director will devote resources to ensuring the smooth playback of the movie. Use the Direct to Stage option for Flash movies that are featured and must play back with the highest priority. It is best to leave this option off for other kinds of movies, such as button interfaces, animated characters, and other elements that must be more flexible as sprites.

Ink effects Ink effects are settings that you can apply to sprites to change their appearance on the Stage. There are four Ink settings that apply to Flash members: Copy, Background Transparent, Transparent, and Blend.

> **Copy** Displays a Flash movie exactly as it was created, pixel for pixel. Copy is the default option.
>
> **Background Transparent** Makes the background color of a sprite invisible (transparent) and allows you to see through to the elements behind the sprite.
>
> **Transparent** Allows some color bleed between a movie and the color of the elements behind it. This effect is more apparent with light colors than with dark.
>
> **Blend** Similar to the _alpha property in ActionScript. Think of it as an opacity setting for each sprite. Blend values and Ink effects can be set in the Sprite Toolbar area of the Score (see Figure 26.4). Blend transitions in Director and _alpha transitions in Flash can be very taxing when a Flash movie is playing inside Director. It is best to avoid these, as the results are often very disappointing.

Macromedia recommends using the Copy setting for most applications because it requires the least amount of memory to display. If possible, a good strategy is to create your movies with the same background color so that knocking out an unwanted background color is unnecessary.

Sound Working with simultaneous audio streams (from both the Flash movie and your Director movie) can be a bit tricky. The difficulty is that Flash and Director are forced to share sound channels. If you are using Windows, you can take advantage of the global property soundMixMedia. When set to true, this property enables Director to mix Score channel sounds with those playing in a Flash cast member. If it is set to false, then Flash and Director sounds must be played at separate times.

Figure 26.4

The Sprite Toolbar area of the Score window allows access to Ink and Blend settings for the sprites in your movies. Ink settings can also be accessed by Cmd/Ctrl+clicking a sprite and choosing an option from the context menu.

> Mixing Flash and Director audio can produce undesirable results throughout your production. We recommend that you implement and control all audio elements within one application or the other.

Communicating Across Movies with Lingo and ActionScript

Now that you are familiar with some of the more technical aspects of working with Flash movies as sprites and cast members, you are ready to begin working with the fun stuff: using one type of media to pass information and commands to the other. This is an essential part of authoring interactive movies. By combining Flash and Director, not only can you combine the best of both worlds, but you can allow them to communicate with one another. This relationship adds yet another layer of interactive possibilities and flexibility to your interactive media productions.

Lingo is an enormous scripting language. If ActionScript is a stream, Lingo is a river; and there are more Lingo topics related to Flash than could possibly be covered in a section of this book. Here, we present some of the more essential elements of Lingo as it pertains to Flash. For a complete listing of Flash-related Lingo, select Help → Lingo Dictionary from Director's main menu bar.

> This section assumes that you have basic familiarity with Director, Lingo, and the conventions of the Director authoring environment. To learn more about these topics, consult the help files that ship with Director (Help → Director Help).

Controlling Flash Playback with Lingo

One of the more common uses of Flash cast members is to use them as movies within movies. In the same way that Movie Clips in Flash are independent animations that can be manipulated via ActionScript, Flash movies can be controlled in Director with Lingo. The Lingo language reserves several special commands to do this. Plus, with a little Lingo know-how, you can create your own scripts for various kinds of custom control options. Start here with some of the basics and then take it from there.

Play Command

To play a Flash cast member, you can use Lingo's `play()` command. This statement tells a specified Flash member sprite to play. For example:

```
on mouseUp
    sprite(1).play()
end
```

This script, attached to some kind of button, will play sprite 1 when the mouse button is released.

> Remember to use the Paused option in the Property Inspector if you don't want a Flash movie to start playing when it's encountered on Director's Stage. Alternately, you can set this property in Lingo by using the pausedAtStart cast member property.

Stop Command

To stop a Flash cast member at its current location, you can use Lingo's stop() command. This statement tells a specified Flash member sprite to stop playing. For example:

```
on mouseUp
    sprite(1).stop()
end
```

This script, also attached to some kind of button, will stop sprite 1 when the mouse button is released.

Rewind Command

Use rewind() to send a Flash sprite back to its first frame, or to use the tape metaphor, *rewind* it.

```
on mouseUp
    sprite(1).rewind()
end
```

This script would serve well attached to a rewind button cast member or as part of a rewind behavior script.

Unfortunately, there is no such thing as a fast-forward command for Flash movies in Lingo. However, it is possible to create one. Consider the following script:

```
on exitFrame
    if gFfwd=true then
        swfFrame=sprite(1).frame
        sprite(1).goToFrame(swfFrame+2)
    end if
end
```

This script stores the current frame of the Flash movie in the variable swfFrame. Then, using the goToFrame() command, it sends the movie ahead two frames. These statements are executed every frame if the variable gFfwd is true. In context, you can use a fast-forward button to toggle the variable off and on, which in turn will control this fast-forward function.

frame and *frameCount* **Properties**

You can use these properties to monitor the playback status of a Flash movie. `frameCount` will get the total length of a Flash movie in terms of frames. For example, this statement:

```
put sprite(1).member.frameCount
```

prints to Director's Message window the total number of frames for the Flash cast member that is sitting in sprite channel 1. If the Flash movie in sprite channel 1 had 19 frames, the Message window would reveal the following:

The `frame` property monitors the current frame number that a Flash cast member sprite is playing. In conjunction with the `frameCount` property, this can be used to create a script that tells your Director movie to perform a function (such as going to a new frame) when the Flash movie has finished playing. For example:

```
on exitFrame
    if sprite(1).frame<sprite(1).member.frameCount then
        go to the frame
    else
        go to "done"
    end if
end
```

This script checks a condition every time a frame loops. The condition uses the `frame` property and checks to see if the current frame playing (`sprite(1).frame`) is less than the total number of frames in the Flash movie member that occupies sprite channel 1 (see line 2). If it is, then the script loops in the current frame. If it is not, meaning that the current frame is probably equal to the total number of frames because it has finished playing, the script sends the Director movie to the marker named `done`.

Toggling ActionScript

Use the `actionsEnabled` property to have Lingo turn a Flash movie's scripts off and on. Consider the following Lingo behavior:

```
on mouseDown
    if sprite(1).actionsEnabled=true then
        sprite(1).actionsEnabled=false
    else
        sprite(1).actionsEnabled=true
    end if
end
```

This behavior script can be attached to a button to create a toggle switch for the Action-Script belonging to the Flash movie in sprite channel 1. Using a simple `if...then` conditional in line 2, this script checks the status of scripts for sprite 1. If they are on, this turns them off; otherwise (if they are off), it turns them on. This property can be helpful if you have a Flash movie containing gotoAndPlay() loops. By setting actionsEnabled=false, you cause the Flash movie to ignore these scripts (and all others, for that matter) and to play through its frames without interruption.

Passing Information from Flash to Director

Depending on the way you use Flash within Director, there might be times when it's necessary to pass information directly from a Flash movie to the Director movie that is hosting it. This kind of functionality would be useful if you had created a Flash navigation bar with animated buttons to be used for controlling the playback of a Director movie. In this situation, it would be helpful to have a means of allowing each Flash button to pass an argument to Director, telling it to which frame it should jump. This can be accomplished using ActionScript's getURL() function. This statement will pass a string of information from the Flash movie (where the function is called) to the Director movie that is hosting it.

To make a button in your Flash movie pass information to Director, select the button and open the Actions panel. Enter the following statements:

```
on (release){
    getURL("directorMarker");
}
```

In this example, directorMarker is a placeholder for the name of a Score marker where you would like to redirect Director's playback head when the Flash button is clicked. Flash will pass the URL information as a string to Director.

Before the button will work completely, however, you have to enter some Lingo that prepares Director to receive the string directorMarker from Flash. In Director, create a behavior script and attach it to the Flash sprite that contains the button. The Lingo for the behavior should read like this:

```
on getURL me, flashStringInfo
    go to frame flashStringInfo
end
```

This Lingo enables the sprite to which it is attached to receive the URL string information and store it in the variable *flashStringInfo*. This variable can be used later in the script. Here, because this string is supposed to help with Director movie navigation, the string holds the name of a marker in your Director movie. If you have a Flash movie with several buttons, each with a different navigation-related string to pass, this behavior will be able to handle each string and route the Director movie accordingly.

The getURL() function also allows you to specify a specific event in Director. An event could be something like a custom handler that you write in Lingo to manage specific kinds of Flash interaction. Take navigation, for instance. Moving around in an interactive movie is something that must be done repeatedly throughout the movie. You could write a custom handler to direct navigation so that every time a Flash button is clicked, it moves the Director movie to the proper location. To do this, you start by assigning the getURL() function to a Flash button. Only this time, you must specify an event and an argument:

```
on(release){
    getURL("event:flashButton \"start\"");
}
```

In this example, the event protocol specifies an event named flashButton. The argument for the event is "start".

> In this example, the argument "start" must include the quotation marks so that Director can interpret the string correctly as the name of a marker. To prevent the quotes from confusing and breaking the ActionScript string, each quote mark is escaped (ignored) by using the backslash character (\).

For this technique to work, the event called in Flash must have a counterpart in Director. Otherwise, the event will not be understood and will fail in your Director movie. You create a counterpart by writing a custom function in Lingo and saving it as a Movie script. For the preceding example, the custom function should be written like this:

```
on flashButton me, swfString
    go to frame swfString
end
```

Here, the name of the event specified in Flash is the name of the handler, flashButton. The argument it passes as a string is stored in swfString, then it gets used later in the script to send the movie to a particular frame. In this example, the script would send the movie to a frame marker named start.

This approach is similar to the previous example that uses on getURL me. There is a difference that is important to understand, however. When using the event protocol, Flash relies on a custom function in your Director movie. The advantage of the function is that you needn't attach a Lingo script to every Flash sprite. Because your function is sitting in a Movie script in your Director cast, it is always available when your Flash movie calls for it.

ActionScript's getURL() function provides yet another way to pass information from Flash to Director. The lingo protocol is probably the most straightforward, but allows the least amount of flexibility because all statements are hard-coded. Using this technique, you specify specific Lingo statements in your Flash movie so that they can be passed directly to a Director host movie. For example:

```
on(release){
    getURL("lingo:go to frame 10");
}
```

This script, when attached to a button in Flash, will pass a message to Director telling it to jump to frame 10. Because the `lingo` protocol uses explicit Lingo statements, there is no need for any additional scripting in Director.

Manipulating Flash Sprites with Lingo

As sprites under the control of Lingo in a Director movie, Flash movies seem to lose some of their "Flash-ness," but you can still manipulate the sprites in much the same way as if they were inside a Flash movie. For basic navigation, you can use `tellTarget()`, `endTell-Target()`, and a handful of basic functions for navigation: `play()`, `stop()`, and `gotoFrame()`. To set and retrieve the attributes of a Flash movie within Director, use `setFlashProperty()` and `getFlashProperty()`. The `getFlashProperty()` function monitors the current attributes of a Flash movie sprite, and `setFlashProperty()` assigns a new value to a component of a Flash movie. For example, if a Flash movie sprite contained a Movie Clip, you could use these functions to monitor the clip's attributes and set them as needed. Their syntax is as follows:

```
sprite(spriteNum).setFlashProperty("targetName",#property,newValue)
sprite(spriteNum).getFlashProperty("targetName",#property,newValue)
```

In each, you must specify the sprite number of the Flash movie. Then you use the function you need and specify the name of the clip you wish to target, the property you need to set or retrieve, and a new value. See the following example:

```
on mouseUp
    if sprite(1).getFlashProperty("topleft",#alpha,"")=100
    then
        sprite(1).setFlashProperty("topleft",#alpha,50)
    else
        sprite(1).setFlashProperty("topleft",#alpha,100)
    end if
end
```

This script can be used to toggle the opacity (`#alpha` in Lingo, `_alpha` in ActionScript) of a Movie Clip instance named `topleft` of the Flash movie in sprite 1. If the `#alpha` value of the target equals 100, then it is set to one-half its value (50). If it is not 100, then it is set back to its full value (100). If you are using `getFlashProperty()` and don't need to set a new value, simply use an empty string (`""`) for that argument.

There are many properties that Lingo can use to manipulate targets and their values in a Flash sprite. See Table 26.2 for a complete listing and description of each.

Table 26.2

Lingo Terms for Manipulating Flash Movie Properties

NAME	TYPE	DESCRIPTION
#posX	R W	Pixel value for the X axis location of a target
#posY	R W	Pixel value for the Y axis location of a target
#scaleX	R W	Pixel value for the X scale of a target
#scaleY	R W	Pixel value for the Y scale of a target
#visible	R W	Determines whether a target is hidden or visible
#rotate	R W	Degree value for a target's rotation
#alpha	R W	Percent value of a target's opacity
#name	R W	Name assigned to a Movie Clip instance
#width	R W	Pixel width of a target
#height	R W	Pixel height of a target
#target	R	Full path in slash notation for a target relative to a movie's main Timeline
#url	R	Full path in HTTP syntax for a target
#dropTarget	R	Full path in slash notation for a target on which a draggable Movie Clip was dropped
#totalFrames	R	Total number of frames in a target
#currentFrame	R	Location of the playback head in a target's Timeline
#lastFrameLoaded	R	Last frame number to be loaded for a Flash sprite to be fully loaded into memory; see _framesLoaded property in ActionScript.
#focusRect	R W G	Controls the visibility of the yellow button focus rectangles in a Flash movie. (These appear over the buttons of a Flash movie when the Tab key is pressed.)
#spriteSoundBufferTime	R W G	Determines how many seconds of sound should preload before playback begins

R = a property that can be read or retrieved; W = write, or a property that can be set; G = global property for an entire Flash movie.

In Table 26.2, there are two global properties that apply to an entire Flash movie. When working with these, enter an empty string (" ") as the target argument—for example, `sprite(1).getFlashProperty("",#focusRect,"")`.

To control the playback of the main Timeline and Movie Clip instances in your Flash movie, use the `tellTarget()` and `endTellTarget()` functions. Although these terms are deprecated in ActionScript, they work within Director to target individual clip instances.

The Lingo syntax is as follows:

```
on mouseDown
    sprite(whichSprite).tellTarget("targetPath")
    --statements to target a clip or Timeline
    sprite(whichSprite).endTellTarget()
end
```

In this script "template," you use the `tellTarget()` and `endTellTarget()` statements as you would use bookends; they enclose the statements that control a clip instance or movie Timeline. In the `tellTarget()` statement, you must specify, using slash syntax (circa Flash 4), the target path to the Timeline or clip you wish to control. Consider the following example:

```
on mouseDown
    sprite(1).tellTarget("/menu")
    sprite(1).play()
    sprite(1).endTellTarget()
end
```

This Lingo example tells the clip menu (which is on the Main Timeline) to start playing. The equivalent ActionScript would look like this:

```
on(press){
    _root.menu.play();
}
```

Here are a few other Lingo terms you can use to target clip instances and Timelines in your Flash movies:

play() Starts the playback of a Movie Clip or Timeline when the statement is called. Comparable to ActionScript's `play()` function.

stop() Halts the playback of a Movie Clip or Timeline when the statement is called. Comparable to ActionScript's `stop()` function.

gotoFrame(frame) Skips the playback head to the specified frame of a Movie Clip or Timeline when the statement is called. Comparable to ActionScript's `gotoAndStop()` function.

If you want `gotoFrame()` to skip to a particular frame *and* resume playback from that point (like `gotoAndPlay()`), you can use the following script, which combines these two terms. This script sends the Timeline of the menu instance ahead to frame 10 and resumes playback from that point.

```
on mouseDown
    sprite(1).tellTarget("/menu")
    sprite(1).gotoFrame(10)
    sprite(1).play()
    sprite(1).endtellTarget()
end
```

This simple technique is the building block of something quite powerful. Remember BubbleBody from Chapter 19? If not, go back to the section "How Flash Manages Multiple Movie Timelines" in that chapter. Consider the idea of a Movie Clip that consists entirely of other nested Movie Clip instances, each of which is a body part of a digital puppet or marionette. Because each clip can be targeted as an individual instance, you can control the animation of any body part through scripting. Now, add this character to a Director movie. Not only can your puppet exist as a scalable, vector-based cast member; it is a cast member that you can control completely through Lingo scripting. You can use Lingo to skip your character ahead to frames and animated loops, to perform lip sync animations, to create facial expressions…the works! To see a real-world example of how this technique was used, see the "Inspirational Design Model" section at the end of this chapter.

Lingo can also be used to manipulate Flash sprites in the same way it does the other elements of Director movies. This means that Flash movies can be scaled, spun, flipped, restacked, and altered just like any other sprite. Lingo sprite properties present you with another option for customizing the performance of a Flash sprite in your Director production. There are many sprite properties that can be set and retrieved in Lingo. First, you should take a look at the basic syntax structure:

```
sprite(spriteNum).property=value
```

In Lingo, you must first identify the sprite that you wish to control. Then you state the property you would like to change, and assign a new value to that property. Consider the following Lingo example:

```
on mouseUp me
    spin=sprite(me.spriteNum).rotation
    sprite(me.spriteNum).rotation=spin+90
end
```

This script works as a behavior to rotate by 90° the sprite to which it is attached each time that sprite is clicked. This script stores the current rotation value in the variable spin. Then it reassigns the sprite's rotation to the current value plus 90°.

There are many Lingo properties that can be used to control the attributes of a sprite. See Table 26.3 for a partial listing and description of sprite properties that can be used to manipulate a Flash movie sprite. For a complete listing and description of sprite properties, see the documentation that ships with Director and the Lingo Dictionary.

While there are many options for controlling Flash cast members within a Director movie, the process and results will not always be as smooth as you would like. The best approach is (unfortunately) one of trial and error. Use the techniques set forth in this chapter as guidelines. They explain what is and is not possible when using Flash inside Director. While you might not find a solution that fits your immediate needs, there's likely a workaround that will enable you to accomplish the goals you have set forth. Be persistent, use your resources, and good luck!

PROPERTY	DESCRIPTION
rotation	Sets the rotation value for a sprite by degrees of rotation.
scale	Scales a sprite relative to its origin point.
locH	The horizontal location of a sprite on the Stage in pixels, measured from the Stage's upper-left corner.
locV	The vertical location of a sprite on the Stage in pixels, measured from the Stage's upper-left corner.
locZ	Controls the layering order of sprites in the Score.
flipV	Determines whether a sprite has been flipped vertically on the Stage; if so, this returns true.
flipH	Determines whether a sprite has been flipped horizontally on the Stage; if so, this returns true.
skew	Sets the skew value for a sprite by degrees of tilt from an upright, vertical position.
blend	Sets the opacity of a sprite; 100 = fully opaque, 0 = transparent.
color	Determines the foreground color of a sprite.

Table 26.3

Lingo Properties for Manipulating Flash Sprites

Inspirational Design Model

The possibilities given to you by Flash and Director—two very powerful authoring applications—are vast. When you discover how each medium cooperates with the other and delivers what you want, the results can be quite exciting.

WSTD-TV (see Figure 26.5) is an educational CD-ROM that was able to find the right balance. It was produced by Academic Edge, Inc. (www.academicedge.com) in the fall of 2002. This project used Flash for all its characters and environments and Director as a container to help manage media assets. The characters you see are "Flash puppets"; each has several states that are controlled by Lingo and ActionScript. By switching their states, characters are brought to life and made to talk, gesture, and interact with other characters they encounter.

© The Academic Edge, Inc.

Figure 26.5

WSTD-TV is an educational CD-ROM produced by the Academic Edge. It uses Director and Flash to lead adolescents on a tour of a television station.

CHAPTER 27

Working with Flash and Dreamweaver

One of the great things about Flash is that you can use many third-party programs to extend its usability and functionality. In many cases, these programs also have native tools for manipulating Flash movies and for creating Flash content.

One of the most notable among these is Macromedia's visual web design program, Dreamweaver. The program allows you to carry out several useful Flash-oriented operations. For instance, you can insert Flash movies into HTML documents by hand and then manipulate the characteristics of the file from within Dreamweaver. In addition, you create, insert, and manipulate Flash text and buttons directly from within Dreamweaver—all of which are cool features indeed!

In this chapter, you'll explore the following topics:

- The dream of Dreamweaver
- Working with Flash movies in Dreamweaver
- Creating Flash text in Dreamweaver
- Inserting and manipulating Flash buttons in Dreamweaver

The Dream of Dreamweaver

In 1989, Tim Berners-Lee of the European Particle Physics Laboratory (CERN) wrote an innocent little document entitled "Information Management: A Proposal," which, among other things, outlined the development of Hypertext Markup Language (HTML). Little did he realize that the modest 18-page document would forever change the way that the world accesses, acquires, and shares information.

HTML caught on like wildfire. By July 1993, hundreds of computers worldwide could deliver HTML documents. Up until that point, however, the majority of people in on this exciting new technology were members of academia and hard-core computer users. Shortly thereafter, a small group of students at the University of Illinois's National Center for Supercomputing Applications (NCSA) decided that the text-based software being used to view HTML just didn't cut it. The result of their work was Mosaic, a nifty program (dubbed a *browser*) that changed everything. Among the browser's most important features was a graphic interface as well as compatibility with the Windows operating system. No longer was the Web the domain of scientists and computer geeks.

Fast-forward to 1997 when Macromedia released Dreamweaver 1.0, a WYSIWYG (What-You-See-Is-What-You-Get) web design tool that made it possible to create web pages visually instead of with the traditional method of writing the HTML manually. No more hand-coding HTML, no more puzzling over cryptic lines of code, and certainly no more head scratching for those who weren't trained programmers. Anyone could conceive, create, and distribute their own web pages. The world had just gotten a whole lot bigger; the possibilities were endless.

Although Dreamweaver certainly wasn't the first WYSIWIG web design tool, it was arguably one of the best. Several years and several versions later, Dreamweaver MX 2004 (which is the current version of the program) is one of the most popular visual web-authoring tools available. Including such features as an intuitive and flexible visual authoring environment, support for dynamic backend database technologies, Roundtrip HTML, and support for Dynamic HTML, Dreamweaver has more than 700,000 users and a market share of more than 75 percent, according to Macromedia. In short, Dreamweaver has made high-level web-page authoring accessible to both professional and amateur designers alike.

 A demo copy of Dreamweaver MX 2004 has been included on this book's companion CD. If you don't have Dreamweaver, you'll need to install this demo version to follow along with these examples.

If you are interested in learning more about Dreamweaver, try *Dreamweaver MX: Design and Technique* (Sybex, 2002) or *Dreamweaver MX 2004 Solutions* (Sybex, 2003), both by Ethan Watrall.

Working with Flash Movies in Dreamweaver

Flash can automatically create an HTML document and embed your movie when it's exported.

For more information on how to embed SWF files into an HTML document upon export, see Chapter 30.

This is great, but what if you run into a situation where you want to manually insert the Flash movie into an HTML file? Say, for instance, you had a web page in which a Flash movie was only a small part of the overall design and you wanted to manipulate the other parts of the document. Well, Dreamweaver has several tools that allow you to manually insert Flash files into a Dreamweaver document. In the following sections, you are first going to explore how to insert Flash files into a Dreamweaver document. Then, you'll look at how to manipulate an inserted Flash movie with Dreamweaver's Property Inspector.

Inserting a Flash Movie into a Dreamweaver Document

Inserting a Flash movie into Dreamweaver is really quite easy. And, as with many things in Dreamweaver, you have a couple of different ways to do it.

To insert a Flash file with the Objects panel, follow these steps:

1. Choose Window → Insert to open the Insert bar.

2. In the Common section of the Insert bar, click the Flash button ●.

The Common section of the Insert bar features nested objects that are grouped based on their type. If the Flash button is not visible, you might have to access it by clicking the down arrow to the right of the Media button group.

3. When the Select File dialog box opens, navigate to the Flash file you want to insert and click the Select button.

Although Dreamweaver allows you to choose any file type, you need to make sure you insert the SWF file (which is the web-ready version of Flash) and not the FLA file (which is the native Flash format).

Alternatively, you can use the main program menu to insert the Flash file:

1. Choose Insert → Media → Flash or use the shortcut Cmd/Ctrl+Option/Alt+**F**.

2. When the Select File dialog box opens, navigate to the Flash file and click the Select button.

When you initially insert a Flash file into Dreamweaver, you'll see a placeholder (a Flash icon in the center of a gray box the size of the Flash file). This saves memory. Don't worry; you'll be able to see your movie from within Dreamweaver by using the Property Inspector.

Manipulating a Flash Movie with the Property Inspector

When it comes to working with Dreamweaver MX 2004, the Property Inspector is indispensable. With it, you can access the characteristics of any object in the Document window (Dreamweaver's version of the Stage). The cool thing about the Property Inspector is that it's a *dynamic* tool. It changes each time you select a new object in the Document window. So, when you select a Flash movie that you've inserted by one of the methods described previously, the Property Inspector displays only properties unique to that Flash movie. You open the Property Inspector by selecting Window → Properties or by using the shortcut Cmd/Ctrl+F3.

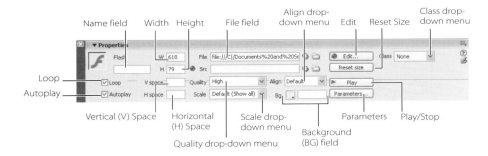

Let's take a detailed look at each of the properties in the Property Inspector:

Name The Name field allows you to enter a unique identifier for the Flash movie for the purpose of scripting.

W and H (Width and Height) Although Dreamweaver inserts a Flash movie with its original dimensions, the W and H fields (Width and Height) let you enter a new value in pixels.

If you want to manually change the Flash movie's dimensions, simply click and drag the resize handles located along the ends of the movie after it has been selected. If you want to constrain the movie's proportions while it's being resized, hold down the Shift key.

File The File field indicates the path of the currently selected Flash movie. If you want to change the path, click the Browse icon (the small folder to the right of the field) and navigate to the new location or simply type in a new path.

Align The Align drop-down menu lets you align the selected Flash movie to other elements on the page (not the page itself). If you want to align the movie to the page, click to the right or left of the movie (so that it's deselected), and then use the three align tools (center, left, or right) located in the Property Inspector.

Bg field When you click the Bg swatch, you can choose a background color for the movie area. This color is also present when the movie isn't playing.

Reset Size If you've changed the size of your movie (and can't remember its original size), click the Reset Size button and your movie automatically reverts to its original size.

Play/Stop The Play button (which turns into a Stop button after it is clicked) allows you to preview your Flash movie from within Dreamweaver.

V Space and H Space The V Space (vertical) and H Space (horizontal) fields allow you to specify an invisible border (in pixels) around the Flash movie.

Quality The Quality drop-down menu allows you to choose from several preset levels of quality for your Flash movie. The settings (Low, Auto Low, High, and Auto High) correlate to the degree of anti-aliasing used during the movie's playback. Although a movie generally appears better with a high setting, it requires a faster processor to render properly. Auto High ensures that both traits—speed and visual quality—are maintained. However, if forced, Auto High first sacrifices speed in favor of visual quality. On the other hand, Low enables the movie to play faster and more smoothly, at the price of decreased visual quality. Auto Low emphasizes speed to begin with but improves appearance when possible.

Scale The options in the Scale drop-down menu define how the movie displays within the area defined for the movie by the values in the Width and Height fields. Show All makes the entire movie visible in the specified area, keeping the aspect ratio of the movie and averting any distortion. No Border is similar to Show All, but it might result in portions of the movie being cropped. Finally, Exact Fit causes the entire movie to fill the specified area, but it sacrifices the aspect ratio, which can result in some distortion.

Loop/Autoplay The Loop and Autoplay check boxes affect how your movie plays. By choosing Loop, your movie loops infinitely. Autoplay, on the other hand, makes sure your movie plays automatically when the page loads.

Parameters The Parameters button opens a dialog box where you can manually insert information passed to the Flash movie through the OBJECT, EMBED, and APPLET HTML tags. For example, you can control the quality of a Flash movie by using the Parameters dialog box.

Class The Class drop-down menu allows you to attach a style sheet to the Flash movie or edit a style sheet that has already been attached.

Edit Clicking the Edit button launches the SWF file in its associated external editor (Flash), allowing you to make many changes to the movie.

Creating Flash Text in Dreamweaver

In Dreamweaver MX 2004, Macromedia has generously given you the ability to create editable vector text with Flash text. By using Flash text, you can avoid all those nasty restrictions (such as font and size limitations) inherent to HTML. In addition, if you use Flash text instead of an image for text, your graphics are scalable, smaller in file size, and look nice and crisp when they're printed.

> Users will need the Flash Player plug-in installed on their computers before they'll be able to view any Flash text you insert into your Dreamweaver document.

Let's take a step-by-step approach to creating Flash text in Dreamweaver:

1. Choose Window → Insert to open the Insert bar.

2. Place your cursor where you want to insert the Flash text. Then, in the Common section of the Insert Bar, click the Flash Text button 🐾. Alternatively, you can choose Insert → Media → Flash Text. At this point, Dreamweaver prompts you to save the file.

> The Common section of the Insert bar features nested objects that are grouped based on their type. If the Flash button is not visible, you might have to access it by clicking the down arrow to the right of the Media button group.

3. When the Insert Flash Text dialog box opens (see Figure 27.1), select a font from the Font drop-down menu. The menu includes all the fonts you have loaded on your system. Remember, you aren't limited to system fonts because you are in HTML.

4. Enter the font size in the Size field. Unlike with normal web text, you use points for Flash text.

5. Click the color swatch to open the Color palette. From here, you can choose the color you want your Flash text to be. If you aren't happy with the available colors, simply click the color wheel in the top-right corner of the Color palette to open the Color Picker. From there, you can mix your own color.

6. If you want your text to change color when the user moves their mouse over it, click the Rollover color swatch and choose the color you want the text to change to.

7. Type the text you want into the Text field. If you select the Show Font check box just below the Text field, the text you enter is displayed in the font you've chosen.

8. If you would like your Flash text to act as a link, enter an absolute URL (for example, www.whatever.com) into the Link field. If the file you want to create the link to is on your hard drive, click the Browse button and navigate to it.

9. Use the Target drop-down menu to set the window location where the link will load.

10. Click the Bg Color swatch to choose a background color for the movie area. This color will also be present when the movie isn't playing.

11. Enter a filename in the Save As field. You can use the default filename (`text1.swf`), but you must enter something in this field. The file is automatically saved to the same directory as the current document.

12. Click Apply and then OK. Depending on what you entered in the Text field, the result should look something like Figure 27.2.

14. To reedit Flash text, double-click the text or hit the Edit button in the Property Inspector (when the text is selected).

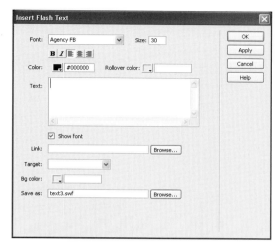

Figure 27.1

The Insert Flash Text dialog box

Inserting and Manipulating Flash Buttons in Dreamweaver

One of the most widely used and popular features in Flash (especially for beginners) is the Button symbol. Buttons are great; you can create all manners of interesting user-responsive navigational tools by using them. This flexibility, coupled with the relative ease in which they're created, gives you a lot of power.

Flash Text Rocks!

Figure 27.2

Flash text gives you a clean and crisp effect, far superior to that of plain HTML text.

Macromedia was quick to recognize the popularity of buttons, and back in Dreamweaver 4, added a way to create them in your Dreamweaver document. Now, don't get too excited. Flash buttons in Dreamweaver MX 2004 are nowhere near as powerful and functional as they are in Flash. Unfortunately, you can't really create buttons from scratch. Instead, you select the different states of the button from a predetermined library of styles. Granted, you can assign text labels and links to these "preforms," but this really isn't the same as making the button from scratch.

To create Flash buttons in Dreamweaver, follow these steps:

1. The first thing you need to do when inserting Flash buttons into Dreamweaver is save your document. To do this, choose File → Save (or Save As).

2. Select Window → Insert to open the Insert bar.

3. Place your cursor where you want to insert the Flash button. Then, in the Common section of the Insert Bar, click the Flash Button button 🎨. Alternatively, you can choose Insert → Media → Flash Button.

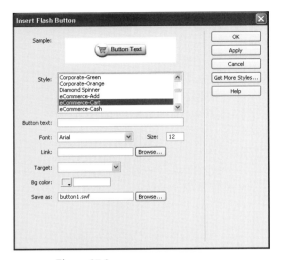

Figure 27.3

The Insert Flash Button dialog box

4. When the Insert Flash Button dialog box opens (see Figure 27.3), select a style from the available list. If you want to test the appearance of the button when the user moves their mouse over it, move your cursor over the button preview in the Sample window.

   If you aren't happy with the styles available, click the Get More Styles button. This loads the Macromedia Exchange in your browser where you'll be able to find additional styles (as well as many other funky Dreamweaver, Flash, and Fireworks widgets).

5. Enter the text you want to appear on the button in the Button Text field. Unfortunately, the Sample window won't display a preview of the button as it will look with your new text.

6. Choose a font for the text from the Font drop-down menu. Then, enter a size (in points) for the text. Remember, because you're working with Flash, you aren't restricted by the usual HTML text limitations.

> The size of the button will not increase if you increase the size of your text. As a result, it's best to leave the font size as the default.

7. If you would like your Flash button to act as a link (which you most likely will), enter an absolute URL into the Link field. If the file to which you want to create the link is on your hard drive, click the Browse button and then navigate to where it's located.

8. Use the Target drop-down menu to set the location in which the link will load.

9. Click the Bg Color swatch to choose a background color for the movie area. This color will also be present when the movie isn't playing or is loading.

10. Just as with Flash text, you need to enter a filename in the Save As field to name the file. You can use the default filename (`text1.swf`), but you must enter something in this field. The file is automatically saved to the same directory as the current document.

11. When you're finished editing your button, click OK (or Apply to see how the text looks without closing the dialog box).

> To reedit a Flash button, double-click the button or hit the Edit button in the Property Inspector (when the text is selected).

Inspirational Design Model

When you're working with Flash and Dreamweaver, it's all about integrating Flash components into an overall HTML-based creation. In a world where, for the most part, total Flash products reign supreme, this can often be a daunting task. Why would you integrate HTML and Flash when you can create slicker, cooler, and far sexier interactive experiences completely in Flash? Ultimately, the answer lies in the desire to balance the proven usability and acceptance of HTML with the cool "wow" factor of Flash.

One of the best examples of Flash/HTML integration is Phireworx (`www.phireworx.com`). The website, which promotes a series of Macromedia Fireworks tools created by Stephen Voisey and Steven Grosvenor, is a wonderful example of stylish and clean HTML design into which a small Flash movie has been inserted (see Figure 27.4). The Flash movie, which functions as a moving advertisement/announcement for their latest product, subtlety injects a sense of life and movement into the overall design.

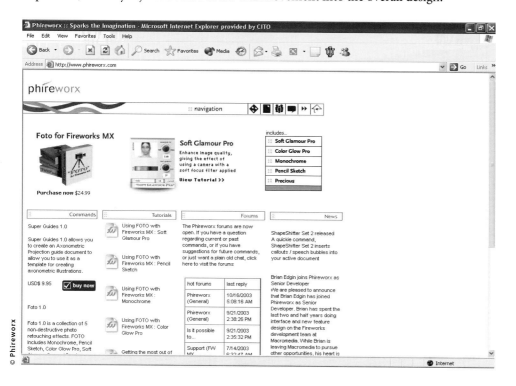

Figure 27.4

The Phireworx site uses both HTML and Flash to create a wonderfully designed self-promotional site.

CHAPTER 28

Working with Flash and Digital Audio Applications

Of all the different types of applications that can be used in conjunction with Flash, digital audio programs are the least similar to Flash itself. In digital audio, there are no animated frames, no movie clips, and no scripting language. It is just you, a sound file or sample, and lots of tools to change the way something sounds. Additionally, audio applications demand a completely different kind of mind-set. You must make the shift from a visual time-based medium to an aural time-based medium. Your ears are most important!

You have learned quite a bit about digital audio in this book, particularly how to prepare sound files for the Flash environment and how to handle them once they get there. Now it's time to step back and look at some of the additional resources you can use outside of Flash to give your movies a great sonic punch. With the right tools and a little know-how, you will discover a world of creative possibilities.

This chapter contains the following topics:

- **Introduction to current multi-track, loop, and wave-editing audio applications**

- **Review of current MIDI sequencing applications**

- **Audio effects and digital processing techniques**

- **Creating your own seamless loops**

- **Flash techniques for adding interactive audio loops to your movies**

Digital Audio Tools

More digital audio applications are available today than ever before. The range of software is enormous: from robust, professional, multi-track systems to smaller, homemade sound gadgets and audio modifiers or creators. Whatever your budget, you are bound to find something that will help you create the music, vocal, or effects soundtrack to accompany your Flash movie.

The overview of software presented here is by no means complete. There are many additional tools that will render excellent results in your Flash soundtrack. This collection is more or less a highlight list of reputable applications that are often used in conjunction with digital multimedia. Choosing the one (or two or three…) that works best for you can take some time. It helps to have a little experience working with audio on your computer so that you know the kinds of features that will be most helpful, based on your working style, your equipment, the size of a typical project, and so on. In most cases, the manufacturers make it easy for you to decide. Many software companies offer free trial downloads of their products. What better way to shop for an application than to test-drive it for free and be absolutely sure that it is right for you? For each entry in this section, you will find a list of online resources where you get additional information about the software, manufacturer, compatibility, and pricing.

This section of the chapter is meant both to inform you about the audio tools that are currently available and to offer some guidance based on the particular strengths and weaknesses of each application. Consequently, it is divided into four parts: multi-track applications, waveform editors, loop editors, and MIDI sequencers. If you are already familiar with these terms, you should have no problem locating the information you need. If this is all very new, then keep reading. With each description, you will find that it's easy to narrow things down based on the demands of your current projects.

Multi-Track Audio Editors

Multi-track applications are used primarily for three things: recording audio, cutting and editing, and mixing together the final song or piece. Because they have great depth and offer a wide range of possibilities, most of them are used for large-scale projects, or projects that require you to combine many different elements into a single song or composition. If you plan to produce your own original music, or assemble a track using narration, dialog, music, and sound effects, then a multi-track audio editor is for you.

Pro Tools

Pro Tools is currently the industry standard for professional-level recording, editing, and mixing of digital audio. Manufactured by Digidesign, this application is built for large audio projects involving many tracks, and it gives you complete control over the performance of each element in your mix. Additionally, Pro Tools offers support for video, MIDI, and both multi-channel and surround sound mixing.

Pro Tools has two types of systems. The primary one is known as TDM, which stands for *time division multiplexing*. With a Pro Tools TDM system, audio information is routed through additional hardware that's installed on your computer. The power of the TDM system lies in this additional hardware, because it manages most of the DSP (*digital signal processing*) and allows the computer to work with multiple simultaneous audio streams in real time. TDM systems provide the greatest amount of power and flexibility, but they demand a substantial financial investment and are recommended for serious users only.

The other kind of Pro Tools system is RTAS, or Real-Time AudioSuite. The main difference is this: RTAS systems use *host processing*, or the CPU of the computer running the software, rather than additional hardware. Consequently, the performance of the system is affected greatly by the speed and efficiency of the computer running the software. RTAS systems (Pro Tools LE) are great for smaller-scale projects and still offer all the editing capabilities of a TDM system. For an illustration of the Pro Tools LE environment, see Figure 28.1.

Currently, Pro Tools is supported on Macintosh (OS 9 and OS X), Windows XP, Windows 2000, Windows 98, and Windows Me computers. Consult Digidesign (www.digidesign.com) for up-to-date information on compatibility and system requirements. If interested, you can try Pro Tools for free. Visit the Digidesign website and follow the link for Pro Tools FREE. This software is a scaled-down but fully functional version of Pro Tools that will give you a taste of the application. Pro Tools FREE is also supported on both Macintosh and Windows platforms, though not for OS X or Windows XP.

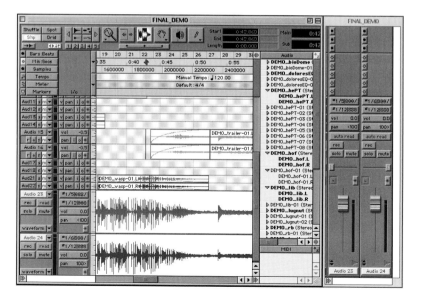

Figure 28.1

Pro Tools LE has all the editing features of regular Pro Tools but depends on the host computer to do any digital signal processing (DSP).

Other Multi-track Audio Options

Many multi-track audio applications also have the capability to work with MIDI (Musical Instrument Digital Interface) data. In a nutshell, MIDI music has two main components: a sequence and a sound bank or module. A *sequence* is a computer file saved in a MIDI-compatible format that serves as a kind of digital piano roll. When it is played back by the computer, it communicates via MIDI with a sound module. The *sound module* reads the MIDI information that is sent by the sequence, provides the correct notes, sounds, and effects, and plays them back in real time. To create MIDI music, you need to have both of these components: a sound module or sampler, and a MIDI sequencer to create MIDI files and send musical information. A MIDI sequence itself isn't music, but rather a list of instructions sent to a sound module or bank. When the sound device receives the instructions, it plays the notes accordingly. As a result, to capture MIDI music, you must record the sounds coming from the device playing your MIDI file as a digital audio file. For this reason, many applications that were at one time "MIDI-only" have added features that allow them to do multi-track audio recording, editing, and mixing. These represent some of the most comprehensive applications available in terms of their functionality. See Table 28.1 for an overview of available applications.

Table 28.1

Multi-Track/Multi-Purpose Audio Applications for Macintosh and Windows

APPLICATION	MANUFACTURER	WEBSITE	OS	FEATURES
Cubase	Steinberg Media Technologies	www.steinberg.net	Mac/Win, VST	MIDI, digital audio
Sonar	Cakewalk	www.cakewalk.com/Products/SONAR	Win, VST	MIDI, digital audio, loop-based composition
Digital Performer	Mark of the Unicorn (MOTU)	www.motu.com	Mac, VST	MIDI, digital audio
Logic	Apple (Emagic)	www.apple.com/software/pro/logic	Mac, VST	MIDI, digital audio
Reason	Propellerhead	www.propellerhead.se	Mac/Win	MIDI, loop-based composition, synthesis

In many cases, expanded features doesn't necessarily mean an expanded price tag. Check each manufacturer's website for details.

Waveform Editors

Waveform editors are a step down from multi-track editors—not because they are less useful, but because they take a different approach to audio editing. In reality, most waveform editors have many of the features found in a multi-track system. The main difference is *size*. Waveform editors are generally geared to handle only one or two simultaneous tracks (mono and stereo files). While this might seem limiting, it has its advantages. It can be easier to work quickly when you have fewer options. Waveform editors might not have all the bells and whistles of a larger audio application, but they do provide a simple, streamlined environment for editing, tweaking, and preparing audio files. Depending on your profession or your role on a Flash development team, it's safe to say that a reliable waveform editor will be able to take care of 85 to 90 percent of the audio work that is required to produce a Flash movie.

Sound Forge

Sound Forge has quickly become one of the staples of the digital media industry. This Windows-only waveform editor provides excellent support for cutting, pasting, trimming, creating fades, recording, doing signal processing, editing loop points, and much more. Sound Forge also includes three kinds of equalizers: graphic, parametric, and paragraphic. It can also be used to encode MP3 files for direct import into Flash. Additionally, Sound Forge offers several DirectX audio plug-ins: Amplitude Modulation, Chorus, Delay, Distortion, Flange, Gapper, Noise Gate, Pitch Bend, Reverb, Vibrato, Time Compression, Wave Hammer, and more. You can see an illustration of Sound Forge in Figure 28.2.

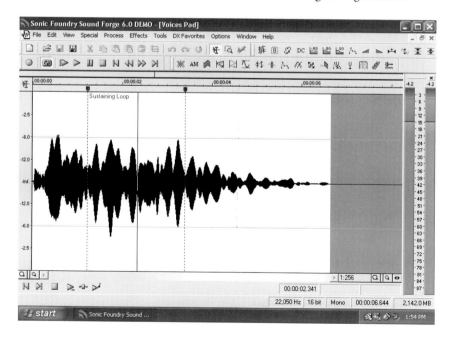

Figure 28.2

Sound Forge is a top-quality, intuitive waveform editor made by Sonic Foundry.

Sound Forge was manufactured by Sonic Foundry (www.sonicfoundry.com). until mid-2003 when Sony Pictures Digital (mediasoftware.sonypictures.com) acquired all of Sonic Foundry's Desktop Software assets. Though it has a new manufacturer, the application is still alive and well, and runs on the following systems: Windows 98SE, Me, 2000, and XP. You can download a demo copy of Sound Forge at http://mediasoftware.sonypictures.com/download.

Peak 4

Peak is manufactured by BIAS, or Berkley Integrated Audio Software. Currently, it is one of the few professional-quality digital audio editing applications made expressly for the Macintosh operating system. As an audio editor, it has the kinds of tools that you would expect: You can cut, paste, fade, cross-fade, change pitch and duration, normalize, and perform stereo-to-mono conversions. Besides the main, detailed waveform display, Peak provides the useful "Audio Waveform Overview," a kind of panoramic display of the entire sound file. If your main window shows a detail of the wave, the Overview window will still display the entire file, along with an indicator of which area you are currently examining (see Figure 28.3).

Figure 28.3

The Peak interface provides two levels of navigation for a sound file, regular (detailed waveform) and Overview, shown in the top-most window.

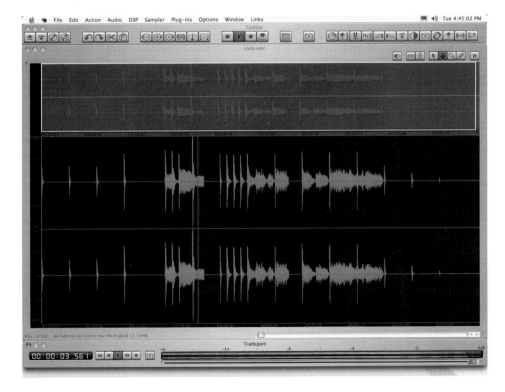

In addition to its editing features, Peak 4 supports Steinberg VST plug-ins. You can use these in a variety of ways to apply equalization, compression, reverb, and many other kinds of processing to a sound file. VST architecture also allows you to take advantage of Freq 4, BIAS's four-band paragraphic equalizer, and their recently released noise-reduction software, SoundSoap (see the section "Noise Reduction" later in this chapter). Peak 4 also offers a batch-processing feature. This asset comes as a huge relief if you have ever had to convert a large collection of files to a different sample rate, file type, and so on. Peak expands the possibilities of a batch processor by also providing an option to apply DSP (normalize, stereo/mono conversion, and so on) to the batch-processed files.

Peak will run on any PowerPC-equipped or G3/G4 Macintosh computer running Mac OS X (10.2 minimum). For additional system requirements and compatibility information, or to download a trial version of Peak, visit BIAS at `www.bias-inc.com`.

Other Waveform Editors for Macintosh and Windows

SoundForge and Peak are certainly not the only two audio editors on the planet. There are many solid alternatives that provide power and flexibility equal to those found in these applications. See Table 28.2 for a partial listing of your alternatives. Some are for Macintosh, others for Windows. We've included a few free programs for students and others on a tight budget.

APPLICATION	MANUFACTURER	WEBSITE	OS	LICENSE
Audition (formerly Cool Edit Pro)	Adobe	`www.adobe.com`	Win	single-user
DSP-Quattro	i3	`www.i3net.it`	Mac	single-user
Spark ME	TC Electronic	`www.tcelectronic.com`	Mac/VST	freeware
Audacity	SourceForge (open source)	`audacity.sourceforge.net`	Mac/Win/VST Linux/Unix	freeware
Goldwave	Goldwave, Inc.	`www.goldwave.com`	Win	shareware

Table 28.2

Digital Audio Waveform Editors for Macintosh and Windows

Loop Creation and Editing

If you are interested in putting together your own music but don't necessarily have the inclination to dive into full-blown composition or song writing, loop software might be a good choice for you. Working with loops is one part composing, one part editing, and features the best of both worlds. When you work with loops, much of the musical material is finished and has been prepared for you as repeatable audio segments known as *loops*. Audio loops can then be cut, layered, mixed, remixed, and combined to produce an entirely new piece of music. Or, using your own music, you can create your own loops and produce remixes or variations to create a different kind of interactive sound experience. Used tastefully, loop software is a great way to produce original music for your Flash movies. To read more about specific uses of looped audio in Flash, see the section "Creating Seamless Audio Loops" later in this chapter.

ACID PRO

ACID PRO is the all-popular application for creating loops and loop-based music. Once made by Sonic Foundry, it (like Sound Forge) is now under the name of Sony Pictures Digital. To use it, you assemble the loops you want to use, arrange them in ACID's time-line, click the Play button, and away you go! Because most loops you encounter are "fin-ished" chunks of music, there is often little work required in terms of editing sound files. ACID PRO allows you to get right into the music and create your musical statements almost instantly (see Figure 28.4).

ACID PRO loop tracks can be manipulated in several ways. You are able to control overall tempo, panning, and volume (envelope), and to create track fades and transitions. And, like most other Sonic Foundry software, ACID PRO supports 18 DirectX plug-ins to add effects and apply processing to your looped creations. ACID PRO ships with a CD that contains a large loop library filled with musical gestures in a variety of styles. Addi-tional audio loop libraries are available from Sony as well as other third-party manufac-turers. One of ACID's best features, though, is that it allows you to bring in original loops (edited in SoundForge and other applications) to add a personal flair to your project. ACID PRO will run on Windows 98SE, Me, 2000, and XP systems.

Figure 28.4

The ACID PRO edit-ing environment allows you to com-pose and produce music using differ-ent combinations of looped sound files.

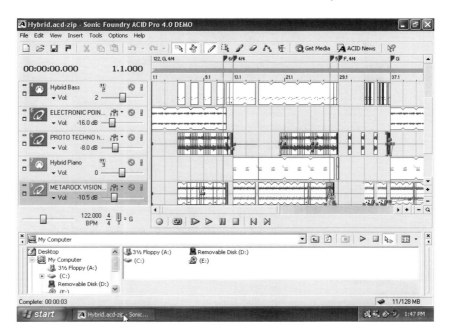

If you use Windows and want to try your hand (and ears) at creating music with ACID, the introductory version of ACID allows you to explore the possibilities of loop-based music at no cost whatsoever. This software is available at `http://mediasoftware` `.sonypictures.com/download`.

Soundtrack

Soundtrack is Apple's answer to ACID Pro. This application (see Figure 28.5) brings the flexibility and speed of loop-based music composition to Macintosh users. Soundtrack ships with a large library of pre-recorded loops to fit a variety of styles and genres. You can browse through the loops, select those that fit your needs, drop them in a Timeline, and instantly hear the results. Soundtrack performs all operations in real time, allowing you to work quickly and efficiently. The best part is that all the Apple loops are 100 percent royalty-free. This means that they can be used for both personal and professional projects without infringing on copyright or paying expensive licensing fees.

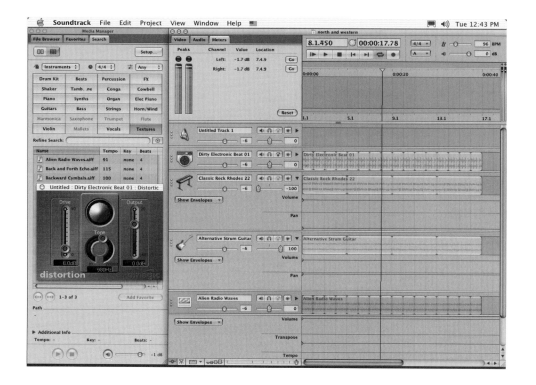

Figure 28.5

Apple's Soundtrack provides a composition environment where you can assign pre-recorded audio loops to individual tracks and then mix them together to create your own songs.

Soundtrack supports Acid, AIFF, and WAV file formats, so it is easy to work with audio material that you already own or have created in another program. Wouldn't it be nice to see your Flash animation while you create its soundtrack? Apple's Soundtrack also allows you to import QuickTime movies for scoring purposes so you can watch a video version of your Flash animation while you compose music to accompany it. Soundtrack also supports a variety of audio effects and plug-ins, which can give your compositions a finished, professional sound.

Soundtrack runs on Macintosh G4 computers with system 10.2.5 or later. Unfortunately no demo version is available. To learn more about Soundtrack, see Apple's website at www.apple.com/soundtrack.

Digital Audio Techniques

So far, you have learned about the vast array of tools that are currently available for creating, editing, mixing, and producing audio for Flash movies and animations. However, selecting a tool for the job is only half the battle. Being able to use it to do the job creatively and professionally is the real trick. And to reach this level, it takes some time to learn how the features of audio editors affect the files they manipulate.

This section of the chapter focuses on different audio editing techniques that are particularly useful in preparing audio for Flash and other kinds of digital media. If you are unfamiliar with digital audio concepts, it might be helpful to refer to Chapter 22 and gain a basic understanding before proceeding with the ideas presented here. Because there are so many different audio applications, the instructions and steps described in this section are general. Each concept or technique is presented in a way that applies to all applications.

Audio Effects and Processing

When working with digital audio, any time you need to change the way something sounds, you can apply digital processing or an effect. Depending on the effect, DSP will perform an operation on the audio waveform to change the way it sounds. Like cutting and pasting, this is part of the editing process.

In the world of digital audio, there are two kinds of editing: destructive and nondestructive. The names are rather self-explanatory. *Destructive* editing means that the wave will be forever changed, unless you undo the operation. *Nondestructive* means that the original will *not* be altered. Generally, a new file is created with the particular edit and used in place of the original. This applies to all kinds of edits, particularly edits that involve processing and effects. Depending on which application you use, you will be doing destructive editing, nondestructive editing, or perhaps a bit of each. Be sure to check before you begin working so that you won't ruin an irreplaceable file by accident. When all else fails, you can usually undo (Cmd/Ctrl+**Z**) an operation to return to the last state of a file. Well, enough of the precautions; let's do some editing.

Normalize

In some respects, *normalization* is the single most important kind of processing you can apply to a digital audio file, especially if you are preparing the audio for computer-based multimedia. The reason is that you never know how loud someone will have their system volume or speakers set to play. And although you have no (or little) control over this, the one thing you can do is ensure that your sounds are set at their highest possible volume. Plus, to avoid possible audio distortion, it's always easier and better sounding to turn something down than to have to turn it up. To learn how to normalize an audio file, see Chapter 22.

Using the Level Meter to Monitor Clipping and Distortion

If you have spent any time at all with a digital audio application, you have undoubtedly encountered the word *clipping*. Clipping means that a sound's level has been boosted beyond the capabilities of the playback system and has been distorted. Clipping (or *distortion*) is characterized by a rough, scratchy, buzzing quality that destroys the clarity of an audio file. While working with a sound, you can monitor its level using the level meter in your digital audio application (see Figure 28.6). These are usually designed to resemble the LEDs (light-emitting diodes) found on many professional mixing boards. The meter tracks the level of a sound as it plays back and gives you a readout of a sound's dynamics. As a sound approaches the point of clipping, the meter generally changes from green to yellow to orange. If the sound goes over the limit, the meter usually displays a red "clip indicator" to let you know that the sound's dynamics are out of range or the sound is distorting.

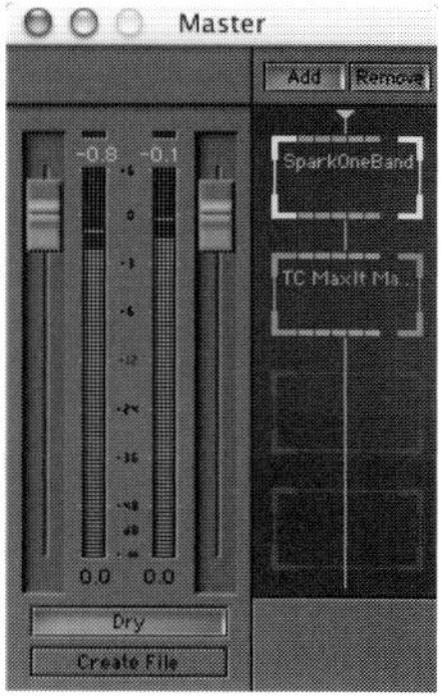

Figure 28.6

This example shows the Master window in TC Electronic's Spark. There are meters for both the right and left channels of a stereo sound.

The Flash Player (particularly the Windows version) can boost the volume of audio in a Flash movie. Consequently, when preparing audio for Flash it is important to be sure that you check the levels for each sound. If the level meter goes above −0.2dB (decibels), you are likely to get distortion when the sound is played back in the Flash Player. An occasional peak above −0.2 dB will probably not cause problems, but frequent levels above this threshold might yield distortion and ruin the effect of your soundtrack. To be on the safe side, try to keep levels around −0.4dB.

Equalizer

An *equalizer* is a tool that is used to alter the frequency balance of a sound file. *Equalization* (also known by the slang term *EQ*) makes adjustments to the frequencies of a sound by either boosting or cutting them. For example, cutting the low frequencies of a sound will take out the "boominess" or "muddy" quality of a sound. Boosting the high range will make a sound "brighter"; too much of this can make a sound shrill or tinny.

Generally, an equalizer is used to make a sound clearer. As with most effects, your ears are the best judge. Work with the equalizer until the file sounds the way you think it should. And as always, monitor the levels of a sound so that you don't clip, or distort, the file. Too much EQ can send a sound flying off the meters!

To apply EQ to a sound file or sample:

1. Select the portion of the file that you want to equalize. This is usually the entire sound file.

2. Choose Equalizer from one of the application's menus (usually Process or Effects). An Equalizer dialog box opens (see Figure 28.7).

3. Using the equalizer's slider controls (this is typical in most interfaces), set values for the various frequencies of a sound. As a general guide to frequency adjustment, see Table 28.3. Chicago-based recording engineer and instructor Bernie Mack developed this chart to help his students match sound characteristics or descriptions with frequency ranges. For example, you might hear a sound and realize that it's "muddy." *Muddy* is a great descriptive word, but it doesn't tell you how to make the sound clearer. Using the chart, you can see that frequencies described as muddy are usually in the range of 200–250Hz. By attenuating (reducing the level of) these frequencies, you can make a sound clearer, or less muddy. Similarly, to adjust the *bass* qualities of a sound you would add to or take away from the frequencies around 60–80Hz. To give a sound more *attack* you could add to the frequencies at 7,000Hz. Realize that these terms offer a general range for adjustment; every sound you work with will yield slightly different results.

Table 28.3

Bernie Mack's Subjective EQ Terms

FREQUENCY OF SOUND (IN HERTZ)	DESCRIPTION OF SOUND
60–80	Bass
200–250	Muddy
350	Pinched, nasal
450	Warm
5,000 (5kHz)	S's
7,000 (7kHz)	Attack
12,000 (12kHz)	High end, bright

4. Some equalizers allow you to preview the new settings. Click Preview to audition the sound. When you have the sound dialed in to where it sounds best, click OK to finalize the edit.

EQUALIZING AUDIO FILES FOR FLASH MP3 COMPRESSION

If you have exported sounds with Flash's internal MP3 compression, you have surely noticed a drop in sound quality of the exported files. Every sound responds to compression differently. For some, the changes rendered by the compression are minimal, while other sounds show a definite difference in their overall character and quality. In general, the lower you set the bit rate, the lower the quality of your sound file will be, and the more drastically a sound will be changed.

These changes in sound quality, however, don't have to be a permanent part of your movie. You can correct the effects of compression by using equalization to bring a sound to a point of equilibrium. By attenuating the frequencies that compression boosts, and boosting the frequencies that compression dampens, you will be able to retain more of a sound's original character after your movie is published.

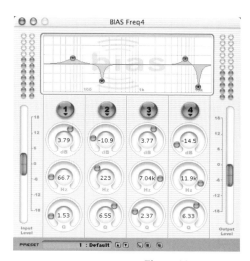

Figure 28.7

Peak 4 features Freq 4, a four-band paragraphic equalizer.

These changes should be applied to the original sound file (or copy of the original file) *before* it is imported into Flash. By doing this, you will compensate ahead of time for the adverse effects MP3 compression has on the sound file. Ideally, when the Flash movie is published, all sounds will be brought back to their original character. A sound will probably never be exactly the same, but it will be a definite improvement over the unequalized alternative.

Use the image to the right as a guideline for your EQ. This EQ setting boosts the low end, cuts the low-to-mid range, and slightly boosts the high-mids and the highs. All EQ settings affect different sounds in different ways, however. Use this example as a starting point. With a little tweaking and experimentation, you should be able to bring your compressed Flash sound files closer to the original.

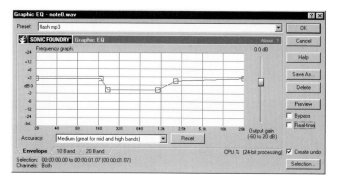

Compression

Compression is like normalization in that it affects the volume of a sound. However, there is more to it than just a change of volume. Whereas normalization boosts the peaks and valleys of a sound and keeps their relationships intact, compression alters the overall dynamics of a sound and can bring its peaks and valleys closer together. If you have a sound with very erratic volume levels, a compressor can level the playing field by cutting the loud parts, bringing them closer to the soft parts. Then, after bringing the levels closer together, a compressor can boost the overall volume of the entire sound file with the new, closer relationship of highs and lows.

To apply compression to a sound or sample:

1. Select the entire sound file or the portion of the file that you need to compress.

2. Choose either Compressor or Dynamics from one of the application's menus (usually Process or Effects). A Dynamics dialog box opens. With most compressors, you are asked to specify five things: Threshold, Ratio, Attack, Release, and Output.

    Threshold Determines at what point the compressor kicks in.

    Ratio Sets the amount of compression. It is usually best to keep this between 2:1 and 6:1. For every 2dB of change, the compressor yields 1dB; for every 6dB of change, the compressor yields 1dB, and so on.

    Attack and Release Set how quickly the compressor kicks in once it is beyond the threshold.

    Output Allows you to boost the final volume of the compressed sound.

3. Once you have made your settings, you can click the Preview option to test the compressor. If the results meet your satisfaction, click OK to compress the sound.

Compression can be a big asset to the production of Flash projects. Use it to compress dialog and narration so that it sounds even and has no "dips" that obscure the meaning or clarity of the words.

Limiter

A *limiter* is another kind of compressor. The difference is that limiters have a set compression ratio of around 10:1. Limiters are used to compress dynamics and boost the overall volume of a final mix. To use a limiter, set the ceiling (or headroom) parameter at the highest acceptable level for your music. For Flash, this means setting the limit no higher than –0.2dB. Sounds will be compressed and sound "louder," but the volume will never exceed the defined ceiling.

Reverb

Reverb is an effect used to make a sound or sample seem as if it is heard in a particular acoustic space. Reverb can make something sound as if it is in a tiled bathroom, long hallway, or cathedral. It is often used to simulate the natural mixing of sounds that occurs in a room with reverberation (see Figure 28.8).

When working with sounds for Flash movies, you can use reverb to create echo effects, sweeten the quality of a vocal line (spoken or sung), add authenticity to environmental sound effects, and much more. Although there are too many different kinds of reverb available today to discuss using them in any kind of detail, here are a few of the parameters you can expect to see:

Room size This causes the effect to simulate the natural acoustics of certain kinds of rooms.

Decay This parameter controls how long the reverb effect persists.

Diffusion This parameter controls the density of the reverberation.

Color This option is a bit more esoteric, but is usually intended to control the character of the reverberated sound.

Figure 28.8
TC Electronic's Native Reverb has a graphic interface that makes reverb parameters easy to understand.

If you like the results of reverb but want something that has more of a bounce or more clear repetitions, you can also try experimenting with echo and delay effects.

Pitch Shift

A *pitch shift* effect can produce wild and humorous results with sound samples, especially when used in the extreme ranges. Pitch shifting basically takes the pitch of a sound and transforms it to a lower or higher pitch; for example, it can make the human voice sound like that of a chipmunk. Pitch shifting is a fabulous technique for modifying sounds to create new and interesting sound effects.

Depending on the sophistication of the software you are using, pitch shifting can be done one of two ways. In many cases, pitch shifting changes the duration of the sound: Pitch shifting up (a higher pitch) makes a sound shorter, while pitch shifting down (a lower pitch) elongates a sound. With newer pitch shift effects, you might have the option to preserve the original duration of the sound or sample.

To apply pitch shifting:

1. Select the entire sample or portion of the sound that you want to pitch-shift.

2. Choose Pitch Shift from the Effects (or similarly titled) menu. The Pitch Shift dialog box opens.

3. Set the pitch shift value and click OK to perform the shift. To shift the pitch to an even greater degree, repeat steps 1–3 several times over. This allows you to "multiply" the effect and create incredibly dramatic results.

Pitch shifting is a sound designer's best friend. With a little experimentation, you will be surprised at how typical, everyday sounds can be transformed into wild sonic oddities. Use this effect liberally in Flash cartoons to create crazy, over-the-top *clanks!, boinks!, and ka-booms!*

Time Shift

Time shift and pitch shift are similar in nature, but they affect different aspects of a sound. Whereas pitch shift can raise or lower the pitch of a particular sound, the *time shift* effect will increase or decrease a sound's duration. And unlike some pitch shift effects that alter the duration of a sound, time shift generally tries to preserve the original pitch of the sound that it is shifting.

To apply a time shift effect:

1. Select the portion of the file or sample that you want to time-shift.

2. Choose Time Shift (or Tempo, Stretch, and so on) from the audio application's Effects menu. The Time Shift dialog box opens.

3. Every interface varies; generally, you either use a slider to set the value, or type in a number for the length of the "shifted" file.

4. If the application provides a Preview option, select it to audition the sound. When you have created the right effect, click OK to apply the time shift.

Time shift effects are particularly good for making sound effects shorter or longer. For example, if you have an explosion sound that you want to sustain for an extended period of time, apply a time shift effect and stretch it to the length you desire.

Noise Reduction

If you're in the habit of recording and producing your own audio and sound effects, you might need a good noise- reduction tool. Unless you have access to a professional-quality recording room, it's nearly impossible to record a sound without some additional (unwanted) noise. While in many cases this is harmless, you might find that you have recordings that need serious "cleaning" to reduce buzz, hum, static, and other undesirable elements that can make their way into a recording.

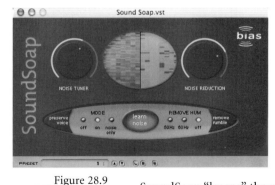

Figure 28.9

BIAS Inc.'s Sound-Soap is an easy-to-use application (or plug-in) that "scours" unwanted noise from digital audio recordings.

Noise-reduction (or audio-restoration) tools can help get rid of annoying scratches, hiss, and other junk that you don't want to hear. BIAS Inc. (maker of Peak 4) has created Sound-Soap to do just this. SoundSoap (see Figure 28.9) is compatible in both Macintosh and Windows environments. One click and SoundSoap "learns" the noise, or identifies what needs to be removed. To double-check for accuracy, you can also toggle between noise-free and noise-only versions of a sound.

SoundSoap can run as a stand-alone application or as a plug-in to an audio application that supports either VST or DirectX.

Creating Seamless Audio Loops

Chapter 22 introduced you to loops, small chunks of music that can be repeated, or looped, continuously. And in Hands On 6, you learned how loops can be cued via Action-Script to ensure accurate beat-timing between repetitions. When you combine loops in different ways throughout the movie, they can serve as the impetus for a highly interactive soundtrack. Yes, loops do carry a negative connotation, but hopefully these techniques illustrate how loops can produce pleasing, musical results. Remember that loops themselves are not always grating or annoying; rather, the unimaginative *application* of loops can make them so.

Whatever creative solution you might devise for working with loops, it is important that they are created in such a way that they sound clean and are free of pops, clicks, and bumps when played back. The best way to do this is to be sure that the loop file has one continuous waveform with no seams or gaps. If the line of the wave ever has to jump or skip, the break in the wave will be unpleasantly audible when you play back the looped file (see Figure 28.10).

So, the key to a smooth-sounding loop is to have one continuous wave that never breaks. Because it's nearly impossible to find a natural sound that is like this, you must edit the file to create the loop. Many audio editing applications offer loop creation tools that assist you with this, and generally they have names like "Loop Tuner." Built-in loop editing tools such as these can be very helpful, but they don't always give you complete

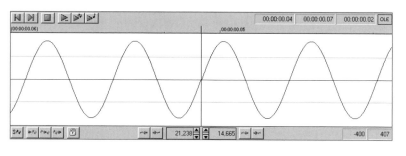

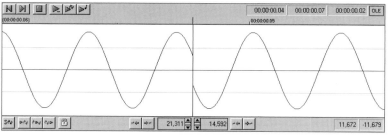

Figure 28.10

The image on top shows a sample with two loop points that meet smoothly; this sound will play back without glitches. The sample on the bottom will pop every time it loops, due to the gap in the waveform.

control over the file while you are defining its loop points. These tools work very well for rhythmic loops, where the beats of the music are clearly defined by the shape of the wave. For ambient, loosely rhythmic, or *rubato* music, though, using the tools can be difficult.

In the following steps, you will learn how to create ambient loops that work as a musical backdrop to your Flash movies. First, though, you should understand what is meant by an ambient loop. An *ambient loop* is a sound, often with no particular rhythm or pulse, which repeats continuously. It sounds boring by definition, but an ambient loop can sound absolutely beautiful. Think of such loops as unobtrusive textures—or soundscapes—that create an environment or sense of "place." Ambient loops serve as excellent musical backdrops for websites and interactive interfaces, because they establish a mood without ever stepping in the way of the other design elements. In a sense, the sound is as integral to the design as the type, colors, and images.

To create a smooth loop for an ambient sound:

1. Open a sound that you think is appropriate for your purpose, and listen to it. Are the beginning and the end drastically different? If so, you might need to do some creative editing to reorder the parts of the music or sound collage that make up the sound. To get the best results from this technique, work with a sound that has an ending that will transition smoothly to the beginning without sounding strange or awkward. Additionally, the sound should be at least 30 seconds long. Looped sounds are most obvious when they are short, so work with the longest sound file your movie can afford in terms of file size.

2. Using your audio editor's selection tool, select the last few seconds of the sound file. (The portion that you select will ultimately have to blend with the audio at the beginning of the file. Try to make a generous selection so that you leave plenty of room to blend. Four to ten seconds is a good, flexible range with which to work.) Let's assume that the sound is stereo and you have selected both tracks. It's critical that your selection starts at a point where the sound wave is crossing the 0 amplitude line (see Figure 28.11). If you make the selection at any other point in the wave, you'll get a glitch when the file loops.

3. Select Edit → Cut (Cmd/Ctrl+X) to cut the audio chunk you selected. Then, create two new tracks (or one stereo pair) in the sound file. Make the new tracks active by dropping your cursor in the tracks. Make sure that the cursor is at the very beginning of the sound file, and then choose Edit → Paste (Cmd/Ctrl+V) to insert the information that you cut from the sound's tail end into the new tracks. Your file should now resemble something like Figure 28.12. Depending on the editor you use, you might need to set the pan position for each of the new tracks.

If you are using an editor such as Sound Forge or Peak that doesn't support multiple tracks, you will still be able to use this technique but with less flexibility. Rather than create two new tracks, perform a crossfade or blend edit to paste the tail-end portion smoothly over the beginning of the file. Set the blend or crossfade so that the pasted information starts at full volume and fades to silence, and the original starts at silence and fades to full volume. Creating this effect with a multi-track editor is much easier and gives you greater control over the outcome.

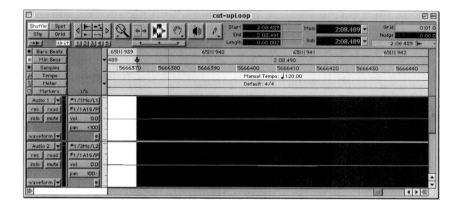

Figure 28.11

When making your loop selection, be sure that the selection begins at a point in the sound wave (or waves, if stereo) where there is a zero crossing.

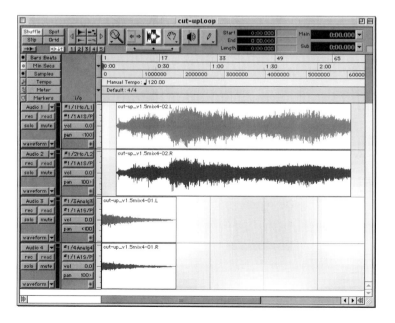

Figure 28.12

The original sound file after cutting the last few seconds and pasting it into two new tracks

4. Now you are ready to blend the newly pasted tracks (the old tail end of the sound) with the beginning of the sound. This can be done in one of two ways:

    •   Create a fade-in for the top stereo pair and a fade-out for the bottom pair. In effect, this is fading out the tail while fading in the head.

    •   Create a crossfade transition (if your audio editor supports this feature). Crossfade between the four tracks so that as two are fading in, the other two are fading out.

> In some situations, you might also find that it is helpful to move the original track slightly to the right to allow more room for the fades to take place.

Whichever method you choose, the idea is to create a seamless transition that blends the various tracks. This final step creates the smooth loop. Because the new beginning of the file *exactly* matches the tail (remember, one used to be attached to the other), there is no glitch or gap in the loop. And because you were able to fade one chunk of the sound into another, there is no longer any differentiation between where the track starts and where it stops (see Figure 28.13).

5. To finalize the process, mix the edited file to a two-track (stereo) file. It's now ready to be imported into a Flash movie.

Figure 28.13

The final file has a fade-out to contour the tracks that you pasted in and a gradual fade-in to raise the volume of the track's original beginning.

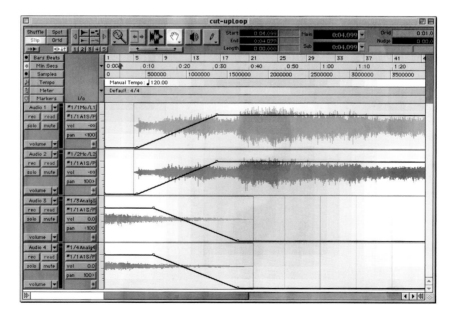

Ambient loops serve as nice background sounds and can loop whimsically due to their loose rhythmic nature. Because they have no one section that sticks out above the others, ambient loops provide a pleasant alternative to rhythmic loops. The absence of repetitive components such as prominent drumbeats and bass or guitar riffs makes the cycles of the loop less obvious.

Ambient Loops in Context

On the companion CD-ROM for this book, there is a file that uses both the ambient loop technique and rhythmic loops. In the Chapter 28 folder, open the file named `loopDesign.html` in your web browser (be sure the Flash plug-in is installed). Here you can hear two different looping techniques in action.

The ambient loop is stored in a sound-only SWF file that is loaded onto `_level1` at the outset of the main movie. This loop is cued as an event sound and uses the techniques described earlier to create a seamless (and continuous) background loop.

Additionally, there are several rhythmic loops that are cued when you interact with the movie. Each of these loops was composed to fit musically with the ambient background and provide a different feel for each section of the movie. The visual and informational content of this movie is incomplete. What is there is intended solely to serve as a navigational structure so that the audio techniques can be tested. The idea is that the ambient piece provides a common thread for the entire movie, while the loops add special flavor to the individual movie sections.

Inspirational Design Model

Flash can do much more with audio than play loops. As evidence of that, we want to present PANSE (`http://130.208.220.190/panse/index.htm`). As stated on their website, it provides "an open platform for the development of audio-visual netart, open to all." The name PANSE is an acronym for Public Access Network Sound Engine.

PANSE (see Figure 28.14) is an MP3 streaming-audio program with a TCP server that allows for multi-user, real-time interaction. It consists of two 16-step sequencers, a monophonic synthesizer, and an effects generator. Many of the sound parameters can be edited over any TCP connection, such as the speed of the sequencers and the number of steps to be played by each; note that the values of the steps can be changed as well as the filters on the sounds. The monophonic synthesizer is playable via messages over TCP and also has a controllable filter; the effects generator is controlled in the same way.

PANSE is open to anyone interested in creating music via the Internet. The best part is that you can use Flash to create an interface that allows your audience to control and manipulate the music that you've composed. Visit the PANSE website to learn how you can connect to the live stream, explore and listen to current exhibits, and submit works to the gallery.

Figure 28.14

PANSE is an open platform for music, art, and interactive exploration.

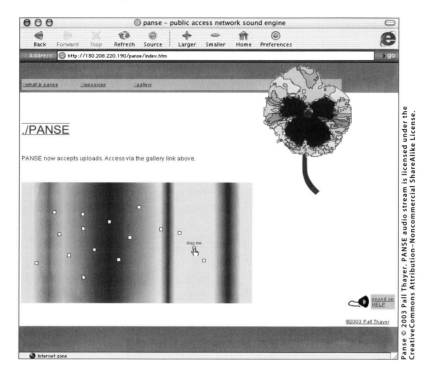

CHAPTER 29

Creating 3D Flash

Up to this point, all your visual creations have existed in two dimensions. You've simulated depth by using some nifty optical tricks such as creating depth in Hands On 2. But they were just that: tricks.

The universe exists in three dimensions: height, width, *and* depth. A whole subset of digital media specializes in creating 3D models and animations for games, television, and movies. Unfortunately, the technology as well as the skills needed to create 3D models and animations is *extremely* specialized. As a result, the worlds of 3D and Flash have remained separate—that is, until recently. As Flash grew in prominence as a tool for authoring 2D visual creations, developers inevitably started looking toward 3D as a new means by which to express their digital vision.

Unfortunately, on its own, Flash's inherently 2D-focused painting and drawing tools are not particularly suited for creating 3D models. But there are many techniques and third-party applications designed specifically to integrate 3D into your Flash creations.

In this chapter, you'll explore the following topics:

- **Simulating 3D in Flash**
- **Using third-party 3D applications to export directly to SWF**

Simulating 3D in Flash

Although Flash is not particularly suited to creating 3D objects or animations, there are some tricks you can use to add the illusion of the third dimension—depth—to your Flash creation. For instance, in Hands On 2, when you inserted some of the fish in the scene, you added them behind other layers so that they appeared to be in the distance. This simulates depth; however, it's nothing more than sleight of hand. The objects are only a two-dimensional drawing that you've manipulated to fool the viewer's eye into believing they're three-dimensional.

> Although it is easy enough to create 3D sleight of hand in Flash, you can create "real" 3D using some fairly complicated and advanced ActionScript that employs pretty scary math—a process well beyond the scope of this book. To see some great examples of "real" Flash 3D, refer to the FLA section of www.ultrashock.com. Alternatively, you can see some wonderful Flash 3D creations at Wireframe Studio (www.wireframe.co.za).

Even though the tricks you'll try out in this chapter aren't designed to create real 3D, don't dismiss them immediately. They have their uses, and in using them, you take your first step on the grand adventure of Flash and 3D. In the following sections, you'll take some of the skills you learned in Chapter 4 and create static 2D objects that look like they're 3D. You'll then create a simulated 3D animation.

Creating Simulated 3D Objects with the Painting and Drawing Tools

If you think back to your high school geometry class, you'll remember that the textbook featured a slew of diagrams that, although appearing to be 3D, were actually 2D. That was a wireframe effect, one of the two basic ways of creating the illusion of depth in a 2D image. The other method is by using shading. In this section, you'll replicate both effects by using Flash's painting and drawing tools.

Creating a Pseudo-3D Sphere

With a rounded object such as a sphere, you suggest the third dimension by adding shading to create the impression of reflected light. To do that in Flash, you create and then modify a gradient fill. Here are the steps:

1. Open a new document by choosing File → New.

2. When the New Document dialog box opens, select the Flash Document option (under the General tab) and click OK.

3. In the middle of the Stage, use the Ellipse tool ○ to draw a circle about 3 centimeters (1.5 inches) in diameter. Make sure you hold down the Shift key while you are drawing the ellipse to ensure it's a perfect circle.

4. Make sure that the circle has a solid color fill by using the Fill Color picker in the Toolbox's Colors section.

5. Now select the circle's fill with the Arrow tool 🖔 .

6. Choose Window → Design Panels → Color Mixer to open the Color Mixer panel.

7. From the Fill Style drop-down menu, choose Radial. At this point, your soon-to-be 3D sphere should look something like the image to the right.

8. You'll notice that, by default, Flash makes the two colors in the gradient black and white, with the white on the outside and the black in the inside. The colors themselves need to be switched, with the light on the inside and the dark on the outside, so that it gives the impression that a light source is reflecting off the curved 3D surface of a sphere. Select the sphere's fill with the Arrow tool 🖔 .

9. Now, with the Color Mixer panel still open, select the right gradient handle (the white one). Next click the color swatch to the left of the Fill Style drop-down menu and choose a dark color (in this example, it's black).

10. From here, click the left gradient handle (the black one). Then click the color swatch to the left of the Fill Style drop-down menu and choose a very light color (in this example, it's white). The sphere should look something like the image to the right.

11. Now you need to manipulate the gradient so that it gives a more realistic impression that a light source is reflecting off the curved 3D surface of the sphere. With the Color Mixer panel still open and the sphere's fill still selected, as illustrated in Figure 29.1, click and drag the right gradient handle toward the center of the Gradient Definition bar. By doing this, you restrict the size of the simulated reflection.

12. Then you need to manipulate the shape and position of the gradient to enhance the look of the simulated reflection. First, make sure the sphere's fill is deselected.

Figure 29.1

By moving the right gradient handle, you restrict the size of the simulated reflection.

> The simulated reflection created by the gradient is what changes the humdrum circle into a magnificent pseudo-3D sphere. Spend some time getting it to look exactly how you want.

13. Select the Fill Transform tool 🖫 from the Toolbox and then click the sphere's fill. By doing this, the gradient's bounding box and associated handles will be displayed. (If you are having trouble remembering how to manipulate a gradient fill using the Fill Transform tool, see Chapter 4.)

14. To change the position of the simulated reflection, move your mouse over the handle in the center of the fill. Notice that your cursor changes. Click and drag to the upper-right area of your sphere. By doing this, you change the center of the circle gradient's position. At this point, your sphere should look something like this.

15. To change the shape of the simulated reflection, move your cursor over the *square* handle on the circle's edge (notice that your cursor changes). Click and drag toward the center of the circle slightly; this "squishes" the gradient, making it more linear.

> If, when you are editing the gradient, it snaps, then you'll need to turn the Snap To Objects feature off (View → Snapping → Snap To Objects).

16. At this point, you want to rotate the simulated reflection so that it looks like light is hitting the sphere from the upper right. With the Transform Fill tool and the circle's fill selected, move your cursor over the bottommost circular handle. Notice that your cursor switches to four arrows arrayed in a circle. Click and drag so that your simulated reflection is slanted at a roughly 45-degree angle.

17. Now click and drag the center handle to reposition your radial gradient's center near the upper-right corner of the sphere.

Congratulations, you've just created a pseudo-3D sphere using a simple circle and radial gradient—which should look something like the image to the left.

You'll employ a sphere such as the one you've just created in the "Animating Simulated 3D Objects" section later in this chapter, so you might want to save this one. Fiddle around with the shape, size, and orientation of the gradient to get different looks for your pseudo-3D sphere.

Creating a Wireframe Cube

In traditional 3D modeling, the term *wireframe* refers to a display mode in which objects are represented by lines, resulting in the object looking as if it's made of a wire mesh. This view, originally a working tool for modelers, is now often seen in advertisements (as a kind of visual shorthand to suggest high-tech engineering). In Flash, you can create simple wireframe images to create the illusion of depth and perhaps to evoke this now-familiar look.

You can create a wireframe cube using Flash's drawing tools by following these steps:

1. Open a new document by choosing File → New.

2. When the New Document dialog box opens, select the Flash Document option (under the General tab) and click OK.

3. Draw a perfectly proportioned square with the Rectangle tool ⬚ (remember to hold down the Shift key to maintain the proportions).

4. Because the pseudo-3D cube you are drawing is wireframe, you need to make sure that it doesn't have a fill. To do this, select the square's fill with the Arrow tool ➤ and delete it.

5. Now select the square (which should simply be a black outline) with the Arrow tool ➤ and group it by choosing Modify → Group.

6. Now that you've created the front face of the pseudo-3D cube, you can create the back face. Select the square, copy it (Edit → Copy), and then paste it (Edit → Paste In Center or Paste In Place).

7. Click and drag the newly pasted square so that it is located slightly up and to the right of the first square. Make sure each square's bottom-left corners line up diagonally. So far, the scene should look something like the image to the right.

8. Now that you've created the front and back face of the pseudo-3D cube, it's time to create all the other faces. To do this, you'll link each of the two square's respective corners with the Line tool. First, you want to turn on Snap To Objects by choosing View → Snapping → Snap To Objects. When you do this, the lines that you draw with the Line tool will snap exactly to the corners of the squares.

9. Now, select the Line tool ╱ from the Toolbox. Position your cursor over the bottom-left corner of the lower square (which will serve at the cube's front face). Click and drag to the bottom-left corner of the upper square (which will serve as the cube's back face). Notice that your line snaps exactly to the square's corner.

10. Now repeat the process for the two cubes' upper-right, bottom-right, and upper-left corners.

Congratulations, you've created a pseudo-wireframe 3D cube that should look something like the image to the right.

Animating Simulated 3D Objects

Now that you've learned how to create pseudo-3D objects using Flash's painting and drawing tools, you can animate them. Because the objects have the illusion of depth, you'll also want to create and maintain that illusion in their animation. To do this, you can use a couple of techniques. The most basic one involves creating an animation in which a single objects moves in front of and behind another object, creating the necessary illusion.

In this section, you'll take the animation skills you already mastered in Part III and create a simple animation in which a pseudo-3D sphere orbits around a second, larger pseudo-3D sphere. To accomplish this, you'll use a little ActionScript trickery; in particular, you'll leverage the power of the setProperty() action.

If you are new to ActionScript, see Parts IV and V.

A working version of this project has been included in the Chapter 29 folder of this book's accompanying CD (in both SWF and FLA formats).

Follow these steps:

1. Open a new document by choosing File → New.

2. When the New Document dialog box opens, select the Flash Document option (under the General tab) and click OK.

3. Open the Document Properties dialog box (Modify → Document) and set the width of the Stage to **600** and the height to **400**.

4. Start off by creating three pseudo-3D spheres using the process described earlier in this chapter. Make one of the spheres small and make the other two (which *must* be exactly identical in size, shape, and color) larger. This is an example of what your three spheres might look like.

5. Now convert each 3D sphere to a Movie Clip. Although the name of the small spheres (which will be doing the orbiting) doesn't really matter, make sure one of the large spheres is named **front** and the other **back**.

The reason you are making these images Movie Clips instead of graphic symbols is that the ActionScript you'll use later in the tutorial works only with Movie Clip symbols.

6. Because you've converted the three spheres to symbols, you can delete the original spheres from the Stage.

7. Next create three additional layers (which would give you a total of four). Name each of the layers, from top to bottom: **actions**, **front**, **small ball**, and **back**.

8. Click the first keyframe in the front layer and drag the Front symbol from the Library onto the Stage.

9. Open the Info panel (Window → Design Panels → Info) and enter **250** for the X value and **150** for the Y value.

Remember, you can also add the X and Y coordinates using the Property Inspector (Window → Properties).

10. Select frame 30 in the front layer and choose Insert → Timeline → Frame (or use the shortcut F5).

11. Select frame 30 in the back layer and choose Insert → Timeline → Frame.

12. Click the first keyframe in the back layer and drag the Back symbol onto the Stage.

13. With the Back symbol still selected, open the Info panel (Window → Info) and enter **250** for the X value and **150** for the Y value. By setting it to the same location as the symbol in front, you make it appear that there is only one large sphere on the Stage while there are actually two.

14. Now select the small ball layer and insert a motion guide by clicking the Add Motion Guide button ✦ at the bottom left of the Timeline or by choosing Insert → Timeline → Motion Guide.

15. Select the first keyframe of the new motion guide layer (which appears just about the small ball layer) and use the Ellipse tool ○ to draw a compressed ellipse. Make sure the newly created ellipse doesn't have any fill. Position the ellipse (which will serve as the motion path for the small orbiting ball) over the large sphere. The result should look something like the image to the right.

16. Now it's time to fiddle with the motion path a bit so that it will function properly in relation to your intended product. Hide the back and front layers by clicking their Show/Hide buttons (represented by the little black dots below the eye icon in the Timeline).

After you've manipulated the motion path, you can turn the back and front layers back on by clicking their Show/Hide buttons.

17. Use the Zoom tool 🔍 to zoom into a section of the motion path that is behind the large sphere (make sure you are at the maximum magnification). With the Lasso tool 🅿, select a small section of the magnified motion path and then delete it. (Once you've cut the small section out of the motion path, you can set the Stage's magnification back to 100 percent.)

By doing this, your motion path will no longer be closed but will have a small break. The result should look something like the image to the right.

18. Now you need to attach the small orbiting sphere to the motion path. With the two large spheres still hidden, click the first keyframe of the small ball layer and drag the small Sphere symbol onto the Stage. With the Library open (Window → Library), click and drag the small Sphere symbol so that it snaps to one end of the motion path. If the sphere doesn't snap, make sure Snap To Objects is on (View → Snapping → Snap To Objects).

19. Select frame 30 in the small ball layer and choose Insert → Timeline → Keyframe.

20. Select the final keyframe in the layer and click and drag the small sphere so that it snaps to the other end of the motion path.

21. Now, to add the motion tween, select the first keyframe in the small ball layer and select Window → Properties. Choose Motion from the Tween drop-down menu.

22. Test your motion tween by hitting the Return/Enter key or by choosing Control → Test Movie. You'll notice that the motion of your small orbiting ball is partially hidden by the Front symbol. In the next few steps, you'll use some ActionScript to dynamically change the visibility of both large spheres to create the illusion that the small sphere is passing in front of and behind the same object.

23. If you haven't already, you need to turn the visibility of the two large spheres back on.

24. Click the front layer and select the Front symbol. Choose Window → Properties and enter **front** in the Instance Name field. Repeat the process for the Back symbol in the back layer (but instead enter **back** in the Instance Name field). By doing this, you are assigning a unique identifier to the instance; this is *absolutely* necessary if you want the ActionScript that you'll write in the next few steps to work properly.

> To select each symbol (remember, they are placed one on top of the other), you could hide the back layer and then select the Front symbol. Then you could hide the front layer and select the Back symbol.

25. Now onto the ActionScript that makes it all possible. Select the first keyframe in the actions layer and open the Actions panel by choosing Window → Development Panels → Actions.

26. Expand the Global Functions category in the ActionScript Toolbox, expand the Movie Clip Control category and double-click the `setProperty()` Global Function to add it to the ActionScript text box.

27. From here, edit the `setProperty()` Global Function so that it looks like this:

```
setProperty("front", _visible, true);
```

28. Add a second `setProperty()` Global Function. In this case, however, edit it so it looks like this:

```
setProperty("back", _visible, false);
```

> If you don't enter the exact same name in the Target field as you put in the Name field of the Property Inspector, the ActionScript simply won't work.

29. Now you need to create the ActionScript that will hide the Front symbol and display the Back symbol, giving the illusion that the orbiting ball is passing in front of the large sphere. First, select frame 10 in the actions layer (or the frame in which the sphere has reached the maximum extent of its orbit).

30. Choose Insert → Timeline → Keyframe.

31. Repeat the process described in steps 26–28. However, switch the value of the Front symbol to **false** and the value of the Back symbol to **true** and change the appropriate values instead of building the script from scratch.

> If you want, you can simply cut and paste the script created in steps 27 and 28.

32. Now that you've allowed the small sphere to pass in "front" of the large one, you'll create a script that will hide the Back symbol and display the Front symbol, allowing the sphere to pass "behind" the large sphere and complete its orbit. First, click frame 28 (or the frame just before the small sphere touches the larger one).

33. Repeat the process described in steps 25–28. Use the exact same script. By doing this, you tell Flash to display the Front symbol and hide the Back symbol, allowing the sphere to pass "behind." In the end, your Timeline should look something like this.

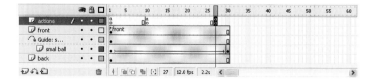

Congratulations, you've just created an animation in which a pseudo-3D sphere revolves around another pseudo-3D sphere. Test your movie by choosing Control → Test Movie. Now that you've mastered the basics, you can play around with the effect. Try adding more orbiting spheres to create a molecule or create an animation that is more than just two spheres.

Using Third-Party 3D Applications to Export Directly to SWF

As the integration of Flash and 3D has become more popular, several astute 3D modeling software companies have caught on and have added the ability to export SWF files from their programs. This is a huge advancement for Flash and 3D. Now there is little need to resort to visual trickery (like that described earlier) to add the illusion of depth to your Flash creations. You can simply create a 3D model or animation (which is exported to a SWF file) and import it directly to Flash.

In the following sections, you'll explore some of the more prominent 3D modeling programs that feature SWF export, including Swift 3D v3, plasma, and Carrara Studio 3. In some cases, such as in the discussion of Swift 3D (designed purely for creating 3D models destined for Flash export), you'll delve deeply into the program.

In other cases, such as in the discussion of middle- to high-end 3D modelers such as plasma and Carrara Studio 3 (which do far more than create models for Flash export), you'll focus on how models are exported as SWF files.

> It's important to realize that the specific programs that are discussed in this chapter are certainly not the only 3D modeling programs that feature SWF export. Quite the contrary. Given the increasing popularity of 3D Flash, there are quite a number of 3D modeling applications that have jumped on the Flash bandwagon. What sets apart the applications discussed here is the fact that they are, in my humble opinion, some of the best tools available for creating 3D Flash.

Swift 3D v3

Electric Rain's Swift 3D (www.erain.com) was one of the first stand-alone programs designed to create 3D models directly exportable to SWF. Although the program can't compare with most of the more robust 3D modeling programs, it does have a hefty set of features, including direct 3DS (3ds max) import, EPS and AI import, complex lighting, and preset animation templates, which allow you to create and optimize 3D models for Flash. Many other programs lack these features. In addition, Swift 3D v3 comes in both Mac and Windows versions. Although cross-platform support should be a given, 3D modeling has traditionally been the domain of the Windows and Unix operating systems; until fairly recently, Mac users have been pretty cut off from the world of 3D modeling, so Swift 3D v3's cross-platform support is a welcome feature for all Mac users.

Despite Swift 3D v3's usefulness, you shouldn't mistake it for a full-featured 3D modeling program. Comparing it with 3D modeling programs such as Maya, 3ds max, LightWave 3D, or Cinema 4D would be inappropriate. Swift 3D v3's ability to create even marginally complex 3D models is limited. If you're interested in experimenting with polygon modeling techniques, Swift 3D v3 is probably not for you. However, this doesn't mean the program isn't useful; Swift 3D v4 is quite easy to learn, unlike most of the full-featured 3D modeling programs (some of which require years of study to learn and a small fortune to acquire). Those who have experience working with high-end 3D modeling programs can use Swift 3D v3 as a filter of sorts to set Flash-specific properties of an imported 3ds max file before exporting it as an SWF file. One of the great things about Swift 3D v3 is its price tag: $169, which is pretty manageable for most people.

In the following sections, you'll explore the Swift 3D v3 creative process. Be aware, however, that although Swift 3D v3 is on the "light" end of 3D modelers, it still has a fair amount of features. As a result, we won't cover Swift 3D v3 in its entirety. To get an in-depth account of the program and all of its options and tools, refer to the documentation that accompanies the program, which is quite good.

> Besides Swift 3D v3, Electric Rain has also recently announced Swift 3D Xpress. Designed as a revolutionary new 3D Extension for Flash MX 2004 and Flash MX Professional 2004, Swift3D Xpress allows users to quickly convert 2D text and artwork to 3D animations without leaving the Flash interface. Vector objects on Flash's stage can be brought into the Swift 3D Xpress interface and customized using pre-built animations, lighting schemes, and materials. The 3D scenes are then rendered and placed in a specialized Movie Clip in Flash's Library for further use or future editing. For more information about Swift3D Xpress, visit www.macromedia.com/software/flash/extensions/swift3d. One of the best things about Swift3D Xpress is its $99 price tag, which is far more manageable for those who only dabble in Flash 3D.

A demo copy of Swift 3D v3 has been included on this book's accompanying CD.

Starting a Swift 3D Project

You have a handful of options for starting a Swift 3D project:

- To start with a new file, choose File → New, or click the New button [icon] in the top-left corner of the program's interface.

- To open an existing document, click the Open button [icon] in the top-left corner of the program's interface. When the Open dialog box is displayed, navigate the location where the file you want to open is located and select it.

- To import Encapsulated Postscript (EPS), Adobe Illustrator (AI) files, or AutoCAD (DXF) files, choose File → Import. When the Import dialog box opens, navigate to the location where the file you want to open is located and select it.

Any Encapsulated Postscript or Adobe Illustrator image imported to Swift 3D is converted to a 3D object, while still retaining its original 2D shape. Any previously applied color will be lost when the file is imported.

- To start a new document based on an existing 3ds max file (.3ds), choose File → New from 3DS.

Working with the Swift 3D Property Toolbox

The Property Toolbox, which is located on the left side of the program's interface, is one of the most vital tools in Swift 3D v3. With it, you can access all the properties of the scene on which you're currently working. As you add objects to your scene, their properties become accessible by clicking the appropriate heading in the Property Toolbox's list box.

SETTING LAYOUT PROPERTIES

The Layout properties (see Figure 29.2) allow you to control various aspects of your scene in Swift 3D. By clicking the Layout heading located in Property Toolbox's list box, you'll see three discrete groups of controls: Layout, Display, Settings.

Layout Lets you set the dimensions of your project. Simply choose a unit of measurement from the Units drop-down menu and then enter values in the Height and Width fields.

Display Lets you manipulate the way in which the objects are displayed in the program's viewport. You have the following options:

- The Shaded option displays your objects as closely as they would appear when exported to SWF, complete with materials and lighting.
- The Fast Shaded option displays the object shaded, but without smooth gradients.
- The Outline option displays your objects as wireframe models.
- The Box option displays each object as a 3D bounding box.
- When checked, the Pivots option displays the object's pivot point, which is kind of like the registration point for a 3D object.
- When checked, the Paths option displays the motion paths in your scene as purple lines.
- The Grid option toggles the XYZ coordinate system on and off.
- The Hidden option lets you either hide or show objects in your scene.

Settings Lets you set the value of several additional settings. You've got the following options:

- The Trace Depth settings controls how deep the EMO Ray Tracer will trace for reflections and refraction (through glass). It is similar to the RAViX III "Reflection Depth" control except that it applies to refraction as well.

Figure 29.2

Swift 3D's Layout properties window

- The Nudge Increment setting controls how far your selected object will move when you nudge it with your keyboard arrow keys. It is set to 1 pixel.

> If your monitor is running at an 800×600 resolution, you will have to undock this toolbar to adjust this increment.

SETTING CAMERA PROPERTIES

The Camera properties (see Figure 29.3), accessible by clicking the Camera header in the Property Toolbox, allow you to access the properties of any selected camera.

You have these options:

- The Name field displays the name of the currently selected camera. When selected, the field becomes live, allowing you to change the camera's name.

- The Lens Length setting (expressed in millimeters) approximates the lens length of a camera. The longer the lens length, the more the camera will zoom in on your scene. The shorter the lens length, the more distant you appear to be from your scene.

Figure 29.3
Swift 3D's Camera properties window

> Just as with a camera lens, if the length is shortened, your image will get distorted as the view becomes more panoramic in nature.

SETTING ENVIRONMENTAL PROPERTIES

Clicking the Environment header in the Property Toolbox's list box gives you access to three important properties: Background Color, Ambient Light Color, and Environment (see Figure 29.4).

The Background Color, as you might have already guessed, is the color of your final rendered image's background. To set the background color, simply click the Background Color swatch to open the Color Picker. From here, you can pick the color you want for the background or mix your own custom color. When you're finished, just click the Apply button.

Ambient light, theoretically speaking, is the cumulative effect of all the light bouncing off of all the objects in a given area. Practically speaking, the Ambient Light option equally illuminates all objects in a given scene. To set the Ambient Light color, simply click the Ambient Light Color swatch to open the Color Picker. From here, you can pick the color you want for the scene's ambient light or mix your own custom color. When you're finished, click the Apply button.

Figure 29.4
Swift 3D's Environment properties window

Adding Primitive Objects

Figure 29.5
The Swift 3D shape primitives

Box   Cone   Torus   Polyhedron

Sphere   Pyramid   Cylinder   Plane

A large part of the modeling you'll do in Swift 3D entails adding and manipulating a series of shape primitives. Once you insert the shape in your scene, you can then manipulate its properties (size, orientation, and so on).

To add a shape primitive to your scene, click the appropriate button, as shown in Figure 29.5. The corresponding shape will be inserted at the intersection of the X, Y, and Z axes.

Using the Object Trackball

Now that you've added an object to your scene, you can manipulate its orientation. Located in the bottom-left corner of the program interface, the Object Trackball (see

Figure 29.6
The Object Trackball

Figure 29.6) lets you adjust the orientation of objects in your scene.

The Object Trackball remains inactive until you select an object in the viewport. Once selected, the object appears within the Object Trackball. From there, you can click and drag the trackball to rotate the object itself.

You can also constrain the direction in which the trackball moves by clicking one of the Lock Axis (Lock Horizontal or Lock Vertical) buttons located to the left of the Object Trackball.

- The Lock Horizontal button ![icon] constrains the movement of the selected object along its horizontal axis.
- The Lock Vertical button ![icon] constrains the movement of the selected object along its vertical axis.
- The Lock Spin button ![icon] constrains the movement of the selected object so that it can rotate only clockwise or counterclockwise.
- By clicking the Rotation Increment button ![icon], you can set the value (in degrees) that the trackball rotates.

Adding and Manipulating 3D Text

Text is a powerful tool in any medium, including 3D. In Swift 3D, text is considered an object, as are all the shape primitives you looked at previously. Let's take a look at a step-by-step approach to adding and manipulating text in Swift 3D:

1. With a new document open, click the Create Text button ![icon]. By doing this, the program inserts a default text object in your current scene.

Remember that you can access the properties only of a currently selected object, so make sure you select the text you're currently working with by clicking it.

2. Click the Text heading in the Property Toolbox's list box.

3. Choose a font from the Font drop-down menu.

4. Enter the desired text in the Text field; notice how the text automatically appears in the viewport.

5. Choose one of the alignment options by clicking the appropriate alignment button.

6. Now click the Bevel heading in the Property Toolbox. From here, you'll be able to manipulate the bevel properties of the text.

7. Choose a bevel style for the Style drop-down menu (to get an idea of your options, experiment with each).

8. Enter a value in the Depth field to set the depth of the bevel. The higher the value, the higher the bevel will be.

9. Choose a Face option. By choosing Front, the bevel will appear only on the front of the text. Choosing Back will display the bevel only on the back of the text. Choosing Both will apply the bevel to both faces of the text.

10. Adjust the Smoothness slider to alter how Swift 3D v3 draws the curves of the text. Moving the slider toward Course makes the text more angular and block and moving it toward Smooth makes the curves smoother.

A higher level of smoothness results in a higher file size and less smoothness results in a smaller file size.

11. Adjust the Mesh Quality slider, which lets you exert some control over the quality of the 3D object's mesh.

12. Now click the Sizing heading in the Property Toolbox's list box.

13. Enter a value in the Height, Width, and Depth fields to adjust the actual size of the 3D text.

14. Enter a value in the Inter Character field to adjust the space between characters.

15. Enter a value in the Inter Line field to adjust the space between lines.

Working with Preset Materials

Although delving too deeply into Swift 3D v3's ability to create and mix custom materials is beyond the scope of this chapter, you'll apply materials from a preset library to the objects within your scene.

Unlike other 3D modeling programs where you've got access to all manner of tools and techniques for creating and mixing materials, Flash's inherent limitations (especially when it comes to bitmaps) limit the types of materials you can apply to objects in Swift 3D v3.

To apply preset materials to your objects, follow these steps:

1. Make sure the object with which you want to work is selected.

2. Click the Show Materials button ▨ in the Gallery (located in the bottom-right corner of the program interface) to open the Materials palette.

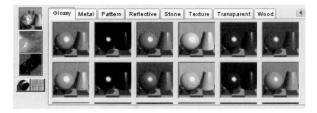

3. Click one of the tabs in the Materials palette to access a particular subset of materials.

4. Simply click and drag the desired material from the Materials palette onto the currently selected object.

> When it comes to text (or complex models imported), you'll need to apply materials to each separate section of the object. For text, this means applying the material to both faces as well as the bevel.

Working with Lights

One of the most important aspects of any 3D creation is lighting. With proper lighting, you can turn a mediocre model into a great model. Don't get too excited, however; because of the Flash medium, your lighting options in Swift 3D v3 are somewhat limited. But this doesn't mean you should spend any less time on lighting your 3D scene. When exported, a well-lit 3D Flash scene can be quite compelling.

Swift 3D v3 gives you two types of lights to work with: Point Lights and Spot Lights, which can be added to a scene in two different ways (with the Lighting Trackball or directly into the scene). Point Lights act somewhat like a light bulb, casting illumination in a more diffuse area, and Spot Lights focus illumination on a specific area.

ADDING AND SUBTRACTING TRACKBALL LIGHTS

You can add any number of lights to your scene by clicking either the Create Trackball Point Light button ![] or the Create Trackball Spot Light button ![], both to the right of the Lighting Trackball at the bottom of the program interface.

As you add lights, they'll be displayed on the Lighting Trackball.

To delete a light from your scene, select the light on the Lighting Trackball (by clicking it) and click the Remove Light button ![].

ADDING AND SUBTRACTING SCENE LIGHTS

You can also add lights directly to the scene. To do so, just click the button for the type of light you want.

When you add a light, it appears in the scene as a small yellow symbol. When you select a light in the scene (by clicking it), the symbol's color changes from yellow to red.

Figure 29.7 illustrates the difference between free and target lights. A free light (Free Point Light or Free Spot Light) acts like any other object in your scene. As such, once you have added one, you can easily select and manipulate it using the Rotation Trackball (left). A target light (Target Point Light or Target Spot Light), on the other hand, always points at the pivot point of the object that was selected when it was inserted in the scene (right).

Free Point Light
Target Point Light
Free Spot Light
Target Spot Light

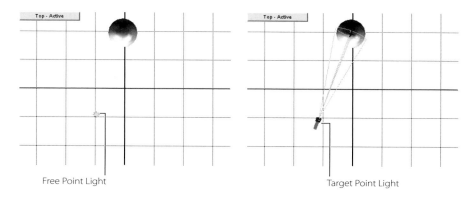

Free Point Light

Target Point Light

Figure 29.7

Free lights and target lights

MANIPULATING THE POSITION OF LIGHTS

Manipulating the position of a light in your scene is extremely easy. In the case of a trackball light, all you need to do is select the light on the Lighting Trackball, and then drag the trackball itself.

Much as with the Object Trackball, you can use one of the three Lock Axis buttons (Lock Horizontal ⬤, Lock Vertical ⬤, and Lock Spin ⬤) to constrain the movement of the light.

You'll notice that as you drag the Lighting Trackball, your scene will dynamically change to reflect the new lighting scheme.

In the case of a scene light, all you need to do is click and drag the Light symbol in the scene (notice that your cursor changes), move it to its new position, and then release your mouse button.

If you are moving the position of a target light, you'll notice that the line that links the Light symbol to the object's pivot point (which represents the direction in which the light itself is pointing) remains no matter where you move the light.

Using Drag-and-Drop Animations

Swift 3D v3 not only functions as a limited modeling program, but also as an animation program. You can create true 3D animations (quite unlike those requiring the kind of visual trickery employed earlier in the chapter) and then export them as SWF.

Swift 3D v3's animation tools use frames and keyframes the same as Flash does. There are, however, some differences in the ways in which the two programs work. Much as with materials in Swift 3D v3, you've got a whole library of preset animations that you can apply to any given object in your scene. These *drag-and-drop animations*, as they are called, are pretty useful for quickly adding moderately sophisticated animations. Follow these steps to put these drag-and-drop animations to work in your scene:

1. Make sure that the object you want to work with is selected.

2. Click the Show Animations button ⬤ in the Gallery (located in the bottom-right corner of the program interface) to open the Animations palette.

3. From here, you see a single tab—Regular Spins—which gives you access to a series of animations you can apply to your objects to make them spin in place.

4. Simply click and drag the desired animation from the Animations palette onto the currently selected object.

5. To test your animation, click the Play button ▶ located just below the Timeline.

Exporting to SWF

Now that you've created your model, applied materials to it, and infused movement in it with animations, you can now output your creation as an SWF file:

1. Click the Preview and Export Editor tab at the top of the program interface.

Preview and Export Editor

2. From here, you have quite a few different options that you can set for the exported animation, all of which are accessible through the Property Toolbox. To start off with, click the General option in the Property Toolbox.

3. Select the file format to which you want to export your Swift 3D v3 project from—in this case, Flash Player (SWF).

> A new feature to Swift 3D v3 is the SWFT file format. Designed to be read only by the Swift 3D Importer (which is installed on your machine when you install Swift 3D—if you have Flash MX), SWFT is a proprietary file type created by Electric Rain. The main advantage that you gain by using the SWFT file format is the ability to render your scene using the SmartLayer Technology, allowing you to import your Swift3D v3 animations to Flash with all the various components broken into separate layers.

4. Choose the version of Flash for your exported SWF from the File Level drop-down menu.

5. Adjust the Curve Fitting slider. When you adjust the slider toward the Curves end, the program will smooth out the irregular curves in your objects.

6. Choose the level of detail for your exported SWF file from the Detail Level drop-down menu. Remember, a higher level of detail means a larger file size. Also, the lower the detail level, the faster your SWF file will render.

7. If you want, select the Combine Edges and Fills option. By doing this, your object will be rendered so that both the line and fill are part of the same object (kind of like being grouped together). If, on the other hand, you leave the option unchecked, the exported SWF file will contain an object (or objects) whose stroke and fill will be able to be manipulated independently without having to break the object apart.

8. Now select Fill Options in the Property Toolbox.

9. If you want the object (or objects) in the exported SWF file to have fill, check the Fill Objects option.

10. From here, select one of the options from the Fill Type drop-down menu. The more colors in an exported SWF, the larger the file will be. Each will affect the way in which your object's fill appears in the exported SWF:

    - When you choose Cartoon Single Color Fill, the diffuse color of an object is sampled and then applied to the entire object, creating objects with solid color.

    - By selecting the Cartoon Average Color Fill, groups of individual polygons that occur on similar surfaces will have the same color in the exported file.

    - Like the Cartoon Average Color Fill, the Cartoon Two Color Fill option colors groups of individual polygons on similar surfaces. The difference is that the Cartoon Two Color Fill option applies two colors, instead of one, to the groups of polygons.

    - By selecting the Cartoon Four Color Fill, four colors, instead of two, will be applied to groups of polygons on similar surfaces.

    - When you choose Cartoon Full Color Fill, a separate color can be applied to each individual polygon.

    Despite that the Cartoon Full Color Fill option results in a relatively detailed image, there is no shading between the color areas.

    - When you select Area Gradient Shading, the program looks for groups of polygons that appear on similar surfaces and applies a radial gradient, creating the appearance of a light reflecting off a surface.

    - The Mesh Gradient Shading option results in the highest quality image by fully merging all the colors in all the model's polygons.

11. If you select the Include Specular Highlights option, the program searches for surfaces perpendicular to the scene's light source and applies a lighter color to them.

    Be aware that turning on the Include Specular Highlights option greatly increases the size of your exported file.

12. If you want your exported scene to include shadows, select the Include Shadows option.

13. If you want the exported file to include any reflections, select the Include Reflections option.

14. Select the Edge Options in the Property Toolbox.

15. If you want the object (or objects) in the exported SWF file to have a stroke, check the Include Edges option.

16. Select an option from the Edge Type drop-down menu:
    - When you choose the Outlines option, the edges of all objects will be outlined with a solid line.
    - By choosing the Entire Mesh option, the edges of all polygons in the 3D object (objects) will be outlined with a solid line, creating a wireframe-like result.

17. If you want the edges on the backside of a 3D object to be visible, select the Include Hidden Edges option.

18. Both the Include Detail Edges and Detail Edge Angle options affect the amount (and detail) of internal edges displayed in the final SWF exported file.

19. Select the width (thickness) of the line from the Line Weight drop-down menu.

20. To set the color of the line, double-click the color within the Line Color box. This opens the Color Picker, from which you can either choose a new color or mix your own.

21. From here, the animation needs to be rendered before it's exported. To render the entire animation, click the Generate All Frames button Generate All Frames . To render a single frame, select the appropriate frame in the Render Preview bar, and then click the Generate Selected Frames button Generate Selected Frames .

22. From here, Swift 3D will render each individual frame. The more frames, the longer it takes to render the animation.

23. When it's finished rendering, click the Export All Frames button Export All Frames... to export the entire animation. To export an individual frame in the animation, select the desired frame in the Render Preview bar and click the Export Selected Frames button Export Selected Frames... .

24. When the Export Vector File dialog box opens, navigate to the location where you want the SWF file exported, enter a name in the File Name field, and click Save.

plasma

Created by Discreet, the same company that makes 3ds Max, plasma is arguably one of the most exciting products for creating 3D Flash content. Not only was it created specifically for exporting 3D content to the Web (in either SWF or Shockwave format), but it also features a very hefty modeling environment (see Figure 29.8) that easily surpasses Swift3D v3 (as well as many other strictly 3D modeling programs available on the market) in terms of scope, scale, and power. In addition, plasma features Havok Dynamics, a tool that allows you to simulate real-world physics in a 3D animation. Animating a rubber ball falling and bouncing off the ground, for example, is a relatively simple task for an experienced animator. However, animating 200 bouncing balls is a monumentally more complicated task. The Havok Dynamics feature in plasma allows you to easily create these kinds of animations, even when the amount of objects, connections, and interactions between them, such as things colliding and bouncing off each other, makes manual animation far too difficult and the result never realistic enough.

> A demo copy of plasma can be downloaded from the Discreet website (www.discreet.com/products/plasma/download_demo.html).

The downside to plasma, at least in terms of 3D Flash, is its hefty modeling environment, which can be somewhat daunting to those who lack the experience in traditional 3D modeling programs. The second downside to plasma is that it costs $650. Now, in the world of 3D modeling programs, this is actually quite a steal. However, for those people who aren't used to shelling out this kind of cash for a program, plasma might not be the first choice for creating 3D Flash content. But for those who are dedicated to creating cutting edge 3D Flash content and want a robust and extremely powerful modeling environment in which to do it, plasma is definitely an excellent choice.

Figure 29.8

The plasma modeling environment

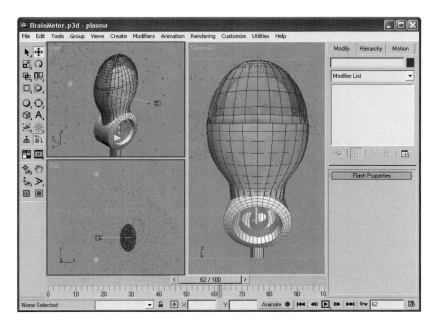

In this section of the chapter, we'll explore how you take a 3D model and export it to SWF format.

> If you are interested in exploring how to use plasma to actually create 3D models, check out the program's documentation (which includes some pretty interesting step-by-step tutorials).

1. With the 3D model you want to export to SWF open in plasma, choose Rendering → Render.

2. When the Render Scene dialog box opens, click the Flash Renderer rollout to get access to the SWF export properties (see Figure 29.9).

3. In the Output section of the Flash Renderer rollout, select the format to which the model is rendered from the File Type drop-down menu.

Figure 29.9

The Flash Renderer section of the Render Scene dialog box

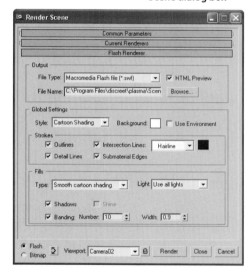

   Screen Only   The Screen Only option renders the model and displays it within the plasma workspace, but does not save the rendered model to file.

   Macromedia Flash File (*.swf)   The Flash option renders the model as an SWF file.

   Swiff-V File (*.swfv)   Exports the model to a Swiff-V file. The Swiff-V file format is supported by the plasma importer, which is automatically installed on your machine when you install plasma.

> The plasma importer allows vector graphic rendered in plasma to be imported directly to Flash MX (or higher). The importer offers plasma users several extra benefits over using the usual (*. swf) import function when bringing their exported 3D models into Flash. First, when the importer is used, all imported files are placed in a single folder in the movie's Library, allowing for greater organization of assets. Second, when Swiff-V files are brought into Flash with the plasma importer, they have a tendency to be smaller in size (which retaining the same visual quality) than regular SWF files.

   Adobe Illustrator File (*.ai)   Exports models to an Adobe Illustrator file format. Given the fact that Adobe Illustrator does not support animation, each frame in an animation exported from plasma are rendered as an individual file.

When you export to Adobe Illustrator, only the object's stroke will be rendered, not the fill.

Figure 29.10

File rendered using the Cartoon Shading style option

4. From here, enter the name of the exported file in the File Name field. If you want to render the file to a specific location on your hard drive, click the Browse button. When the Save As dialog box opens, navigate to the location to which you want to save the exported file, enter the filename in the File Name field, and click Save.

5. If you want plasma to also create an HTML file in which the exported Flash file is displayed, click the HTML Preview check box.

The HTML Preview option is available only if you are exporting to an .swf or .swfv file.

6. From here, select one of following options from the Style drop-down menu:

    Cartoon Shading As illustrated in Figure 29.10, the Cartoon Shading option produces flat, filled renderings with the addition of cartoon-style lighting effects.

Figure 29.11

File rendered using the Gradient Shading style option

    Gradient Shading As illustrated in Figure 29.11, the Gradient Shading option produces a Flash file with either linear or radial gradient shading (depending on the option you select from the Type drop-down menu in the Fills section, which will be discussed shortly).

    Flat Shading As illustrated in Figure 29.12, the Flat Shading option produces a Flash file in which a single color has been used as a fill for each individual 3D object.

    Wireframe As illustrated in Figure 29.13, the Wireframe Shading option produces a Flash file in which all of the objects in the scene are rendered without any fill.

7. To set the background color of the exported Flash file, click the Background color swatch. When the Color Selector opens, select the desired color.

8. If you want the background of the exported Flash movie to be the same as the Environment background color (which is set by choosing Rendering → Environment), click the Use Environment check box.

9. From here, you need to determine how the 3D object's stroke is rendered. In the Stroke section, select the Outline check box if you want the edges of your 3D object to have an outline.

Figure 29.12

File rendered using the Flat Shading style option

10. If you want the object's internal edges to be visible, select the Detail Lines check box.

11. If you want the point at which 3D objects intersect to be visible, select the Intersection Lines check box.

The Strokes drop-down list, which is to the left of the Intersection Lines check box, lets you set the thickness of the stroke intersections. In addition, clicking the color swatch to the left of the Strokes drop-down menu opens a Color Selector from which you can set the stroke color for intersections.

Figure 29.13

File rendered using the Wireframe style option

12. From here, you need to set the fill properties for the style you selected in step 6. It's important to remember that each Style has a different set of fill properties, all of which are accessible in the Type drop-down menu and are listed next:

There are no fill Type options for the Wireframe style.

Cartoon Shading For the Cartoon Shading style, you have these options:

- Faceted, Bi-Level produces a flat, filled, and faceted representation of the objects in the scene. This option renders fills in two-color iterations.

- Faceted, Quad-Level produces a flat, filled, and faceted representation of the objects in the scene. Unlike the Faceted, Bi-Level option, fills are rendered in four-color iterations.

- Faceted, Full Color produces a flat, filled, and faceted representation of the objects in the scene. This option rendered the scene's fills with separate colors for each facet of an object.

- Smooth Cartoon Shading produces a flat, filled image with smoothed cartoon-like bands of color.

Gradient Shading For Gradient Shading, you have these options:

- Radial applies a single Flash radial fill to each 2D area in the scene. The positions of the radii are based on the positions of lights in the scene.

- Linear applies a single Flash linear fill to each triangle in the mesh representation of the scene. The direction and length of the gradient is determined by the positions of lights in the scene.

Flat Shading For Flat Shading, you have these options:

- Flat renders all fills of the same material as a single color, regardless of any lights in the scene.

- Averaged renders each fill, based on any lights in the scene and the diffuse color of the object's material, as an averaged color.

13. If you want the shadows in your scene to be included in the exported Flash file, select the Shadows check box in the Fills section.

> If you've selected the Wireframe fill type option, your exported scene cannot include shadows.

14. If you have selected the Smooth Cartoon Shading fill type, you can add shine to your rendered scene by selecting the Shine check box.

15. If you have selected the Smooth Cartoon Shading fill type, you can turn on banding (as well as manipulate the number and thickness of the bands) by selecting the Banding check box.

> When Banding is turned on, the borders between lit and shaded surfaces are replaced with bands of appropriate intermediate colors. The direction of the banding is determined by the selection made from the Light drop-down menu in the Fills section.

16. When you are finished setting the Flash export properties of the file, click the Render button [Render]. The Rendering dialog box will open and display the progress of the rendering process. If you've chosen a specific file type (as opposed to the Screen Only option), it will be saved to the same directory in which the original file is locates.

Carrara 3 Studio

Originally developed by MetaCreations, Carrara Studio 3 (originally called Carrara) was in danger of disappearing into that great processor in the sky when the company divested itself of all its creative 3D and 2D software. Fortunately, the original development team got together, formed a company called Eovia (www.eovia.com), and snatched up Carrara. They released a minor bug-fix upgrade and then, in June 2001, released Carrara Studio.

The most recent version of the program, Carrara Studio 3, is designed to be an accessible, middle-range, one-stop rendering and animation solution. Perhaps one of the most interesting features of the program is its highly unorthodox and intuitive interface (see Figure 29.14), which is divided into "rooms," each with its own toolset. Carrara Studio has five such rooms: Assemble, Storyboard, Model, Texture, and Render, which are accessed via a set of icons located in the top-right corner of the screen. The setup allows you to flip between rooms, creating a model in one, adding texture in another, and then rendering in another.

The focus of the workflow is the Assemble room, where you place and animate models, lights, and cameras. The most interesting feature of the Assemble room is the 3D work area, where you'll find three intersecting planes (X, Y, and Z) forming an open box. Any models you import are displayed as solids with projections on the box "walls." These projections enable you to locate the object in 3D space and can also be used to select, reposition, and resize the object. This feature alone is quite interesting and diverges from the traditional 3D modeling workspace.

Carrara features several modeling systems, each of which allows you to create objects using splines, subdivision surfaces, vertices, text, and MetaBall. The spline and vertex modelers are graphically enhanced versions of those found in MetaCreation's old modeling package, Infini-D, and the MetaBall modeler traces its origin back to Ray Dream. Boolean modeling is also fully supported in Carrara Studio. If you're mathematically inclined (or particularly masochistic), you can also create models with mathematical formulas. The program features a whole host of modifiers that you can apply to models to change their physical shape or movement.

In the grand scheme of things, Carrara Studio 3 fits somewhere between Swift3D v3 and plasma. It's quite a bit more powerful than Swift3D in terms of 3D modeling (due to the fact that Carrara Studio 3 is designed for traditional 3D modeling). And with a price tag of somewhere around $399, it's cheaper than plasma.

The kicker is that Carrara Studio 3 doesn't actually feature native Flash export. The good thing is that the folks at Eovia have developed a plug-in (which actually uses technology developed by Electric Rain, the company that makes Swift 3D v3) called VectorStyle that lets you export 3D models made in Carrara Studio 3 to SWF.

Figure 29.14

The Carrara Studio 3 interface

In this section of the chapter, you'll explore how to take a 3D model created in Carrara Studio 3 and export it to Flash using VectorStyle.

1. With the 3D model that you want to export to SWF open, choose File → Save As.

2. When the Save As dialog box opens, enter the name for the exported file in the File Name field.

3. Select Flash (*.swf) from the Save As Type drop-down menu.

4. Make sure the Options check box is selected.

5. Click Save. The Flash Export dialog box (see Figure 29.15) opens.

6. From the File Version drop-down menu, select the version of Flash to which you want the SWF file to be exported.

7. In the Layout section of the Flash Export dialog box, enter the dimensions of the exported SWF file (in pixels) in the Width and Height fields.

8. If you are exporting an entire animation (as opposed to a static image), select the Export Animation check box.

9. If you want the object's fill to be included in the exported file, select the Fill Objects check box.

10. From here, you can select the object's fill style from the drop-down menu just below the Fill Objects check box. The options include the following:

    - Cartoon Shading Single Color fills the objects within your exported movie with a single color. While this results in low color detail, it also gives you a small file size.

    - Cartoon Shading Average Color separates your objects into groups of polygons that occur on similar surfaces and, based on their angle relative to the scene's light source, applies a flat color fill to each.

Figure 29.15

Carrara Studio's Flash Export dialog box

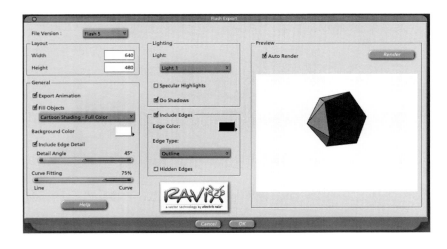

- Cartoon Shading 2 Colors fills your object with two colors. The location of each is determined by the position and angle of your scene's light.

- Cartoon Shading 4 Color calculates each surface's relative angle to the light sources and fills in four different colors according to the calculations.

- Cartoon Shading Full Color applies a different color (based on the position and angle of your scene's light source) to each polygon in the model, creating a far more detailed result.

- Area Gradient Shading looks for groups of polygons that occur on similar surfaces and applies one radial gradient to each surface.

- Mesh Gradient Shading applies a linear gradient to each one of the model's polygons. While this option results in the most realistic result, it also results in the largest file size.

11. To set the background color of the exported Flash movie, click the Background Color swatch and choose an appropriate color from the Color Picker.

12. Select the Include Edge Detail check box to gain access to the exported movie's level of internal edge detail.

13. Adjust the Detail Angle slider to control the level of internal edges that are visible in the exported Flash file. The lower the detail angle, the lower the number of internal edges.

14. Adjust the Curve Fitting slider to control the degree to which the curves of your object are optimized. While a higher value results in a smaller file size, it also can result in the edges of your model being distorted.

15. In the Lighting section of the Flash Export dialog box, select the scene's primary light from the Light drop-down menu.

16. If you want the exported Flash movie to include specular highlights, select the Specular Highlights check box.

Specular highlights are what make objects look shiny. Unlike diffuse illumination, where light scatters equally when it hits a surface, specular illumination goes in a particular direction. When it goes directly into the eye, it results in a highlight.

17. If you want the exported Flash movie to include shadows, select the Do Shadows check box in the Lighting section.

18. If you want the external edges (as opposed to the internal edges) of the model to be visible, select the Include Edges check box.

19. To set the edge color of the object within the exported Flash movie, click the Edge Color swatch and choose an appropriate color from the Color Picker.

20. Select the specific type of edge from the Edge Type drop-down menu.

21. By selecting the Hidden Edges option, the edges on the back side of the model will become visible, giving the exported Flash movie a "transparent Wireframe" look.

22. Click the Render button to get a preview of the way the exported movie will look.

23. When you are finished, click OK and Carrara Studio 3 will export the file to SWF.

Inspirational Design Model

Though 3D Flash is a relatively young creative enterprise, quite a few motivating examples exist. One of the most interesting is Penguin Chat (see Figure 29.16).

Created by RocketSnail (www.rocketsnail.com), a small, innovative online Flash-based game developer based in Kelowna, British Columbia, Penguin Chat (www.rocketsnail .com/chat/penguin) is a cute little Flash-based chat application in which you assume the persona of a 3D penguin, which was modeled using Carrara Studio and VectorStyle.

Figure 29.16

RocketSnail's Penguin Chat

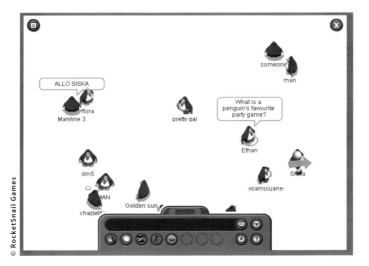

© RocketSnail Games

Creating an Animated 3D Flash Preloader

Throughout Part VII, you looked at how you can integrate Flash with other programs. For this tutorial, you'll take some of the skills you've mastered (as well as some ActionScript skills covered in Parts IV and V) and create an animated 3D Flash preloader for one of your Flash files.

> The process by which you make the Flash movie that the animated 3D preloader will preload is not covered in this tutorial. You can simply use any of your own movies to try out the preloader.

You'll start off by taking the 3D model (which has already been created) and importing it into Swift3D v3. From there, you'll export the 3D Flash animation as an SWF file, which can then be imported into Flash to be incorporated with the other elements of the preloader. To finish up, you'll take the preloader (which will be exported as an SWF) and place it in a Dreamweaver HTML document.

 You'll find demo copies of both Electric Rain's Swift3D v3 and Macromedia's Dreamweaver MX 2004 on this book's accompanying CD. In addition, you can find all the files used in this tutorial in the Hands On 7 directory on the CD. You will also find a copy of the finished files (so you can get an idea of what the final product might look like). However, as with all the tutorials in this book, the process is far more important than the final product.

Working with the 3D Model in Swift3D v3

To start off with, you'll take the static 3D model (which has already been created for you) and import it into Swift 3D v3 so that it can be converted into an animated SWF file that can then be brought into Flash.

1. Make sure you have Swift3D v3 open.
2. Choose File → New from 3DS.

3. When the Import 3DS File dialog box opens, navigate to the Hands On 7 directory on this book's accompanying CD, select the spheres.3ds file, and click the Import button.

4. After Swift 3D v3 has finished importing the model (see Figure H7.1), select it.

5. From there, select the Scale option in the Toolbox (which is located on the left side of the interface) and enter **.5** in the X Factor field, **.5** in the Y Factor field, and **.5** in the Z Factor field. This scales the model down to half its original size.

6. Click the Show Animations button ![icon] in the Gallery (located in the bottom-right corner of the program interface) to open the Animations palette.

7. Click and drag the Right 45 Degrees animation preset from the Gallery onto the spheres model.

8. Click the Preview and Export Editor tab at the top of the program's interface.

9. Select the General option from the Property Toolbox.

10. Choose Flash Player (SWF) from the Target File Type drop-down menu.

11. Select the Fill Options option from the Property Toolbox and make sure the Cartoon Average Fill option is selected from the Fill Type drop-down menu.

Figure H7.1

The Swift3D interface with the imported model

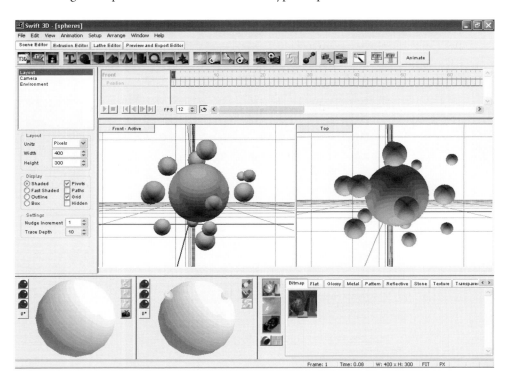

12. Select the Edge Options option from the Property Toolbox (see Figure H7.2) and make sure the Include Edges check box is selected.

13. Choose Outlines from the Edge Type drop-down menu, select 3.00 pt from the Line Weight drop-down menu, and set the edge color to any color except black (which can be done by double-clicking the Line Color swatch and choosing a color from the Color Picker).

14. Now that you've set the properties of the Flash file, click the Generate All Frames button [Generate All Frames].

15. After Swift3D v3 has finished rendering all the frames in the animation (and you are happy with the result), click the Export All Frames button [Export All Frames...].

16. When the Export Vector File dialog box opens, navigate to where you want to save the exported SWF file, enter a name in the File Name field, and click Save.

Working with 3D Animation in Flash

Now that you've converted the static 3D model into an animated 3D SWF file, it's time to create the actual preloader in Flash.

1. Open a movie (of your own creation) that you want to add the preloader to.

2. Open the Scene panel by choosing Window → Scene. (For the purposes of this tutorial, we'll assume your entire movie resides in a single scene.)

3. Rename the existing scene to **main movie**.

4. Before you continue, select the final frame in your main movie, open the Property Inspector (Window → Properties), and enter **final** into the Label field. The reason for this will become apparent a number of steps down the line.

5. Now, add a second scene (by clicking the Add Scene button **+**) and call it **preloader**. Make sure the preloader scene is *above* the main movie scene in the Scene panel.

6. Select the preloader scene.

7. Select the single layer (Layer 1) and rename it to **actions**.

8. Select frame 5 in the newly named actions layer and enter a keyframe by choosing Insert → Timeline → Keyframe.

9. With the newly created blank keyframe selected and the keyframe still selected, open the Property Inspector (Window → Properties).

10. Enter **check** into the Label field.

11. Now, select frame 10 in the actions layer and add another keyframe.

12. With the Property Inspector, add the label **loop** to the newly created keyframe.

Figure H7.2

The Edge Options section of the Property Toolbox

13. Select frame 5 (check), and open the Actions panel (Window → Development Panels → Actions).

14. Enter the following script into the ActionScript text box:

```
if (_framesloaded<_totalframes) {
    gotoAndPlay("loop");
} else {
    gotoAndPlay("Main Movie", 1);
}
```

Remember that all the scene and frames names are case sensitive, so you need to enter them *exactly* as you see here.

Essentially, this script checks the number of frames loaded against the total frames in the movie. If the total number of frames loaded at the point the script executes is less than the total number of frames in the movie, the playhead goes back to the loop frame. On the other hand, if the total number of frames loaded at the point the script executes is equal to the total number of frames in the movie, the playhead skips to frame 1 in the main movie scene.

15. Now it's time to insert the necessary ActionScript that will make sure the movie continues to recheck whether the main movie has loaded (after the initial check). Select frame 10 (loop).

16. Open the Actions panel and enter the following script into the ActionScript text box:

```
gotoAndPlay(1);
```

By doing this, the movie automatically jumps back to the first frame in the movie. From there, the playhead progresses to frame 5 and reexecutes the script that checks to see if all the frames have been loaded.

17. Now that you've set up the necessary scripts to check whether the main movie has loaded, you'll take the 3D Flash file you exported from Swift3D v3 and bring it into Flash to serve as the preloader animation. Choose Insert → New Symbol.

18. When the Create New Symbol dialog box opens, enter **preloader animation** into the Name field, make sure the Movie Clip radio button is selected, and click OK.

19. When the Symbol Editor opens, choose Import → Import To Stage.

20. When the Import dialog box opens, navigate to the location where you save the exported animated 3D SWF file, select it, and click Open.

If you want, you can use the spheres.swf file located in the Hands On 7 directory of this book's accompanying CD.

By doing this, the 3D sphere animation will be imported as a series of discrete frames in the movie clip.

If you want, you can center the animation on the Symbol Editor's Stage—though it isn't really necessary.

21. Now, return to the main Timeline in the preloader scene.

22. Create a new layer and call it **preloader animation**.

23. Click and drag the preloader animation layer so that it is below the actions layer.

24. Now, with the first keyframe in the preloader animation layer selected, click and drag your animation Movie Clip from the Library onto the Stage. From here, you can position it exactly where you want.

25. Add a stop() action to the final keyframe of the main movie scene so that, once it plays through, the playhead won't go back to frame 1 in the first scene (the preloader scene). To do this, switch to the main movie scene, add a new layer, and call it **actions**.

26. Now you can test out the logo by selecting Control → Test Movie.

27. Before you start the final stage of the project (placing your 3D Flash animated logo into an HTML document using Dreamweaver), you need to export the movie as a SWF file. To do this, choose File → Export → Export Movie.

Although it might seem a little elementary, it's important to remember that the native Flash file format (FLA) is not readable by web browsers with the Flash plug-in. Instead, the SWF file format is what you'll ultimately want to export.

28. When the Export Movie dialog box opens, type **preloader** in the Name field, navigate to the location on your hard drive where you want to save the SWF file, and click Save.

29. When the Export Flash Player dialog box is displayed, leave everything at its default setting and click OK.

Inserting Your Flash Movie into a Dreamweaver Document

Now that you've created your Flash movie (complete with 3D animated preloader) and exported it as an SWF file, you can use Dreamweaver to insert it into an HTML file.

 You'll find a demo copy of Dreamweaver MX 2004 on this book's accompanying CD for your use.

1. With a blank document open in the Document window, you need to insert the animated Flash logo. To do this, select Insert → Media → Flash.

2. When the Select File dialog box opens, navigate to the location where you saved the SWF file, select it, and hit Select.

3. Before Dreamweaver inserts the Flash movie into your page, you'll be faced with a series of prompts. For the first, which suggests that you save your file to make the Flash file's path document relative, you can choose OK. For the second, which asks you whether you want to copy the Flash file to your local site, choose No.

> Dreamweaver is as much a website creation and management tool as it is a web-page creation tool. The program is designed to help you create, manipulate, and manage entire sites. All these tools revolve around the initial creation of a local site, which will ultimately include all the files in your site and reside in a specific location (usually a single folder) on your hard drive. There are a couple reasons for creating a local site, the most important of which is that when you get to the point where you want to upload your site to a web server, you'll just upload the entire site's folder. By doing this, you ensure that you're not missing any components. When you set up your local site, you'll also be able to track and maintain your links.

When it's initially placed in the Dreamweaver document, the Flash file is represented by a gray box with a Flash icon in the center. Don't worry, because this is quite normal. You'll be able to preview the Flash movie from within Dreamweaver—something we'll explore a little later.

4. After your SWF file has been inserted into the Dreamweaver document, it's time to position it so that the overall page is a little more aesthetically pleasing. Click your mouse just to the right of the Flash file (so that the file is no longer selected). From there, choose Window → Properties to open the Property Inspector.

5. Now, click the Align Center button ≣ , which is the center button in the group of three alignment buttons located in the top-right corner of the Property Inspector. This aligns the Flash file to the center of the page.

6. Now that you've positioned the Flash movie, it's time to use the Property Inspector to do some final tweaking. Select the Flash movie. Open the Property Inspector (Window → Property Inspector).

7. If it isn't selected already, choose High from the Quality drop-down menu.

8. Select the Autoplay check box located in the expanded section of the Property Inspector. This ensures that the Flash movie will automatically play when the page is located.

9. Select Default (Show All) from the Scale drop-down menu.

10. To preview the Flash movie, click the Play button ▶ Play .

11. Now save the document by selecting File → Save. When the Save As dialog box opens, navigate to the location in which you want to save the HTML file (which should be in the same folder in which you saved the SWF file), enter a name of your choice into the Name field, and hit Save.

> If you haven't saved the HTML document in the same location as the SWF file, you'll have some problems. Essentially, when you try to view the HTML file, the browser won't be able to locate the SWF file and therefore won't display it.

12. Finally, to preview your creation in a browser, hit F12 or choose File → Preview In Browser.

> If you haven't gone through the process of setting up a Target Browser, refer to Dreamweaver's Help files (Help → Using Dreamweaver).

PART VIII

Publishing and Distributing Your Flash Movies

So, *you've spent hours creating your Flash masterpiece. You've created cool images, crafted groovy animation, and added amazing interactivity with ActionScript. What's next? Well, after a bit of a breather and a good pat on the back, it's time to start thinking about what to do with this amazing piece of brain sweat. Yeah, that's right, it isn't finished yet. The whole point of creating interactive media of any kind is so that other people can enjoy, experience, and explore your creative vision.*

In this part of the book, you'll explore the various ways you can get your masterpiece out there. First, you'll explore how to take your native Flash FLA file and convert it to a wide variety of file formats (the chief among them being SWF) suitable for distribution. From there, you'll delve into integrating Flash with video. Next, you'll investigate all the issues involved in distributing your Flash movie on a CD. Finally, you'll explore creating movies destined for the Pocket PC.

Publishing Your Flash Movie

You've spent hours creating beautiful graphics, prodding your animation, and tweaking your ActionScript, so what's next? Well, all your hard work is for naught if others can't experience your beautiful creation.

The process of converting an FLA file (the native type of Flash) into a format that can be distributed over the Web or via another medium is called *publishing*. Although publishing your movie is pretty straightforward, you need to make sure the file's settings maximize your movie for its intended audience and file format. As a result, it behooves you to become familiar with the various file types available as well as their often copious publishing settings.

Through the course of this chapter, you'll explore the following topics:

- Testing your movie
- Working with Flash publishing settings
- Manipulating individual publish format settings
- Working with publishing profiles
- Previewing your Flash movie
- Publishing your Flash movie
- Publishing accessible Flash movies
- Creating printable Flash movies

Testing Your Flash Movie

Before you need to even start thinking about the format you'll publish your grand Flash creation in, you need to make sure everything is functioning as it should be and see how it will look in the Flash player in SWF format.

> When you're working in Flash, the vast majority of the work that you will publish will be in SWF format. This is why, when you want to test your movie (before you actually set any of the publishing properties), you do so in the Flash Player as a SWF file. If your movie will ultimately be published in a different format, you can also test it from within the Flash environment; however, you first need to set the file's publishing settings, and then test it (see the section "Working with Flash Publishing Settings" later in this chapter).

To do this, you've got a few options:

- Choose Control → Test Movie to view the entire movie in SWF format with the Flash Player.
- Choose Control → Test Scene to view the current scene in SWF format with the Flash Player.
- If you're working in Flash MX Professional 2004 and want to test the Project you're currently working on, select Control → Test Project.

When you do any of these procedures, Flash opens the movie within the workspace using the Flash Player. When you're finished testing the movie, choose File → Close, and you'll be returned to your original document.

Testing Download Performance

Given the fact that the vast majority of Flash movies are destined to be delivered over the Web in SWF format, Macromedia has included a way for you to simulate the download process over an Internet connection—as opposed to the almost instantaneous performance you get from running the movie directly from your hard drive.

To test your movie's download performance, follow these steps:

1. Choose Control → Test Movie or Control → Test Scene.

2. When the movie opens in the Flash Player, choose View → Download Settings and select the specific connection over which you want to simulate your movie's download. Your choices range from a slow 14.4 modem to a super-fast T1 dedicated connection.

3. If you want to view a graph displaying a frame-by-frame download performance, choose View → Bandwidth Profiler from within the previewed SWF file.

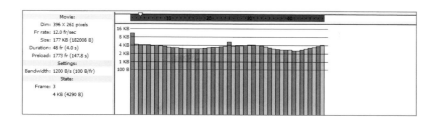

Figure 30.1

The Bandwidth Profiler

The left side of the Bandwidth Profiler (see Figure 30.1) displays information about the document. The right side shows a graph in which each vertical bar represents an individual frame in the movie. The size of the bar corresponds to that frame's size in bytes. The red line beneath the Timeline header indicates whether a given frame streams in real time with the current modem speed that you set. If a bar extends above the red line, the document must wait for that frame to load. As the green bar along the top of the Bandwidth Profiler extends, it indicates when each individual frame is loaded.

4. To turn the download simulation on and off, choose View → Simulate Download.

5. When you're finished viewing your movie over a simulated Internet connection, select File → Close, and you'll be returned to the original document.

Working with Flash Publishing Settings

The majority of the time, you'll publish your movies as SWF files (the format viewable by browsers with the Flash Player). However, Macromedia has provided a series of other file formats for publishing your movie. This enables you to tailor your Flash creation so you can reach the maximum number of people. For instance, if you created a series of non-interactive animated shorts, you could publish them as both SWF and QuickTime files to take advantage of those two formats' wide installation base. The cool thing about publishing your movie is that you can do so in a number of other different formats simultaneously. As you might have guessed, each of the various file types has quite a few settings that allow you to further manipulate a movie's ultimate look and behavior.

In the following sections, you'll explore each of these various file types. You'll then look at the individual publishing settings for each of the file types.

Although the process of publishing your movie is relatively simple, it actually involves two separate tasks. The first task, inputting the publishing settings, will be discussed after you've thoroughly explored all the file types to which a Flash movie can be outputted. The second task, telling Flash to publish your creation based on the settings, will be discussed in the section "Publishing Your Flash Movie" later in this chapter.

Publishing Formats

Flash offers a series of file types to which your creation can be published. Each has its own particular strengths and weaknesses. You should learn about each one so that you know which to use.

Flash

Most of the time, you'll publish your Flash creations as SWF files. The default publishing format, SWF, is viewable only if your intended audience has installed the Flash Player on their computers. It's definitely important to know that, of all the possible file types, SWF is the only one that fully supports all ActionScript and animation; other formats such as QuickTime don't fully support these features. So if you want to leverage the full power of Flash, use SWF.

> If you plan to distribute your SWF movie over the Web (as opposed to creating a stand-alone SWF that is played by the Flash Player), you'll need to publish an HTML file as well—a process discussed in the section "Manipulating HTML Settings" later in this chapter.

HTML

Playing an SWF movie in a web browser requires an HTML document in which the Flash movie is embedded. The HTML file serves to activate the movie, specify browser settings, and to a certain degree, determine how the SWF file appears. As a result, if your SWF file is destined for distribution on the Web, you must publish it with an HTML file.

The Flash Player (placed on the user's computer when they install the Flash plug-in) can display SWF files without the help of an HTML file. As a result, if your movie is not destined to be viewed in a web browser, you don't have to worrying about publishing an HTML file along with your movie.

GIF

GIF stands for Graphic Interchange Format. Developed originally by CompuServe back in the late 1980s, GIFs are the workhorse images of the Web. The format itself can display a maximum of only 256 colors. As a result, GIFs are best used for relatively simple images with flat colors and are generally smaller in size (in terms of kilobytes) than other formats such as JPEG. One of the great things about GIFs is that they come in a few different forms:

- Transparent GIFs are partially transparent, causing the background they're placed on to be visible.

- Interlaced GIFs are structured so they come into focus slowly as the browser loads the image.

- Animated GIFs are simply a series of images saved in the same file. When an animated image is loaded by a browser, all the images in the file are displayed in sequence, creating an animation—sort of like a digital flipbook.

You can export a Flash movie as an animated GIF for distribution to users who don't have the Flash plug-in installed on their computer. A Flash movie published as an animated GIF is generally larger in size than if it had been published as a SWF file. In addition, any interactivity in a Flash movie exported to an animated GIF will be lost.

JPEG

JPEG stands for Joint Photographic Experts Group. JPEGs came along after GIFs and were designed specifically to display photographic or continuous color images. Their main strength is that they can display millions of colors. As a result, JPEGs tend to have larger file sizes than GIFs. A good way to think about it is that as the quality of the JPEG increases, so does its file size. Unfortunately, JPEGs come in only one flavor—no transparency, no interlacing, and definitely no animation.

By default, Flash exports the first frame of a movie as a static JPEG. There is, however, a trick for forcing Flash to export an alternative frame (as opposed to the first one). This is covered in the section "Setting JPEG Publish Options" later in this chapter.

PNG

PNG stands for Portable Network Group. Developed in part by Macromedia and established as a web standard by the World Wide Web Consortium, PNGs are a little less straightforward than GIFs or JPEGs. They were designed to combine the best of both GIFs and JPEGs. As a result, they can support indexed-color (256 colors), grayscale, and true-color images (millions of colors), and transparency. The problem with PNGs is that they have spotty browser support. Microsoft Internet Explorer (4.0 and later) and Netscape Navigator (4.04 and later) partially support the display of PNG images. Because PNG is the native file type of Fireworks, Flash MX has some sophisticated tools geared specifically toward their manipulation and management.

Much as in the case of JPEGs, Flash exports a single static PNG image.

Windows Projector

A Windows Projector is probably one of the coolest formats available. Basically, it's a self-executing EXE file that doesn't need a browser or a plug-in to view it. This has some definite advantages over the other file types. First, you can distribute the Windows Projector without having to worry whether the intended audience has the necessary Flash plug-in, a compatible web browser, or even an Internet connection. They are self-contained little packages that are great for distribution of media such as CD-ROMs or DVDs.

Macintosh Projector

The Macintosh Projector is the Mac equivalent of the Windows Projector. A self-executing HQX file, the Macintosh Projector doesn't need the Flash plug-in or a browser to be viewed.

QuickTime

> If you don't have QuickTime (version 4 or later) installed on your computer, you won't be able to publish your Flash movie in QuickTime format.

Publishing your Flash movie to QuickTime creates a MOV file that plays in the Quick-Time Player. This format retains the vast majority of your movie's interactive features. However, users need to have the QuickTime plug-in installed to view Flash files published as MOV files.

> When rendered, your Flash creation occupies a single track in the QuickTime movie.

Manipulating Individual Publish Format Settings

Now that you've explored each of the various file formats that your Flash movie can be published in, let's look at the publishing settings of those various file formats. All the work you'll do in this section is through the Publish Settings dialog box (see Figure 30.2), which you access by choosing File → Publish Settings.

As you select individual file types in the Formats tab of the Publish Settings dialog box, you'll notice that additional tabs (labeled with the specific file type) are added. By clicking any of these tabs, you get access to that file type's settings. When you're finished manipulating the settings of all the file types that you're publishing your Flash movie in, click OK.

By selecting the Use Default Names option [Use Default Names], your file is published with the same name you assigned to your FLA file. If you deselect this option, you can name the file uniquely.

> Because neither the Windows Projector nor the Macintosh Projector has any unique publishing settings, they aren't discussed in the following sections. However, when you export a movie to Windows Projector or Macintosh Projector, its properties are set by the choices you make under the Flash tab.

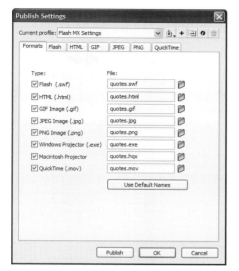

Figure 30.2

The Publish Settings dialog box

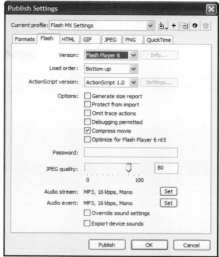

Figure 30.3

The Flash tab of the Publish Settings dialog box

Working with Flash Settings

After you select Flash (.swf) in the Formats tab of the Publish Settings dialog box (see Figure 30.3), you can click the Flash tab to access those settings.

The options include the following:

Version Specifies the version of Flash Player (1, 2, 3, 4, 5, 6, 7, or Flash Lite 1.0) that your published movie will be compatible with.

> Macromedia Flash Lite is a profile for use in NTT DoCoMo handsets that uses Flash 5 objects and Flash 4 ActionScript.

You'll have to be careful about which version you're publishing in if you've used newer Flash features not supported in older Flash Player versions. For the most part, when it comes to backward compatibility with older plug-ins, you need to be most concerned with the ActionScript you're using.

Load Order Sets the order (either Bottom Up or Top Down) in which the layers in each individual frame load (and are displayed). Your choice is particularly important if the Flash file is being loaded over a slow Internet connection. In that case, you might want to set the load order to reflect the position of the larger elements (large graphics, audio, and so on) so that they load first. If, for instance, you set the load order to Top Down, and the top layer in your movie is occupied by your ActionScript (which will load extremely quickly), you'll find that script layer will load and run before some of the more bandwidth-intensive elements (that occupy lower layers in the movie) even get a chance to load.

If, on the other hand, the movie is being accessed over a fast connection, your choice really won't matter that much because the layers will load so fast that there won't be any perceivable difference between the options.

ActionScript Version   The ActionScript Version drop-down menu lets you set the specific version of ActionScript used in your published movie. For Versions 1 through 5 (as well as Flash Lite v1), your only choice is ActionScript 1.0. However, if you're publishing for Version 6 or 7, you can choose between ActionScript 1.0 and ActionScript 2.0.

For more information on the differences between ActionScript 1.0 and 2.0, see Chapter 18.

Generate Size Report   Tells Flash to output a SimpleText (Mac) or TXT (Win) file that reports on the bandwidth intensity of the various portions of the movie.

Protect from Import   Prevents your published SWF file from being imported back into Flash—a handy option for those conscious about their work being digitally plagiarized.

Omit Trace Actions   Ignores any trace actions (which automatically opens the Output window) that you've added to your movie. For more information on the trace function, refer to Chapter 21.

Debugging Permitted   Allows the Debugger to work on the published file. In addition, when selected, this option also allows remote debugging via a browser using the Flash Debug Player plug-in or ActiveX control.

Compress Movie   Compresses the movie so that its file size and download time are reduced. Beware, however, that movies that have been compressed using this option can be played only with the Flash 6 Player or above.

Password   Allows you to enter the password needed to either open the Debugger (remotely or locally) or import the movie back into Flash. This option is enabled only if you selected either the Protect from Import or Debugging Permitted option.

JPEG Quality   Lets you adjust the level of compression applied to all bitmaps in your Flash movie. Alternatively, you can also enter a value (from 0 to 100) into the field to the right of the slider. The lower the value you set, the more compression will result. The kicker is that although lower quality means smaller image size, it also means that the images will have a lower visual quality. The trick is finding the right balance between appearance and file size.

Audio Stream By clicking the Set button , you access the Sound Settings dialog box (see Figure 30.4). From here, you can manipulate the settings of your movie's audio. The Compression drop-down menu lets you set the type of compression used on your audio. Each of the options (MP3, ADPCM, RAW, Disable, and Speech) has unique options that you can manipulate.

> For the theory behind audio (compression, bit rate, sample rate, and so on), see Chapter 22. You can also refer to Chapter 23 for a more in-depth look at the various compression options.

Audio Event By clicking the Set button 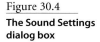, you open the Sound Settings dialog box (see Figure 30.4). From here, you can set the various compression properties of any event sounds in your movie.

> For a refresher on event and stream audio, see Chapter 24.

Override Sound Settings Uses the settings you established in the Flash tab of the Publish Settings dialog box, automatically overriding any compression schemes set in the Library.

Export Device Sound If you're working with Flash MX Professional 2004, select the Export Device Sound option to export your audio in a format suitable for mobile devices.

Manipulating HTML Settings

If your Flash movie is destined for distribution over the Web, it needs to be embedded in an HTML file. Before Flash 5 came along, you had to use another program, called Aftershock, to generate an HTML file into which your Flash movie was embedded. However, with Flash 5, Macromedia integrated the functionality of Aftershock into the Publish Settings dialog box, which is your one-stop tool for creating the HTML file that accompanies a published SWF file.

If you don't have the Flash option selected in the Formats tab of the Publish Settings dialog box, you don't have access to HTML as a file type. Likewise, if you select HTML from the Formats tab, Flash is automatically selected.

After you select HTML in the Formats tab of the Publish Settings dialog box, you'll be able to click the HTML tab to access the HTML-related settings (Figure 30.5).

Figure 30.4

The Sound Settings dialog box

The settings include the following:

Template Lets you choose from a set of predefined HTML templates that will be used to display the Flash movie.

Most of the time, you won't need to choose anything but the Flash Only (Default) template. However, some of the other templates are geared toward alternative file types, such as QuickTime, and will be useful in other situations. (For more information on each of the specific templates, see Flash MX's help feature.)

> To get information about a specific template, select it from the drop-down menu and then click the Info button (to the right of the drop-down menu).

Detect Flash Version You can configure your document to detect your users' Flash Player version. By selecting the Detect Flash Version option, users who access your Flash application are transparently directed to an HTML file that contains a SWF file designed to detect the version of their Flash Player. If they have the specified version or later, the SWF file again redirects the user to your content HTML file, and your SWF file plays as designed. If users don't have the specified version, they're redirected to an alternative HTML file that Flash creates or that you've created.

By clicking on the Settings button `Settings...`, you get access to the Version Detection Settings dialog box (see Figure 30.6), where you'll be able to set the file that detects the version of the user's Flash Player, the file they'll be sent to if they have the necessary version, and the file they'll be sent to if they don't have the right version.

Figure 30.5

The HTML tab of the Publish Settings dialog box

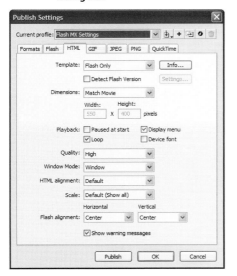

Dimensions Controls the HTML document's WIDTH and HEIGHT values in the OBJECT and EMBED tags. It's important to understand that the value you enter in the Width and Height fields (just below the Dimensions drop-down menu) doesn't actually affect that size of your Flash movie, just the area of the web page through which your movie is viewed. The way the movie fits in this area is determined by the Scale setting (discussed later). These are the options in the Dimensions drop-down menu:

- Match Movie retains the same width and height of the actual movie.

- To enter a width and height value in pixels, choose Pixels from the drop-down menu and then enter a value in the Width and Height fields.

- By choosing Percent and entering a value in the width and height fields, you set a percentage of the browser window that the movie fills.

Playback Controls how the Flash movie plays when it's downloaded:

- By choosing the Paused at Start option, your movie automatically stops at the first frame. A button with a play() action can restart the movie. In addition, selecting Play from the movie's Ctrl+click (Mac) or right-click (Win) menu can restart the movie.

- When selected, the Loop option forces the movie to loop *ad infinitum*.

- The Display Menu option lets you determine whether the movie's Ctrl+click (Mac) or right-click (Win) menu is active.

- When selected, the Device Font option, which applies to movies only when they're played on a Windows machine, replaces any font that the user doesn't have installed on their system with anti-aliased system fonts. This increases the legibility of small text and decreases the overall size of the movie.

Figure 30.6

The Version Detection Settings dialog box

Quality Determines the quality at which your movie is played. Basically, the options determine whether your movie sacrifices speed for quality or vice versa:

- By turning off any anti-aliasing, Low sacrifices speed over visual quality.

- Auto Low starts the movie playing without anti-aliasing but bumps the quality up to High if the user's computer can cope with the improved quality while still maintaining quick playback.

- Auto High begins playback at High quality but shifts into Low mode if the user's computer can't cope with the increased visual quality and playback speed.

- By choosing Medium, your movie is partially anti-aliased with no bitmap smoothing. The option results in a higher visual quality than Low, but a lower visual quality than High.

- When you select High, you force your movie to be anti-aliased. If the movie contains bitmaps that aren't animated, they are smoothed. On the other hand, if the bitmaps are animated in any way, they won't be smoothed.

- When you choose Best, you force your movie to be played at the highest visual quality possible with little regard for playback speed.

Window Mode Sets options for movies played in Internet Explorer 4.0 (and later) with the Flash ActiveX control:

- By choosing Window, your movie is played in its own rectangular window on a web page. It's important to note that this option results in the fastest animation speed.

- The Opaque Windowless option pushes any Dynamic HTML elements (specifically, layers) behind, so they don't appear over the Flash movie.
- The Transparent Windowless option displays the background of the HTML page on which the movie is embedded through all transparent areas of the movie.

The Transparent Windowless option often results in slower playback.

HTML Alignment Positions your Flash movie within the web page. The default option centers the Flash movie horizontally and vertically within the web page. The other options align the Flash movie along the left, right, top, and bottom edges of the browser window.

Scale Works in conjunction with the option you set with the Dimensions drop-down menu:

- The Default (Show All) option expands the size of your movie (without distortion) to fit the entire specified area while still maintaining the movie's aspect ratio. As a result, even if you choose this option, you might have borders appear on either of the movie's two sides.

- By choosing No Border, your movie is expanded (without distortion) to fill the entire area defined by the Dimensions setting. As with the Show All option, the movie maintains its aspect ratio. However, the difference is that when you choose No Border, your movie might actually expand to be larger than the area defined by the Dimensions settings to maintain the movie's aspect ratio. As a result, the edges of your movie might appear as if they've been cut off.

- Exact Fit displays the entire movie in the specified area without reserving the original aspect ratio. As a result, your movie might be somewhat distorted.

Flash Alignment Determines the placement of the movie within the Dimensions area. You set it by choosing an option from the Horizontal and the Vertical drop-down menus.

Show Warning Messages Tells Flash to alert you to any conflicts created by your various publishing settings.

Working with GIF Settings

By selecting the GIF option from the Formats tab and then clicking the GIF tab, you can set GIF-specific options (see Figure 30.7).

The settings include the following:

Dimensions Allows you to set the dimensions of the static image or animated GIF that is published by entering values (in pixels) in the Width and Height fields. If you want the dimensions of the GIF to match those of the Flash movie, select the Match Movie option.

Playback If you want to export a single frame of the Flash movie, select the Static option. By default, Flash exports the first frame of your movie as the static GIF image. If you want to force Flash to export an alternative frame, attach a #Static frame label to the desired frame by using the Property Inspector. (For a refresher on how to attach frame labels, see Chapter 10.)

If you want to export the Flash movie as a GIF animation, select the Animated option. If you want to avoid publishing the entire movie as an animated GIF, attach a #First label to the initial frame in the range you want to publish and a #Last frame label to the final frame in the range.

From there, you can select Loop Continuously (to have the animation play over and over again without stopping) or enter the number of repetitions for the animation in the Repeat field.

Optimize Colors Tells Flash to remove any unused colors from the GIF's color table. This can reduce the final file size.

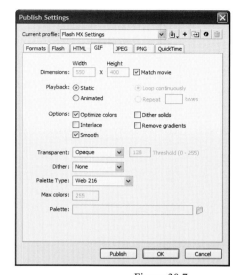

Figure 30.7

The GIF tab of the Publish Settings dialog box

If you have chosen Adaptive from the Palette drop-down menu, selecting the Optimize Color option has no effect.

Interlace Publishes the movie as an interlaced GIF. An interlaced GIF is structured so that it comes into focus slowly as the browser loads the image.

Smooth Anti-aliases all the artwork in the movie when it's published to GIF format. Be advised that this option results in a larger file size.

Dither Solids Applies dithering to both colors and gradients.

Remove Gradients Converts all your gradients to solid colors. Because gradients don't translate well to GIF format, leaving this option unchecked could result in some odd (and visually unappealing) results.

Transparent Determines the level at which the background of the movie is transparent, as well as how the Flash movie's Alpha settings are converted:

- By choosing Opaque, the movie is published as a GIF with a solid background.
- By choosing Transparent, the movie is published as a GIF with a transparent background.

Choosing the Transparent option in conjunction with the Smooth option can result in semi-transparent halos around all objects.

- By choosing the Alpha option, you control the transparency of individual objects. By entering a Threshold value between 0 and 255, you make all colors below the value completely transparent and colors above the threshold partially transparent. A value of 128 corresponds to 50 percent Alpha.

Dither Generates colors not in the current palette by combining pixels from a 256-color palette into patterns that approximate other colors. The options in the Dither drop-down menu let you set the method by which the pixels are combined when the movie is exported to GIF:

- By choosing None, dithering is turned off and colors not in the basic color table are replaced with solid colors from the table that most closely approximate the specified color. Although not dithering can produce smaller files, it often results in strange colors.
- Choosing Ordered results in good-quality images with a relatively small file size.
- Choosing Diffusion results in the best-quality image. However, file size and load time are increased.

Palette Type Lets you choose the type of palette that's used when the GIF is published:

- The Web 216 palette is composed of 216 colors that are identical on both Windows and Macintosh computers.
- By choosing Adaptive, you set a custom palette of colors derived from the actual colors in the image. When you choose Adaptive, you can also limit the number of colors by entering a value (up to 256) in the Max Colors field.
- The Web Snap Adaptive palette is almost the same as the Adaptive palette. The only difference is that it converts similar colors to the Web 216 color palette.
- By selecting the Custom option, you can specify a custom-created palette by clicking the ellipses (…) button just to the right of the Palette field and browsing for an ACT file.

Setting JPEG Publish Options

If you want to publish a single frame of your Flash movie as a JPEG file, select JPEG Image from the Formats tab, and click the JPEG tab to manipulate its publishing settings (see Figure 30.8). Much as in the case of a GIF, you can force Flash to export a frame other than the first one by attaching a #Static frame label to the desired frame with the Property Inspector.

> Because the Dimensions option in the JPEG tab is exactly the same as that in the GIF tab, we'll skip them in this section. For a refresher, see the previous section.

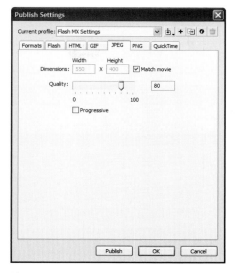

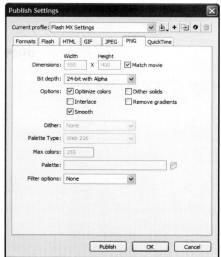

Figure 30.8

The JPEG tab of the Publish Settings dialog box

Figure 30.9

The PNG tab of the Publish Settings dialog box

You can also set the following additional options:

Quality Adjusts the level of compression applied to the published JPEG. Alternatively, you can also enter a value (from 0 to 100) in the field to the right of the slider. The lower the value you set, the greater compression will result.

Progressive Creates a JPEG similar to an interlaced GIF.

Working with PNG Publishing Settings

If you want to publish a single frame of your Flash movie as a PNG file, select PNG Image from the Formats tab and click the PNG tab to manipulate its publishing settings (see Figure 30.9). Much as in the case of GIFs and JPEGs, you can force Flash to export a frame other than the first one by attaching a #Static frame label to the desired frame with the Property Inspector.

> Because the majority of options for PNG are the same as those for publishing a GIF, we won't go over them again. For a refresher, see the section "Working with GIF Settings" earlier in this chapter.

You have the following additional options:

Bit Depth Determines the amount of colors in the published PNG image:

- Choosing the 8-bit option results in an image with a maximum of 256 colors.

- The 24-bit option results in an image that can display a maximum of 16.7 million colors. As one would expect, this produces larger file sizes but renders your Flash movie far more accurately.

- The 24-bit with Alpha includes support for 16.7 million colors as well as an additional 8-bit channel for transparency support. When you choose this option, the unfilled areas in a PNG image turn transparent when the file is published.

Filter Options Determines the compression algorithm used on the PNG image:

- By choosing None, no compression algorithm is applied to the image. This results in a significantly larger image.

- The Sub option, which transmits the difference between each byte and the value of the corresponding byte of the prior pixel, works best on images that have repeating information (such as stripes or checks) along the horizontal axis.

- The Up option works in the opposite manner from the Sub option and is most effective on images that feature vertically repeating information.

- The Average option, which uses a pixel's two adjacent neighbors to predict its value, works best on images that have a mix of both horizontally and vertically repeating information.

- The Path option generates a linear function of the pixels above, to the left, and to the upper left, and then makes a prediction based on the neighboring pixel closest to the computed value.

Setting QuickTime Publish Options

If you want to publish your Flash creation as a QuickTime movie (MOV), select the Quick-Time option from the Formats tab and click the QuickTime tab (see Figure 30.10).

You can then manipulate the following options:

Dimensions Allows you to set the dimensions of the QuickTime movie that is published by entering values (in pixels) in the Width and Height fields. If you want the dimensions of the QuickTime movie to match those of the actual Flash movie, select the Match Movie option.

Alpha Lets you control the transparency of the Flash information in the QuickTime movie:

- By choosing Auto, the Flash movie becomes transparent if it is on top of any other tracks in the QuickTime movie (such as additional QuickTime video tracks), but it becomes opaque if it is the bottom or the only track in the movie.

- The Alpha-Transparent option makes the Flash track transparent, displaying the contents of any additional lower tracks.

- When you choose the Copy option, the Flash track is rendered as completely opaque, blocking all lower tracks.

Layer Controls the position of your Flash content relative to any QuickTime content in the exported movie. Choose Top if you want the Flash content to occupy the top layer and Bottom if you want it to occupy the bottom layer. When you choose Auto, the Flash track is placed in front of other tracks in the QuickTime file if the Flash objects in the movie itself are in front of video objects. If they aren't, the Flash track is placed behind all other tracks in the QuickTime file.

Streaming Sound Forces Flash to export all the streaming audio in the movie to a Quick-Time soundtrack. In the process, the audio recompresses using the standard QuickTime audio settings. To manipulate the default settings, click the Settings button [Settings...] to open the Sound Settings dialog box.

From here, you can set the compressor used, the bit rate, and the audio to mono or stereo.

> For the theory behind audio (compression, bit rate, sample rate, and so on), see Chapter 22.

Controller If you've ever viewed a QuickTime file, you probably noticed that it had an interactive controller at the bottom of the player. With it, you can do such things as pause, play, and adjust volume. The Controller drop-down menu lets you determine whether you want the standard controller to be displayed (by choosing Standard), no controller (None), or the QuickTime VR controller (QuickTime VR).

Loop Sets the QuickTime movie to loop indefinitely.

Paused at Start Sets the QuickTime movie to not automatically play. The user can begin playback by clicking the Play button in the controller.

Play Every Frame Overrides the frame rate and plays every frame without any of the skipping characteristics of QuickTime's attempt to maintain time. It's important to note that when this option is selected, the audio track is turned off.

Flatten (Make Self-Contained) If this option is unselected, the Flash content won't be combined with the QuickTime movie itself. Instead, the file content is published as a separate file and referenced separately by QuickTime. If all the files are not in the same place, the QuickTime movie cannot display the Flash content. When you select the Flatten (Make Self-Contained) option, all the content is combined into one file.

Figure 30.10

The QuickTime tab of the Publish Settings dialog box

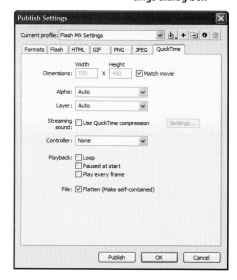

Previewing Your Flash Movie

If you've gone to the trouble of painstakingly manipulating the publishing settings of each of the file types your Flash movie will be published in, it would be a shame if you couldn't preview your movie to see how it looks. To preview your movie in any of the various file types you selected in the Formats section of the Publish Settings dialog box, select File → Publish Preview and choose from the available list of file types.

> You'll be able to access only those file types that were selected in the Formats section of the Publish Settings dialog box.

Flash automatically loads the selected file type.

Publishing Your Flash Movie

Now that you've manipulated the publishing settings of your various file types and previewed those files (and done any necessary tweaking), you can publish your Flash movie. Having gone to all the trouble to get here, the publishing process is rather anticlimactic. All you have to do is choose File → Publish, and Flash does all the work. All the various file types you set in the Publish Settings dialog box will be published simultaneously to the folder on your hard drive where you saved the FLA file they're based on.

Besides the Publish command, there's also an Export command in the File menu. Export is almost the same as Publish; the difference is that, by using Export, you bypass the Publish Settings dialog box and are faced with an Export Movie dialog box where you set the file type and export location. The drawback of exporting is that you don't have access to the file type's publishing settings.

Working with Publish Profiles

When it comes to publishing your movie, Publish Profiles are easily one of the coolest time-saving new features in Flash MX 2004 and Flash MX Pro 2004. Basically, Publish Profiles are a group of publish settings (such as those you explored in the previous section of this chapter) that are saved under one name. The joy of Publish Profiles is that they can be created and then applied to any of your projects, saving you the time of having set all the publish settings manually. You can also export the profiles and use them across projects to publish consistently under different conditions.

> The real drawback to working with Publish Profiles is that once you create one, it is not instantaneously available in another document. Don't worry, you can use a single Publish Profile across multiple documents. However, you'll need to export it from the document in which it was originally created and import it into the document you want to use it in.

Applying a Publish Profile is really quite easy. Select the Profile you want to use form the Current Profile drop-down menu at the top of the Publish Settings dialog box (File → Publish Settings) and click OK.

In the following sections of this chapter, you will learn how to create a Publish Profile, import and export a Publish Profile, duplicate a Publish Profile, change a Publish Profile's name, edit an existing Publish Profile, and delete a Publish Profile.

Figure 30.11

The Create New Profile dialog box

Creating a Publish Profile

The process by which you create a Publish Profile is easy; just follow these steps:

1. Choose File → Publish Settings.

2. When the Publish Settings dialog box opens, click the Create New Profile button ＋ .

3. When the Create New Profile dialog box opens (see Figure 30.11), enter the name for the profile into the Profile Name field.

> From there, you'll need to set the properties of the Publish Profile (by following the steps outlined in the previous section of this chapter).

4. When you're finished, click OK.

Importing and Exporting Publish Profiles

As already mentioned, a Publish Profile that you create in one document is not instantaneously accessible in other document. This is where importing and exporting your Publish Profile comes in.

> Publish Profiles are exported as XML files.

To export a Publish Profile, follow these steps:

1. Make sure the Publish Settings dialog box is open (File → Publish Settings).

2. Select the Publish Profile that you want to export from the Profile Name drop-down menu at the top of the Publish Settings dialog box.

3. Click the Import/Export Profile button 🔄, and choose Export from the drop-down menu.

4. When the Export Profile dialog box opens, enter a name for the exported profile in the Name field, navigate to the location where you want the profile exported, and click Save.

Once a Publish Profile has been exported, it can then be imported and used in another document entirely. To do so, follow these steps:

1. Make sure the Publish Settings dialog box is open (File → Publish Settings).
2. Click the Import/Export Profile button 🔧 and choose Import from the drop-down menu.
3. When the Import Profile dialog box opens, navigate to the location of the Publish Profile that you want to import, select it, and click OK.

Duplicating a Publish Profile

What happens if you want to create a new Publish Profile that is almost identical to an existing Publish Profile, but you don't want to go through the process of creating the new Publish Profile from scratch? Thankfully, you can duplicate an existing profile and then make any changes you want to the copy.

To do so, follow these steps:

1. Make sure the Publish Settings dialog box is open (File → Publish Settings).
2. Select the Publish Profile that you want to duplicate from the Current Profile drop-down menu.
3. Click the Duplicate Profile button ⊞.
4. When the Duplicate Profile dialog box opens (see Figure 30.12), enter a name for the duplicate profile into the Duplicate Name field.
5. You'll notice that the duplicate profile now appears in the Current Profile drop-down menu. You can select it and make any changes you want. When you're finished, click OK.

Changing the Name of a Publish Profile

You can easily change a Publish Profiles name; here's how:

1. Make sure the Publish Settings dialog box is open (File → Publish Settings).
2. Select the Publish Profile whose name you want to change from the Current Profile drop-down menu.
3. Click the Profile Properties button ⚙.
4. When the Profile Properties dialog box opens (see Figure 30.13), enter a new name into the Profile Name field and click OK.

Figure 30.12

The Duplicate Profile dialog box

Figure 30.13

The Profile Properties dialog box

Deleting a Publish Profile

At some point, you might want to delete a Publish Profile that you've created. To do so, follow these steps:

1. Make sure the Publish Settings dialog box is open (File → Publish Settings).

2. Select the Publish Profile you want to delete from the Current Profile drop-down menu.

3. Click the Delete Profile button 🗑 .

4. When the alert appears, click OK to delete the Profile.

Publishing Accessible Flash Movies

Although there are a myriad of file types you can publish your movie in—all of which extend the scope of your audience—there is one aspect of publishing and distributing Flash movies that we haven't discussed yet.

In recent years, there has been a growing desire to make web content accessible, that is, usable for individuals with a variety of disabilities. One of the most pressing concerns is that, up until now, Flash movies couldn't be interpreted by screen reader—a type of software the "reads" the contents of a computer screen and then "speaks" it back to a visually impaired user. This problem derives from the fact that visual information (as opposed to text) involves a subjective interpretation. In other words, one person's description of an image will probably differ from another's. As a result, screen readers, which are simple pieces of software, are completely incapable of describing visual imagery. So visually impaired individuals are not only cut off from visual content, but they are often also cut off from navigation schemes, many of which depend heavily on graphical interface elements (buttons, menus, and so on).

So, where does this leave visually impaired individuals who want to access Flash content? In Flash MX 2004 and Flash MX Pro 2004, you can attach information to certain elements in your movie that can then be interpreted by screen readers—cool, huh? That way, *you* determine how your visual creation will be described.

There are, however, some pretty heavy caveats that need to be addressed. First, to make an object accessible to screen readers, it must have an instance name. As a result, there are a limited number of objects that can be made accessible to a screen reader: dynamic text, text-input fields, buttons, Movie Clips, and entire movies.

To make Static Text accessible, you must first convert it to Dynamic Text.

Second, and perhaps most importantly, users must be running a Windows operating system, complete with screen reader software and the Flash 7 plug-in, to access accessible content created in Flash MX 2004 and Flash MX Pro 2004.

Figure 30.14

The Accessibility panel

This having been said, let's take a look at how you go about making your movie accessible so that you don't exclude a portion of your potential audience:

1. Select the object that you want to make accessible to the screen reader.

2. Choose Window → Other Panels → Accessibility to open the Accessibility panel (see Figure 30.14).

If the object you've selected cannot be made accessible, you won't have access to any options in the Accessibility panel.

3. If you want to make the currently selected object accessible, click the Make Object Accessible option.

4. If the object you selected is a Movie Clip, you'll also see a Make Child Objects Accessible option. If you select this, all the various elements within the Movie Clip will also become accessible.

5. Enter a name into the Name field. The name, which will be read and vocalized by the screen reader, is the most basic aspect of making your object accessible.

If you make some Dynamic Text accessible, you won't have access to its Name. The actual text will be automatically used.

6. Enter a description for the selected element into the Description field.

7. If you want to add a keystroke to individual buttons, Movie Clips, or text-input fields, enter a shortcut in the Shortcut field. There are, however, a few guidelines you need to follow:

   - Spell out the abbreviations of key names such as Shift, Ctrl, and Alt.

   - Use capitals for letters of the alphabet.

   - Use the plus (+) sign between key names, for example, Alt+5, Ctrl+H, or Shift+9.

> To provide a keyboard shortcut, you must use the ActionScript Key object to detect user keypresses during movie playback. For more information on how to capture user keypresses, see Chapter 19.

8. Enter a value into the Tab Index field. This determines the order in which the user's screen reader cycles through the accessible objects in your movie when the Tab key is pressed.

9. When you've finished setting the accessibility options, simply close the Accessibility panel.

This process is good for making certain objects accessible to a screen reader (a process that is sometimes also referred to as *exposing*), but what if you want to make the entire movie accessible? All you need to do is follow these steps:

1. Make sure you deselect all the elements on the Stage.

2. Choose Window → Accessibility (see Figure 30.15).

3. Select the Make Movie Accessible option.

4. If you want all the accessible objects within the movie to be exposed to screen readers, select the Make Child Objects Accessible option.

5. Enter a name for the movie into the Name field.

6. Enter a description for the movie into the Description field.

7. If you want, select the Auto Label option. By doing this, Flash will use text that's integrated into buttons or text-input fields as the object's name.

8. When you're finished, close the Accessibility panel.

Figure 30.15

The Accessibility panel displaying the movie's accessibility option

Creating Printable Movies

By this point, you're probably convinced that Flash content, because it's based on vectors, looks pretty cool. You've heard it all: based on mathematical computations, scalable, incredibly crisp—yadda, yadda, yadda. What you probably haven't realized is that because it's vector-based, Flash movies look equally cool when they're printed. Wow, this is great! You can create all sorts of content that looks just as good on a screen as it does when printed.

> The processes described in this section set your movie so that it is printed as vectors, maintaining the crisp, clean appearance. If you elect to skip this section, your movie can still be printed. However, it will print like any other 72dpi image—very low quality.

There are two methods you can use to configure your movie so that it prints as vectors. First, you can designate specific frames in the Timeline that will print; all the frames that aren't designated as printable will not print. Second, you can designate certain areas within certain frames that will print; all the space outside of the printable area will not print.

> The kicker about creating a printable movie is that you're only controlling how your content is being printed using the right-click context menu. Users can still print your movie using their browser's Print command—you've got no control over that.

Before you learn how to configure your movie to be printable, there are a couple of important details you should be aware of:

- All elements must be fully loaded to be printed.
- For a Movie Clip to be printed, it must be either on the Stage or in the work area, and it must have an instance name.
- Flash Players earlier than 4.025 (Win) or 4.020 (Mac) do not support frame printing.

This having been said, let's take a look at how you go about configuring your Flash movie so that it's printable.

Designating Printable Frames

To designate specific frames as printable, follow these steps:

1. In the Timeline, select the specific frame that you want to make printable.
2. If it isn't open already, open the Property Inspector by choosing Window → Properties.

3. Enter **#p** into the Frame Label field to set that frame as printable.

4. Repeats steps 1 and 3 on any additional frames that you want to make printable.

Specifying a Printable Area

To designate a specific area in a frame as printable, follow these steps:

1. Select the frame that you want to designate as a printable area. The frame itself must not have already been designated as printable with the #p label.

2. Select the frame that contains the object you want to use to designate the frame as printable.

3. If it isn't open already, open the Property Inspector by choosing Window → Properties.

4. Enter **#b** into the Label field.

Inspirational Design Model

Based in Portland, Oregon, Second Story Interactive (www.secondstory.com) has created a string of Flash-based kiosks that range from the educational and entertaining to the highly compelling.

Figure 30.16

Inventions & Inspirations: History of Recorded Sound kiosk

Arguably one of their most entertaining (as well as educational) was the *Inventions &Inspirations: History of Recorded Sound* kiosk (see Figure 30.16). From Thomas Edison to Public Enemy, from gramophones to digital sampling, this interactive kiosk tells the epic story of the individuals and innovations that transformed how we create and experience music. Housed in the Sound Lab of Seattle's Experience Music Project, *Inventions & Inspirations* traces the evolution of making and capturing sound, and features visionaries with their inventions and influential musicians who embraced invention in their artistry, as well as each innovation's impact on audience experience. The kiosk also includes interactive modules that demonstrate what sound is, and how we're able to record it.

CHAPTER 31

Working with Flash and Video

It is standard practice now to develop software applications that are *versatile*. Not only do you expect them to perform their particular job, but you also expect them to work cooperatively with other applications. This increases their effectiveness as well as your creative possibilities. It's this kind of versatility that puts the *multi* in multimedia.

Flash is no exception to this standard. In fact, due to its popularity as well as the SWF file format's wide applicability, Flash is one of the most portable programs available today. Not only can Flash incorporate many kinds of media into an animation or interactive movie, but it can also create and work with files that are usable in a variety of non-Flash applications.

This chapter explores the possibilities of Flash in a very different kind of setting: video. Flash movies can be exported as video. Or vice versa, videos can be imported into the Flash environment and controlled interactively like any other part of a Flash production. Video and Flash are fundamentally unlike. Video has no vectors, no tweening, no painting tools, and above all else, no interactivity. However, video does have its own advantages. Whereas Flash is great at displaying stylized, cartoon-like images, video can show your audience images that are very lifelike and realistic. And unlike Flash, video can be broadcast on television and incorporated into movies. This chapter discusses the many ways you can combine video with Flash, including:

- **Importing video into Flash**
- **The Sorenson Spark codec**
- **Exporting FLV video**
- **Using the Video Import wizard**
- **Using ActionScript to control video playback**
- **Preparing the elements of a Flash animation for video or DV tape**
- **Working with Flash video and audio tracks**
- **Exporting Flash animations for use in video applications**

Understanding Video in the Flash Environment

One of the most sweeping changes originally introduced in Flash MX was the addition of support for digital video. When using previous releases of Flash, developers had to simulate video. They usually did this by putting still-image sequences inside a Movie Clip to create a sort of digital flipbook. From a functional standpoint, this technique worked fairly well, but it tended to increase the size of the final movie appreciably because there was no way to compress (reduce the file size of) the "video."

Luckily for us, this has long since changed. Flash MX started the trend and Flash MX 2004 continues with support for video that represents a significant step forward for both the application and its community of users. What was once the best means of delivering animated content on the Web is now also one of the best means of distributing video content. Anyone whose browser is equipped with the Flash plug-in (version 6 or higher) is now able to see both traditional Flash movies *and* Flash movies that contain real video footage. One plug-in covers it all! Now that we've got your attention, let's take a closer look at how all this works in Flash MX 2004 and MX Professional 2004.

Sorenson Spark Codec

The "wizard behind the curtain" responsible for video in Flash MX is a video compression/decompression codec named Spark. Developed by Sorenson Media (`www.sorenson.com`), Spark enables you to put high-quality video into your Flash movies without entailing significant cost in terms of bandwidth or file size.

When you bring video into Flash, Spark will compress it in FLV (Macromedia Flash Video) format. The codec is actually part of Flash MX 2004; any video files that are imported and embedded in a Flash document must have this compression applied to them. If you are using Flash MX Professional 2004, you can now export video files in FLV format from video-editing applications such as Adobe Premiere and Final Cut Pro. This new feature can significantly increase your workflow because you no longer need to wait for a video to be compressed upon importing it into Flash.

Spark applies *temporal* compression to your video. This type of compression looks at areas of change in a video file and encodes each frame based on the amount of change from one frame to the next. If a frame doesn't exhibit a significant change, its information is simply copied from the preceding frame. This kind of encoding is also known as *interframe*. When the change between video frames *is* significant, however, Sorenson Spark automatically inserts a video *keyframe* into the video file. A keyframe is a complete picture of a frame, and like the keyframes in your Flash Timeline, marks a significant change in content. So, to put it all in perspective, Spark uses a combination of keyframes and interframes (temporal compression) to deliver high-quality video while maintaining smaller video file sizes.

The version of Spark included in Flash MX 2004 and Flash Player 7 is known as *Sorenson Spark Standard Edition*. If you enjoy working with Spark, you might be interested in upgrading to Sorenson Spark Pro. This expanded codec offers several advantages over the basic codec. Spark Pro is available to you within the application Sorenson Squeeze. Squeeze can compress your video files in Macromedia Flash Video format (FLV). This application is especially helpful to users with Flash MX 2004 who don't have access to the FLV encoder that ships with the Professional version of Flash MX 2004. Additionally, Squeeze and the Spark Pro codec present a clear advantage over standard Spark because they allow you to compress your video using a Variable Bit Rate (VBR). Files compressed with VBR are generally much smaller because they are compressed "intelligently." Video frames that contain complex changes in color or motion are allowed more bandwidth than simple frames. This allows the file to use compression where it needs it most, yielding a video file that's much smaller overall. Visit www.sorenson.com/content.php?cats=2/3&nav=2 for more details on Sorenson Squeeze.

Exporting FLV Video Files from Other Applications

Users of Flash MX Professional 2004 can take advantage of the FLV Export plug-in that ships with the Pro edition. With the help of QuickTime 6.1.1, the FLV Export plug-in allows you to compress videos with the Spark codec and save them from the native application as FLV files. In turn, FLV files can be imported directly into Flash or accessed remotely over the Web. This can be a huge timesaver for designers and developers working with a large amount of video content in their Flash projects.

The FLV Exporter plug-in isn't directly integrated with Flash MX Pro 2004. It must be installed as a separate application. To install the Exporter, insert the Flash MX 2004 CD into your computer, double-click the Flash_Video_Exporter installer icon, and follow the on-screen instructions. During installation, the exporter is placed in your computer's QuickTime folder, making it accessible to any application that uses QuickTime 6.1.1, even those that are installed later. Once the FLV exporter has been installed, you will be able to use it with many different video-editing applications for both Macintosh and Windows. For a list of supported applications, see Table 31.1.

WINDOWS AND MACINTOSH	WINDOWS	MACINTOSH	
Adobe After Effects	Anystream Agility	Apple Final Cut Pro	**Table 31.1**
Avid Xpress DV		Apple Final Cut Express	**Video-Editing Applications That Support the FLV Export Plug-In**
Discreet Cleaner		Apple QuickTime Pro	
Discreet Cleaner XL			

Exporting video with the FLV Export plug-in is a simple but long process. It will leave you with a file that is immediately ready to be used in a Flash movie.

To export an FLV video file:

1. The video you wish to export should be open in a video-editing application that supports QuickTime 6.1.1. See Table 31.1 for a list of possible applications. Choose File → Export → Quicktime.

2. A dialog box opens. For Export, select Macromedia Flash Video (FLV) and click the Options button. The FLV Exporter dialog box is displayed (see Figure 31.1). Here you will select options that affect how your video is compressed.

3. Select from the Encoding Method drop-down list:

   • Baseline (1 Pass) can be used to produce a "rough draft" of a video or for simple video files such as talking heads and other clips with little motion.

   • Better (1 Pass VBR) is better for producing a final FLV clip. It takes longer to compress, but it dynamically applies compression frame by frame. Each frame is considered and encoded with as little data as possible to yield smaller overall file sizes.

   • Screen Recording Codec is best for clips with a limited color palette, such as video captured from a computer screen. This makes it perfect for compressing the video used in interactive tutorials that demonstrates the steps involved in using a piece of software.

4. Set the frames per second. Best results can be obtained by keeping the video's original frame rate. If you have to reduce the frame rate, cut it by half, a third, or a quarter of the original. For video shot at 30fps (frames per second), you can drop the frame rate to 15, 10, or 7.5fps.

Figure 31.1

With Flash MX Pro 2004, you can use the FLV Exporter plug-in to export video in FLV format from a Quicktime-enabled video-editing application.

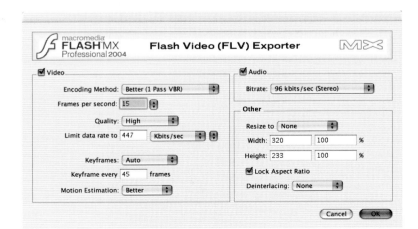

5. Data rate determines the rate (in bits per second) at which video information is transmitted. You can set a maximum data rate that allows the video to play within the limits of your audience's network connection speed. For Limit Data Rate, do one of the following:

   - Choose Low, Medium, or High. The exporter determines a generic setting based on your video's resolution and frame rate.

   - Choose a preset value between 5 and 500 Kbps.

   - Enter a value in the field to set a custom data rate. To cope with network congestion, you need to set a data rate that is lower than the speed of your audience's connection. For 56kb modems, set a data rate between 36 and 40kbps; for CD-ROM, set a data rate of 250kbps. For a higher bandwidth connection such as cable modem, you can set the data rate to around 500kbps, which is closer to the device's actual bandwidth in a world of busy network connections.

   - For a list of maximum bandwidth you can expect over a variety of connections, see this article at the Indiana University Knowledge Base: `http://kb.indiana.edu/data/aijg.html?cust=199853.98885.131`.

6. For Keyframes, select Auto to let the exporter choose the number of keyframes or select Custom and enter a keyframe value in the field. Remember, a keyframe is a complete picture of a frame. The more complete (uncompressed) frames you have, the more you can expect quality and file size to increase. To keep file size down, set large keyframe intervals between frames to reduce the number of total keyframes in the compressed clip.

7. For Motion Estimation, select Best for slower encoding and better quality or Faster for quicker encoding and lower quality.

8. Check the Audio box to export your video with sound. Choose a setting for bit rate and number of channels. Higher bit rates will yield better-sounding results at the cost of larger file size, while lower bit rates decrease file size and quality. To learn about the differences between stereo and mono, see Chapter 22.

9. Use the options in the Other section to change the size of the video:

   - Select a preset size from the Resize To menu.

   - Enter a pixel value or percentage for Width and Height.

   - Check Lock Aspect Ratio to preserve the clip's original dimensions.

10. Choose an option for Deinterlacing. If a clip was originally produced for television, it might have an interlaced signal. Deinterlacing will clean up the noise and jagged edges produced by interlacing.

    - Select None if the video is not interlaced.
    - Lower deinterlaces video produced for television in the United States (NTSC format).
    - Upper deinterlaces video produced for television in Europe (PAL format).

11. Click OK. Then choose a destination for the compressed video and click Save. The video will be compressed in FLV format and placed in the specified location.

Depending upon the length of the video you compress, the time it takes to complete the process will vary. Video clips with large dimensions and clips of long duration take longer to compress than smaller, shorter clips. Getting a video to compress correctly is a process of trial and error. Every video will compress differently based on the scene or event it portrays. Ultimately, you strive to strike a delicate balance between file size, acceptable quality, and smooth playback. Experiment with different settings and test the final FLV files side by side to compare for quality. Your final, compressed FLV file can now be imported into Flash.

Importing Video

To get video into the Flash authoring environment, you must first import it—just as you do sounds, bitmap images, and other media. Flash supports a wide variety of digital video formats. For both Macintosh and Windows platforms, you must have QuickTime 4 (or higher) installed on your computer to import most kinds of video into Flash MX. If you are a Windows user, you can benefit from the added support of DirectX 7 (or higher), which allows you to import additional Windows-specific video formats.

Table 31.2 gives you a summary of video import file formats supported by Flash MX 2004.

Table 31.2

Video File Formats Supported for Import to Flash MX 2004

FILE TYPE	PLATFORMS
Audio Video Interleaved (.avi)*	Macintosh, Windows
Digital Video (.dv)	Macintosh, Windows
Moving Picture Experts Group (.mpg, .mpeg)*	Macintosh, Windows
QuickTime Movie (.mov)	Macintosh, Windows
Windows Media File (.wmv, .asf)*	Windows
Macromedia Flash Video (.flv)**	Macintosh, Windows

These formats are supported in Windows only if DirectX 7 (or higher) is installed.

**Macromedia Flash Video (.flv) files can be imported directly into Flash MX 2004 without the help of QuickTime or DirectX, but they must be compressed using the FLV Exporter plug-in or Sorenson Squeeze.*

If Flash is unable to import a particular video format, it will display a message alerting you to the fact. In some situations, you might be able to import the video but not the audio. In that case, you do have the option to import the video without sound.

> Even with Sorenson Spark and the other great advances in video compression technology, you should still take steps to ensure that you have made your video as "compression friendly" as possible. This means optimizing video and audio content and targeting the video to the bandwidth requirements of your audience. To read more about this, see "Tips for Creating Flash Video with Sorenson Spark" in the Help panel (F1).

Importing Embedded Video Files

When you import a video into a Flash document, it becomes part of that document, or is *embedded* in the document. Embedding a video file is the most direct way to include it in a Flash movie. However, if you prefer to keep your Flash movie and the video separate, you have other options. With the help of the new media components (Flash MX Pro 2004 only) you can also stream external FLV video files into your movie. These videos can be saved locally or posted on the Internet. To learn more about streaming video in the Pro version of Flash MX 2004, see Hands On 8.

To import a video into Flash and embed it in a document:

1. Choose either File → Import to Stage (Cmd/Ctrl+**R**), which will import your video and place it directly onto your movie's Stage, or File → Import to Library, which will drop the video into the Library of the current document and leave you with the task of placing it in the Flash document yourself.

2. In the Import dialog box, choose All Video Formats from the Show (Mac)/ Files of Type (Win) drop-down menu (see Figure 31.2). This option will act as a filter, displaying only the video files that are available to Flash (see Table 31.2, shown earlier). Select the video you want to import and click Import.

3. If you chose to import an FLV video file directly to the Stage, a warning appears, asking if you want to expand the frame count of the main Timeline to accommodate the length of the video. Do one of the following:

   - Click Yes so that the frame count extends to fit the length of your video.

   - Click No to leave the frame count as is. You can add frames later as needed.

Figure 31.2

Only video files available to Flash are available in the Import dialog box. Other files appear grayed out.

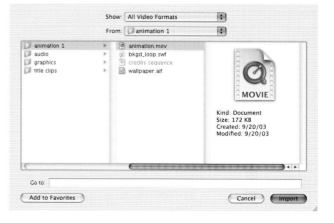

If you chose to import an FLV video to the Library, it will appear in your movie's Library. Because FLV video has already been compressed, there is no further configuration required. You can stop here and begin working with your video inside Flash. If you chose to import one of the other video file formats, the Video Import wizard opens. In the wizard, select Embed Video In Macromedia Flash Document. Click Next and proceed to step 4.

4. Select Import Entire Video to import the clip without editing, or select Edit the Video First to perform basic edits on the clip. To learn more about editing video with the wizard, see the section "Editing Video Clips as You Import Them" later in this chapter. Click Next to continue or click Back to return to the previous step.

5. Select a Compression profile from the drop-down menu. To learn how to edit existing profiles or create new profiles, see the section "Setting and Creating Compression Profiles" later in this chapter. Click Next to continue or click Back to return to the previous step.

6. To apply advanced settings that affect the color, dimensions, audio track, and Timeline destination of the imported video, choose an option from the Advanced Settings menu. To learn more about these options, see the section "Working with Advanced Video Settings" later in this chapter.

7. Click Finish to complete the import process. A progress bar shows you the length of time it will take to compress and import the video.

   If you chose to import the video directly to the Stage, a warning appears asking if you want to expand the frame count of the main Timeline to accommodate the length of the video. Do one of the following:

   • Click Yes so that the frame count extends to fit the length of your video.

   • Click No to leave the frame count as is. You can add frames later as needed.

The imported video file appears in your movie's Library with a video icon beside its filename. Once the video is in the Library, you can incorporate it into your movie. To read about how this is done, see the section "Using ActionScript to Control Video Playback" later in this chapter.

Using the Video Import Wizard

The Video Import wizard enables you import videos in Flash MX 2004 and embed them in a Flash document. As part of the import process, the wizard provides options that allow you to edit, compress, and apply advanced color settings to the video clips you import. The wizard also allows you to save individual import settings as Compression Profiles. This helps avoid the hassle of setting import options every time you need to import a video.

Editing Video Clips as You Import Them

If you are working with raw, unedited video footage and know that there are few adjustments you need to make to the video, you can use the Video Import wizard to perform basic edits to the clip. This includes trimming the size of the clip and breaking it into smaller components to create a new, abridged version of the source video.

To edit a video clip in the Video Import wizard:

1. If you chose Edit the Video First when importing the video clip, the wizard takes you to a new screen (see Figure 31.3), where you can edit your clip.

   Editing a video is a fairly simple process. You set an *in point,* the location where you want the edit to begin, and an *out point,* the spot where you want the edit to end. The clip between the in and out points has been *edited,* or separated from the original. It can be treated as a single clip or combined with other edited clips to create a new clip sequence.

2. Begin by viewing the clip. Click Play to play the clip from its current position; click Stop to halt the video. To scan through the clip quickly, click and drag the playback head from left to right. To advance one frame at a time, click the Step Back or Step Forward button.

3. Once you have isolated the section you want to edit, you can set in and out points. Move the playback head to the position where you want to start your edit and click Set In Point Position. The in point triangle snaps to that location on the playback Timeline. To set an out point, move the playback head to the position where you want to end your edit and click Set Out Point Position. You can also drag the in and out point triangles along the Timeline. Click Preview Clip to see the edited clip from start to finish.

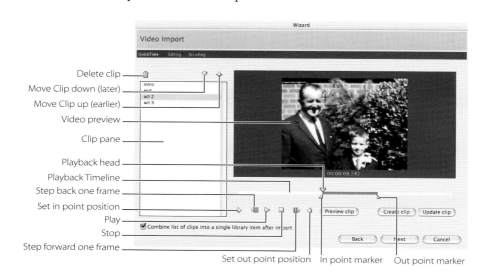

Figure 31.3

The Video Import wizard provides an interface for editing a video clip before it is imported into a Flash document.

4. After in and out points have been set, click Create Clip. This creates a new, edited clip starting at your in point and ending at your out point. The clip appears in the Clip pane at the side of the Wizard window. Enter a name for the newly created clip. To create additional clips, repeat the process outlined in steps 2 and 3.

5. To re-edit a clip, select it in the Clip pane. Set new in and out points for the clip and click Update Clip.

6. One of the best features of the wizard is that it allows you to combine all your edited clips into a single, longer, composite sequence. This is great because you can take an edited segment that was originally at the end of a video and put it at the beginning or vice versa.

   Click the Combine List of Clips check box in the lower corner of the wizard to put the clips together in a sequence. The sequence of clips is ordered from top to bottom in the Clip pane. To change the order of the edited clips, select the clip you want to move and click the Up or Down buttons. Up places a clip earlier in the sequence; down sets it to appear later. To delete a clip, click the Trash icon.

7. When you have finished editing the clip, click Next to continue the import process.

Setting and Creating Compression Profiles

When you import a video in Flash MX 2004, the video is compressed by the Spark codec. By setting a compression profile, you determine the amount of compression applied to a particular clip. These settings are very important. They allow you to fine-tune a clip for delivery to a particular audience by setting parameters for bandwidth, quality, keyframe frequency, and synchronization within the Flash document. The Video Import wizard allows you to select a preset compression profile or define a custom profile to suit your particular needs.

To use a preset compression profile, select from the drop-down menu. Bandwidth options range from 56kbps for dial-up modem to 786kbps for DSL and cable modem. Select a profile that matches the playback capabilities of your audience.

To create a custom compression profile:

1. Select Create New Profile from the Compression Profile drop-down menu.

2. The wizard switches to a new screen, where you can create your new profile (see Figure 31.4). Choose either Bandwidth or Quality. If you select Bandwidth, you will set the clip's data rate. Drag the slider across the range of 0 to 750kbps. See the section "Exporting FLV Video from Other Applications" earlier in this chapter to learn more about setting data rates.

   If you select Quality, drag the slider to set a value between 0 and 100. Higher settings afford better video quality but produce larger file sizes. Low settings do the opposite, yielding smaller files at the expense of quality. Settings at 60 or higher for Quality generally give good results.

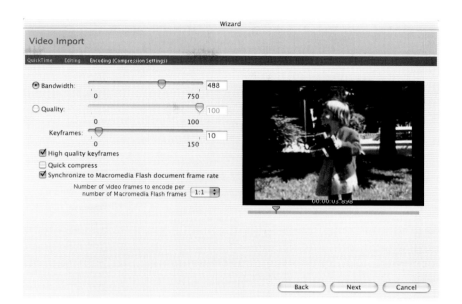

Figure 31.4

The compression settings screen of the Video Import wizard allows you to create a custom compression profile.

3. Set the frequency of keyframes using the Keyframes slider. Generally, you want to use as few keyframes as possible because a keyframe is a complete picture of a frame. The more complete (uncompressed) frames you have, the more quality and file size increase. To keep file size down, set large keyframe intervals between frames to reduce the number of total keyframes in the compressed clip.

4. Select High Quality Keyframes if you are using the Bandwidth slider. When bandwidth is fixed, keyframes can lose their sharpness and clarity. This will create better-quality keyframes in the compressed file.

5. Select Quick Compress to reduce overall compression time. This setting might reduce quality; use it only for temporary or low-quality files.

6. Select Synchronize to Macromedia Flash Document Frame Rate to lock video playback speed with that of your movie's Timeline. To let the video and your movie play with their individual frame rates intact, deselect this option.

7. Select a ratio for Number of Video Frames to Encode per Number of Macromedia Flash Frames. This specifies the ratio of imported video frames to main Flash Timeline frames. For example, to play one video frame per one Flash Timeline frame, select 1:1; to play one video frame for every four Timeline frames, choose 1:4; and so on.

8. When you have finished, click Next. Give your newly created profile a name and enter a description to help identify its unique properties. Click Next again and continue with the process of importing your video clip.

To edit an existing compression profile, select the profile in the drop-down menu and click Edit. Follow steps 2–8 to change the profile's properties. To remove a compression profile, select the profile in the menu and click Delete.

Working with Advanced Video Settings

If you want to make more significant changes to a clip as it is imported, you can use Advanced Settings. These parameters allow you to perform color corrections, change a clip's dimensions, and choose options that determine what kind of object the video will be in your Flash document: a Movie Clip or graphic symbol. You can also distill a clip's audio track or remove it altogether. Advanced settings can be saved as individual profiles that are easy to reuse in future Flash video projects.

To create an Advanced Settings profile:

1. Choose Create New Profile from the Advanced Settings menu.

2. The wizard switches to a new screen, where you can create your new profile (see Figure 31.5). Here you have options to modify a clip's color, dimensions, and track options.

3. In the Color section, enter values or use the sliders to set the following parameters that will adjust the color of a video clip:

   Hue Determines a color based on a position within the color wheel. Set a clip's hue between −180° and 180°.

Figure 31.5

The Advanced Settings screen of the Video Import wizard

Saturation The strength of the color. It represents the amount of gray in proportion to the hue. Set saturation values between −100 (gray) and +100 (fully saturated with the hue).

Brightness The relative lightness or darkness. Set brightness as a value between −100 (black) and +100 (white).

Contrast Determines the difference between light and dark areas of an image. Set values between −100 (no contrast) and +100 (most contrast).

Gamma Determines overall lightness and darkness. Set values between 0.1 (dark) and 1.8 (light). Larger Gamma values tend to send the colors of an image to their extremes: dark areas become very dark and light areas become very light.

4. In the Dimensions section, enter values to affect the size and scaling of a video clip:

   - For Scale, drag the slider down to reduce the scaling of a video clip from 100% to 0%. The values for Width and Height are updated accordingly.

   - For Crop, enter values or drag the sliders to set a new position for the top, left, right, and bottom of the clip. Crop position is measured in pixels; look at the video preview for a white box that shows the boundaries of the cropped video image.

5. In the Track Options section, choose a value for the Import Into parameter. This determines what kind of object will hold the imported video clip.

   Current Timeline Imports the clip into the Timeline that is currently active in your Flash document. In most cases, this will be the Main Timeline. However, try to avoid placing video files on your movie's Main Timeline. The high number of frames required to play the video will make it cumbersome when you try to create video navigation controls and other interface elements for your Flash movie.

   Movie Clip Imports the clip into a new Movie Clip symbol. This is the best option to use as it provides the greatest flexibility. When held inside a Movie Clip, you can use ActionScript to control the playback of the video's parent Timeline from buttons and other interface elements. To learn more about controlling video with ActionScript, see the section "Using ActionScript to Control Video Playback" later in this chapter.

   Graphic Symbol Imports the clip into a Graphic symbol. This option is useful for videos that need to remain separate from the Main Timeline, but don't require any ActionScript. Graphic symbols will play only if their parent Timeline has enough frames to fit the length of the video inside the symbol. For example, if your video requires 200 frames in the Graphic Symbol Timeline, but the main Timeline has only 100 frames, only the first half of the video will be seen in the final movie.

6. Choose a value for the Audio Track parameter. This determines how a clip's audio will be imported.

   Separate Divides audio and video components of a clip and imports the audio track as a separate audio file.

   Integrated Imports the audio track as part of the video clip.

   None Removes a video's audio track from the imported file.

   Unless you specifically need to remove or separate audio from a video file, use the Integrated option.

7. When you have finished, click Next. Give your newly created profile a name and enter a description to help identify its unique properties. Click Finish to complete the process of importing your video clip.

To edit an existing Advanced Settings profile, select the profile in the drop-down "menu and click Edit. Follow steps 3–7 to change the profile's properties. To remove an Advanced profile, select the profile in the menu and click Delete.

Using ActionScript to Control Video Playback

Now that you've brought a video into your Flash movie, you might be wondering how to manage its playback—how to make the video start, stop, rewind, skip ahead, and so on. The good news is that the imported video will behave like other elements within the Flash environment.

The best way to control your video is through a video Movie Clip. Such a clip is a lot like an ordinary Movie Clip, except that it has the frames of the video stretched across its Timeline. Also, like ordinary Movie Clips, a video Movie Clip can be controlled via ActionScript. This means that you can use scripting commands within Flash to dictate the playback of the video Movie Clip's Timeline.

> If ActionScript isn't for you, you're still in luck. See Chapter 14 to learn about ActionScript behaviors that will allow you to control the playback of video. You can also check out Hands On 8 to learn about controlling video with components and synchronizing the video with other elements of your movie or application.

If you use the Advanced Settings when you import a video, you can have Flash automatically put it in a Movie Clip Timeline. To learn how to do this, see the earlier section "Working with Advanced Video Settings." If your video is already inside a Movie Clip, skip ahead to the section "Controlling a Video with ActionScript." If it is in the Library, follow the steps here to create a clip that holds your video.

To create a video Movie Clip, you must have a video imported into your movie's Library. If you don't have a video of your own, we have provided a few that you can use. Open the Chapter 31 folder on this book's companion CD. If you want to use a QuickTime video, you can use mxVideo.mov. If you want to try using an FLV video, use mxVideo.flv. You will also want to have a few buttons on hand for use as controls to start and stop the video playback.

To create a video Movie Clip:

1. Choose Insert → New Symbol (Cmd/Ctrl+F8). Name the symbol **video_mc**, select Movie Clip as its behavior, and click OK.

2. Flash switches to Symbol Editing mode. In the Movie Clip Timeline, rename Layer 1 as **video**. Then insert a new layer and name it **code**.

3. Highlight the Video layer and drag your video clip from the Library onto the Stage. Flash is likely to warn you that the current Timeline doesn't have enough frames to display your entire video and ask you if you would like to add frames. Click Yes to add the necessary number of frames. Your video should now appear on the Stage, and your Timeline should have new frames stretching far enough to accommodate the length of the video (see Figure 31.6).

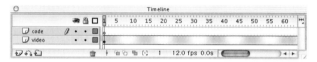

Figure 31.6

Frames are added to accommodate the video.

4. Use the Property Inspector (Cmd/Ctrl+F3) to position the upper-left corner of the video at X-Y coordinates (0, 0). Now that your clip is in place, you can add some ActionScript to help monitor its playback.

5. Select the first keyframe in the code layer and open the Actions panel. Enter a stop() function and close the panel. At the very least, this is the only command your video Movie Clip requires. With stop() placed at frame 1 of its Timeline, the clip won't start playing until prompted to do so.

6. Save your movie and return to the main Timeline.

Controlling a Video with ActionScript

Once a video has been imported into your Flash document and placed in a Movie Clip Timeline, you will be able to write ActionScript to control the playback of the video. In this section, you will learn how to write scripts that play, stop, and fast-forward the video.

To write ActionScript that controls a video:

1. Drag an instance of video_mc to the Stage and use the Property Inspector to assign it the instance name **trailer** (or something different if you prefer). This lesson uses trailer throughout.

2. Now that your clip has a unique name, you can add buttons that will allow you to interactively control the playback of the Movie Clip. Drag two buttons from your Library to the Stage: one for Play and one for Stop. Select the Play button, open the Actions panel, and enter the following statements:

```
on(press){
    trailer.play();
}
```

The function of this script should be fairly self-explanatory. When the button is pressed, it plays the `trailer` clip from its current location.

3. Select the Stop button, open the Actions panel (if it's not open already), and enter the following statements:

```
on(press){
    trailer.gotoAndStop(1);
}
```

Again, a very straightforward script. When pressed, this button sends the clip instance back to frame 1 of its Timeline and stops it there.

4. Select Control → Test Movie or press Cmd+Return (Mac) or Ctrl+Enter (Win) to give these buttons a try. You will notice that the Play button sets the clip in motion and the Stop button both halts it and sends it back to frame 1.

Additionally, you can add all sorts of controls to manipulate video playback. Here are just a few samples:

Pause Attaches the following to a button to pause the video:

```
on(press){
    trailer.stop();
}
```

Fast Forward This example involves a few more elements. Attached to a Fast Forward button, you have two handlers that toggle the variable *ffwd* on and off:

```
on(press){
    ffwd = true;
}
on(release){
    ffwd = false;
}
```

Then, to respond to the change in variable value, you assign a function for the video Movie Clip instance `trailer`. This script is attached to frame 1 of the main Timeline.

When `ffwd` is "on," it sends the clip ahead by four frames. This number can be increased or decreased to change the speed of the fast-forward:

```
ffwd = false;
trailer.onEnterFrame = function(){
   if(ffwd == true){
        frame = trailer._currentframe;
        trailer.gotoAndPlay(frame+4);
   }
}
```

There is a lot you can do to control the playback of a video within Flash. Using built-in functions and methods of the Movie Clip object, you should be able to invent all sorts of interesting techniques and video shuttle widgets. For example, the previous function will fast-forward the video until the end and loop back to the beginning. It would be nice to make the clip stop when the video reaches the end. For this and other video-scripting solutions, check out the file(s) named `video2MX.fla` or `video2MX.swf` in the Chapter 31 folder on this book's companion CD. They'll show you this and other examples in the context of an actual movie.

Managing Video Files in Your Movie

There are a few techniques that can be helpful for managing your video media inside and outside a Flash document. After you edit or change an embedded video file outside Flash, you can update the file rather than re-import it.

To update an embedded video clip:

1. Select the video clip in the Library.

2. Ctrl+click (Mac) or right-click (Win) the video in the Library and choose Properties from the context menu.

3. Click Update in the Update Video Properties dialog box. The embedded clip is updated with the edited file.

Alternatively, you can replace the selected clip with an entirely different video clip. Click Import and choose a different clip in the Import dialog box. That clip will replace the embedded clip in your Library.

You might also want to replace the embedded video clip that is used for an embedded video instance or change the clip's properties. To perform either of these tasks:

1. Select the clip on the Stage that you want to change.

2. Open the Property Inspector (Cmd/Ctrl+F3) to display the instance information for the selected clip.

3. Depending upon your needs, do any of the following:

- Click Swap and choose the clip you want to exchange for the clip on the Stage. Click OK and the clip instance is updated accordingly.

- Enter values for W and H to change the width and height of a clip. Realize that increasing the size of the video can produce an ugly, "blocky" appearance. If a video needs to be larger, the best approach is to return to the source and re-export the video at a larger size.

- Enter values for X and Y to set the Stage position of the video instance's upper-left corner.

When publishing a Flash movie as an SWF file, the soundtrack of any embedded video clip(s) will be exported using the Stream sound settings. (These are the settings for Stream in the Flash tab of the Publish Settings dialog box.) Be sure that these options are set at the appropriate rate for your target audience. To read more about audio compression settings in Flash, see Chapter 23.

Publishing a Flash Movie on Videotape

Given the power and flexibility of the Flash authoring application, you might wonder why anyone would even consider putting their SWF masterpiece on videotape. After all, video is a noninteractive, linear medium. One of Flash's greatest assets is its ability to deliver animations and information in an audience-directed format: Your viewers can decide how the piece is presented. Plus, with the visibility of the Flash plug-in on the Web, your pieces are available to a worldwide audience of unprecedented size.

Video can be helpful in several situations, however. It might not provide the kind of interactivity found on the Web, but video does allow you to use Flash for applications in which the computer and interactivity are not part of the media equation. If you want to use Flash to create animated shorts or cartoon for television, you have to go to video. Flash can be transferred to video for projected playback at concert venues and art galleries and used as source material for video-mix artists and performers. If you are involved in any kind of video postproduction work, you can use Flash to animate title sequences or special effects and to composite the Flash animation with your video footage to create interesting layered effects. As always, Flash gives you an endless variety of possibilities.

The steps for transferring a Flash animation to video are outlined in this chapter. Depending on the specific kind of video you want to produce, you might find that some modifications are needed to get the best results for your particular project. In general, the process includes the following steps:

- Prepare the Flash Timeline graphics, including Movie Clips.
- Prepare the audio tracks if you plan to use the Flash audio.

- Export the Flash animation as QuickTime video (Mac) or AVI (Win).
- Import the animation to a video editing application and make any needed adjustments or edits depending on your specific goals.

That's the process in a nutshell. Let's dive into the specifics and get things under way.

Preparing the Flash Timeline

The first part of the transfer-to-video process involves preparing your movie's Timeline. In this case, *preparing* means simplifying so that the Timeline is free of ActionScript, Movie Clips, and any other items in your work that would not apply to a linear medium (such as navigational buttons).

ActionScript statements must usually be cut simply because they can interrupt the flow of a linear animation. For example, if you have any kind of gotoAndPlay() loops that send the movie back to a previous frame, you need to delete these from your Timeline. If the statements are somehow integral to the overall animation, you can work around this situation by copying and pasting the frames in the loop. For instance, if you have an animation of a knock-knock joke, you might have a gotoAndPlay() function that sends the movie back to frame 1 to repeat the "Knock, knock! Who's there?" part of the joke. Because this statement won't work when you transfer to video, your best strategy is to copy and paste the frames that you need to repeat. Choose Edit → Timeline → Copy Frames, then choose Edit → Timeline → Paste Frames to reconstruct the animation structure as needed. To learn more about manipulating frames in the Timeline, see Chapter 10.

> It's okay to use this technique with a Flash animation that uses scenes. The animation will be exported in the order the scenes are listed in the Scene panel (select Window → Design Panels → Scene or press Shift+F2).

Additionally, if your animation uses Movie Clips, you will need to do some tweaking. As self-contained animations, Movie Clips work fine in the Flash Player or in QuickTime Flash movies but are not supported in linear video applications. Consequently, you have to include them on their own layer(s) in the main Timeline. Using the same copy-and-paste technique described earlier, you can move animated components out of a Movie Clip Timeline and into your main Timeline.

To transfer a Movie Clip animation to the main Timeline:

1. Open the Movie Clip's Timeline by using the Edit Symbols pop-up menu or by double-clicking the Movie Clip's icon in the Library. Flash jumps into Symbol Editing mode.

2. While pressing Shift, click each layer's name or label to select the frames that make up the Movie Clip animation. Take note of how many layers are used in the Movie Clip.

Figure 31.7

You can copy all frames of a Movie Clip to the Clipboard.

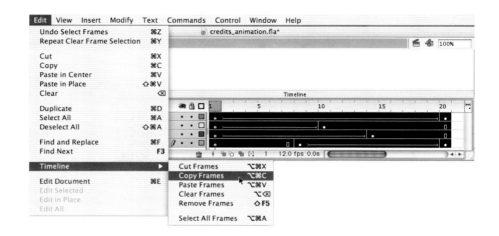

3. Choose Edit → Timeline → Copy Frames to copy the frames to the Clipboard (see Figure 31.7). Return to Movie Editing mode.

4. Now you're ready to add the elements of the Movie Clip to your main Timeline. Insert new layers as needed to accommodate the components of the Movie Clip. If your Movie Clip used four layers, insert four new layers.

5. Click the frame in the topmost new layer where you want to paste the Movie Clip. Then, Shift+click the lowest new layer to select the first frame for each, as shown at the top of Figure 31.8.

6. Choose Edit → Timeline → Paste Frames to paste the Movie Clip frames into the new layers, starting at the frame you just highlighted. See bottom of Figure 31.8 for the results.

   This is a fairly simple process, but it might require some additional tweaking depending on how you used the Movie Clip in the original animation.

Figure 31.8

Movie Clip frames pasted into the main Timeline

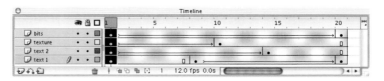

Some Advice about Monitors

Another point to consider if you are planning to display your video on a television monitor is the *aspect ratio*. The aspect ratio for television is 4:3, meaning that for every 4 units of width, there are 3 units of height. The standard size for television and video is 640×480 pixels. You can adjust your Flash movie to a 4:3 aspect ratio by choosing Modify → Document to set the width and height accordingly. Or, if your movie already conforms to this ratio but is smaller (for example, 160×120), you can make the adjustments when you export the video.

Concerning screen size and television monitors, be aware that not all monitors will play a video in exactly the same way. On some, information at the edge of the screen might be lost; for this reason, you want to be sure that your animation contains nothing of vital importance at the edge of the Stage. There are two "safe zones" that will help you avoid problems with inconsistent monitors: the *action-safe zone* and the *title-safe zone*. The action-safe zone is exactly 90% of the total screen size; so for a 640×480 animation, you'll want to keep important images and animation within the area 576×432. The title-safe zone is reserved for text and is exactly 80% of the total screen size. This translates to an area of 512×384. Both these safe zones are centered within the total area of the Stage (see Figure 31.9).

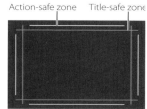

Action-safe zone   Title-safe zone

Figure 31.9

To prepare a Flash animation for playback on a television monitor, be sure that important elements fall within the action-safe and title-safe zones.

Preparing the Flash Audio

Flash can work as an animator alone, and dealing with audio at this point might not be a concern. If your plan is to bring an animation in and composite or edit it together with existing video footage, it's probably best not to incorporate sound in the Flash movie itself, but to wait and add your audio elements in the video application. However, if you plan to deliver your entire Flash animation (including the soundtrack) as a video, you'll need to follow some additional steps to prepare your movie.

When you export a Flash movie as video, there are several sound-related issues that you should be aware of:

Mixing When you created your Flash animation, chances are you used the Edit Envelope dialog box (shown here) to adjust the relative volume level of each sound in your movie. This is a crucial step because it allows you to assign each sound its proper place in the audio spectrum. Some sounds, such as narration and dialog, are important and need to be heard clearly whenever they are present. Other sounds, such as music and sound effects, can be adjusted accordingly so that they don't impede on other audio elements.

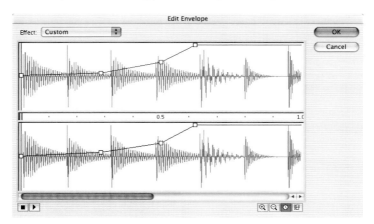

Your goal is to use the envelopes to create an ideal sound balance for your movie's audio components. Before you export to video, revisit these settings and be sure that your levels are correct. Once the Flash animation has been exported, the audio track is permanently mixed and cannot be changed. To tweak the audio, you would have to go back to your Flash file, readjust the audio, and re-export the movie. To learn more about options concerning the Edit Envelope window, see Chapter 23.

Synchronization Sync is a big topic when it comes to discussions of audio and video. It's very important because, if these elements lose sync, your animation will begin to look like a poorly dubbed monster movie. Regardless of the sync settings in your original animation, when you prepare to export to video, you should use the Property Inspector (Cmd/Ctrl+F3) to set all of the audio to Stream sync. This will lock your audio to the movie's frame rate and ensure tight synchronization. Also, be sure that each sound has enough frames to play in its entirety. Stream sounds will be heard only for the duration of the frames they occupy. To learn more about Flash synchronization options, see Chapter 24.

A Word of Caution about Embedded Audio

Exporting sound from your Flash movie has its pros and cons. One of the benefits is that your synchronization will be preserved and you don't have to worry about reconstructing your audio track in a separate application later. Another plus is that your final video will be complete, with all its audio and visual elements neatly packed in a single digital video file.

However, if you plan to take your Flash video into another application such as Final Cut Pro or Adobe Premiere for more editing, you should take an additional step to prepare the audio. The streaming audio tracks that are embedded within a Flash video file don't always work in video editors. Often, any audio included with your Flash video will be distorted beyond recognition when brought into a video application. Not all video editing applications experience this, but you should test the situation first by importing a video. If the sound is distorted, you will need to take a few additional steps.

Audio distortion in your video can be avoided when you bring the audio and video elements into the application *separately*. In the Mac OS, you can use QuickTime Pro (www.apple.com/quicktime/buy) to extract the audio track from your video by exporting the video file with the Sound to AIFF option. In Windows, you can export two separate versions of your Flash movie: one that is silent and one that is sound-only. For details, see the section "Exporting Your Movie as a WAV File" later in this chapter.

Exporting Flash as Video

After completing all of the previously outlined steps, you are ready for the next phase of production: exporting your movie as video. If you are working on a Macintosh, you have the option to export your animation as QuickTime video. If you are a Windows user, Flash allows you to export under the AVI format. Both processes convert your vector-based animation to a raster-based video file that can be opened and manipulated in a video editing application.

QuickTime Video (Macintosh)

If you work on a Macintosh, Flash allows you to export your animation as a QuickTime video file. You should note the fundamental difference between the different QuickTime file types, QuickTime Flash and QuickTime video. One of the enhancements in version 4 of QuickTime was its support for Flash files. Consequently, Flash can be exported as *QuickTime Flash*, which allows the movie to retain all of its interactive properties and act like a regular Flash file. To learn more about publishing interactive QuickTime Flash movies for both Macintosh and Windows, see Chapter 30.

Of all Flash's export options, the QuickTime video format is the least like Flash itself. It is raster-based (composed entirely of pixels) and has no interactive properties. However, it is the easiest format for transferring a Flash animation to video. Assuming that you have followed the steps outlined in the preceding section, your animation should be ready to export.

To export a Flash animation as QuickTime video:

1. Select File → Export → Export Movie. The Export Movie window opens, asking you to name the exported movie and browse to the location where you would like to save it (see Figure 31.10). Select QuickTime Video from the Format drop-down menu and give the file a name. Note that in the Name field, Flash appends a filename extension of .mov to the untitled file to signify that it will be a digital video file.

Figure 31.10

When you export a movie, you will be prompted to choose an export format and location for the exported file.

2. Click Save and the Export QuickTime Video dialog box opens (see Figure 31.11). This interface is where you set all the options for your exported video.

   Dimensions Use these fields to specify width and height for the final video. Unless your Flash animation contains bitmap images, it can be scaled up or down without distortion to produce the final video. When the Maintain Aspect Ratio box is checked, your movie will be constrained to the proportions defined in the Document Properties dialog box.

   Format Choose from the following color options for your movie:

   • Black and white: very low quality

   • 4-bit color: low quality

   • 8-bit color: 256 colors (marginal quality)

   • 16-bit color: comparable to the Macintosh "Thousands of Colors" setting

   • 24-bit color: comparable to the Macintosh "Millions of Colors" setting

   • 32-bit color: same as 24-bit color, plus it supports Alpha Channel information for transparency effects

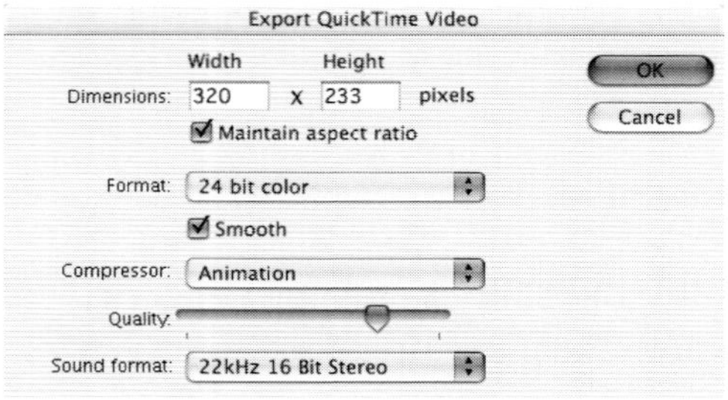

Figure 31.11

Export options

Smooth   The Smooth option applies anti-aliasing to the exported QuickTime movie. Smooth can produce a higher-quality video image but might also lead to some distortion. Deselect this option if any unacceptable changes occur to your video.

Compressor   These options allow you to take advantage of one of QuickTime's video-compression codecs. For vector-only Flash movies, you will experience good results with the Animation compression option. The Cinepak and Sorenson codecs are good for CD-ROM distribution. To learn more about individual QuickTime codecs, see the QuickTime website: `www.apple.com/quicktime/products/qt/specifications.html`.

Quality   This slider controls how much compression is applied to the video. If you position the slider to the far right, the compression is minimal, affording better quality. As you move the slider to the left, more compression is added and quality suffers.

Sound Format   Use this drop-down menu to set the parameters for the quality of sound exported from your movie. To learn more about sampling rates, bit depths, and other sound-related issues, see Chapter 22. This option can also be set to Disable if you wish to export your movie without its sound components.

If you plan to bring the exported video into another application outside of Flash, your best bet is to export the audio at the highest possible quality. It can always be downsampled later if necessary.

3. Once you've set all your options, click OK, and Flash will begin the exporting process. This can sometimes take a while, especially if you are exporting a long animation or a complex soundtrack or you are applying compression.

Your final QuickTime file will appear in the location you set; you'll see the capital-Q filmstrip icon and the filename extension of `.mov`. This file is suited for distribution as digital video on a CD-ROM or the Internet or as source material for a video project, depending on what settings you applied.

Audio Video Interleaved (Windows)

If you're working with Flash on the Windows platform, you'll need to export your video in Audio Video Interleaved (AVI) format. Like QuickTime video, AVI is a raster-based video format that will transfer nicely into a video editing application.

To export a Flash animation as an AVI:

1. Select File → Export → Export Movie. A window opens, asking you to name the exported movie and browse to the location where you want to save it. Give the file a name and select Windows AVI from the Save as Type drop-down menu. When finished with these choices, click Save.

2. The Export Windows AVI dialog box opens (see Figure 31.12). This is where you set all the options for your exported video.

Figure 31.12

The Export Windows AVI dialog box

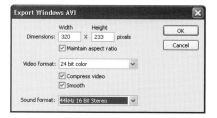

Dimensions Use these Width and Height fields to specify dimensions for the final video. Unless your Flash animation contains bitmap images, a video file can be scaled up or down without distortion. When the Maintain Aspect Ratio box is checked, your movie is constrained to the proportions defined in the Movie Properties dialog box.

Video Format Choose from the following color options for your movie:

- 8-bit color: low quality.

- 16-bit color: Windows High Color setting.

- 24-bit color: Windows True Color setting.

- 32-bit color: like 24-bit color, plus it supports Alpha Channel information for transparency effects. This feature is not widely supported. Check the documentation for your video software before exporting a 32-bit video file.

Compress Video When checked, this opens an additional dialog box (after you've pressed OK in the current dialog box) that allows you to apply compression to your video. In this format, compression is recommended to help keep file sizes down.

Smooth Check the Smooth box to turn on anti-aliasing. Note that this might add unwanted pixels or noise to the final video image.

Sound Format Use this drop-down list to set the parameters for the quality of sound exported from your movie. To learn more about sampling rates, bit depths, and other sound-related issues, see Chapter 22. This option can also be set to Disable when you wish to export your movie without its sound components.

If you plan to do additional editing of your video in another application such as Adobe Premiere, we recommend that you select Disable as the Sound Format option. The soundtrack of an AVI video that has been exported from Flash doesn't perform well in video applications (see the section "A Word of Caution about Embedded Audio" earlier in this chapter). Namely, the Flash audio track gets distorted to the point of being unrecognizable. To have a clear-sounding audio track, you must export separate versions of your Flash movie: one as a silent AVI video and one as a sound-only WAV file. To learn how to export a WAV version of your Flash movie, see the next section, "Exporting Your Movie as a WAV File (Windows)."

3. Click OK to acknowledge all these video settings and to export your animation as an AVI video.

4. If you enabled compression in step 2, an additional dialog box opens (see Figure 31.13) in which you can set the following options:

Compressor   Choose the compression codec that best suits the video equipment and software with which you are working. Consult the documentation that ships with your video editing system (or software) for specifics on working with compressed AVI footage. If you intend to view or distribute the animation as a stand-alone AVI, the Cinepak codec is a good choice.

Compression Quality   This slider sets the amount of compression applied to a file.

Key Frame Every   To insert a keyframe at regular intervals, check this box and enter a number in the field. Keyframes help the compressor handle video information. Adding a keyframe at an interval equal to your movie's frame rate can be helpful. For example, a movie at 30 frames/second should have one keyframe every 30 frames.

Data Rate   Checking this setting limits the amount of data a video generates when it plays back. A data rate of 150KB/second can help video stream smoothly from a CD-ROM drive.

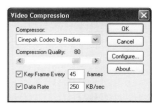

Figure 31.13

The Video Compression dialog box offers a list of possible compressors.

5. Click OK when you are finished with the compression settings. Flash will export the AVI to the location you defined back in step 1.

When exporting is completed, you'll have a digital video file that is ready for use in a video editing application or as part of a CD-ROM. If you want to go one step further and transfer your video to tape, see the upcoming section on preparing your video.

Exporting Your Movie as a WAV File (Windows)

If you plan to bring your Flash video into Adobe Premiere or another video editor, you must import it as two separate elements: a silent AVI video and a sound-only WAV file. This allows you to avoid the distortion that happens to Flash video soundtracks inside Premiere.

> To be certain that your movie is ready to be exported as a WAV, see the earlier section "Preparing the Flash Audio" before proceeding.

To export your Flash movie as a WAV file:

1. Select File → Export → Export Movie. A window opens, asking you to name the exported movie and browse to the location where you want to save it. Name the file and select WAV Audio from the Save as Type drop-down menu. When finished with these choices, click Save.

2. The Export Windows WAV dialog box opens. This is where you set all the options for your exported soundtrack. Choose the highest possible sampling rate and bit depth

from the Sound Format menu (you can always lower the quality later) and select the Ignore Event Sounds check box.

3. Click OK, and Flash exports the sound as a WAV file to the location you specified in step 1. You now have all the elements you need to produce a video. Later, while working with a video editor, you must remove your Flash video's original soundtrack and replace it with this file.

Next Steps to Give Your Video a Life Beyond Flash

And now, for our next trick…You might feel like a circus performer jumping between so many different windows, rearranging frames, and setting video compression options. The process can indeed be a bit crazy, but you're almost finished.

Your Flash animation has been saved as a digital video file: `.mov` for Macintosh or `.avi` for Windows. At this point, all the pieces are in place. You have many options, most of which go beyond the scope of this book. Here are a few of the possibilities you might wish to consider.

- Import your video to a video editing application. It can be used as a scene in a movie or as part of a title sequence. Use the Print to Video (or similar) option to transfer your Flash animation to VHS or DV tape.

- Import your video into a compositing application. Programs such as Adobe After Effects will allow you to do layering and create special effects that aren't possible (or easy to achieve) in Flash.

- Distribute your video as a stand-alone movie, viewable in either QuickTime or Windows Media Player.

Inspirational Design Model

The new advances in video with Flash MX 2004 and MX Pro 2004 leave you with tons of video-related options, and for that Flash designers should be grateful. However, Macromedia tends to focus on the business-to-business applications of this feature. And while these are perfectly useful, we want our readers to know that there are a lot more possibilities afforded by the medium. For instance, you can think of Flash as a means to create your very own movie theater in cyberspace. Flash makes it possible to create a personalized interface for screening features, documentaries, or videos of your cousin Louis's wedding. If you have something you want to express on video, Flash can help you get it out to the world.

A great example is the interactive tour of Wildcat Creek in Richmond, California (`www.redstartstudio.com/wildcat/wildcat.html`). The piece (see Figure 31.14) is part of a site plan analysis project initiated through the Landscape Architecture program at the University of California at Berkeley in the fall of 2002. The analysis focuses on Wildcat Creek as it flows through the densely populated cities of Richmond and San Pablo, California. Despite the strong urban overlay, pockets of natural wildness still exist in and around Wildcat Creek. Several of these localities are represented in the interactive map, which incorporates video, sound, and digital images gathered by Lauri Twitchell and Peter Suchecki. Flash is used here as a supplement to the traditional modes of presentation used by landscape architects.

© Lauri Twitchell and Peter Suchecki

Figure 31.14

This walking tour of Wildcat Creek was produced in Flash by Peter Suchecki and Lauri Twitchell.

CHAPTER 32

Using Flash for CD-ROM Development

One of Flash's greatest strengths is its ability to deliver high-quality audio and animation in a single, compact file. This characteristic makes Flash ideally suited for the Internet and other applications in which bandwidth is a major concern. What is often forgotten, though, is that Flash can also be distributed in ways that are not limited by download-time or plug-in issues.

One of the best ways to distribute your Flash movies is to pass them to your audience on a CD-ROM as stand-alone or self-contained applications. In this format, Flash can either rely on the stand-alone Flash Player or be completely independent and run on both Macintosh and Windows platforms without additional software. Plus, with the capacity of a CD-ROM, you are able to deliver a greater amount of information without the concerns of bandwidth that you encounter on the Web.

While no single delivery method can do it all, you will find that each has its particular advantages and allows you to distribute your movies in new ways that open the door to many new possibilities. This chapter will cover the following topics:

- **Stand-alone Flash Player movies**
- **Self-contained Flash projectors**
- **Publishing movies for CD-ROM delivery**
- **Using ActionScript FSCommands**
- **Designing and scripting interface elements for a Flash-based CD-ROM**

Stand-Alone Flash Files

Although Flash most commonly appears on the Internet in the context of a website, don't forget that there are other options that help you to reach your audience. Flash can produce two types of stand-alone movies that enable you to share your work without requiring that your audience go to the Web. The first is a standard SWF file. If your audience has the stand-alone Flash Player application, they will be able to see your movie without the aid of a web browser. The other type of stand-alone movie is a self-contained *Flash projector*. This is a self-running application that allows your movie to run on any computer, whether the Flash Player is installed or not.

One of the best advantages of both stand-alone options is that you can create all your movies so that they will run on all platforms. Regardless of the operating system that you use to run Flash, you'll be able to create final files that match the playback capabilities of your audience. This characteristic makes Flash one of the most portable multimedia applications currently available.

Distributing Movies with the Flash Player

The Flash Player application 🅕 comes with Flash. It can be used to play any SWF file without the assistance of a web browser. The Flash Player (see Figure 32.1) offers several menu options with which you control the playback and appearance of a movie. You can find the application in the Players folder, inside the folder where Flash resides on your computer's hard drive. For Macintosh users, the stand-alone player is named *SAFlash-Player*; for Windows folks, it's named *SAFlashPlayer.exe*.

Because the Flash Player will play any SWF file, it's very easy to distribute your movies in a compact manner, over a variety of platforms, and with minimal fuss. The average computer user won't have this application, however. Thus, it isn't the best delivery option if you're trying to target a large number of people—unless you're sure they all have the Flash Player application installed (meaning that they already own the Flash authoring application). To make your movie deliverable to the widest possible audience, use a self-contained Flash projector.

Figure 32.1

A movie running on a local computer with the Flash Player application

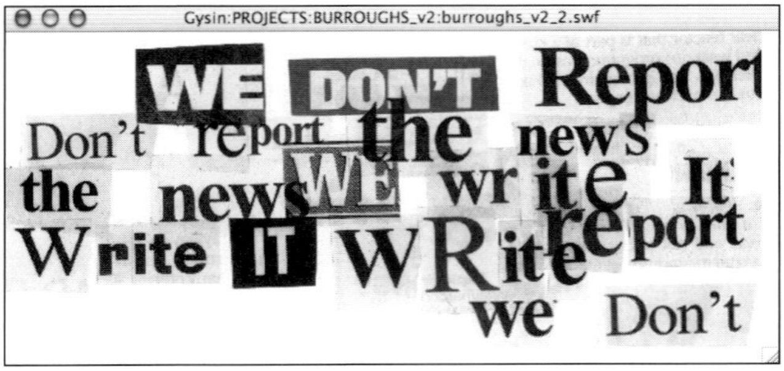

Delivering Movies as Self-Contained Flash Projectors

Self-contained Flash projectors are quite possibly the best way to distribute your movies outside the Web. A self-contained projector is an executable file—a self-contained application that will run your movie just as you created it on either Windows or a Macintosh operating system. Anyone using Windows or a Mac (which is just about everybody) will

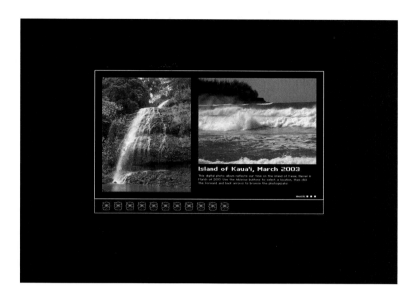

Figure 32.2

A self-contained projector can run in its own window or on the full screen (as shown here).

be able to see your Flash masterpiece without the help of any additional software or web-browser plug-in. Fantastic! Plus, by putting a self-contained projector on a CD-ROM, you're able to hand it out to fans, clients, customers, students, and so on, in a format that is easily accessible on any computer with a CD-ROM drive. Figure 32.2 shows a Flash projector in context.

Creating Flash Projectors

Creating, or, more appropriately, *publishing,* a Flash projector is very simple. And because Flash allows you to create both Macintosh and Windows projectors, you can take care of creating both files in a single step. One minor disadvantage is that the self-contained projector will be a few hundred kilobytes larger than the SWF version of the same movie. This is because the projector file must contain information necessary for playing your movie using the resources of the operating system on which the projector is running.

Figure 32.3

The Publish Settings dialog box contains the options for creating self-contained projectors.

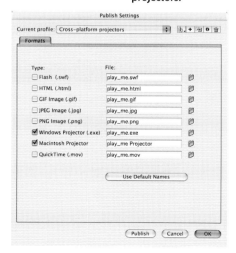

To publish a self-contained Flash projector:

1. When you've finished creating the movie, choose File → Save to save it with any final changes in place.

2. Choose File → Publish Settings. The Publish Settings dialog box opens (see Figure 32.3).

3. Check the box next to Windows Projector or Macintosh Projector depending on what kind of projector you need to create. Check both boxes if you want to create both varieties. You can give each version a name in the adjacent File field. Be sure to leave the .exe suffix on the name of your Windows projector.

4. As an optional step, you can take advantage of two new publishing-related features in Flash MX 2004 and MX Pro 2004:

   - Click the Select Publish Destination button to save each published projector to a unique location. In this case, you could put one in a *Mac* folder and the other in a folder named *Windows*.

   - Use the Current Profile menu (see Figure 33.3) to create a "projectors only" profile. To learn how to create publishing profiles, see Chapter 30.

5. To finally publish the projector, do one of the following:

   - Click the Publish button. This will publish your projector immediately. This option is helpful if you need to publish several different kinds of movies in one sitting.

   - Click OK to accept the selections you've just made in the Publish Settings dialog box. Then select File → Publish (Shift+F12) to publish your projector(s).

   The Publishing window opens, showing the progress made toward publishing your movie. When it is finished, your projector file(s) should be sitting in the same folder as the Flash file you are currently using.

6. Quit Flash (File → Quit/Exit). After being published, Flash stand-alone projectors are given a circular icon showing the Flash MX *f* 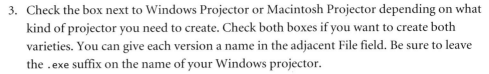. Double-click the projector's circular icon to launch the self-contained projector application. The file is now ready to be burned onto a CD-ROM.

Using Flash to Create CD-ROM Interfaces

Although publishing your self-contained projector is the final step of the process, there are many additional things you can do with your movie to make it look and act more like a self-sufficient application. With the help of a few ActionScript commands, you can take your Flash movie and turn it into an independent multimedia production that is controlled in precisely the ways you define. Not only does this give your piece a more professional look and feel, but it allows you to set the stage for the ways in which your audience chooses to view your work.

FSCommands

FSCommands are an element of ActionScript that allow Flash and the Flash Player to communicate with the application that is hosting your movie. In the context of this chapter, that application is either the Macintosh or Windows operating system. By issuing

FSCommands in your movie, you can set many different parameters for the movie's presentation, and the options available to the audience who is viewing it. The syntax for `fscommand()` is as follows:

```
fscommand("command","argument");
```

The available commands for `fscommand()` are:

fullscreen This command takes one of two arguments, `true` or `false`. When set to `true`, the projector fills the entire monitor window and displays no menu bar at the top of the screen. When set to `false`, the projector appears in a window whose size is set by the dimensions specified in the Movie Properties dialog box.

allowscale This command, when set to `true`, allows the movie to stretch to fit the size of the window (or monitor) playing it. When set to `false`, the window that contains the movie can be stretched as needed, but the movie itself is not scaled.

showmenu When set to `true`, this command enables the options in the context menu (Ctrl+click/right-click) for a projector file. These options allow your audience to play, stop, rewind, zoom, and change the display quality of the projector file. When set to `false`, all options are grayed out or removed, with the exception of the Settings option and the About Macromedia Flash Player option.

trapallkeys This command, when set to `true`, will disable the keyboard. When set to `false` (the default), the movie can accept input from the keyboard. Watch out—by setting `trapallkeys` to `true`, you are effectively cutting off the keyboard. If you do this to prevent nonscripted interaction with your movie, be sure to include a button or other element with the `fscommand("quit")` statement for shutting down the projector.

exec Use the exec command to launch another application from the Flash projector. The new application will appear over the projector file. The argument for this command is specified as a string containing the relative path to the application you want to launch. For example:

```
on(release){
    fscommand("exec", "TimeMe");
}
```

For the exec command to work, the application that you wish to launch must be in a separate folder named `fscommand`. In the previous example, if the SWF were in a folder named `/files`, the path to the application `TimeMe` is required to be `/files/fscommand/`. Note however, that the path is not included in the second parameter of the function.

quit This command takes no arguments. When it's issued, your computer will close the projector file.

All FSCommands (`quit`, `exec`, and so on) and their arguments are entered as strings. For example:

```
fscommand ("fullscreen", "true");
```

This statement sets a projector to play in full-screen mode. The command `fullscreen` and its argument `true` are listed in quotation marks, making each a text string. If you don't enter the arguments as strings, Flash won't be able to communicate properly with the operating system and perform the actions you specify.

The best place for FSCommands is in a frame on the main Timeline. Put them in the first frame of the movie so that they are executed before any other scripts are called. If you place your FSCommands in your movie's first frame, they will require no handler and will be one of the first movie parameters loaded into memory.

Letterbox Projectors and CD Interface Elements

Using FSCommands is the first step toward creating a truly unique CD-ROM for your Flash movie. This section introduces you to a few design-related techniques that you can employ to create a stylish and functional movie for cross-platform distribution.

The first technique involves creating a letterbox-style projector. *Letterbox* is a term used to describe the appearance of a full-screen video image. When you go to a movie theater, you see films on a screen that is quite different from the monitor on your television or computer. Rather than the standard 4:3 aspect ratio, movie screens have a 16:9 aspect ratio. These screens are much wider than they are tall and accommodate a broader field of view. Consequently, when studio films are re-released on video and DVD for consumers' televisions and VCRs, they are often modified to fit the 4:3 aspect ratio.

In some cases, though, this isn't done. To preserve the 16:9 cinematic aspect ratio, videos and DVDs can be released in letterbox (or *widescreen*) format. Roughly the top one-third and the bottom one-third of the screen are left black, and the image fills the entire width of the display. Ultimately, this format makes the image smaller than if it were in the 4:3 ratio but preserves the original proportions of the film. Although letterbox is used as a technical convention, it has a very stylish look and can lend an interesting visual quality to Flash projector files.

Creating the letterbox effect is very simple and involves only a few small modifications to your movie:

1. Select Modify → Document. The Document Properties dialog box opens. Set your movie dimensions so that they conform to the 16:9 aspect ratio (such as 320 × 180 or 640 × 360).

> Changing the movie dimensions of a finished animation often creates problems with the alignment and position of movie elements. So it's best to adjust the dimensions *before* you create the Flash movie.

2. Set the background color of the movie to black, even if you want your movie to have a different background color. When you create a self-contained projector, the background color of the movie is used to determine the color of the monitor when you play the movie in full-screen mode. Click OK to close the Document Properties dialog box.

3. Create a new layer in your movie and name it **letterbox**. Drag this layer so that it's at the bottom of all other layers in the Timeline. Select Insert → New Symbol and create a new graphic symbol that is a rectangle exactly the same size as your Stage. Make the rectangle whatever color you want for your movie background. Drag the rectangle onto the **letterbox** layer, positioning it in the center of the Stage. Lock the layer once it's in position.

4. Create another new layer and name it **code**. Insert a new keyframe in frame 1 of this layer, highlight it, and press F9 to display the Actions panel. Enter the following statements:

```
fscommand ("allowscale", "false");
fscommand ("fullscreen", "true");
```

The first statement in this script prohibits the movie from being scaled, and preserves the dimensions set in the movie's properties. To scale the movie so that it fills the width of the screen, you can set "allowscale" to true, but the letterbox effect is more pronounced when it is false.

The second statement in the script, sets your projector so that it plays back fullscreen—meaning that it fills the entire monitor, covering the computer's desktop and any applications that are running. The "fullscreen" statement is crucial to the success of the letterbox technique, because it uses the background color of your movie (black) to create the matte that surrounds the 16:9 area of your Stage.

5. Publish your movie as a self-contained projector and see the letterbox effect in context.

By setting the movie dimensions to a 16:9 ratio, you established the initial effect. The black background color created the black mask. Then, by using a symbol as a colored backdrop for the movie, you created the impression that the Stage's color is something other than black. The size of the backdrop matches your Stage size, and the letterbox effect is complete. See Figure 32.4 for an illustration.

Figure 32.4

A letterbox projector playing in full-screen mode

This technique treats the rectangular symbol like background scenery in a theater production. In the same way that a stage crew might change props during a play, you can change the color or other attributes of the background symbol in your movie.

You can also create custom menus for your movie. Using the button techniques outlined in Chapter 15, you can create a series of buttons (menu bar) to serve as navigational controls for your projector. Then, with some basic ActionScript, you can attach commands to the buttons that will start, stop, rewind, skip, and perform all the necessary behaviors you require for navigation and other kinds of interactivity. To learn more about ActionScript commands that allow your audience to interactively navigate through your movie, see Chapter 19 or the ActionScript Reference on this book's companion CD.

Something interesting that you can do with a menu bar is allow your audience to toggle it off and on—it's there when they want it, and gone when they don't. This is especially useful for full-screen projectors, where you don't want a permanent menu or other navigational element cluttering your screen and distracting from your movie. There are many ways to toggle something off and on; consider the following example:

```
_root.menu._visible=false;
keyWatcher = new Object();
```

```
keyWatcher.onKeyDown=function(){
    if(Key.getCode()==Key.SPACE){
        _root.menu._visible=true;
    }
}
keyWatcher.onKeyUp=function(){
    if(Key.getCode()==Key.SPACE){
        _root.menu._visible=false;
    }
}
Key.addListener(keyWatcher);
```

This script creates a simple toggle behavior for a Movie Clip instance called `menu`. Any time a key is pressed, events are broadcast to the Listener object `keyWatcher`. When the events are either `keyDown` or `keyUp`, the script tests to see whether the key creating the event happens to be the spacebar. If it is, then `menu` is shown while the spacebar is down, and hidden when it is up. Of course, while `menu` is visible, all the navigation buttons it contains are available. This allows your audience to toggle the menu "on" with the spacebar, and then click the buttons within the Movie Clip that make your movie do whatever it is that the users need to do: rewind, skip to another section, quit, and so on. To work properly, `menu` must be invisible when the movie is first played. This is handled by the first line of the script.

To see both the letterbox projector technique and a spacebar menu toggle in a self-contained projector, see the file `projectorDemo` (Macintosh) or `projectorDemo.exe` (Windows) in the Chapter 32 folder on this book's companion CD. To examine the source file and to witness these scripts in context, see `projectorDemo.fla` in the same folder.

Inspirational Design Model

One of the best ways to find the inspiration needed to produce your own CD-ROM is to see just how easy it is to create the disc. A task that might have once seemed daunting and mysterious is actually very doable, provided that you have the necessary resources. The following list provides a good variety of information and advice for all your CD-ROM burning needs.

www.roxio.com Roxio is the manufacturer of Toast 6 Titanium, the premiere tool for cross-platform (hybrid) CD burning in a Macintosh environment. To learn more about using Toast 6 Titanium, see Bonus Hands On, "CD Burning for Cross-platform Flash Movies" on this book's companion CD.

www.apple.com/creative/resources/superdrive If you have an Apple G4 or G5, your computer is probably equipped with a SuperDrive. A SuperDrive is an all-in-one CD/DVD authoring device available in many Apple computers. This resource on the Apple website offers many technical specifics about the SuperDrive as well as links to helpful articles about CD and DVD authoring in a Macintosh environment.

www.nero.com Nero 6 is the Windows-compatible CD-burning tool for creating hybrid CDs in a Windows environment. This PC-only burning application is manufactured by Ahead Software. To read more about Nero 6, see the section "Beyond Burning Basics" in Bonus Hands On, "CD Burning for Cross-platform Flash Movies" on this book's companion CD.

www.microsoft.com/windowsxp/expertzone/focuson/cdburning.asp This article on the Microsoft website fields a variety of issues concerning CD burning in a Windows XP environment. See this resource to learn more about CD burning basics, troubleshooting tips, and a list of Windows XP–compatible devices.

CHAPTER 33

Creating Mobile Flash Content for the Pocket PC

As computers continue to become smaller, mobile, and more communicative, Flash is right there in the forefront of the handheld device revolution. The Flash Player is poised to deliver content to a wide variety of consumer gadgets and mobile devices. This includes business applications news services, games, educational applications, maps and geographical aids, event guides, entertainment, wireless applications, and so much more—the works!

In this chapter, you'll learn the basic techniques for creating Flash content for Pocket PC (PPC) devices. The following topics will be covered:

- **Introduction to Flash and the Pocket PC**

- **Performance issues**

- **Creating for your Pocket PC Flash movie**

- **Working with the Pocket PC input methods**

- **Testing your Pocket PC Flash movie**

- **Publishing for the Pocket PC**

Introduction to Flash and Pocket PC

Flash is not just for desktop computers anymore. Flash is pushing its way into broadcast media, WebTV, game consoles, and most importantly (at least in terms of this chapter), Pocket PC handheld devices.

More than just simple organizers, Pocket PC devices are increasingly powerful, easy-to-use mobile platforms that can display all sorts of rich media content, including Flash movies. The great thing is that handheld devices that run the Pocket PC operating system (manufacturers include Dell, Toshiba, HP, and Viewsonic) all ship with the Flash Player. As a result, you can confidently develop Flash content and not worry about whether or not your intended audience can play it.

> For more information on the Pocket PC operating system and Pocket PC handheld devices, check out www.microsoft.com/windowsmobile/products/pocketpc.

While different devices have different specifications, the vast majority of handheld devices running the Pocket PC operating system (at press time, the current edition is Pocket PC 2003) at the very least share the following characteristics:

- Intel StrongARM Processor
- 32–64mb of RAM
- 240×320, 64,000-color screen
- Built-in expansion slot(s) for CompactFlash, SD, and MMC

> The cool thing is that the Pocket PC operating system is not unique to consumer handheld devices. There is also a version of the Pocket PC operating system designed for mobile phones.

The powerful features in the Pocket PC operating system as well as the inherent mobility of Pocket PC devices make them excellent platforms for creative, nontraditional Flash applications, such as conference guides.

However, the marriage of Flash and Pocket PC devices isn't all sunshine and roses. First off, as you will see shortly (in the next section, "Performance Issues"), Pocket PC devices have nowhere near the level of power or memory that we've become accustomed to in our desktop computers. As a result, there are special performance considerations that you need to take into account when you are creating a Flash movie destined for Pocket PC devices. Second, by default, when you create Flash content for Pocket PC devices, you display it by placing the SWF file in an HTML page and using Pocket Internet Explorer (PIE) to view the page. The kicker is that, as you will learn later in this chapter, there are some frustrating limitations to using Pocket Internet Explorer. There are some ways around this problem—as you will learn in the section "Publishing Your Pocket PC Flash Movie" later in this chapter—but they often carry additional problems of their own.

Performance Issues

Unfortunately, despite their ever-increasing sophistication, Pocket PC devices still don't measure up to desktop or laptop computers in terms of speed and power. As a result, when you are creating Flash content specifically destined for a Pocket PC device, there are some things you should be aware of for your grand mobile Flash creation to perform at its best.

Device Speed and Frame Rate

Back in Chapter 10, you explored the whole notion of frame rate. You learned that the higher the frame rate, the higher the ultimate quality of your Flash movie. However, with increased frame rate comes increased file size (and an increased demand on the computer's processor). The problem becomes even more of an issue when it comes to developing Flash content for Pocket PCs. Realistically speaking, due to the hardware limitations of the Pocket PC platform, you'll get an adequate level of playback only with a frame rate of between 12 and 15fps.

> While devices running the Pocket PC operating system are nowhere near as powerful as desktop systems, new devices with faster processors that can handle higher frame rates are constantly being released. As a result, you need to remain aware of the optimum frame rate on the device you're developing your Flash content for.

Optimizing ActionScript

ActionScript is not often thought of as an element that might cause performance issues in your Flash movie. Well, it is. ActionScript, like any other kind of data, needs to be dealt with by the processor in the user's computer. The more ActionScript there is, the more information the user's computer has to process. Now, in the grand scheme of things, when someone is viewing a Flash movie on a desktop or laptop, the ActionScript is the least of your concerns—in terms of the movie slowing down. However, when you are developing Flash content for Pocket PC, given the fact that mobile devices have far slower processors than desktops or laptops, you have to make absolutely sure that your movie is as lean as possible. The more bloated your movie's ActionScript, the more likely your movie will suffer a slowdown. To avoid this, here are some suggestions to optimize your ActionScript:

- Avoid any unnecessary characters.
- Keep your movie's variable, method, instance, and function names as short and as compact as possible.
- Use Functions for menu and button events.
- Use Functions for repetitive events in your movie.

Audio

Audio in a Flash movie consumes a great deal of your Pocket PC device's system resources. As a result, you really need to think about whether or not your movie actually needs sound. The other thing you need to realize about content that runs on a Pocket PC device is that, given the nature of the device itself, most people don't actually expect sound to be part of their experience. As a result, if you are conscious of the limitations imposed by slow processors and low memory (relatively speaking), you probably won't encounter the kind of high demand for audio in a Pocket PC Flash movie than you would in a Flash movie destined for viewing on a desktop or laptop.

However, if you do decide to include audio in your Pocket PC Flash movie, there are some guidelines you should follow:

- Always include a built-in method for turning the audio off. This is especially important if your movie is full screen.

> When a Flash movie is full screen on a PPC device, the user doesn't have access to PPC UI volume controls.

- Make absolutely sure that when you publish the movie, the audio is at the lowest possible quality (while still maintaining its intended sound).

Creating Content for Your Pocket PC Flash Movie

When you create a Flash movie destined for distribution to a PPC device, you aren't using a different authoring environment than you would use if you were creating Flash content destined for distribution to the Web. All the skills you've learned throughout the course of this book are applicable. The only real difference is that there are some added issues and specialized techniques you should be aware of if you want your PPC Flash movie to be the best that it can be.

In this section, you'll spend the time exploring the full range of specialized issues and topics involved in created a Flash movie destined for a Pocket PC device.

Setting Screen Size

One of the most obvious design issues when you are creating Flash content for a Pocket PC device is the screen size. While not all Pocket PC devices have the same screen size, the overwhelming majority of them have a screen size of 240×320. If you are creating a Flash movie that will play full screen, you can use all this space. However, if you are using Pocket Internet Explorer (with the help of the Flash Player) to display your content, you'll have some additional size constraints.

First, the Pocket PC 2002 user interface has two areas (see Figure 33.1) in which absolutely no content can be placed.

Caption bar

Menu bar

Figure 33.1

When you are creating a Flash movie that will be viewed in Pocket Internet Explorer, no content can be displayed in either the menu bar or the caption bar.

> The user can choose to switch off the address bar—a decision that ultimately provides you with an extra 23 pixels of space in your design. However, because turning off the address bar is optional, you can't initially design your page to use that space.

Each bar removes 26 pixels from the vertical resolution of your screen. Therefore, if you design content for a Pocket Internet Explorer that fits on one page, the page cannot exceed 240×263 pixels.

> Pocket Internet Explorer has a scroll bug that allows you to use only 263 pixels of the available height, not the real 268 pixels—bummer.

After a page exceeds 263 vertical pixels, a vertical scroll bar appears. A vertical scrollbar, which takes up 11 additional pixels, means that your screen width gets reduced even further to 229 pixels. Likewise, if your movie requires a horizontal scrollbar, you will lose an additional 11 pixels from the screen's height. So, if you want to maximize the amount of space you have for your Flash creation, you'll want to do your best to make sure that the movie is compact enough that it doesn't actually require either a vertical or horizontal scrollbar.

> If you are planning to let your user enter information into your movie, you need to shave an additional 80 pixels off the height of your screen to accommodate the interface's SIP (the area that pops up at the bottom of the Pocket PC interface which has the keyboard and block recognizer).

Ultimately, if you are absolutely sure that your movie won't require any scroll bars, the optimum size for your Flash movie should be somewhere around 240×260 pixels.

Manually Setting Screen Size

To manually set the size of your movie to work within the screen size constraints of Pocket PC devices is easy; just follow these steps:

1. Choose File → New.

2. When the New Document dialog box opens, select the Flash Document option in the Type list box and click OK.

3. Choose Modify → Document.

4. When the Document Properties dialog box opens, enter **240** in the Width field and **260** in the Height field.

> If you are creating a Flash movie that will play back in full screen, enter **240** in the Width field and **320** in the Height field. Likewise, if you are creating a Flash movie for a Pocket PC device that has a different screen size, enter the correct width and height.

Using a Pocket PC Template to Set Screen Size

One of the great features in Flash MX 2004 and Flash MX Professional 2004 is that there are a series of starter templates with sizes geared toward a specific Pocket PC device. So if you are developing for a specific device and are not entirely sure of the screen size, you can use one of the handy-dandy templates to set the size of your Stage.

The ultra-cool thing about the mobile device starter templates is that they not only configure your Stage to the screen size of the particular device for which you are creating the Flash movie, but they also display an image of the device itself (see Figure 33.2), allowing you to see how your overall movie will appear on the device.

To set the screen size of your movie with a mobile device starter template, just follow these steps:

1. Choose File → New.

2. When the New From Template dialog box opens, click the Templates tab.

3. Choose Mobile Devices from the Category list to display a list of the available device templates (see Figure 33.3).

4. Select one of the specific templates from the Templates list. Notice that a preview of the document size appears in the Preview box.

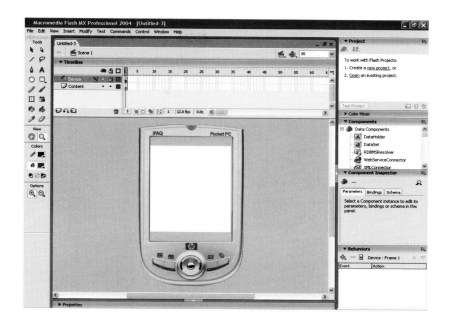

Figure 33.2

Using one of the mobile device starter templates displays an image of the specific device itself on the Stage.

You have access not only to specific Pocket PC devices, but to a series of other mobile devices that also support the Flash Player.

5. When you are finished, click OK.

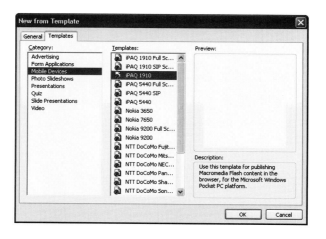

Figure 33.3

The Mobile Devices category in the Templates section of the New From Template dialog box lets you access a series of specific device templates.

Working with Type

When you are working with text in a Flash movie destined for display on a Pocket PC device, there are some extremely important issues that you should be aware of. Given the fact that the screen size on Pocket PC devices is so much smaller than it is on a regular desktop or laptop, the type you use will be relatively small. The problem with Flash is that, by default, all text is anti-aliased. Here's the problem: The vast majority of fonts are not

> This is what happens to small text in Flash. This particular text is Arial, 10 point.

designed to be anti-aliased at a small size. They appear blurry and are difficult to read, such as the example shown to the left.

So, what happens when you need the text in your Pocket PC Flash movie to be crisp and legible? As you'll see in the following two sections, you can either use pixel fonts or optimize the text using Alias Text.

Using Pixel Fonts

Because they automatically display without any anti-aliasing, pixel fonts are specifically designed to be viewed at small point sizes, and therefore are a great choice to use when you are creating a Flash movie for Pocket PC devices. Here's an example shown to the left.

Pixel fonts use the smallest unit of screen measure: the pixel. Because these fonts use pixels to create each character, they remain crisp and easily read regardless of screen size and resolution. There are, however, a few things about pixel fonts that you need to be aware of:

Regular font

> This is a regular anti-aliased font at a small size (10 points)

> This is an example of a Pixel Font at 8 points.

Pixel font

- Pixel fonts need to be used in increments of 8 points (8, 16, 24, and so on).

- Pixels fonts must be placed on whole X and Y coordinates (50, instead of 50.5). You can make sure they are sitting on whole X and Y coordinates by using the Info panel (Window → Design Panels → Info) or the Property Inspector (Window → Properties).

- If you are using an input or dynamic text, make sure you embed the fonts. Otherwise, your Flash movie will use the default Pocket PC system fonts.

> Pixel fonts are not normally included in the collection of fonts that are shipped with a new computer. You need to purchase them separately. Here are some Pixel Font creators/vendors: www.miniml.com, www.fontsforflash.com, and www.atomicmedia.com.

Optimizing Small Fonts

One of the best new features in Flash MX 2004 and Flash MX Professional 2004, at least when it comes to creating content for Pocket PCs, is the ability to increase the readability of small text in Flash by using the Alias Text feature. Essentially, the Alias Text option makes small text more readable by aligning its outlines along pixel boundaries, making the text appear aliased even when anti-aliasing is enabled, as shown in the image to the right.

The great thing about using the Alias Text feature is that, unlike when you are using pixel fonts, the text itself doesn't have to be placed on whole X and Y coordinates. Also, you don't have to go out and buy a specific font; the Alias Text feature works on all the fonts installed on your machine. However, on the other hand, pixel fonts are custom-designed fonts that each has their own artistic flair. As a result, you can pick one that is best suited for your project.

There are, however, a few things about aliasing text that you should be aware of:

- If the user has version 7 of the Flash Player installed on their machine, the Aliased Text option works with Static Text, Dynamic Text, and Input Text. However, if they have a previous version of the Flash Player, the Aliased Text option works only with Static Text.

- If you are using very a very small font size (below 8 points), the Aliased Text feature probably won't improve the readability of your text.

- In the case of some fonts, using bold or italics will actually reduce the readability of aliased text.

- Sans-serif fonts (such as Arial or Helvetica) tend to look clearer when they are aliased than serif fonts (such as Times or Times New Roman).

To use the Aliased Text feature to increase the readability of the fonts in your Pocket PC Flash movie, just follow these steps:

1. Select the text block of small text that you want to alias.

> For how to create and manipulate text, refer back to Chapter 5.

2. If it isn't open already, open the Property Inspector (Window → Properties).
3. Click the Alias Text button ![icon].

Opening External Files from within your Pocket PC Flash Movie

When you create your Pocket PC Flash movie, you might find that you want to call external assets (such as an additional SWF or JPEG file) to play or display within the movie itself. You might also want to load an external file (such as a Word or PDF document) that cannot natively display within a Flash movie. In this case, you would need to rely on the specific program (such as Acrobat Reader or Pocket Microsoft Word) installed on the user's Pocket PC that is associated with the external file you want to open.

Granted, in Flash MX 2004 and Flash MX Pro 2004, you've got a host of really cool options for integrating media (such as digital video and audio) into your Flash movie. However, no matter how well any embedded media can be compressed and optimized when it's brought into Flash, it always increases the overall size of your movie—sometimes drastically so. And as we saw earlier in this chapter, given the slower processor and reduced memory of any Pocket PC device, performance is a huge issue. As a result, you might decide to call an external media file instead of actually embedding it in your Flash movie. By doing this, you can reduce the overall size of the Flash movie itself. In addition, by doing so, you can actually create a certain amount of modular dynamism to your Flash movie by creating content that can be updated.

> If you are calling an external file to play or display within the Flash movie or by the Pocket PC's default application for that file, you have to make absolutely sure that when you publish, package, and distribute the movie, you include the file itself. Otherwise, there won't be anything for the movie to play or display when it's run on the user's Pocket PC.

In either case, with the help of a little simple ActionScript, you can call external files from within your Flash movie. In this section, you'll explore how to call several different types of external files from your Flash movie.

> For more information on working with the kind of (relatively) simple ActionScript described in the following sections, check out Chapter 14.

Windows Media Player Files

Because the Pocket PC operating system is a Microsoft product, it's no great surprise that its default media application is a stripped-down version of Windows Media Player. Given this, you know that everyone who is viewing your movie has a copy of the program and can therefore play Windows Media video (WMV) files.

> Remember that one feature of Flash MX 2004 and Flash MX Pro 2004 is increased support for video import, optimization, and compression. As a result, you might want to explore embedding your video file instead of displaying it with the Pocket PC Windows Media Player. For more information on working with video in Flash, check out Chapter 31.

To play an external Windows Media Player video file, you need to use the `getURL` Global Function. Here is an example in which a WMV file (called `myvideofile.wmv`) will open in the Windows Media Player when a button is pressed:

```
on (press) {
getURL("myvideofile.wmv");
}
```

Notice that a relative path was used to target the video clip. If you wanted, you could easily use an absolute path instead.

> Windows Media Player can be used to play other media files such as Intel Indio video files, AIFF audio files, WAV audio files, MPEG files, MIDI files, AU audio files, and MP3 files.

MP3 Files

The MP3 file format is a popular one for audio because it offers high quality within a relatively small file size. While, as in the case of video, you can easily embed audio in your Pocket PC Flash movie, there are situations in which you might want to call an external MP3 instead.

To do so, you'll use the `getURL` Global Function. Here is an example in which an MP3 (called `music.mp3`) will open in the user's default player when a button is clicked:

```
on (press) {
getURL("music.mp3");
}
```

> In most cases, Windows Media Player is the default application that will open external MP3 files.

HTML files

Any external HTML file that you call (whether it's physically on the Pocket PC device or on the Internet and being accessed through a wireless connection) will open in Pocket Internet Explorer (PIE).

As with many other external files, you do so using the `getURL` Global Function. Here is an example of an external HTML file (called `pictures.html`) that resides in the same directory as the actual Flash movie that is calling it being opened when the user clicks a button:

```
on (press) {
getURL("pictures.html");
}
```

On the other hand, here is an example of the ActionScript necessary to open a specific website:

```
on (press) {
getURL("http://www.vonflashenstein.com");
}
```

Remember, if your user isn't connected to the Internet (through either a physical or a wireless connection), the website won't open.

JPEG and SWF files

As you've probably figured out, the getUrl() Global Function is used in many cases to load external files into a default Player (usually Pocket Internet Explorer or Windows Media Player). However, there are several kinds of files that you can load directly into your Flash movie without having to resort to an external application. Well, that's where loadMovie() and loadMovieNum() (which are both Global Functions of the Movie Clip object) enter the picture. By using the loadMovie() and loadMovieNum() Global Functions, you can dynamically load JPEG images or external SWF files into a target Movie Clip (using loadMovie()) or a level within the main Timeline (using loadMovieNum()).

What exactly is the difference between loadMovie() and loadMovieNum()? Well, loadMovie() loads a JPEG (or SWF) into a specific Movie Clip, while loadMovieNum() loads the JPEF (or SWF) into a specific level. For more information on levels, check out Chapter 20.

Here is an example of the ActionScript required to load an external JPEG (or SWF file) when a user clicks a button:

```
on (press) {
    loadMovie("someimage.jpeg", "somemovieclipinstance");
}
```

If the file is in the same directory as the Flash movie, you really only have to enter the image name. However, if it isn't located in the same directory, you'll have to enter the exact path (either as an absolute or relative URL) so that the Flash movie can locate it.

If you use loadMovieNum(), your script should look like this:

```
on (press) {
    loadMovieNum("somemovie.swf", 2);
}
```

If the Movie Clip you are loading the JPEG or SWF file into is not a direct child of the current Timeline, you'll need to enter the proper target path using dot syntax. For more information on targeting Movie Clips in a multiple-Timeline movie, refer to Chapter 20.

Although using `loadMovie()` or `loadMovieNum()` to dynamically load a JPEG or SWF is pretty easy, there are two things you need to realize. First, when it comes to using `load-Movie()`, all the contents of the target Movie Clip will be replaced by the loaded file. Second, only one file can occupy a given level in the Flash movie. As a result, if you load a second file into `_level1`, the first one you loaded will be automatically replaced.

Older Pocket PC devices that are running Flash Player 5 will not be able to dynamically load JPEGs and SWFs.

Using the Flash Pocket PC Components for Interface Development

Under normal circumstances, due to the memory and processor speed limitations of Pocket PC devices, interface components (such as radio buttons and check boxes) that would have no real effect on a normal Flash movie tend to have a harmful performance effect when used in a Pocket PC Flash movie. As a result, Macromedia has developed a series of UI components that are specifically designed to run well in a Pocket PC Flash movie.

They include the following components:

- The CheckBox component adds a check box to your Flash movie.
- The RadioButton component adds a radio button to your Flash movie.
- The ListBox component adds a list box to your Flash movie.
- The DropDown component adds a drop-down menu to your Flash movie.
- The ScrollBar component adds a scrollbar to your Flash movie.

The great thing about all these components is that, except when it comes to the decreased level of stress they place on the Pocket PC device's system resources, they are identical to their counterparts found in the Flash UI components.

To learn more about the parameters of the Pocket PC UI components, check out the coverage of the regular Flash UI components in Chapter 16.

Unfortunately, the Pocket PC UI components don't ship with Flash MX 2004 or Flash MX Pro 2004. However, they are freely downloadable at www.macromedia.com/devnet/devices/pocket_pc.html.

> To make the Pocket PC components available for use in Flash, you have to manually place them in the Components subdirectory, located in the First Run subdirectory of the directory in which you installed Flash MX 2004 and Flash MX Pro 2004.

Testing Your Pocket PC Flash Movie

As with a regular Flash movie, you need to test your Pocket PC Flash movie to ensure that it doesn't have any problems and functions exactly as it's supposed to before you publish it.

Unfortunately, Flash MX 2004 and Flash MX Pro 2004 don't ship with any device emulators that can be used to test your movie to see how it would perform on its intended Pocket PC device.

> An *emulator* is a piece of software that runs on a desktop and allows you to test applications in a virtual environment that reproduces the specific platform (in this case, Pocket PC) for which you are developing.

Unfortunately, despite the increasing popularity of Pocket PC devices, the only real emulator available comes packaged with Microsoft's Pocket PC Software Development Kit (SDK), which can be downloaded at www.microsoft.com/windowsmobile/information/devprograms/default.mspx. However, because the emulator is designed to test full-fledged Pocket PC applications developed in a programmed language such as eMbedded Visual C++, it's overkill (as well as amazingly complicated to use) for those wanting to test their humble Pocket PC Flash movies.

Given these issues, you have only a couple of options for testing your movie on its target device:

- If you don't have one of the devices for which you're targeting your movie, go out and buy one. This is a pretty unreasonable solution, especially if you want to test your movie out on multiple devices.

- Post a request on a discussion group (such as the Macromedia Flash Handhelds Online Forum) asking for developers to test your movie on their device. For the most part, other developers will be more than happy to test out your movie and provide feedback about its content and performance.

Publishing Your Pocket PC Flash Movie

After you've spent hours and hours developing your elegant Pocket PC Flash movie, it's time to publish it. The way you publish your Pocket PC flash movie is actually relatively simple and not much different from publishing a regular Flash movie. In this section, you'll explore how to publish a Pocket PC Flash movie that is intended to be viewed in Pocket Internet Explorer (PIE) using the Flash Player. From there, you'll learn how to create a stand-alone, full-screen movie using a groovy third-party program called FlashPack.

Publishing a Pocket PC Flash Movie for Pocket Internet Explorer

If you cast your mind back to the beginning of this chapter, you'll remember that all Pocket PC devices come with a version of the Flash Player. The kicker is that the standard Flash Player on all Pocket PC devices cannot display a Flash movie in the same way that the Flash Player on a desktop or laptop can. Instead, it must use Pocket Internet Explorer to display the Flash movie. As a result, when you are publishing a Pocket PC Flash movie, you also need to publish an HTML file.

So to publish a Pocket PC Flash movie for Pocket Internet Explorer, just follow these steps:

1. With the movie open that you want to publish, choose File → Publish Settings.

2. When the Publish Settings dialog box opens, make sure that the Flash and the HTML file types are selected in the Formats tab.

3. From there, set all the publish properties of your SWF file.

> Its important to note that, as of the time of this writing, Macromedia had yet to announce Flash Player 7 for the Pocket PC. As a result, you need to make sure you select Flash Player 6 (or below) for the version of your movie.

4. Set all the publish properties of the associated HTML file. The only thing that you need to be sure of is that you select Flash for Pocket PC 2003 from the Templates drop-down menu.

> For a refresher on the publish settings of the associated HTML file, see Chapter 30.

5. When you are finished, click Publish.

Creating a Stand-Alone Flash Projector with FlashPack

Easily one of the biggest drawbacks of creating Pocket PC Flash movies is that you cannot create a stand-alone projector. This is a huge bummer, because a stand-alone projector would allow you to partially sidestep the screen-size restrictions that come with having to display your Flash content from within Pocket Internet Explorer.

There are, however, a couple of ways around this problem. The first is to use the Macromedia Flash Standalone Player (SAP). The SAP is a client side (meaning it installs on your machine) that allows you to create Flash projectors that run on Pocket PC devices. Sounds good, right? Well, first off, it will cost you $499 to license the SAP. We're talking about licensing here, not purchase. And after one year, you need to renew your license—which will cost you another $499 (or whatever the price tag has risen to).

> To learn more about the Flash Standalone Player—though, honestly, there isn't much more to learn—check out www.macromedia.com/software/devices/products/pocketpc/faq/.

The second way to bypass the inherent problems of the Pocket PC Flash Player is to purchase a third-party program that allows you to convert your SWF file into a true, stand-alone executable file (.exe) that can play full screen and doesn't actually require that any version of the Flash player is installed on the user's device. Easily one of the best of these programs is FlashPack. Created by HandSmart (www.handsmart.com), FlashPack, which also comes in a stripped-down version called FlashPack Jr. and a professional version called FlashPack Pro, is designed to allow you to create full-screen, stand-alone executable files (.exe) out of your Flash SWF movie without any programming knowledge. The great thing about FlashPack is that its price tag is a reasonable $89.95 (for the Standard Edition)—which is a far cry from the whopping $499 yearly licensing fee that you would have to pay for the Flash Standalone Player.

> The only real drawback of using FlashPack is that, for your executable file to work properly, the Flash Player (not the Flash Standalone Player) must be installed on the target device. Given the fact that the vast majority of all Pocket PC devices have the Flash Player, this isn't such a big deal.

 A demo version of FlashPack has been included on this book's accompanying CD. To create a stand-alone executable file (.exe) from your Flash movie, just follow these steps:

1. Make sure that you have already published your movie as a SWF file.

> Given the fact that you aren't using Pocket Internet Explorer to view your Flash movie, you don't need to publish an accompanying HTML file.

2. Open FlashPack.

3. Make sure you are working in the Source Movie section, which is accessible by clicking the Source Movie tab at the top of the interface (see Figure 33.4).

4. Click the Browse button Browse... . When the Select File dialog box opens, navigate to where your SWF file is located, select it, and click Open.

5. From here, select one of the options from the Dimensions drop-down menu, located in the Movie Appearance section. If you select either Custom Pixels or Custom Percent, you'll be able to enter your values in the Width and Height fields, just below the Dimensions drop-down menu.

6. From here, select one of the options from the Alignment drop-down menu to determine where on the Pocket PC device's screen the movie will be aligned.

7. Select one of the options from the Scale drop-down menu to determine how your movie is cropped/scaled to fit within the dimensions you designated.

8. If you want your movie to pause at the start and wait for a command to play, click the Paused at Start check box.

9. If you want your movie to loop continuously, click the Loop check box.

10. If you want the movie to use the Pocket PC device's system fonts (as opposed to those used in the movie itself), click the Device Font check box.

11. If you want the full Flash right-click menu to be visible, click the Device Menu check box.

12. Select an option from the Quality drop-down menu. Remember, the higher the quality, the larger the file and the more of a drain the movie will have on the device's system resources.

13. If you want to change the default background color of the movie, click the Background Color swatch. When the Color Picker is displayed, select a new color.

14. To see how the changes you made affect the look of your movie, click the Reload Preview button Reload Preview .

15. Click the Publish tab to access the Publish settings of the movie (see Figure 33.5).

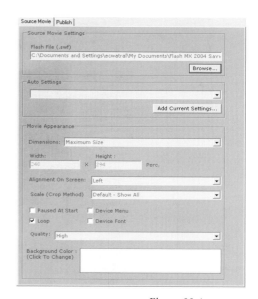

Figure 33.4

The Source Movie tab in FlashPack

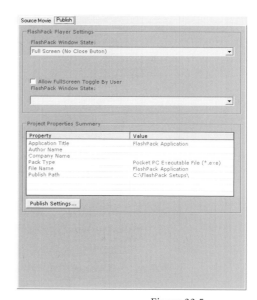

Figure 33.5

The Publish tab in FlashPack

Figure 33.6

**The example on the
left illustrates the
Full Screen option,
while the example
on the right illus-
trates the Win-
dowed option.**

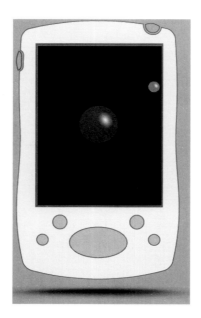
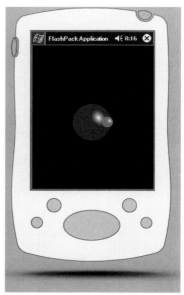

16. Select one of the options from the FlashPack Window State drop-down menu (see Figure 33.6): Full Screen or Windowed.

17. If you've chosen the Windowed option and you want your user to be able to toggle the Full Screen option, select the Allow Full Screen Toggle by User check box. Then, from the FlashPack Window State drop-down menu, select the specific button on the device that you want to act as a toggle for Full Screen mode.

18. Click the Publish Settings button `Publish Settings...` to access the FlashPack Preferences dialog box (see Figure 33.7), where you'll manipulate some of the properties of the file itself.

19. To set the location of FlashPack's output, click the Browse button to the right of the Output Directory field. When the dialog box opens, locate and select the directory into which you want the movie to be exported.

20. Enter the name of the exported file in the Setup File Name field.

21. Select an option for the type of exported file from the Pack Type drop-down menu.

22. Click the Setup Appearance tab (see Figure 33.8).

23. Enter a name in the Application Title field. This name will appear during the setup process.

Figure 33.7

The Output Setup Files tab in the FlashPack Preferences dialog box

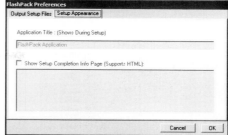

Figure 33.8

The Setup Appearance tab in the FlashPack Preferences dialog box

24. If you want to include some information that appears after the setup process has finished, click the Show Setup Completion Info Page check box, and then enter the text that you want to show in the text field. The Show Setup Completion Info Page field supports HTML.

25. When you are finished, click OK. You'll notice that properties of your movie are displayed in the Project Properties Summary list box.

26. When you are finished setting all the properties of the file, click the Publish button Publish , and your movie is published as an executable file to the location you set and with the properties you set.

> We didn't have room to cover all the new features in Flash MX 2004 and Flash MX Pro 2004 related to mobile devices. Most notable among these additional features is support for creating and manipulating MIDI device tones—a feature that is used when authoring Flash content for certain types of mobile phones.

Inspirational Design Model

Pocket PC devices are…well…mobile. So as one would expect, they are great for carrying around. Given this, Pocket PC applications are best when they can replace books, papers, and other general space-consuming miscellanea. Take conference materials, for example. Most people have been to conferences (trade shows, fan fests, and so on) in which multiple booklets, schedules, abstracts, and other documents are needed to know what is going on, when it's going on, and where it's going on. What if all of it could all be in a Flash application that runs on a Pocket PC device? This is exactly what happened in the case of the Pocket PC Summit 2002 Philadelphia Event Guide (see Figure 33.9).

Figure 33.9

**The Pocket PC
Summit 2002
Philadelphia
Event Guide**

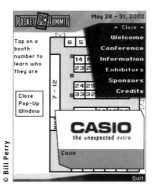

Created entirely in Flash by Bill Perry, the full-screen guide had immediate purposes. The first was to enable conference attendees to have all relevant information about the conference available to them on their Pocket PC, allowing them to be mobile and to access the content any time and anywhere. The second purpose was to show attendees the benefits of using Macromedia Flash to create a full-screen guide and to present the content in a rich and engaging user interface.

Synchronizing Streaming Video with Flash Animations

If you have ever worked with digital video in the context of a multimedia application, you know how difficult it can be to get your video to synchronize with other elements. While other authoring applications might struggle with this task, Flash MX Professional 2004 provides an integrated solution that makes synchronizing video with both static and animated elements an easy, straightforward process.

The secret of its success is in the MediaPlayback component. This new component uses cue points to facilitate close synchronization between a video and other elements of a Flash movie. *Cue points* are flags or markers that you assign to specific points in time across the duration of a video. As a video plays, it passes the cue points you defined for it. When that happens, each cue point is linked to a frame in your Flash movie where you can display a graphic, cue an animation or sound, send an ActionScript command, or include any other events you require. The beauty is that cue points are locked to the time-code of a video: When the video reaches a cue point, it initiates the specified event and maintains tight synchronization.

When you work with the MediaPlayback component, you can also take advantage of video streaming. *Streaming* describes a video that can begin playing before it has completely loaded into the Flash Player. This can be a huge benefit for your audience, as they will have to wait only a few moments before a video starts to play. As they watch the first segments of your presentation, the remainder is loading quietly in the background. Using the MediaPlayback component, you can stream FLV video and MP3 files that are either saved locally or posted to a URL on the Internet.

To begin this lesson, go to the Hands On 8 folder of this book's companion CD-ROM and copy the file `family.flv` to your computer's desktop. This is the video you will stream into your movie. You can also preview the finished file, `family_photos.swf`, or examine the final Flash document, `family_photos.fla`. If you want to play either of these files, be sure they are in the same directory as `family.flv` when you open them. `family.flv` is an external, streaming video file. If its host movie can't locate it, the video will not be displayed.

Once the external files are in order, choose File → New and select Flash Document from the New Document dialog box. Click OK. Press Cmd/Ctrl+F3 to open the Property Inspector. You will need it several times throughout this lesson and it's helpful to make it available at the outset.

> This lesson requires Flash MX Professional 2004. It uses components that ship only with the Pro edition.

Phase 1: Preparing the Stage

Figure H8.1

The MediaPlayback component is in the Media Components category of the Components panel.

To prepare your movie for a video with cue points:

1. Choose Modify → Document. Set the width to 500 pixels and the height to 400 pixels. Click OK.

2. Choose Window → Development Panels → Components to open the Components panel. Click the handle beside the Components icon to expand the Media Components category. Double-click the MediaPlayback Component icon (see Figure H8.1). This places an instance of the component in the center of the Stage. The MediaPlayback component can play FLV video or MP3 audio. It includes controls to start, stop, preview, and monitor the progress of these media files.

3. Use the Property Inspector to set the attributes of the component. Assign the instance name `my_movie`; enter 500 for W, 400 for H, 0 for X, and 0 for Y. If you start with your cursor in the Instance Name field, you can use the Tab key to move to the other fields.

4. To configure the component, you must use the Component Inspector. To open it, do either of the following:

   - Choose Window → Development Panels → Component Inspector.

   - Select the MediaPlayback component on the Stage and click the Launch Component Inspector button in the Property Inspector.

   The Component Inspector opens (see Figure H8.2). Whereas the Parameters tab of the Property Inspector is sufficient for configuring more basic components, MediaPlayback has a greater variety of settings and requires a more robust interface.

Phase 2: Configuring the MediaPlayback Component

Once the component has been placed on the Stage, you must link it to a video and define its parameters in the Component Inspector. This process includes defining cue points for the video.

To configure a MediaPlayback component and assign cue points:

1. In the Component Inspector panel, check FLV to control streaming video compressed with the Spark codec. To learn more about Spark and video compression in Flash MX Pro 2004, see Chapter 31.

2. Use the four Video Length fields to specify the duration of your video in the following time-code format:

   Hours:Minutes:Seconds:Frames

3. Enter **0:0:23:14**. Choose 30 in the FPS drop-down menu. This allows you to specify your video's frame rate.

4. Unlike embedded videos that are part of your final SWF file, the MediaPlayback component works with external video files and streams them into your movie. The URL field allows the component to locate the external video. This can be a file on your local computer, on a CD-ROM, or on the Internet. Do either of the following to specify a URL:

   - Enter `family.flv` in the URL field. This causes the component to look for the local version of the video you copied to your computer's desktop from this book's accompanying CD.

   - Enter `http://www.vonflashenstein.com/resources/family.flv`. This is the absolute path to a copy of the same FLV video on our website. Feel free to try this exercise by streaming the video from the Web. However, this video was optimized for DSL and cable modem users. If you are using a 56K dial-up connection, you won't get the best results.

5. Put a check mark in the Automatically Play box. This allows the video to begin playback as soon as enough is loaded into the Flash Player. When unchecked, your audience must initiate playback on their own.

6. Put a check mark in the Use Preferred Media Size box. This preserves the original size of the video. When unchecked, the size of the video is determined by the size of the MediaPlayback component. To prevent any weird stretching or scaling, be sure that the Respect Aspect Ratio box is also checked.

7. In the Control Placement section, click the Bottom radio button to position the video control buttons at the bottom of the component. The other parameters will position the control buttons at the top, left, or right of the component.

8. Select On in the Control Visibility section. When set to Off, the controls are hidden; when set to Auto, they are displayed only when the mouse moves over the controller area.

Figure H8.2

The Component Inspector provides a more comprehensive interface for setting the parameters of a MediaPlayback component.

9. With the main parameters in place, you can now set your cue points. Click the Add Cue Point button (+). In the Name field, enter **start**, the name for your first cue point. Then for the four fields labeled Position, enter the time-code value **0:0:1:15**. This creates a cue point named start at 1 second and 15 frames into the video.

10. Repeat this process for each additional cue point. You will need to insert 10 additional cue points for this lesson. See Table H8.1 for a complete list of cue point names and their corresponding time-codes. Use these cue point names and time-code values to create cue points for the my_movie instance of the MediaPlayback component.

If at any point you make a mistake, click the Remove Cue Point button (–) to delete a cue point. Though it can be helpful to put the cue points in chronological order, it's not absolutely necessary. If you forget one on the list, simply add it to the end. Flash reads the time-code for each cue point, not the order in which it appears on the list in the Component Inspector.

Table H8.1

Cue Point Names and Time-Code Values

NAME	TIME-CODE
start	0:0:1:15
jim	0:0:5:0
off	0:0:9:0
gpa	0:0:10:0
off	0:0:12:0
sis	0:0:14:4
off	0:0:15:26
photo	0:0:18:0
off	0:0:19:20
bye	0:0:20:0
off	0:0:22:14

In this lesson, we've provided the cue points for you. When you do this on your own in the future, you will need to retrieve them yourself. A video-editing application or media viewer such as QuickTime or Windows Media Player will allow you to do this.

11. Once you've completely configured the component, choose File → Save to save your movie. Entering cue points can be tedious, and you don't want to do it again if you can avoid it!

Phase 3: Syncing the Cue Points with Your Movie

The hardest part of the process is behind you. You have a Media component on the Stage and it's been configured to link to an external video. You have also defined cue points that are associated with a specific point in time during the video. Your next steps are to create the elements that will synchronize to the cue points and to add the ActionScript that will allow one to work with the other.

To add synchronized content to go with your video:

1. Return to your movie's main Timeline. Add two new layers; name the first **text** and the second **labels**.

2. Click to select frame 8 of Layer 1 and press F5. This extends the frames of the layer holding the MediaPlayback component to frame 8.

3. Click to select frame 8 in the text layer. Hold down the Shift key and click frame 2 of the labels layer. This should select all the empty frames in these two layers.

4. Press F7. The empty frames are converted to empty keyframes (see Figure H8.3).

Figure H8.3

You must create 14 blank keyframes in the text and labels layers (7 keyframes per layer). These will be used to hold chunks of text, frame labels, and ActionScript.

5. Click to select the first keyframe of the labels layer and press F9 to open the Actions panel. Enter the following statement:

   ```
   stop();
   ```

   Now that the main Timeline has more than one frame, it's necessary to stop it at frame 1 and prevent it from playing the additional frames too early.

6. When you define cue points for a MediaPlayback instance, those cue points must coincide with frame labels in your movie. That way, when a cue point is reached in the video, your Flash movie's Timeline will skip to the frame whose label matches the name of the cue point. You need to enter seven frame labels for the seven empty keyframes of the labels layer. See Table H8.2 to pair frame numbers with their appropriate labels and enter the frame labels in the Property Inspector. Each frame in the labels layer must have a frame label to match one of the cue points defined for your video.

FRAME NUMBER	FRAME LABEL
2	off
3	start
4	jim
5	gpa
6	sis
7	photo
8	bye

Table H8.2

Frame Numbers and Labels

7. Click to select frame 3 of the text layer. Use the Text tool and insert a block of static text.

8. Use the Property Inspector to set the size to 40 and the alignment to center. Type the phrase **Here she goes....** Because this movie has a whimsical feel, we used a font that looks as if it were written in a felt-tip marker.

9. With the text block still selected, open the Align panel (Cmd/Ctrl+**K**). Make sure the To Stage option is selected, then click Align To Top Edge and Align Horizontal Center. This aligns the text block to the top-middle of the Stage (see Figure H8.4).

10. Select the block of text in frame 3 and press Cmd/Ctrl+**C** to copy it.

11. Click to select keyframe 4 of the text layer and press Cmd/Ctrl+Shift+**V** (Edit → Paste In Place). This pastes the text into the keyframe at exactly the same position.

12. Change the new text in keyframe 5 to read **Hi! I'm Jim**.

13. Repeat the process of copying text from one keyframe and pasting it in place in another keyframe for frames 5 through 8. Use Table H8.3 to see what the text should read for each keyframe. Each remaining keyframe in the text layer has a different phrase in its block of text.

    The completed Timeline should look like Figure H8.5.

14. At this point, you have a component with a linked video and a series of keyframes that match the video's cue points. There is one more step you must complete to allow these elements to work together. You must attach a behavior that enables the MediaPlayback component to navigate to the appropriate frame label when a cue point is passed.

    Click the MediaPlayback instance to select it on the Stage. Then choose Window → Development Panels → Behaviors to open the Behaviors panel.

Figure H8.5

The final Timeline has three layers: one for the MediaPlayback component, one for text, and one for frame labels.

15. Click the Add Behavior button (+) and choose Media → Labeled Frame CuePoint Navigation. The Labeled Frame CuePoint Navigation dialog box opens.

16. Choose the Absolute radio button, select _root in the Select Clip With Labeled Frames list box, and check the Go To And Stop box (see Figure H8.6). This tells the behavior script three things: use an absolute path, the cue point frame labels are on the _root Timeline, and use a `gotoAndStop()` function when skipping from frame to frame.

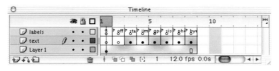

17. Click OK and choose File → Save to save your movie.

18. Everything is finally ready! Select Control → Test Movie to see how your movie performs.

First, the video will take a few seconds to load. Once it is ready, playback will commence. As the video plays, the various phrases of text that you inserted will be displayed on the screen. This shows you the cue points in action. When a cue point is passed in the video, the Cue Point behavior tells the movie to jump to a frame label by the same name.

KEYFRAME	TEXT
5	This is Grandpa.
6	That's my sister, Margaret.
7	We're posing for her.
8	Will she ever take the picture?

Table H8.3

Keyframes and Text

As the video starts to play, take notice of the streaming progress indicator in the Media-Playback component (see Figure H8.7). Even though you video starts to play, the file is still in the process of loading into your movie.

You might wonder why the second keyframe of the text layer remains empty. This is the same frame that has the frame label off. The reason is that in some cases, you might not want a chunk of text to linger for too long. Every time you want to clear the screen and make the text disappear, you can define a cue point that points to off. When this cue point is reached, the Timeline jumps to keyframe 2, where there is no text.

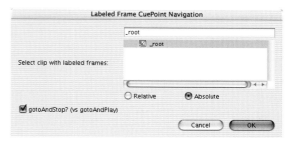

Figure H8.6

The Labeled Frame CuePoint Navigation dialog box

Did you find that the Component Inspector panel is a little cumbersome for setting cue points? If so, select frame 1 of the labels layer, press F9 to open the Actions panel, and enter the following statements:

```
my_movie.addCuePoint("start",1.5);
my_movie.addCuePoint("jim",5);
my_movie.addCuePoint("off",9);
my_movie.addCuePoint("gpa",10);
my_movie.addCuePoint("off",12);
my_movie.addCuePoint("sis",14.06);
my_movie.addCuePoint("off",15.86);
my_movie.addCuePoint("photo",17.06);
my_movie.addCuePoint("off",19.06);
my_movie.addCuePoint("bye",20);
my_movie.addCuePoint("off",22.46);
```

Use addCuePoint() to define cue points via ActionScript. This method takes two arguments: the name of the cue point (as a string) and the time (in seconds) at which the cue occurs.

Next Steps

If you found this lesson to be helpful, you'll be glad to know that it is just the tip of the iceberg. You can expand on these techniques and do a great deal more once you've mastered the basics. Consider the following suggestions:

Playback position arrow   Stream progress bar

Figure H8.7

The MediaPlayback component tracks the progress of the streaming video. See how the Stream progress bar and playback position arrow are in different locations.

- Rather than show static images or text at each cue point, have each cue skip to a frame where an animation begins.

- In lieu of graphics, use audio. Put an audio file at the same frame as the frame label for each new cue point. Use this technique to include a voice-over in several different languages for a single video file.

- The MediaPlayback component also accepts MP3 files. Use the Component Inspector panel to set cue points for a streaming MP3 audio file.

- The MediaPlayback component is an all-in-one component for streaming media in Flash. For something with fewer parameters that affords more flexibility, see the MediaDisplay and MediaController components. They work in an identical fashion but allow more leeway for integrating components into existing movies and applications.

Index

Note to the Reader: Throughout this index **boldfaced** page numbers indicate primary discussions of a topic. *Italicized* page numbers indicate illustrations.

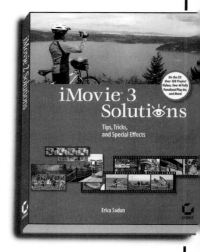
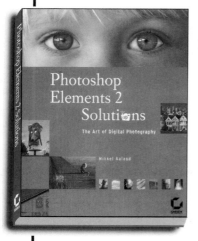